AUTOMOTIVE TECHNOLOGY

AUTOMOTIVE TECHNOLOGY

Frederick C. Nash
Head, Automotive Mechanics
R. S. McLaughlin Collegiate and
Vocational Institute
Oshawa, Ontario

Kalman Banitz
Illustrator
Whitby   Ontario

McGRAW-HILL RYERSON LIMITED
Toronto   Montreal   New York   London
Sydney   Mexico   Johannesburg   Panama
Düsseldorf   Singapore   Rio de Janeiro
New Delhi   Kuala Lumpur

PREFACE

This text has been prepared to provide the student with a thorough understanding of the *principles, construction,* and *operation* of automotive components. The current technical and service literature prepared by the automotive manufacturers was carefully analyzed during the preparation of this text in order to ensure the inclusion of the latest technical advances in the industry.

The layout of the text is such that it can be easily adapted to either a full coverage of the automotive programme or to the unit type of automotive options. Each section of the text covers the theory of construction and operation for the components of that section. The relevant principles of Mathematics, Physics, Chemistry, and Hydraulics are covered in this text where they apply to the topic being discussed.

Hundreds of especially drawn illustrations have been prepared for this text. A second colour has been used to emphasize the important points being discussed. Nonrelated, unimportant features have been minimized or eliminated from the illustrations to improve their clarity and understanding.

The review questions at the end of each chapter are intended as homework or review assignments.

Due to the wide variation in the service procedures of the various automotive and equipment manufacturers, only general repair and service procedures are covered. It is the authors' opinion that these procedures are best outlined in the manufacturers' service manual as required for the make, model, year, and vehicle.

CONTENTS

UNIT ONE
Shop Practice

Chapter 1
INTRODUCTION

1-1 HISTORY OF THE AUTOMOBILE INDUSTRY

The progress of transportation has always been closely related to the progress of civilization. Transportation on water has evolved from the simple raft to the modern ocean liner; in the air, from the first balloon to the supersonic aircraft; and on land, from the unhurried oxcart to the high-speed automobile.

The evolution of the automobile has met with many obstacles including severe legal action and disapproval from the general public. For example, in Great Britain, laws were passed in 1865 which required that at least three people should be in charge of the motor vehicle while it was moving. One person carrying a red flag was to precede the vehicle on foot by at least sixty yards, to warn

(A) 1896 FORD'S FIRST CAR

(B) 1903 MODEL "A" FORD

(C) 1915 MODEL "T"

(D) 1928 MODEL "A" FORD

(E) 1932 V8 TUDOR

(F) 1938 FORDOR

(G) 1949 CUSTOM FORDOR

(H) 1955 MERCURY HARDTOP

(I) 1973 THUNDERBIRD

Fig. 1-1   Evolution of the Automobile

Ford of Canada

(A) A TYPICAL SERVICE STATION IN 1916

(B) A TYPICAL SERVICE STATION OF TODAY

Fig. 1-2   Automotive Service Stations   Imperial Oil Limited

drivers and riders of horses of the approaching danger. A speed limit was enforced of two miles per hour in the city and four miles per hour in the country. This act was enforced until 1896.

In 1885, Carl Benz of Germany introduced the first road vehicle powered by an internal combustion engine. In 1891, C. E. Duryea produced the first American made gasoline-powered automobiles, and in 1896 Henry Ford built his first car.

Around the turn of the century, gasoline-powered vehicles had stiff competition from steam and electric automobiles. The steam and electrically powered vehicles had the advantage of an abundance of power at low speed, making a transmission unnecessary. The danger of high-pressure steam boilers and the inconvenience of recharging the electric car's batteries reduced their popularity.

The gasoline-powered vehicle, despite the necessity of the transmission, had many advantages:

(a) Producing a large amount of power from a small quantity of fuel
(b) The ability to travel farther without stopping for fuel or water, in contrast to the steam-powered unit or recharging of the batteries in the electric unit
(c) The fuel required could be replenished easily and quickly

1-2 AUTOMOBILES OF TODAY

The modern automobile is the result of the accumulation of many years of pioneering, research and development. The result is seen in the manufacturing of an efficient, dependable low-cost means of mass transportation. Today's automobile is a highly complicated machine involving numerous mechanical and electrical devices employing many scientific principles.

The servicing of the automobile has also changed greatly to keep in step with the engineering advances of the industry. The early automobile repairer was usually the local blacksmith, since he was frequently the only man in the community who had any experience, or the facilities to make repairs to the running gear of the early vehicles. However, he lacked the knowledge and experience required to make repairs to the engine or drive line. When these units required repair, the vehicle could not be used until a factory-employed mechanic arrived to service the vehicle.

From 1910 to 1930, the men who called themselves mechanics were self-trained. They gained their knowledge from books and trial-and-error experiences while on the job. Their place of employment was usually some small, dirty dark converted building, located in an off-street lane. By the late 1920s the first especially designed repair garages were constructed.

The tools and equipment which the early mechanic used were poor compared to today's standard, and in many cases, made by the mechanic.

Today's automotive mechanic is well trained and works in a clean, bright, well-ventilated specially designed automotive service centre.

Automotive service work falls into two categories; preventive service, and breakdown or repair service. The trend today is to prevent breakdowns rather than to repair them.

A thorough knowledge of the parts, and an understanding of the mechanisms are essential in order that faulty conditions in any part of the automotive mechanism may be detected and corrected. As a result, the mechanic must possess the knowledge, skill, and experience in this field to be successful.

You can only gain experience over a period of time by putting your best effort into every possible situation that may arise. Experience consists of practising the different small operations over and over again, and mastering the difficulties and problems as they arise. A fully trained mechanic can tackle with confidence what appears to be a new mechanical problem. After an inspection and analysis of the job to be done, he may discover that the job simply involves a series of small operations with which he is already familiar. Here again, knowledge is important in order to determine the sequence of the known operations in dealing with the new problem.

One of the most important habits to form, in order to become a thorough mechanic, is to make a final inspection of every job. Cotter pins, patent locking devices, lock washers, loose screws, spacers, small defects, the lubrication of parts, the proper assembly of parts in new positions, and the proper marking of parts are a few of the many

Imperial Oil Limited

Fig. 1-3 Equipment Required for Modern Automobile

small details that are easily overlooked or forgotten. Any one of these may be important when doing a good job. Returned work quickly pulls down a mechanic's reputation, and he should strive to prevent it.

1-3 AUTOMOBILE DIVISIONS

The modern automobile can be divided into two distinct sections known as the *body* and the *chassis*.

1-4 THE BODY

The body gives the vehicle its lines and finished appearance. Its chief purpose is to provide comfort and protection for the passengers.

The body section includes the passenger compartment, trunk, bumpers, fenders, radiator grille, hood, interior trim, glass, and paint. A wide variety of body styles, such as two-door and four-door sedans or hard tops, convertibles and station wagons, are available for each chassis model. Various types of interior and exterior trim packages are also available to transform any body style from a plain austerity model to a glamorous show piece of luxury and splendour. Automobile manufacturers offer a greater selection of models by offering at least three types of trim packages with each model.

The interior of the body is covered with various types of upholstering materials such as cloth, vinyl, and leatherette. Protective padding, placed under the upholstery of the dashboard, roof, and on the seat springs, adds to the comfort and safety of the passengers and driver.

Safety glass must be used for all windshields and windows of the vehicle. Safety glass, when broken, does not shatter into sharp splinters. Instead, it has a tendency to crumble into small rectangular shapes.

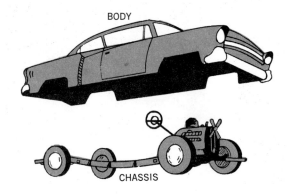

Fig. 1-4   Sections of an Automobile

Windshields are extremely strong when struck from the outside of the vehicle, but will crumble when hit by a moderate blow from the inside. This feature helps reduce injury to the passengers should they be thrown against the windshield by a sudden stop.

Many new passenger safety devices are now incorporated in body construction. Seat belts, breakaway ash trays, concealed interior door and window handles, padded dash and sun visors, and concealed control knobs are now required by law.

The exterior of the body is protected from rusting and weathering by being either dipped or sprayed with rust inhibitors, then sprayed with several coats of enamel or acrilic paint. Bright metal parts are protected by chromium plating or anodizing.

Repairs to the body of a vehicle are the job of the *Automobile Body Repair Mechanic*.

1-5 THE CHASSIS

The chassis is a complete operating unit which can be driven under its own power. It does not include the body parts.

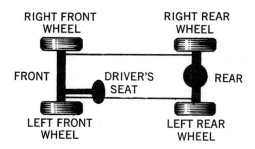

Fig. 1-5   Chassis and Wheel Location

The right and left sides and the front and rear of a chassis are determined from the driver's seat. The right front wheel, for example, is in front of the driver and to his right.

The chassis can be divided into four sections as illustrated in Figure 1-5.

Repairs to the mechanical parts of the chassis are performed by the *Motor Mechanic*, although he will also be called upon to do minor repairs to the body. The modern motor mechanic can specialize in any one of the subsections of the chassis.

1-6 BODY AND CHASSIS CONSTRUCTION

There are two methods of body and chassis construction; the separate body and chassis method, and unibody construction.

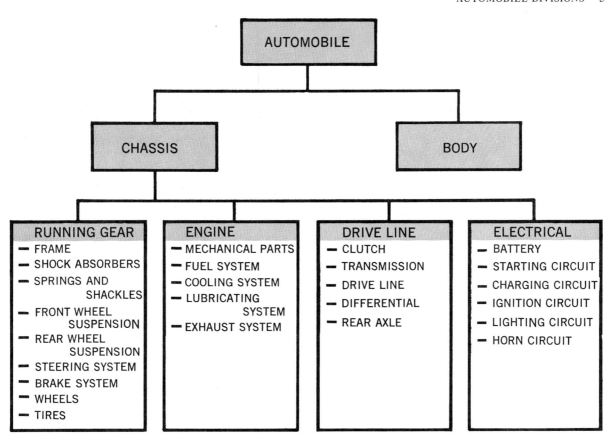

Fig. 1-6 Divisions of the Automobile

In the separate body and chassis construction, the body is held to the frame of the chassis by means of a number of body bolts, passing through the sill or base of the body and the upper part of the frame. To prevent squeaks and rattles, pads of anti-squeak or vibration materials, such as rubber, are placed between the body and the frame where each body bolt is located.

In the unibody construction, the body and the frame of the chassis are combined, thus eliminating the mounting squeaks and rattles.

1-7 CHASSIS MEASUREMENTS

In order to make comparisons between different makes and models of automobiles as to their size, riding qualities, and handling ease, definite areas of measurement have been established. The measurements used are called wheel base, wheel tread, and road clearance.

Wheel Base. The wheel base is the distance in inches between the centre of the rear wheel and the centre of the front wheel on the same side of

the automobile. The front wheels must be in the straight-ahead position. Vehicles with longer wheel bases usually have better riding qualities, whereas those with shorter wheel bases are easier to park

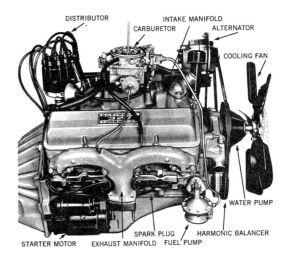

Courtesy of General Motors

Fig. 1-7 Automobile Engine

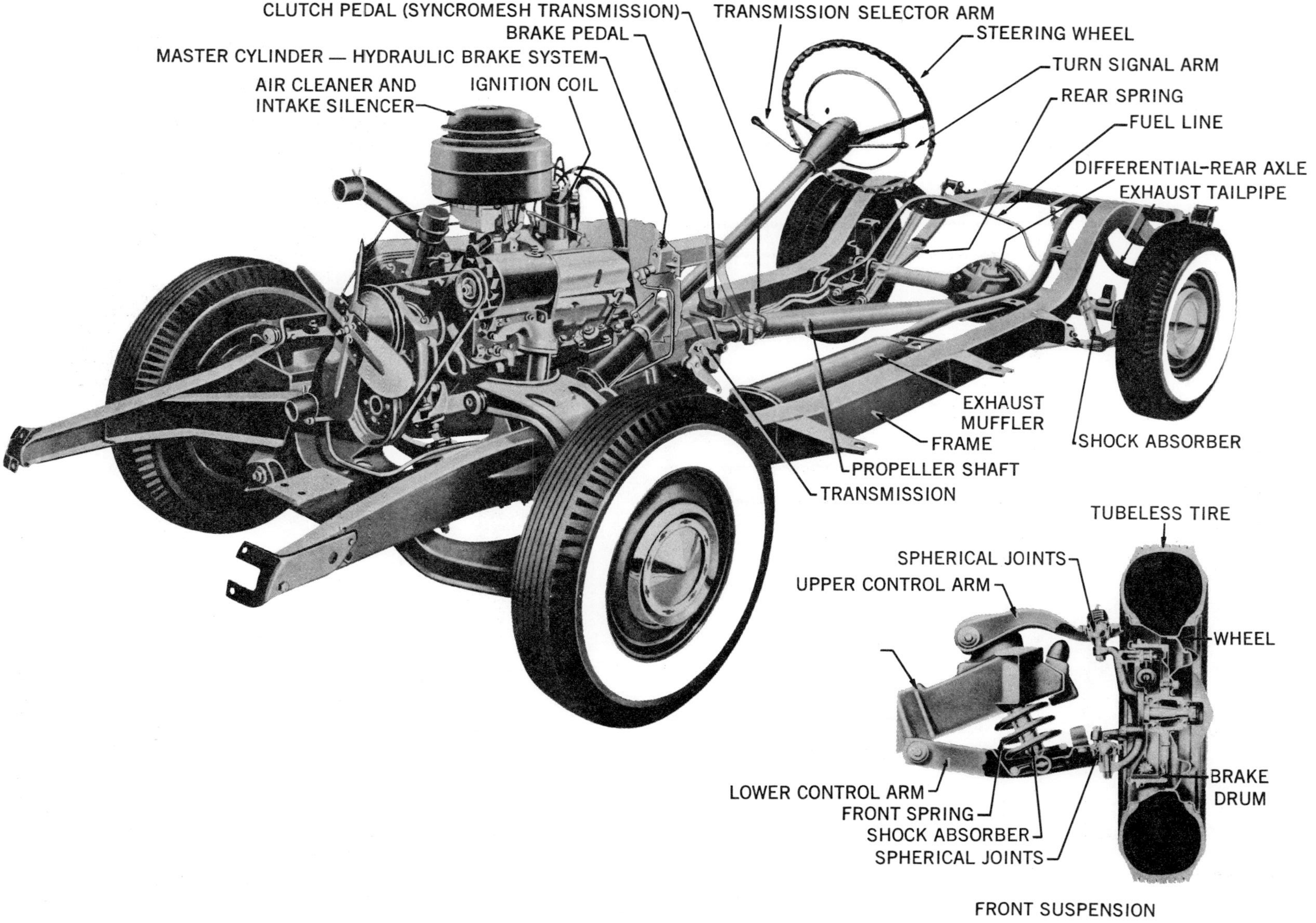

CLUTCH PEDAL (SYNCROMESH TRANSMISSION)

TRANSMISSION SELECTOR ARM

STEERING WHEEL

TURN SIGNAL ARM

REAR SPRING

FUEL LINE

DIFFERENTIAL–REAR AXLE

EXHAUST TAILPIPE

SHOCK ABSORBER

EXHAUST

MUFFLER

FRAME

PROPELLER SHAFT

TRANSMISSION

BRAKE PEDAL

MASTER CYLINDER — HYDRAULIC BRAKE SYSTEM

IGNITION COIL

AIR CLEANER AND
INTAKE SILENCER

TUBELESS TIRE

WHEEL

BRAKE
DRUM

SPHERICAL JOINTS

UPPER CONTROL ARM

LOWER CONTROL ARM

FRONT SPRING

SHOCK ABSORBER

SPHERICAL JOINTS

FRONT SUSPENSION

Courtesy of General Motors

Fig. 1-8   *Automobile Chassis*

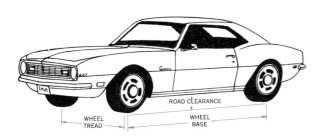

Fig. 1-9   Chassis Measurements

or manoeuvre. The wheel base measurements may vary between 80" and 130".

Wheel Tread. The wheel tread is the distance in inches between the centre of the left tire and the centre of the right tire on either the front or rear axle of the automobile. The wheel-tread measurement indicates the width of the automobile. It is a general rule that the longer the wheel base, the wider the tread.

Road Clearance. Road clearance is the distance in inches from the lowest part of the automobile to the road. The lowest part of an automobile is usually the differential housing.

The overall length and width of a motor vehicle is governed by the body design rather than wheel base and wheel-tread measurements.

REVIEW QUESTIONS

1. Name three early manufacturers of automobiles and state the date of their first vehicle.
2. Name and give one advantage and one disadvantage of three types of automobiles manufactured around the turn of the century.
3. Why was the local blacksmith also the local auto repairer?
4. How were mechanics trained in the period (a) 1919-1930, (b) 1930 to today?
5. Compare the working conditions of the early automotive mechanic to today's service man.
6. State the two basic categories of automotive service work.
7. State the requirements of a good automotive mechanic.
8. List the small details which, if overlooked, can result in poor workmanship.
9. Name the two basic divisions of an automobile and state the purpose of each.
10. Name the two classifications of automotive repair mechanics and the areas in which one of these may specialize.
11. What is a chassis?
12. List all of the parts on the chassis and engine diagrams Figs. 1-7 and 1-8 according to the chassis classification in which they belong.
13. How do you determine which is the right front wheel?
14. Name the two methods of body and chassis construction and state the difference between them.
15. State the major chassis measurements and explain how each is obtained.
16. What are the advantages of (a) a long-wheel base (b) a short-wheel base?

Chapter 2
SHOP PRACTICE

This chapter describes the common hand tools, fastenings, bearings, gaskets, and safety practices that are used in the servicing and repair of the modern automobile.

2-1 USE OF TOOLS

Many kinds, types, and sizes of tools are used in automobile work. The progressive and efficient

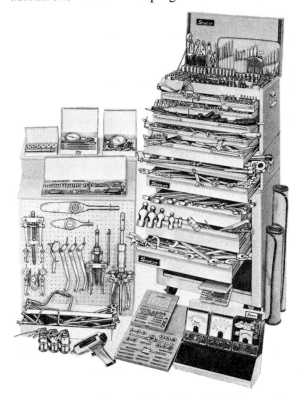

Snap-on Tools of Canada Ltd., Toronto, Ont.

Fig. 2-1   Typical Mechanic's Tool Set

mechanic and engineer learns to use them intelligently. Using the proper tool in the correct way is the first and most important step towards doing successful work. Use each tool for the job for which it is intended. Select the right kind and size of tool for each operation. Do not abuse tools.

2-2 HAND TOOLS

Hand tools are the tools owned by the mechanic. They include wrenches of various types and assorted pliers, screwdrivers, punches, chisels, files, gauges, and hammers.

2-3 WRENCHES AND ACCESSORIES

There are many types of wrenches available (Figs. 2-2 and 2-3), such as sockets and handles, open end, combination, and tappet. Each type has a special use. The mechanic should always make sure that the wrench fits the bolt head or nut exactly, thereby preventing injury to himself or damage to the nut or bolt head.

A pull on a wrench is preferable to a push, as pulling lessens the possibility of a wrench slipping and causing injury.

The pressure applied to a wrench used to tighten a nut or bolt increases in direct proportion as the diameter of the bolt increases. Learn to judge the amount of pressure required for each size of bolt. The wrench-handle leverage is generally 12″ for every 1″ of socket size.

Socket Wrench. The socket and handle wrench is the most efficient type and should be used in preference to other wrenches wherever possible. *Sockets* are cylindrical in shape and have a square opening at one end for the driving handles and either a single or double hexagonal opening at the other end. Sockets are made with either single or double hexagonal positions, are available in standard or deep lengths, and can be used interchangeably with a variety of handles. The opening in a socket is designed to fit snugly over the hexagonal shape of a bolt head or nut. The possibility of the socket slipping off the bolt head or nut is very small and injury to the mechanic is, therefore, unlikely.

Sockets and handles are available in four different sizes of drives:

(a) The ¼″ drive or Midget drive for small light work
(b) The ⅜″ drive or Ferret drive for loosening and tightening nuts, bolts or cap screws up to ⅜″ diameter

9

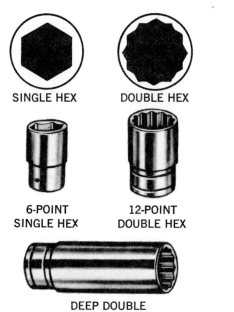

SINGLE HEX   DOUBLE HEX

6-POINT SINGLE HEX   12-POINT DOUBLE HEX

DEEP DOUBLE

Snap-on Tools of Canada Ltd., Toronto, Ont.

Fig. 2-2   Sockets

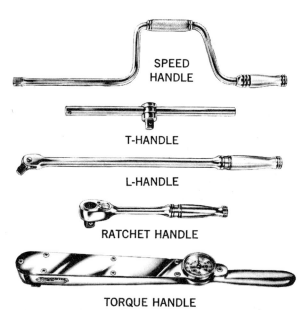

SPEED HANDLE

T-HANDLE

L-HANDLE

RATCHET HANDLE

TORQUE HANDLE

Snap-on Tools of Canada, Ltd., Toronto, Ontario

Fig. 2-3   Socket-Wrench Handles

(c) The ½″ drive or Standard drive for loosening and tightening nuts, bolts or cap screws ⅜″ to ⁹⁄₁₆″ diameter

(d) The ¾″ drive or Heavy-Duty drive for nuts, bolts or cap screws larger than ⁹⁄₁₆″ diameter

Socket-Wrench Handles. Sockets are provided with various types of handles which serve different purposes.

The *speed handle* is in the shape of a crank or a carpenter's brace. It is a fast handle but has not sufficient leverage for large nuts and bolts. The speed handle is recommended, therefore, for use on sockets ⅝″ or smaller.

The *T-handle* is also a fast handle, but it too has little leverage. It is also used on sockets ⅝″ and smaller.

The *L-handle, flex-handle* or *nut spinner* is used to tighten bolts or nuts when the socket is larger than ⅝″. It has greater leverage than the above two, but its operation is very slow.

The *rachet handle* is the same as the *L-handle*, except that it has a built-in ratchet, a device that permits the socket to rotate in one direction only, yet allows the handle to turn in the opposite direction. As a result, it is much faster than the L-handle.

The *torque handle* is also similar to the L-handle. It has a measuring device that indicates, in pound-feet, the amount of torque (twist) put on the fastening. A *pound-foot* is a force of one pound

applied to the wrench handle one foot from the socket.

Socket Accessories. *Extensions* are placed between the sockets and the handle to facilitate more convenient operation of the handle when the socket is in a confined area. Rigid extensions are available in various lengths from 2″ to 24″ in all four sizes of drivers. Flexible extensions are available in ¼″ and ⅜″ drivers to assist in reaching awkwardly placed nuts or cap screws. They are not intended for breaking loose or final tightening of nuts, bolts or cap screws.

Universal joints are placed between the socket and the handle when the handle must be used at an angle to the socket. Flex sockets, a combination of

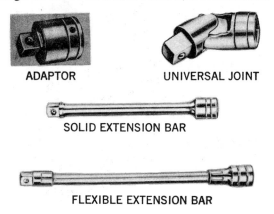

ADAPTOR   UNIVERSAL JOINT

SOLID EXTENSION BAR

FLEXIBLE EXTENSION BAR

Snap-on Tools of Canada, Ltd., Toronto, Ont.

Fig. 2-4   Socket-Wrench Accessories

a socket and universal joint, are also available for this purpose

Adaptors are used when it is necessary to join a socket of one size drive with a handle of a different size drive.

Open-End Wrench. An open-end wrench is not as convenient to use as a socket wrench and is used when a socket wrench cannot be placed over the bolt or nut. The open-end wrench has a U-shaped opening at each end. This opening is machined to specific size to fit a bolt head or nut and the opening is usually at an angle of 15° to the body of the wrench. This angle assists the working of the wrench in close quarters. Turning the wrench over so that the other face is down will enable the wrench to fit the next two flats of the hexagon-shaped nut, bolt or cap screw head, even though the swing of the wrench may be limited to 30°.

Be sure to select the proper size of wrench in order to avoid spreading the wrench sides or damaging the bolt, cap screw or nut.

Tappet Wrench. A tappet wrench is similar in appearance to an open-end wrench, except that it is longer and thinner. It is used for adjusting valve tappets and must not be used for any other purpose.

Box Socket Wrench. The box socket wrench has a socket on each end and is used under similar conditions to the open-end wrench. It is safer than the open-end wrench and is used in places where a socket wrench cannot be used easily.

Combination Wrench. This is a combination of two types of wrenches. It has an open-end wrench on one end and a box socket wrench of the same size on the other end.

Adjustable Wrench. Adjustable wrenches are equipped with movable, smooth jaws. They should

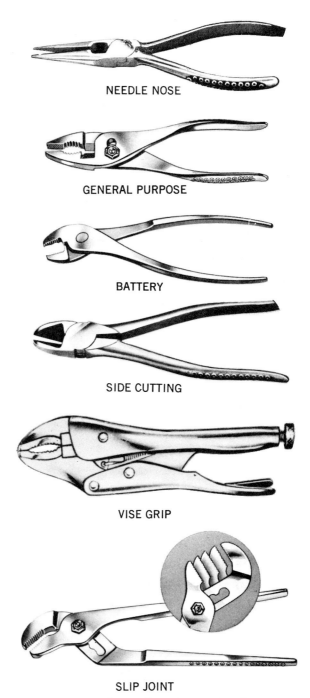

NEEDLE NOSE

GENERAL PURPOSE

BATTERY

SIDE CUTTING

VISE GRIP

SLIP JOINT

Snap-on Tools of Canada Ltd., Toronto, Ont.

Fig. 2-6 Pliers

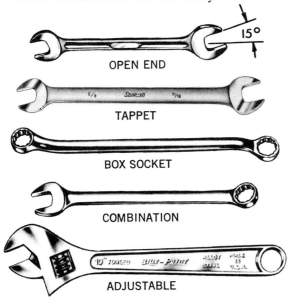

OPEN END

TAPPET

BOX SOCKET

COMBINATION

ADJUSTABLE

Snap-on Tools of Canada Ltd., Toronto, Ont.

Fig. 2-5 Wrenches

be used only when no other wrench will fit because the jaws do not form as snug a fit as those of other wrenches.

2-4 PLIERS

Side-cutting or diagonal pliers—have hardened steel cutting jaws set at an angle and are used for cutting electrical wire, sheet metal, and for pulling out cotter pins.

Combination or slip-joint pliers—are made with a slip joint at the hinge pin. This permits the jaws to close tightly in one position or to open wider in the other. The pliers are used for gripping round stock, but in so doing, they leave teeth marks. Therefore, they should not be used on finished surfaces, which may be spoiled by such marks. Never use pliers on nut or bolt heads.

Needle-nose pliers—are used for fine work on instruments, radios, and other electrical equipment.

Vise-grip pliers—are special lever-action, adjustable pliers that can be clamped tightly onto an unfinished surface. Vise-grip pliers may be substituted for other pliers, a vise clamp or pipe wrench, but should not be used to loosen or tighten nuts, bolts or cap screws.

Battery pliers—have specially shaped jaws designed to loosen or tighten battery terminal nuts that have been corroded by acid action.

Special pliers—are designed to do a specific job such as removing brake retraction springs, snap rings, wire-type hose clamps, etc. When used properly, these pliers make the job easier and safer.

Snap-on Tools of Canada Ltd., Toronto, Ont.
Fig. 2-7   Special Pliers

2-5 SCREWDRIVERS

A screwdriver is designed to turn screws. If the blade is used for prying or chiseling, the stem will bend or the blade will be damaged.

Screwdrivers are available in various sizes and lengths. The blade width and thickness are proportional; the wider the blade the thicker the blade.

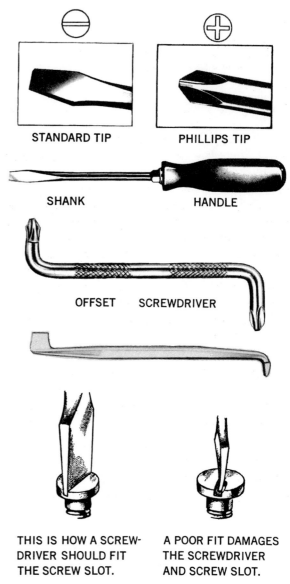

STANDARD TIP   PHILLIPS TIP

SHANK   HANDLE

OFFSET   SCREWDRIVER

THIS IS HOW A SCREW-DRIVER SHOULD FIT THE SCREW SLOT.   A POOR FIT DAMAGES THE SCREWDRIVER AND SCREW SLOT.

Snap-on Tools of Canada, Ltd., Toronto, Ontario
Fig. 2-8   Screwdrivers

When a standard type screwdriver is required, the blade width should be approximately the same as the diameter of the screw head. When a Phillips screwdriver is required, the cross should be the size of the slot in the screw head. The length chosen should be sufficient to enable the screwdriver to be turned conveniently on the centre line of the screw.

To prevent damage to screw heads, always choose the proper size screwdriver, maintain proper alignment between the screwdriver and the screw, and be sure the end of the standard screwdriver blade sits flat and square in the screw slot.

Standard screwdrivers—have flat blades that fit into the slots in the screw head. The shank may be round or square and the handle made of wood or plastic. The square-shank type is designed so that a wrench may be used to assist in turning the screwdriver.

The width of the blade and the shank length are usually given when specifying the screwdriver size. Generally speaking, the longer the shank length, the wider the blade, although many special long- or short-shank narrow-bladed screwdrivers are available for special purposes.

Phillips screw heads—have two slots that cross at the centre and are used to attach body and trim parts. The cross-type slots prevent the screwdriver from slipping out of the slots and scratching or damaging the finished surface.

Phillips screwdrivers are available in four sizes numbered from 1 to 4, number 1 being the smallest, number 4 the largest. The diameter of the screw determines the depth, width and thickness of the cross; the larger the diameter, the larger the cross. Shank lengths of from 2″ to 12″ are available.

Offset screwdrivers—are designed for use in limited space. They are available with either straight or Phillips-shaped ends. In an offset screwdriver the blades are at right angles to the shank and are set 90° from each other. The arrangement of the blades permits continuous turning of the screw when space is limited.

2-6 OTHER USEFUL TOOLS

Hammers. A steel *ball peen hammer* is used for striking a punch or cold chisel. A *lead* or *plastic hammer* is used to strike soft metal parts of finished surfaces which would be damaged by a steel hammer. A *rubber-tipped hammer* is frequently used in tire work for replacing hub caps. (See Fig. 2-9.) Always grip any hammer handle near the end.

Punches. Three punches are commonly used in the automotive trade. (See Fig. 2-10.)

The *starter* punch is tapered and is used to free a pin or shaft.

The *drift* or *pin* punch is used to drive out a shaft or pin. Drift punches come in various sizes, such as ¼″, ⁵⁄₁₆″, and ⅜″.

The *centre* punch is a sharp steel punch used for marking or making holes to start drills.

Cold chisels. The cold chisel is used to cut rivets and bolts or sheet metal. It should never be used

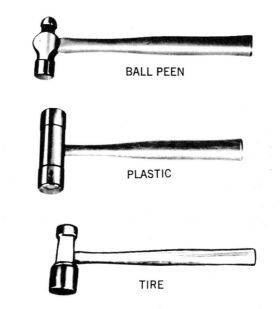

BALL PEEN

PLASTIC

TIRE

Snap-on Tools of Canada, Ltd., Toronto, Ontario

Fig. 2-9   Hammers

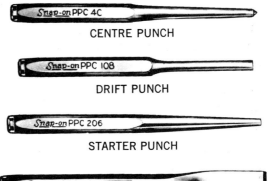

CENTRE PUNCH

DRIFT PUNCH

STARTER PUNCH

FLAT CHISEL

Snap-on Tools of Canada, Ltd., Toronto, Ontario

Fig. 2-10   Punches and Chisels

in place of a drift punch. Cold chisels are available in various shapes and sizes to suit specific jobs.

Files. Files are available in various types of cut, degrees of coarseness, shapes and sizes.

The degree of cut and coarseness is determined by the number of rows of teeth angled across the face of the file. They may have single rows (single cut) or two rows criss crossing (double cut). The spacing and size of the teeth determines the coarseness of the file; the larger the teeth and the greater the spacing, the coarser the file. Four degrees of coarseness are available; coarse, bastard, second cut, and fine.

Files are available in *flat, round, half-round,*

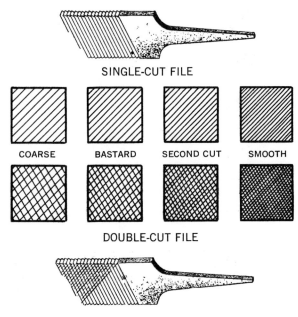

SINGLE-CUT FILE

COARSE   BASTARD   SECOND CUT   SMOOTH

DOUBLE-CUT FILE

Courtesy of General Motors

Fig. 2-11   Files

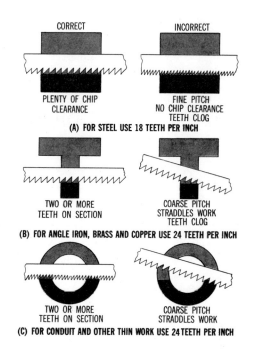

CORRECT   INCORRECT

PLENTY OF CHIP CLEARANCE   FINE PITCH NO CHIP CLEARANCE TEETH CLOG

(A) FOR STEEL USE 18 TEETH PER INCH

TWO OR MORE TEETH ON SECTION   COARSE PITCH STRADDLES WORK TEETH CLOG

(B) FOR ANGLE IRON, BRASS AND COPPER USE 24 TEETH PER INCH

TWO OR MORE TEETH ON SECTION   COARSE PITCH STRADDLES WORK

(C) FOR CONDUIT AND OTHER THIN WORK USE 24 TEETH PER INCH

(D) HACKSAW

The L. S. Starrett Company

Fig. 2-12   Hacksaw Blade Spacing

square, and *three-cornered* shapes. A file should be fitted with a tight-fitting handle to prevent injury to the user and should be cleaned frequently with a file card to preserve the life of the file and prevent scratching of the work.

Coarse files are used when a considerable amount of metal is to be removed. A fine file is used to smooth a surface.

Hacksaws. A hacksaw consists of a frame and a blade which is placed in the frame with the teeth pointing forward. See Fig. 2-12. A thumbscrew is tightened sufficiently to keep tension on the blade. When using the hacksaw, take great care not to twist the blade, as this would cause it to break. A slight pressure should be applied on the forward stroke, and released with the return stroke. Operate with a slow, steady motion, passing the entire length of the blade over the work.

Blades with 14, 18, 24 and 32 teeth-per-inch are available. The selection of the right type of blade depends upon the type and shape of the material to

be cut. The 18-tooth blade is used by automotive mechanics to cut most materials. The 32-tooth blade is used to cut thin metal and tubing.

Cleaning Tools. The cleaning of automotive parts which require repairs is an important part of automotive service work. Cleaning tools include a variety of different brushes and scrapers. The brushes include bristle brushes for use with suitable solvents, hand and power driven wire brushes. The power wire brushes are usually driven by a ¼″ electric drill. *CAUTION*: Always wear safety eye protection when using power grinders or wire wheels.

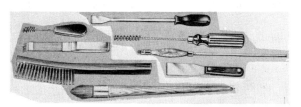

Snap-on Tools of Canada Ltd., Toronto, Ont.

Fig. 2-13   Cleaning Tools

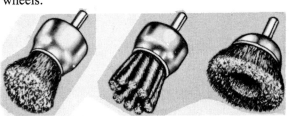

Snap-on Tools of Canada Ltd., Toronto, Ont.

Fig. 2-14   Carbon Brushes

The scrapers include both the solid blade and flexible blade types. Each is designed for certain cleaning jobs.

2-7 SPECIAL TOOLS AND POWER TOOLS

Valve-Spring Compressors. Valve-spring compressors or lifters are used to compress the valve spring to facilitate the removal of the valve retainer lock or keeper from the valve stem. A C-type valve-spring compressor is used when the valves are located in the cylinder head. A standard expansion-type compressor is used when the valves are in the block.

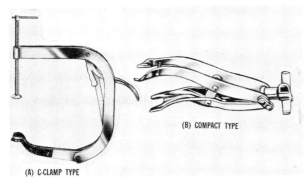

(B) COMPACT TYPE

(A) C-CLAMP TYPE

Snap-on Tools of Canada Ltd., Toronto, Ont.

Fig. 2-15   Valve-Spring Compressors

Piston-Ring Compressors. Piston-ring compressors are placed around the piston, covering the rings. As the compressor is tightened, it compresses the piston rings into their grooves on the piston. Then the piston and rod assembly is installed into the cylinder.

Snap-on Tools of Canada Ltd., Toronto, Ont.

Fig. 2-16   Piston Ring Compressor

Taps and Dies. Taps and dies are used for cutting threads. The tap is used to cut inside threads, such as threading a hole in a casting, while dies are used

TAPER

PLUG

BOTTOMING

TAPS   DIE

Fig. 2-17   Taps and Dies

to cut outside threads on pieces of round stock. Taps are available in various types. The *taper tap* is used for starting a thread, the *plug tap* is used for threading near the bottom of a hole after a taper tap has been used, and a *bottoming tap* is used to thread to the bottom of a blind hole. Both taps and dies are available in all thread types and sizes. Special handles are used to hold both taps and dies during the threading operation.

Pullers. Pullers come in a variety of types and sizes and are used to remove wheels, gears, and bearings from shafts, or to remove shafts from housings. Each pulling operation differs from the other and care must be exercised to prevent damage to the parts.

(A) PULLER   (B) SLIDE HAMMER PULLER

Snap-on Tools of Canada Ltd., Toronto, Ont.

Fig. 2-18   Pullers

Stud Removers. Special stud removers lock on the unthreaded portion of the stud to facilitate their removal or installation. If the special tool is not available, removal or installation of the stud can be accomplished by locking two nuts together similar to a locknut. Turn the lower nut with a wrench to remove the stud, turn the upper nut to install the stud.

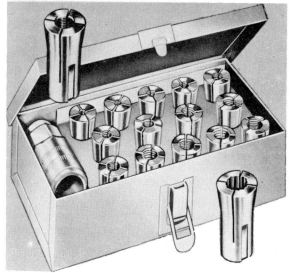

MULTISPLINE TYPE

TAPER-BIT TYPE

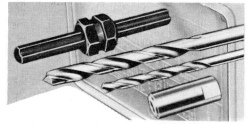

(A) FOR SERVICEABLE STUDS

(B) FOR BROKEN STUDS OR CAP SCREWS

Fig. 2-19   Stud Removers and Resetters

Snap-on Tools of Canada Ltd., Toronto, Ont.

Occasionally studs or cap screws will break leaving the threaded portion in the casting. If the break is above the surface, the sides of the stud can be filed flat and a wrench used for removal, or a slot may be cut in the top and a screwdriver used. When the break is below the surface, a type of screw or stud extractor may be used. Many types of extractors are available; two common types are the "Ezy-Out," and the fluted type. Both are used in a similar

manner; centre punch the broken part, drill a hole of the correct size, insert the extractor in the hole and turn it in a clockwise direction. The extractor binds in the hole in the stud. To remove the stud, turn the extractor counterclockwise.

Vises. Vises are used to hold parts firmly while they are being worked on. Many types of vises are available; some are designed for special purposes, such as the piston vise. Standard vises have hard

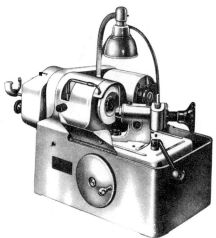

(A) POST HOIST

(B) HYDRAULIC JACK

(C) VALVE REFACER

(A) Canadian Curtiss-Wright, Limited
(B) Hein-Werner Corporation
(C) Snap-on Tools of Canada Ltd., Toronto, Ont.

Fig. 2-21   Power Tools

steel jaws which can damage finished surfaces. To prevent damage, soft lead or copper inserts are placed between the jaws of the vise and the part before the vise is tightened.

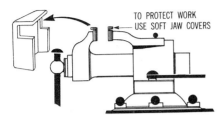

Fig. 2-20 Automotive Vise

Power Tools. These are tools such as: a valve refacing machine, valve-seat refacing machine, honing machine, electric drills, hydraulic jacks, and hoisting equipment. Since most of this equipment is highly specialized, no one should operate any power tool without first receiving complete instruction, or until after very careful reading of the operating instructions.

2-8 MEASURING INSTRUMENTS

Measuring is a basic rudiment of automotive service work. Various measuring devices are used depending upon the degree of accuracy required. The scale or ruler, inside and outside caliper, feeler gauge, the micrometer, and the dial gauge are examples.

Feeler Gauges. There are two common types of feeler gauges, the *flat-strip* type and the *wire* type.

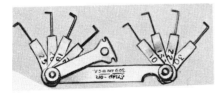

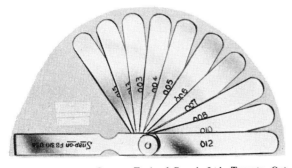

Snap-on Tools of Canada Ltd., Toronto, Ont.

Fig. 2-22 Feeler Gauges

Both are made of hardened steel and are accurately ground or rolled to a given size. They vary in thickness ranging from .001″ to .050″ and are usually supplied in sets.

The go, or no-go, gauge consists of two accurately sized areas. One area is of the minimum allowable size, the other of the maximum. For example: if a hole was to be of a specified size of 1″ plus or minus .001″ then one end of the gauge would measure .999″ and should pass through the hole while the other end would measure 1.0001″ and should not enter the hole.

Specified measurement gauges are designed to measure or set distances between irregular surfaces. The carburetor-float setting gauge is one example.

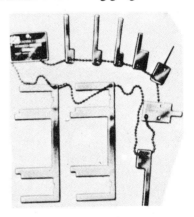

Courtesy of General Motors

Fig. 2-23 Specified Measurement Gauges

Scale or Ruler. The scale or ruler is used to measure in-line distances when a high degree of accuracy is not required. Scales may be graduated in divisions as small as $\frac{1}{64}$″ although $\frac{1}{16}$″ is the most common.

Calipers. To measure circular distances, calipers are used. The outside caliper is adjusted so that it slips just over the diameter of the shaft, the inside caliper so that it slips into the hole. The distance between the legs of the caliper is then measured with a scale. Calipers are used only when a *low degree of accuracy* is required.

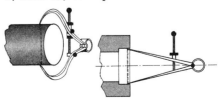

OUTSIDE CALIPER   INSIDE CALIPER

Fig. 2-24 Calipers

Micrometers. Inside and outside micrometers are precision measuring instruments and are used when a *high degree of accuracy* is required. The commonest micrometers are graduated to read in thousandths of an inch.

The accuracy of a micrometer or "mike" is wholly dependent upon the accuracy of a 40 thread per inch thread cut between the barrel and spindle and the thimble assembly. Since $\frac{1}{40}$ of an inch equals 25 thousands (.025) of an inch, therefore one revolution of the spindle and thimble assembly will move the assembly .025″ along the barrel. When one revolution of the thimble equals 25 thousandths of an inch movement along the barrel, the circumference of the thimble is divided into equal spaces numbered 0 to 24, each space being equivalent to one-thousandth (.001) of an inch.

A lateral line 1″ in length and divided into 40 equal parts, each part representing .025″, is scribed along the length of the barrel. Starting from 0, each fourth line is numbered consecutively 1, 2, 3 to 9, each number representing one hundred-thousandths (.100) of an inch.

When the spindle is against the anvil the zero line of the thimble is aligned with the zero mark on the barrel. Rotating the thimble until there is a clearance of .005″ between the anvil and the spindle will bring the 5 mark on the thimble opposite the lateral line and represent .005″. One complete revolution of the thimble will uncover the first mark on the barrel and represent .025″. Four revolutions of the thimble will uncover the number 1 on the barrel and represent .100″.

Note the number of divisions visible beyond the last figure and multiply this number by .025″. Next note the line of the thimble which is adjacent to the lateral line on the barrel; since each thimble line represents .001″ this line indicates thousandths of an inch.

Example:

Last figure visible on the barrel 5 =	$5 \times .100 = .500″$
Number of divisions visible beyond 5 is 3 =	$3 \times .025 = .075″$
Thimble line adjacent to the lateral line of the barrel is 12 =	$12 \times .001 = .012″$
Total reading	$12 \times .001 = .587″$

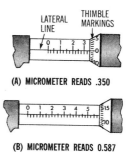

(A) MICROMETER READS .350

(B) MICROMETER READS 0.587

Fig. 2-26   Reading a Micrometer

Inside micrometers, although different in construction, are read in the same manner as outside micrometers. Many pieces of automotive machine equipment, such as valve refacers, hones and boring equipment, are equipped with micrometer-type adjustments and each is read in a similar fashion.

A micrometer is a delicate instrument and should be handled with care. A micrometer should be

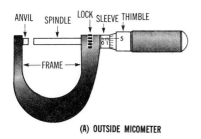

(A) OUTSIDE MICOMETER

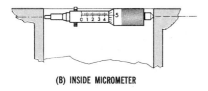

(B) INSIDE MICROMETER

Fig. 2-25   Micrometers

To read a micrometer, note the last figure visible on the barrel scale; each figure represents .100″.

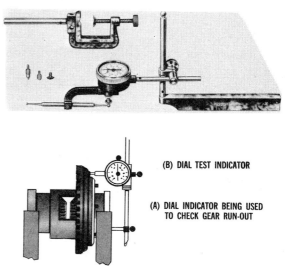

(B) DIAL TEST INDICATOR

(A) DIAL INDICATOR BEING USED TO CHECK GEAR RUN-OUT

The L. S. Starrett Co.

Fig. 2-27   Dial Indicators

tightened only enough to cause a slight drag as it is removed from the part being measured. NEVER use a micrometer as a clamp.

Dial Indicators. Dial indicators are accurate precision instruments measuring in thousandths of an inch. They utilize a dial face and needle to register measurements. Dial indicators are used to measure gear lash, the amount of run out or wobble of a gear, and the trueness of a shaft.

Special dial indicators, such as an Ames gauge, are provided with the adapters necessary to measure engine cylinders for truth.

2-9 CARE OF TOOLS AND EQUIPMENT

2-10 HAND TOOLS

Hand tools should be clean, because greasy or oily tools are difficult to hold and use. They should be wiped clean and returned to their proper storage place immediately after use. Adoption of this policy will reduce the loss of tools and speed up work.

A good mechanic keeps his tools in good repair. Punches and chisels should have mushroom ends removed as soon as they appear; chisels and drills should always be sharp; screwdrivers correctly ground; hammers inspected before use to ensure that the head is not loose nor the handle cracked. Worn or loose ratchets should not be used, as personal injury could result.

2-11 SHOP EQUIPMENT

Shop equipment and special tools should be cleaned and returned to their proper storage place immediately after use, as other mechanics may require them. Power equipment should be lubricated and serviced as required, and electrical cords and plugs should be inspected and serviced frequently.

As a mechanic is judged by his tools, a repair shop is judged by its cleanliness and equipment.

A cluttered, dirty shop is neither a pleasant nor safe place to work, nor does it appeal to clients. Customers prefer to do business with an organization that has a clean, neat appearance and employs mechanics who show proper respect and care for tools and shop equipment.

Develop a sense of responsibility toward the tools and equipment that you own or use. This is one of the important steps in becoming a successful mechanic.

2-12 AUTOMOTIVE FASTENINGS

An automobile is made up of a number of units and parts, securely fastened together in such a manner that each unit or part may be removed for repairs or inspection.

Threads. Most of the fastenings that join the mechanical parts of an automobile together are threaded. Threads are classified by the number of threads per inch (pitch), thread series (the shape and number of threads per inch), and by class (quality of finish and fit). Two main types are used for automotive work; the *Unified National Fine* (unf) and the *Unified National Coarse* (unc).

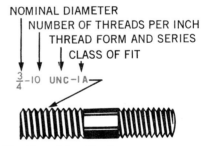

Fig. 2-29   Thread Specifications

The Unified National Fine thread is the more popular because it does not tend to work loose with vibration. It makes a stronger bolt because of the shallowness of the thread. The other type used is the Unified National Coarse thread which, because of its depth, is not easily stripped or cross-threaded.

GROUND RIGHT   GROUND WRONG

(A) SCREWDRIVERS

HAMMER HEAD IS WEDGED ON HANDLE IN BOTH DIRECTIONS

(B) HAMMERS

BEFORE AND AFTER DRESSING

(C) CHISELS

Fig. 2-28   Care of Hand Tools

The Unified National Coarse thread is always used in cast iron and aluminum, where a deep thread is necessary to take hold (Fig. 2-29).

The addition of the term "Unified" to the terms National Coarse or National Fine threads is the outcome of meetings held by standardization committees of the United Kingdom, the United States, and Canada. Nuts and bolts of the Unified type, made in these countries, are interchangeable.

2-13 SCREWS

Cap Screws. The cap screw is similar to a bolt, but it does not require a nut. It is screwed, instead, into a threaded hole. Either the Unified National Coarse or Unified National Fine thread is used, depending on the type of material into which it is to be screwed.

Machine Screws. Machine screws come in a variety of screw slot and head designs and are available in sizes ranging up to 3⁄8″ in diameter. When the stem diameter is less than 3⁄16″, it is designated by the wire size numbers 2, 4, 6, 8, 10, and 12. They are available in either coarse or fine threads. Identity is by number 10-32 (10 is the wire size, 32 is the number of threads per inch). Machine screws may be threaded into a threaded hole or used with a nut.

Sheet Metal and Self-Tapping Screws. These screws are case-hardened screws that cut or form a thread in metal, plastic, and other materials without pretapped holes. They permit rapid installation, since nuts are not required and access is required from only one side of the joint. Various head and screw-slot designs are available.

2-14 BOLTS

Several types of bolts with either square, round or hexagonal heads are used as fasteners. The hexagon head type is the one most commonly used in automotive work. The stem of the bolt is threaded to a sufficient length to enable a nut to tighten the parts sufficiently and complete the fastening.

Stove Bolts. Stove bolts have round heads with screwdriver slots. They are threaded the entire length of the stem, and are available only in the coarse thread series and in sizes of 3⁄16″, 1⁄4″, 5⁄16″, and 3⁄8″. The fastening is completed with a square or hexagon nut.

Studs. Studs are steel rods with threads at each end, usually a unf thread at one end and a unc thread at the other. The coarse end is screwed into a threaded hole in a casting, because the coarse thread holds better in cast iron; the other end passes through a hole in the part to be attached. A nut on the outside end completes the fastening.

Nuts. Several types of nuts are used in the automotive industry. The majority are hexagonal in shape. Some of the common types are plain, castle (castellated), slotted, and self-locking. Slotted and castle nuts have slotted tops, so that a cotter pin may be installed for locking purposes. There are several types of self-locking nuts. One type has the upper threads slightly distorted. When this nut is tightened, the sections are drawn together, creating friction and locking the nut in position. Another type of self-locking nut is called the interference type, which uses a fibre or soft metal insert near the top; as the nut is tightened new threads are cut in the insert, creating friction which holds the nut in place. A third type (which is illustrated) has

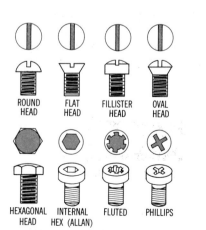

(A) MACHINE SCREWS AND STOVE BOLTS

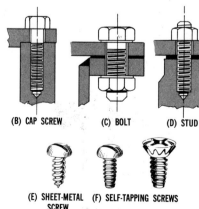

Fig. 2-30 Common Automotive Threaded Fasteners

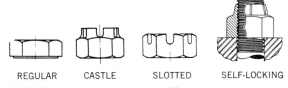

REGULAR   CASTLE   SLOTTED   SELF-LOCKING

Fig. 2-31   Common Automotive Nuts

thin vertical slots cut in the upper portion of the nut. This upper portion of the nut is smaller in diameter than the bolt. As a result the slotted portion presses tightly against the bolt, holding the nut in place.

NOTE: Self-locking nuts are not reusable.

Flat Washers. This type of washer is used under the head of a bolt, cap screw or nut, to protect the surface of the parts being joined. The flat washer also helps to distribute the pressure of the fastening over a larger area.

2-15 CAP-SCREW, BOLT, NUT, AND WRENCH SIZES

Bolt and cap-screw sizes are calculated by measuring the diameter of the stem and the length from under the head to the end of the stem (Figure 2-32). The nut size is the internal diameter of the thread. The thread in a nut of specific size will fit the thread on a bolt of the size named. For example, a ½″ bolt will measure ½″ in diameter over the thread, and a ½″ nut will have a ½″ threaded hole. A knowledge of the standard bolt head and nut sizes will greatly help the student in his selection of the proper wrench. The diameter of the head on bolts from ¼ to $\frac{7}{16}$ inch is $\frac{3}{16}$ inch greater than the bolt stem diameter; on bolts ½ to ¾ inch, the head is ¼ inch greater than the stem diameter. For example, a ¼″ bolt requires a $\frac{7}{16}$″ wrench, and a ½″ bolt requires a ¾″ wrench. The

nut sizes are the same as the bolt head sizes. The table below for nut, bolt, and wrench sizes should be memorized.

BOLT & NUT SIZE	WRENCH SIZE
¼″	$\frac{7}{16}$″
$\frac{5}{16}$″	½″
⅜″	$\frac{9}{16}$″
$\frac{7}{16}$″	⅝″
½″	¾″

2-16 OTHER FASTENERS

Set Screws. Set screws are used to hold collars and gears to shafts. A set screw has a pointed end; when the set screw is tightened this pointed end bites into the shaft, thereby holding the part to the shaft in its proper position.

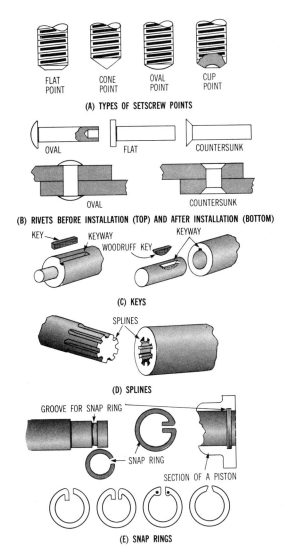

FLAT POINT   CONE POINT   OVAL POINT   CUP POINT

(A) TYPES OF SETSCREW POINTS

OVAL   FLAT   COUNTERSUNK

OVAL   COUNTERSUNK

(B) RIVETS BEFORE INSTALLATION (TOP) AND AFTER INSTALLATION (BOTTOM)

KEY   KEYWAY   KEYWAY   WOODRUFF KEY

(C) KEYS

SPLINES

(D) SPLINES

GROOVE FOR SNAP RING   SNAP RING   SECTION OF A PISTON

(E) SNAP RINGS

Fig. 2-33   Other Types of Fastenings

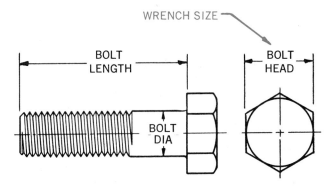

WRENCH SIZE

BOLT LENGTH   BOLT HEAD

BOLT DIA

Fig. 2-32   Bolt Measurements

Keys. When considerable torque or twist is to be transferred between a gear or pulley and its shaft, keys of various shapes are frequently used. The **half-moon, or woodruff, key** and the **rectangular, or Gibb, key** are most common types used in the automotive industry. The shaft is machined with a recess of the proper shape to receive the key and a corresponding groove is cut in the pulley or gear. When the parts are assembled the key transmits the drive, and frequently the fit is such that it also is used to hold the pulley or gear in its proper position.

Splines. When considerable torque is to be transmitted between a pulley or a gear and a shaft, and the pulley or gear must be free to slide along the shaft, external and internal splines are used. Splines resemble gears in appearance. The external splines cut on the shaft fit loosely into the internal splines of the gear or pulley, transmitting the torque, yet allowing back-and-forth movement along the length of the spline.

Snap-rings. When a shaft is free to rotate in a housing or a gear or pulley to rotate on a shaft, internal and external snap-rings are frequently used to prevent endwise movement of the shaft or gear. The external snap-ring fits into a groove in the shaft; its larger outside diameter holds the gear or shaft in position. It must be expanded with special snap-ring pliers during removal or replacement.

The internal snap-ring fits into a groove cut in the circumference of the hole in the housing. Its smaller inside diameter holds the shaft in position. To remove or replace this type, special snap-ring pliers are used to contract the ring. In some special applications, combination external-internal snap-rings are used. In these cases the snap-ring is contracted to place it in the groove of the hole. The groove in the hole is of a large enough diameter to permit expansion of the snap-ring so that the shaft may be installed. When the groove in the shaft is in line with the snap-ring, the snap-ring contracts and is wide enough to fit in both the groove in the shaft and the housing, thus holding the shaft in place.

2-17 LOCKING DEVICES

Locking devices are used to prevent bolts and nuts from working loose with vibration. Every bolt or nut should have a locking device on it to prevent possible accident. It has been said that the locking

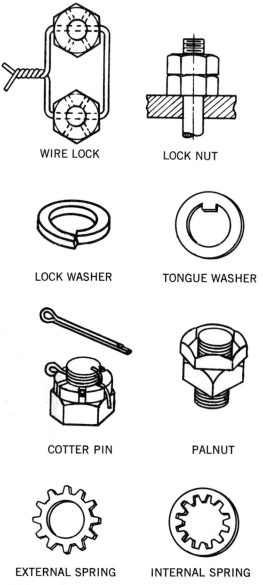

WIRE LOCK   LOCK NUT

LOCK WASHER   TONGUE WASHER

COTTER PIN   PALNUT

EXTERNAL SPRING   INTERNAL SPRING

Fig. 2-34   Locking Devices

device is the most important device in the automobile. (See Figure 2-34.)

The most commonly used locking devices are:

Cotter Pins. These are long, slender, split metal pins with rounded heads. They are placed through the slots in castellated nuts and through holes in bolts; the split ends are then bent apart. This type of lock is one of the best.

Lock Washers and Shakeproof Washers. Both types are of spring steel and have one or more offset ends. When the nut is tightened, the offset ends are drawn together, creating a great pressure under the nut and forming a tight lock.

Lock Nuts and Palnuts. When two nuts are drawn tightly against each other, a great pressure is exerted on the threads. This pressure prevents their loosening. The lock nut is a plain nut that is tightened against the nut already in place.

A palnut is a thin, steel, one-thread nut that is frequently used instead of a second plain nut. To lock properly, the palnut should be tightened until the flat side just touches the first nut, then tightened a half-turn more. Palnuts should not be reused.

Tongue Washers. These are flat washers with a small tongue-like projection on the inner edge. The tongue fits into a groove in the bolt or shaft and the washer is prevented from turning. This lock is used in places where the turning motion of a bearing might loosen the nut. For example, the front-wheel spindle has a tongue washer between the outer wheel bearing and the spindle nut.

Wire. Sometimes wire is placed through a bolt head when space does not permit the use of other locking devices. Wire may be placed through holes in two or more bolt heads, binding them together and making an adequate locking device.

2-18 BEARINGS

Every part of an automobile that moves with a rotary or sliding motion is supported in bearings, which reduce friction and wear, if lubricated properly.

Bearings are called upon to do three kinds of work: to take a *radial load*, a *thrust load*, or a *combination* of both. A radial load exerts pressure at right angles to a shaft. A thrust load exerts pressure parallel to or in the direction of the shaft (Fig. 2-35).

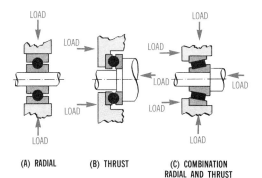

Fig. 2-35   *Bearing Loads*

2-19 PLAIN BEARINGS

A plain bearing is a bearing with no moving parts. It acts as a lining between a housing and a shaft and is made of metal which is softer than the shaft it supports. Alloys of lead and tin, called *babbitt*, or copper and tin, called *bronze*, are the two most common types of bearing materials. Since most bearing metal is soft and weak, it must be fused to a steel backing for strength. Plain bearings can be either made in one piece or split in two pieces for convenience of assembly. *Piston-pin bushings* and *camshaft bearings* are examples of one-piece plain bearings; *crankshaft main bearings* and *connecting-rod bearings* are examples of the split type. Plain bearings can be designed with flanges that will enable them to support a combination of both radial and thrust loads (Figure 2-36). At least one crankshaft main bearing is designed to support a combination of the radial load and the end thrust load of the crankshaft.

RADIAL   THRUST   COMBINATION   BUSHING

Fig. 2-36   *Plain Bearings*

2-20 ANTIFRICTION BEARINGS

There are five popular types of antifriction bearings, namely, the annular ball bearing, the ball-

ANNULAR
BALLBEARING

CUP-AND-CONE
BALLBEARING

CYLINDRICAL
ROLLER
BEARING

TAPERED
ROLLER BEARING

BALL THRUST
BEARING

Canadian SKF Company Limited

Fig. 2-37   *Antifriction Bearings*

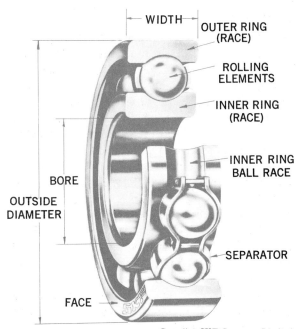

Fig. 2-38 Bearing Nomenclature

Canadian SKF Company Limited

Orange Roller Bearing Co., Inc.

Fig. 2-39 Needle Bearings

thrust bearing, the cup-and-cone ball bearing, the straight roller bearing, the tapered roller bearing, and the needle roller bearing.

Antifriction bearings consist of four principal parts; the *cone*, or inner race, which fits over the shaft or spindle; the *cup*, or outer race, which fits inside the wheel hub or other carrier; a series of *balls* or *rollers* which revolves between the cone and cup; and a *cage* or other device to keep the balls or rollers in position between the cup and cone (Fig. 2-38).

When *needle roller bearings* are used, the rollers may or may not be held by a cage, and the bore in the housing serves as the cup and the hardened shafts serves as the cone (Fig. 2-39).

In bearing design, several different methods are used to take care of the different kinds of load. One method uses a separate bearing for each; a second method uses annular ball bearings or straight roller bearings, equipping them with plain thrust washers to carry the thrust load; a third method uses tapered roller bearings or cup-and-cone bearings. The third type is most suitable and most efficient because it supports both kinds of load, takes up less room, and is adjustable.

There are three types of adjustable bearings, the split type of plain bearing, the cup-and-cone ball bearing, and the tapered roller bearing.

2-21 GASKETS

Gaskets are used on many parts of the automobile, such as the engine, transmission, and differential.

GENERAL TYPES		INDIVIDUAL TYPE	TYPE OF LOAD
Plain		Babbitt Bearings Bronze Bushings	Radial, Thrust & Combination Radial, Thrust & Combination
Ball		Annular Ball Ball Thrust Cup and Cone	Radial Thrust Combination
Roller	Standard	Straight Tapered	Radial Combination
	Needle	Straight	Radial

Fig. 2-40A Bearing Chart

TYPE OF MATERIAL	AMOUNT OF HEAT	LOCATION OR USE
Asbestos Copper Asbestos Steel Asbestos	Large Amount	cylinder head, manifold, exhaust pipe
Cork Neoprene (Synthetic Rubber)	No Heat	rocker cover, tappet cover, oil pan, fuel-pump cover, timing-gear cover, transmission cover, and differential cover
Vellumoid	No Heat	carburetor, fuel pump, transmission, water pump, oil pan, differential, and rear-axle flange
Fibre	Some Heat	where a sealing washer is required

Fig. 2-40B   Gasket Chart

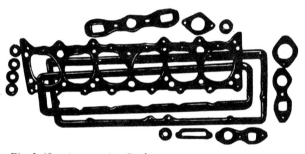

Fig. 2-40   Automotive Gaskets

The purpose of gaskets is to provide a seal between two connecting metal surface. To make a metal-to-metal sealed joint without gaskets would require expensive grinding and lapping, in order to make both surfaces smooth enough to resist the leaking of either air or oil pressure. It is for this reason that some sort of soft or flexible material is placed between the surfaces. (See Fig 2-40.)

There are many types of gasket materials used for different purposes. Gaskets are made of special paper, fibre, cork, neoprene, asbestos, copper, copper lined with asbestos, or steel lined with asbestos. Special gasket papers are known by various trade names such as *Vellumoid*. They are paper or cardboard-like materials treated with oil to make them soft and flexible. Gasket pastes are sometimes used, either in place of gaskets or in addition to gaskets, to improve their sealing ability.

Oil and grease seals. Oil and grease seals are used to prevent leaks between stationary and moving parts and to exclude foreign matter. The seal most commonly used in the automotive industry is the radial seal, which is often referred to as a shaft seal. This type of seal applies a sealing pressure to a rotating shaft to retain the fluid. The sealing insert, made of materials such as leather, neoprene or felt, is held in a metal retainer.

Most automotive oil seals are of the metal encased spring-loaded single-lip type, although dual-lip types are used when two different lubricants are to be sealed apart or when a lubricant is to be sealed in and dirt excluded.

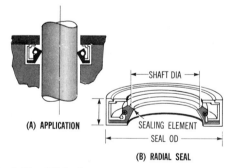

Fig. 2-41   Oil Seals

Sealing is accomplished by having the sealing lip held tightly against the shaft by a uniform pressure. This pressure is created by a garter spring located between the sealing lip and the outer case.

Oil seals should never be stored by being dumped loosely into a bin, hung over rods, nails, or anything which can contact the sealing lip. Seals should be kept clean. Many seals are damaged just before assembly by being placed in unclean work boxes or on benches. The seal should be left in its protective covering until time for assembly. Damage can occur during assembly. A defect in the sealing lip can be caused very easily and every precaution should be taken to prevent damage.

The shaft on which the seal is to be installed should be checked for wear, marks, nicks or scratches. Insignificant as these may appear, they can cause the sealing lip to wear prematurely or tear the lip causing leakage.

The seal must be installed so that the lip faces the lubricant to be sealed. When installing, use proper installation tools. If the proper tool is not available, do not use materials which will splinter or break and leave chips around the sealing-lip area. The entering edge of the seal and the bore should have a rounded corner or chamfer to facilitate installation. Be sure the plane of the seal is at right angles to the shaft axis to assure that the seal will bottom in the bore; this also prevents distortion of the seal.

Oil seals should not be reused after being removed.

Chicago Rawhide Products Canada Ltd.

Fig. 2-42   Installing Oil Seal

O-Rings. Static O-ring seals are classified as gasket-type seals. When an O-ring is used, a groove is machined in one or both surfaces to be sealed. The O-ring fits into the groove and is compressed, which provides the seal when the parts are tightened together.

O-rings are also used to provide a seal between a stationary and a moving part. In this case the groove is cut in one surface only.

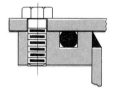

Fig. 2-43   O-Ring Seal

2-22 TUBING, CONNECTORS, AND FITTINGS

Various types of leakproof tubing are needed in automobiles, for purposes such as:
1. To transfer fuel from the gasoline tank to the fuel pump, then to the carburetor
2. To transmit hydraulic pressure from the master cylinder to the wheel cylinder of the hydraulic brake system

These lines are connected to the units by a variety of connectors and fittings, which eliminates the soldering of connections. Three types of tubing materials are used in the automotive service industry: steel, copper, and flexible hoses.

2-23 TUBING

Steel Tubing. Steel tubing is used by all automotive manufacturers as original equipment for fuel, oil, brake, and vacuum lines. It is formed to the assorted shapes required to join the various units. Steel tubing is difficult to rework or to bend to a different shape.

Copper Tubing. Copper tubing is soft and pliable when new and can be formed into any desired shape. Copper tubing work hardens (becomes less flareable and more brittle, due to the vibration of the automobile), and a used piece must be annealed before is can be reworked.

Flexible Rubber Tubing. Flexible tubing consists of three separate layers; a neoprene (synthetic rubber) inner layer, a fabric reinforcement layer, and an outer cover of neoprene. The number of reinforcement layers or plies varies from one to six, depending upon the pressure requirements. The necessary fittings or couplings are permanently

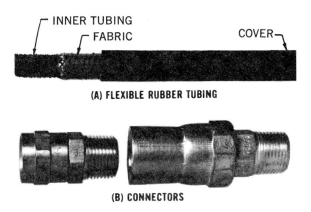

(A) FLEXIBLE RUBBER TUBING

(B) CONNECTORS

The Weatherhead Company of Canada Ltd.

Fig. 2-44   Flexible Rubber Tubing and Connections

attached to the hose. Flexible lines are used where the movement or vibration of the line would cause a rigid line to break. For example, a flexible hose is always used between the frame and the wheel cylinder of the braking system.

Tubing Sizes. The outside diameter of a tube indicates the size. Various wall thicknesses are used in copper and steel tubing to enable the tubing to withstand the required amount of pressure.

Tubing Flares. In order to use certain types of connectors, it is necessary to flare or spread the end of the tubing. Two methods of flaring are used, the single flare and the double flare. (Fig. 2-45). The flare is the part of the tubing that is squeezed between the fitting and the nut to form the seal. The single flare is usually used with copper tubing

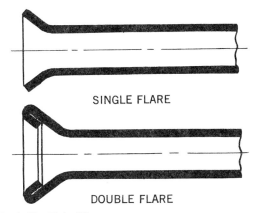

SINGLE FLARE

DOUBLE FLARE

Fig. 2-45   Tube Flares

because single-flared steel tubing has a tendency to split at the end of the flare; the double flare is used with steel tubing.

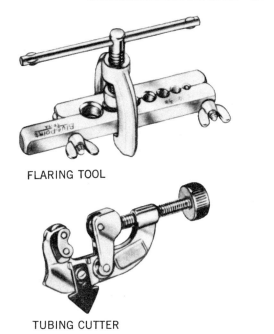

FLARING TOOL

TUBING CUTTER

Snap-on Tools of Canada Ltd., Toronto, Ont.

Fig. 2-46   Flaring Tool and Tubing Cutter

2-24 CONNECTORS AND FITTINGS

To connect the lines to their units, connectors or fittings of various types are used: SAE 45° Flared, Inverted Flared, Compression, and Double Compression. There are also a number of shapes used, such as straight, 45° and 90° elbows, and tees (Fig. 2-47).

Each of these types consists of a male fitting, a seal, and a female nut. The male fitting is usually threaded on both ends, one end having a pipe thread that is threaded into the unit, the other end having a special fitting thread. Each type of fitting has its own unique thread, which prevents mismating of the connectors.

To prevent damage to the seal when tightening or loosening a connection, hold the fitting with one wrench while turning the nut with another.

To prevent damage to the fittings, a special flare nut wrench is used (Fig. 2-48). This wrench eliminates the possibility of rounding the corners or collapsing the centre of the fitting.

SAE 45° Flared Fittings. The male portion of this fitting is threaded tightly into the unit, whereas the female or nut portion is placed on the tubing before flaring takes place. The seal is obtained by compressing the flare on the tubing between the tapered faces of the male and female connectors.

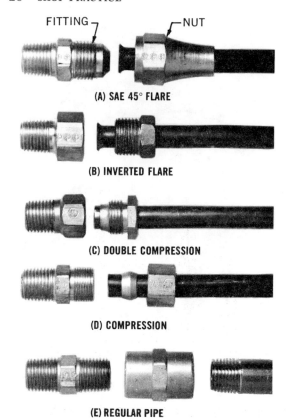

(A) SAE 45° FLARE

(B) INVERTED FLARE

(C) DOUBLE COMPRESSION

(D) COMPRESSION

(E) REGULAR PIPE

The Weatherhead Company of Canada Ltd.

Fig. 2-47   Tube Fittings

Inverted Flared Fittings. In this type of fitting, the female connector has an external pipe thread, which is threaded into the unit; the male portion is placed on the tubing before flaring takes place. The seal is produced by compressing the flare on the tubing in the same manner as the SAE 45° fitting. This type of connector provides the best seal and is used in brakeline connections.

SAE Compression Fittings. This type of fitting does not require a flared tubing, but uses instead a compression sleeve or olive. The sleeve is placed on the tubing between the nut and the fitting, and the seal is produced by compressing the sleeve tightly onto the tubing as the connection is tightened.

SAE Double Compression Fittings. This connection requires neither flared tubing nor compression

Snap-on Tools of Canada Ltd., Toronto, Ont.

Fig. 2-48   Flare Nut Wrench

sleeves. The seal is produced when the tubing is crimped by the male fitting as it is forced against the female nut.

Hose Clamps. Some low-pressure neoprene or rubber hoses, such as gasoline lines or radiator hoses, do not have permanently attached end-fittings. Instead, the end of the hose is placed over the plain neck of the fitting, held in place and prevented from leaking by a hose clamp. These clamps are tightened by stove bolts, worm screws, or by the spring tension of the clamp (Fig. 2-49).

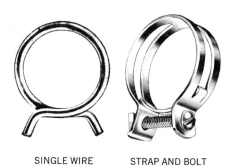

SINGLE WIRE   STRAP AND BOLT

WORM GEAR

H. Paulin & Co. Limited 1963

Fig. 2-49   Hose Clamps

2-25 SPECIFICATIONS

The term specifications refer to the *measurements*, *settings*, and *clearances* that the designing engineers, production men, and the factory service men establish as correct for the manufacture and satisfactory operation of the motor vehicle. These specifications vary from year to year and from manufacturer to manufacturer.

When the mechanic wishes to know the correct setting, clearance, or capacity of a particular unit, he refers to the tables of specifications in the manufacturer's manual for the particular make, model, and year of the vehicle upon which he is working. For example, if he were setting the ignition timing, the specifications would provide the location of the timing marks, the number of degrees before or after top dead centre that the spark should occur, and any other pertinent information. If he were overhauling the differential, the specifications would provide the setting for the backlash between the ring and drive pinion gears.

Specifications provide the measurements for standard size parts. By comparing the measurements taken from worn parts with those of the specifications, the amount of wear that has taken place can be easily calculated. The mechanic can then decide whether the parts require adjustment, re-machining or replacement, and can make the necessary corrections.

2-26 SAFETY PRACTICES

Safety is everyone's business, and safe work habits are another important step towards becoming a successful automotive mechanic. Listed below are a few important safety habits for the beginning student. Study the list and add any other rules that will apply to your particular situation.

1. Fire is a constant threat in any automotive shop. Therefore, use gasoline only as a fuel. Do not, under any circumstances, use it as a cleaning agent. If gasoline is spilled, wipe it up immediately, and place the wiping cloths outside or in a safe place to dry.

    Oily rags and waste are other potential fire hazards and *must* be kept in covered metal containers.

    Fire extinguishers are available for use on various classes of fires. The most common type of extinguisher for gasoline or oil fires is CO_2 (carbon dioxide). Know the location of the fire extinguishers in your shop and how to operate them.

2. Exhaust fumes from internal-combustion engines contain carbon monoxide fumes. These fumes are poisonous and can cause asphyxiation and death. Do not run an engine in a shop or garage unless a suitable pipe is connected to the exhaust system to conduct the fumes out of the building. An exception to this rule is when enough ventilation is provided to remove the deadly gas. At least three large windows, or two windows and one door, should be wide open while the engine is running and for some time after the engine has stopped.

3. If it is necessary to work under a car, make certain that the jack is properly in place. Solid

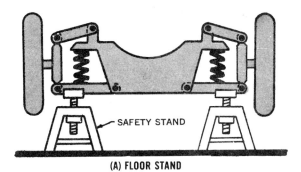

(A) FLOOR STAND

(B) HOIST STAND

Courtesy of General Motors

Fig. 2-50   The Use of Safety Stands

safety stands must always be placed under the car in case the jack should slip.

4. Wear safety glasses at all times when you are working in any type of shop. Be sure to wear safety glasses, goggles, or shields when you are using grinding wheels (bench, valve, or disc

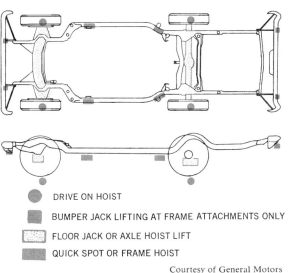

● DRIVE ON HOIST

■ BUMPER JACK LIFTING AT FRAME ATTACHMENTS ONLY

▢ FLOOR JACK OR AXLE HOIST LIFT

▨ QUICK SPOT OR FRAME HOIST

Courtesy of General Motors

Fig. 2-51   Valve Lifting Points

machines) and any other pieces of equipment that may cause eye injury.

5. Before starting an engine, be sure that the engine is in a safe operating condition. Check the oil and coolant levels. Check for loose parts, tools, trouble lights, and test equipment that might become caught in the fan. Check the location and operation of the controls, particularly to make sure that the gear-shift lever or automatic transmission selector is in the neutral position. If the vehicle is to be moved, brakes and steering must be in a safe operating condition.

6. When loosening nuts or bolts, make sure that your fingers are not in a position to be jammed if the wrench slips or the nut gives suddenly. A pull on the wrench is always preferred to a push as it lessens the possibility of the wrench slipping and causing injury.

7. When a hoist is to be used, be sure that the support plates between the hoist and the vehicle are so placed as to support the vehicle safely, but not damage any of the vehicle's parts. If the vehicle is to be left up on the hoist for a long period of time, special safety stands should be placed under the vehicle.

REVIEW QUESTIONS

1. What is the general rule of wrench-handle leverage?
2. State the advantage of a socket wrench over other types of wrenches.
3. What is the purpose of a torque wrench?
4. Why is adding additional leverage to a wrench poor policy?
5. Why should adjustable wrenches not be used?
6. What damage can be caused to finished parts through the use of pliers?
7. Name three things that can damage a screwdriver.
8. Describe an offset screwdriver.
9. When should the pressure be applied and released while using a hacksaw?
10. State the purpose of (a) valve-spring compressors (b) piston-ring compressors.
11. **Explain the difference between a go, or no-go, gauge and a specified measurement gauge.**
12. When are micrometers used in preference to calipers?
13. What is an "Ames" gauge?
14. Name three types of taps and state when each should be used.
15. Give briefly the procedure for removing a stud broken off below the surface of a casting.

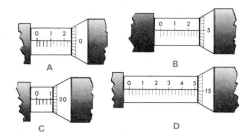

16. Give the micrometer reading shown above.
17. State when a dial gauge should be used.
18. How may finished surfaces be protected from jaw marks when a vise is used?
19. What precautions should be followed before using a piece of power equipment?
20. State five service operations necessary to help keep hand tools in good repair.
21. Give three reasons why you as a customer would prefer to have your automobile serviced in a clean neat shop in preference to a dirty cluttered one.
22. Define each of the terms in the following bolt classification: $\frac{1}{4}'' \times 2\frac{1}{2}''$ — 28 unf — 2A.
23. Why should self-locking nuts not be reused?
24. State the size wrench required for each of the following: (a) $\frac{1}{4}''$ unc nut, (b) $\frac{5}{16}'' \times 2''$ unc cap screw, (c) $\frac{3}{8}'' \times 1\frac{1}{2}''$ unf bolt.
25. What advantage does a spline have over a key?
26. Explain how a combination internal-external snap-ring holds a shaft in place.
27. Name and describe four types of locking devices.
28. Describe three types of bearing loads.
29. What are the advantages of combination bearings?
30. Why are gaskets necessary?
31. Name three gasket materials and give two locations where each is used.
32. Why should copper tubing not be used to repair steel brake lines?
33. How is mismating of brass fittings prevented?
34. What is a tubing flare?
35. Why must steel tubing be double flared?
36. What type of fitting is usually used for brake line connections?
37. What produces the seal when an SAE compression fitting is used?
38. When is an oil seal used?
39. Why should an oil seal not be removed from its protective covering until just before installation?
40. What checks should be performed on a shaft before installing a new oil seal?
41. Which way should the lip of an oil seal face?
42. What is meant by the term *automotive specifications*?
43. How can specifications be used by the mechanic to determine the amount of wear that has taken place on a particular part?

UNIT TWO
The Running Gear

Chapter 3
FRAME AND SUSPENSION SYSTEMS

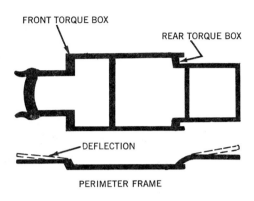

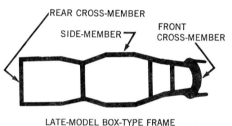

Fig. 3-1   Automobile Frames

The modern automobile handles well because of its ability to negotiate rough roads and turns at most speed ranges. It can be brought to a safe, smooth stop quickly. This is as a direct result of well-designed suspension, steering, and braking systems.

3-1 THE FRAME

The frame is used to support all of the various units of the chassis and body, and to keep these units in correct alignment with one another. It usually extends the entire length of the automobile. The frame must be strong enough to withstand the many twists, shocks, vibrations, and distortions which occur when the car is standing or running on uneven roads.

Maximum strength and minimum weight are the essential characteristics of an automobile frame. An exceptionally strong frame could be made if solid steel beams were used, but such a frame would be far too heavy to be practical. To make the strong, light frame needed for an automobile, *channel section* is used. It is a specially constructed U-shaped beam made of light, but tough, steel alloy.

The frame consists of two long pieces of channel section called *side-members* connected near each end by *cross-members.* At the rear, the side-members are arched upwards over the rear axle to provide clearance for the vertical movement of the axle, and to keep the frame in a low-slung position. In addition to the two cross-members, diagonal cross-members were often used on older type automobiles to provide extra bracing effect. These diagonal members were located about midway along the frame and form an X- or K-pattern.

Small triangular plates or brackets known as *gussets* are riveted at points where cross-members and side-members intersect. Gussets serve as additional braces and help keep the frame in correct alignment.

In some late-model automobiles the manufacturers have completely eliminated the frame side-members from the passenger compartment area, permitting fewer humps in the floor. This type of frame depends entirely upon the strength of the X-members.

Another popular frame is the *box-girder* type. With this design, resistance to twists and distortion depends upon the box-like construction of the two side-members. In some automobiles the box-girder type side-members are placed at the outer edges of the body compartment and are angled in to permit a narrow frame over the front and rear wheels. This type of construction also reduces the humps in the floor of the passenger compartment.

The *perimeter frame* incorporates the use of torque boxes on each side of the frame, located at either, or both, the cowl and rear door areas. This permits the front and rear frame sections to deflect as the wheels move across uneven road surfaces.

Some automobiles do not have a separate frame. Instead, certain of the body members have been greatly reinforced and these, along with the body panels, serve as the automobile frame. The advantages of this type of construction are a reduction in body rattles and squeaks and a higher degree of safety. This type of construction is called integral body and frame construction, or *unibody*.

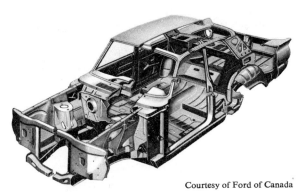

Courtesy of Ford of Canada

Fig. 3-2 Integral Body and Frame Construction (Unibody)

3-2 SUSPENSION SYSTEMS

The wheels and axles are suspended by springs that support the weight of the vehicle. The springs absorb the road shock as the wheels encounter holes or bumps and keep the jarring up-and-down action of the axle from being carried through to the frame and body.

Only the parts of the automobile attached to the frame benefit from the spring action. The weight carried by the springs is called *sprung weight*. *Unsprung weight* is the name given to the parts of the automobile not protected by the spring action and depends only on the tires for the reduction of road shock. Front and rear axles are examples of unsprung weight parts.

Engineers endeavour to keep unsprung weight

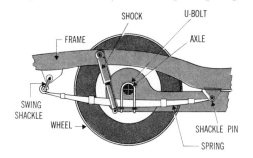

Fig. 3-3 Springs, Shackles, and Shocks

as low as possible, because as unsprung weight increases, so does the roughness of the ride. For example, if the unsprung and sprung weights were equal there would be no spring action. Therefore it is desirable to keep unsprung weight as small a percentage of the vehicle weight as possible.

3-3 SPRING CHARACTERISTICS

The ride of a vehicle depends for the most part on the spring action. Springs that are too soft allow too much movement, and springs that are too stiff allow too little movement. Both conditions would produce poor riding qualities.

The softness or stiffness of a spring is referred to as its *deflection rate*. Deflection rate is the force required to cause 1″ of spring deflection and is expressed as so many pounds-per-inch deflection. For example, an 80 pound-per-inch spring would require a force of 80 lb. to deflect the spring 1″; a 160-pound-per-inch spring would require 160 lb. to deflect 1″ and would be classed as a stiffer spring.

Elasticity of materials is the property of materials to return to their original shape after they have been forced out of shape, or distorted. Materials have a limit of elasticity. Beyond this point the material will return to its original shape, and its elasticity is no longer proportional to the load. Hooke's Law states "that a force applied to a coil spring will cause the spring to compress in direct proportion to the force applied," that is, if 100 lb. compresses a spring 2″, then 200 lb. will compress it 4″.

Engineers design automotive springs to remain within the material's elastic limit and to have a deflection rate that is about constant throughout their operating range.

The most satisfactory riding qualities are obtained by using a fairly soft spring and a shock absorber.

The springs may be of the *single-* or *multileaf*, *coil*, or *torsion-bar type*.

Leaf Springs.

The *multileaf spring* is an assembly of flat steel plates of graduated lengths, called leaves. The spring assembly acts as a flexible beam and is usually fastened at both ends to the car frame by spring hangers and shackles, and at the centre to the axle, by U-bolts. To provide flexibility and strength to reduce flattening out, the spring leaves are made of a specially heat-treated steel alloy known as

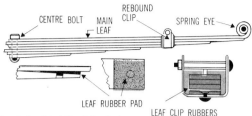

Fig. 3-4 Multileaf Spring

spring steel. The longest leaf is called the *main leaf* and has what is known as a *spring eye* at each end, fitted with a bronze or rubber bushing to reduce friction and wear. The remaining leaves are known as numbers 2, 3, 4, etc.

To prevent squeaks and to ease spring action when the spring bends, special neoprene rubber inserts are often placed between the ends of the spring leaves. The springs then flex on the small rubber pads. Other springs are encased with metal casings and are filled with grease. Rubber pads are also used between the spring and the axle to prevent vibration transfer.

A bolt called the *spring centre bolt* passes through the centre of the leaves to hold them together and in place lengthwise. The head of the centre bolt fits into the spring seat portion of the rear axle, thus preventing the spring from moving out of position after the U-bolts, which hold the spring to the axle, have been tightened.

Rebound clips are placed around the spring leaves at various places to prevent their separating when the spring flexes upwards or rebounds.

The *single-leaf* spring replaces the multileaf spring assembly on some automobiles. The single leaf is shaped like the multileaf assembly, thin at the ends and thicker in the centre. Its action is the same as the multileaf type.

Fig. 3-5 Single-Leaf Spring

If the spring is attached to the top of the axle, it is said to be overslung; if the spring is attached to the under side of the axle, it is said to be *underslung*. Usually front leaf springs are overslung, and rear leaf springs are underslung.

Rear leaf springs are also required to absorb rear-end torque when a Hotchkiss-type drive shaft is used, to keep the rear axle in alignment with the frame, and to absorb side thrusts when the vehicle rounds a curve.

Leaf springs may be mounted parallel to the frame or cross-wise on the frame. In the cross-wise,

or transverse, method the centre of the spring is attached to the frame. The outer ends are attached to the control arms or axles through a spring shackle. Radius rods are used to maintain axle-to-frame alignment and a rear-end torque rod is required if a Hotchkiss-type drive shaft is used.

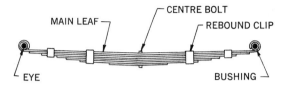

Fig. 3-6 Transverse Type Spring

Coil Springs.

A coil spring is a heavy coil spring steel formed at high temperatures, cooled, and heat-treated to the proper tension. The coil is placed between the frame and the suspension device, in such a way that it supports the weight of the car. The vehicle

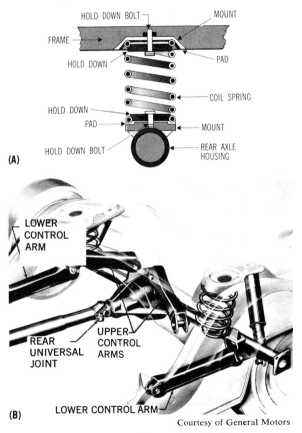

Courtesy of General Motors

Fig. 3-7 Typical Rear Coil-Spring Installations

weight puts the spring under an initial compression. The spring will further compress as the wheel passes over a bump in the road, or will expand if the wheel encounters a hole. Rubber pads are placed between the ends of the coil spring and the frame, or suspension device, to prevent vibration transfer. Coil springs may be used in either front- or rear-suspension systems. When coil springs are used in rear-suspension systems, additional rods are required. Radius rods or control arms are used to keep the axle in alignment with the frame and torque rods to absorb rear-axle torque.

Torsion Bars.

The torsion-bar suspension system utilizes the flexibility of a steel bar twisting lengthwise to absorb road shock and to cushion the ride. The twisting of the torsion bar exerts resistance to the up-and-down movement of the wheel; therefore it can be used to replace the flexing action of the leaf spring, or the compressing-and-extending action of the coil spring. Torsion bars may be mounted parallel to or laterally to the frame side members.

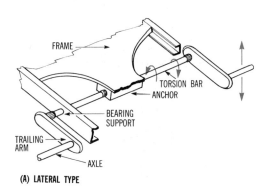

(A) LATERAL TYPE

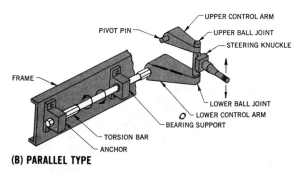

(B) PARALLEL TYPE

Fig. 3-8   Torsion-Bar Suspension

Parallel-Mounted Type Torsion-Bar Suspension.

When this type of torsion bar is used, the bar usually has hexagon-shaped ends. The rear hexagon of the bar is rigidly attached to the frame, usually through a car levelling device. This device can be adjusted to compensate for any sag in the suspension system which may occur because of loss of tension in the bar.

The front hexagon of the torsion bar is attached

to the pivot points of the lower control arm. The bar twists as a result of the up-and-down movement of the lower control arm as the wheel goes over a bump. This results in a spring action.

Lateral-Type Torsion-Bar Suspension. Lateral-type torsion bars can be used to provide the spring action for front and/or rear wheel independent suspension systems. When a lateral-type torsion bar is used, the inner end of the bar is attached rigidly to the frame ahead of the wheel it is to support in such a manner that the wheel trails the torsion bar. The outer end of the bar is attached to one end of the trailing arm. The other end of the trailing arm is attached to the wheel support mechanism. When the wheel goes over a bump it causes the trailing arm to swing up and down in an arc. As the trailing arm swings, it twists the torsion bar, creating the necessary resistance and spring action.

Air Suspension Systems.

In the *air-bag suspension*, heavy rubber bags encased in a metal dome or girdle hold air pressure and replace the conventional spring. The vehicle weight is supported by the bag which is filled with compressed air from an engine-driven air compressor. As the wheel goes over a bump or hole in the road, the air in the bag further compresses or expands in the same manner as does a coil spring. With this type of suspension it is possible to vary, either manually or automatically, through a series of special level control valves, the riding qualities of the car to compensate for heavy or uneven loading, or to increase the road clearance as the driver wishes. Therefore the riding quality of the vehicle can be adjusted by altering the amount of air pressure in the bags.

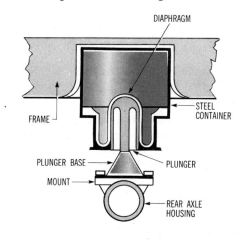

Fig. 3-9   Air-Bag Unit

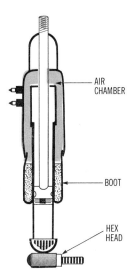

Fig. 3-10   *Typical Air Absorber Suspension Unit*

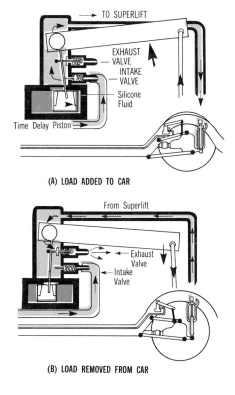

(A) LOAD ADDED TO CAR

(B) LOAD REMOVED FROM CAR

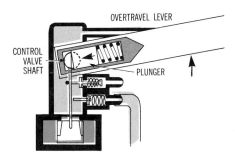

(C) RAPID MOVEMENT OF OVERTRAVEL LEVER

Courtesy of General Motors

Fig. 3-11   *Typical Air Suspension Control Valve*

Another type of air suspension, called *automatic level control*, uses a type of rear shock absorber that contains a compressed air chamber. The level and the riding qualities of the vehicle can be varied by increasing or decreasing the amount of compressed air in the shock-absorber chambers.

In both the air-bag and air-shock type of suspension, the control valves are attached to the frame and connected by linkage to the axle. When a load is added to the vehicle and the curb height is decreased, it causes the overtravel lever to move upward, thus opening the intake valve and allowing compressed air into the air chambers of the air bags or air shock absorbers. When the load is removed, the overtravel lever moves in the opposite direction to open the exhaust valve, releasing compressed air from the air bag or air shock.

Rapid movement of the overtravel lever, such as when the vehicle goes over a bump, cannot revolve the control-valve shaft because of a time delay mechanism built into the control valve. This mechanism allows rapid movement of the overcontrol lever without it rotating the control-valve shaft. The shaft, in order to turn, must move a control piston through a chamber containing a silicone fluid. The piston retards the rapid movement of the control-valve shaft preventing the control valves from opening. Since the piston will move slowly through the silicone fluid, changes in vehicle height because of load changes are not restricted by the action of the piston.

Air bags are also available as an accessory which can be used in addition to the conventional suspension system of the vehicle. They are usually installed on vehicles that occasionally carry a heavy load or tow a trailer. This type of installation does not have its own air compressor. It is inflated with compressed air from an external source. When the vehicle is loaded or the trailer is attached the vehicle is driven to a source of compressed air and the bags are filled with compressed air until the vehicle reaches its normal unloaded height. When the load has been removed the compressed air is manually released from the air bags to lower the height of the vehicle.

3-4 SPRING SHACKLES

When a load is placed on the frame, the single-leaf or multileaf spring flattens out, increasing the distance between the spring eyes. If the spring eyes were rigidly fastened to the frame, the distance between the eyes could not change; therefore, there would be no spring action. To allow the springs to lengthen and shorten, the rear end of the spring is attached to the frame by means of a pair of swing links known as a *spring shackle*. The other end of the spring is attached by a spring bolt to a bracket on the frame called a *spring hanger*. This pin and hanger prevent the spring from moving fore or aft.

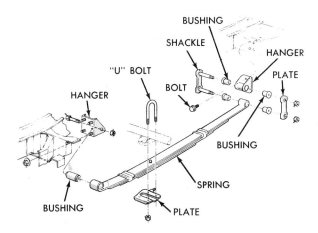

Chrysler Canada Ltd.

Fig. 3-13   Typical Rear-Spring Shackle Assembly

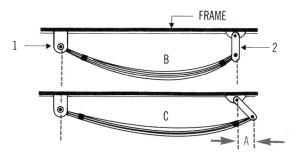

Fig. 3-12   Spring Shackle Action

The spring shackle must be free to oscillate; therefore the spring bolt is not clamped tightly. If clamped tightly, proper spring action would be prevented and spring breakage would occur.

Most spring shackles are similar in design but use different materials to reduce friction. One type uses a rubber bushing between the spring and the shackle bolt. The spring and shackle bolt do not touch. The turning motion of the pin is absorbed by the flexible rubber bushing and, since it is rubber, it requires no lubrication. This type of shackle uses separate shackle bars to connect the spring-shackle bolt to the spring-hanger bolt. The bars are usually forced onto a serrated portion of the shackle bolts to prevent the bar from turning on the bolt. Nuts threaded onto one end of the bolt prevent the bars from separating.

Bronze bushings sometimes replace the rubber. In this type, the twisting motion is between the bushing and the shackle bolt. Frequent lubrication is required to prevent wear.

Another type of shackle uses a U-shaped shackle bolt. The U-bolt passes through the spring eye and the hanger bracket. The two legs of the U-bolts

are threaded full length. A steel bushing, threaded inside and out, is screwed onto the bolt and into the spring eye until it tightens in the spring. The twisting motion is between the bushing and the U-bolt. This type of shackle requires frequent lubrication to prevent premature wear.

3-5 SHOCK ABSORBERS

The best riding qualities for an automobile can be obtained through the use of fairly soft springs. A soft spring requires little weight to cause it to deflect. Therefore, when a vehicle goes over a bump, the spring compresses, expands, or flexes and will continue to compress, expand, or flex several times before returning to its original position. A similar action is seen when a rubber ball is dropped on the floor. This oscillating action is undesirable and results in an uncomfortable ride. On a bumpy road or especially on a curve, this oscillation could become serious enough to cause the driver to lose control of the vehicle. To reduce this action as

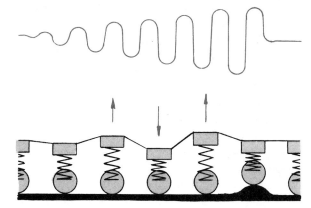

Fig. 3-14   Spring Oscillation

quickly as possible, shock absorbers or *shocks* are placed between the axles and the frame.

Various types of shocks have been used, friction, air, and hydraulic, to name a few. The hydraulic type is in common use today. The direct-acting, or telescopic-type hydraulic, shock absorber is most widely used on both front and rear installations.

In the direct-acting hydraulic shock absorber, a telescoping tube is partially filled with a fluid that can pass through a restricted passage from one part of the tube to the other. When the tube is compressed or expanded, the fluid flows through the restricted opening causing a slowing down action on the telescoping tube. The rate of flow through the opening varies depending upon the severity of the road shock, and as a result it dampens the additional flexing action of the spring.

Two methods of attaching the shock absorber to the frame and suspension system are in common use: the bayonet, or *pin-mount* type, consists of a threaded rod attached to the ends of the shock absorber which passes through holes in the mounting brackets; and the *eye-end* type, which has an

eye attached to the ends of the shock absorbers and a bolt and nut passes through the mounting bracket and the eye. Rubber bushings are used between the metal parts of both types of mounts.

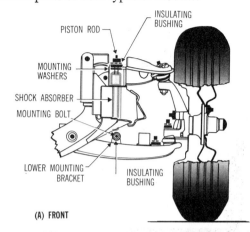

(A) FRONT

(B) REAR

Courtesy of General Motors

Fig. 3-16   Typical Shock Absorber Installation

3-6 FRONT SUSPENSION

Front-suspension systems must be designed to provide for both spring action (up-and-down motion) and for steering motion (the change of angle between the wheel and the frame). This chapter will consider only the spring action. Chapter 5 will describe the steering system.

Two basic front-suspension systems are used: the *solid I-beam*, or rigid axle leaf-spring type, and the *independent-wheel suspension* system using long and short swing arms. The passenger car uses the independent front-wheel suspension system. Light trucks may be equipped with either solid

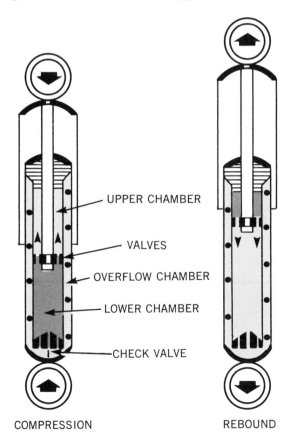

COMPRESSION   REBOUND

Fig. 3-15   Shock Absorbers

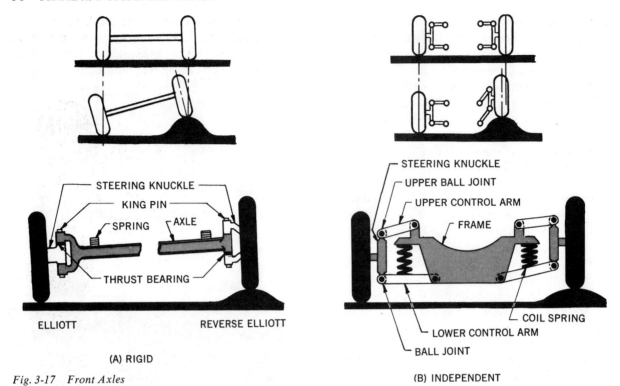

STEERING KNUCKLE
KING PIN
SPRING
AXLE
THRUST BEARING

ELLIOTT   REVERSE ELLIOTT

(A) RIGID

Fig. 3-17   Front Axles

STEERING KNUCKLE
UPPER BALL JOINT
UPPER CONTROL ARM
FRAME
COIL SPRING
LOWER CONTROL ARM
BALL JOINT

(B) INDEPENDENT

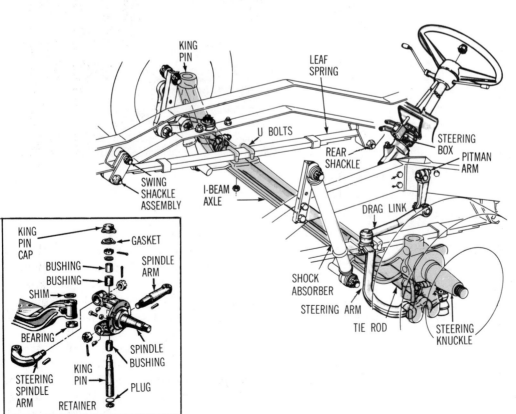

KING PIN
LEAF SPRING
U BOLTS
REAR SHACKLE
STEERING BOX
PITMAN ARM
SWING SHACKLE ASSEMBLY
I-BEAM AXLE
DRAG LINK
SHOCK ABSORBER
STEERING ARM
TIE ROD
STEERING KNUCKLE

KING PIN CAP
GASKET
BUSHING
BUSHING
SPINDLE ARM
SHIM
BEARING
SPINDLE BUSHING
STEERING SPINDLE ARM
KING PIN
PLUG
RETAINER

Fig. 3-18   1-Beam Front Axle and Steering Assembly

Ford of Canada
Chrysler Canada Ltd.

I-beam axles or independent front-wheel suspension systems. Heavy trucks usually have solid I-beam front axles.

Solid I-Beam Axles.

Solid I-beam axles are made from drop-forged steel, a special steel which is heated and hammered into shape. Leaf springs are attached near each end of the I-beam to provide the spring action. Any up-and-down movement of either front wheel causes a vertical tipping effect in both wheels because they are connected by a common axle. This tipping effect has a tendency to upset steering geometry, and to twist the springs and frame, resulting in uncomfortable riding qualities. However, since these axles are used largely in heavy trucks, this is not considered a great disadvantage. A variation of the solid I-beam axle is the *Twin I-Beam* front axle. This type uses two I-beams and each one can pivot independently. Radius rods or control arms are required and coil-type springs are used.

In both types the wheels pivot for steering purposes on a king pin mounted between the steering knuckle and the axle. Antifriction ball-thrust bearings are mounted between the steering knuckle and the axle I-beam to reduce the friction between these parts when the steering knuckles are pivoted for steering purposes.

Independent Front-Wheel Suspension.

Most modern automobiles use independent front-wheel suspension. The weight may be supported by either a coil spring, torsion bar, or air bag. In all cases the basic construction of the system is similar.

The principle of operation is the short and long arm (SLA) principle. The short arms are called the upper control arms, while the long arms are

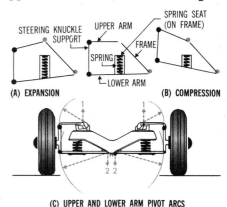

Fig. 3-20   *SLA Principle*

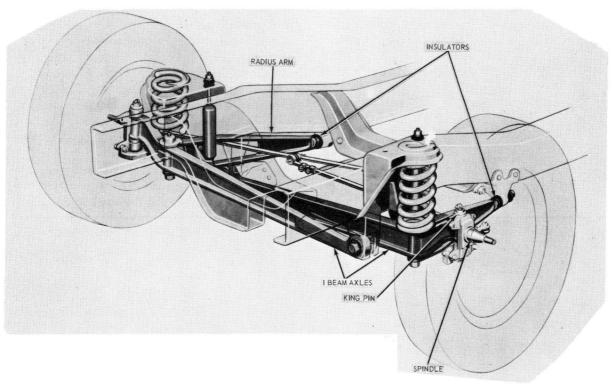

Fig. 3-19   Twin I-Beam Front Axle

Ford of Canada

called the lower control arms. The action between these two arms, as the wheel goes over a bump, is such that it will allow the coil spring or air bag to compress or expand, or the torsion bar to twist, while maintaining almost vertical alignment of the steering knuckle and wheel.

An important factor controlling the steering stability of independent front-wheel suspension systems is the location of the *instant centre*. The instant centre for any one position of the wheel is the point of intersection of lines drawn through the upper and lower control-arm attaching points. If the vertical distance between the inner pivot points of the upper and lower control arms is less than the vertical distance between the outer pivot points, the instant centre will be inside the vehicle. This will result in a small amount of negative camber developing as the wheel goes over a bump.

When the inner pivot distance is larger than the outer pivot distance, the instant centre for any one position of the wheel will be outside the vehicle and will result in a small amount of positive camber being developed when the wheel goes over a bump. This tends to produce an outward thrust which counteracts the inward thrust created by the bump. When the vehicle rounds a curve and centrifugal force throws more force on to the outer wheel, then if a small amount of additional positive camber can be produced, an additional bracing effect will result. The positive cambered position of the

wheel will help to overcome the centrifugal force. At the same time, the outward tilting of the wheel results in an inward shift of the vehicle's centre of gravity which also helps to counteract the centrifugal force.

In the common type of the independent front-wheel suspension, the coil spring is placed between the lower control-arm spring seat and the frame spring seat. The inner ends of both upper and lower control arms are pivoted through rubber mounts to shafts which are bolted to the frame. The outer ends of the control arms are attached to ball or spherical joints. These joints are attached to the steering knuckles and allow for the up-and-down spring action and the swivel action required for steering purposes. The design and position of the control arms aids in the controlling of brake dive by a weight transfer counterreaction. Provision is made in the construction of the upper control arm-to-frame mounting to provide a means of adjusting the steering geometry angles of caster and camber.

In some coil-spring type suspension systems the coil spring is located between the upper ends of the steering knuckle pins and seats in the wheel house panel. All other units of this system are similar to the common coil-spring type.

When air bags are used, the air bag is substituted for the coil spring.

When torsion-bar type suspension is used, the inner ends of the lower control arm are attached to the front hexagon of the torsion bar, instead of the pivot shaft. The up-and-down movement of the wheel end of the control arm causes a twisting action in the torsion bar. The torsion bar resists this twisting action, thereby providing the spring effect.

To prevent any fore-or-aft movement of the lower control arm, a strut is placed between the outer end of the lower control arm and the frame.

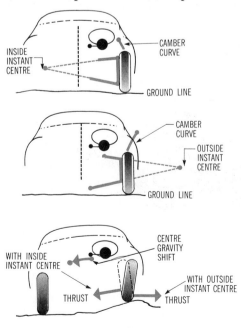

Fig. 3-21   Instant Centre Principle

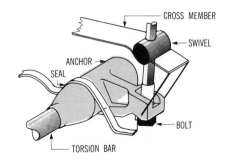

Fig. 3-23   Torsion Bar Adjusting Assembly

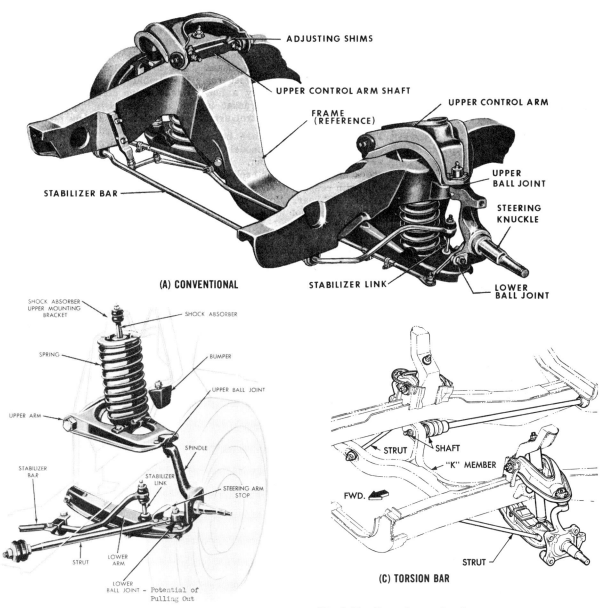

(A) CONVENTIONAL

(B) COIL SPRING MOUNTED OVER UPPER CONTROL ARM

(C) TORSION BAR

Fig. 3-22   Front Suspension System

(A) Courtesy of General Motors
(B) Ford of Canada
(C) Chrysler of Canada Ltd.

The rear hexagon of the torsion bar is attached to the car frame through a car-levelling device, which can be adjusted to compensate for any sag in the suspension system because of loss of tension in the bar.

To adjust the height of the car it is necessary to turn the adjusting bolt of the levelling device which in turn turns the hub and anchor assembly. This rotates the rear end of the torsion bar, increasing or decreasing the tension, and results in the raising or lowering of the front end of the car.

Rubber bumpers are placed between the lower control arms and the frame to prevent metal-to-metal contact of the these parts in case the spring should compress beyond its normal range. The shock absorber is attached to the frame and lower control arm.

Stabilizer Bars. A stabilizer bar is usually included in a suspension system to overcome the tendency of the vehicle's body to lean outwards on corners. As long as the movement is in a normal manner,

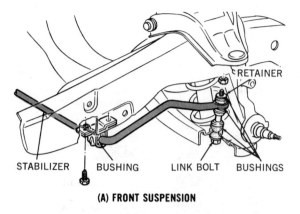

(A) FRONT SUSPENSION

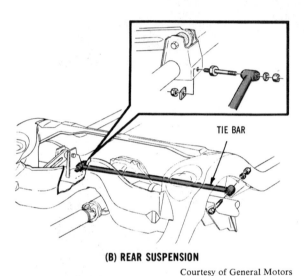

(B) REAR SUSPENSION

Courtesy of General Motors

Fig. 3-24   Stabilizer Bar

up and down, the stabilizer bar is ineffective. When the body attempts to lean to one side, as in cornering, one end of the bar must be bent down while the other end bends upward. This produces a torsional effect in the bar as it resists the rolling, tipping action, and helps keep the vehicle body level.

Stabilizer bars are made of spring steel and are supported in two places by rubber bushings as they pass across the frame. The outer ends are bent around and back and are attached to the lower control arms of the front-suspension system through rubber-mounted short links.

3-7 REAR SUSPENSION

The rear suspension system is required to transmit the driving forces of the rear axle to the car frame. It is particularly important to transmit the rear-end torque from the axle to the frame when a

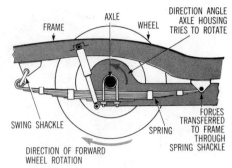

Fig. 3-25   Driving Force Reaction

Hotchkiss-type drive shaft is used. The rear suspension system must absorb the side thrusts produced when the vehicle turns a corner and at the same time maintain proper alignment between the axle and the frame. When parallel leaf springs are used no additional bracing is required. The spring and shackles are capable of withstanding the rear-end torque of the axle, the side thrusts, and maintaining proper alignment. If the leaf spring is transverse mounted, then control rods, or radius rods, and a torque rod, or torque-tube type drive shaft, are required to absorb these forces.

When coil springs are used in the rear-suspension system, control rods and torque rods are required. The coil spring is assembled between the spring seats on the control rods and the frame spring seats. The two control rods are mounted through rubber bushings and bolts to the frame and the axle brackets. The control arms are free

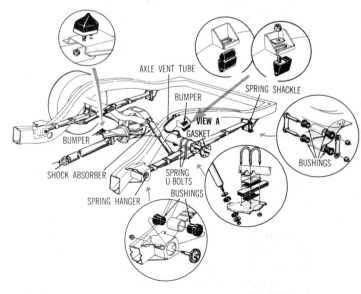

Fig. 3-26   Leaf Spring Rear Suspension   Ford of Canada

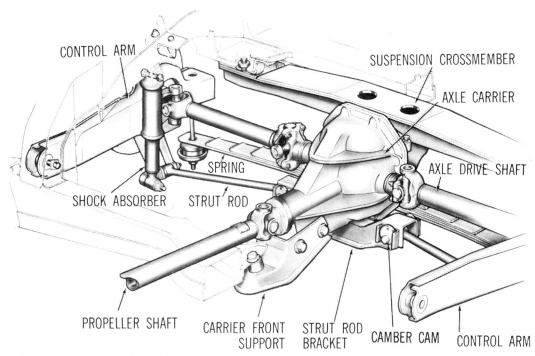

CONTROL ARM
SUSPENSION CROSSMEMBER
AXLE CARRIER
SPRING
AXLE DRIVE SHAFT
SHOCK ABSORBER
STRUT ROD
PROPELLER SHAFT
CARRIER FRONT SUPPORT
STRUT ROD BRACKET
CAMBER CAM
CONTROL ARM

Fig. 3-27   Transverse Spring Suspension

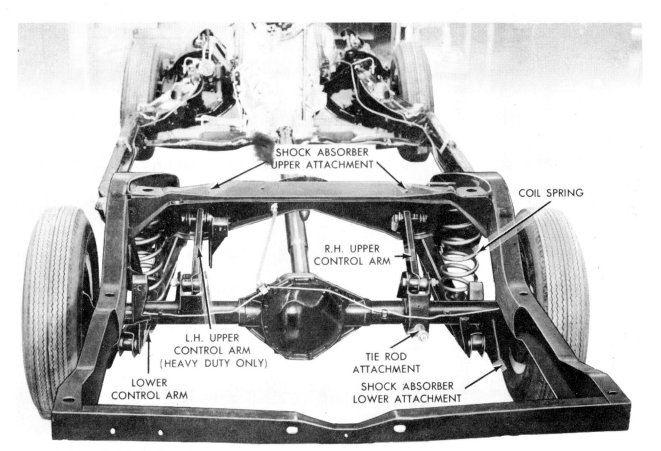

SHOCK ABSORBER UPPER ATTACHMENT
COIL SPRING
R.H. UPPER CONTROL ARM
L.H. UPPER CONTROL ARM (HEAVY DUTY ONLY)
TIE ROD ATTACHMENT
LOWER CONTROL ARM
SHOCK ABSORBER LOWER ATTACHMENT

Fig. 3-28   Coil Spring Rear Suspension

to move up and down with the spring action yet they prevent any fore-or-aft movement of the axle. **The torque arm is rubber-mounted vertically between the frame and the axle to absorb the rear-end torque.** A track or stabilizer bar is rubber-mounted diagonally crosswise between the axle and the frame to prevent any sideways motion between the frame and axle.

Telescoping hydraulic shock absorbers are mounted between the frame and axle on all types.

REVIEW QUESTIONS

1. What is the purpose of the vehicle frame?
2. State the essential characteristics of an automobile frame.
3. What is a frame gusset?
4. Describe a perimeter frame.
5. What are the advantages of integral body and frame construction?
6. Define the terms: (a) sprung weight (b) unsprung weight (c) overslung springs.
7. Explain the terms: (a) deflection rate (b) limit of elasticity (c) Hooke's Law.
8. List three other functions besides the absorption of road shock that the rear leaf spring must perform.
9. Explain how a torsion-bar type of suspension absorbs road shock.
10. What is the purpose of a spring shackle?
11. Why are shock absorbers used?
12. Describe the operation of a telescoping type of shock absorber.
13. Describe how the air shock-absorber type of automatic level control operates.
14. What is the disadvantage of a solid I-beam type of front axle?
15. What is the advantage of independent front-wheel suspension?
16. Make a sketch of a coil-spring type of front-suspension system and identify all major components.
17. Describe: (a) the short and long arm principle of suspension (b) instant centre principle.
18. How may the loss of torsion-bar tension be compensated?
19. Explain how a stabilizer bar keeps the vehicle level when rounding a curve.
20. Why are (a) control rods (b) torque rods required when coil springs are used in the rear-suspension system?

Chapter 4
SUSPENSION-SYSTEM SERVICE

4-1 SUSPENSION-SYSTEM SERVICE

Suspension-system service usually arises from the following complaints: hard or rough riding qualities, sway on turns, floating, spring breakage, sagging springs, or noises.

Hard or Rough Ride. Hard or rough riding qualities are usually caused by too high tire pressure, excessive friction in the suspension system (caused by lack of lubrication or misaligned parts), or ineffective shock absorbers.

To reduce the excessive friction, lubricate the parts as specified by the manufacturer, using the specified lubricants. Correcting the misaligned parts requires loosening of the shock-absorber arm linkage, shackle bolts, and U-bolts. This allows realignment of the parts, thereby reducing the excess friction. Retighten the parts in the reverse order.

Shock-absorber action on most vehicles may be checked by pushing up and down several times on the bumper near each corner of the vehicle. If the shock absorbers are operating normally, the vehicle should come to rest as soon as the pushing action is stopped. Some Chrysler products are equipped with shock absorbers which are valved to permit slow spring oscillation for a soft ride and, as a result, the vehicle will not come to rest quickly.

Shock absorbers may be more accurately checked after the linkage has been disconnected. Operate the shock absorber, noting the resistance to movement. If the resistance is small, or not uniform throughout the full stroke, or if the resistance is very slight, the unit requires replacement. Most

modern type shock absorbers cannot be repaired.

On some vehicles the front shock-absorber arms form part of the upper control arm of the suspension system. This type of shock absorber should not be disconnected unless the front-end alignment is to be checked.

Sway on Turns or Floating on Rough Roads. Sway on turns or floating on rough roads may be caused by a loose or broken stabilizer bar or shaft, ineffective shock absorbers, excessive positive caster angle, or weak springs.

Stabilizer bars or shafts should be firmly attached to the axle or suspension arms and to the frame; excessive movement at these points reduces the stabilizer bar's efficiency. Ineffective shock absorbers or weak springs permit excessive spring flexing which causes floating, and pitching or swaying, particularly on rough roads. High positive caster angle will cause the vehicle to roll or lean out on turns (see Fig. 6-3). This requires realignment of the front wheels.

Spring Breakage. Springs break for many reasons. Some of the most common reasons are: excessive overloading, ineffective shock-absorber action, loose U-bolts or centre bolts, defective rebound clips, or tight shackles.

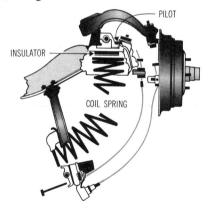

Courtesy of General Motors

Fig. 4-1 When Dismantling Front Suspension System, Be Careful

If the main leaf breaks near the spring eye, a tight shackle is usually the cause. If the main leaf is broken in the centre between the eye and the centre bolt, excessive overloading or ineffective shock absorbers are the cause. Breakage of any leaf near the centre bolt is usually caused by loose U-bolts. Breakage at the centre-bolt hole is caused by loose centre bolts. One or more new leaves may be installed and the other leaves re-arched, or new springs installed. Frequently the unbroken spring must be removed and re-arched in order to maintain a level vehicle. Unlevel vehicles frequently are difficult to steer at higher road speeds.

Sagging Springs. Sagging springs are commonly caused by overuse and overloading. Continual flexing of the spring causes the spring to lose some of its elasticity. A spring's elasticity may be restored by re-tempering or re-arching the spring leaves or the coil spring. On some vehicles with coil springs, spring sag sometimes results from the loss of the spring-seat shim. Defective shock absorbers may tend to restrict spring action thus making the springs appear to sag.

Many manufacturers provide specifications giving the proper spring heights for their vehicles. These heights must be checked before checking front-end alignment, as sagging springs tend to change the alignment angles.

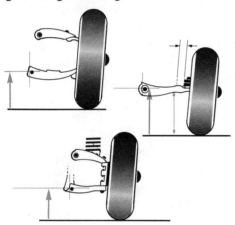

Courtesy of General Motors

Fig. 4-2   Checking Riding Height

Suspension System Noises. Suspension noises are commonly caused by rattles and squeaks. Rattles are caused by loose parts or worn bushings on the springs, shock absorbers, or stabilizer shafts or bars. Squeaks are caused by lack of necessary lubrication.

4-2 CHECKING BALL-JOINT WEAR

Before checking ball joints for wear, it is necessary to determine if (1) the joint is of the preloaded or unloaded type, (2) the joint is a load bearing or nonload bearing joint. Usually preloaded ball joints are nonload-bearing joints. The location of the coil spring determines how the vehicle weight will be transferred to the steering knuckle. When the

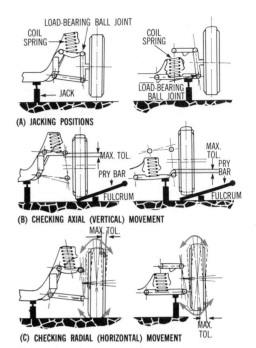

Fig. 4-3   Checking Ball Joint Wear

coil spring is mounted above the upper control arm, the upper ball joint will be the load-bearing joint. When the coil spring is mounted on the lower control arm, the lower ball joint will be the load bearing joint.

To relieve the vehicle weight from the load-bearing joint the vehicle must be jacked up as shown in **Fig. 4-3.**

To check the radial (horizontal) play of a non-preloaded load-bearing joint, place the plunger of a dial indicator against the wheel flange and attach the body of the dial indicator to the appropriate control arm. Grasp the tire at the top and bottom and move the tire in and out. Note the reading on the dial indicator. If the reading exceeds specifications, replace the joint.

To check axial (vertical) play of a nonpreloaded load-bearing joint, place the plunger of a dial indicator against the wheel flange and attach the body of the indicator to the appropriate control arm. Place a pry-bar between the floor and the tire, and using a fulcrum placed just at the outer edge of the tire tread, pry up and down. If the up-and-down movement between the ball stud and its housing exceeds specifications, replace the joint.

Preloaded ball joints are usually checked for play by disconnecting the ball joint from the control arm, re-installing the retaining nut, and locking it with a lock nut. Then, with a socket and torque wrench measure the amount of torque required to rotate the ball stud in its socket. Readings above or below specifications indicate joint replacement is required.

Some manufacturers state replacement of preloaded ball joints is required if any lateral movement is visible in the joint.

REVIEW QUESTIONS

1. List three causes of hard or rough ride.
2. How may shock absorbers be checked?
3. List three causes of sway on turns or floating on rough roads.
4. How may sagging springs be corrected?

flected, regardless of how the driver held on to the steering wheel.

The amount of steering gear ratio found in various steering boxes depends on the type or use of the vehicle, vehicle weight, and steering characteristics (fast or slow) desired. Steering gear ratios for standard manual steering boxes range between 15 to 1 and 24 to 1, resulting in steering-wheel movement of from 4 to 6 revolutions from extreme right to extreme left position. Vehicles equipped with power steering frequently have steering gear ratios of less than 15 to 1.

5-2 STEERING LINKAGE

The steering linkage is used to connect the steering knuckle to the pitman-arm shaft of the steering box. The parallelogram (called this because of its shape when viewed from the top) type of linkage is the most common in use today, although centre point and solid tie-rod types are used sometimes.

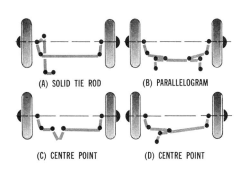

(A) SOLID TIE ROD   (B) PARALLELOGRAM

(C) CENTRE POINT   (D) CENTRE POINT

Fig. 5-2   Typical Steering Linkages

The steering linkage may be placed ahead or behind the suspension assembly. Various linkage combinations are used to produce the desired effects. The steering linkage consists of the following parts: steering arms, tie rods, ball joints, centre links, idler arms, and the pitman arm.

Steering Knuckle. The steering knuckle includes the wheel spindle or stub axle, with facilities to attach the knuckle to the axle I-beam or upper and lower control arms. It is designed so that the brake backing plate and steering arms may be attached easily.

When an I-beam front axle or the older type independent front-suspension systems are used, kingpins are required. The knuckles may be of the

---

Chapter 5
STEERING SYSTEMS

The steering system is comprised of two major units: the *steering gear box* with the steering wheel and shaft, and the *linkage* including the knuckles, steering arms, and the rods necessary to transfer the steering-box motion to the front wheels.

The combination of the steering gear box and the linkage produces a mechanical advantage that is known as steering gear ratio or steering gear reduction.

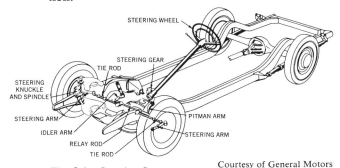

Fig. 5-1   Steering System

Courtesy of General Motors

5-1 STEERING GEAR RATIO

Steering gear ratio refers to the amount the steering wheel is turned compared to the amount the wheels are turned. Steering gear ratio assists the driver in turning the steering knuckles in any desired direction, and aids him in holding the front wheels in position. Without a proper steering system and steering gear ratio, any irregularities in the road would cause the front wheels to be turned or de-

Elliott or *Reverse Elliott* type. The king-pin is usually fixed in the I-beam, or steering knuckle support, and the knuckle is free to pivot. Bushings and lubrication between the steering knuckle and the king-pin help reduce friction and wear. An anti-friction ballthrust bearing is placed between the knuckle and the axle, or support ends, to reduce friction when the knuckles are pivoted for steering purposes.

When ball joints or spherical joints are used, king-pins and thrust bearings are not required. The ball joint is designed so that the knuckles may pivot for steering purposes, or may move up and down with the spring action. These knuckles provide ease of movement while overcoming the friction of the thrust load imposed by the weight of the vehicle.

Steering Arms. Steering arms are usually made of forged steel and are either bolted to the knuckle assembly or forged as an integral part of the knuckle. The outer ends of the arms have a tapered hole to which the tie-rod ball sockets are attached.

When the steering arms are moved in either direction, they force the steering knuckle to pivot on the king-pins or ball joints.

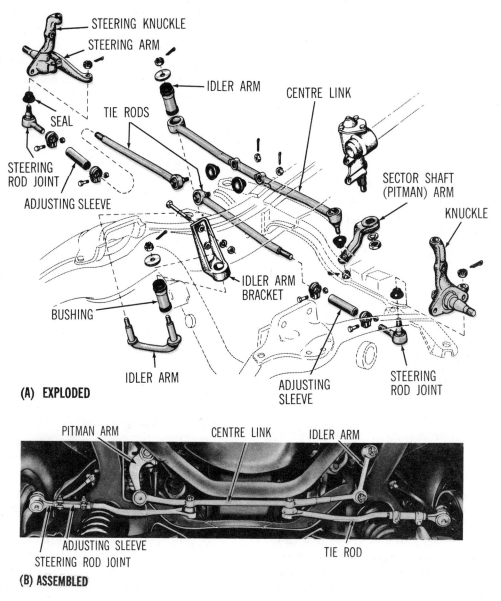

(A) **EXPLODED**

(B) **ASSEMBLED**

Fig. 5-3   Steering Linkage Components

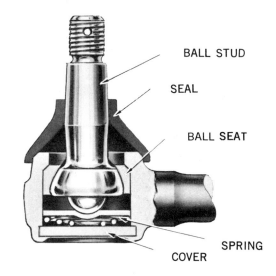

(A) SEALED NONADJUSTABLE TYPE

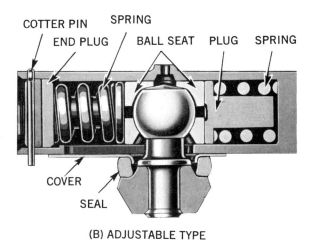

(B) ADJUSTABLE TYPE

Courtesy of General Motors

Fig. 5-4 Steering Rod Joints

Steering Rod Joints. Since all steering rods must pivot in all directions, it is necessary to have some type of flexible joint at their ends. Two common types are the *ball-stud* type and the *integral* type.

In the ball-stud type, the shaft of the ball stud is tapered to fit the tapered hole in the steering arm or other steering rod. A nut and cotter pin complete the fastening. The ball stud is encased in a ball socket, one end of which is threaded to the steering rod to be attached. The ball and socket allow freedom of movement over a wide variety of angles. A spring placed under the ball removes the slackness between the ball and the socket. When the spring can no longer compensate for the wear, a loose fit becomes evident and replacement of the joint is required.

When the integral type is used, the ball stud is placed between two halves of the socket. The sockets are placed inside the end of the steering rod and are held tightly against the ball stud by springs and plugs. The outer plug is threaded into the rod, compressing the springs, to assure a snug fit between the sockets and the ball. A limited amount of wear can be compensated for by tightening the outer plug.

Tie Rods. Tie rods are used to connect the steering arms to the centre link. Ball joints at each end provide the necessary flexibility. The ball joints are threaded into each end of the tie rod to provide a means of adjusting toe-in. The rods are usually of equal length in order to minimize the change in toe-in or toe-out caused by the up-and-down motion of the spring action. The tie rods are usually about the same length as the lower control arms and are as parallel as possible to the centre link when viewed from the front. One-piece tie rods are usually used in I-beam front axles.

Centre Link. The centre link is a long rod placed crosswise to the frame and attached at one end to the pitman arm and at the other end to the idler arm. The tie rod is attached to the centre of the centre link. Its purpose is to transfer the pitman-arm motion to the tie rods. On some linkage types, the centre link is replaced by a drag link. A drag link performs the same function but is usually placed parallel to the frame. Centre links are not required on centre-point type steering systems.

Idler Arm. The idler arm is attached to one end of the centre link by a ball joint and is free to pivot on a bracket which is attached to the frame. The idler arm and pitman arm must be parallel. Idler arms are not required on centre point or I-beam steering systems.

Pitman Arm. The pitman arm is connected by a ball joint to the centre link, and by means of a spline and retaining nut to the pitman-arm shaft or sector shaft of the steering box. The pitman arm can be made to swing from side to side (cross steering) or front to back (fore-and-aft) by rotating the pitman-arm shaft. The pitman-arm movement is from side to side in parallelogram-type steering, and front to back in the centre point or solid I-beam axle-type of steering.

5-3 STEERING COLUMNS

The steering-column assembly connects the steering wheel to the steering gear box. It consists of the

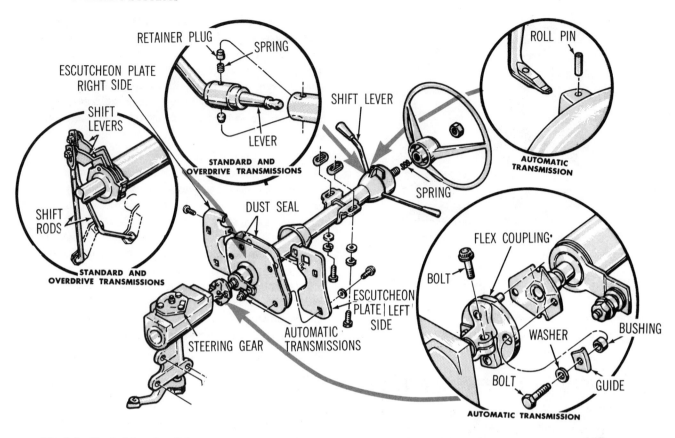

Fig. 5-5   Typical Steering Column

Ford of Canada

steering wheel and shaft, and a jacket tube and bushing assembly. Frequently standard transmission and automatic transmission gear selectors are attached to, or integral with, the steering column.

The electric horn button or ring connections, as well as directional signal controls, also are built into the steering column.

Steering Wheel and Shaft. The steering wheel and shaft transfer the driver's steering motions to the steering box. The shaft may be of one-piece construction, or contain one or more universal joints when the steering box and steering wheel must be offset. The shaft may include special devices to tilt the steering wheel up and down or sideways, or it may contain a device to lengthen or shorten the shaft. Both are used for ease of driver entrance or to accommodate variations in driver posture. Special safety devices are included which prevent the tilting, lengthening, or shortening of the shaft unless the gear selector is in the park position.

The steering wheel is attached to the tapered end of the steering shaft, locked to the shaft by means of *splines* or a *key*, and secured by a nut. The

steering shaft is enclosed in a tube called the *steering mast* or *jacket tube*. The assembly is known as the *steering column*. A jacket-tube bushing or bearing supports the upper end of the shaft. The hub of the steering wheel exerts pressure on a spring, which in turn presses against a sleeve, which presses against the inner bearing race to maintain the proper fit. A rattle will develop should the fit between the bearing and the shaft become loose.

5-4 ENERGY-ABSORBING STEERING COLUMN

The energy-absorbing or collapsible steering column is a protective device that will collapse upon impact. If, as a result of an accident, the driver is thrown forward against the steering wheel, the steering column will collapse and in doing so absorbs the energy of the driver's forward movement and thus greatly reduces the possibility of injury to the driver.

The two-piece steering worm shaft of an energy-absorbing steering assembly is designed so that it not only transmits the turning action of the steering

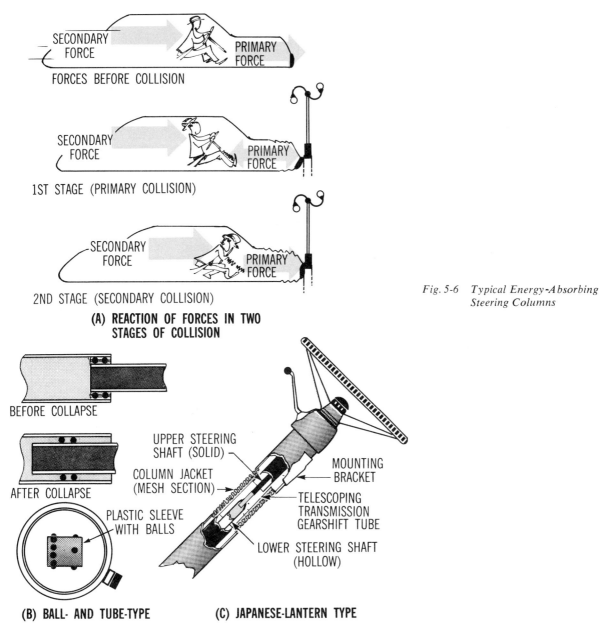

SECONDARY FORCE   PRIMARY FORCE

FORCES BEFORE COLLISION

SECONDARY FORCE   PRIMARY FORCE

1ST STAGE (PRIMARY COLLISION)

SECONDARY FORCE   PRIMARY FORCE

2ND STAGE (SECONDARY COLLISION)

(A) REACTION OF FORCES IN TWO STAGES OF COLLISION

Fig. 5-6 Typical Energy-Absorbing Steering Columns

BEFORE COLLAPSE

AFTER COLLAPSE

PLASTIC SLEEVE WITH BALLS

UPPER STEERING SHAFT (SOLID)
COLUMN JACKET (MESH SECTION)
MOUNTING BRACKET
TELESCOPING TRANSMISSION GEARSHIFT TUBE
LOWER STEERING SHAFT (HOLLOW)

(B) BALL- AND TUBE-TYPE   **(C) JAPANESE-LANTERN TYPE**

wheel but can also telescope as the steering column collapses.

One type of energy-absorbing steering-column jacket tube is called the *Japanese-lantern* type. In this type a plastic lattice-work insert several inches in length joins the upper and lower sections of the jacket tube. Upon impact this plastic insert collapses and folds up like a Japanese lantern.

Another type of energy-absorbing steering column is the *ball-and-tube* type. In this design the upper and lower sections of the jacket tube are placed one inside the other with tight fitting ball bearings located between the two sections. Upon impact the two tubes are forced to telescope and the ball bearings must plow furrows in each of the tubes in order to permit collapse. The plowing action of the ball bearings results in a more uniform rate of collapse.

5-5 TILT- AND TELESCOPING-TYPE STEERING WHEELS

The tilt-type steering wheel permits the driver to change the normal angle of the steering wheel a few degrees, either to a more vertical or horizontal position. The telescoping-type steering wheel permits the driver to move the steering wheel toward

(A) TILT STEERING WHEEL

TILT WHEEL
RELEASE LEVER

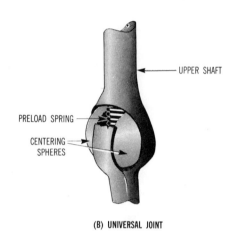

UPPER SHAFT

PRELOAD SPRING

CENTERING
SPHERES

(B) UNIVERSAL JOINT

Courtesy of General Motors

Fig. 5-7   Tilt Steering

or away from the instrument panel. A combination of both types is also available.

The changing of the position of the steering wheel permits easier entrance and exit for the driver, and enables him to adjust the postion of the steering wheel to suit his stature or driving position.

In this type of construction the steering worm shaft is in two sections joined by a universal joint (tilt type) or a universal slip joint (tilt and telescoping type).

The steering wheel is locked into position by a control knob on the side of the steering column. The position of some steering wheels may only be changed when the transmission selector lever is in park position.

5-6 STEERING LOCK

As a deterrent to car theft, manufacturers place the ignition lock on the steering column and incorporate with it a steering locking device.

The steering locking device consists of a *gear and rack strip* and a *spring-loaded plunger* which enters a notch in a disc attached to the worm shaft. The position of the plunger (locked or unlocked) is controlled by the gear attached to the ignition-lock cylinder and meshed with the rack strip. When the ignition switch is turned on, the gear rotates and pulls the rack strip, which in turn pulls the plunger out of the notch in the worm-shaft disc, thus releasing the steering. When the ignition switch is turned off, the gear rotates moving the rack strip and plunger into the locked position. If the plunger and the notch in the worm disc are not properly aligned the plunger spring is compressed. When the steering wheel is turned, and the notch in the disc and the plunger are in alignment, the spring forces the plunger into the notch, thereby locking the steering wheel.

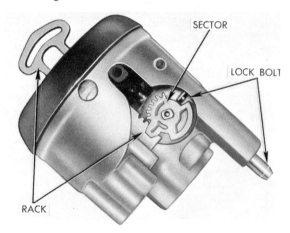

SECTOR

LOCK BOLT

RACK

Courtesy of General Motors

Fig. 5-8   Steering Lock

5-7 STEERING GEAR BOXES

The steering gear box serves two basic purposes: it produces a large portion of the mechanical advantage required to provide easy and safe steering; and it provides a convenient means of converting the turning motion of the steering wheel into the side-to-side or fore-and-aft motion required to operate the steering linkage.

5-8 STANDARD OR MANUAL
STEERING GEARS

Several types of standard steering gear are used:

the *recirculating-ball* type, the *worm-and-roller* type, the *cam-and-roller* type, and the *rack-and-pinion* type. The recirculating-ball type and the worm-and-sector type are the most popular today.

Each type uses a steering shaft with the steering worm on one end and the steering wheel on the other. A pitman-arm shaft passes at right angles to the worm gear. The inner end of the pitman shaft engages the worm through either a sector roller, lever studs, or tapered peg, or a large ball nut that rides on the worm.

The worm-gear end of the steering shaft is supported by roller or ball bearings placed at each end of the worm. These bearings are adjustable in order to remove side or end play. The pitman-arm shaft or sector shaft is mounted in bushings or needle bearings. Adjustments are provided to assure proper pitman-arm shaft-to-worm clearance.

A casting called a steering box encloses all the parts and keeps them in proper alignment. The steering box is partially filled with gear oil to provide the necessary lubrication. Oil seals around the shafts prevent leakage of the lubricant and the entry of dirt and grit. The steering box is bolted to the frame or some rigid area.

Recirculating-Ball Type Steering Gear Box.

In the recirculating-ball type steering box, the sector roller and lever stud are replaced by a large ball nut assembly or gear rack which is mounted on the worm. The nut is driven by two separate closed circuits of hardened steel ball bearings which circulate in the spiral grooves ground in the ball nut and the worm. When the worm is turned, the ball bearings are rotated, forcing the ball nut to move along the worm gear. As the balls rotate in the grooves in the ball nut, they will come one by one to the end of the grooves, Return tubes carry the balls diagonally across the back of the ball nut so that they re-enter the ball nut at the opposite end. In this way the balls recirculate through the two circuits, reducing the friction between the worm and nut to a very low level.

One side of the ball nut has tapered gear teeth cut into it. The pitman-arm sector gear has tapered gear teeth which engage the ball-nut teeth. When the worm gear rotates, the ball nut travels up or down, rotating the pitman-arm shaft.

When the steering is in the straight-ahead position, the pitman-arm shaft sector gear meshes

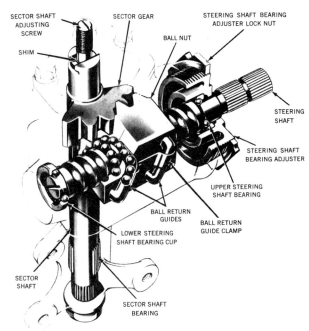

Ford of Canada

Fig. 5-9   Recirculating-Ball Type Steering Gear

snugly with the teeth on the ball nut to provide minimum clearance in this area.

As the pitman-arm shaft is turned, the pitman-arm shaft sector gear travels in an arc away from the centre line of the worm and ball nut. This provides the necessary clearance at the extreme right and left, and a convenient means of adjustment to compensate for the wear that takes place in the straight-ahead driving position. This adjustment is accomplished by moving the pitman-arm shaft along its axis toward the worm and ball nut by means of a thrust screw.

The worm gear and its shaft and the pitman-arm shaft are mounted in bearings. Adjustments to compensate for wear are accomplished in the usual manner.

Worm-and-Sector Roller-Type Steering Box.

In the worm-and-sector roller-type of steering gear, the pitman-arm shaft roller and worm are made of heat-treated alloy steel and are accurately machined. The sector roller is mounted on double row ball bearings, supported by a through bolt that attaches the roller to the sector or pitman-arm shaft. The sector roller, being free to rotate, provides a rotating engagement with the worm. When the worm is rotated by the steering wheel, the sector roller rotates and at the same time is moved toward or away from one end of the worm gear. This action of the sector roller results in the pitman-arm shaft

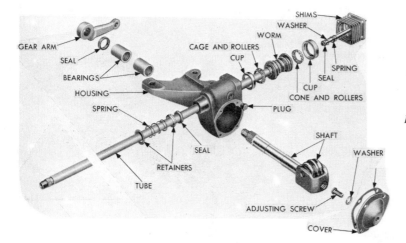

Fig. 5-10   Worm-and-Sector Steering Gear

rotating on its axis, causing the pitman arm to swing and operate the steering linkage.

Cam-and-Lever Steering Gear Box.

The cam-and-lever steering uses one or two lever studs mounted into tapered roller bearings which ride in the worm gear grooves. When the worm is revolved, it causes the studs to follow along with the worm gear grooves, imparting a turning motion to the pitman-arm shaft.

When the steering is in the straight-ahead position, the lever studs fit snugly into the worm gear grooves to provide minimum clearance in this area. As the pitman-arm shaft is turned, the stud travels in an arc away from the centre line of the worm. This provides the necessary clearance at the extreme right or left end and also a convenient means of adjustment to compensate for the wear that takes place in the straight-ahead driving position. This adjustment is accomplished by moving the pitman-arm shaft along its axis toward the worm gear by means of a thrust screw.

The worm gear and its shaft and the pitman-arm shaft are mounted in bearings. Adjustments to compensate for wear are accomplished in a similar manner to the worm-and-sector roller-type steering box.

Pinion and Rack Steering Gears.

In this type of steering the pinion gear is attached to the steering-wheel shaft and the rack strip is integral with the steering linkage. When the pinion gear is turned it moves the rack strip to the right or left to provide steering control.

Fig. 5-11   Rack and Pinion Steering Gear

5-9 STEERING HIGH SPOT

Since most driving is done in a straight-ahead position, the sector gear or roller is in contact with the centre portion of the ball nut or worm gear most of the time, which results in extreme wear in this area. In order to compensate for wear and to provide ease of steering from the extreme right or left positions, the sector gear or roller and the ball nut or worm gear are designed with different arcs.

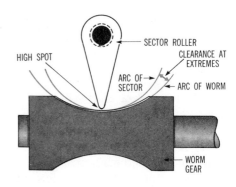

Fig. 5-12   Arcs of Steering High Spot

The arc formed by the pivoting pitman-arm shaft and sector gear or roller is of a smaller radius than the arc used on the ball nut or worm gear. The sector gear or roller is closer to the ball nut or worm gear in the centre position than at the two extremes. As a result it is possible to move the sector gear or roller closer to the centre of the ball nut or worm gear as wear takes place in this area, and still have sufficient clearance at the two ends of the ball nut or worm gear.

This adjustment is accomplished by means of a *thrust screw* or *lash adjustor* which moves the sector gear or roller and shaft along its axis toward the ball nut or worm gear. As the sector gear or roller is moved in towards the ball nut or worm gear, it meshes deeper, reducing the clearance between them. The point of contact between the two arcs is known as the *steering high spot*, and should be one-half of the number of turns of the steering wheel between the extremes.

5-10 POWER STEERING

Power steering is a hydraulic and mechanical booster device used to reduce the steering wheel turning effort applied by the driver. When the steering wheel is turned, the power steering unit is set into operation and takes over most of the work of steering. While power steering does most of the work, it must be designed so that the driver can retain some road feel.

Road feel is the feeling transferred to the steering wheel by the wheels of a car in motion. This enables a driver to determine the correct steering response, such as the amount of turning effort required to stabilize the car body on turns, or the resistance when encountering cross winds. Road feel is maintained in most power steering units when the driver applies an effort of between 2 and 3 lbs on the steering-wheel rim before the power-steering unit takes over.

Power-steering systems are of two general types, the linkage type and the integral type. The *linkage type* uses a hydraulic piston and cylinder and a control valve attached to the steering linkage. A standard-type steering gear box is used.

In the *integral type* the hydraulic piston and cylinder and control valve are built into or part of the steering gear box. The hydraulic pressure required for both systems is produced by a hydraulic pump, belt driven from the engine.

The basic operation of both types is similar.

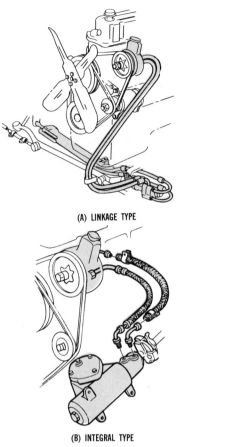

(A) LINKAGE TYPE

(B) INTEGRAL TYPE

Courtesy of General Motors

Fig. 5-13   Typical Power Steering Systems

When the control valve is actuated by the driver's steering effort, oil under pressure is admitted to one side or the other of the hydraulic piston. This pressure is transferred mechanically to the pitman-arm shaft in the integral type, or to the linkage in the linkage type, thus assisting the driver in manipulating the front wheels.

It should be noted here that in the event of pump pressure failure for any reason, power-steering systems can be operated manually. However, to do so, more effort is required to manipulate the unit than is required for conventional steering systems.

Power Steering Pumps.

Two types of power steering pumps are in common use today, the vane-type pump and the rotor-type pump. In the *vane type*, vanes slide in and out of the driving rotor to contact the inner surface of an oval-shaped chamber in the pump body. As the rotor rotates, the vanes slide out to contact the face of the larger diameter of the oval, and the size of the pockets between the vanes increases. During

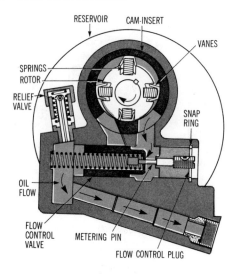

Chrysler Canada Ltd.

Fig. 5-14   Typical Vane-Type Pump

this increase, oil enters the pockets through the inlet port from the oil reservoir. As the vanes approach the smaller diameter of the oval, they slide into the rotor and the size of the pocket decreases. The oil is forced, under pressure, out the outlet port.

In the *rotor type*, an inner-drive rotor meshes

with an outer-drive rotor. As the rotors rotate, the pockets increase and decrease in size. As the pockets increase in size, oil enters through the inlet port from the reservoir. As they decrease in size, oil is forced out through the outlet port under pressure. Both pumps are equipped with a pressure-regulating valve which prevents the development of excessive pressure.

Type-A automatic-transmission fluid is used in most power-steering units because it is ideal for the transmission of pressure, and the lubrication and cleanliness of the pump, control valve, and power piston.

In-Line Self-Contained Power Steering.

This type of power steering is very compact because the power-steering gear, steering shaft, hydraulic valves, worm, and rack-piston are all in a line. The basic steering box uses all of the elements of the conventional steering gear. The pitman-arm shaft engages a recirculating ball nut that rides on a typical worm gear. The reaction unit, a pivot lever, and a valve body have been added to the basic steering box. The ball nut has been changed to enable it to be used as a power piston.

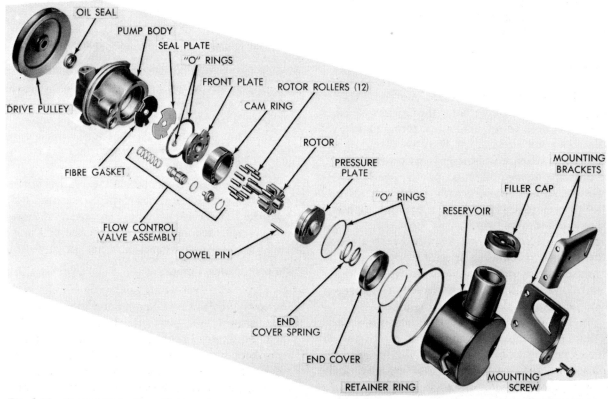

Fig. 5-15   Typical Rotor-Type Pump

Courtesy of General Motors

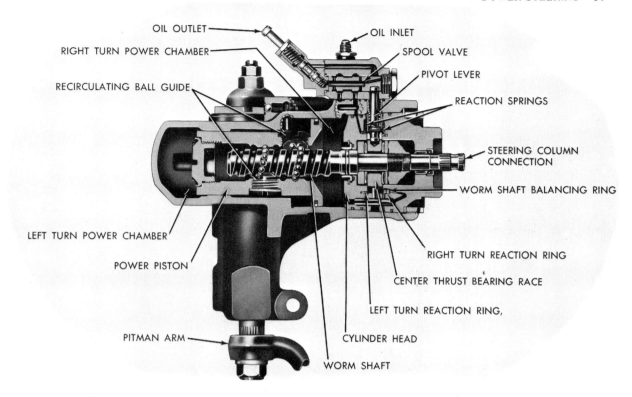

OIL OUTLET

RIGHT TURN POWER CHAMBER

RECIRCULATING BALL GUIDE

OIL INLET

SPOOL VALVE

PIVOT LEVER

REACTION SPRINGS

STEERING COLUMN CONNECTION

WORM SHAFT BALANCING RING

LEFT TURN POWER CHAMBER

POWER PISTON

RIGHT TURN REACTION RING

CENTER THRUST BEARING RACE

LEFT TURN REACTION RING,

PITMAN ARM

CYLINDER HEAD

WORM SHAFT

Fig. 5-16   Typical In-Line Self-Contained Power Steering Gear Unit   Courtesy of General Motors

When little pressure (about 1 to 3 lb) is being applied to the steering wheel, the reaction unit is centered, the pivot lever is straight up and down, and the spool valve is in neutral position. When a pressure of more than 1 to 3 lb is required to turn the steering wheel, because of the resistance to pivoting of the front wheels, the worm shifts endwise slightly. This movement of the worm moves the reaction unit causing the pivot lever to tilt, moving the spool valve, and admitting oil at high pressure from the pump to one side or the other of the piston. This results in an assisting action to the turning effort. The higher the resistance to the turning of the steering wheel, the more the worm moves endwise, and the more the pivot lever tilts and opens the spool valve. This results in higher pressures being applied to the piston to give additional assistance in the turning of the steering wheel. This assistance is in direct proportion to the effort required. Most of the turning effort is handled by the oil pressure on the piston.

When a turn is made in the opposite direction, the worm moves toward the other end of the steering box, moving the reaction unit, pivot lever, and spool valve in the opposite direction. This opens the passageways which direct the high-pressure oil to the opposite side of the power piston.

The spool valve also opens the necessary passageways to direct the returning oil from the power piston to the reservoir.

In some types of in-line self-contained power-steering units, the reaction unit, the pivot lever, and spool valve are replaced by a rotary valve and spool valve attached to a torsion bar. In this type, the twisting of the torsion bar moves the spool valve in relation to an open-centre, three-way, rotary-type valve.

In the straight-ahead position the spool valve is held in a neutral or centre position. Since one side of the spool valve is attached to the rotary valve body, and the other end is attached to the torsion bar, twisting of the torsion bar turns the spool slightly in relationship to the rotary valve. This turning of the spool valve opens passageways which direct the oil pressure to one end of the piston, assisting the turning effort of the driver. The greater the effort required to turn the steering wheel, the more the torsion bar twists, the more the spool valve turns, and the more high-pressure oil is admitted to the piston. Therefore, the assistance given

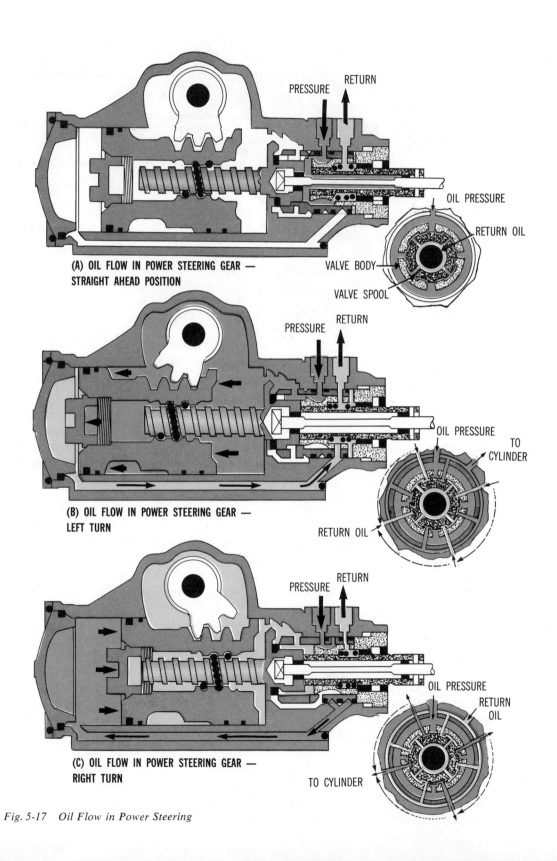

PRESSURE   RETURN

OIL PRESSURE

RETURN OIL

VALVE BODY

VALVE SPOOL

**(A) OIL FLOW IN POWER STEERING GEAR —
STRAIGHT AHEAD POSITION**

PRESSURE   RETURN

OIL PRESSURE

TO
CYLINDER

RETURN OIL

**(B) OIL FLOW IN POWER STEERING GEAR —
LEFT TURN**

PRESSURE   RETURN

OIL PRESSURE

RETURN
OIL

TO CYLINDER

**(C) OIL FLOW IN POWER STEERING GEAR —
RIGHT TURN**

Fig. 5-17   Oil Flow in Power Steering

by the power-steering unit is proportional to the driver's turning effort. As a result the driver is always aware of the variations in steering effort.

Self-Contained Off-Set Power Steering.

In this type of power steering the basic conventional-type steering gear and the control valve are located in the steering box. A separate power piston and cylinder assembly is attached to the side of the steering box. The piston has a rack gear that meshes with a second set of pitman sector teeth. The recirculating-ball nut applies its force to the first set of sector teeth and the power piston gear applies force to the second set. When oil pressure is applied to one side or the other of the piston, the piston moves, moving the rack gear which in turn rotates the pitman-arm shaft, providing the power assist.

The control valve may be either the rotary valve, spool valve, and torsion-bar type or it may utilize the endwise movement of the worm to operate the reaction unit, pivot arm, and spool valve. In each case the construction and operation is similar to the in-line type of control valve.

Linkage-Type Power Steering.

This system uses a conventional manual steering gear box. The power, or booster, cylinder is attached between the steering-gear linkage and the car frame. The control valve is operated by the pitman arm.

The ball end of the pitman arm is placed in a spring-loaded ball socket in the control valve. When the pressure on the pitman arm is greater than 1 to 3 lb, the reaction springs compress and the spool valve moves. This directs oil pressure to one side or the other of the power-cylinder piston. Since the power piston is attached to the car frame and the power cylinder to the steering gear linkage, the entrance of oil under pressure to one end of the cylinder moves the cylinder one way or the other to provide most of the effort to pivot the front wheels.

The control valve may be a separate unit or may be integral with the power piston.

(A) TYPICAL INSTALLATION

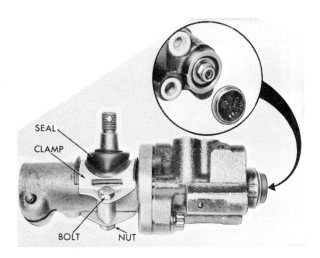

(B) CONTROL VALVE

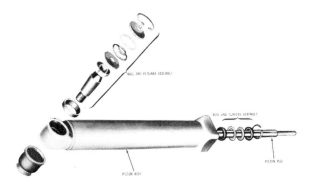

(C) POWER CYLINDER

Chrysler of Canada

Fig. 5-18   Linkage-Type Power Steering

REVIEW QUESTIONS

1. What is (a) a steering knuckle (b) a steering arm?
2. Why are king-pins not necessary when ball or spherical joints are used in the front-suspension system?
3. Name and describe two types of steering rod joints.
4. What is the purpose of the steering linkage?
5. Make a sketch of the steering linkage and identify each of the components.
6. What is meant by the terms (a) mechanical advantage (b) steering gear ratio (c) steering high-spot.
7. Why is steering high-spot necessary?
8. Describe the construction of a recirculating-ball type of steering box.

9. Describe the basic operation of a power-steering system.
10. What safety precaution is built into a power-steering system?
11. Describe the operation of a vane-type power steering pump.
12. Why is automatic transmission fluid used in most power-steering assemblies?
13. How is the sense of road feel obtained in (a) linkage type (b) in-line integral-type power-steering systems?
14. Describe two methods of moving the spool valve to control the operating fluid in an integral-type power-steering system.
15. How is the movement of the spool valve controlled in a linkage-type power-steering system?

Chapter 6

ALIGNMENT AND WHEEL BALANCE

It is not enough to merely place the front wheels on hubs, stand them up vertically, and provide a method of swinging them from right to left. If a vehicle's front wheels were to be attached in this manner, the vehicle could be driven, but it would steer poorly, and at higher speeds it would become dangerous. Tire life would be short.

In order to assure stability and ease of steering, and to minimize tire wear, the wheels must be in correct alignment.

6-1 THE ACKERMAN PRINCIPLE

The automobile uses the *Ackerman Principle* of steering. Only the wheels and the steering knuckles swing, instead of the whole axle as in a horse-drawn vehicle. With this steering principle, the steering-knuckle arms are placed at the angle of 100 to 105° instead of 90° to the wheel spindle. As a result of this arrangement, the inner wheel turns at a greater angle than the outer wheel when the vehicle makes a turn. When the vehicle is being driven in a straight line the wheels are parallel. The Ackerman Principle of steering is used with both solid and independent front axles.

The Ackerman Principle locates the centre line of the steering-knuckle arms on a line drawn between the steering axis and the centre of the rear axle. The angle between the wheel spindle and the steering-knuckle arms ranges between 100 and 105° instead of 90°. This places the steering-knuckle arms in different arcs of the circle.

In Fig. 6-2 distance 1 is greater than distance 2, 2 is greater than 3, and 3 greater than 4, even

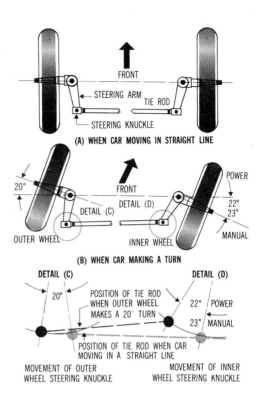

Fig. 6-1   Ackerman Principle of Steering

though the arc is 20° in each case. Therefore, when arm A moves through distance 1, it will move arm B through 2 and part of 3. Distance 1 being larger than distance 2, the extra distance coming from part 3, the steering arm B will rotate more than steering arm A. This results in a different angle of steering for each spindle.

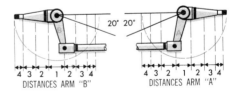

Fig. 6-2

6-2 STEERING GEOMETRY

Front end, or steering geometry, is the term given to the inter-related angles between the axles, wheels, other front-end parts, and the frame. The names of the angles used in steering geometry are: *caster, camber, king-pin inclination, toe-in* and *toe-out* on turns.

Caster Angle.

Caster angle is the tilt of the spindle pivot towards

the front or rear of the vehicle. Because of "caster," the wheels contact the road behind the weight line or centre line of the spindle pivot. This produces a trailing effect, similar to a furniture caster. In a furniture caster the caster wheel always follows its pivot. The front wheel fork of a bicycle is another example of the caster principle. In both of these examples, the wheel tends to maintain its straight-ahead position because of the fact that the centre line of the pivot intersects the ground ahead of the wheel's point of contact. In effect, the wheel is being pulled; consequently the wheel must follow. When the pivot centre line intersects the road ahead of the wheel contact point, caster is positive. When the pivot centre line contacts the road behind the contact point, caster is negative, and the wheel has a tendency to turn away from the straight-ahead position. Therefore, caster angle may be defined as the number of degrees that the spindle pivot centre line (the top of the axle, king-pin, or ball-joints) tilts from the vertical toward either the front (negative caster) or rear (postive caster) of the vehicle.

Positive caster tends to force the wheels to travel in a straight-ahead position and assists in turning the wheels back to the straight-ahead position after making a turn. Consequently, it makes it more difficult to swivel the wheels from the straight-ahead. It also results in a mild tipping effect when cornering. When turning to the right, the right wheel will cause the steering knuckle to rise slightly, while the left wheel will lower the left knuckle slightly. This tipping effect is the opposite to what is desirable for safe cornering. Because of these undesirable features, most modern vehicles have little or no positive caster.

Negative caster, on the other hand, eases the swivelling of the front wheels and tends to produce a desirable, mild banking effect when cornering. That is, the side of the car on the inside of the turn will lower slightly, while the other side will rise, adding to the stability of the vehicle during the turn. Many modern vehicles use negative caster and utilize steering-knuckle inclination to assist in maintaining steering ease while driving straight-ahead.

Excessive positive caster, which requires excessive effort to turn the wheels and to hold the vehicle in a turn, can result in slow speed shimmy, as is sometimes seen when pushing furniture. *Excessive negative caster* can result in road wander and loss

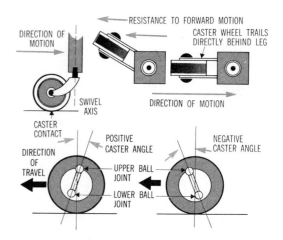

(A) POSITIVE CASTER SIDE VIEW (B) NEGATIVE CASTER SIDE VIEW

Fig. 6-3   Caster Angle

of directional stability because the turning forces of the negative caster might be sufficient to overcome the other inherent directional forces. Improper or negative caster settings cannot, in themselves, cause excessive tire wear. A vehicle will tend to lead or pull to the side with the least amount of positive caster. However, caster variations almost always cause variations in camber.

Camber Angle.

Camber angle is the tilt of the front wheels away from the vertical which tends to bring the point of contact between the tire and the road more directly under the load line. An outward tilt is called positive camber while an inward tilt is called negative camber.

Positive camber gives the wheels a slight outward tilt to start with. When the vehicle is loaded, the load brings the wheels closer to the vertical. Positive camber also assists in reducing the tendency of the front wheels to spread apart at the front (toe-out) as the vehicle rolls forward, and materially lessens the road shock to the steering system.

If camber were set at 0°, any hole or bump in the road might cause the wheel to turn around the spindle pivot. Steering effort would also tend to increase because of the large radius between the spindle pivot and the tire contact point, through which the wheel must turn. This radius is called *scrub radius* because, in effect, the tire has to scrub through this radius when turning the wheels at the stand-still. The larger the cross section of the tire, the larger the scrub radius. Low-pressure, wide

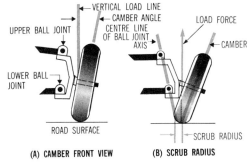

Fig. 6-4   *Camber Angle*

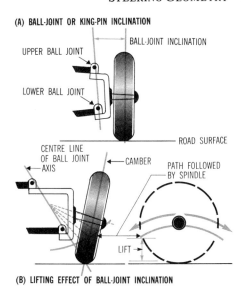

Fig. 6-5   *Ball-Joint Inclination*

cross-sectional tires restrict the amount of camber that can be successfully used.

Positive camber reduces the scrub radius by reducing the distance between the spindle pivot centre line and the tire contact point.

Most modern vehicles use a small amount of camber, usually less than 1°. When a large camber angle is used, the tire cross section will contact the road in a conical pattern. This results in increased tire wear on the edges of the tire tread because the outer part of the tread is rotating in a smaller radius circle than the inner part of the tread. The circumference of a circle is proportional to the radius. Because the tread on a tire is rotating through more than one radius, one portion of the tire must slip while rotating with the other. Excessive positive camber results in rapid wear on the outer edge of the tread, excessive negative camber on the inner edge of the tread.

King-Pin or Steering-Axis Inclination.

King-pin, or steering-axis inclination is the angle between a line drawn through the centre of the upper and lower ball joints and a vertical line. Its purpose is to provide steering stability by returning the wheels to the straight-ahead position after a turn has been made. It also helps to reduce steering effort, particularly when the vehicle is stationary. Tire wear is reduced and road shock is transmitted in such a manner as to cause it to be absorbed by the heavy inner spindle and knuckle assembly.

Steering-axis inclination assists steering stability. When the wheels are turned from the straight-ahead position the vehicle is actually lifted. This is because the wheel spindle, when turned, is moved about the steering axis, and as the axis is tilted, the spindle will move in a downward direction. Since downward movement is impossible because the spindle is supported by the wheel, the steering

knuckle is forced upward, thus raising the vehicle. The weight of the vehicle will tend to force the spindle to swivel back, thus returning the wheels to the straight-ahead position.

King-pin inclination also helps to reduce the scrub radius, and helps to place the spindle-pivot centre line directly over the tire contact point.

By using king-pin inclination, camber can be reduced. However, the benefits of high camber, easier steering, and reduced road shock can be retained.

Included Angle.

Included or combined angle is the steering-axis angle plus the camber angle. It determines the point of intersection of the wheel and steering-axis centre lines.

When the point of intersection is below the road

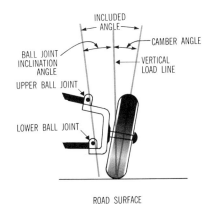

Fig. 6-6   *Included Angle*

surface, the wheels have a tendency to toe-out (to be farther apart at the front than the rear). This results from the fact that the forward push of the vehicle is transferred to the wheels through the steering axis, and this axis is inside the centre line of the wheel. When the point of intersection is above the road, the steering axis is outside the centre line of the wheel, resulting in the wheel toeing in. In the modern vehicle the point of inter-section is usually slightly below the surface of the road and the tendency of the wheels to toe-out is overcome by setting the wheels with a small amount of toe-in. Since king-pin inclination is fixed by the design of the steering knuckle, any changes in included angle must be made by changing the camber angle.

Toe-In.

Toe-in occurs when wheels are angled towards one another so that they are closer together at the front than at the back when viewed from the top. It is the difference between the centre-to-centre dis-tances. (A — B = Toe-in as shown in Fig. 6-7.)

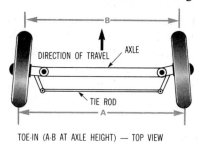

Fig. 6-7   *Toe-In Measurement*

The purpose of toe-in is to offset the undesirable cone-rolling effect caused by the included angle, and by the natural forces that tend to compress the clearances built into the steering linkage which cause the wheels to toe-out when the vehicle is moving. By setting the wheels to toe-in ⅛ to ¼″ when the vehicle is standing, the forces of motion will cause the wheels to operate at 0° toe-in and the wheels will remain parallel.

Proper toe-in will allow the tires to move forward without scrubbing, a scraping action between the tire and the road. Excessive toe-in causes the outer edge of the tire to wear rapidly, while too much toe-out wears the inner edge of the tread.

Toe-Out on Turns.

Toe-out on turns is the amount of spread, or dif-ference, in angles steered by the inner and outer

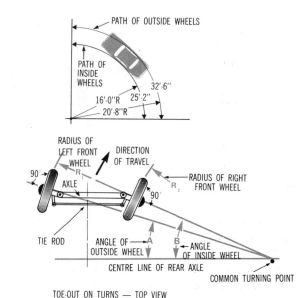

Fig. 6-8   *Steering Geometry*

wheels when the vehicle makes a turn. Since the inner wheel follows a smaller radius circle than the outer wheel, the inner wheel must steer at a sharper angle than the outer wheel, hence the wheels must spread apart at the front during turns. For example, if the inner wheel turns to an angle of 23° from the car frame, the outer wheel turns only 20°. The circles formed by the inner and outer wheels will have a common centre.

6-3 REAR-WHEEL ALIGNMENT

Rear-wheel alignment is comparatively simple since, except in rear engine vehicles, there is little or no camber or toe-in. It is important, however, that the relationship of the rear wheels to the front wheels be correct. This is called *tracking*.

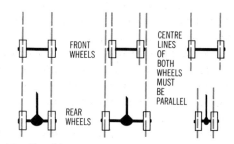

Fig. 6-9   *Tracking*

Tracking means having the rear wheels follow the front wheels in a parallel position; the point equidistant between the centres of the front wheels being perpendicular to the point equidistant between the centres of the rear wheels.

The rear wheels will not necessarily follow the same tracks as the front wheels because many modern vehicles have a different front and rear tread measurement.

There are four distinct causes of improper tracking: swung rear end, swung front end, swayed frame, and diamond frame. Each type will cause tire wear and difficult steering.

6-4 WHEEL BALANCE

Proper tire and wheel balance is necessary for good steering. An unbalanced tire and wheel can result in shimmy and erratic steering, particularly at higher road speeds.

There are two conditions of balance: static, considered as stationary or still balance; and dynamic, or rotating balance.

Static balance is when the weight is equally distributed around the circumference of a wheel in such a manner that there is no tendency for the wheel to rotate when it hangs free. When a tire and wheel are in balance, a reference mark can be placed on a tire, the tire rotated to several different positions, and the tire will stay in the position in which it is placed. An unbalanced tire, however, when moved to different positions, will rotate itself until the heaviest portion of the tire is always at

the lowest point. In operation, a statically unbalanced tire and wheel has a tendency to *hop* up and down at high speed. This is because of the greater centrifugal force, created by the heavy spot trying to move the rotating axis.

To correct this type of unbalanced condition, it is necessary to place a balancing weight 180° from the heavy spot. The centrifugal force of the balancing weight cancels the centrifugal force of the heavy spot. This, therefore, cancels the force trying to move the wheel-rotating axis. A wheel in static balance is not necessarily in dynamic balance.

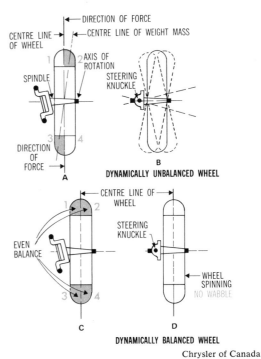

Fig. 6-11 *Dynamic Balance*

Chrysler of Canada

Dynamic balance is obtained only when the weight of a tire and wheel is equally distributed on each side of the centre plane of the assembly.

A wheel may have a centre of gravity of one-half of the wheel on the right side of the centre plane of the assembly. The other half of the wheel's centre of gravity could be to the left of the centre plane. This condition would not affect static balance. However, when the wheel is rotated, the centrifugal forces of the two halves of the wheel act in opposite directions and along different lines to form a couple action. Each time the heavy spots pass the horizontal, they produce a force which tends to turn the wheel inward or outward. This force takes place in opposite directions every 180°.

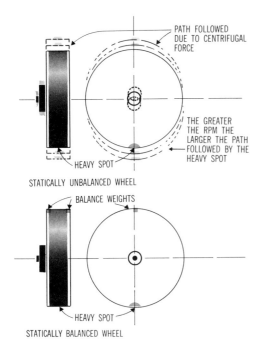

Fig. 6-10 *Static Balance*

Dynamic unbalance, therefore, causes the wheels to vibrate rapidly sideways, producing rapid wear on tires, wheel bearings, and steering linkage.

Wheels are balanced dynamically only after static balance has been corrected. Weights must be added to the rim in the correct position to eliminate the couple action, yet maintain correct static balance.

Similar unbalance conditions can exist in the rear wheels, but as they are held more rigidly the condition is not as readily noticed. However, balancing rear wheels, especially on models with coil springs or extremely flexible rear springs, will increase driving ease and tire mileage.

REVIEW QUESTIONS

1. Why is it necessary to turn the front wheels at different angles when the vehicle rounds a corner?
2. Describe briefly the Ackerman Principle of steering.
3. Give three reasons why front-end alignment must be correct.
4. By means of sketches, illustrate the angles used in steering geometry.
5. What is the purpose of positive caster?
6. Give three disadvantages of excessive caster.
7. What would result from unequal caster settings between the right and left front wheels?
8. What is the purpose of camber?
9. Explain the term "scrub radius."
10. What portion of the tire tread will show excessive wear because of excessive positive camber?
11. Explain how king-pin inclination returns the wheels to the straight-ahead position upon completion of a turn.
12. How does king-pin inclination help reduce scrub radius?
13. What is meant by the term "included angle"?
14. How does toe-in offset the undesirable effect of the included angle?
15. Why is toe-out on turns necessary?
16. What is meant by the term "tracking"?
17. Define (a) static (b) dynamic balance.
18. How may (a) static unbalance (b) dynamic unbalance be corrected? State the procedure to be followed in each case.
19. Which state of unbalance should be corrected first? Why?

Chapter 7
STEERING-SYSTEM SERVICE

Having discussed wheel-alignment angles, their purpose and effect upon steering and tire wear, and the component parts of the steering assembly, this chapter will outline some common steering problems. Steering problems may be listed as: excessive play in the steering system, shimmy, wander or weaving, hard steering, vehicle pulling to one side, road shock or steering kickback, and abnormal tire wear.

7-1 STEERING PROBLEMS

Excessive Play in the Steering System. Before any alignment checks can be made, the steering system must be checked for excessive play or free movement of the component. A small amount of play is desirable in order to provide easy steering. When this play becomes excessive, it is impossible to maintain correct front-wheel alignment, and the

Fig. 7-1   *Checking Tie Rods and Linkage for Looseness*

steering wheel must be turned a considerable distance before any corresponding movement of the front wheels takes place. This excessive turning of the steering wheel makes driving difficult and dangerous.

Excessive play may be caused by: wear or improper adjustment in the steering gear or linkage, worn steering-knuckle parts, or loose wheel bearings.

Steering gears may be quickly checked by having a second person turn the steering wheel to the left and then to the right while the wheels of the car are on the floor. If the steering wheel can be turned a considerable distance before the pitman arm starts to turn, then the steering gear requires adjustment or replacement of worn parts.

Steering linkage may be checked for wear by jacking up the front end of the vehicle and grasping the two front wheels and alternately pushing and pulling on both front wheels at the same time. Any looseness will be evident in the free movement of the wheels.

While the vehicle is jacked up, worn *steering knuckles* or *wheel bearings* may be checked by grasping the top and bottom of the wheel and pushing and pulling alternately on the top and bottom. Excessive looseness indicates worn or loose parts. Checking the wheel-bearing adjustment will indicate whether the wear is in the wheel bearings or steering-knuckle parts.

Fig. 7-2   *Checking for Wear in the Steering Knuckle and Wheel Bearing*

Shimmy. Shimmy is an abnormal vibration of the wheels in a lateral or vertical motion causing a jerky motion to be felt at the steering wheel. There are several types of shimmy.

Low-speed shimmy, usually noticeable under

30 mph, is the lateral oscillation of the front wheel around the steering-knuckle pin, causing the front end of the car to shake from side to side. Common causes of low-speed shimmy are: loose or worn steering linkage, low or uneven tire pressure, weak springs, uneven camber, excessive caster, or irregularities in the tire treads.

High-speed shimmy, or front wheel tramp, usually noticeable between 40 to 60 mph, is the vertical oscillation of the front wheels, which in severe cases results in the front wheel actually lifting off the road surface. In less severe cases the portion of the tire in contact with the road rapidly flexes and unflexes. It first appears deflated as the wheel moves down and inflated as the wheel moves up. High-speed shimmy is frequently caused by the centrifugal force created by either static or dynamically unbalanced wheels, or defective shock absorbers which fail to control natural spring movements.

Wander or Weaving. Wander or weaving is the name given to the driving condition which requires frequent steering-wheel movements in order to keep the vehicle travelling in a straight line and to prevent the vehicle from wandering from one side of the road to the other. It can be caused by:
1. Low or uneven caster angle.
2. Low or uneven tire pressure.
3. Any condition of tightness in the steering system which prevents the wheels from seeking the straight-ahead position as a result of proper caster and king-pin inclination.
4. Improper wheel alignment.
5. Any play in the steering system which would allow the wheels to wander slightly from the straight-ahead position.

Hard Steering. On vehicles with standard steering, hard steering could result from:
1. Low or uneven tire pressures.

2. Lack of lubrication of the steering-linkage joints.
3. Tight steering connections or steering gear.
4. Improper wheel alignment, particularly excessive positive caster angle.
5. Sagging springs or misaligned frame.

If tight steering connections are suspected, disconnecting the pitman arm from the linkage can isolate the trouble to either the linkage or the steering gear.

On vehicles equipped with power steering, failure of any of the power-steering units, the pump, control valve, or actuating piston causes the steering to revert to manual steering. Additional effort is required to steer the vehicle as some of the power units must be operated manually.

Vehicle Pulls to One Side. When this condition occurs during normal driving, it is usually caused by anything which tends to make one wheel drag more than the other. Common causes are: uneven tire pressure, uneven caster or camber angles, tight wheel bearing, uneven brake adjustment, uneven springs, or improper tracking.

When the condition occurs only during braking, it is usually caused by defective brakes (see chapter 12) or uneven tire pressure or tire-tread wear.

Road Shock, or Steering Kick-Back. Road shock, or steering kick-back, is a series of quick successive jerks that may be felt at the steering wheel while driving over a rough stretch of road. Although similar to a shimmy condition, it is easily distinguished, since the jerk action takes place only on rough roads or when passing over a bump.

Normally some road shock will be transferred through the steering system to the steering wheel. But if the jarring becomes excessive, the following conditions could be responsible: incorrect or uneven tire pressure, worn or improperly adjusted steering linkage or gear, sagging springs, or defective shock absorbers.

CONDITION	RAPID WEAR AT SHOULDERS	RAPID WEAR AT CENTRE	CRACKED TREADS	WEAR ON ONE SIDE	FEATHERED EDGE	BALD SPOTS
CAUSE	UNDER-INFLATION	OVER-INFLATION	UNDER-INFLATION OR EXCESSIVE SPEED	EXCESSIVE CAMBER	INCORRECT TOE	WHEEL UNBALANCED
CORRECTION	ADJUST PRESSURE TO SPECIFICATIONS WHEN TIRES ARE COOL			ADJUST CAMBER TO SPECIFICATIONS	ADJUST FOR TOE-IN ⅛ INCH	DYNAMIC OR STATIC BALANCE WHEELS

Fig. 7-3   Tire Wear Patterns

Abnormal Tire Wear. Abnormal or uneven tire wear can result from various causes: improper wheel alignment, improper tire inflation, improper braking, poor driving habits (such as jack-rabbit starts), severe braking, turning corners too fast, and high-speed driving. Only tire wear caused by improper wheel alignment will be discussed in this section.

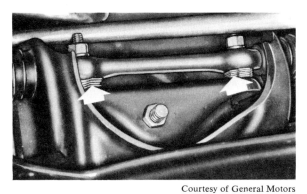

Courtesy of General Motors

Fig. 7-4   Caster and Camber Adjustment—Shim Method

Too much positive camber causes excessive tire wear on the outer edge of the tire, while excessive negative camber results in rapid wear of the inner edge of the tire.

Improper toe-in setting results in the tire being dragged sideways along the road. A ¼″ excessive toe-in causes the tire to be dragged sideways along the road about 38′ in every mile travelled. This

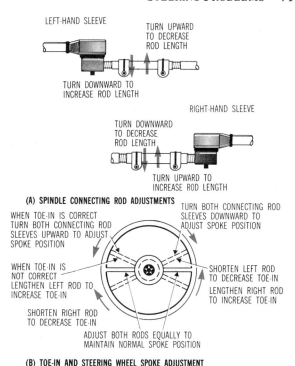

(A) SPINDLE CONNECTING ROD ADJUSTMENTS

(B) TOE-IN AND STEERING WHEEL SPOKE ADJUSTMENT

Ford of Canada

Fig. 7-6   Toe-In Adjustments

sideways drag scuffs the rubber from the tread. Too much toe-in causes the outer edges of the two front tires to be scuffed, while excessive toe-out causes scuffing on the inner edges. If only one tire shows scuffing on either the inner or outer edge the cause

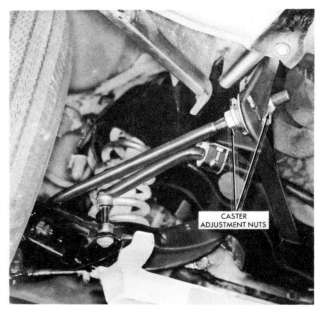

Fig. 7-5   Caster and Camber Adjusting Points

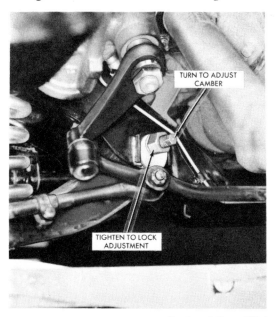

Courtesy of General Motors

(A) ON THE CAR BALANCING

(B) OFF THE CAR BALANCING

John Bean Manufacturing Co.

Fig. 7-7   Alignment Equipment

is usually a bent steering arm which causes one wheel to toe-in more than the other.

Tire wear from toe-in can be identified from camber wear because of the feather edges on the tread.

High-speed cornering causes a diagonal type of wear on the outside shoulder of the tire, with fins or sharp edges to be found on the inner edges of the tread.

Uneven or spotty tire wear is usually caused by unbalanced wheels, improper brake action, or mis-alignment.

7-2 FRONT-END ALIGNMENT

Front-end alignment is the term given to the service operation of checking and setting the caster, camber, ball-joint inclination, toe-in, and toe-out on turns. Various types of equipment are used for this purpose. Always follow the equipment manufacturers' procedures when using alignment equipment.

Before front-end alignment can be checked, the following items must first be checked and corrected as required.

1. Tire inflation	5. Ball-joints
2. Wheel bearings	6. Steering linkage
3. Wheel run-out	7. Shock absorbers
4. Wheel balance	8. Tracking
9. Vehicle spring height	

Unless the above items are satisfactory, realignment of the front end would mean very little, because as soon as the vehicle went out on the highway any of the above conditions could cause steering problems.

REVIEW QUESTIONS

1. List three causes of excessive play in the steering system.
2. What effect will excessive play in the steering system have on vehicle control?
3. How may excessive play in the steering system be checked?
4. List three causes each for (a) low-speed (b) high-speed shimmy.
5. How may hard steering be corrected?
6. What causes a vehicle to pull to one side?
7. List four types of abnormal tire wear and give one cause for each type.

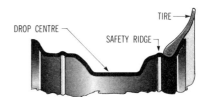

Fig. 8-2   Safety Rim

Chapter 8
WHEELS, HUBS, AND TIRES

8-1 WHEELS

The most common type of wheel in use today is the drop-centre steel disc-type wheel. It is made in two sections; the outer part forms the rim, while the inner or centre section forms the disc, or wheel, and is either riveted or spot welded to the rim. Four, five, or six holes drilled in the disc are used to mount the wheel to the hub or axle flange.

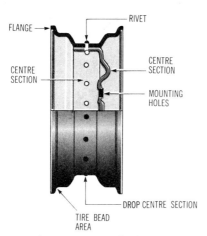

Fig. 8-1   Typical Drop Centre Wheel

The centre section of the rim is smaller in diameter than the outside edges. The centre, or dropped, portion of the rim makes it possible to remove the tire from the rim. When one side of the tire is placed in the dropped area, it is then possible to lift the outside of the tire over the rim flange.

Late model rims are equipped with safety ridges on the inside of the bead seat. These ridges tend to keep the tire bead from moving into the dropped centre portion of the rim and coming off the rim in the event of a tire blow-out.

Many truck wheels or rims do not have a drop centre. Instead, a demountable rim flange, which locks in a groove around the rim, locks the tire in position. To remove the tire, the rim flange or lock ring must first be removed.

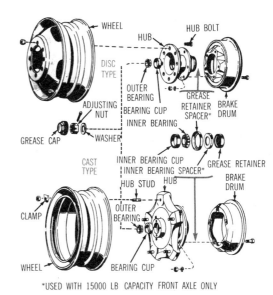

*USED WITH 15000 LB CAPACITY FRONT AXLE ONLY

Ford of Canada

Fig. 8-3   Typical Truck Front Hubs, Bearings and Wheels

Wheels must be very true and when mounted, must be within acceptable run-out limits.

The wheel is bolted to the front hub or rear-axle flange by either lug bolts that pass through the holes in the wheel and are threaded into the hub or flange, or by studs which protrude from the hub or flange. Special nuts with a tapered side are used with these studs. The tapered portion of the nut fitting into the tapered portion of the wheel hole provides a larger area to transfer the vehicle weight or driving torque from one unit to the other.

Some manufacturers use right-hand threads to mount the wheels on the passenger side, and left-

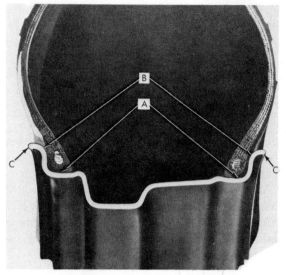

Chrysler Canada Ltd.

Fig. 8-4 Wheel Run-Out Checking Areas

hand threads to mount the wheels on the driver side. Other manufacturers use right-hand threads on both sides. Wheel nuts or bolts must be tightened using a criss-cross pattern to assure that the wheel fits truly on the hub or flange.

Some sports cars use a quick-change type of wire wheel. When this type of wheel is used, wire spokes replace the centre-pressed steel disc. The wheel slides onto a splined hub and is held in position by a large, single knock-off spinner-type nut. To remove the wheel it is necessary to strike only the spinner-nut flange and spin it off. The wheel then pulls off.

Fig. 8-5 Typical Quick-Change Type Wheel

8-2 HUBS

Front-Wheel Hubs. Front-wheel hubs revolve about the steering-knuckle spindle on either cup-and-cone ball bearings or tapered roller bearings. A castellated or slotted nut on the end of the

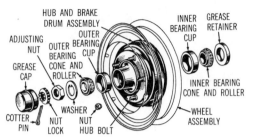

Ford of Canada

Fig. 8-6 Typical Front Hub Assembly

spindle adjusts the bearings to remove any play between the bearings and the hub. Most manufacturers specify a tightening procedure and a torque specification for adjusting front-wheel bearings.

A tongue washer placed between the outer bearing and the nut prevents the rotating motion of the bearing being transferred to the nut. A cotter pin is always passed through the castellated nut and the spindle.

Front-wheel bearings require a special stringy, fibrous wheel-bearing grease which is not affected by the heat produced during braking.

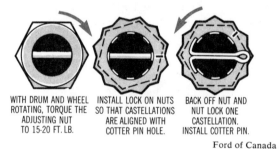

WITH DRUM AND WHEEL ROTATING, TORQUE THE ADJUSTING NUT TO 15-20 FT. LB.

INSTALL LOCK ON NUTS SO THAT CASTELLATIONS ARE ALIGNED WITH COTTER PIN HOLE.

BACK OFF NUT AND NUT LOCK ONE CASTELLATION. INSTALL COTTER PIN.

Ford of Canada

Fig. 8-7 Typical Front-Wheel Adjustment

Rear Hubs. Two types of rear hubs are in use today. The detachable-type hub is secured to the tapered axle end by means of a nut and a key. The key passes through a groove cut in both the axle shaft and the hub and is used to transmit the driving

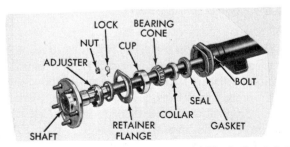

Chrysler Canada Ltd.

Fig. 8-8 Typical Rear Hub

torque. This type of hub requires a special puller in order to remove the hub and brake-drum assembly from the axle shaft.

In the other type, a flange is forged as part of the axle shaft. The wheel is then bolted directly to this flange. No special puller is required to remove the brake drum.

8-3 TIRES

Pneumatic (air-filled) tires are used today on all automobiles. The tires have two functions. They provide the necessary traction to move the car and keep it from skidding, and they absorb a certain amount of road shock. Shock is absorbed by the flexing action of the tread pressing inward against the cushion of air as the tire hits small bumps in the road. In effect, an automobile rides on a cushion of air.

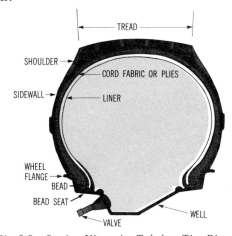

Fig. 8-9   Section View of a Tubeless Tire Rim

The outer casing of the tire takes the wear and tear of travelling over the road. This casing is an outside coating of rubber of varying thicknesses, baked or vulcanized onto the plies. The term *vulcanized* describes the process of heating rubber under pressure. This process moulds the rubber into the desired form and tread pattern, and at the same time gives the rubber the characteristics required for flexibility and long wear.

The rubber tread of the tire that makes contact with the road is thicker than the casing and is supplied in a number of different patterns to provide good frictional contact with the road, particularly when the road is wet, snow covered, or muddy.

Tire Plies. The tire ply or plies form the tough, flexible inner structure of a tire. A ply may be made of rayon, nylon, polyester, etc., and is impregnated (filled) with rubber. The carcass plies of the tire are wrapped around a series of steel bead wires to prevent the tire from opening up and leaving the wheel.

There are two general methods of arranging the casing ply or plies—on the *bias* or *radially*.

In the bias-ply tire the carcass plies are laid down in a criss-cross pattern. This has been the conventional method of tire construction for many years. In the radial-ply tire the carcass plies are laid down at right angles to the tread centre line. When radial plies are used, extra plies called *tread plies* are required. These plies are placed directly under the tread area. Some radial-ply tires have a layer or two of fine steel mesh embedded in the tread plies to add extra protection against tire damage.

The radial-ply design allows the tire to flex with a minimal amount of tread distortion which results in longer tread life, better traction, and less rolling resistance; but they are harder to mount, require greater steering effort, and have an appearance of being underinflated.

The belted-bias tire is made up of criss-crossed carcass plies and additional tread plies similar to the radial-ply tire. This type of tire has many of the advantages of the radial-ply tire without many of its disadvantages.

Many new tires use carcass plies of polyester with tread plies of fibreglass.

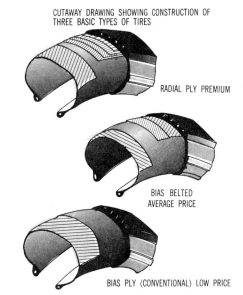

Fig. 8-10   Types of Tire Plies

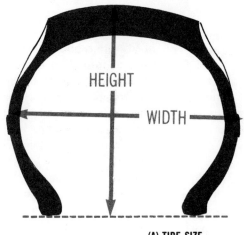

(A) TIRE SIZE

SIZE—In this area may be found the size of the tire. In the example we find it is marked GR70 x 15.

G   Load carrying capacity (1620 lbs. at 32 psi maximum pressure).

R   Radial ply construction.

70   Series (Height to width ratio). The height of the tire — 70% of the width.

15   Rim size diameter.

LOAD AND INFLATION—In this area of the tire may be found the maximum load and inflation limits of a tire. In the example, we can see that this tire when inflated to a maximum air pressure of 32 pounds per square inch will support a maximum load of 1620 lbs.

MANUFACTURING NUMBER—Every tire manufacturer is assigned a specific identification number which is placed upon all tires it produces.
This is required by the Department of Transportation (DOT).

LOAD RANGE—On the sidewall of every tire may be found the words "load range" followed by a letter. Load range letters are used to identify load and inflation limits and replace the ply rating term. Load range B is for any 4-ply rating tire. Load range C — any 6-ply rating tire. Load range D = any 8-ply rating tire.

CONSTRUCTION TYPE—In this area we may find the type of construction of any tire. In our example, it is readily identified as a radial ply construction.

PLY AND MATERIAL IDENTIFICATION—In this area may be found information describing the ply construction and material used. See the example above, on it the following information may be found:

Sidewall information appearing on today's tires is explained in the above illustration. Note that the manufacturing number is different for each tire maker.

(B) TIRE INFORMATION

Fig. 8-11   Tire Size and Information   Rubber Manufacturers Association

Ply Ratings. The ply rating is an indication of the tire load-carrying capacity. The load-carrying capacity not only depends upon the number of plies used but to a great extent upon the type of material from which each ply is made. For example: in the modern two-ply/four-ply rated tire, the ply cords are thicker and stronger and as a result produce a tire with the same load-carrying capacity as the older type of four-ply/four-ply rated tire. The two-ply type has the advantage of running cooler, rolling easier, providing better traction and a superior ride.

Because of the increase in ply strength the use of the standard "ply rating" is being replaced by a "load range" that will actually indicate the tire's weight-carrying capacity.

Tubeless Tires. The older type of tires required an inner tube. The inner tube, made of rubber, was the heart of the tire, since it retained the pressurized air. When air was pumped into the tube, it expanded outward against the inner surface of the tire casing, supplying the cushion of air inside the tire.

Late-model vehicles are equipped with tubeless tires, which do not require a separate inner tube. The rim must be sealed and must have a sealed-in tire valve. A thin rubber liner is frequently bonded to the inner surface of the tire casing to prevent air leaks into the ply. The bead, the outside edge of the tire that presses against the wheel, is so constructed that it seals tightly against the rim flange; thus the air is kept within the tire when the tire is inflated.

Tire Sizes. All types of tires are made in a wide variety of sizes ranging from the 6.00 × 13 for passenger cars to 12.00 × 20 for large trucks and buses. For many years the 6.00 or 12.00 indicated the width of the tire in inches while the 13 or 20 indicated in inches the inside diameter of the tire or the size of wheel the tire would fit.

The introduction of the low-profile or wide-oval type of tire has made it necessary to alter the tire size designations so as to indicate the correct load ratings.

The low-profile or wide-oval tire which is extremely wide in relation to section height uses a series designation that indicates the relationship between the section height and the width. A "70 series" designation means that the average section height is 70% of the width. The basic width of the tire is indicated by a prefix letter (D, E, F, G, etc). This letter replaces the numerical (7.35, 7.75, etc.) used to indicate the width of standard-type tires. The basic width of the tire increases according to

the alphabetical listing (E being wider than D, etc.). The tire size D70-14 therefore indicates that the tire is D width or size section, that the height is 70% of the section width, and it has a 14″ diameter across the beads.

Tire Run-Out. All tires must be reasonably true to prevent vibration and unbalance. Since the tire is flexible, it can absorb some of its own inaccuracy; therefore, tire run-out is not as critical as wheel run-out.

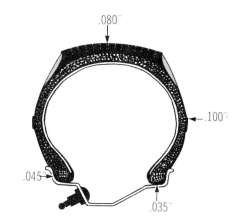

Fig. 8-12   Typical Wheel and Tire Run-Out

Tire Inflation. Tire inflation pressures vary from 22 to 30 psi for passenger cars and up to 120 psi for large trucks and buses. It is very important that the tire be inflated to its correct pressure. Too little pressure will cause the side walls of the tire to fail and the outside edges of the tread to wear rapidly; too much tire pressure will cause rapid tread wear.

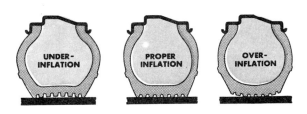

Fig. 8-13   Tire Inflation

AUTOMOBILE TIRE SIZE CONVERSION CHART
(Rubber Manufacturers Assn.)

CONVENTIONAL BIAS PLY		BIAS AND BELTED BIAS PLY			RADIAL PLY		
1965 On	REPLACES Pre-1965	"78 Series"	"70 Series"	"60 Series"	Metric	"78 Series"	"70 Series"
6.00-13					165R13		
		A78-13	A70-13			AR78-13	AR70-13
6.50-13		B78-13	B70-13		175R13	BR78-13	BR70-13
7.00-13		C78-13	C70-13		185R13	CR78-13	CR70-13
			D70-13			DR78-13	DR70-13
			E70-13		195R13	ER78-13	ER70-13
			A70-14		155R14		AR70-14
6.45-14	6.00-14	B78-14	B70-14		165R14	BR78-14	BR70-14
6.95-14	6.50-14	C78-14	C70-14		175R14	CR78-14	CR70-14
		D78-14	D70-14			DR78-14	DR70-14
7.35-14	7.00-14	E78-14	E70-14		185R14	ER78-14	ER70-14
7.75-14	7.50-14	F78-14	F70-14		195R14	FR78-14	FR70-14
8.25-14	8.00-14	G78-14	G70-14		205R14	GR78-14	GR70-14
8.55-14	8.50-14	H78-14	H70-14		215R14	HR78-14	HR70-14
8.85-14	9.00-14	J78-14	J-70-14		225R14	JR78-14	JR70-14
			K70-14				KR70-14
			L70-14				LR70-14
	6.00-15				165R15	BR78-15	
6.85-15	6.50-15	C78-15	C70-15		175R15	CR78-15	CR70-15
		D78-15	D70-15			DR78-15	DR70-15
7.35-15		E78-15	E70-15	E60-15	185R-15	ER78-15	ER70-15
7.75-15	6.70-15	F78-15	F70-15	F60-15	195R15	FR78-15	FR70-15
8.25-15 (8.15-15)	7.10-15	G78-15	G70-15	G60-15	205R15	GR78-15	GR70-15
8.55-15 (8.45-15)	7.60-15	H78-15	H70-15		215R15	HR78-15	HR70-15
8.85-15	8.00-15	J78-15	J70-15		225R15	JR78-15	JR70-15
9.00-15	8.20-15		K70-15				KR70-15
9.15-15		L78-15	L70-15		235R15	LR78-15	LR70-15
	8.90-15	N78-15					

NOTE: Since interchangeability is not always possible for equivalent tires due to differences in load ratings, tire dimensions, fender clearances, and rim sizes, automobile manufacturer's recommendations should be checked. Due to differences in handling characteristics, radial ply tires should not be mixed with bias ply tires on the same vehicle. In the case of "70 Series" and "60 Series" tires, mixing with conventional tires is permitted but only if used in pairs on the same axle.

High speeds and heavy loads produce excessive tire heat and tire wear. Normal tire life is figured for speeds at about 50 mph with normal loads. Under these conditions the tire temperature will remain below the critical temperature of approximately 240° When tires operate at 250 to 270° they lose a great deal of strength and wear resistance. For example, a vehicle driven at 80 mph, or over-loaded, will receive only about 20% of normal expected tire mileage.

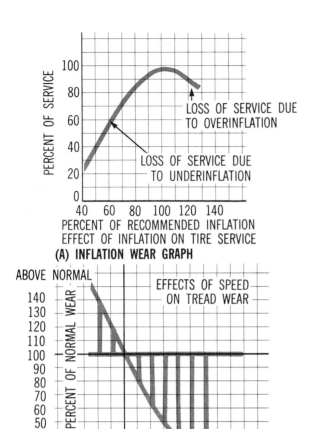

(A) INFLATION WEAR GRAPH

(B) SPEED AND TIRE WEAR GRAPH

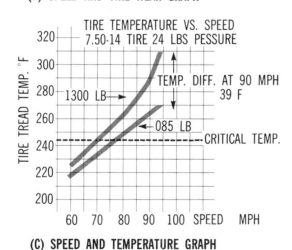

(C) SPEED AND TEMPERATURE GRAPH

Fig. 8-14   Speed and Temperature Graph

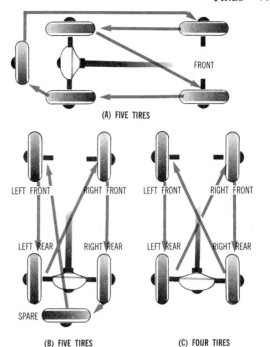

Fig. 8-15   Tire Rotation Patterns

correctly set). To equalize the amount of wear on each tire, the tires should be rotated. Rotating the tires every 5,000 miles not only increases the total mileage of a set of tires but also provides an excellent opportunity to inspect the tires for defects.

Tire-Tread Wear Indicators. The potential driving cornering and braking traction decreases as tires wear. Furthermore, as the tread depth is decreased the tire has less resistance to road hazards and is

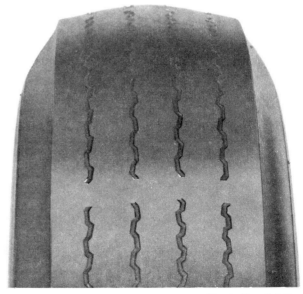

Chrysler Canada Ltd.

Fig. 8-16   Tire-Tread Wear Indicator

Tire Rotation. Tires wear according to their location on the vehicle. The right-rear tire on most vehicles wears most; the left-rear tire is next, followed by the right front and left front which wears the least (assuming that front-end alignment is

more likely to hydroplane on wet pavement. Tread-wear indicators are provided to assist in determining when tires are worn so as to require replacement. These indicators are moulded into the bottom of the tread grooves and will appear as approximately $\frac{1}{2}''$ wide bands when the tread depth has been reduced to $\frac{1}{16}''$. Tire replacement because of tread wear is necessary when these indicators appear in two or more adjacent grooves or a localized worn spot eliminates all the tread.

REVIEW QUESTIONS

1. What is meant by the term "drop-centre rim"?
2. Why is the drop centre necessary?
3. What is the purpose of the safety ridges on the modern rim?
4. Why do wheel nuts have tapered faces?
5. What two functions do tires perform?
6. What is a ply?
7. Describe the construction of (a) a radial ply, (b) bias-belted type tire.
8. What is meant by the tire term "load rating"?
9. What is the significance of the (a) D, (b) 70, (c) 14 in the tire size D70-14?
10. What determines the number of plies a tire will have?
11. Why does high-speed operation decrease tire life?
12. How does improper tire inflation pressure increase tire wear?

Fig. 9-1   Tire Spreader

Chrysler Canada Ltd.

Chapter 9
TIRE SERVICE

Tire service includes periodic inflation, periodic tire inspection, tire removal, repair, and replacement.

9-1 TIRE INFLATION

It has been pointed out that incorrect tire inflation can cause various types of steering and braking difficulty. Low tire pressure causes hard steering, front-wheel shimmy, road shock, and tire squeal on turns. Low pressure reduces tire life by causing excessive wear on the outside tire treads, excessive flexing of the side walls resulting in ply separation and rim bruises, which could cut the plies resulting in a blow-out.

Too high a tire pressure causes the centre of the tread to wear rapidly and produces a hard ride. High pressures do not let the tire flex normally. Thus, when the tire meets a rut or hole the plies take the shock. This could result in rupture of the plies.

Uneven tire pressures cause the vehicle to pull toward the side of the lower pressure.

Check tire pressures when the tire is cold. Never inflate a tire when it is hot. The increase in temperature causes a corresponding increase in air pressure inside the tire. Never bleed off excessive pressure in a hot tire as this will result in low cold tire pressure. Pressures specified by the tire manufacturers are for cold tires.

Tire valves should always be protected by a valve cap to prevent dirt and moisture from entering the valve or air from escaping.

9-2 TIRE INSPECTION

Visual inspection of the tire treads can denote steering or brake defects and under- or over-inflation, depending on the type of wear shown. Dangerous cuts from glass or stones can easily be seen, along with cracks in the shoulder or side walls. These cuts or cracks can cause ply separation or rupture, resulting in premature failure of the tire.

Less obvious are the internal damages from rim bruises or ply breaks. Frequently a tire can be

Chrysler Canada Ltd.

Fig. 9-2   Filling Hole with Sealing Gun

Chrysler Canada Ltd.

Fig. 9-3 Plug and Needle Installed in Puncture (sectional view)

Chrysler Canada Ltd.

Fig. 9-4 Sealing Plug Correctly Installed

bruised badly enough to break the plies, yet appear quite satisfactory when viewed from the outside. To inspect a tire thoroughly, remove it from the rim and spread the bead so that the casing may be examined inside and out.

9-3 TIRE REPAIRS

A variety of repairs may be made on tires. Small holes, punctures, or cuts may be patched; larger damaged areas may be vulcanized. If the tire tread is badly worn and the casing shows no damage to the plies, a new tread may be vulcanized to the casing. This process is known as *recapping*.

Chapter 10
PHYSICAL PROPERTIES OF BRAKES

Once an automobile is set in motion, it possesses momentum. Brakes are necessary to bring it to an abrupt stop or to slow it down. In early wheeled vehicles, a wedge was frequently pulled ahead of the wheel to slow the vehicle or used to block the wheel when the vehicle was stopped. As the block was pulled, friction between the wheel, road, and the block resulted in rapid wear of the block. Man

Fig. 10-1 Early Types of Brakes

soon learned that he could stop the roll of a wheel through the use of friction, and that friction could be increased through the use of levers. Because of engineering developments, braking systems have progressively improved in design to meet today's driving conditions. The physical properties of brakes include the physical characteristics of the hydraulic principle, and the principles of friction and heat.

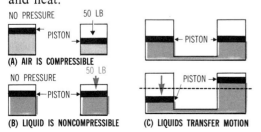

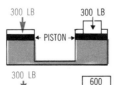

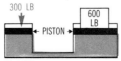

10-1 HYDRAULIC PRINCIPLE

Air, when confined and under pressure, will compress, reducing its volume. Liquids on the other hand cannot be compressed. A liquid in a closed container can be used to transmit pressure, increase or decrease pressure, and transmit motion.

If two partially liquid-filled cylinder and piston assemblies of the same size are connected together by a tube, any movement of one piston results in similar movement of the other piston. If a force is placed on one piston the other piston will support a similar force. If force is applied to one piston and cylinder assembly that is smaller than the other, movement of the larger piston will be less, but it will support a greater force.

The operation of any hydraulic system is based on *Pascal's Law*, which states that a pressure exerted upon a mass of liquid in a closed container is transmitted without loss in all directions.

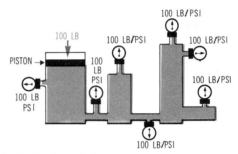

Fig. 10-3 Pascal's Law

This type of system must be sealed against the entrance of air. If there is enough air in the system, the pistons will not move at all because the compression of the air will utilize the entire volume of the fluid movement.

There are various ratios built into the master brake cylinder, wheel cylinders, and brake pedal linkage which permit the application and the development of from 700 to 1,000 pounds per square inch fluid pressure manually, and up to 1,500 pounds per square inch fluid pressure on vehicles equipped with power brakes.

Fig. 10-2 Hydraulic Forces

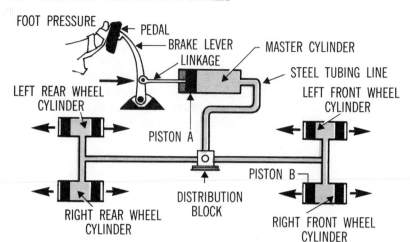

Fig. 10-4 *Schematic of a Simple Hydraulic Brake System*

Mechanical advantage may be obtained hydraulically by using differently sized piston and cylinder assemblies in a hydraulic system. For example: if a pressure of 800 pounds were applied to the piston of a master cylinder with an area of .8 square inches, then the pressure on the liquid in the system would be 800 ÷ .8 = 1,000 pounds per square inch (psi). Transmitting this 1,000 psi hydraulic pressure to a wheel cylinder piston with an area of .7 square inches would produce an output force of 1,000 × .7 = 700 pounds. Transmitting it to a wheel cylinder piston with an area of .9 square inches would produce an output force of 1,000 × .9 = 900 pounds. Therefore, an applied force of 800 pounds can be converted hydraulically to forces of 700 pounds and 900 pounds by varying the size of the piston and cylinder assemblies used. Front-wheel cylinders are usually larger in diameter than rear wheel cylinders, in order to take advantage of the greater weight upon the front

wheels, and the forward shift of the centre of gravity of the vehicle during braking.

10-2 FRICTION

Friction is that force which acts upon the surface of two bodies to keep them from sliding upon each other. (As a result of friction man is able to walk. The friction between his feet and the floor allows him to step forward.) Without friction, braking force could not be developed within the brakes, nor could the tire grip the road.

Static friction is one type of friction, kinetic friction is another. Static means at rest; kinetic means in motion. Therefore *static friction* is the friction of an object at rest, while *kinetic friction* is the friction of an object in motion.

From experiments we learn that it requires more force to start an object in motion than it does to keep it in motion. Therefore, the static friction of

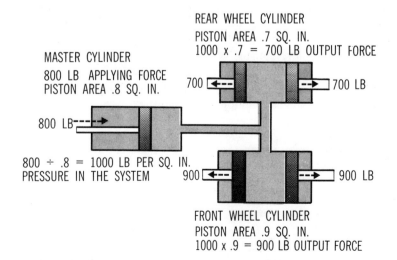

Fig. 10-5 *Hydraulic Force Multiplication*

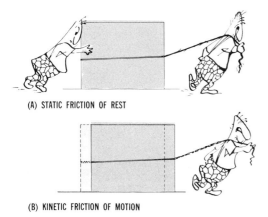

(A) STATIC FRICTION OF REST

(B) KINETIC FRICTION OF MOTION

Fig. 10-6   Types of Friction

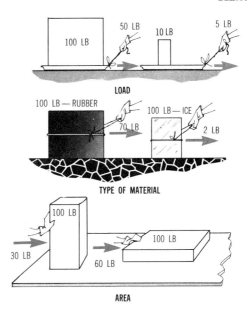

Fig. 10-7   Factors of Friction

an object at rest is greater than the kinetic friction of an object in motion.

Factors of Friction. There are three factors which govern the amount of friction produced: the pressure applied, the amount of frictional surface in contact, and the nature of the materials used in making up the frictional surfaces.

When pressure is applied to two frictional surfaces it will cause these surfaces to grip each other and resist movement. The greater the pressure, the greater the resistance.

The larger the frictional surface in contact, the greater the frictional resistance. For example, the pressure applied on a revolving shaft by two hands will bring the shaft to a stop faster than the pressure applied by one hand.

Some materials require more force to move them over a surface than others, even though the area and the pressure applied are the same. Each material has its own frictional characteristics. The frictional characteristics of a material has been defined as the material's "coefficient of friction."

The coefficient of friction of a material may be calculated by dividing the force required to slide the object over a surface by the weight of the object. For example: it requires a 3-lb pull to slide a 5-lb iron block over a wooden table. The coefficient of friction, there, equals 3 lb ÷ 5 lb = .6.

If the coefficient of friction used in automobile brakes is too high, the brakes may grab and cause the wheels to skid. If the coefficient of friction is too low, excessive brake pedal pressure will be required to bring the vehicle to a stop. Engineers select materials which provide a balance between these two extremes.

The modern automobile brake has the capacity

to skid the tires on a dry road. The stopping ability of a vehicle is determined by the tire–road coefficient. The lower the tire–road coefficient the greater the stopping distance. For example, a vehicle requires a greater distance to stop on a wet road than it does on a dry road.

There are several things that can affect the frictional characteristics of materials. Some of these are accidental, such as water, grease, brake fluid, dust, etc. These factors are beyond the control of the brake designer and manufacturer, but are frequent causes of brake-system malfunction.

10-3 HEAT

In order to stop the car, automobile brakes change horsepower into heat. Heat may be expressed as British Thermal Units (Btu). The speed and weight of the vehicle determines the amount of power that must be converted into heat. For example, the heat equivalent of stopping a car travelling at maximum speed (kinetic energy 1,500,000 foot-pounds) would be approximately 1,925 Btu's. This is sufficient to melt a 2⅜-inch cube of iron weighing 3½ pounds.

In the 5 to 6 seconds required to stop a vehicle, the temperature of the brake drums could rise to between 200 and 400° F. It will take 15 to 20 minutes of normal driving, with average braking, for the brakes to cool to normal temperatures.

Brakes are generally more powerful than the automobile engine. For example, a vehicle weighing 3,500 lb may be accelerated to a speed of 60 mph in 750′ by a 100-hp engine. The same vehicle could probably be brought to a stop in 150′. Therefore, the brakes of the vehicle are approximately 5 times as powerful as the engine.

When extremely high temperatures are produced during braking, such as when descending a mountain or long hill, the brake drums expand, and the coefficient of friction of the brake lining decreases to a very low level. This reduction in braking efficiency is sometimes known as brake "fade." The design of the modern braking system provides sufficient cooling facilities to produce efficient braking for today's high-speed highway driving, for the frequent stops during city driving, and reducing brake fade to a minimum.

REVIEW QUESTIONS

1. Name two methods used to stop early vehicles.
2. Name and explain the primary use of the two types of braking systems used on motor vehicles.
3. Name and state the law which applies to the hydraulic portion of the braking system.
4. How is mechanical advantage obtained through the use of hydraulics?
5. Why are front-wheel brake cylinders usually larger in size than rear-wheel brake cylinders?
6. Explain the terms (a) static friction (b) kinetic friction.
7. Name four factors of friction and state how each is applied to the braking system.
8. Why is the coefficient of friction an important factor in brake design?
9. Name four things that can affect the frictional characteristics of a material.
10. How is the heat produced by braking dissipated?
11. What effect does heat have on brake efficiency?

Chapter 11
THE BRAKE SYSTEM

Automobiles are fitted with two sets of brakes, the service, or foot brake, and the emergency, hand, or parking brake. The foot brake is used for stopping the moving vehicle and is applied by pressure supplied by the driver's foot to the brake pedal. The emergency, hand, or parking brake is applied by a separate lever operated by the foot or hand and is used to keep the vehicle from moving when parked.

The braking system consists of the hydraulic system and the frictional system. The hydraulic system is made up of the *master cylinder*, the *wheel cylinders, connecting lines* and *brake fluid*. The frictional system consists of *brake shoes* and *linkage*, and the *brake drums*.

11-1 BRAKE HYDRAULIC SYSTEM

11-2 MASTER CYLINDER
The master cylinder has four functions to perform: 1. It displaces the fluid necessary to actuate the wheel cylinders. 2. It develops the required pressure. 3. It compensates for changes in temperature. thus permitting the fluid in the system to expand or contract. 4. It compensates for fluid seepage from the system from a reservoir which is an integral part of the cylinder body. It is designed to recharge the system upon each release of the brakes and, in the process of this recharging operation, to return any surplus fluid to the fluid reservoir.

Single Master Cylinder. Manual brakes usually use a piston with a rubber primary cup at one end to prevent fluid and pressure leakage. As pressure is applied to the piston it moves ahead and the primary cup traps the fluid ahead of the piston. Some types of power brake units use a displacement type of piston or hydraulic plunger (slave cylinder). As pressure is applied to this hydraulic plunger, it moves further into the cylinder, displacing the fluid in the system.

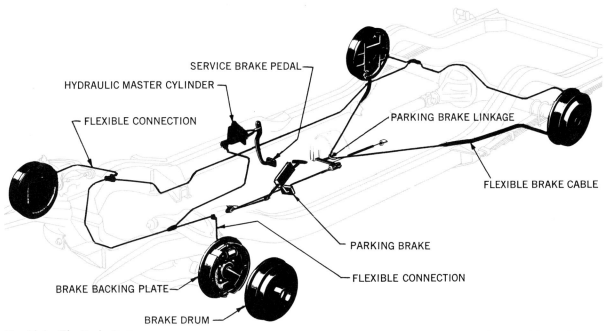

Fig. 11-1   The Brake System

As the piston in either type is forced forward in the cylinder, it pushes brake fluid ahead of it. Because the brake lines and wheel cylinders are filled with brake fluid, the piston is acting upon a solid column of fluid.

When the brake shoes have been expanded against the brake drum by the wheel cylinders, the fluid movement ceases, and the pressure in the system rises according to the force on the master-cylinder piston.

Most master cylinders are made of cast iron and are mounted on the fire wall between the driver and engine compartments. In older vehicles, the master cylinder was frequently mounted below the floor boards. (Fire-wall mounting facilitates service and inspection and reduces the possibility of dirt and water entering the master cylinder reservoir.)

The master cylinder incorporates a fluid reservoir to provide additional fluid, when needed, to compensate for tiny leaks, or for the additional fluid movement required as the brake lining wears. This reservoir is filled with authorized brake fluid

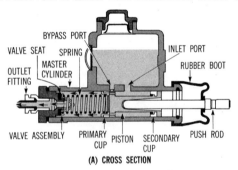

(A) CROSS SECTION

to within ¼ to ½″ of the filler cap. The reservoir filler cap is vented to the atmosphere to allow for fluid expansion and contraction without creating a pressure or vacuum in the system.

A very smooth walled cylinder is machined in the master cylinder casting. The cylinder is connected to the reservoir by two holes or ports: the compensating port and the breather port. The breather port is the closest to the brake push rod.

The cylinder is fitted with an aluminum piston, the inner end of which presses against the rubber primary cup. The primary cup prevents fluid and pressure leakage past the piston. A rubber secondary cup is attached around the other end of the piston to prevent external leakage of the fluid. The primary-cup head of the piston has several small bleeder holes. These holes allow the brake fluid to pass through the piston head to the base of the rubber primary cup. This provides the extra brake fluid required in the system when the brake pedal is pumped. The piston assembly is prevented from coming out the rear of the cylinder by a *stop plate* and *snap ring*.

When a hydraulic-type plunger is used, the only seal required is around the plunger where it enters the master-cylinder housing. This seal prevents both pressure and external leaks. Pressure is applied to the piston or the plunger by means of a push rod attached to the brake pedal linkage or the power booster cylinder.

The *check valve* is located at opposite end of the cylinder to the piston. The valve is held against a rubber seal by a coil spring. One end of the spring

(B) EXPLODED

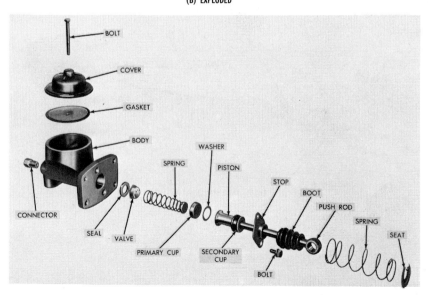

Chrysler Canada Ltd.

Fig. 11-2   Single Master Cylinder

presses against the check valve while the other end presses against the piston primary cup. The valve is of a two-way design. When the brakes are applied, the piston forces fluid through one part of the valve into the brake lines. When the brakes are released, the brake-shoe return-springs create pressure on the wheel-cylinder pistons, forcing the fluid back against the check valve. This pressure compresses the check-valve spring, lifting the check valve off its seat and allowing the fluid to return to the master cylinder.

When the return pressure becomes less than approximately 10 lb, the spring returns the valve to its seat, retaining this pressure in the brake lines and wheel cylinders. This pressure will prevent the entry of air, dust, etc., into the brake system, and assures a solid column of fluid in the system. Any

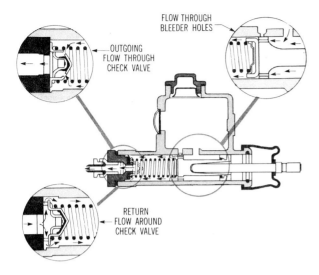

Fig. 11-3   Master Cylinder Check Valve and Bleeder Hole Operation

Chrysler Canada Ltd.

Fig. 11-4   Dual-Type Master Cylinder

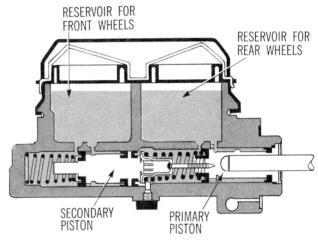

(A) CROSS-SECTION VIEW

(B) EXPLODED VIEW

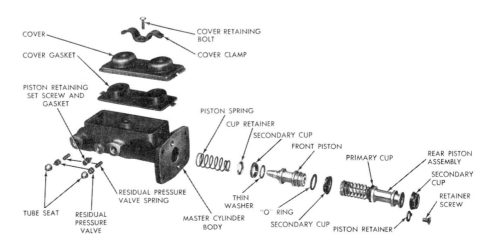

movement of the master-cylinder piston will be transmitted immediately to the wheel-cylinder piston and the brake shoes.

A rubber boot between the master-cylinder housing and the brake push rod helps prevent the entry of dust, water, etc., into the open end of the cylinder.

Dual Master Cylinders.

The modern automobile is equipped with a dual master-cylinder assembly. One cylinder operates the front brakes while the other operates the rear brakes. Failure of either system does not affect the operation of the other. This is a desirable feature from a safety standpoint.

The dual master cylinder places two pistons, the primary and secondary, in a single cylinder and both are operated by a common brake push rod. Each piston has a separate reservoir and inlet and bypass port, and is kept in the released position by its own return spring. When used on a shoe-type braking system, both the primary and secondary outlet ports have residual check valves. When the cylinder is used in conjunction with front disc brakes, no check valve is used in the disc brake outlet port.

The operation of a dual master cylinder is as follows: when the brake pedal is in the released position, both pistons are held in the retracted position by the return springs. Each piston has brake fluid in front of it and the bypass ports are open. When pedal pressure is applied to the primary piston, the piston moves forward and blocks off the bypass port, thus sealing the fluid in front of it. As the piston continues to move forward, it will transmit fluid pressure to the rear wheel cylinders and to the base of the secondary piston. This pressure causes the secondary piston to move forward, blocking off its bypass port and applying pressure to the front wheel cylinder. The brake pedal pressure, therefore, has moved both pistons and has created pressure to both front and rear wheel cylinders.

A failure in the rear wheel portion of the braking system would allow fluid to escape from that part of the system and thus prevent any pressure buildup. As the primary piston moves in, it forces fluid from the burst portion of the system, until the primary piston strikes the secondary piston. Additional pedal movement will cause the primary piston to physically move the secondary piston forward,

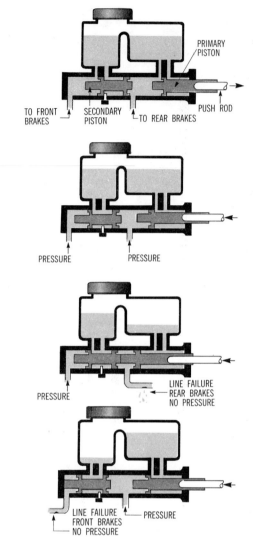

Fig. 11-5   Operation of Dual Master Cylinder

thereby transmitting normal brake operating pressure to the front wheel cylinder.

If the front brake hydraulic system fails, the primary piston will force the secondary piston to move inward until the secondary piston strikes the end of the cylinder. The primary piston will then apply normal brake operating pressure to the rear wheel cylinders.

The dual master cylinder, by providing separate systems for the front and rear wheel cylinders, will provide some braking force regardless of line failure. Although both front and rear systems could fail at the same time, such an event is highly unlikely.

Brake Warning Lights. Brake warning lights are required when dual braking systems are used. They warn the driver of failure in either the front-wheel or rear-wheel brake system. The light is controlled by a switch which is activated by a pressure-differential valve connected between the brake lines of the front and rear systems. The valve contains a piston which is centered when both systems are operating normally. Should either system fail, then there will be low pressure on one side of the valve piston and high pressure on the other. The higher pressure causes the piston to move causing it to actuate the light switch.

In most vehicles the warning light is also lit when the parking brake is applied.

11-3 WHEEL CYLINDERS

The wheel cylinders perform two important functions: they move the shoes outward to contact the brake drum, and they convert the hydraulic pressures of 0 to 1,500 pounds per square inch into comparable mechanical force. This exerts pressure mechanically against the brake shoes, thereby making a contact of lining to the brake drum.

The *wheel cylinder assembly* consists of a cast-iron housing, enclosing an accurately finished cylinder, two aluminum pistons, two rubber cups, a light-weight coil spring, two rubber boots and two push rods to transfer the motion of the pistons to the brake shoes. The casting is drilled and

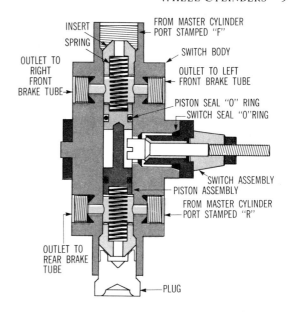

Chrysler Canada Ltd.

Fig. 11-6   Brake Warning Light Switch

threaded to provide facilities to attach a bleeder screw, (to remove air trapped in the system) and the brake lines.

Some wheel cylinders have both pistons of the same size. Other cylinders, called *step cylinders*, have one-half of the cylinder one diameter and the other half of the cylinder a different diameter. This type of cylinder is used to apply more force to one

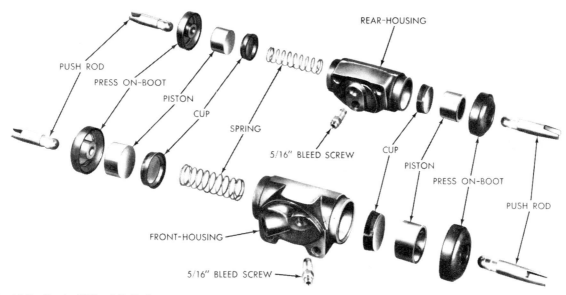

Fig. 11-7   Typical Wheel Cylinders

brake shoe (usually the primary shoe) than the other. Some types of brake design use two single-piston-type wheel cylinders, each cylinder operating one brake shoe.

11-4 BRAKE LINES AND FLUID

The brake fluid is transmitted from the master cylinder to the wheel cylinders via high-quality, double-thickness steel tubing. The tubing is frequently copper plated and lead coated to prevent corrosion. Copper tubing must *never* be used in brake lines as it cannot withstand the hydraulic pressures produced in the system.

Whenever a flexible connection is required, such as between the front wheels and the frame, high pressure neoprene-cloth flexible hoses are used.

The entire system is filled with only high-quality authorized brake fluid. Any type of mineral oil, such as kerosene, gasoline, coal oil, etc., even in minute quantities, will swell and destroy the rubber cups in the system.

11-5 OPERATION OF HYDRAULIC BRAKES

When the brake pedal is in the release position, the piston of the master cylinder is back against the piston stop. Atmospheric pressure on the fluid in the reservoir causes the fluid to flow through the compensating and breather ports to fill the cylinder.

When the pedal is depressed, the pressure is transmitted through the push rod to the piston. As the piston and primary cup move forward, the compensating port is closed and the fluid is forced through the check valve, out of the outlet fitting, and through the brake pipe lines to the wheel cylinders. The fluid enters the wheel cylinders between the two cups. The pressure forces the pistons outward against the brake shoes; the brake shoes are expanded, thus making contact with the brake drums.

When the brake pedal is released, the return spring in the master cylinder pushes the piston and primary cup back against the piston stop. At the wheels, the brake-shoe return springs pull the shoes back together. This forces the pistons inward, and the fluid is forced back to the master cylinder. This returning fluid must have sufficient pressure to force the check valve from its seat. As this return of fluid is much slower than the return of the master-cylinder piston, a vacuum is created in the fluid between the piston and the check valve. This vacuum is relieved by fluid which passes in the

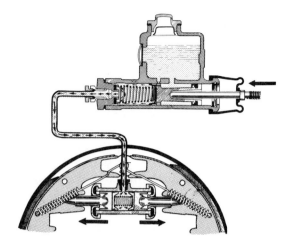

Fig. 11-8   Service Brakes Applied   Courtesy of General Motors

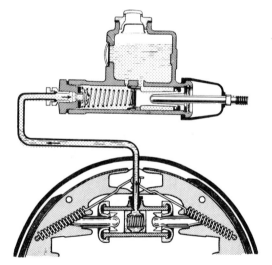

Courtesy of General Motors

Fig. 11-9   Service Brakes Released

breather port, through the holes in the piston, and past the lip of the primary cup. As more fluid returns from the wheel cylinder, it enters the master cylinder, and any excess fluid returns to the reservoir through the compensating port. This system keeps the cylinder full of fluid at all times and ready for application of the brakes.

Bleeding Brakes. Air, unlike liquids, can be compressed and could create a very dangerous situation if allowed to enter the brake system. Should this occur, the wheel cylinders would not move out because the compression of the air would utilize the entire volume of the fluid movement. A hydraulic brake system with air in it results in a spongy brake pedal. Each wheel cylinder is provided with a *bleeder screw* which is threaded into a hole leading to the centre of the cylinder.

11-6 BRAKE FRICTION SYSTEM

11-7 WHEEL BRAKE ASSEMBLY

The hydraulic system can be classed as the actuating device, and the wheel brake assembly as the device which produces the friction necessary to stop or slow the vehicle. Each wheel assembly consists of a *brake backing plate*, a *set of brake shoes*, *attaching clips*, *return springs*, and a *brake drum*.

Brake Backing Plate. The backing plate is a round, stamped steel disc bolted rigidly to either the steering knuckle or the rear-axle housing. The brake shoes and wheel cylinders are attached to the backing plate.

Brake Shoes. Most wheel brake assemblies use two brake shoes. Each shoe is made of stamped steel and has a brake lining of a special asbestos compound attached to its face either by rivets or by bonding (high temperature glueing). All brake shoes are similar in design and utilize a T-shaped cross section. The web of the T is used to give the shoe rigidity so that when the shoe is forced against the drum it will exert braking pressure over the full lining, length and width.

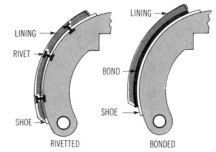

Fig. 11-11   Brake Shoes and Lining

Brake shoes differ greatly in the method in which they are attached to the backing plate. The shoe may be free-floating, or one end may be attached to a brake anchor pin. The end of the brake shoe which first contacts the drum when pressure is applied is called the *toe*; the other end is called the *heel*. The brake shoe which is ahead of the wheel cylinder when the wheel is rotating forwards is called the *primary*, or *leading brake shoe*. The one behind the cylinder is called the *secondary brake shoe*.

Brake return or retraction springs pull the shoes away from the brake drum when the hydraulic pressure is released. Various types of small clips keep the shoes against the backing plate to ensure proper brake shoe-to-brake drum alignment and to prevent rattles.

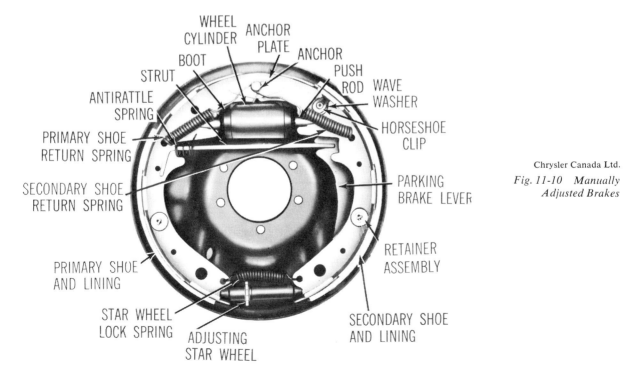

Chrysler Canada Ltd.
Fig. 11-10   Manually Adjusted Brakes

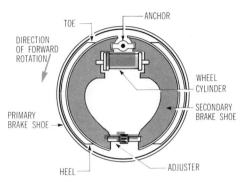

Fig. 11-12   Brake Shoe Identification

Brake Lining. There are two general types of brake lining, *woven* and *moulded*. Both are made of asbestos impregnated with special compounds to bind the asbestos together. The woven type consists of asbestos threads and fine copper wire which are woven together, cured, then cut and drilled to fit the brake shoes. The organic moulded lining consists of asbestos fibres and special compounds ground up and pressed into shape. Moulded lining is most commonly in use today.

There are two types of moulded organic lining, the dry mix, and the wet mix. *Organic dry mix* is basically a gray-white compound of asbestos, filler materials, and powdered resins which is thoroughly mixed, preformed to shape, and placed under heat and pressure until it forms a hard, slate-like board. Then it is cut and formed into individual, accurate segments and attached to the brake shoe.

Organic wet mix is a compound of asbestos, organic fillers, and liquid resins that has a gray-brown colour when blended. The compound is processed by any one of several methods, which include high-pressure extruding, screw extruding, calendering, and other processes.

Organic linings are generally compounded of six basic ingredients: asbestos to give heat resistance and a high coefficient of friction; friction modifiers, such as oil of the cashew nut shell to give the desired friction qualities; fillers, such as rubber chips to control noise; curing agents to produce the required chemical reactions in the ingredients; materials such as powdered lead, brass chips, and aluminum powders to improve the overall braking performance; and binders, such as phenolic resins, to hold the other ingredients together. This combination of ingredients produces a brake lining with the following characteristics: low wear rate; high yet even coefficient of friction to prevent pull and

erratic braking conditions; resistance to high temperatures and fading; prevents excessive wear or heat checking of the drums; engages smoothly with low effort; and operates efficiently with both standard and power brakes; quietness of operation and low cost.

Metallic-type brake linings sometimes replace the asbestos-type lining on sports or racing cars. They will withstand more severe braking, higher temperatures, and have less tendency to fade. When this type of lining is used, the metallic pads are attached to the brake shoes in place of the asbestos lining.

Brake Drums. The brake drum consists of an outer braking rim of cast iron or aluminum, cast to a pressed-steel centre disc. The assembly is mounted on the wheel bolts between the hub and the wheel and revolves with the wheel. The brake drum surrounds the brake-shoe assembly and comes very close to the brake backing plate. This prevents water and dust from entering. The braking surface of the rim must be smooth, round, and parallel to the shoe surface.

In addition to providing the necessary friction surface for the brake shoes, the brake drum is used to dissipate the heat produced by this friction. Aluminum drums and cooling fins aid in heat dissipation. When aluminum is used, a cast-iron braking surface is fused to the aluminum rim. Frequently, a stiff spring is stretched around the brake drum to help reduce drum vibration and brake squeal.

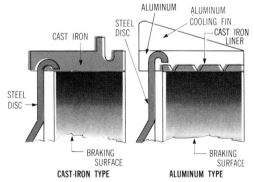

Fig. 11-13   Brake Drum Construction

Servo and Self-Energizing Actions. In order to reduce the braking efforts supplied by the driver, most modern brake systems utilize the *self-energizing principle*. In the operation of this principle, a wedging action is produced between the brake shoe

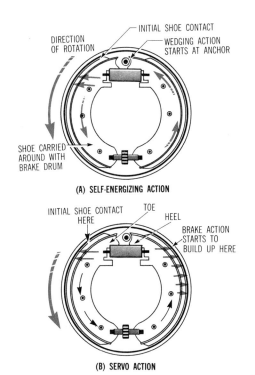

Fig. 11-14 Servo and Self-Energizing Action of Brake Shoes

and the drum. When the brakes are applied, it is the toe of the brake shoe that contacts the drum first. The friction created between these two surfaces tries to rotate the shoe with the drum. Since the heel end of the shoe is pivoted upon a thick anchor, the shoe cannot rotate with the drum. Instead it is forced outward, creating a wedging action between the shoe and the brake drum. The more the shoe tries to rotate, the greater the wedging action. This forces the shoe tighter against the drum, creating more friction, thereby slowing or stopping the vehicle with little increase in driver effort.

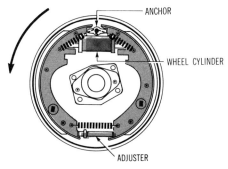

Fig. 11-15 Servo Action Self-Energizing-Type Brake

The *servo principle* is defined as one shoe helping to apply the other. The action is produced by connecting the toe of the secondary shoe to the heel of the primary shoe, placing the anchor pin between the heel of the secondary shoe and the toe of the primary shoe.

When the brakes are applied, the toe of the primary shoe contacts the revolving brake drum, and tries to rotate with it. As the primary shoe attempts to revolve, it jams the heel of the secondary shoe against the anchor. This produces a self-energizing action in both shoes. When the servo principle is used, equal self-energizing action is produced when the vehicle is moving either forward or reverse.

11-8 TYPES OF BRAKE-SHOE ARRANGEMENT

Servo Action, Self-Energizing-Type Brake (Bendix). In the servo action, self-energizing-type brake, the anchor pin is mounted to the backing plate above the wheel cylinder and between the toe of the primary shoe and the heel of the secondary. The brake adjusting mechanism is used to connect the heel of the primary shoe to the toe of the secondary. The wheel-cylinder push rods contact the shoes near the anchor ends of the shoe. The primary shoe usually has a shorter lining than the secondary shoe. The secondary shoe does most of the braking, and therefore usually wears faster. Brake adjustment is accomplished by expanding the star-wheel adjuster which connects the primary and secondary shoes.

Double-Anchor Brake (Lockheed). In the double-anchor brake the heel of each shoe is fastened to a separate anchor. The toe of each shoe is connected to the push rods of a stepped wheel cylinder, the larger step actuating the primary shoe. In this type of brake, only the primary shoe is self-energized when the vehicle moves forward, and therefore usually has the larger lining as it does most of the braking. A retraction spring between the toes of the shoes pulls the shoes away from the drum when the brake is released. Hold-down clips keep the brake shoes against the backing plate to reduce rattle. Proper shoe-drum alignment is secured by moving cam-like anchors. Shoe-drum adjustment is provided by cam adjustors near the toes of the shoes. During a minor brake adjustment only the toe of the shoes is adjusted. A major adjustment

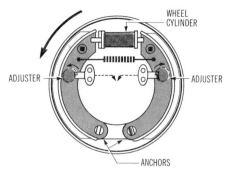

Fig. 11-16   Double-Anchor Brake (Lockheed)

requires readjusting of both toes and heels of the shoes.

Single-Anchor, Self-Centering (Centre Plane) Brake. In this type of brake the shoes are not attached to the anchor. Instead, the ends of the shoes butt against the anchor block and are free to move up or down and automatically align with the drum. A stepped-wheel cylinder is connected by push rods to the toe ends of the shoes. Only the primary shoe is self-energized when the vehicle is moving forward. Therefore it has a longer lining as it does most of the braking. Each shoe is provided with an eccentric cam adjuster, located mid-way along the shoe, to compensate for wear. Retraction springs and shoe clips are provided to return the shoes and to prevent rattles.

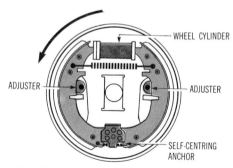

Fig. 11-17   Single-Anchor Self-Centering Brake (Centre Plane)

Double-Anchor, Double-Cylinder (Lockheed) Brake. In this type of brake, each shoe has a separate anchor and wheel cylinder. The anchor for one shoe is placed beside the wheel cylinder of the other. The toe end of each shoe is actuated toward the direction of the forward rotation of the wheel. This results in both shoes being self-energized, both classed as primary shoes, both equal in area, and both doing equal braking. Adjustments are made

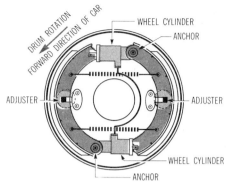

Fig. 11-18   Double-Anchor Double Cylinder (Lockheed) Brake

in a similar manner to the double-anchor single-cylinder brake.

Self-Adjusting Brakes. Most late-model automobiles are equipped with self-adjusting brakes. Two types are in use: the plug type, which adjusts the primary shoe, and the automatic star-wheel adjustor type. The latter is the most popular.

When the *plug type* is used, a plug or plunger is mounted in the primary shoe. One end of the plug contacts the drum, the other end operates a taper wedge that is placed between the shoe and the eccentric adjustment. As the lining wears, the plug is forced inward, moving the wedge upward and forcing the shoe away from the eccentric, thus maintaining constant drum-shoe clearance for the primary shoe. Since only the primary shoe is self-energized in this type of brake, the primary lining wears faster. When the taper wedge completes its

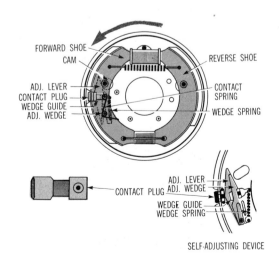

Fig. 11-19   Plug-Type Self-Adjusting Brake Shoes

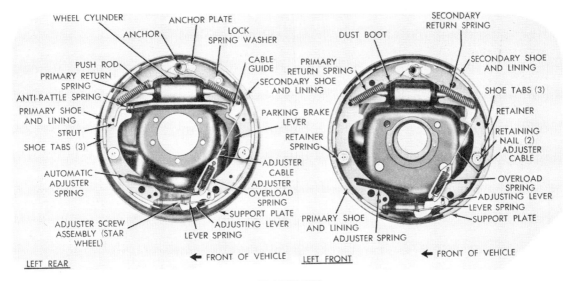

Fig. 11-20 Self-Adjusting Brakes

Chrysler Canada Ltd.

(B) CABLE TYPE

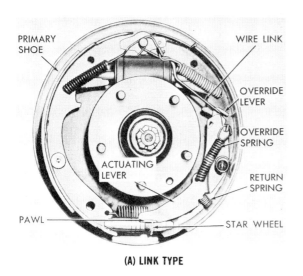

(A) LINK TYPE

travel, no further adjustment takes place. The brake shoes then need relining.

The *automatic star-wheel adjustor type* adjusts the brakes only when the automobile is moving backwards and the brakes are applied. The adjustment depends upon the reverse movement of the shoes created by the self-energizing action. When the brakes are applied, this movement of the brake shoes results in the adjusting lever being pulled up by either a line or cable. If the lining has worn sufficiently, the lever will be pulled up far enough to mesh with the next tooth of the star wheel. When the brakes are released, the adjusting lever return spring will draw the lever down, advancing the star wheel and expanding the brake shoes. This procedure is repeated as the linings wear. When the automobile is moving forward and the brakes

are applied, the self-energizing action is in the opposite direction. Therefore, it does not move the adjusting lever and no adjustment is made.

11-9 DISC OR CALIPER BRAKES

When disc or caliper brakes are used, they usually replace the conventional drum-type brakes on the front wheels only, although some manufacturers offer disc brakes on all four wheels.

The disc- or caliper-type brake replaces the conventional brake drum with an open disc that rotates with the wheel. The open disc is exposed to the air; therefore it can quickly dissipate the heat produced by braking, thus preventing brake fade. The conventional curved brake shoes are replaced by flat blocks or pads. The brake pad or pads and their hydraulic piston and cylinder assemblies are mounted in a U-shaped caliper assembly which surrounds one portion of the disc. Both fixed and floating caliper-type brakes are used.

Fixed Caliper-Type Disc Brakes. This type of disc brake uses a rigid caliper assembly that surrounds one portion of the disc. This caliper usually contains four hydraulic applying cylinders, two on each side of the disc, and two brake pad assemblies. When the brakes are applied, fluid from the master cylinder enters the caliper cylinders, forcing the

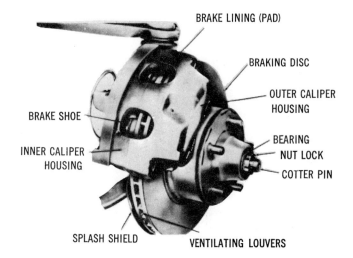

BRAKE LINING (PAD)

BRAKING DISC

OUTER CALIPER HOUSING

BEARING

NUT LOCK

COTTER PIN

BRAKE SHOE

INNER CALIPER HOUSING

SPLASH SHIELD

VENTILATING LOUVERS

Fig. 11-21   Typical Disc Brake Assembly

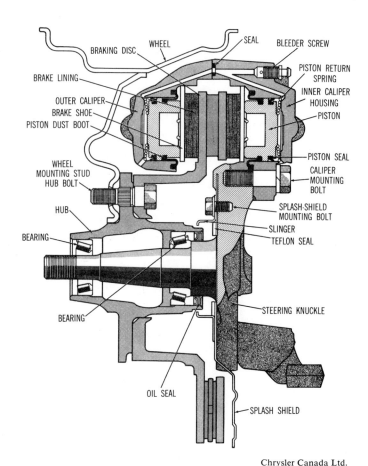

BRAKING DISC   WHEEL   SEAL   BLEEDER SCREW

PISTON RETURN SPRING

BRAKE LINING

INNER CALIPER HOUSING

OUTER CALIPER BRAKE SHOE
PISTON DUST BOOT

PISTON

PISTON SEAL

WHEEL MOUNTING STUD HUB BOLT

CALIPER MOUNTING BOLT

HUB

SPLASH-SHIELD MOUNTING BOLT

BEARING

SLINGER

TEFLON SEAL

BEARING

STEERING KNUCKLE

OIL SEAL

SPLASH SHIELD

Chrysler Canada Ltd.

Fig. 11-22   Typical Fixed Caliper-Type Disc Brake

brake pads inward against each side of the disc. The friction between the braking pads and the disc produces the braking action.

The Floating Caliper-Type Disc Brake. In this type of disc brake the caliper can pivot, or swing, in or out from the disc. Floating caliper brakes require only one piston and cylinder assembly and two brake pads. One pad is attached to the piston, the other to the caliper on the opposite side of the disc. When hydraulic pressure is applied to the piston, it

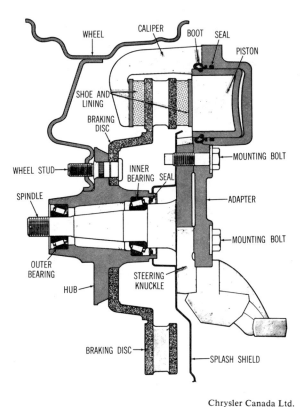

WHEEL   CALIPER   BOOT   SEAL

PISTON

SHOE AND LINING

BRAKING DISC

MOUNTING BOLT

WHEEL STUD

INNER BEARING   SEAL

SPINDLE

ADAPTER

MOUNTING BOLT

OUTER BEARING

STEERING KNUCKLE

HUB

BRAKING DISC

SPLASH SHIELD

Chrysler Canada Ltd.

Fig. 11-23   Typical Floating Caliper-Type Disc Brake

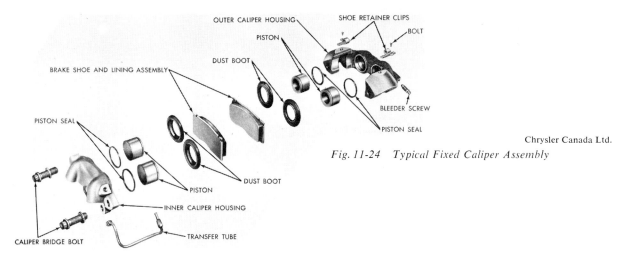

Chrysler Canada Ltd.

Fig. 11-24   Typical Fixed Caliper Assembly

forces its shoe against the disc. At the same time, the pressure of the shoe against the disc causes the caliper to pivot so that the brake shoe attached to the caliper is brought into contact with the other side of the disc. The friction between the brake pads and the disc produces the braking action.

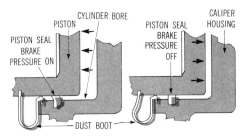

Fig. 11-25   Piston Seal Function

Metering and Proportioning Valves. Since disc brakes use relatively small friction areas, and use either the self-energizing or servo actions of the conventional drum-type brakes, they require much higher hydraulic operating pressures. In order to obtain the desired amount of braking effort between the front and rear wheels, a metering and/or a proportioning valve is included in the hydraulic system.

The metering valve prevents brake fluid movement until a specified pressure has been built up in the system. This ensures that the rear brakes will apply at the same time as the front brakes.

The proportioning valve regulates the hydraulic pressure applied to the rear wheel brakes, thus preventing rear wheel skid by limiting the rear-brake action when high pressure is required at the front wheel.

No residual check valve is required in the master

cylinder or brake lines which operate disc brakes, because no heavy brake-shoe retraction springs are used on the brake pads. Any residual line pressure would maintain brake application.

11-10 POWER BRAKES

Power brakes are used to reduce the amount of driver effort required to stop a vehicle. Several common types of power brakes are: *compressed air*, *vacuum*, and *electrical*. Large trucks, tractor trailers, and buses are usually equipped with compressed-air type power brakes, smaller trucks and many automobiles are equipped with vacuum type power brakes, and some travel-trailers are equipped with electrical-type power brakes.

Power brakes not only reduce the amount of driver effort, but also reduce the brake pedal travel. This allows the brake pedal and the accelerator pedal to be placed approximately the same height from the floor boards. To apply the brakes, the driver need only shift his foot slightly from the accelerator to the brake.

11-11 VACUUM-TYPE POWER BRAKES

Vacuum-type power brakes consist of two main units; the *vacuum power cylinder* and the *hydraulic master cylinder*. The hydraulic master cylinder has been discussed previously.

Vacuum Power Cylinder. If a piston or a diaphragm is placed in the centre of a cylinder, and the pressures on each side of the piston are different, the piston will move toward the side having the lower pressure. The amount, rate, and force of this movement depend upon the pressure difference and the size of the area affected. Power brakes utilize

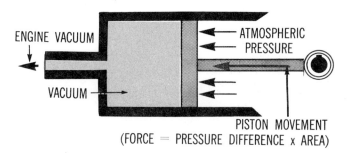

Fig. 11-26   Basic Vacuum Cylinder

this type of movement. Vacuum from the intake manifold of the engine is connected through a control valve to one side of the piston and cylinder assembly, while the other side of the assembly is open to atmospheric pressure of approximately 14.7 psi.

When the driver depresses the brake pedal, the control valve opens to admit engine vacuum to one side of the piston and cylinder assembly. The pressure on the vacuum side of the assembly drops below 14.7 psi. The piston moves toward the vacuum or low pressure side, and compresses a return spring. The piston movement is used to apply the brakes. The amount of movement depends upon the amount the control valve is opened to create a vacuum, and therefore a pressure difference. To return the piston to its normal position, it is necessary only to close the control valve. In the closed position the control valve opens the vacuum side of the piston and cylinder assembly to atmospheric pressure, cancelling the pressure difference, and allowing the return spring to centralize the piston in the cylinder.

On the outside of the cylinder housing there is an air filter and a fitting which is connected to the source of vacuum.

Frequently a vacuum reservoir tank is included in the system. This is to provide the necessary vacuum for several brake applications should the engine stop running. A vacuum check valve keeps a constant vacuum in the reservoir and the lines up to the floating-valve assembly in the power-brake cylinder. As long as the engine is running, the check valve is open. If the engine stops, the check valve closes, trapping the vacuum in the reservoir and lines.

There are two types of vacuum cylinder assemblies, the *air suspended* and the *vacuum suspended*. In the air-suspended type, atmospheric pressure is on both sides of the piston in the released, or off, position. Vacuum is applied to one side to apply

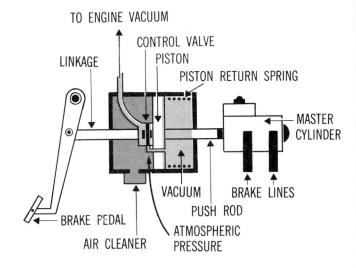

Fig. 11-27   Basic Power Brake Unit

the brakes. In the vacuum-suspended type, engine vacuum is applied to both sides of the piston in the released, or off, position and atmospheric pressure is admitted to one side to apply the brakes.

11-12   TYPES OF VACUUM POWER BRAKES

There are three common types of vacuum power brakes: the *assist*, *integral*, and *multiplier*.

Assist Type. In this type of power brake the hydraulic master cylinder and the vacuum cylinder are separate units. The vacuum cylinder assists in applying the brakes through a mechanical linkage. When the brakes are applied, linkage to the vacuum cylinder is actuated, causing the control valve to open, thus admitting vacuum to one side of the piston. Atmospheric pressure on the opposite side of the piston produces movement, which is carried through additional linkage to the master cylinder, thereby increasing the total braking force.

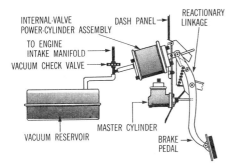

Fig. 11-28   Typical Assist-Type Power Brake Unit

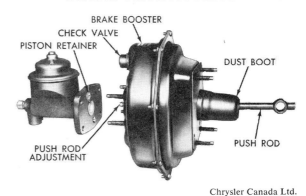

Chrysler Canada Ltd.

Fig. 11-29   Typical Integral Power Brake Unit

Integral Type. This is the most common type and is used on most automobiles. In this type of power-brake unit, the hydraulic master cylinder and the vacuum cylinder are combined in one unit. The assembly consists of the master cylinder, vacuum cylinder and piston assembly, the control valve, and reaction mechanisms. The power piston which is connected to the piston or plunger of the master cylinder also houses the control valve and reaction mechanism. The control valve consists of a plunger, an air valve, and a floating control-valve assembly. The reaction mechanism is made up of a hydraulic piston-reaction plate, a series of levers and a valve-reaction plate. A push rod, which operates the valves and transfers the brake reaction, or feel, to the driver, projects from the end of the assembly through a boot to the brake pedal. When the brakes are applied, the pedal action is transferred to the control valve, to the vacuum cylinder, to the master cylinder, to provide the necessary braking action.

Multiplier Type. In this type of power-brake system a conventional master cylinder is joined by brake lines to a vacuum-cylinder and master-cylinder assembly. This type of system multiplies the pressure produced by the conventional master cylinder. When the brakes are applied, the pressure developed in the fluid from the conventional master cylinder actuates the vacuum-cylinder control valve, resulting in movement of the vacuum piston. This movement moves a piston in the vacuum-cylinder and master cylinder, thus producing high hydraulic pressures which can be used for brake application.

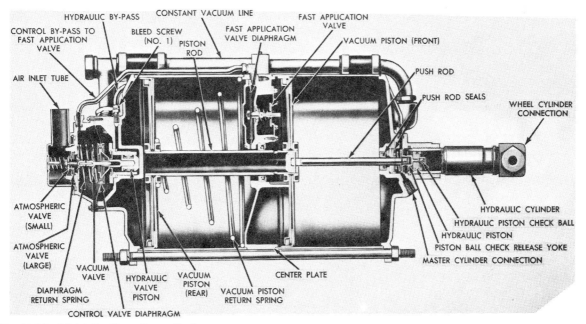

Fig. 11-30   Multiplier-Type Power Brakes

11-13 POWER-BRAKE OPERATION (INTEGRAL TYPE)

The operating procedure for a vacuum-suspended type will be given. For air-suspended types read atmospheric for vacuum, and vacuum for atmospheric.

Power-brake operation can be divided into three stages: releasing the brakes, applying the brakes, and maintaining constant brake pressure.

In the brake release position—and with the engine running, the push rod and valve plunger have moved toward the rear, closing the atmospheric port and opening the vacuum port to admit vacuum to both sides of the power piston. The power-piston return spring moves the assembly to the rear, releasing any pressure upon the master-cylinder piston.

When the brakes are applied—the push rod is moved forward by depressing the brake pedal. The valve plunger moves with the push rod to close off the vacuum valve. Further movement of the push rod causes the plunger to move the floating valve off its seat, thereby opening the atmospheric port and allowing air pressure to be applied to the rear side of the piston.

With vacuum on the front of the piston and atmospheric pressure on the rear, the power-piston assembly moves forward, applying pressure to the master-cylinder rod and piston.

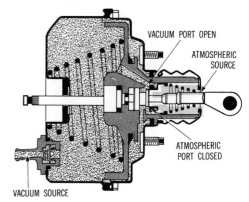

Fig. 11-32   Power Brakes in Released Position

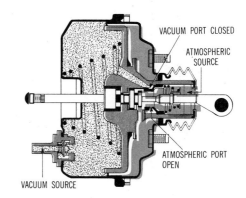

Fig. 11-33   Power Brakes in Applied Position

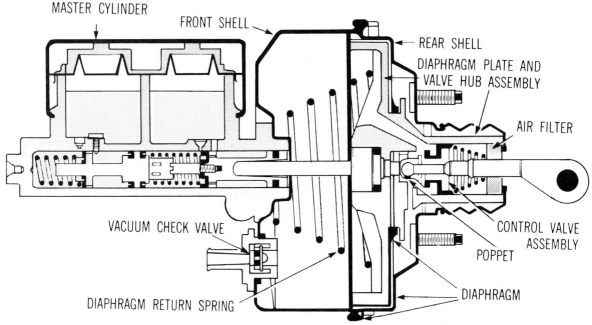

Fig. 11-31   Cut-a-Way View of Typical Integral Power Brake Unit

As hydraulic pressure is built up in the braking system, a reaction pressure is transmitted back through the master-cylinder push rod. This pressure is applied to a reaction disc. This disc, usually made of rubber, is located between the master-cylinder push rod and the power piston. The reaction pressure compresses the disc. As the disc compresses, it will attempt to bulge through a small hole in the centre of the power piston, thereby applying pressure to the end of the valve plunger. This tends to move the plunger rearward and shut off the atmospheric port. This transmits a reaction pressure, commonly called "brake feel," to the driver that is directly proportional to the pressure built up in the brake system.

With heavy braking it is possible to reach a point where full atmospheric pressure has been admitted to the back of the power piston, and maximum pressure is being produced by the power-brake assembly. This point is called "run-out point." If the driver requires more brake pressure, he can exert additional pressure on the brake pedal. This additional pressure will hold the atmospheric port wide open and brake-pedal pressure will be transmitted directly to the master-cylinder piston. Usually, the wheels will lock up and skid the tires before the run-out point is reached.

Should the power-booster unit fail to operate for any reason, the driver can apply the brakes by increasing his pedal pressure. This forces the power piston to move manually, and to transmit this manual pressure through the reaction disc to the master cylinder rod.

In the brake-hold position—when the desired braking effect has been reached and the brake-pedal pressure is not increasing, the valve plunger movement will cease. The reaction pressure will cause the reaction disc to bulge through the hole in the power piston to move the valve plunger slightly to the rear. This closes the atmospheric port. The vacuum port also remains closed. The pressure difference between both sides of the power piston remains constant, retaining, but not increasing, the force applied to the master cylinder.

Should additional pedal pressure be applied, the atmospheric port will be reopened in order to increase the pressure difference and to apply more force to the master-cylinder piston, until the applying and reaction pressures balance again.

When the brake-pedal pressure is released—the vacuum port will open and the atmospheric port will remain closed. Vacuum will be admitted to both sides of the power piston. This cancels the force produced by the pressure difference and allows the power-piston return spring to move the power piston and valve assembly toward the rear. This releases the pressure on the master-cylinder piston and releases the brakes.

There are many variations in power-brake design. However, the operating principles of all are very similar.

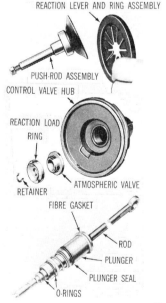

Ford of Canada

Fig. 11-35   Typical Control Valve and Reaction Assembly

11-14 AIR BRAKES

Air brakes use compressed air pressures of 100 psi or more to operate pressure cylinders. These cylinders are connected through linkage to the brake

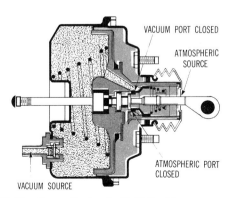

Fig. 11-34   Power Brakes in Hold Position

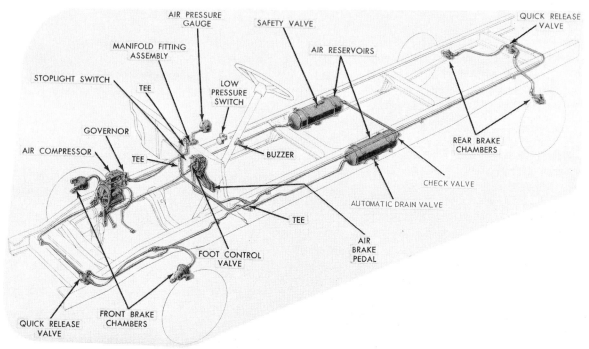

Fig. 11-36   Typical Air Brake System

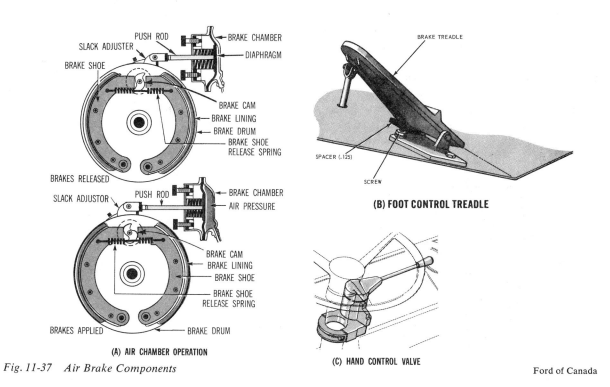

(A) AIR CHAMBER OPERATION

(B) FOOT CONTROL TREADLE

(C) HAND CONTROL VALVE

Fig. 11-37   Air Brake Components

Ford of Canada

shoes. When air pressure is admitted into the cylinders, the shoes are forced outward against the brake drums.

The system consists of an engine-driven *air compressor*, compressed air *storage tanks*, a *governor*, *pressure cylinders* or *diaphragm chambers* at each wheel, suitable *control valves*, and the necessary *piping* and *connectors*. The control valve may be either foot or hand operated. When the system is used on tractor-trailer applications, separate controls and systems are frequently used: a foot control for the tractor system and a hand control for the trailer system. The pressure chambers operate and increase the brake application pressures in a similar manner to the vacuum-type cylinder.

11-15 ELECTRIC BRAKES

This type of braking system is frequently used on travel-trailers. Electric brakes use electromagnets to produce the movement and pressure necessary for brake application. The armature of the electromagnet is attached to a lever and cam assembly that, when rotated, forces the shoes outward against the brake drum. The amount of braking effort is determined by the strength of the electromagnet. Magnetic strength is controlled by the amount of current flowing through the electromagnet. The amount of current flowing is controlled by a driver-operated rheostat which may be connected to the vehicle foot brake or mounted on the dash for hand control.

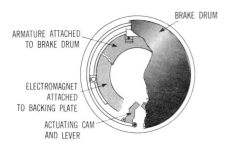

Fig. 11-38   Typical Electric Brake

11-16 PARKING OR EMERGENCY BRAKES

Two types of parking or emergency brakes are in use today, the drive-shaft type and the mechanically operated shoe type using the brake shoes of the rear hydraulic system.

The *drive-shaft type* uses a brake drum attached to the output shaft of the transmission. The brake

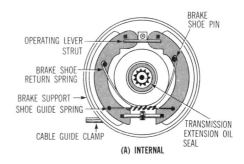

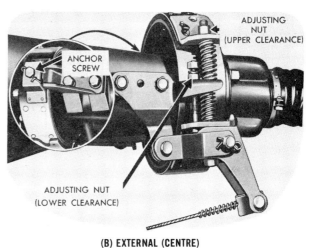

(B) EXTERNAL (CENTRE)

Chrysler Canada Ltd.

Fig. 11-39   Driveshaft Brakes

shoes may be mounted inside the drum, or a brake band may be placed around the outside of the drum. A mechanical linkage, operated by a hand lever under the dash, or a foot pedal located to the left of the clutch pedal, either expands the internal shoes or contracts the outside brake band against the drum. When the drum is stopped, the drive line and rear axle cannot rotate as long as both rear wheels are on the ground; therefore, the vehicle cannot move.

When the *mechanically operated shoe type* is used, a hand lever or foot pedal is connected to the brake shoes of the rear wheels by mechanical linkage and cables. When the brake is applied, the linkage expands the rear brake shoes against the brake drums.

Inside the rear-brake assembly, the brake cable is attached to the lower end of a lever that is pivoted near the top of the secondary brake shoe. A brake strut is notched into the lever just below the pivot; the opposite end of the strut is notched into the primary shoe. When the brake is applied, the brake cable pulls the lever, which moves the strut forward, pushing the primary shoe against the drum. Continued movement of the lever causes it to pivot on the strut, forcing the secondary shoe against the drum. Additional movement forces both brake shoes against the drum, preventing the wheel from rotating.

REVIEW QUESTIONS

1. State the purpose of the following brake parts: (a) master cylinder (b) wheel cylinder (c) master-cylinder primary cup (d) master-cylinder secondary cup (e) master-cylinder check valve.
2. What is the location and purpose of the master cylinder (a) compensating port (b) breather port?
3. What is the purpose of the series of holes drilled in the primary cup head of the master cylinder piston?
4. State the advantage of a step-type wheel cylinder.
5. Why must copper tubing not be used as a brake line?
6. What damage to the hydraulic system would result if any petroleum product was added to the brake fluid?
7. Describe the operation of a hydraulic brake system (a) when the brakes are applied (b) when the brakes are released.
8. Why must the lip of both the master-cylinder and the wheel-cylinder rubber cups face toward the fluid?
9. Explain how the cylinder of the master cylinder is kept full of fluid at all times, ready for an application of the brakes.
10. Why does air in the hydraulic system result in a spongy brake pedal feel?
11. Why are T-shaped brake shoes used?
12. How is (a) the primary brake shoe (b) the toe of a brake shoe determined?
13. Describe in detail the two general types of brake lining material.
14. Describe (a) wet mix (b) dry mix organic-type brake lining compounds.

15. What are the essential characteristics of brake lining?
16. What is the advantage of metallic-type brake linings?
17. State two purposes of the brake drum.
18. Explain how the braking action is increased because of the self-energizing action of the brake shoes.
19. Explain why the servo principle of brake design is used.
20. Explain why the secondary shoe of a servo action, self-energizing type brake wears down faster than the primary shoe of the same type of brake.
21. Describe briefly three different types of brake shoe arrangements and identify which shoe (primary or secondary) would wear down fastest in each type.
22. Explain why brake pedal height decreases as brake lining wears.
23. Describe how the star-wheel type of self-adjusting brakes adjusts the brakes during normal vehicle operation.
24. State the major advantage of disc-type brakes.
25. What is a disc-brake caliper assembly?
26. Explain how the braking action is produced when disc brakes are used.
27. Describe briefly the construction and operation of two types of parking or emergency brakes.
28. Name three types of power-brake systems.
29. Describe the basic construction and operation of a vacuum booster brake unit.
30. Explain the terms (a) air-suspended (b) vacuum-suspended types of power-brake cylinder assemblies.
31. Why is a vacuum reservoir sometimes included in the power-brake system?
32. Explain the term "brake feel."
33. How is brake feel produced and transmitted to the driver's foot?
34. When the desired braking effect has been reached and the brake pedal pressure is maintained, why does the braking effect not increase as long as pressure is applied to the brake pedal?

Chapter 12
BRAKE SERVICE

There are many types of brake system malfunction; brake pedal goes to the floor, brakes drag, brakes pull, brake pedal soft, pedal hard, etc. The following will deal with some of the causes and correction of brake problems.

12-1 BRAKE PROBLEMS

1. *Too much brake travel*—can be caused by: worn brake lining, brake shoes out of adjustment, low master-cylinder fluid level, leaking brake lines, air in the brake system, or lack of pressure buildup because of a defective master-cylinder piston or cup.
2. *Brake pedal soft or spongy*—can be caused by: air in the system, improper anchor adjustment, warped or distorted brake shoes, or thin brake drum.
3. *Stiff brake pedal*—can be caused by: the wrong type of brake lining; glazed or too smooth brake lining or drums reducing brake friction; brake lining soaked with oil because of leaking wheel or axle oil seals or over-filling of the differential; brake lining soaked with brake fluid because of leaking wheel-cylinder cups; or mechanical resistance at either the pedal, linkage, or brake shoes. A temporarily hard brake pedal and poor braking can be caused by: water-soaked linings, because of driving during a hard rain or through deep puddles; or overheated brakes after a long hard application as in descending a long steep hill. In both cases the brakes return to normal after they have dried out or cooled.
4. *Brakes pulling to one side*—can be caused by:

uneven tire pressure, tread design, or wear; improper adjustment of the brake shoes; different types of lining on some shoes; defective or sticking wheel cylinders producing uneven braking pressures on the shoes; oil- or brake-fluid soaked linings causing the vehicle to pull to the opposite side; or loose wheel bearings.

5. *Dragging brakes*—can be caused by: incorrect shoe adjustment; insufficient clearance between the master-cylinder push rod and the master-cylinder piston (this prevents the master-cylinder primary cup from clearing the compensating port and thereby traps hydraulic pressure in the system and retains brake-shoe application); mineral oil in the system causing the primary brake cup to swell and cover the compensating port; wrong or defective check valve creating too high a residual pressure in the brake lines and wheel cylinders.

  Only one brake dragging could be caused by: incorrect shoe adjustment; clogged brake line; weak shoe return spring; sticking wheel-cylinder piston; or brake shoe binding on the backing plate. When both rear wheels drag, sticking emergency brake cables are usually the cause.

6. *Grabbing brakes*—on one or more wheels is usually caused by: a light coating of grease or brake fluid on the linings (a light coating of grease causes grabbing, soaking causes hard braking); wrong type of lining; rough or scored brake drums; or primary and secondary shoes reversed.

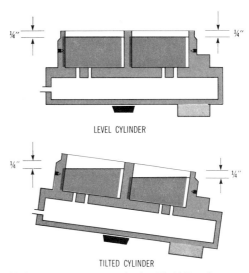

LEVEL CYLINDER

TILTED CYLINDER

Fig. 12-1   Correct Main Cylinder Fluid Level

12-2 BRAKE ADJUSTMENTS

Before performing a brake adjustment, check the following brake items and make corrections as required: fill the master cylinder to the proper fluid level; adjust the brake pedal toe-board clearance as required; remove one front-wheel brake drum to inspect the brake linings for wear, or the drums for roughness. (Since the front brakes do the largest percentage of the braking, they wear the fastest. Badly worn front linings usually indicate that all brake linings require replacement.) If the owner mentions any other brake complaints check to find the cause of the complaint before the brakes are adjusted.

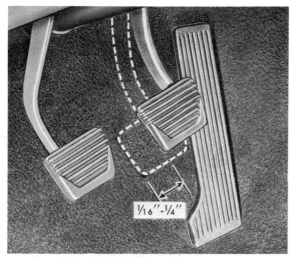

Courtesy of General Motors

Fig. 12-2   Brake Pedal Travel

Minor Brake Adjustments. Minor brake adjustments compensate for brake lining wear only and are usually made through slots cut in the brake backing plate (Bendix type only), or by turning the heads of the adjusting cams which protrude through the backing plate (Lockheed type). Very rarely is

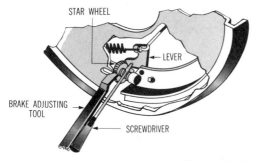

Chrysler Canada Ltd.

Fig. 12-3   Adjusting Brakes

it necessary to remove the brake drum to perform a minor brake adjustment.

Normally self-adjusting brakes will not require manual adjustment but in the event of a brake reline it may be advisable to make the initial adjustment manually to speed up adjusting time. (Follow manufacturer's instructions when performing a minor brake adjustment.)

Major Brake Adjustments. Major brake adjustments are performed on some types of brakes. A major brake adjustment necessitates the realigning of both the toe and heel of the brake shoe, and is

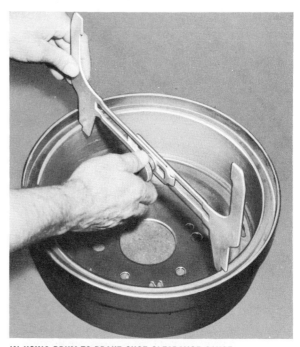

(A) USING DRUM-TO-BRAKE SHOE CLEARANCE GAUGE

(B) CHECKING BRAKE SHOE LINING CLEARANCE

Courtesy of General Motors

Fig. 12-4   Measuring Brake Lining Clearance

usually done after the brake shoes have been re-lined or disturbed during other repairs.

To perform a major brake adjustment, it is necessary to remove the brake drums and, in some cases, to install a brake-shoe adjusting jig or drum in order to adjust the brake anchors and adjusting cams to the correct setting. Follow the manufacturer's instructions to adjust brakes.

After the brake adjustment has been completed, pump the brake pedal several times to expand the wheel-cylinder pistons out against the new expanded position of the brake shoes.

As the wheel-cylinder pistons are expanded outwards, less brake fluid will return to the master cylinder, thereby lowering the master-cylinder fluid level. The fluid should be topped up to the proper level.

12-3 RELINING BRAKES

If brake linings are excessively worn, new brake lining is required. On some types of vehicles the new lining may be riveted to the original shoes. On other vehicles it is necessary to install replacement shoes to which the new lining has been bonded (high-pressure, high-temperature glueing).

To establish good brake shoe-to-drum contact, some manufacturers recommend a preliminary contour grinding of the brake shoes either before or after the new brake shoe is installed. Follow the manufacturer's instructions regarding the removal and replacement of brake shoes.

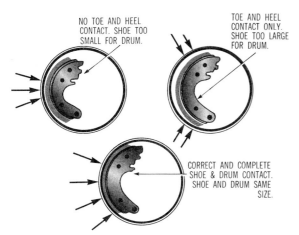

Fig. 12-5   Brake Shoe-to-Drum Contact

If brake drums are scored, rough, or excessively glazed, repair the braking surface by turning, or grinding, the brake drum on a brake-drum lathe. If more than 25 percent of the total thickness of the

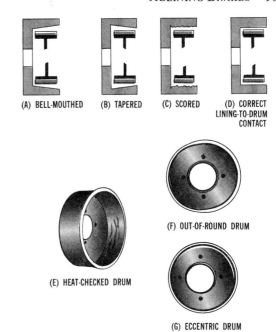

Fig. 12-6   Brake Drum Problems

drum is removed during the lathe operation, replace the drum. (Replacement is necessary because the drum may be weakened by the grinding to the extent that it may crack or break during heavy braking; or over-heating may warp the drum, causing faulty brake action.)

If brake drums have been cut over-size, place a special shim of the correct thickness between the lining and the brake shoe to retain maximum brake adjustment. This compensates for the amount removed from the brake drum.

When the brakes are being relined, check the wheel cylinders and master cylinder for leaks or faulty operation. If either condition is apparent, remove the unit for repairs or replacement.

When making repairs to the hydraulic system, exercise extreme care to prevent any petroleum

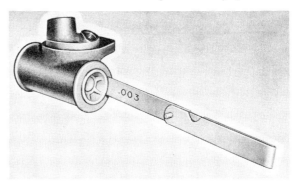

Fig. 12-7   Checking Wheel Cylinder Piston Fit

product, such as grease, oil, or dirt from entering the system. Replace all rubber parts. Remove small scratches in the hydraulic cylinders by using crocus cloth (a fine type of grinding cloth) ONLY. Remove large scores by honing, providing the diameter of the cylinder is not enlarged by more than a few thousandths of an inch. Check piston-to-cylinder clearances against manufacturer's specification to maintain proper fit. Excessive clearances necessitate replacement of the piston or piston and cylinder assembly. During reassembly lubricate all rubber parts with brake fluid before installation. Follow manufacturers' instructions to remove, overhaul, and replace defective cylinders. Check all wheel and axle grease and oil seals for possible leakage and replace if found defective.

If any dirt or damaging fluid, such as mineral oil, has been introduced into the hydraulic system, flush the system with a special brake system flushing compound.

12-4 BLEEDING BRAKES

After any portion of the hydraulic system has been opened to the atmosphere, or if the fluid level has become so low that air has been pumped into the system by the master-cylinder piston, it is necessary to bleed the brakes to remove this air.

Courtesy of General Motors

Fig. 12-9   Bleeding Brakes With Pressure Bottle

When pressure is applied to the master cylinder and the bleeder screw is loosened, the trapped air can escape. The bleeder screw must be retightened before the pressure is released. This procedure is repeated at each cylinder until all of the air has been removed from the system. The most common method of bleeding brakes is to attach one end of a small rubber hose to the bleeder screw and to place the other end in a jar partially filled with brake fluid. Loosen the screw and apply pressure to the master cylinder, either manually or by a brake-bleeder bottle. This bottle contains brake fluid under air pressure. When the bleeder screw is opened, the pressure in the master cylinder forces the air trapped in the system out through the hose attached to the bleeder screw. As the air leaves the end of the hose, you will see bubbles in the jar of fluid. When the bubbles stop, tighten the bleeder screw. All the air in that cylinder has been removed. Repeat this procedure for all wheel cylinders.

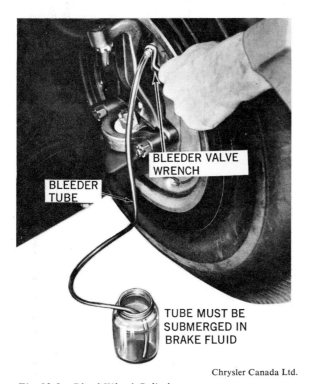

Fig. 12-8   Bleed Wheel Cylinder

Chrysler Canada Ltd.

Fig. 12-10   Bleeding Sequence

12-5 POWER BRAKE SERVICE

Power brake complaints consist of: hard pedal, caused by a vacuum leak anywhere in the system; faulty check valve; collapsed vacuum hose, or low engine vacuum; intermittent power assist caused by sticking air valve, or dented or distorted power-cylinder housing; too much pedal travel caused by brakes out of adjustment, low brake fluid, air in the system, fluid leaks, or defective master cylinder; brakes failing to release caused by broken power-piston return spring, air valves blocked or sticking, clogged air cleaner, or excessive friction in any part of the linkage. All of the manual brake-system troubles apply to the power-brake system and these should be checked and corrected first.

To determine whether the hydraulic system or the power-brake units are defective, the following tests may be used. With the engine stopped, apply the brakes several times to exhaust all the vacuum retained in the system. Maintain a light pressure on the brake pedal, and start the engine. If the brake pedal tends to fall away under the foot pressure, and less pressure is required to hold the brake pedal in the applied position, the power booster portion of the assembly is in satisfactory condition. If no assist is felt, then the power booster portion is defective.

To determine leaks in the hydraulic system, exhaust all the vacuum reserve in the system and apply a heavy pressure on the brake pedal. If the pedal slowly falls away, the hydraulic system is leaking externally or has back-passed the master-cylinder piston.

To check for vacuum leaks, run the engine at a medium speed for a few minutes. Stop the engine and after 90 seconds try the brake action. If there is no assist for two or three applications of the brakes, there is a leak, or the vacuum check valve is defective.

If the brake pedal travels to within 1″ of the floor boards, the brakes require adjusting or re-lining. For all repairs follow the manufacturers' instructions.

REVIEW QUESTIONS

1. Give two causes for each of the following brake system problems: (a) too much pedal travel (b) brakes pull to one side (c) brake pedal hard (d) grabbing brakes.
2. Why do front wheel brake shoes wear faster than rear wheel shoes?
3. What is the difference between a minor and major brake adjustment?
4. What is contour grinding? Why is it used?
5. What is the maximum amount of material that can be removed from a brake drum during the turning process? Why is the amount limited?
6. How may small scratches or scores be removed from the hydraulic cylinder surfaces?
7. When should the hydraulic system be flushed?
8. Explain how to determine whether the hydraulic or power-brake units are defective in a power-braking system.

UNIT THREE
The Drive Line

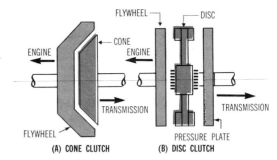

Fig. 13-1   Mechanical Clutches

Chapter 13
THE CLUTCH

A clutch is a mechanism designed to connect or disconnect the transmission of power from one working unit to another. Clutches may be of various types: the cone type is used in the synchromesh unit of a standard transmission; the disc type is used on most modern automobiles with standard transmissions; the multiple-disc type is used in many automatic transmission assemblies; and the one-way clutch, or sprag, is used in overdrive and automatic-type transmissions. On vehicles equipped with automatic transmissions, fluid clutches or torque converters are used in place of a mechanical-type clutch.

The power of an automobile engine may be transferred to the transmission through either a disc clutch, a fluid coupling, or a torque converter. These units will also allow the engine to idle without transmitting power. Since the engine develops little power or torque at low rpm, and since more effort is required to start a body in motion than to keep it in motion, it is desirable to allow the engine to attain increased speed before it is required to put the vehicle in motion. A sudden connection of the power to the rear wheels would result in violent shock. All three types allow a gradual application of the load along with some slowing of the engine speed in order to provide reasonable and comfortable starts.

13-1 MECHANICAL CLUTCHES

The *cone*, *disc* (single or multiple, wet or dry), and the *one-way* clutch are classed as mechanical units and use friction to transmit power. The cone and disc types will transmit power in either direction. One-way clutches transmit power in one direction only. Clutches that run in oil are called wet-type clutches. If the disc-type clutch has only one driven disc, it is classed as a single-disc type, while those with more than one driven disc are classed as multiple-disc clutches.

13-2 SINGLE DRY-DISC CLUTCH

The single dry-disc clutch in use today consists of

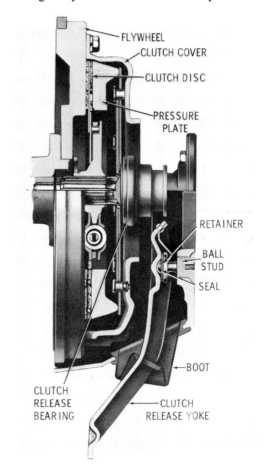

Courtesy of General Motors

Fig. 13-2   Typical Clutch Assembly

113

the following major parts: *flywheel, clutch disc, pressure-plate springs, pressure-plate housing* or *cover, clutch housing* and the *linkage* necessary to operate the clutch.

Flywheel

The flywheel forms a base to which the entire clutch assembly is attached. In addition, it provides momentum to smooth out engine operation, and as a base for the starter ring gear.

The flywheel, attached to the engine crankshaft, is the drive member of the clutch. The clutch side of the flywheel is machined smooth to provide a friction surface for the clutch disc. Tapped holes in the flywheel provide a means of attaching the clutch assembly. A ball bearing or a bronze bushing, called a *pilot bearing*, is placed in a drilled hole in the centre of the flywheel. Sometimes this hole is actually in the end of the crankshaft. The pilot bearing is used to support the end of the transmission clutch or front shaft. It may be lubricated during manufacture, or, if not, it must be lubricated before installation.

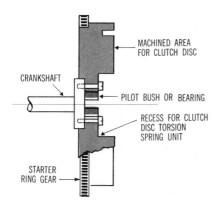

Fig. 13-3 Typical Flywheel Construction

The Clutch Disc

When the clutch is engaged, the clutch disc is forced to revolve as a unit with the flywheel and pressure-plate assembly. All the power developed by the engine is transmitted through the clutch disc to the transmission front shaft. The power is picked up by the lined faces of the clutch disc and transmitted through the steel hub, which is splined to the transmission front shaft.

The clutch-disc facings are of two main types: moulded and woven. Their composition is similar to that of brake lining.

The moulded facings—are made of short asbestos

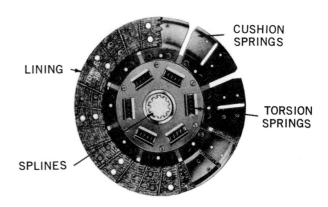

Fig. 13-4 Clutch Disc

fibres and a binder. The facings are moulded to size under pressure and cured at high temperatures. The surfaces are then ground flat and parallel. Some moulded linings have brass chips in the mixture to add to lining life.

Woven linings—are made from sheets of long-fibre asbestos and copper wire, encased in a binder. The facings are wound into a flat ring and moulded to size under high pressure and cured at high temperatures.

The facing surfaces must be smooth, and the assembly uniform in thickness. The facings must be kept free of even a trace of grease or oil or a "grabbing" or chattering clutch could result.

The linings or facings are riveted or bonded to a disc which includes a cushioning device and a torsional vibration-dampening unit.

The cushioning device—between the two faces, is necessary to permit smooth engagement of the clutch and eliminate clutch chatter. The cushioning effect is produced by splitting and cupping the outer edges of the disc. As the clutch is engaged, the cupped segments act as a spring-like cushion.

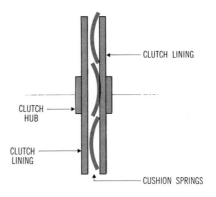

Fig. 13-5 Clutch Cushion Springs

A torsional device—is located near the centre of the hub. This device absorbs the torsional vibrations of the crankshaft and prevents such vibrations from reaching the transmission. The inner hub and outer disc are fastened together in such a manner as to allow a certain amount of radial movement. This radial movement is limited by *stop pins*. The drive between the outer disc and inner hub is transferred through stiff coil springs. These coil springs absorb the torsional thrust, act as a dampening device, and transmit the thrust to the inner hub. The torsional vibration is controlled by a moulded friction washer placed between the inner hub and the outer disc.

The centre of the hub is fitted with splines to allow the disc to both slide along and transmit the power to the transmission front shaft.

Courtesy of General Motors

Fig. 13-6   Clutch Torsion Assembly

13-3 PRESSURE PLATE

The pressure plate is usually made of cast iron and is slightly larger in diameter than the clutch disc. The side of the pressure plate which faces the clutch disc and presses it against the flywheel is machined smooth. The other side has various shapes to which the pressure springs and release levers may be attached.

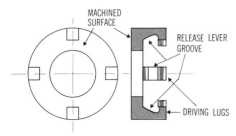

Fig. 13-7   Typical Pressure Plate

Heat checks, created by the heat produced from a slipping clutch, and scores, caused by worn clutch facings, are the enemies of the pressure plate. Pressure plates may be re-machined smooth to remove scores and surface heat checks.

Pressure-Plate Assembly

The pressure-plate assembly includes the pressure plate itself, a series of coil springs or a diaphragm, a cover, and a series of release levers or fingers. During manufacture, the pressure-plate assembly and the flywheel are usually balanced. After balancing they are marked so that the balance may be maintained.

There are two types of clutch pressure-plate assemblies used in automobiles, the *coil pressure-spring type* and the *diaphragm-spring* type.

When the clutch is engaged, the pressure coil springs or the diaphragm spring push the pressure plate forward, forcing the clutch disc firmly against the flywheel. Consequently, these springs must be strong enough to hold the pressure disc against the flywheel and transmit the engine horsepower at speeds up to 5,000 rpm. The pressure plate requires over 1,000 lbs pressure to hold the clutch disc against the flywheel. Insufficient pressure in these springs would cause loss of power, since all the power would not be picked up by the clutch and carried to the transmission. It would also cause a slipping clutch which could overheat, resulting in possible failure.

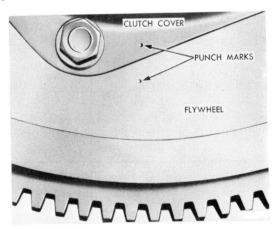

Chrysler Canada Ltd.

Fig. 13-8   Marking Clutch and Flywheel

Coil Pressure-Spring Type

The coil pressure-spring type of pressure-plate assembly is made up of coil springs, a pressure

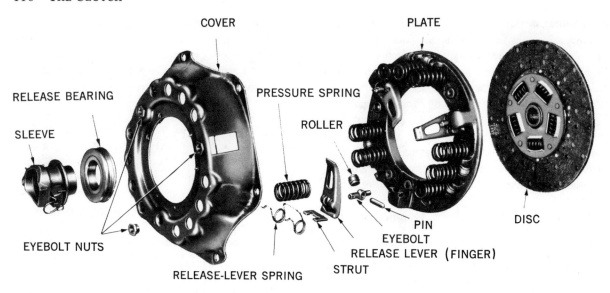

COVER PLATE

RELEASE BEARING PRESSURE SPRING

SLEEVE ROLLER

DISC

EYEBOLT NUTS

PIN
EYEBOLT
RELEASE LEVER (FINGER)

RELEASE-LEVER SPRING STRUT

Fig. 13-9 Coil Spring-Type Clutch (Exploded View) Chrysler Canada Ltd.

plate, release levers, and a cover. These parts are assembled inside the cover, and the cover, in turn, is attached by bolts to the flywheel. The assembly rotates with the flywheel.

Most coil-spring pressure plates use several coil springs, which are spaced around the pressure plate and inside the cover. When the cover is bolted to the flywheel, these springs are compressed and exert pressure between the pressure plate and the cover.

The pressure springs must be of equal length and strength. Any deviation in length or strength

will make it difficult for the clutch disc to seat evenly between the flywheel and the pressure plate. This results in lower pressure at some point on the friction surface, and the possibility of slippage.

To disconnect the transmission from the engine it is necessary to move the clutch disc away from the flywheel. To accomplish this, it is necessary to relieve the pressure on the pressure plate so that the clutch disc no longer revolves with the flywheel. Depressing the clutch pedal causes the release bearing to move forward toward the flywheel. In doing so, it pushes on the inner ends of three clutch

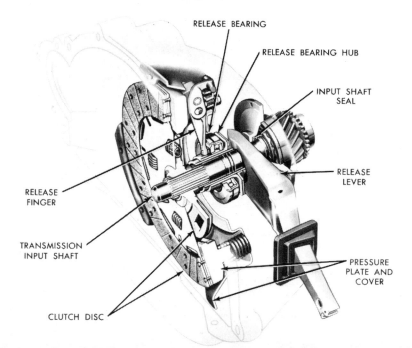

RELEASE BEARING

RELEASE BEARING HUB

INPUT SHAFT SEAL

RELEASE LEVER

RELEASE FINGER

TRANSMISSION INPUT SHAFT

PRESSURE PLATE AND COVER

CLUTCH DISC

Ford of Canada

Fig. 13-10   Coil-Spring Clutch Assembly

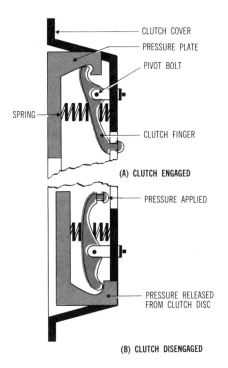

it is then disengaged. In order to overcome the
great pressure of the pressure-plate springs, the
fulcrum of the clutch release levers is at a point
which would produce a six-to-one ratio. Therefore
the inner end of the lever must be moved three-
eighths of an inch to pull back the pressure plate
one-sixteenth of an inch. It is of the utmost importance that these levers be adjusted properly. Each
must have the same amount of clearance and movement to ensure that the pressure plate remains
parallel to the flywheel at all times.

Semi-Centrifugal Coil-Spring Type

In the *semi-centrifugal* type of coil-spring clutch,
the release levers have weights placed on their
outer ends. As the pressure plate rotates, centrifugal
force acts upon the weights and fingers in such a
manner as to assist the coil springs in applying

Fig. 13-11   Clutch Finger Action Coil Spring Type

release levers, or fingers, that are equally spaced
around the centre of the pressure-plate assembly.
Through the leverage action, the outer ends of
these release levers pull back the pressure plate
from the clutch disc. This compresses the springs in
the pressure plate and thereby relieves the pressure which is forcing the clutch disc against the flywheel. This allows the clutch disc to spin freely
without transmitting any power from the engine;

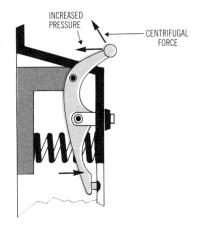

Fig. 13-12   Semi-centrifugal Clutch Finger Action

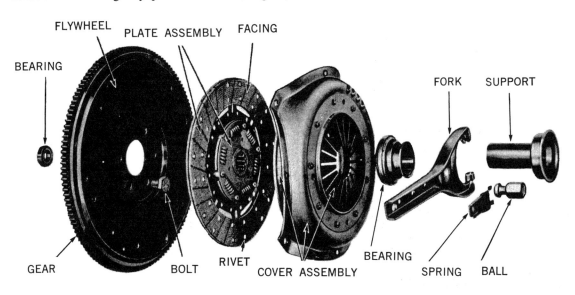

Fig. 13-13   Clutch Assembly Diaphragm Type

Courtesy of General Motors

pressure to the pressure plate. The higher the rpm of the assembly, the greater the pressure applied. When the pressure plate is not rotating, the weights have no effect, and it is only necessary to compress the coil springs to disengage the clutch.

Diaphragm-Spring Type Clutch

The diaphragm-type of clutch incorporates a diaphragm spring that not only provides the spring pressure required to hold the clutch disc against the flywheel, but also acts as the release lever to release the spring pressure when the clutch is disengaged. The diaphragm spring is a solid ring on the outer diameter which has a series of tapered fingers pointed inward toward the centre of the clutch. In the engaged position, the diaphragm spring is slightly dished, with the tapered fingers pointed away from the flywheel. In the disengaged position, the diaphragm spring is dished in the opposite direction. This flexing action is similar to the action of an oil can when the bottom is depressed. Since the diaphragm is pivoted on pivot rings near the outer circumference, it acts as a first-class lever. In the engaged position, the dished design of the spring places pressure around the entire circumference of the pressure plate. This pressure is sufficient to transmit the driving torque of the engine.

In the disengaged position, the throwout bearing is moved inward against the spring fingers. The diaphragm spring is forced to pivot around the inner pivot ring, causing the plate to dish in the opposite direction. The outer circumference of the diaphragm spring now lifts the pressure plate away by means of a series of retracting springs which are located around the circumference of the pressure plate. This allows the clutch disc to spin freely between the flywheel and the pressure plate, breaking the connection between the engine and the transmission.

13-4 CLUTCH PEDAL AND LINKAGE

The clutch pedal is connected through its linkage to the *release bearing* so that pressure on the pedal moves the bearing in against the release levers to disengage the clutch.

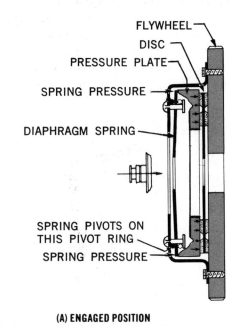

(A) ENGAGED POSITION

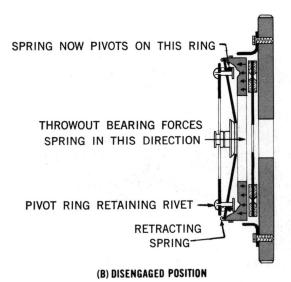

(B) DISENGAGED POSITION

Fig. 13-14   Clutch Finger Action Diaphragm Type

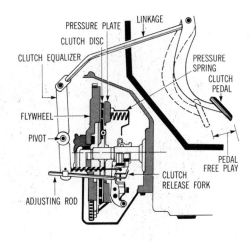

Fig. 13-15   Clutch Pedal and Linkage

13-5 RELEASE BEARINGS

A ball thrust bearing called a *clutch release* or *throwout bearing* is pressed on the release-bearing sleeve, or collar. This allows inner race to remain stationary while the outer race can revolve when it makes contact with the rotating release fingers which are fastened to the clutch cover. This type of bearing is filled with grease at the factory and ordinarily need not be serviced during its normal life.

Some vehicles use a graphite or carbon ring, or collar, instead of a thrust ball-type bearing. This ring remains stationary on the release sleeve; the clutch fingers rotate against the ring.

Ordinarily clutch release bearings cause little trouble, unless the driver has the bad habit of "riding the clutch pedal." Should the driver ride with his foot resting on the clutch pedal, this weight may be sufficient to depress the pedal far enough to cause continuous rotation of the release bearing. Since this bearing rotates at engine speed, a ball-type bearing will become over-heated, lose its lubricant, and consequently be damaged; and a carbon or graphite bearing will wear down rapidly.

The release bearing and sleeve are free to slide forward and backward on an extension which is

part of the front-transmission bearing retainer. The release bearing is moved by the inner end of the clutch *throwout fork*. This fork is usually pivoted on a ball-head stud attached to the clutch housing. A return spring pulls the fork back toward the transmission when the clutch is released. The outer end of the clutch fork is attached to the clutch-pedal linkage. When the outer end of the fork is moved rearward, the inner end pushes the release bearing against the fingers to disengage the clutch.

13-6 CLUTCH HOUSING AND CLUTCH SHAFT

A clutch housing made of cast iron or aluminum bolts onto the engine. This clutch housing surrounds the clutch assembly and flywheel. Some clutch housings are an integral part of the transmission case, while others are bolted to the transmission case. Some housings are designed with openings to allow for heat dissipation, while others have light metal covers which may be removed to facilitate the removal of the clutch mechanism.

The front transmission shaft or clutch shaft passes through the clutch housing and the clutch mechanism. The front or splined end of this shaft is supported in the clutch pilot bearing. The clutch-disc hub rides on the spline. The power from the engine is transmitted through the clutch disc to the hub to the clutch shaft to the transmission clutch gear.

13-7 CLUTCH PEDAL AND LINKAGE METHODS OF CONNECTING

The clutch pedal may be mounted beneath the toe-board or hung from brackets mounted between the

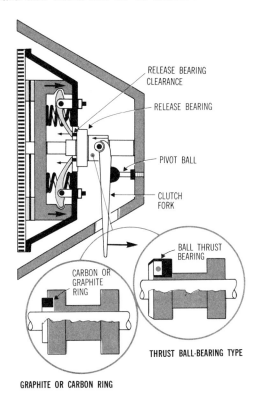

Fig. 13-16   Clutch Fork and Release Bearing Action

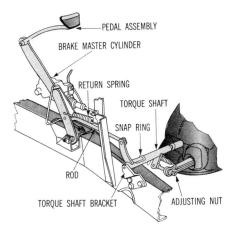

Chrysler Canada Ltd.

Fig. 13-17   Clutch Linkage Toe Board Mounting

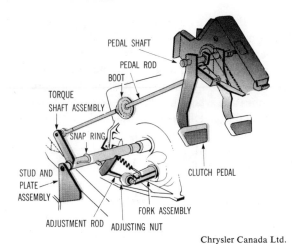

PEDAL SHAFT
PEDAL ROD
BOOT
TORQUE
SHAFT ASSEMBLY
SNAP RING
STUD AND
PLATE
ASSEMBLY
CLUTCH PEDAL
ADJUSTMENT ROD   ADJUSTING NUT
FORK ASSEMBLY

Chrysler Canada Ltd.

Fig. 13-18   Clutch Linkage Overhung Type

firewall and the dashboard. Two principal methods are used to connect the pedal to the clutch fork, the *mechanical* method and the *hydraulic* method.

The mechanical method uses a system of links, levers, and rods. When the clutch pedal is depressed, the force is increased by the mechanical advantage of the linkage and is transmitted to the clutch fork. A means of adjusting the clutch pedal free play is included in the linkage.

The hydraulic method is used on vehicles which, because of lack of space or design, require a very complicated mechanism. The hydraulic system simplifies the job.

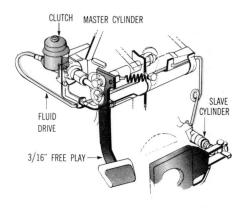

CLUTCH   MASTER CYLINDER
FLUID
DRIVE
SLAVE
CYLINDER
3/16" FREE PLAY

Chrysler Canada Ltd.

Fig. 13-19   Clutch

The hydraulic-clutch principle is the same as the principle used in hydraulic-brake systems. When the clutch pedal is depressed, it actuates a small master-cylinder piston. The pressure created on the liquid in the cylinder is transmitted through tubing to a "slave" cylinder which is bolted to the clutch housing near the clutch fork. A short, adjustable rod connects the slave cylinder piston to the clutch fork. When pressure is applied to the slave cylinder, the rod operates the clutch fork. A small reservoir attached to the clutch master cylinder stores the necessary hydraulic fluid. After service the system must be bled in a similar manner to the hydraulic-brake system. Clutch-pedal free play may be altered by changing the length of the adjustable rod between the slave cylinder and the fork.

REVIEW QUESTIONS

1. What is the purpose of the clutch?
2. What are the two basic characteristics of a clutch?
3. What function do each of the following parts perform in the operation of the clutch: (a) the flywheel (b) clutch disc (c) pressure-plate assembly (d) release bearing (e) pedal and linkage?
4. Describe the two types of clutch-disc facings.
5. State the purpose of (a) torsion springs (b) cushion springs of the clutch disc.
6. Describe the construction and operation of (a) the coil-spring type (b) the diaphragm-spring type of pressure-plate assembly.
7. Why is it of the utmost importance that the clutch fingers of a coil-spring type pressure plate be properly adjusted?
8. What is the advantage of a semi-centrifugal clutch?
9. What is the main cause of premature clutch release bearing failure?
10. What is the purpose and location of the clutch pilot bearing?
11. What is the advantage of a hydraulic-clutch control system?
12. How are (a) the mechanical (b) the hydraulic clutch control systems adjusted to compensate for clutch disc wear?

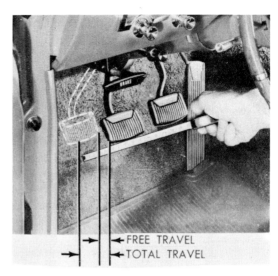

Ford of Canada

Fig. 14-1   Clutch Pedal Travel

Chapter 14
CLUTCH SERVICE

14-1 CLUTCH TROUBLE SHOOTING

Clutch troubles fall into several categories. Some of the common ones are: slipping—failure to transmit full power; dragging—failure to disengage promptly and fully, thus making gear shifting difficult; grabbing—violent and sudden engagement; chattering, especially in low or reverse gears; failure to transmit power at all; noises—squeaks or rattles.

Slipping Clutch

A slipping clutch develops frictional heat. This heat will destroy the temper in the pressure springs, reducing the pressure and squeezing the disc between the pressure plate and the flywheel, thus increasing slippage. Eventually, the clutch disc and, sometimes the pressure plate and flywheel are burned beyond further use.

Three common causes of clutch slippage are improper clutch-pedal free-play adjustment, riding the clutch, and sticking linkage.

The clutch pedal travel may be divided into thirds. The top third is pedal free-play to prevent slippage. Engagement takes place in the centre third. The bottom third is for clearance to prevent clutch drag.

14-2 CLUTCH-PEDAL FREE-PLAY

Clutch-pedal free-play is the amount the pedal may be depressed before the release bearing contacts the clutch-release levers. Free-play is easily checked. Depress the clutch pedal with one finger. It moves easily for about one to one-and-a-half inches. Then it becomes harder to move. The hard point is reached when the release bearing contacted the release fingers. The distance the pedal moved easily is called *clutch-pedal free-play*, or *toe-board clearance*.

All manufacturers specify the amount of free-play that must be allowed. One inch of free-play will move the release bearing one-eighth of an inch.

Proper clutch-pedal free-play is necessary to compensate for the wear on the clutch facings. As the facings wear, the pressure plate moves in toward the flywheel, and the outer ends of the pivoted release levers move out toward the release bearing. Once the fingers contact the release bearing, it is impossible for the pressure plate to move further forward. Consequently, full spring pressure no longer squeezes the disc between the pressure plate and the flywheel and slipping occurs. If the readjustment is made soon enough, clutch-disc life may be prolonged.

14-3 RAPID CLUTCH-DISC WEAR

Rapid clutch-disc wear and its resulting slipping is frequently caused by the driver riding with his foot on the clutch pedal, particularly in first and second gear. This habit prevents full pressure-plate spring pressure and slipping may take place. Too frequent use of the clutch or slow release of the clutch will also cause rapid facing wear and clutch slippage. In either case the remedy is for the driver to use the clutch properly.

Any binding or stiffness in the linkage which prohibits the application of full pressure-spring pressure may cause clutch slippage, even though the pedal may return to the normal position. To correct it, it is necessary to readjust the clutch pedal free-play and lubricate all points of friction.

14-4 CLUTCH DRAG OR SPIN

The condition known as clutch drag, or spin, occurs when the clutch disc does not come to rest after the clutch pedal has been depressed for a few seconds. When a clutch drags, the disc is not being completely released and continues to rotate with or rub against the pressure plate or flywheel. A common cause of clutch drag is excessive clutch-pedal free-play.

When free-play is excessive, complete depression of the pedal will not move the release bearing and release levers far enough to release the pressure plate from the disc. If, after adjusting the linkage to the correct free-play specifications, clutch drag continues, the clutch assembly must be removed for service.

When servicing the assembly for drag, a warped friction disc or pressure plate, a loose friction-disc facing, or binding of the hub spline on the clutch shaft, are possible causes.

14-5 CLUTCH GRABBING

Clutch grab is usually caused by: oil or grease on the clutch facings; loose or glazed facings; binding of the hub spline on the clutch shaft; or broken parts such as facings, cushion or torsion springs. Usually the trouble is in the clutch mechanism, and the assembly must be removed for service.

Sometimes clutch grab is caused by sticking linkage. This stickiness allows the clutch to engage suddenly, resulting in a heavy jerk. Freeing up and lubricating of friction points should correct the trouble.

14-6 CLUTCH CHATTER

A chattering clutch may be caused by such things as: worn or loose engine mounts on a vehicle equipped with a torque-tube type drive shaft; worn or loose rear-spring front shackles on a vehicle equipped with a Hotchkiss-type drive shaft; worn or loose radius rods and torque bar on a vehicle with a coil-spring rear-suspension system; or from wear or looseness in the universal joints, differential, or axles. Check these components to ascertain the cause of the chatter. Repairs or replacement of such worn parts will eliminate clutch chatter.

Internal problems such as: oil or grease on the facings; glazed or worn facings; worn or loose splines on the clutch hub or shaft; broken or loose torsion springs; and a warped disc or pressure plate cause clutch chatter. The assembly must be removed to correct all of these complaints.

14-7 COMPLETE FAILURE TO TRANSMIT DRIVE

Complete failure to transmit drive can be caused by: friction discs torn off or worn out; disc hub torn out; or broken pressure plate springs. In any case, remove the assembly for repair.

14-8 CLUTCH NOISES

Clutch noises are usually most noticeable when the engine is idling. If a squealing noise occurs when the pedal is depressed, it is usually caused by a worn or binding release bearing. A bearing that has lost its lubricant squeals when the pedal is depressed, and the bearing comes into operation. Replace the bearing and readjust the clutch-pedal free-play to prevent continuous operation of the bearing.

If a squealing noise is only audible when the clutch is depressed, the transmission in gear, but the vehicle stationary, it is usually the pilot bearing that is worn or lacks lubricant. Replace the bearing to eliminate the noise.

On vehicles equipped with a diaphragm-spring type clutch, worn or weak retracting springs frequently cause a rattle when the clutch pedal is depressed and the engine is idling. Replace the springs to eliminate the noise.

Noises that occur when the clutch is engaged, or in the process of being engaged, are usually caused by very badly worn linings. Therefore, there is metal-to-metal contact between the pressure plate, flywheel, and the metal parts of the disc. Weak or broken torsion springs, or a worn or loose disc hub-to-clutch-shaft spline can create clutch rattles or noise. Misalignment of the engine and transmission which allows the disc to move back and forth on the clutch spline can also be responsible. Correction of these faults can only be made by replacing the damaged disc as required, or by correcting the engine-to-transmission alignment.

14-9 SERVICING THE CLUTCH

The usual clutch servicing procedures are: adjusting the linkage to obtain the correct clutch-pedal free-play—this will frequently correct a slipping or dragging clutch; lubrication of the linkage friction points to correct a stiff or binding clutch; and clutch overhaul to correct complete failure to transmit power, or a grabbing and chattering condition.

The method of adjusting clutch-pedal free-play varies from manufacturer to manufacturer. Therefore, it is necessary to refer to the manufacturer's service manual for details and specifications.

The removal, overhaul, and replacement of clutch assemblies also varies with different manufacturers. Manufacturers' manuals give the procedure in detail. The general procedure is to disconnect the pedal linkage from the clutch fork and remove the drive shaft, transmission, clutch housing or lower clutch housing, and flywheel cover. The assembly may now be unbolted from the flywheel and removed. When the assembly is removed, carefully inspect the parts to determine necessary repairs or replacements.

The clutch disc should be checked for facing wear. Today, it is not considered good policy to reline clutch discs because, as the facings wear, the heat generated causes the cushion springs to lose their tension, and the torsion springs and hub splines become worn. Instead most manufacturers suggest installation of a new clutch disc.

Check the pressure-plate assembly for scores and heat checks. The heat generated, even in normal operation, is sufficient to cause the pressure-plate coil springs or the diaphragm spring to lose tension.

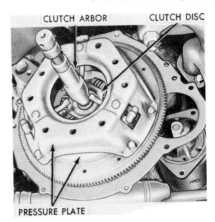

Ford of Canada

Fig. 14-3   Clutch Arbor or Pilot

Again, most manufacturers suggest replacement with either a new or *rebuilt* assembly.

A rebuilt assembly is one that has been completely disassembled. The pressure-plate surface is refaced, pressure springs are tested for tension and length and replaced as required, and clutch-finger contact surfaces are refaced. These are then reassembled and adjusted to manufacturer's specification.

Inspect the release bearing and pilot bearing for wear, noise, and ease of operation. If there are any signs of a defect, replace the bearing. Prelubricated bearings should not be cleaned in any solvent or degreasing compound, since this would remove the lubricant and ruin the bearing. If a bushing-type pilot bearing is used, place a small amount of fibre grease in the bushing before reassembly.

During reassembly, be sure that the flywheel, pressure plate, and disc are completely free of even

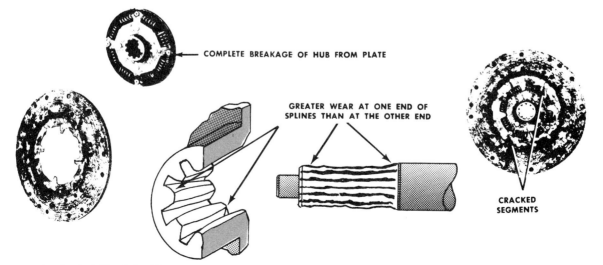

Fig. 14-2   Typical Clutch Problems

a trace of oil or grease; otherwise the clutch is likely to chatter or grab. The clutch disc is usually mounted with the torsion spring assembly away from the flywheel. Place a clutch-disc aligning tool or a pilot shaft through the disc hub and into the pilot bearing to centralize the disc and keep it in proper alignment with the pilot bearing. Remove this pilot shaft once the pressure-plate-to-flywheel bolts are tight. After reassembly is completed, adjust the operating linkage to provide proper clutch-pedal free-play.

REVIEW QUESTIONS

1. Give two causes for each of the following clutch problems: (a) a slipping clutch (b) rapid clutch-disc wear (c) clutch drag (d) clutch chatter.
2. Why is it not considered good policy to reline clutch discs?
3. Why is it good policy to replace the pressure plate, release bearing, and pilot bearing each time the clutch disc is replaced?
4. What is the purpose of a clutch pilot shaft?
5. Describe a rebuilt clutch pressure-plate assembly.

Chapter 15
TRANSMISSION PRINCIPLES

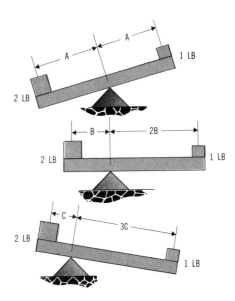

Fig. 15-1   Mechanical Advantage

15-1 PURPOSE OF TRANSMISSION

A great deal more power is required to get an automobile from rest to motion than is required to keep it in motion. Considerably more power is necessary to propel a vehicle up a hill than along a level road. By means of the transmission, the engine obtains the necessary mechanical advantage over the rear wheels to get the automobile into action and to take it up steep hills. The transmission provides a reverse gear for backing up. It also provides a means of disconnecting the motor from the rear wheels so that the engine may be operated with the vehicle parked and no operator at the controls.

15-2 MECHANICAL ADVANTAGE

Mechanical advantage occurs when a weight in one place lifts a heavier weight in another place; or a force applied at one point on a lever produces a greater force at another point. Two examples of mechanical advantage are the teeter-totter and the windlass.

The teeter-totter shows how mechanical advantage can be applied. If a 1-lb weight is placed on one end of a teeter-totter and a 2-lb weight is placed on the other end, the 1-lb weight goes up and the 2-lb weight goes down when both weights are placed equal distance from the fulcrum.

If the fulcrum is moved so that the distance from the 1-pound weight to the fulcrum is twice that of the distance between the fulcrum and the 2-lb weight, the weights remain balanced. If the fulcrum is moved still closer to the 2-lb weight, the 1-lb

weight goes down and the 2-lb weight goes up. You will notice that as the distance between the fulcrum and the 1-lb weight increases, the distance that the 1-lb weight moves must increase proportionately to maintain the same movement of the 2-lb weight. Thus, a light weight can move a heavier weight but, in doing so, the smaller weight must travel a greater distance than does the larger weight.

The wheel and axle is usually just a wheel

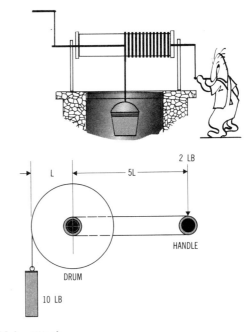

Fig. 15-2   Winch

fastened to a rod. A force applied to the outside of the big wheel produces a greater twisting force on the small rod than if the rod itself were twisted. In the windlass, for example, the hand will move a distance of several feet when turning the crank once. This will turn the rod once which will wind up the rope only a few inches. A greater force can be lifted with a windlass than by just pulling a rope. A twisting force is known as a *torque* and is that force which produces, or tends to produce, rotation or torsion.

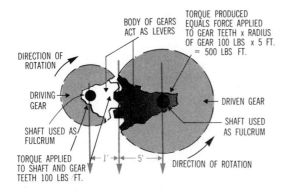

Fig. 15-3   Principle of Gear Torque Multiplication

The wheel and axle principle also applies to gears. A force applied at the outside of a gear will exert a twist, or torque, on its shaft. The bigger the gear, the greater will be the torque. The shaft with the largest gear will have the greatest torque. The same rule applies as in levers; namely, what is gained in torque is lost in speed. If the diameter of one gear is twice the diameter of the other, then one gear must have twice as many teeth as the other. For example, if the small driving gear has 12 teeth and the large driven gear has 24 teeth, then 1 revolution of the driving gear would mesh with 12 teeth of the large gear, or rotate it ½ a revolution. As the speed is decreased the torque is increased.

From the study of the simple lever and windlass it is possible to make the following deductions:

1. If the speed of an engine remains constant and its torque is multiplied through mechanical advantage, it will lift more weight but it will take longer to do it.
2. If the speed of an engine remains constant and its torque is reduced through mechanical advantage, it will lift less weight but will lift it faster.

15-3 GEAR RATIO

Gear ratio may be defined as the relationship between the number of turns made by a driving gear to complete 1 full turn of a driven gear. If the driving gear turns 2 revolutions to turn the driven gear one revolution, the gear ratio is said to be 2 to 1.

When several gears are combined to give this ratio, it is not necessary to consider the speeds of each pair of gears separately. The gear ratio may be found by using the following formula:

$$\frac{\text{Product of the teeth on all of the driven gears}}{\text{Product of the teeth on all of the driving gears}} = \text{Gear Ratio}$$

For example:

A transmission has a clutch gear with 14 teeth connected to a countershaft drive gear with 24 teeth. The low-speed countershaft gear has 18 teeth and the low-reverse sliding gear has 27 teeth. What is the ratio between the engine and the drive shaft in low gear?

Solution:

$$\text{Ratio (in low gear)} = \frac{24 \times 27}{14 \times 18}$$
$$= \frac{2.57}{1}$$

or 2.57 to 1 ratio

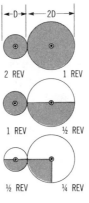

Fig. 15-4   Gear Ratios

In the three-speed transmission, the gear ratios are usually approximately 3 to 1 for first or low gear, approximately 2 to 1 for second gear, and 1 to 1 for high, or direct drive. Reverse-gear ratio is approximately the same as low gear.

The ratios used vary from car to car depending upon the horsepower of the engine and the vehicle weight.

15-4 TRANSMISSION GEARS

Gears are made of high quality steel and drop forged (machine hammered into shape) while at a red-heat. The teeth and other precision areas are finished on precision machinery. The gear teeth are case hardened to produce a smooth hard surface with a soft but very tough interior. Two principal types of gear tooth design are used, the *spur* and the *helical*.

The spur gear—is the simplest and a common type of gear. Its teeth are cut straight across the edge. Spur gears are used to connect parallel shafts which rotate in opposite directions. Because this type of gear is inclined to be noisy in its operation, other types of gears have become more popular in the transportation field.

The helical gear—is similar to the spur gear, except that its teeth are cut at an angle on its edge. The teeth of the gear it meshes with must be cut on the same angle if the shafts are parallel. It is quieter when operating than the ordinary spur gear, is

STRAIGHT-TOOTH SPUR GEARS

HELICAL PINION AND INTERNAL GEAR

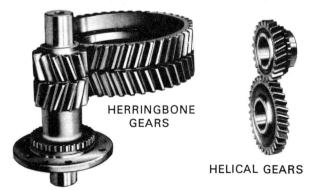

HERRINGBONE GEARS

HELICAL GEARS

Courtesy of General Motors

Fig. 15-5   Transmission Gears

stronger because more tooth area is in contact and for these reasons is usually preferred.

Helical gears must be firmly mounted to prevent end-play, as there is a tendency for them to slide apart when a load is applied. This is because of the angle of the teeth.

Gear Nomenclature

Elementary gear-tooth nomenclature includes: outside circle, which is the full diameter of the gear; root circle, which is the minimum diameter of the gear; pitch line or pitch diameter, which is midway between the outside circle and the root circle; tooth face, which is between the pitch line and the outside circle; and tooth flank which is between the pitch line and the root circle.

Backlash is the distance a tooth of the driven gear can be rotated before it contacts a tooth on the driven gear. *Clearance* is the distance between the outside circle of one gear and the root circle of the other gear when the gears are in mesh.

There must be some clearance and backlash between gear teeth. This clearance is only a few thousandths of an inch and is necessary to allow for expansion and lubrication.

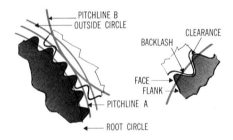

Fig. 15-6   Elementary Gear Tooth Nomenclature

15-5 PLANETARY GEARS

A planetary-gear set consists of a sun gear, a set of planetary gears mounted on a carrier, and an internal ring gear. The planetary gears rotate on their axes while they and their carrier orbit around the sun gear—as the planets in the solar system revolve around the sun. Five gear combinations are possible: *neutral*, *direct drive*, *reverse*, *reduction*, and *overdrive*. Planetary-gear sets are used in multiple sets when more than two forward speeds are required.

In a planetary-gear set the gears are in mesh at all times. The gears are arranged so that they will function as driving units or driven units. In order to transmit power through a planetary-gear set,

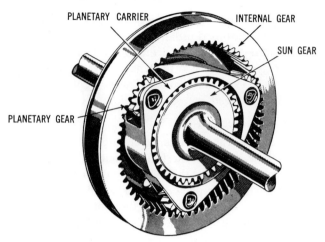

PLANETARY CARRIER — INTERNAL GEAR

SUN GEAR

PLANETARY GEAR

Courtesy of General Motors

Fig. 15-7   Planetary Gears

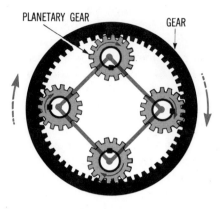

PLANETARY GEAR   GEAR

(A) RING GEAR DRIVING

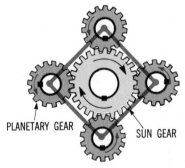

PLANETARY GEAR   SUN GEAR

(B) SUN GEAR DRIVING

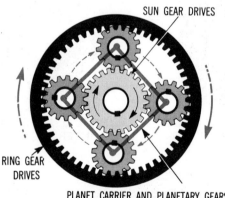

SUN GEAR DRIVES

RING GEAR DRIVES

PLANET CARRIER AND PLANETARY GEARS
ROTATE WITH RING AND SUN GEARS

(C)

Fig. 15-8   Planetary Gears Set in Direct

either one unit must be held stationary or two units locked together. The five various combinations of drive are obtained by driving or holding different components.

15-6 NEUTRAL

Neutral is obtained by not holding any unit, or locking two units together. Under these conditions the input gear rotates the other gears, but no power is transmitted to the output member.

15-7 DIRECT DRIVE

Direct drive is obtained by driving two members of a planetary-gear set at the same relative speed and in the same direction. For example: when clockwise power is applied to the ring gear, the power will be transmitted to the planetary gears, rotating them clockwise. When clockwise power is applied to the sun gear, it will be transmitted to the planetary gears rotating them counterclockwise. When power is applied to both the sun gear and the ring gear at the same time, the power will meet at the planetary gears, preventing them from rotating on their axes. Therefore, the planetary gears and the planetary carrier must be carried around between the ring gear and the sun gear in the same direction and at the same relative speed, thus producing direct drive.

15-8 SPEED INCREASE

There are two methods of obtaining speed increase. The first and most common method is to drive the planet carrier, hold the sun gear, and use the ring

gear as the output member. When the planetary carrier rotates as the drive member, the planet gears must rotate on their axes since they are in mesh with the stationary sun gear. While the planetary gears are rotating on their axes or "walking around"

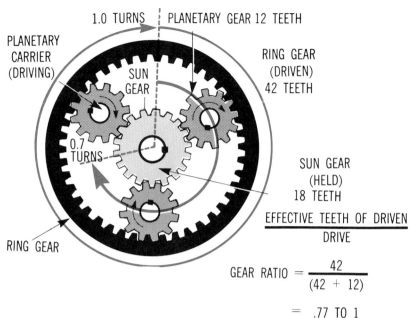

1.0 TURNS | PLANETARY GEAR 12 TEETH

PLANETARY CARRIER (DRIVING)

SUN GEAR

RING GEAR (DRIVEN) 42 TEETH

0.7 TURNS

SUN GEAR (HELD) 18 TEETH

RING GEAR

$$\text{GEAR RATIO} = \frac{\text{EFFECTIVE TEETH OF DRIVEN}}{\text{DRIVE}}$$

$$\text{GEAR RATIO} = \frac{42}{(42 + 12)}$$

$$= .77 \text{ TO } 1$$

Fig. 15-9   Planetary Gears in Overdrive

the sun gear, they and their carrier are also revolving around the sun gear. Since the planetary gears are also in mesh with the ring gear, the ring gear rotates at the speed of the rotating planetary carrier, plus the speed of the planet gears as they rotate on their axes.

For example, one revolution of the planet carrier would rotate the ring gear one revolution. The amount that the planet gears rotated about their axes would rotate the ring gear an additional amount. The extra amount that the ring gear would rotate would depend upon the sizes of the gears.

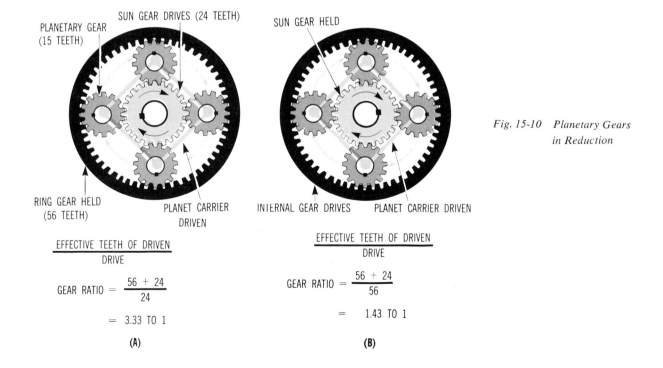

PLANETARY GEAR (15 TEETH)

SUN GEAR DRIVES (24 TEETH)

RING GEAR HELD (56 TEETH)

PLANET CARRIER DRIVEN

$$\text{GEAR RATIO} = \frac{\text{EFFECTIVE TEETH OF DRIVEN}}{\text{DRIVE}}$$

$$\text{GEAR RATIO} = \frac{56 + 24}{24}$$

$$= 3.33 \text{ TO } 1$$

(A)

SUN GEAR HELD

INTERNAL GEAR DRIVES

PLANET CARRIER DRIVEN

$$\text{GEAR RATIO} = \frac{\text{EFFECTIVE TEETH OF DRIVEN}}{\text{DRIVE}}$$

$$\text{GEAR RATIO} = \frac{56 + 24}{56}$$

$$= 1.43 \text{ TO } 1$$

(B)

Fig. 15-10   Planetary Gears in Reduction

Most overdrive units have a ratio of approximately .7 to 1. This means .7 of a revolution of the planet carrier, plus the rotation of the planet gears on their axes, equals one revolution of the ring gear.

The other method of obtaining overdrive uses the same principle but changes the held and driven members. The drive member is still the planet carrier, but the ring gear is now held, and the sun gear becomes the output member. The planet gears now walk around the ring gear to drive the sun gear faster.

15-9 SPEED REDUCTION

Two methods of obtaining speed reduction are available. One method uses the sun gear as the drive member, the ring gear is held, and the planet carrier is the output member. As the sun gear is rotated, it rotates the planet gears. As the planet gears rotate on their axes, they walk around the ring gear, carrying the planet carrier around with them. The carrier therefore rotates, but at a speed less than the sun gear.

In the other method the ring gear is the driving member, and the sun gear is held. The planet gears walk around the sun gear, carrying the planet carrier around at a slower speed than the ring gear.

In both methods, the amount of speed reduction depends upon the size of the gears used.

15-10 REVERSE

Reverse is obtained by holding the planet carrier, driving the sun gear, and using the ring gear as the output member. In this case the planet gears act as idler gears and therefore rotate the ring gear in the opposite direction to the sun gear at a reduced speed.

Reverse may also be obtained by driving the ring gear and holding the carrier—the planet gears act as idler gears to rotate the sun gear in the opposite direction faster than the ring gear.

The method used to hold or lock the various components for the different gear combinations will vary according to application and to manufacturer. The early Model T Ford planetary transmission was controlled by pedals. Today, hydraulic pressure, in combination with mechanical governors and vacuum diaphragms, or electric solenoids, are used. Their construction and operation will be discussed in succeeding chapters.

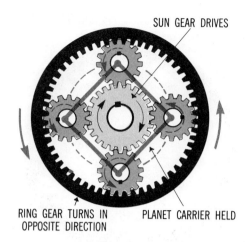

Fig. 15-11   Planetary Gears in Reverse

15-11 GEAR RATIO FOR PLANETARY GEAR SETS

In order to calculate the gear ratio for a set of planetary gears the basic gear ratio formula is modified slightly. For standard gears the formula is driven/drive. For planetary gear sets the formula is effective teeth of driven/drive when the effective teeth equals the sum of the teeth in the sun and ring gears.

In a planetary gear set using a sun gear with 20 teeth, planetary gears with 16 teeth, and a ring gear with 60 teeth then:

A. Reduction with ring gear held, the sun gear driving and the planetary carrier as the output member the ratio equals:

$$\frac{20 + 60}{20} \quad \frac{80}{20} = 4 \text{ to } 1$$

B. Reduction with the sun gear held, the ring gear driving, and the planetary carrier as the output member the ratio equals:

$$\frac{20 + 60}{60} \quad \frac{80}{60} = 1.3 \text{ to } 1$$

C. Overdrive with the sun gear held, the planetary carrier as the drive unit, and the ring gear as the output unit the gear ratio equals:

$$\frac{60}{60 + 20} \quad \frac{60}{80} = .75 \text{ to } 1.$$

D. Reverse with the carrier held, the sun gear as the drive unit, and the ring gear as the output unit the gear ratio equals: (since no movement of the carrier is involved, it is not necessary to use the effective teeth of the driven; therefore, the standard gear formula is used)

$$\frac{60}{20} = 3 \text{ to } 1.$$

15-12 OVERRUNNING CLUTCHES AND SPRAGS

Overrunning, or *one-way*, *clutches* and *sprags* are coupling devices. They will transmit power between two in-line shafts as long as the two shafts revolve at the same speed. Should the driving shaft slow down or stop, the driven shaft could still turn faster or overrun the driving shaft. Under these conditions the clutch "uncouples" the two shafts and the driven shaft overruns.

For example, the overrunning clutch is placed in the drive line of a vehicle. The drive of the coupling is attached to the transmission rear main shaft; the driven side of the coupling is attached to the propeller side. As the engine drives the car, the clutch will lock up and transmit the power. When the accelerator is released and the engine slows down, the propeller shaft now rotates faster than the transmission shaft. The clutch releases, or overruns, and the vehicle will coast.

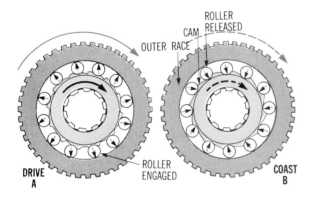

Fig. 15-12 Typical Overrunning Clutch

An overrunning, or one-way clutch—consists of: an inner race, or clutch cam, which has a series of evenly spaced, inclined planes or ramps around its outer circumference; a series of hardened steel rollers, one for each ramp; a roller retainer to keep the rollers in their proper relative positions; and an outer race. The inner race is the driving member and the outer race is the driven member.

When the inner race is driving and turning the outer race at the same speed, the rollers roll up their ramps and jam between the two races. The outer race now turns with the inner race and the overrunning clutch acts as a solid drive.

When the inner race turns more slowly than the outer race, the rollers are forced down into the lower part of the ramp and the outer race overruns. The rollers now act as a roller bearing. When the inner race speeds up again, the rollers roll up the ramp and jam, to form a solid coupling.

A sprag clutch—performs the same function as an overrunning clutch. It consists of an inner and outer race and a series of special sprag segments instead of rollers. The sprag segments are designed so that one diagonal dimension is larger than the distance between the two races, while the other diagonal dimension is smaller.

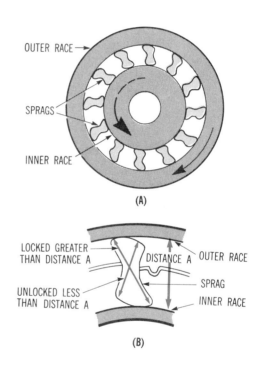

Fig. 15-13 Typical Sprag Unit

When the inner race is driving, the sprags pivot about their centres, and the larger dimension produces a wedging action which locks the two races together. If the inner race slows down, the sprags pivot in the opposite direction, placing the smaller diagonal dimension between the races. The outer race now overruns the inner. The sprags act as a bearing between the two races.

Overrunning clutches and sprags can be used to permit a shaft to rotate in one direction only. They overrun in one direction and lock the shaft stationary when a reversed force is applied.

REVIEW QUESTIONS

1. Why does the internal combustion engine require a transmission, when an electric motor does not?
2. State the three purposes of a transmission in a motor vehicle.
3. What is mechanical advantage?
4. Define the term "torque".
5. How is torque increased through use of the wheel and axle principle?
6. How is torque increased through the use of gears?
7. What is the relationship between speed and torque when the input is the same?
8. What is meant by the term "gear ratio"?
9. How is gear ratio calculated?
10. What determines the selection of the gear ratios for the various gears of a transmission?
11. Determine the gear ratio for first, second and third gear of a transmission using the following gears: clutch gear 16 teeth, countershaft drive gear 32 teeth, countershaft low gear 18 teeth, second-speed gear 21 teeth, low-reverse sliding gear 28 teeth, countershaft second gear 27 teeth.
12. Describe the manufacture of a gear.
13. Why are helical gears superior to spur gears?
14. Define the gear terms (a) backlash (b) clearance.
15. Why is backlash and clearance required between two meshing gears?
16. Make a sketch of a planetary-gear set and label all components.
17. How are the following gear combinations obtained through the use of a planetary gear set: (a) neutral (b) reduction (c) direct or 1-1, (d) overdrive?
18. What is the purpose of a sprag or overrunning clutch?
19. By means of sketches, show the principle of operation of (a) an overrunning clutch (b) a sprag.

Chapter 16
STANDARD TRANSMISSIONS AND OVERDRIVES

Ford of Canada

Fig. 16-1   Typical Three-Speed Semi-Synchronized Transmission

16-1 STANDARD TRANSMISSIONS

A standard transmission provides a means of manually varying the gear ratio or speeds between the engine and the rear wheels. The number of speeds depends upon the application. A heavy truck may have from 4 to 8 speeds. Most small imported automobiles and many Canadian and American sport options use 4-speed transmissions. The conventional standard transmission in most automobiles is a 3-speed transmission.

The transmission consists of: a cast iron or aluminum *case*, four *shafts*, a series of *gears*, *synchronizing devices*, *bearings*, and a *shifting mechanism*.

The clutch shaft and clutch drive gear, sometimes called the front main shaft, is supported in the transmission case by the front transmission bearings; the other end is supported by the clutch pilot bearing. Whenever the clutch is engaged and the engine is running, the clutch gear rotates at engine speed. The clutch drive gear is in constant mesh with the countershaft *cluster gear*. The cluster

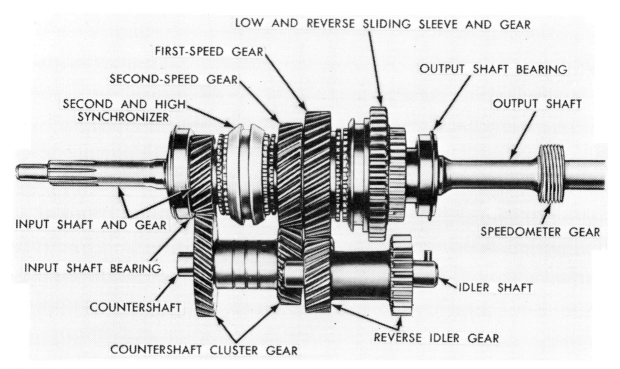

Fig. 16-2   Typical Three-Speed Fully Synchronized Transmission Gears

Chrysler Canada Ltd.

133

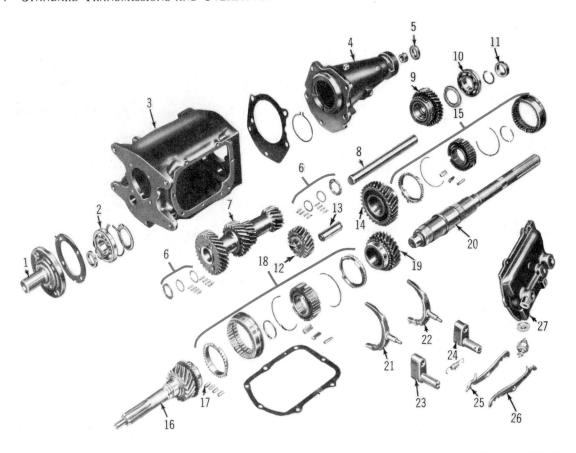

Fig. 16-3   Transmission Components

Courtesy of General Motors

1.	Bearing Retainer	11.	Speedometer Drive Gear	19.	2nd Speed Gear
2.	Main Drive Gear Bearing	12.	Reverse Idler Gear	20.	Mainshaft
3.	Case	13.	Reverse Idler Shaft	21.	2nd and 3rd Shifter Fork
4.	Extension	14.	1st Speed Gear	22.	1st and Reverse Shifter Fork
5.	Oil Seal	15.	1st and Reverse Synchro-	23.	2-3 Shifter Shaft Assembly
6.	Needle Bearings		nizer Hub Assembly	24.	1st and Reverse Shifter Shaft
7.	Countergear	16.	Main Drive Gear		Assembly
8.	Countershaft	17.	Pilot Bearings	25.	1st and Reverse Detent Cam
9.	Reverse Gear	18.	2nd and 3rd Synchronizer	26.	2nd and 3rd Detent Cam
10.	Rear Bearing		Hub Assembly	27.	Side Cover

gear revolves on roller bearings and is supported in the case by the countershaft.

The cluster-gear assembly has three or four gears cut on the same steel blank. They are the countershaft drive gear (the largest), the second-speed gear (next largest), the low gear (the second smallest), and reverse gear (the smallest). Some transmissions use the same cluster gear for both low and reverse; thus, the countershaft has one less gear in this type of transmission.

Since the cluster drive gear is always in mesh with the clutch gear, the assembly rotates in the opposite direction and at a reduced speed, which is in proportion to the gear ratio between the two gears.

The reverse-idler gear rotates on a bushing between it and the reverse idler shaft, which is supported by the transmission case. The reverse-idler gear is in constant mesh with the cluster gear. It rotates in the opposite direction to the cluster gear but in the same direction as the engine.

The rear-transmission main shaft is supported in the rear of the case by a ball bearing. The front of the shaft is supported by a roller bearing placed

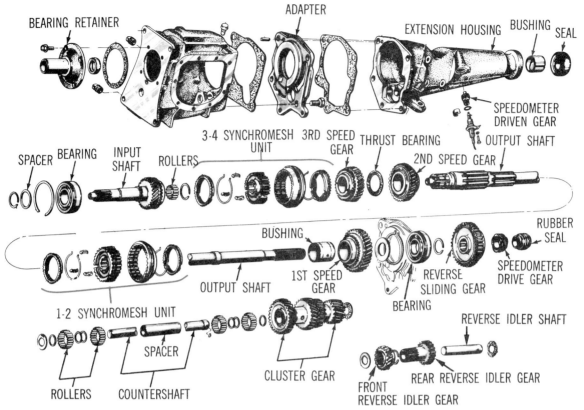

Fig. 16-4   *Four-Speed Transmission Disassembled*   Ford of Canada

in a recess in the centre of the clutch gear. This shaft has two or three gears and one or two synchromesh units mounted on it. In a fully synchronized transmission the low, reverse, and second-speed gears are not allowed to slide but are free to spin on the rear-transmission shaft. The low- and second-speed gears are in constant mesh with their respective gears of the cluster gear, and the reverse gear is meshed with the reverse idler gear. The second and high, and low synchromesh units are attached to the shaft by means of splines. Each unit can be moved back and forth to mesh with splined hubs on their respective gears, thereby connecting the gears to the rear transmission shaft.

When only one synchromesh unit is used (the second and high unit) the second-speed gear is not allowed to slide but is free to spin on the transmission rear main shaft. The low-reverse sliding gear and the synchromesh unit are splined to the rear main shaft. The low and reverse sliding gear can be moved to mesh with either the countershaft low gear or the reverse idler gear. The synchromesh unit can be moved to mesh with splined hubs, which are part of the second-speed gear and the clutch gear.

16-2 NEUTRAL GEAR

Neutral gear position is obtained by moving either the low-reverse sliding gear or the low synchromesh unit and the second and high synchromesh unit to a position where they are not in mesh with their respective gears. The connection between the engine and the rear wheels is broken; this allows the engine to run without driving the rear wheels.

16-3 LOW OR FIRST-SPEED GEAR

In low, or first speed, a set of gears is required which will allow the engine to run at a high rpm, while the automobile moves very slowly. When the operator shifts the gearshift lever into the low-gear position, the mechanism moves either the low-reverse sliding gear into mesh with the countershaft low-speed gear, or the low synchromesh unit into mesh with the splines of the low speed gear. The low gear has a greater number of teeth than the countershaft low-speed gear. Therefore, the rear wheels turn at a slower speed but with increased power. The countershaft revolves when the engine is running because its large drive gear is always in mesh with the smaller clutch-shaft gear. Since the driving gear of this set has fewer teeth

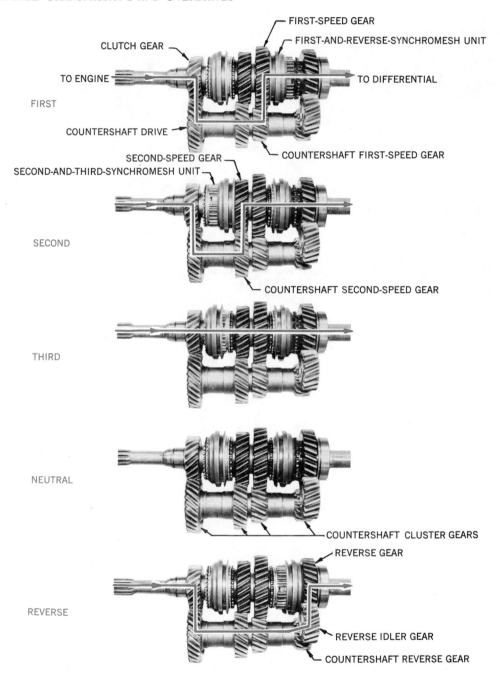

Fig. 16-5   Power Flow in Transmission

Courtesy of General Motors

than the driven gear of the countershaft, the countershaft revolves at a slower speed, but with more torque than the engine crankshaft. The two sets of gears give a combined ratio of approximately 3 to 1.

16-4 INTERMEDIATE, OR SECOND GEAR

When the operator shifts the gear lever from low to second-speed position, the shifter mechanism moves either the low-reverse sliding gear or the low synchromesh unit into neutral position, and engages the synchromesh unit with the second-speed gear on the transmission shaft. The second-speed gear is always in mesh with the countershaft second-speed gear. These two gears have approximately the same number of teeth and their gear ratio is very low. Therefore, in second gear the gear ratio is equal to the products of the gear ratio between the clutch gear and the countershaft gear, and the ratio between the countershaft second-speed gear and the main shaft second-speed gear. This total ratio is approximately 2 to 1.

16-5 HIGH OR THIRD-SPEED GEAR

When the operator shifts from second gear to high gear, the synchromesh unit disengages from the main-shaft second-speed gear and meshes with a spline on the clutch-shaft gear. Since the clutch-shaft gear is revolving at engine speed, and the synchromesh unit connects this gear directly to the rear transmission shaft, no reduction gears are in operation. The speed of the output shaft of the transmission is the same as the speed of the input shaft, and there is no increase in torque, or decrease in speed. Therefore, high gear ratio is 1 to 1.

16-6 REVERSE GEAR

When the operator shifts to reverse gear, the synchromesh unit is placed in the neutral position and the low-reverse sliding gear meshes with the reverse-idler gear, which is in constant mesh with the countershaft reverse gear. This puts an extra set of gears in the gear train and opposite direction in rotation is achieved. Since the same gear is used in reverse as is used in low gear, both have the same approximate ratio of 3 to 1.

When a four-speed type of transmission is used, the shift mentioned in the previous paragraph would engage the lowest forward gear of the transmission, not reverse gear. In a four-speed transmission, reverse gear can be obtained either by sliding a separate reverse gear, which is splined to the output shaft, into mesh with the reverse idler gear or by sliding the reverse idler gear into mesh with the first-speed gear. Simultaneously, the re-

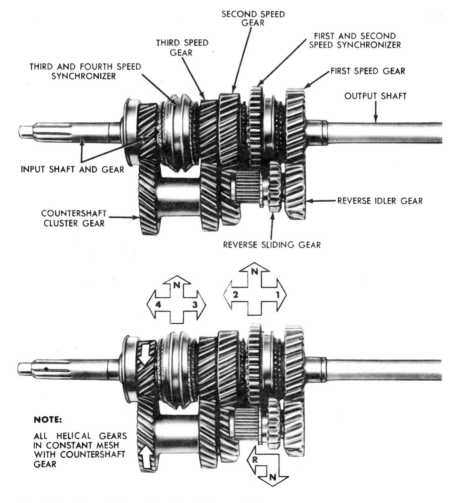

Fig. 16-6   Power Flow—Four-Speed Transmission

verse idler gear meshes with a special spline on the first and second gear synchromesh unit, thereby locking the gear and the synchromesh unit together without moving the synchromesh unit.

16-7 SYNCHROMESH UNIT

When gears were shifted in the older type of transmissions, they frequently clashed and broken or damaged gears resulted. The synchromesh unit was designed to do away with this trouble. The synchromesh is the combination of two words—synchronize and mesh. *Synchronize* means "to do" or "happen" at the same time and *mesh* means to interlace, or join. The synchromesh unit in the transmission combines these two operations. It synchronizes the speed of the clutch shaft with the main shaft and, in doing so, it quietly meshes the second-speed gear with the main drive gear.

Many synchromesh units use cone-type clutches. A cone clutch consists of an external cone that slides into an internal cone. With light pressure, the two cones slip. As the external cone is forced more tightly into the internal cone the two units rotate together. The external cones are attached to and driven by both the clutch gear and the second-speed gear. The internal cones are machined into each end of the synchronizer sliding sleeve or drum. The sliding sleeve frequently includes small-ball and spring assemblies to assist in the cone clutch action and to help lock the synchromesh unit in the desired position.

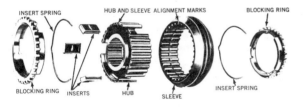

Fig. 16-7A   Second and Third Syncromesh Unit

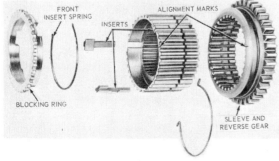

Ford of Canada

Fig. 16-7B   First and Reverse Syncromesh Unit

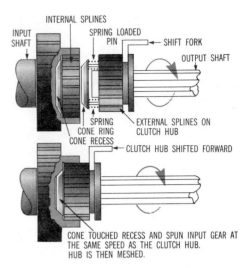

Fig. 16-7C   Simplified Syncromesh Operation

Before shifting, the clutch gear, the second-speed gear, and the synchromesh unit are rotating at different speeds. When the shifter lever is moved, the sliding sleeve of the synchromesh unit moves until the cone on the gear comes in contact with the cone of the sliding sleeve. This contact synchronizes the speed of both units. As the shifter lever is moved farther, the sliding sleeve depresses the synchronizing balls and slides into mesh with the splined hub of the second-speed gear or the clutch gear. This locks the synchromesh unit and the gear together. As both are turning at the same speed, meshing is silent.

16-8 TRANSMISSION SHIFT MECHANISMS

Two types of manual shift mechanisms are in general use on standard transmissions—the *remote control*, or steering-column type, and the *direct*, or floor type. Regardless of the type used, the shift pattern on three-speed transmissions follows the standard (H) pattern: low and reverse on the left, second and high gears on the right. Four-speed transmissions use various shift patterns. Common types are illustrated in Fig. 16-10.

It can be seen that two separate motions are required. The first motion sometimes referred to as the cross-shift is sideways, and it selects the proper gear assembly to be moved, either the low-reverse gear or the synchromesh unit. The second motion, a forward or backward one, moves the gear assembly into mesh with the proper gear.

The motions of the steering column gear-shift

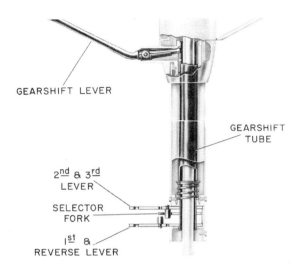

GEARSHIFT LEVER

GEARSHIFT TUBE

2nd & 3rd LEVER

SELECTOR FORK

1st & REVERSE LEVER

(A) COLUMN ASSEMBLY

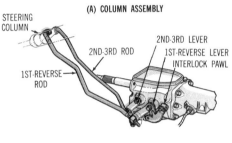

STEERING COLUMN

2ND-3RD LEVER

2ND-3RD ROD

1ST-REVERSE LEVER INTERLOCK PAWL

1ST-REVERSE ROD

(B) TRANSMISSION LINKAGE

Fig. 16-8   Steering Column Gearshift Linkage

lever are transmitted to the transmission mechanism through linkage. The motions of a floor shift may be transmitted to the transmission mechanism through linkage, or the lever may be connected directly into the top of the transmission.

The transmission shifter unit consists of shifter forks that ride in grooves cut into the synchromesh unit, and the low-reverse sliding gear. The forks are attached to a cam and shaft assembly or to

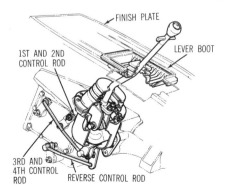

FINISH PLATE

LEVER BOOT

1ST AND 2ND CONTROL ROD

3RD AND 4TH CONTROL ROD

REVERSE CONTROL ROD

Fig. 16-9   Typical Four-Speed Floor-Type Gearshift Assembly

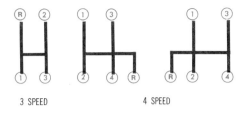

3 SPEED   4 SPEED

Fig. 16-10   Transmission Shift Patterns

shifter rails. Spring-loaded balls, called *poppet balls*, pop into notches cut in the cam or shifter rails to hold the shift mechanism in the position selected. An interlocking ball and spring prevents one lever or rail from moving when the other lever has placed a set of gears in mesh.

The shafts pass through the housing, or cover, and are attached to the shifter-lever linkage.

16-9   OVERDRIVE TRANSMISSIONS

An overdrive transmission is an automatic, two-speed, planetary-type gear transmission which is attached to the rear of the conventional three-speed transmission. The conventional transmission output shaft drives the overdrive unit. The output shaft of the overdrive unit turns the driveshaft at a faster speed than the output shaft of the conventional transmission. The gear ratio of most overdrive units is approximately .7 to 1.

The advantages of the overdrive transmission are: a reduction of approximately 30% in engine speed while maintaining the same road speed; increased gas mileage; a reduction in engine wear and engine noise; and prolonged engine life.

An overdrive transmission works satisfactorily providing the engine is developing sufficient power to propel the vehicle without lugging or straining. Most overdrive units will not up-shift below 30 mph which help prevent lugging. The vehicle must be operated at a reasonable road speed. An overdrive transmission does not usually increase the maximum road speed because as the car speed increases, wind resistance increases rapidly. This increase in wind resistance is comparable to climbing a long hill. As pointed out in the chapter on standard transmissions, an increase in speed through gearing results in a decrease in output-shaft power. Therefore, when the transmission is in overdrive, less power is delivered to the drive shaft. This reduction in power can upset the advantage of a higher gear ratio and, as a result, the top speed in conventional

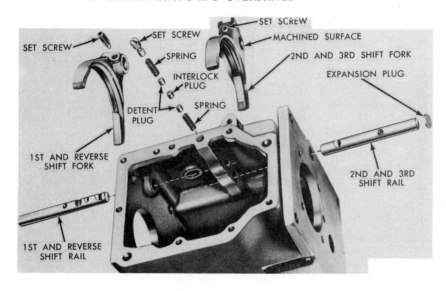

(A) SHIFTER FORKS AND RAILS

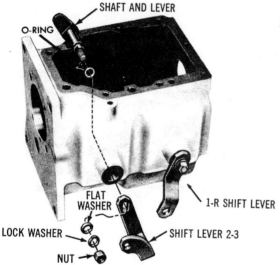

(B) SHIFT LEVER AND SHAFT

Ford of Canada

Fig. 16-11   Transmission Shifter Mechanisms

high gear and in overdrive are usually the same. When in overdrive, the road must be fairly level. Hill climbing requires increased power and therefore could cause the engine to lug.

16-10 OVERDRIVE CONSTRUCTION

The overdrive unit consists of a *planetary gear set*, an *overrunning clutch* or *sprag*, a *balk ring* and *gear plate*, and *control devices*.

When the manual-control lever on the dash is in the overdrive position, direct drive is through the overrunning clutch. The inner, or driving, race of

this clutch is splined to the end of the extended rear-transmission shaft. The outer race is part of the planetary-gear ring housing. As long as the transmission is trying to turn faster than the drive shaft, the clutch is locked. Should the drive shaft turn faster, the clutch overruns.

The planetary-gear set used in an overdrive unit has the ring gear attached to the output shaft; the planetary carrier is splined to the rear transmission shaft. The sun gear is mounted in such a manner that it may be locked in a stationary position or be free to turn. When the sun gear is held stationary, the ring gear and output shaft rotate faster than the transmission shaft and planetary carrier.

To hold the sun gear stationary, a solenoid-controlled pawl engages with the gear plate of the gear-plate and balk-ring assembly. The balk ring is loosely assembled to the gear plate so that it can turn a few degrees one way or the other. This balk ring prevents the pawl from entering a slot on the gear ring until the vehicle reaches approximately 35 mph. Then the governor makes the necessary electrical connections to energize the pawl solenoid,

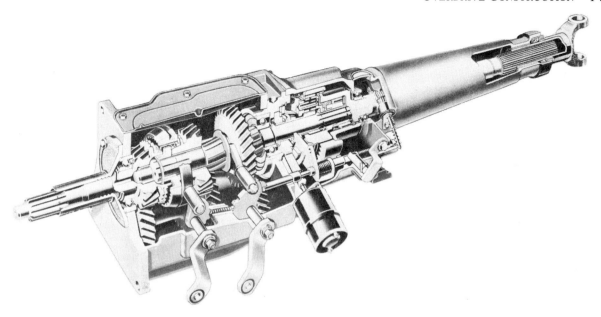

Fig. 16-12 Overdrive Transmission

Ford of Canada

and the driver momentarily releases the accelerator pedal. As the engine slows down, the overrunning clutch allows the drive shaft to overrun the transmission rear main shaft. As a result, the sun gear stops and reverses direction. This sun gear reversal moves the blocker ring around a few degrees into a position which allows the solenoid to push the pawl into the next notch of the ring-gear plate that comes around. This locks the gear plate and sun gear together.

The planet gears now rotate on their axis as the carrier is rotating. Carrier rotation, plus the rotation of the planet gears on their axis, drives the ring gear faster.

When the car speed falls below approximately 22 mph, the governor opens the electric circuit which de-energizes the solenoid and allows the pawl return spring to pull the pawl out of the gear ring. This unlocks the sun gear, allowing it to rotate freely. The unit is again in direct drive, the drive being through the overrunning clutch.

A forced downshift out of overdrive into direct drive may be made at speeds above 35 mph by depressing the accelerator pedal to the floor board. This actuates a switch which breaks the governor-to-solenoid circuit and also momentarily breaks the connection from the ignition system. This releases the pawl from the balk ring, causing the unit to return to direct drive. When the accelerator is released, the unit upshifts again into overdrive.

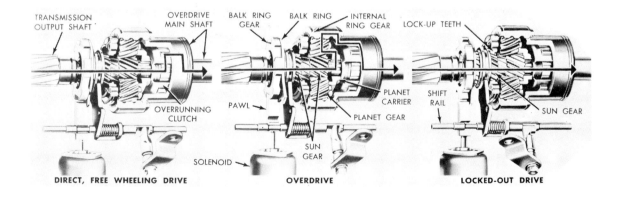

Fig. 16-14 Overdrive Power Flow

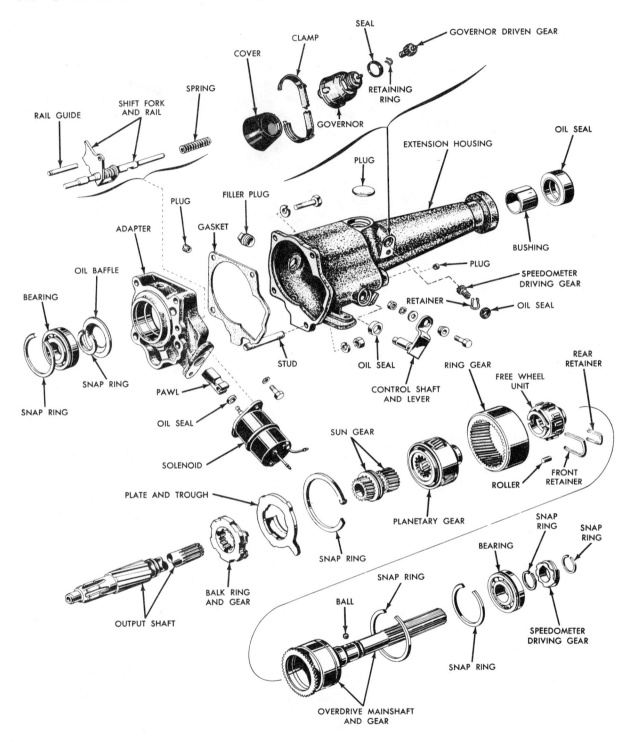

Fig. 16-13   Overdrive Unit Disassembled

16-11 OVERDRIVE ELECTRICAL CONTROLS

Solenoid. A solenoid is an electromagnetic device used to convert electric energy to mechanical energy. A solenoid consists of a soft iron plunger surrounded by coils of wire. When the electric current flows through the coils of wire, magnetism is produced. This magnetism attracts the plunger, moving it endwise to push the pawl into engagement.

Usually solenoids contain two separate coils of wire—a heavy, or *pull-in*, winding to move the plunger, and a lighter, or *hold in*, winding to hold the plunger in place after it has moved. Both coils are used to move the plunger into position. As the plunger moves down, the contacts for operating the pull-in winding are opened, leaving only the hold-in winding operating.

Governor. To upshift and downshift the overdrive unit at the proper speeds, a drive-shaft driven mechanical centrifugal governor is used to control the flow of electricity to the solenoid.

The governor consists of a shaft to which a set of movable counterweights have been attached. Centrifugal force causes the weights to tend to fly outward and upward. This action raises a floating shaft which closes the contact points that are mounted in the governor cover. The governor is designed to close the contact points when it is rotating at a speed equal to approximately 35 mph. It opens contacts again when it slows down to a speed equal to approximately 22 mph. This dif-ferent closing and opening speed is necessary to prevent continuous opening and closing of the contacts if the vehicle were operated around the closing speed.

Forced Downshift or Kick-Down Switch. Under certain driving conditions, such as passing or climbing a hill, it is desirable to be able to shift the transmission from overdrive to direct drive even though the road speed is above 35 mph. An electrical switch is located under the accelerator pedal for this purpose. If the pedal is pushed all the way down, this switch will break the circuit between the governor and the solenoid, and will momentarily short out the current flowing through the primary ignition circuit. The momentary interrupting of the engine ignition slows down the engine, releases the pressure on the pawl, and allows the pawl return spring to pull the pawl out of the gear ring. The movement of the pawl and its plunger reconnects the primary ignition circuit. The ignition-system grounding circuit is completed through a set of contacts which remain together long enough to permit the pawl return spring to retract the pawl. The length of time required for this sequence of events is so short, about one second, that the interruption of the flow of power is not noticeable.

16-12 OVERDRIVE MANUAL CONTROLS

The manual control is operated by a lever mounted on the dash. If this lever is moved to the lock-out position, it moves the sun gear control plate and

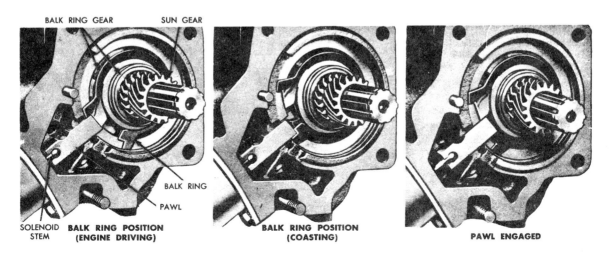

Fig. 16-15 Pawl and Balk Ring Positions

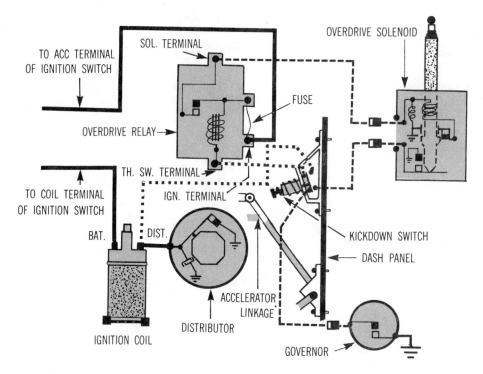

Fig. 16-16　Overdrive Electrical System

sun gear so that the teeth of the sun gear enter into mesh with the internal teeth of the planetary-gear carrier. This locks the sun gear and carrier together. The sun gear and planetary carrier must now rotate together. The sun gear, planetary carrier, and ring gear now rotate as one unit with no increase in speed. Movement of the manual control rod also locks out the sun-gear pawl and, on some models, it operates a switch which opens the solenoid electric circuit, rendering it inoperative.

With the manual lever in overdrive position, the sun gear is moved out of mesh with the planet carrier, direct drive is through the overrunning clutch, and the unit is free to upshift into overdrive when the proper road speed is attained.

When the conventional transmission is shifted into reverse, the gear-shifting mechanism moves the overdrive manual control rod to lock out the overdrive unit.

REVIEW QUESTIONS

1. What is (a) a cluster gear (b) reverse idler gear (c) transmission rear main shaft?

2. How are the gears in the transmission arranged to obtain: (a) neutral position (b) low gear (c) high gear?
3. What is the purpose of a synchromesh unit?
4. Explain the operation of a synchromesh unit.
5. Describe the two separate motions required to select a particular gear by the gearshift lever.
6. How is the gearshifter mechanism held in the selected gear position?
7. What is the advantage of an overdrive transmission?
8. Why should the transmission not shift-up below 30 mph?
9. Why does an overdrive type transmission not materially increase the top road speed of a vehicle?
10. How is an overdrive gear ratio obtained through the use of a planetary gear set?
11. How is the sun gear held stationary?
12. Describe the actions that take place in order to upshift the transmission into overdrive.
13. What is meant by the term "forced downshift"?
14. Why is a forced downshift device required?
15. What is the purpose of the manual control?

Chapter 17
STANDARD TRANSMISSION AND OVERDRIVE SERVICE

17-1 STANDARD TRANSMISSIONS

Standard transmission problems fall into four general classes: bearing or gear noise, clashing of gears when shifting, failure to stay in gear mesh, and oil leaks.

17-2 TRANSMISSION NOISE

Transmission noises should be traced before the transmission is disassembled. To determine if the noise is in the transmission, operate the engine at idling speed and depress the clutch. If the noise does not disappear, it is probably in the clutch assembly or release mechanism. If the noise stops, it is usually in the transmission and can be localized by driving the vehicle in each gear position.

Bearing noise is usually continuous, regardless of the gear position; whereas gear noise, except for a damaged clutch gear or countershaft drive gear, is noticeable only in one gear position. Countershaft drive-gear and clutch-gear noise is noticeable in all gears, but less noticeable in high gear. No power is transmitted through these gears in this gear position, even though the gears are still in mesh.

17-3 CLASHING OF GEARS WHEN SHIFTING

Gear clash when shifting can be caused by clutch drag, clutch not completely releasing when the pedal is depressed, or by a defective synchromesh unit. If the clutch action seems to be normal, remove the transmission and repair or replace the synchromesh unit.

17-4 TRANSMISSION SLIPS OUT OF GEAR

The transmission can slip out of gear if the gearshift linkage is out of adjustment. This prevents the gears from moving far enough to mesh properly. Worn poppet balls or lockout grooves or weak or broken poppet springs can result in insufficient pressure being applied to hold the linkage and gears in the desired gear position. Excessive end-play in the rear transmission main shaft, or end-play in the gears, misalignment, or worn bearings can cause improper meshing of the gears which results in their slipping out of mesh.

17-5 OIL LEAKS

Oil leaks are caused by too high a lubricant level, damaged gaskets, worn oil seals, damaged or improperly installed oil slingers, or loose bearing retainer bolts.

To locate the leak, clean the transmission case of excess oil, and operate the engine with the clutch engaged and the transmission in neutral until the transmission lubricant is at normal operating temperature. Observe the location of the leak. Replace the defective parts.

When the transmission must be removed for service, it is necessary on many models to install an engine support, as the rear engine mounts are frequently placed at the rear of the transmission. Also, many vehicles require the substitution of two pilot, or guide, pins in place of the mounting bolts. These pins prevent damage to the clutch friction discs when the transmission is removed or replaced.

17-6 OVERDRIVE TRANSMISSION SERVICE

When analyzing overdrive transmission troubles, do not blame the overdrive unit for transmission troubles, or vice versa. Hard shifting into reverse gear, for example, could be caused by a defective mechanism in the overdrive and not in the transmission. If the overdrive unit must be removed for repair, follow the precautions listed for transmission removal in reference to engine support and the use of guide pins.

17-7 WILL NOT GO INTO OVERDRIVE

When the unit will not go into overdrive, the trouble is frequently found in the electric controls. Check the control circuit with the ignition switch on and the overdrive control handle in overdrive position, by grounding the units in the following order: governor, lock-out switch, kickdown switch, and relay. If the relay and solenoid operate when any of these units are grounded, repair or replace the defective unit.

Another possible cause is improper adjustment of the manual control cable. With the manual control in, the shifter rail should be against the rear stop to allow the pawl to engage in the slots of the rear ring.

17-8 WON'T COME OUT OF OVERDRIVE

If the unit will not come out of overdrive, the trouble may be either electrical or mechanical. To check, place the transmission in neutral and with the ignition switch off, try to roll the vehicle backward manually. If the vehicle does not roll, do not attempt to force it. Remove the solenoid and check the pawl action. If the pawl does not move freely, the overdrive unit is damaged internally and must be removed for repairs. If the pawl moves freely, the solenoid is defective.

If the vehicle rolls freely, turn the ignition switch on and off. If the relay and solenoid click, the trouble is in the control system. Check each unit by disconnecting each unit in sequence.

If the relay and solenoid do not click, check the wiring for an intermittant short. Also, the governor could be the cause if it does not cut out until the vehicle speed is far below that established by the manufacturer.

17-9 WILL NOT SHIFT INTO REVERSE IN OVERDRIVE POSITION

This condition can be caused by defective electric units. Check the operation of each unit as outlined previously and replace or repair as required. The trouble can be caused by internal troubles which jam the pawl or sun gear. In this case the unit must be removed for repair.

The control mechanism may be out of adjustment, preventing the gear shift linkage from locking out the overdrive.

17-12 OIL LEAKS

Oil leaks are caused by excessive lubricant, defective gaskets or oil seals, or by loose mounting. Run unit at operating temperature and observe the location of the leak. Replace the defective parts.

17-11 NOISY OVERDRIVE

Noisy overdrive is caused by worn, chipped, or broken gears, worn or scored main-shaft bearing, or overrunning clutch. Remove the unit for repairs.

17-10 NO POWER THROUGH OVERDRIVE

This is caused by either a defective overrunning clutch or planetary-gear set. The transmission must be removed for repair.

REVIEW QUESTIONS

1. Give two causes for each of the following transmission problems: (a) transmission noises (b) transmission slips out of gear (c) gear clash.
2. What is the purpose of transmission pilot or guide pins?
3. Give two causes of the following overdrive transmission problems: (a) will not go into overdrive (b) will not come out of overdrive.

Chapter 18
TORQUE CONVERTERS AND FLUID COUPLINGS

Fluid couplings and torque converters are used in conjunction with automatic transmissions. Each uses a special light-weight oil to transmit engine power from one unit to another. The power flows through a liquid instead of through a mechanical device, such as a clutch. Therefore, torsional vibration from the engine, as well as roughness resulting from gear ratio changes, are smoothed out.

NOTE: Manufacturers identify the components of fluid couplings and torque convertors by various names, fluid couplings or torus, driving member or driving torus, driven member or driven torus. For simplicity in the fluid coupling section of this text the driving member will be referred to as the pump and the driven member as the turbine.

18-1 FLUID COUPLINGS
18-2 FLUID-COUPLING CONSTRUCTION
A fluid coupling consists of two basic units; a driving member called a *pump* and a driven member called a *turbine*. Each half, or member, is sometimes called a *torus*.

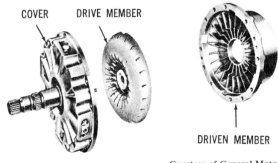

COVER   DRIVE MEMBER

DRIVEN MEMBER

Courtesy of General Motors

Fig. 18-1   Fluid Coupling

When they are assembled, they resemble a hollow steel donut. Inside each member equally spaced fins or veins which have no pitch are positioned radially from the member's axis. These are designed to import thrust upon, rather than movement to, the fluid. The pump member is attached to the input shaft or flywheel, the other is attached to the output shaft leading to the transmission. They are placed face to face with a slight clearance between them. A thin housing from the flywheel also extends around the assembly. An oil seal is placed between the output, or transmission, shaft and this housing. The housing is filled with automatic transmission fluid.

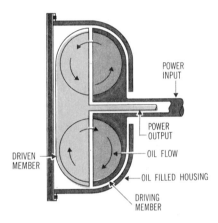

POWER INPUT

POWER OUTPUT

DRIVEN MEMBER

OIL FLOW

OIL FILLED HOUSING

DRIVING MEMBER

Fig. 18-2   Fluid Coupling Power Transfer

The output, or transmission shaft, is supported by a pilot bushing or bearing in the end of the crankshaft. When the crankshaft turns the flywheel, the pump member and housing will turn. The turbine is entirely free as there is no mechanical connection between it and the pump.

18-3 FLUID-COUPLING OPERATION
The operating principle of a fluid coupling can be best illustrated by replacing two electric fans a few inches apart and facing each other. If one fan is turned on, the ensuing air blast causes the other fan to rotate. In this case, air, not fluid, is the medium of power transfer. Since the two fans are not in an enclosed area or closely coupled, the transfer of power would be very inefficient. In a fluid coupling oil is used instead of air, and the driving and driven members are close together and enclosed, resulting in an excellent method of transferring power.

Another aspect of fluid-coupling operation can

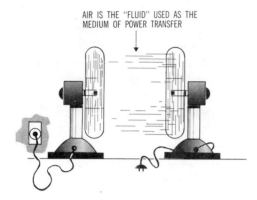

Fig. 18-3   Using Air to Transfer Power

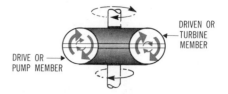

Fig. 18-5   Oil Flow Between Drive and Driven Members

be illustrated by the following: if a person wades slowly through deep water, there is little resistance to his motion from the water. If, however, the person tries to walk fast, he immediately finds terrific resistance to his progress. In the same manner a fluid coupling transmits little power at slow speeds. The instant the pump member is speeded up, it forces fluid against the veins of the turbine member with ever increasing force.

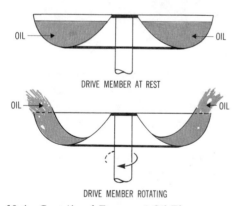

Fig. 18-4   Centrifugal Force and Oil Flow

When oil is placed in a horizontal pump member and is rotated, the veins would carry the oil around at the same speed as the torus. This motion of the oil is called the *rotary motion*. The rotating of the torus also produces centrifugal force. The centrifugal force causes oil to move outward and upward Placing a turbine above the pump member causes the oil that is thrown out of the pump by centrifugal force to strike the veins of the turbine. After striking the veins of the turbine the oil travels up, over, and back into the pump only to be thrown out again by centrifugal force. This round and round motion of the oil is called the *vortex flow*.

The combination of the vortex and rotary oil flow causes the oil to strike the veins of the driven torus at an angle, thereby imparting torque, or turning effort, to the driven member. The faster the pump member turns with the turbine stationary, the harder the oil strikes the veins of the turbine. The greater the force striking the veins of the turbine, the greater the turning effort transmitted. This will cause the turbine to turn faster and faster. As the speed of the turbine approaches the speed of the pump, the effects of the vortex flow against the veins of the driven torus is reduced. When the two units are rotating at equal speeds, there is very little, if any, vortex flow, because both members will produce centrifugal force to throw the oil into the other. This cancels out any transfer of oil from one unit to the other, and no power would be transmitted. This same speed condition will not transmit power. The pump member must always rotate faster than the turbine to transmit power to propel the vehicle. When the speed of the two units is about the same, the unit is said to be "locked up."

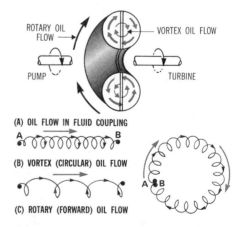

Fig. 18-6   Vortex and Rotary Oil Flows in Fluid Coupling

If the vehicle's speed is higher than the engine's speed, the turbine will temporarily become the driving member. It will force oil against the veins of the member attached to the flywheel, attempting to rotate it faster. Under these conditions the engine acts as a brake, slowing the vehicle.

The circulation of the oil in a fluid coupling takes place in the same manner whether the fluid coupling is in a horizontal or vertical position. When the coupling is used in conjunction with an automatic transmission, it is always placed in a vertical position.

Guide Rings

To increase the efficiency of a fluid coupling by maintaining a smooth vortex flow and to decrease turbulance (the violent, random motion or agitation of the oil), a split guide ring is sometimes placed in each torus member. The oil is then guided around and there is less tendency for the turbulance to have an undesirable effect, particularly in the centre area when there is a considerable difference in speed between the two members.

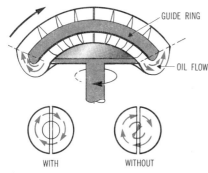

Fig. 18-7   Effect of Guide Ring on Oil Flow

Fluid-Coupling Efficiency

A fluid coupling operates at maximum efficiency at high engine speed and when the turbine is rotating at about the same speed as the pump member. The greater the difference in speed of the two units, the less efficient the coupling. At low engine speed there is very little power transfer. This allows the fluid coupling to act as a clutch, enabling the engine to run without transmitting power to the transmission. As the engine speed increases, power transfer becomes more and more effective, thus eliminating all jerkiness and roughness and producing a smooth takeoff.

A fluid coupling cannot increase torque above that produced by the crankshaft. It is usually used in conjunction with a form of transmission to vary the gear ratios between the engine and the rear wheels. This transmission will enable the driving and driven torus to rotate at their most efficient point as quickly as possible.

18-4 TORQUE CONVERTERS

18-5 TORQUE-CONVERTER CONSTRUCTION

A torque converter consists of three basic units: a driving member called a *pump*; a driven member called a *turbine*; and a *stator*.

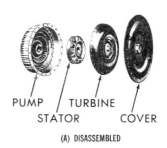

(A) DISASSEMBLED

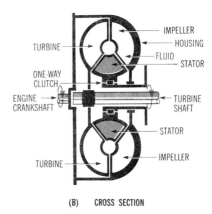

(B)   CROSS SECTION

Fig. 18-8   Torque Converter

The pump is attached to the flywheel, the turbine to the transmission input shaft, and the stator is attached through an overrunning clutch or sprag to an extension of the front transmission case. These units are surrounded by a housing which is attached to the flywheel and filled to the proper level with automatic transmission fluid. A seal in the housing prevents the fluid leaking between the housing and the transmission shaft.

The blades of the converter components are curved to represent an inclined plane in order to produce the proper vortex flow. In the pump this curvature, inclined plane, or pitch effect causes movement of the fluid. In the turbine, the movement of the fluid against the inclined plane causes the turbine to move. The stator blades are curved to redirect the fluid back to the pump in the proper manner. The fluid acting against the stator blades has a tendency to try and rotate the stator in the opposite direction to the pump whenever there is

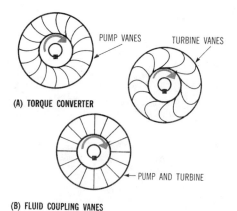

Fig. 18-9   Vane Comparison

18-6 TORQUE-CONVERTER OPERATION

Whereas the fluid coupling was designed to impart thrust rather than movement to the oil, a torque converter is designed to do the opposite. It imparts movement rather than thrust to the oil. Because of this fluid movement a torque converter cannot be "locked up" like a fluid coupling. A torque converter, unlike a fluid coupling, can and does multiply engine torque. The amount of multiplication depends upon the type and design. The greater the variation in speed between the driving and driven members, the greater the torque multiplication. A torque converter's ability to increase engine torque makes it possible to reduce the number of gear ratios required in the transmission.

a difference in speed between the pump and the turbine. The overrunning clutch locks the stator to the transmission extension to prevent this rotation. When there is little or no difference in speed between the pump and the turbine, the returning fluid strikes the opposite side of the stator blades, causing it to rotate in the same direction as the pump. This causes the clutch to overrun.

Torque converters vary greatly in construction and performance. Some use only one turbine and stator, others use two or more. One torque-converter type uses a variable-pitch stator.

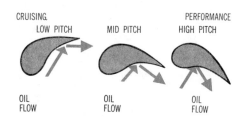

Fig. 18-10   Variable-Pitch Stator Angles

In the variable-pitch stator type of converter a means is provided to automatically change the angle, or pitch, of the stator blades in accordance to the load or speed difference between the pump and turbine. The greater the load on the engine or speed difference, the greater the stator blade angle—thus increased vortex flow. The lesser the load or speed difference, the lesser the angle and vortex flow. The blades of the stator are each equipped with a crank. The crank provides a means by which the blade angle may be changed to suit load and speed requirements.

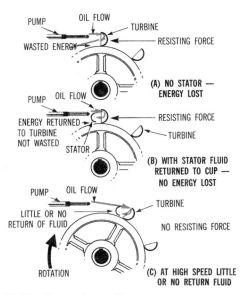

Fig. 18-11   Torque Multiplication by Using a Stator

To illustrate the torque multiplication features of a torque converter, we will use a wheel with several cups attached to its rim and a pressure pump. When oil is forced into the cup by the pressure pump, and the wheel and cup are not allowed to rotate, the oil strikes the curved surface of the cup, imparting a turning effort. Since the cup cannot move, the oil striking one side of the cup is directed around the inner surface of the cup and out the opposite side. This is called the vortex flow. Obviously, there is still a great deal of potential force of the oil not being used. If a curved plate, called a stator, were to be placed in such a manner as to redirect the oil back into the cup, the oil will now strike the cup again, adding extra torque or turning effort to the cup.

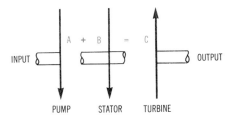

Fig. 18-12   Newton's Law Applied to Torque Converters

In order to understand this principle we must point out *Newton's Law*. Newton's Law states for every action there is an equal and opposite reaction. Applying Newton's Law to the oil stream, we find the force applied to the cup being equal to the force created by the pump, plus the reaction force created by the stator.

When the combined force of the pump and stator becomes greater than the force holding the cup, the cup and wheel will rotate faster and faster. It will finally approach the speed of the oil stream. When this happens, the oil will not fly out of the opposite side of the cup and therefore cannot be redirected back to the cup by the stator to increase torque. Torque multiplication is only possible when there is a great difference in speed between the pump and the turbine. The greater the difference, the greater the multiplication.

In actual torque-converter operation, the fluid is not redirected directly back into the turbine but is recirculated through the pump.

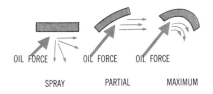

Fig. 18-13   Oil Stream Deflection

In order to get torque multiplication, the blades of the pump, turbine, and stator must be curved in such a manner as to direct the flow of the fluid leaving the vanes of one unit in a direction that will exert as much force as possible upon the next unit.

The leading, or inner edge, of the pump vanes are curved to assist smooth re-entry of the oil being discharged by the stator. The turbine blades are curved in the opposite direction to the pump blades. As a result, the curve on the leading edge of the turbine blades assists the smooth entry of the oil stream. It also prevents a buildup, or damming effect, that reduces oil entry velocity. The curved

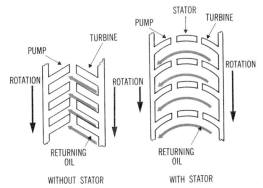

Fig. 18-14   Stator Action

trailing edge of the turbine blades increases the turbine energy absorption by deflecting the oil stream as much as possible. The more the oil stream is deflected, the more energy the oil will give up to the deflecting object. The stator blades are curved in the opposite direction to the turbine blades and in the same direction as the pump blades. This curvature is necessary to intercept the oil leaving the turbine and redirect it in the direction which allows it to enter the pump blades smoothly.

The stator blades are held stationary during the torque multiplication period. The reaction of these blades on the oil flow is such as to direct the force of the oil flow into the pump in the same direction,

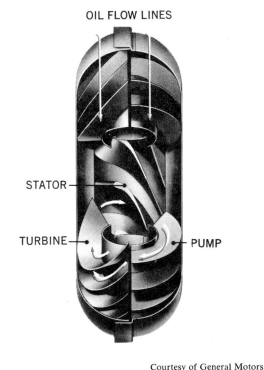

Fig. 18-15   Oil Flow Through Torque Converter

in order to assist in pump rotation. This increases the force of the oil leaving the pump.

This will increase vortex flow. The higher the vortex flow velocity, the greater the torque transfer. The greatest torque multiplication and vortex flow occurs when the pump reaches its highest velocity and the turbine is standing still or at the stall. Torque multiplication obtained through the use of a torque converter at the stall is approximately 2.5 to 1.

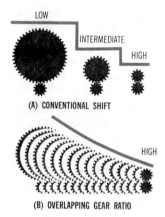

Fig. 18-16   Torque Graduations

As the speed of the output shaft increases and the difference between the pump speed and turbine speed decreases, the vortex flow slows down. The oil leaving the turbine now strikes the back-side of the stator blades, causing the stator to rotate in the same direction as the pump. This reduces torque multiplication, and the converter is now acting like a fluid coupling. The point when the pump and turbine approach approximately the same speeds is known as the "coupling point."

Torque multiplication and vortex flow gradually drop off between the stall and the coupling points.

REVIEW QUESTIONS

1. What is the advantage of transmitting a drive by fluid means over mechanical means?
2. What is the advantage of a torque converter over a fluid coupling?
3. Describe the principle of operation of a fluid coupling.
4. Why must the driving torus rotate faster than the driven torus in order to transmit power?
5. Describe the (a) rotary (b) vortex flow through a fluid coupling.
6. How is torque increased through the use of a stator in a torque converter unit?
7. Why does a fluid coupling require a transmission with more different gear ratios than the transmission used with a torque converter?
8. State Newton's Law.
9. Why are the turbine blades of a torque converter curved in the opposite direction to the pump blades?
10. What is the relationship between the vortex flow and the torque transfer?
11. When is the greatest torque multiplication obtained from a torque converter? Why?

Chapter 19
AUTOMATIC TRANSMISSIONS

Most modern automatic transmissions use planetary gear sets to obtain the desired number of gear ratios. The change from one gear ratio to another is accomplished by a *hydraulic control system*. The hydraulic control system may be operated by the manual selector, the speed of the vehicle, or by throttle opening. Thus, any requirement of load and/or speed can be met automatically.

Automatic transmissions coupled to torque converters take advantage of the torque multiplication of the torque converter, and usually do not have as many gear ratios as automatic transmissions driven by fluid couplings.

One-, two-, and three-speed automatic transmissions usually use a torque converter, while four-speed automatic transmissions use a fluid coupling.

19-1 AUTOMATIC TRANSMISSION COMPONENTS AND SYSTEMS

19-2 PLANETARY-GEAR SETS

Note: Manufacturers identify the components of planetary-gear sets by various names, planet gears or planet pinions, planet-pinion cage or planet-pinion carrier or planet carrier, ring gear or internal gear. In this text the names planet gear, planet carrier, and ring gear will be used.

One or more planetary-gear sets are used in automatic transmissions. In its basic concept only one planetary-gear set is required for a two-speed transmission; a three-speed unit requires one complete set of planetary gears plus a second sun gear of a different size and a matching set of planet

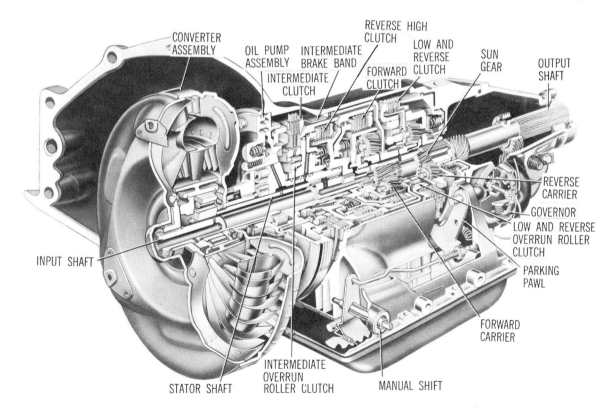

Fig. 19-1 Typical Automatic Transmission

Courtesy of General Motors

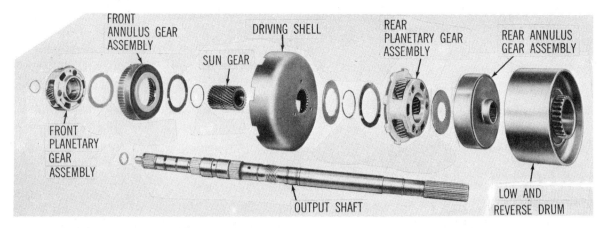

FRONT ANNULUS GEAR ASSEMBLY DRIVING SHELL SUN GEAR REAR PLANETARY GEAR ASSEMBLY REAR ANNULUS GEAR ASSEMBLY FRONT PLANETARY GEAR ASSEMBLY OUTPUT SHAFT LOW AND REVERSE DRUM

Chrysler Canada Ltd.

Fig. 19-2 Typical Planetary Gear Arrangement

gears, which are attached to the original carrier. The second sun gear and its planet gears provide a different gear ratio than those of the basic planetary-gear set. A four-speed transmission requires two complete sets of planetary-gears, each of a different gear ratio. Reverse gear may be obtained by driving and/or holding the necessary components of the forward planetary-gear sets or through the use of a separate planetary-gear set.

The manner in which reduction is obtained varies. In some cases the sun gear is driving, the ring gear is held, and the planet carrier is the output member; in other units the ring gear drives, the sun gear is held, and the planet carrier is the output member.

In three-speed transmissions one method of obtaining reduction may be used for low range and the other for intermediate range. In most cases, direct drive is obtained by driving two different members at the same time and at the same speed, which causes the planetary-gear set to lock up and rotate at a 1 to 1 ratio.

The method of interconnecting the various components of the planetary-gear sets varies between different manufacturers; hydraulically operated multiple-disc clutches, sprags, or overrunning clutches are used to transmit the driving torque; to hold the necessary components hydraulically operated multiple-disc clutches, brake bands, sprags, or overrunning clutches are used.

19-3 OIL PUMP

As the planetary-gear bands and all controls are operated hydraulically, an oil pump is required to produce the necessary oil pressure. These pumps

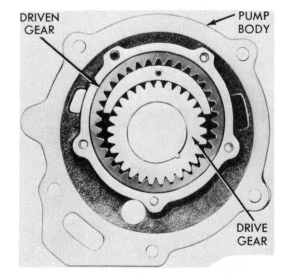

DRIVEN GEAR PUMP BODY DRIVE GEAR

(A) PUMP GEARS

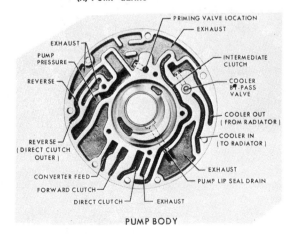

PRIMING VALVE LOCATION EXHAUST PUMP PRESSURE INTERMEDIATE CLUTCH REVERSE COOLER BY-PASS VALVE COOLER OUT (FROM RADIATOR) COOLER IN (TO RADIATOR) REVERSE (DIRECT CLUTCH OUTER) EXHAUST PUMP LIP SEAL DRAIN CONVERTER FEED FORWARD CLUTCH DIRECT CLUTCH EXHAUST PUMP BODY

(B) PUMP BODY AND PASSAGEWAYS
(A) Ford of Canada
(B) Courtesy of General Motors

Fig. 19-3 Typical Gear-Type Pump

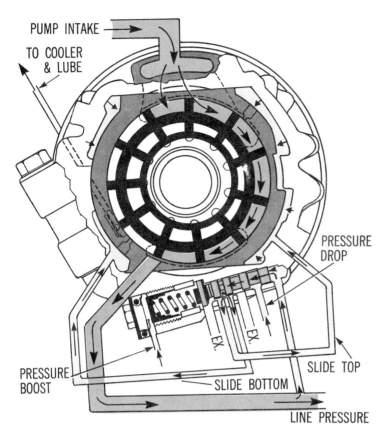

Courtesy of General Motors

Fig. 19-4   Typical Variable Pressure Valve-Type Pump

are usually of the gear type, although the variable-output vane type pump has been used. Earlier automatic transmissions used two pumps, one driven by the engine, the other by the drive shaft. The drive-shaft pump was used in order to produce the necessary pressure to operate the transmission if the vehicle had to be pushed to be started. Late model transmissions use only the engine driven pump; it is not recommended to start most modern vehicles with a push.

The pump maintains pressure in order to circulate oil through the fluid coupling or torque converter, to the cooling system, to the manual and automatic control valves, and for lubrication of the parts.

19-4 PRESSURE-REGULATOR VALVE

Since the oil pressure in the system must be maintained between a low and high limit regardless of engine speed, a pressure-regulating valve is connected into the system near the oil pump.

19-5 SERVOS

A hydraulic piston, called a servo, is used to convert hydraulic pressure to mechanical pressure in order to apply the brake band which holds the ring gear stationary. A servo consists of a cylinder in which a piston is placed. An opening is provided to admit oil under pressure. The piston is held in the released position by a return spring.

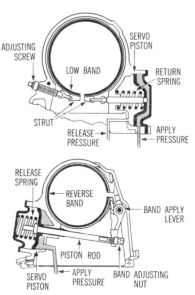

Ford of Canada

Fig. 19-5   Typical Band and Servo Assemblies

When oil under pressure is admitted to the cylinder, the piston moves forward to apply the brake band. When the oil pressure is reduced, the band is released by the return spring.

Some servos have openings on both sides of the piston. In this case oil can be used to apply the piston and also to assist in its release. Other servos are applied by the pressure of the spring and held in the release position by oil pressure.

Some servos use a pushing action to apply the band, while others use a pulling action.

To assist the servo in engaging the band quickly and smoothly, an *accumulator* piston is sometimes used. An accumulator consists of a small check valve and an accumulator piston. These units are built into the centre of the servo piston. Since the servo piston is held in the release position by the return spring and oil pressure is admitted into the cylinder, the oil enters the small check valve first and pushes on the accumulator piston. As the accumulator piston is smaller in diameter than the

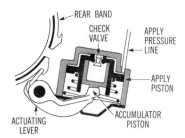

Ford of Canada

Fig. 19-6   Accumulator-Type Servo

return spring it moves the actuating linkage to apply the band rapidly, but with light pressure. Once the band has contacted the drum, it takes more pressure to provide further application. The large servo

piston now applies the additional pressure required to hold the drum from turning. The accumulator piston provides fast, soft application of the brake band, followed immediately by additional heavy pressure to hold the brake drum firmly.

19-6 BRAKE BANDS

A brake band is a steel band lined with a friction lining that surrounds the brake drum. The drum is attached to the component to be held stationary. One end of the band is secured; the other end is attached to a servo actuating rod. When the band is tightened by the servo, the drum will stop rotating.

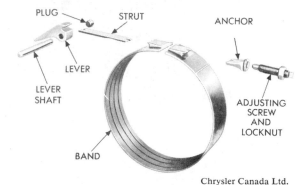

Chrysler Canada Ltd.

Fig. 19-7   Typical Brake Band and Linkage

19-7 CLUTCHES

In order to lock certain rotating components together or to lock certain components stationary to provide the proper gear ratios, one or more multiple-disc clutches are used in an automatic transmission. These clutches are applied and released by hydraulic pressure.

A multiple-disc clutch consists of a stack of clutch discs (the number varies) which are ar-

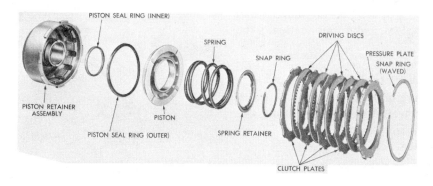

Chrysler Canada Ltd.

Fig. 19-8   Typical Clutch Assembly

ranged in an alternate fashion so that the driving discs are splined to the clutch hub and the driven discs are splined to the clutch drum. Thin discs of a special friction material are bonded to both sides of one set of clutch discs.

The clutch is engaged by a piston in the clutch drum. When oil pressure from the control valve is applied to the piston, it squeezes the discs together. This locks the clutch hub and drum together. A heavy spring releases the discs when the oil pressure is reduced. The clutch is used to lock the planetary-gear set in direct drive by locking two components together. This stops all gear action, and the parts revolve as a solid unit.

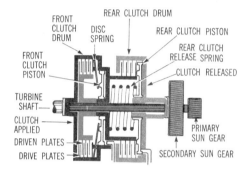

Fig. 19-9   Clutch Operation

19-8 SPOOL VALVE

A spool valve is essentially a solid cylinder with an undercut section. The valve spool moves back and forth in a valve body. As the spool moves back and forth, the lands (undercut sections) cover or uncover holes in the valve body to allow the fluid to pass from one opening in the valve body, through the cylinder, around the undercut portions of the valve, and out another hole in the valve body. These passageways lead to the servos and clutches to select the proper gear ratio.

The openings in the valve body are arranged so that when the spool is in one position, oil pressure is directed to apply the servo or clutch. In another position the oil may be exhausted from the servo or clutch as required.

The movement of the spool can be accomplished by applying pressure to one end of the spool by the gear selector lever, in the case of the manual valve; by the throttle linkage, in the case of the throttle valve; or by oil pressure, as in the case of the shifter valves. The return of the valve to its original position is accomplished by a return spring

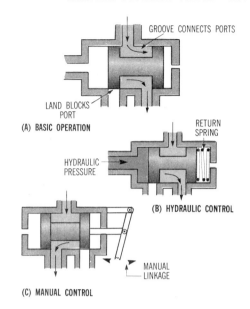

Fig. 19-10   Spool Valves

at the other end of the spool. The pressure applied to move the valve must be greater than the return-spring pressure.

19-9 BALANCED VALVES

Balanced valves are spool valves that are used to produce pressure changes that are proportional to the amount of movement of a mechanical linkage, or to variations in return-spring pressure.

In a balanced valve a regulator plug is placed between the return spring and the base of the valve body. Applying pressure, either mechanically or hydraulically, to the regulator plug will compress the return spring thus increasing its pressure. Higher pressure must now be applied to the other end of the spool in order to cause it to move. This type of valve is ideal in controlling the shift points of the transmission, since the movement of the spool can be timed in accordance with road speed, engine load, and throttle opening.

19-10 MANUAL-CONTROL VALVE

The manual control valve is a spool-type valve that is operated by the driver to select the driving range he wishes: park, neutral, low, drive, or reverse. The valve opens or closes the main-line pressure. When open, this valve directs main-line pressure from the pump to the various clutches or servos to select the gear ratio desired. The valve also directs main-line pressure to the throttle control valve and

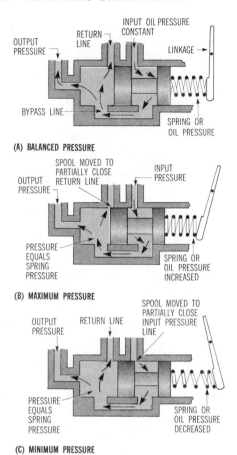

Fig. 19-11   Balanced Valve

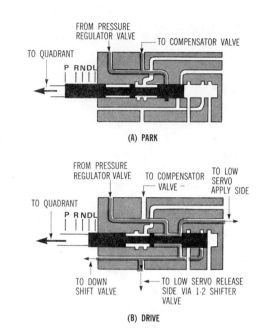

Fig. 19-12   Manual Valve

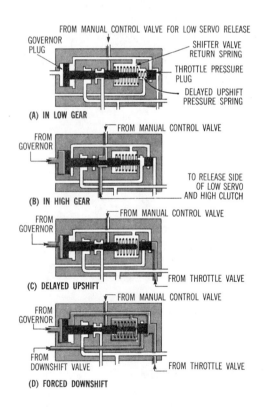

Fig. 19-13   Shifter-Valve Operation

the governor valve preparatory to automatic up-shifting.

19-11 SHIFTER VALVES

Shifter valves are balanced valves. They are used to direct main-line pressure to the servos and clutches which operate gear ratios other than first or low gear. When the shifter valve is moved, it directs oil pressure to release the servos or clutches required for low gear and to apply those required for the next highest gear. To move the shifter valve, pressure from the governor is applied to one end of the shifter-valve spool. This pressure moves the spool and compresses the return spring. When governor pressure drops, the spring returns the valve to its original position. In the original position the oil pressure is exhausted from the second-speed clutches or servos.

The transmission shifter-valve body contains a shift valve for each forward gear ratio other than first gear. Two-speed automatics have one shifter valve, three-speed units have two shifter valves, and four-speed transmissions have three.

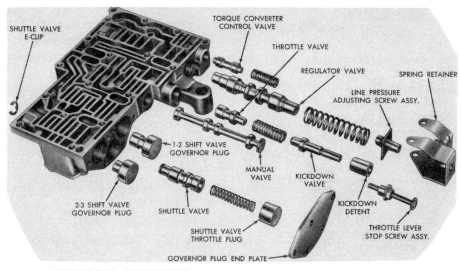

(A) LEVER SIDE — DISASSEMBLED

Chrysler Canada Ltd.
Fig. 19-14   Valve Body Assembly

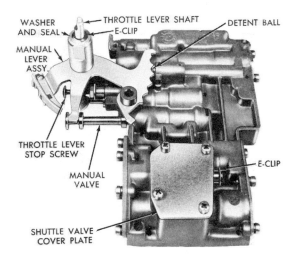

(B) VALVE BODY CONTROLS — ASSEMBLED

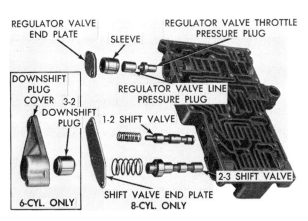

(C) SHIFT VALVE — DISASSEMBLED

Each shifter valve has a regulator plug placed beneath the return spring to increase spring pressure, in order to vary the shift points of the transmission according to driving conditions.

19-12 GOVERNOR

The governor is driven by the drive shaft and controls the upshift points in accordance with road speed. The governor operates on centrifugal force. The faster the governor shaft rotates, the more the fly-weights will move.

In one type of governor the fly-weight movement is connected by linkage to the control valve in such a manner that as the fly-weights move outward they move the valve to open the necessary passageways. In another type of governor the fly-weights are also designed to act as spool valves. In this type of governor as the fly-weights (spool valves) move outward they open the necessary passageways. The movement of the governor valve directs oil pressure to the shifter valve.

With the vehicle stopped, the fly-weights are in the "in position", and the valve is closed. As the vehicle gathers road speed, the governor unit will rotate faster and faster. The fly-weights fly out and, at a predetermined speed, the valve will open and oil pressure will travel to the shifter valve.

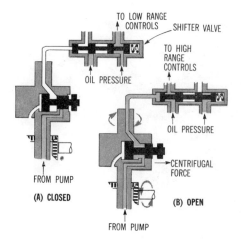

(A) CLOSED   (B) OPEN

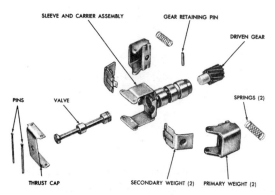

(C) LINKAGE TYPE

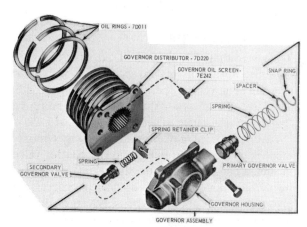

(D) FLYWEIGHT TYPE

(C) Courtesy of General Motors
(D) Ford of Canada

Fig. 19-15   Transmission Governors

19-13 THROTTLE VALVE

The throttle valve is used to delay the upshift points of the transmission. It does this by increasing the shifter-valve return-spring pressure. Three methods are used in different types of transmissions.

In one type, the throttle linkage is connected

directly to the regulator plug of the shifter valve. When the accelerator pedal is depressed beyond a given point, the linkage moves the regulator plug to increase shifter-valve return-spring pressure. The more the accelerator is depressed, the more the regulator plug compresses the return spring, increasing return spring pressure.

A second type of throttle valve utilizes engine vacuum to move a spool valve, which in turn directs oil pressure to the regulator plug. When the engine load is light, engine vacuum is high. This high vacuum compresses the throttle-valve return spring, keeping the spool in the closed position. As a load is placed on the engine, as during acceleration, engine vacuum drops. The drop in vacuum allows the return spring to expand and move the spool valve to the open position. In the open position, oil is directed to the shifter-valve regulator plug, compressing the return spring to increase its pressure. The greater the drop in engine vacuum, the more the throttle valve opens and greater pressure is placed on the regulator plug.

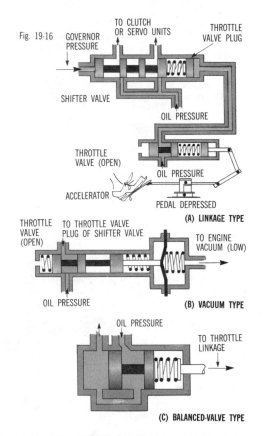

(A) LINKAGE TYPE

(B) VACUUM TYPE

(C) BALANCED-VALVE TYPE

Fig. 19-16   Throttle Control Valves

The third type of throttle valve uses a balanced valve. The pressure of the return spring is controlled by the throttle linkage. When the accelerator pedal is depressed slightly, the spring pressure is light, and only light pressure is directed to the shifter-valve regulator plug. The further the pedal is depressed, the greater is the spring pressure, and the greater the oil pressure that is required to balanced the spring. As a result, more pressure is directed to the shifter-valve regulator plug to compress the shifter-valve return spring.

In all three cases, the increase of shifter-valve return-spring pressure requires more governor pressure to move the spool to the position required to upshift the transmission. In order to increase governor pressure, the governor must rotate at higher rpm to open the governor valve wider. The wider the governor valve opens, the higher the governor pressure.

19-14 DELAYED UPSHIFTS

The throttle valve is used to create a condition known as a *delayed upshift*. Under normal driving conditions the point where the transmission upshifts or downshifts is controlled by governor pressure acting on one end of the shifter-valve spool. This pressure acts against the shifter-valve return-spring pressure. Since the governor is related to road speed, the shifts would always occur at the same speed.

It is very desirable to have the shift points vary according to load requirements. For rapid acceleration, the transmission should remain in low range longer.

The action of the throttle valve, as it increases the pressure on the shifter-valve spring, means that a higher road speed must be attained before the governor valve is opened sufficiently to allow enough pressure through to cause the shifter valve to move and direct pressure to the units required for the next highest gear ratio.

In some transmissions the throttle valve also is used to downshift the transmission. When a heavy load is placed on the engine at low speeds just above the upshift point, the throttle pressure on the shifter-valve regulator plug increases the shifter-valve return-spring pressure above that of the governor pressure. This forces the shifter-valve to move back to its original position and causes the transmission to downshift to a lower gear.

19-15 FORCED DOWNSHIFT

When the transmission is in high ratio and travelling at a reasonable rate of speed (approximately 50 mph), the governor pressure will be higher than the throttle-valve pressure. Frequently, it is desirable to change the transmission to a lower gear ratio for acceleration, such as when passing. Since the governor pressure is now greater than throttle-valve pressure, some other means must be employed to cause the transmission to downshift. A *forced downshift valve* is used.

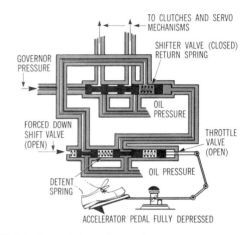

Fig. 19-17 Forced Downshift Valve

The forced downshift valve is a T-type valve. A T-type valve is an undercut portion of a round rod. The rod can slide sideways to open a passageway. When the valve is closed, the large diameter of the rod blocks the passageway. When the rod is moved sideways, the undercut portion moves into the passageway, allowing the oil to pass through. The forced downshift valve may be separate or an extension of the throttle valve.

When the driver depresses the accelerator almost to the floor, the throttle valve is opened and it also strikes a detent plug and spring. Pressing the accelerator beyond this point compresses the detent spring and moves the forced downshift T valve to the open position.

Opening of the T valve directs main-line oil pressure to the return-spring side of the shifter valve. The combination of return-spring pressure, throttle-valve pressure and main-line pressure will be greater than the governor pressure. Therefore, the shifter valve will move to its original position, and the transmission will downshift. When the accelerator pedal is released, the forced downshift valve closes. Governor pressure is now higher than return-spring and throttle pressures, and the transmission upshifts.

19-16 COMPENSATOR VALVE

To add additional pressure to the band servos during heavy acceleration, a *compensator valve* is frequently used. This valve is operated by the throttle valve. When the compensator valve is opened, main-line pressure is directed to a second piston incorporated in the servo. Both compensator and main-line pressures are now being used to apply the band.

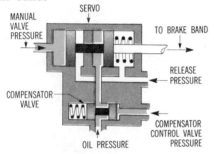

Fig. 19-18   Compensator-Type Servo and Control Valve

19-17 TRANSMISSION CIRCUITS, COOLING AND LUBRICATION

The various clutches, servos, valves, etc., require a complex and compact system of oil passageways. Since compactness is essential, every means possible is used to avoid open-tubing type lines. Many of the shafts and other units are drilled to carry oil. Neoprene oil seals and metal sealing rings are used as required to separate the different systems.

Most of the control valves are housed in one compact control-valve body and are interconnected by drilled passageways.

The oil-operating temperature is maintained at a reasonable level by circulating the transmission fluid via tubes to a cooler housed in the lower radiator tank.

Air cooling of the torque converter is also used. The outer design of the converter housing is such that as the converter is rotated, air is drawn in, circulated around the converter, and exhausted through special ducts.

The transmission moving parts are lubricated by the transmission fluid as it circulates through the unit. Only the special automatic transmission fluid should be used in all automatics.

19-18 POWER FLOW THROUGH AUTOMATIC TRANSMISSIONS

The planetary-gear train of an automatic transmission is much more complicated than the simple gear sets previously discussed. The input shaft is usually connected to the drive units of the gear set through hydraulic clutches. Some planetary-gear sets contain both long and short planet gears and the output member could be the ring gear, or the planet carrier, or both, depending upon the gear ratio being used.

19-19 TYPICAL TWO-SPEED TYPE AUTOMATIC TRANSMISSION

In this type of transmission the forward clutch hub is splined to the input shaft and rotates with it. The forward clutch drum is splined to and rotates with the low sun gear. When this clutch is in the released position, the clutch drum and low sun gear rotate freely on the input shaft. The low sun gear meshes with a set of short planet gears.

Splined directly to the inner end of the input shaft is a second sun gear. This sun gear meshes with the long planet gear. Both the long and short planet gears are mounted on a common planet carrier which is splined to the output shaft.

Neutral Range. In neutral the clutches or bands are not applied and therefore no power is transmitted to the output shaft.

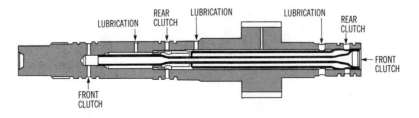

Ford of Canada

Fig. 19-19   Oil Passages in Primary Sun Gear Shaft

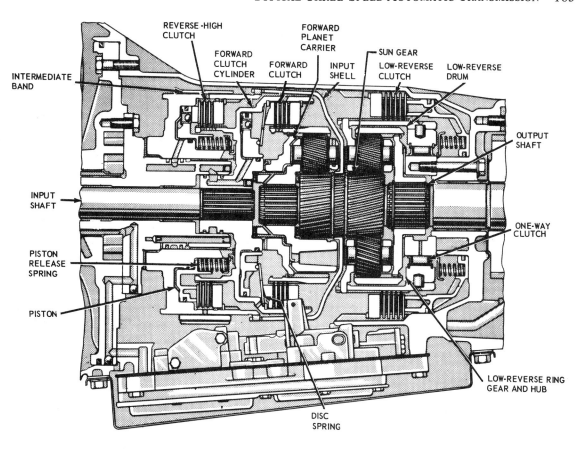

Fig. 19-20   Typical Three-Speed Gear Train, Clutches and Bands

Ford of Canada

Low Range. When the transmission is in low range, the forward clutch is released and a brake band is applied to hold the clutch drum and the low sun gear stationary. The power flow is through the input sun gear, through the long planet gears, and through the short planet gears. Since the short planet gears are meshed with the stationary low sun gear, they must walk around this gear as they rotate. As they walk around the low sun gear, they carry the planet carrier and the output shaft around with them. The rotation of the planet carrier and the output shaft is at a reduced speed and with increased torque.

Drive Range. When the transmission is in drive range, the forward clutch is applied and the low band is released. The forward clutch locks the low sun gear to the input shaft. As a result the low sun gear is trying to drive the short planet gears at one speed, while the input sun gear is trying to drive the long planet gears at a different speed. This locks the planetary-gear set so that it must rotate as a unit at the same speed as the input shaft.

Reverse Range. When the transmission is in reverse range, both the forward clutch and the low band are released, and the reverse clutch is applied. The reverse clutch holds the ring gear stationary. The power flow is through the input sun gear, through the long planet gears and through the short planet gears. With the ring gear stationary, the short planet gears must walk around the ring gear, rotating the planet carrier and the output shaft in a reversed direction.

19-20 TYPICAL THREE-SPEED AUTOMATIC TRANSMISSION

In this type of transmission the input shaft is splined to the front clutch cylinder. This clutch cylinder drives the forward clutch drum and the reverse-high clutch drum. The forward clutch hub is attached to the ring gear and the reverse-high clutch drum is splined to the sun gear.

The sun gear is meshed with both the forward and reverse planet gears.

The reverse planet carrier is splined to the low-reverse clutch hub. The low-reverse clutch drum

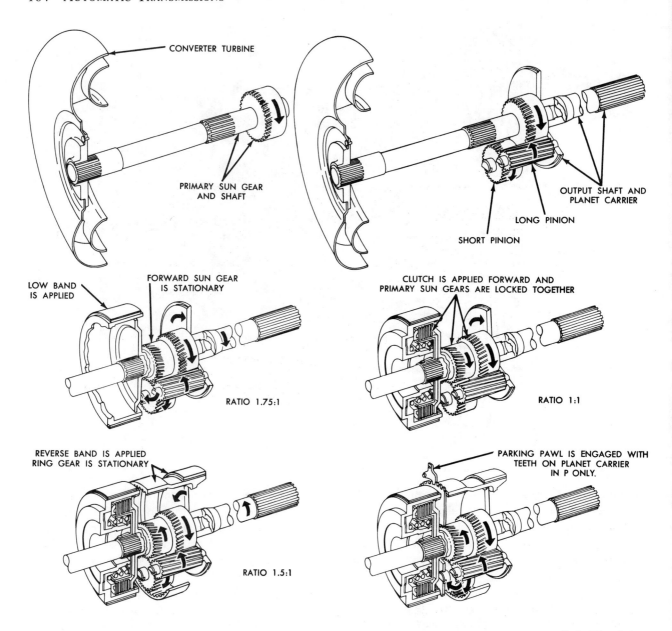

Fig. 19-21   Typical Power Flow Through a Two-Speed Automatic Transmission

Ford of Canada

is held stationary in the transmission case by splines. The low-reverse clutch hub is also held stationary by an overrunning clutch. Both the forward planet carrier and the reverse ring gear are splined to the output shaft.

Neutral Range. In neutral, no clutches or bands are applied; therefore, no power is transmitted to the output shaft.

Low Range. In low range, the forward clutch is applied and the low-reverse overrunning clutch (drive 1) or the low-reverse clutch (low range) is

holding the reverse planet carrier from rotating. The power flow is from the input shaft to the forward clutch cylinder to the forward ring gear, through the forward planet gears to the sun gear. Since the sun gear is meshed with both the forward and reverse planet gears, they all rotate together. From the sun gear the power flows into the reverse planet gears whose carrier is held stationary by the overrunning clutch (drive 1) or the low-reverse clutch (low range). This results in the reverse ring gear and output shaft being rotated at a reduced speed but with increased torque. The reduced speed

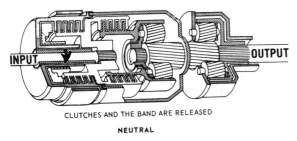

CLUTCHES AND THE BAND ARE RELEASED

NEUTRAL

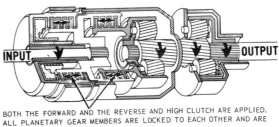

BOTH THE FORWARD AND THE REVERSE AND HIGH CLUTCH ARE APPLIED. ALL PLANETARY GEAR MEMBERS ARE LOCKED TO EACH OTHER AND ARE LOCKED TO THE OUTPUT SHAFT.

HIGH GEAR

THE FORWARD CLUTCH IS APPLIED. THE FRONT PLANETARY UNIT RING GEAR IS LOCKED TO THE INPUT SHAFT.

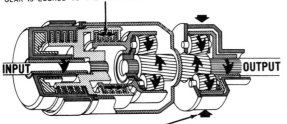

THE LOW AND REVERSE CLUTCH (LOW RANGE) OR THE ONE-WAY CLUTCH (D1 RANGE) IS HOLDING THE REVERSE UNIT PLANET CARRIER STATIONARY.

FIRST GEAR

THE REVERSE AND HIGH CLUTCH IS APPLIED. THE INPUT SHAFT IS LOCKED TO THE REVERSE AND HIGH CLUTCH DRUM, THE INPUT SHELL AND THE SUN GEAR.

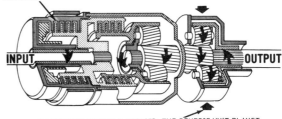

THE LOW AND REVERSE CLUTCH IS APPLIED. THE REVERSE UNIT PLANET CARRIER IS HELD STATIONARY.

REVERSE

THE INTERMEDIATE BAND IS APPLIED. THE REVERSE AND HIGH CLUTCH DRUM, THE INPUT SHELL AND THE SUN GEAR ARE HELD STATIONARY.

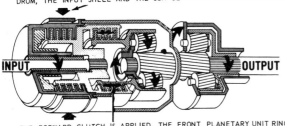

THE FORWARD CLUTCH IS APPLIED. THE FRONT PLANETARY UNIT RING GEAR IS LOCKED TO THE INPUT SHAFT.

SECOND GEAR

Ford of Canada

Fig. 19-22   Typical Power Flow Through Three-Speed Automatic Transmission

and increased torque are provided by the combined gear ratios of the forward and reverse planetary-gear assembly.

Intermediate Range. In intermediate range the forward clutch is applied, and the intermediate brake band is applied to prevent the reverse-high clutch drum and sun gear from turning. The power flow is through the input shaft into the forward clutch and the ring gear of the forward planetary-gear set. The sun gear of this set is held stationary by the intermediate brake band; therefore the planet gears of the forward planetary-gear set must walk around the stationary sun gear carrying the forward planet carrier with them. This carrier is splined to the output shaft and rotates at a reduced speed but with increased torque provided by the gear ratio of the forward planetary-gear assembly.

High Range. In high range both the forward and reverse-high clutches are applied. The forward clutch drives the ring gear and the reverse-high clutch drives the sun gear; both are trying to rotate the planet gears at the same time but at different speeds. This causes the planetary-gear set to lock up and rotate as a unit. In doing so the planet carrier and output shaft are rotated at the same speed and torque as the input shaft.

Reverse Range. In reverse range both the reverse-high and reverse-low clutches are applied. The power flow is through the input shaft to the reverse-high clutch to the sun gear, to the reverse planet gears, whose carrier is held stationary. Therefore the reverse planet gears rotate the reverse ring gear which is splined to the output shaft in a reversed direction.

19-21 AUTOMATIC TRANSMISSION OPERATION

Since all automatic transmissions operate on similar principles, a general description will be given.

In order to start the engine, it is necessary to place the transmission selector in either neutral or park position. Every automatic transmission is equipped with a starting safety switch. This switch is operated by the manual linkage and unless the selector is in either park or neutral position, the electric circuit to the starter solenoid is not complete. Therefore, the engine will not crank over.

Once the engine is started and power is delivered to the transmission front main shaft, the transmission oil pump is driven to produce the oil pressure necessary to operate the transmission hydraulic system. This oil pressure is directed to the proper servos or clutches to ensure that the planetary-gear sets cannot transmit drive.

The oil pressure is directed to the manual valve. Since the manual valve is closed in either park or neutral position, main-line pressure goes no farther.

When a driving gear is selected by the driver, the manual valve is opened to direct main-line pressure to the necessary clutches or servos to produce the required gear ratio. At the same time it directs the pressure to the governor, the shifter-valve body, and the throttle valve, preparatory to upshifting.

If normal acceleration is desired, the throttle valve will remain closed. As the vehicle increases speed, the governor will open the governor valve to direct pressure to the shifter valve. When this pressure overcomes shifter-valve return-spring pressure, the shifter valve moves. This movement directs main-line pressure to release the clutches or servos required for first gear and applies those required to give the next highest gear ratio.

If rapid acceleration is desired, the accelerator pedal will be depressed far enough to open the throttle valve. Throttle-valve pressure is then directed to the shifter-valve regulator plug. This compresses the shifter-valve return spring, thus increasing the spring tension. The vehicle must now increase road speed before the governor valve opens far enough to admit sufficient pressure to overcome the combined shifter-valve return-spring and throttle-valve pressure.

If the transmission has more than two forward-gear ratios, the second-to-third and the third-to-fourth shifter-valve return springs are progressively stronger. Thus they require more governor pressure to cause the shifter valve to move. Therefore, a progressively higher road speed is required to open the governor valve sufficiently to provide the necessary pressure to cause the third and then the fourth shifter valves to move and upshift the transmission.

During heavy acceleration throttle pressure is also directed to the regulator plugs of all shifter valves, thereby delaying each upshift.

The transmission valves are so designed that as the vehicle speed is slowly decreased, the transmission will not downshift unless throttle pressure is increased. If the vehicle is brought to a stop, the valving is designed to downshift the transmission to its lowest gear ready to set the vehicle in motion again.

The driver, by changing the position of the manual control lever, can prevent the transmission from upshifting automatically. With the lever at the low-gear position, the transmission will remain in its lowest gear ratio until the lever is shifted to drive position. In the low position oil pressure is either cut off from the shifter valve, or very high pressure is directed to the return-spring side of the shifter spool to prevent upshifting.

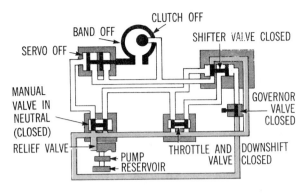

(A) NEUTRAL

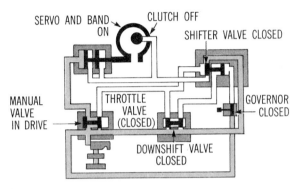

(B) LOW-RANGE SELECTOR IN DRIVE

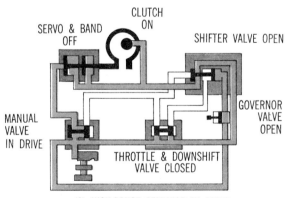

(C) HIGH-RANGE SELECTOR IN DRIVE

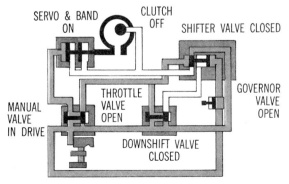

(D) LOW-RANGE DELAYED UPSHIFT SELECTOR IN DRIVE

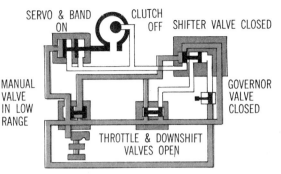

(E) LOW-RANGE SELECTOR IN LOW RANGE

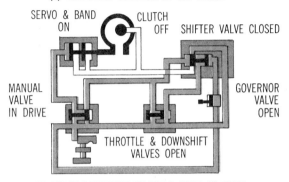

(F) FORCE DOWNSHIFT SELECTOR LEVER IN DRIVE

Fig. 19-23   Automatic Transmission Hydraulic System

In three-speed transmissions not only is it possible to select low gear only, but it is also possible on some units to start the vehicle in intermediate gear and then to have it upshift automatically into high gear. When the manual lever is moved to this position, oil pressure is directed to the servos or clutches required for intermediate gear instead of low gear. The transmission upshifts from intermediate, or second, gear to high gear in the normal manner.

On other types of three-speed transmissions, when the selector lever is moved to the intermediate or second speed position the transmission is automatically placed in low range and will upshift to second speed range normally. However, this type of transmission will not upshift to high range until the manual selector lever is moved to the high or drive position. With the manual lever in the second speed position governor pressure is not applied to move the second-to-third shifter valve to the high range, regardless of road speed.

In four-speed units it is also possible to prevent the transmission from upshifting into fourth gear. When the manual lever is in the correct position, oil pressure is directed to the return-spring side of the third-to-fourth shifter valve to prevent it upshifting.

In all types of automatic transmissions it is possible for the driver to force the transmission to downshift from its highest gear ratio to the next lowest gear ratio. This is accomplished by depressing the accelerator pedal far enough to operate the throttle valve or T-valve. This valve directs oil

pressure to the return-spring side of the shifter valve. The combination of throttle-valve, T-valve, and return-spring pressures are greater than the governor pressure; therefore, the shifter valve returns to the position which will direct oil pressure to operate the clutches or servos necessary for the

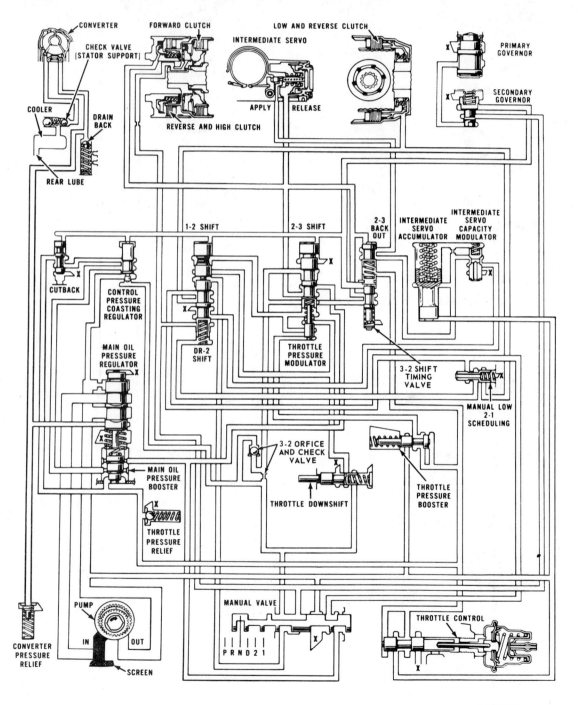

X EXHAUST

Fig. 19-24   Typical Automatic Hydraulic Control System

Chrysler Canada Ltd.

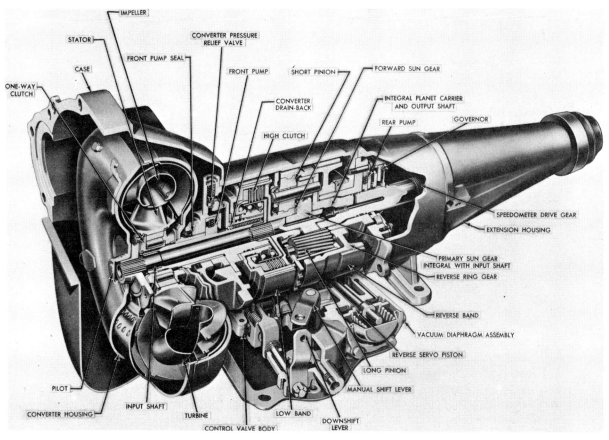

Fig. 19-27   Ford Two-Speed Automatic Transmission   Ford of Canada

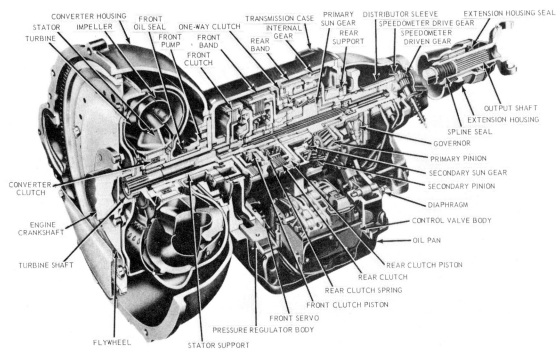

Fig. 19-28   Ford FMX Three-Speed Automatic Transmission   Ford of Canada

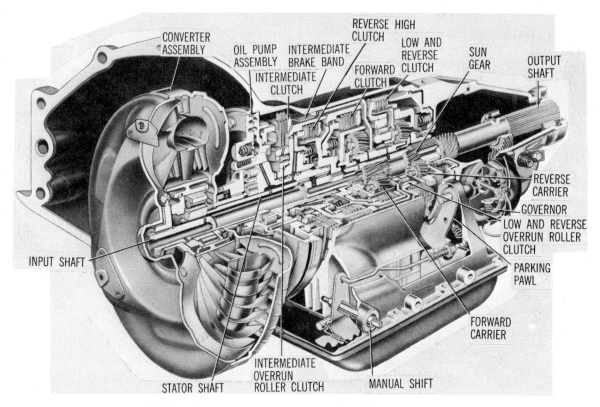

Fig. 19-29 *General Motors Turbo-Hydramatic Three-Speed Transmission*   Courtesy of **General Motors**

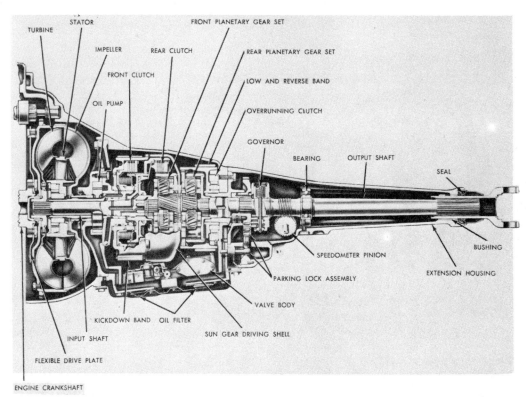

Fig. 19-30 *Chrysler Torqueflight Three-Speed Automatic Transmission*   Chrysler Canada Ltd.

next lowest gear ratio. When the accelerator pedal is released the throttle valve and T valve close, cutting off the pressure to the return spring side of the shifter valve. Governor pressure now moves the shifter valve to the highest gear ratio possible.

19-22 MANUAL CONTROL MECHANISMS

Many types of manual controls have been used. The most common is the quadrant and lever. The quadrant indicates the gear position in which the lever has been placed. The quadrant and lever are mounted on the steering column in a manner similar to that of the standard transmission steering-column gear shift. Some manufacturers have used a set of push buttons, one for each gear ratio, mounted on the dashboard and connected to the manual control valve by cables. When the button is pushed, the manual control spool valve moves to the correct position to select the proper gear ratio.

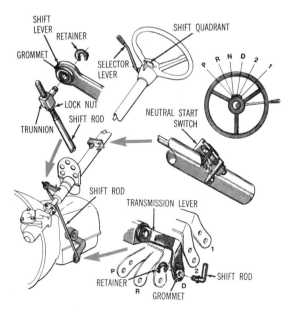

Fig. 19-25   Gearshift Column Assembly

Many modern sports models use a floor console gear selector. This is mounted on the floor between the front seats. In most cases, when this type is used, there is a position for each forward speed. The driver may manually select each gear as he chooses. To prevent the transmission from up-shifting, the main-line oil pressure is directed to the return-spring side of the shifter-valve spools. When the lever is moved to the next highest position, this main-line oil pressure is cut off from the

shifter valve, and the transmission upshifts. The transmission will upshift automatically through the gears below the one selected by the lever. If the lever is moved to a lower gear position, the main-line oil pressure is again directed to the return-spring side of the necessary shifter valve, forcing it to downshift the transmission.

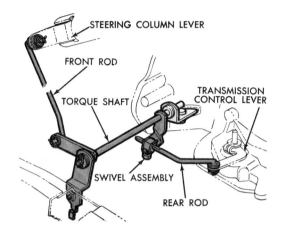

(A) COLUMN GEARSHIFT LINKAGE

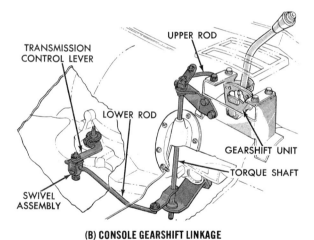

(B) CONSOLE GEARSHIFT LINKAGE

Ford of Canada

Fig. 19-26   Gearshift Linkage

19-23 SEMI-AUTOMATIC TRANSMISSION SYSTEMS

A semi-automatic transmission system (such as the Volkswagon Automatic Stick-Shift) consists of a torque converter, a vacuum-operated disc clutch and a standard fully synchronized gear-type three-speed transmission. The transmission does not shift automatically from one speed range to another according to engine load, road speed, or throttle position. Instead the driver selects the required gear ("L" for steep inclines, "1" for starting or city driving "2" for cruising, "R" for reverse, or "N"

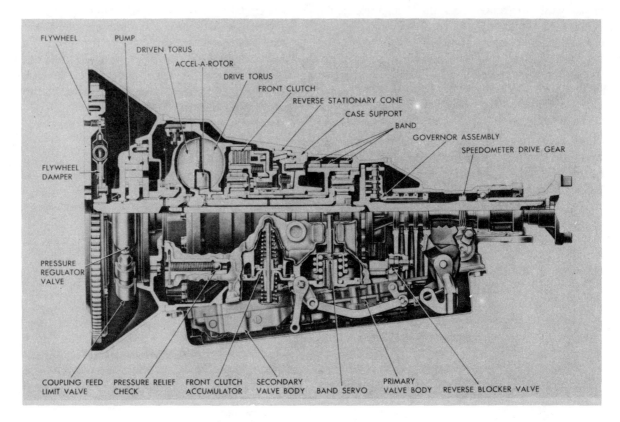

Fig. 19-31   General Motors Four-Speed Hydramatic Automatic Transmission   Courtesy of General Motors

neutral). When the driver desires to shift from one range to another, or is required to bring the vehicle to a stop, he is not required to depress the clutch pedal.

To change from one forward gear to another the driver simply moves the shift lever to the desired position. This action closes electrical contacts, located in the shifter-lever base, completing the electric circuit to a solenoid. When the solenoid is energized, it opens a vacuum valve which, when open, directs engine vacuum into one side of a vacuum diaphragm. Atmospheric pressure on the opposite side of the vacuum diaphragm causes the diaphragm to move toward the vacuum side. This movement operates the clutch release lever to disengage the clutch. With the clutch disengaged the transmission can be shifted into the desired speed range. When the driver releases the gear-shift lever the solenoid circuit is broken. The breaking of the solenoid circuit allows the vacuum valve to close, thereby engaging the clutch.

A vacuum reservoir is included in the system to ensure that the transmission can be shifted even

though the engine has been switched off, or if there is not sufficient vacuum in the intake manifold, such as when the engine is under heavy load.

The system includes a temperature warning lamp. This lamp lights when the torque convertor fluid exceeds the permissable operating temperature. Should this light go on, it is an indication to shift the transmission to the next lower gear ratio. The resulting higher engine speed and reduced torque converter load and faster fluid circulation will reduce the fluid temperature and the lamp will go out.

Another type of semi-automatic transmission is a manually operated power shift transmission which does not require a clutch or clutch pedal. The transmission is similar to the fully automatic-type transmission except for changes in the control valve body and the elimination of the vacuum diaphragm, throttle rod, governor, and inner and outer downshift lever assemblies.

To select the necessary gear ratios, the transmission must be shifted manually by moving the transmission selector lever to the desired position.

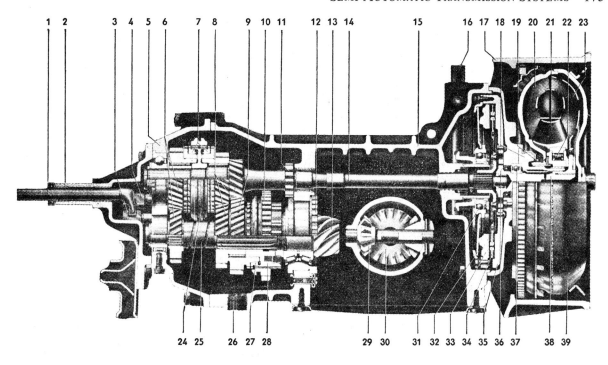

1 - Inner shift lever	14 - Drive shaft	27 - 1st gear synchronizer ring
2 - Gearshift housing	15 - Transmission case	28 - Synchronizer hub 1st/reverse gear
3 - 1st/reverse shift rod	16 - Shift clutch release shaft	29 - Differential pinion
4 - 2nd/3rd shift rod	17 - Converter housing	30 - Differential side gear
5 - Gear carrier	18 - Support tube for one-way clutch	31 - Shift clutch release bearing
6 - 3rd speed gears	19 - Oil seal for converter	32 - Diaphragm spring
7 - 2nd/3rd gear synchronizer rings	20 - Impeller	33 - Pressure plate
8 - 2nd speed gears	21 - Stator	34 - Clutch plate
9 - 1st speed gears	22 - One-way clutch	35 - Carrier plate
10 - Operating sleeve for 1st/reverse gear	23 - Turbine	36 - Oil seal for converter housing
11 - Reverse gear drive	24 - 2nd/3rd gear operating sleeve	37 - Bearing for turbine shaft
12 - Retaining ring for pinion	25 - 2nd/3rd gear spacer spring	38 - Turbine shaft
13 - Pinion	26 - Magnetic oil drain plug	39 - Torque converter

Volkswagon Canada Ltd.

Fig. 19-32   Automatic Stick Shift (Volkswagon)

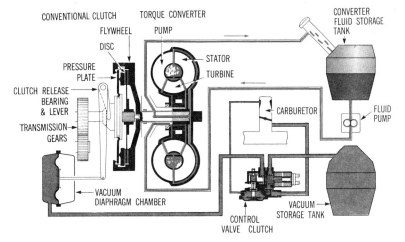

Fig. 19-33   Semi-Automatic Transmission

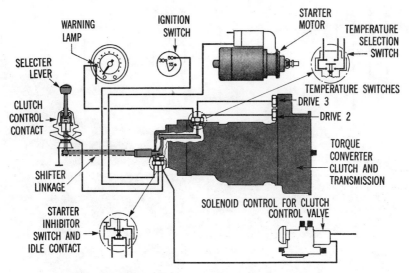

Fig. 19-34 Semi-Automatic Transmission Clutch

The transmission consists of a torque convertor, planetary-gear train, two multiple-disc clutches, a one-way clutch, and a hydraulic control system.

REVIEW QUESTIONS

1. What is the basic difference between an automatic transmission that is coupled to a fluid coupling and an automatic transmission that is coupled to a torque converter? Why?
2. How are the planetary-gear sets combined to give (a) a two-speed (b) three-speed (c) four-speed automatic transmission?
3. Describe briefly how (a) reduction (b) direct drive (c) neutral are obtained through the use of a planetary-gear set as used in an automatic transmission.
4. Why is oil pump pressure required to operate the automatic transmission?
5. What is a servo? What is its purpose?
6. What is the advantage of accumulator-equipped servos?
7. Describe the operation of the hydraulic multi-disc automatic-transmission clutch assembly.
8. Sketch a spool-valve assembly.
9. Explain the operation of a spool valve.
10. State two methods of controlling spool-valve movement.
11. What is the purpose of a balanced valve?
12. How can the movement of a balanced valve be controlled?
13. Why is the manual-control valve necessary?
14. What determines the number of shifter valves required?

15. What other automatic transmission components does the shifter valve control?
16. What does the automatic-transmission governor control? Why is it necessary?
17. What is the purpose of the automatic-transmission throttle valve?
18. State two methods of automatic-transmission throttle valve operation.
19. Explain the following terms and state how each is accomplished: (a) delayed upshift (b) forced downshift.
20. Describe two methods of automatic transmission fluid heat dissipation.
21. Describe briefly the operating conditions and the step-by-step operation of an automatic transmission as it shifts from first gear to second gear under normal accelerating conditions.
22. What control does the driver have of an automatic transmission?
23. Explain how individual gear selection is controlled in some automatic transmissions that are installed in sport-type vehicles.
24. Describe the path of power flow through a two-speed automatic transmission when it is operating in low range.
25. Describe the path of power flow through a three-speed automatic transmission when it is operating in (a) intermediate (b) high range.
26. Describe the actions that take place when a driver changes from one transmission range to another in a stick shift semi-automatic transmission.
27. What causes the warning lamp to light in a stick shift semi-automatic transmission?
28. What should the driver do when the warning lamp lights in a stick shift semi-automatic transmission? Why?

Chapter 20
AUTOMATIC-TRANSMISSION SERVICE

Automatic transmission troubles can be divided into two general classes: linkage problems and defective internal components. It should be noted too that an engine that lacks power frequently gives the impression of transmission troubles.

20-1 OIL LEVEL AND CLEANLINESS

Before any test is performed to determine automatic transmission troubles, check the fluid to ascertain if it is clean and at the proper level. Dirty or wrong type of fluid can cause malfunction of the components. (See dirt, below.)

If the fluid level is low, the fluid coupling or torque converter will not transmit all of the power applied to it. Servos and clutches will not apply full pressure if they are not completely filled. Since the fluid is also used for lubrication and cooling of the transmission, excessive wear and temperatures could result.

20-2 DIRT

Since the hydraulic components of the transmission are fitted to very close tolerances, tiny particles of dirt or grit can cause serious malfunction and damage to the components. One particle of dirt could cause a shifter valve to stick so that the transmission would not shift normally.

20-3 STALL TEST

The stall test is used to determine whether the engine is developing sufficient power or if the clutches or bands are holding securely.

This test must be used with moderation because considerable strain is exerted on the drive line, differential gears, and axles. A tremendous amount of heat is also generated in the fluid coupling or torque converter.

To perform a stall test the engine should be at the normal operating temperature. Attach a tachometer to the engine and firmly apply the parking and service brakes. Place the transmission in drive range and depress the accelerator to the floor board.

If the engine does not reach a speed of approximately 1,800 rpm, it should be tuned up and then retested. If the engine rpm goes higher than 2,000 rpm, the transmission clutches, bands, or sprags are slipping.

In order to keep drive-line strains and converter heat to a minimum, never hold the throttle open for more than one minute during the test. Should the engine speed increase above 2,000 rpm, close the throttle immediately to avoid damaging the transmission.

20-4 THROTTLE AND CONTROL LINKAGES

Since the manual-valve and throttle-valve movement is very small between the different ranges, the linkage between the manual-control valve lever, the accelerator pedal, and the transmission must be properly adjusted. Incorrect manual-control linkage adjustment could prevent the transmission from operating in the range selected.

Incorrect throttle-linkage adjustment can prevent the transmission from upshifting at the right time according to speed and load conditions, or prevent the transmission from upshifting at all.

Most manufacturers provide setting measurements or special gauges to ensure proper linkage adjustments.

20-5 AUTOMATIC TRANSMISSION REPAIRS

Sometimes it is possible to make repairs to the valve body and governor and to adjust the bands without removing the transmission from the vehicle. But most repairs necessitate transmission removal.

The bands are adjusted in different ways on different transmissions. Special gauges are frequently required to obtain the proper adjustment. When the bands are properly adjusted, they will not slip on a stall test but will release fully under proper operating conditions.

When repairing automatic transmissions, follow the manufacturers' instructions as given in the shop manuals. Cleanliness is of special importance when repairing any part of an automatic transmission.

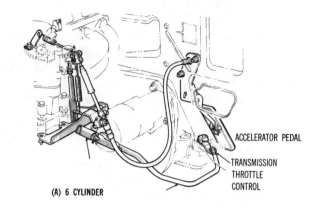

(A) 6 CYLINDER

ACCELERATOR PEDAL

TRANSMISSION
THROTTLE
CONTROL

Chrysler of Canada
Fig. 20-1   Typical Throttle Control Valve Linkages

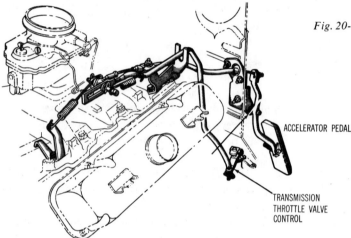

ACCELERATOR PEDAL

TRANSMISSION
THROTTLE VALVE
CONTROL

(B) 8 CYLINDER

20-6 TOWING OR PUSHING A VEHICLE WITH AUTOMATIC TRANSMISSION

Generally speaking, it is not good policy to push-start a vehicle with an automatic transmission. Many late models cannot be started by pushing since they do not have a rear pressure pump that is driven by the drive shaft. Consequently, no pressure will be built up in the transmission hydraulic system to operate the clutches or bands. Older models with rear pumps could be push-started. Observe the special instructions supplied by the manufacturers.

A vehicle equipped with an automatic transmission can usually be towed short distances at low speed with the selector lever in neutral position without damaging the transmission. However, on some vehicles the transmission may not receive normal lubrication. Thus, it could be ruined in a short distance, particularly if it is towed at high speed. With this type of vehicle, it is recommended that the rear of the vehicle be lifted or that the drive shaft be removed. Any vehicle equipped with an automatic transmission that is to be towed a great distance should be lifted at the rear or have the drive shaft removed.

Always observe manufacturers' recommendations when towing or pushing an automatic-transmission equipped vehicle.

REVIEW QUESTIONS

1. Why must the proper automatic-transmission fluid level be maintained?
2. What is the purpose of a stall test?
3. Why should the stall test be used in moderation?
4. Why is the throttle and control valve linkage adjustment of critical importance?
5. Give three precautions that are good policy when an automatic-transmission equipped vehicle must be towed.

Chapter 21
DRIVE SHAFTS

21-1 PURPOSE OF DRIVE SHAFTS

In order to connect the output shaft of the transmission to the drive pinion of the differential, a drive, or propeller, shaft must be used. In order to compensate for the up-and-down motion of the differential and rear axle (as the wheels encounter irregularities in the road) and load conditions, the drive shaft must be connected to the transmission or differential by at least one flexible or universal joint.

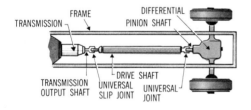

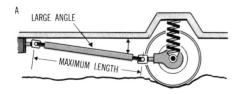

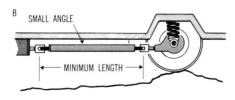

Fig. 21-1   Drive Shaft and Drive Angles

In addition to changes because of road irregularities and load variations, there is a further change in drive-shaft angles caused by the application of engine torque. This torque is called *rear-end torque.*

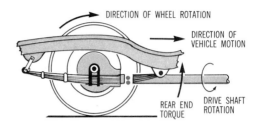

Fig. 21-2   Rear-End Torque

Rear-end torque—is the tendency of the drive shaft to rotate around the rear axle in the opposite direction to the axle shaft and wheel. Rear-end torque is of considerable force. This is illustrated by the tendency of the front end of a vehicle to rise when power is suddenly applied to the rear wheels.

Rear-end torque is transferred from the pinion shaft, to the axle housing, to the leaf springs or, when coil springs are used, to the torque rods. Both the springs and torque rods are anchored to the frame. When the leaf springs are used to transfer rear-end torque to the frame, flexing and distortion of the spring results. This flexing and distortion will allow the front end of the pinion shaft to lower, thus changing the angle between the pinion shaft and the drive shaft.

The drive shaft is made of quality steel tubing

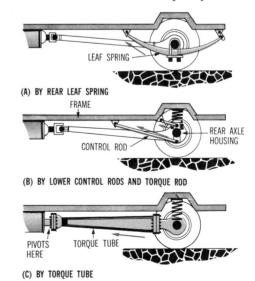

Fig. 21-3   Methods of Transferring Rear-End Torque to Frame

to promote light weight, and has a diameter large enough to impart great strength. Two universal yokes or a yoke and a spline stub are welded to the ends of the tube. The assembly must run true and be carefully balanced to avoid vibration. Since the drive shaft can turn at engine speed, a great deal of damage can be done if the shaft is bent or unbalanced, or if the universal joints are worn.

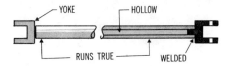

Fig. 21-4   Drive Shaft Tubes

21-2 TYPES OF DRIVE SHAFT

21-3 THE HOTCHKISS DRIVE SHAFT

The Hotchkiss drive shaft is a hollow steel tube with a universal or flexible joint attached to each end. The shaft is not encased in any cover; hence the term *open drive shaft*. One universal joint, usually the front, is designed to compensate for changes of length in the drive shaft. Both universal joints are used to compensate for the changes in the drive-shaft angle as the wheel encounters irregularities in the road. This type of drive shaft is not designed to absorb any rear-end torque. Instead, this action is transferred to the frame through the rear-spring front shackle and the rear springs.

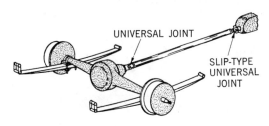

(A) HOTCHKISS DRIVE SHAFT

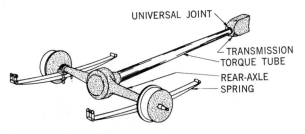

(B) TORQUE-TUBE DRIVE SHAFT

Fig. 21-5   Types of Drive Shafts

21-4 THE TORQUE-TUBE DRIVE SHAFT

In the torque-tube drive shaft the propeller shaft is enclosed in a hollow steel tube. This tube is bolted to the differential housing and is attached to the transmission case by a flexible or universal joint. This universal joint is free to slide on the propeller shaft to compensate for the changes in length, as well as changes in the angle between the drive shaft and the differential housing as the rear wheels encounter irregularities in the road. The torque tube absorbs the rear-end torque action and transfers this action through the transmission, motor, and motor mounts, to the frame.

With a torque-tube drive the engine is usually mounted as low as possible in the frame, or mounted on an angle with the front of the engine higher than the rear. Some vehicles using Hotchkiss drives also have the engine tilted in the same manner. The tilting is used to obtain as straight a line as possible for power transmission. Power is always lost by any angularity in the drive line.

21-5 TWO-PIECE DRIVE SHAFTS

The introduction of the automobiles with longer wheel bases made it necessary to adopt the truck-type two-piece drive shaft, with its centre support bearing. Long drive shafts have a tendency to vibrate and whip. Dividing the shaft in two and adding the centre support reduces this tendency. The two halves of the drive shaft are joined together by a *slip joint*.

The centre support bearing consists of a ball bearing held in a dust-proof housing. The housing is attached to the frame. Rubber is usually incorporated in the mount to reduce noise and vibration. The rubber will also allow some movement of the shaft without binding.

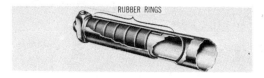

Ford of Canada

Fig. 21-7   Rubber-Element Drive Shaft

21-6 RUBBER-ELEMENT DRIVE SHAFT

In the rubber-element type drive shaft, one of the universal-joint yokes is not welded to the drive tube. Instead, the yoke is welded to a separate piece of steel tubing. This tubing, which has several rubber rings bonded to it, is slightly smaller in diameter than the drive-shaft tube. The smaller

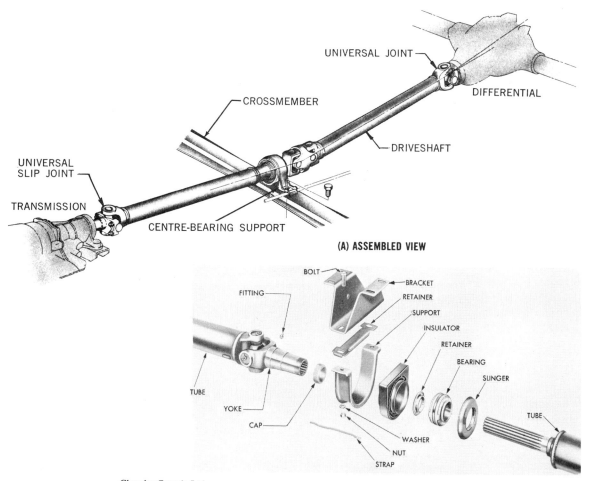

(A) ASSEMBLED VIEW

(B) CENTRE BEARING DETAIL

Fig. 21-6   Drive Shaft   Chrysler Canada Ltd.

tube and yoke are then pressed into one end of the drive shaft. The rubber rings between the two tubes are now under so much compression that the two tubes are locked together but isolated from one another. The rubber element prevents noise from "telegraphing" up and down the drive shaft.

21-7 UNIVERSAL JOINTS

21-8 CROSS-AND-ROLLER UNIVERSAL JOINT

This joint is basically a double-hinged joint. It consists of two yokes and a cross-shaped centre joint. The yokes are attached to the driving and driven units and are connected together by the centre joint. The drive is transferred from the first yoke to the cross-shaped piece, or spider, and then to the second yoke. Small roller bearings are usually placed between the arms, or trunnions, of the spider and the yokes. These bearings not only transmit the

drive, but also permit the yokes to turn freely on the spider as the joint rotates when the driving shaft is at different angle to the driven shaft.

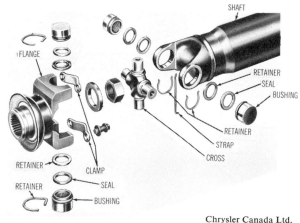

Chrysler Canada Ltd.

Fig. 21-8   Typical Rear Cross and Roller Universal Joint

21-9 BALL-AND-TRUNNION UNIVERSAL JOINT

This type of joint will transmit torque through an angle and will also act as a slip joint to allow slight variations in drive-shaft length.

The joint consists of two ball-and-roller assemblies that are mounted on each end of a cross pin which in turn is inserted in a hole in a ball on the end of the propeller shaft. The outer body of the joint is attached to the output shaft of the transmission and extends over the propeller shaft ball. The outer body contains longitudinal grooves into which the ball-and-roller assemblies are placed. The torque is transferred from the outer body through the ball-and-roller assemblies and cross pin to the ball on the end of the drive shaft. The ball-and-roller assemblies are also free to slide back and forth in the longitudinal grooves in the outer body, thus permitting slight variations in drive-shaft length.

21-10 SLIP JOINTS

Slip joints are used to compensate for the changes in drive-shaft length that result from the up-and-down movement of the rear axle as it encounters irregularities in the road or varying load conditions.

When the axle moves up and down, it swings on an arc that is different from that of the drive line. This difference in arcs results in slight changes in the distance between the transmission and the differential.

A slip joint is a universal joint in which one yoke is not rigidly attached to one of the rotating members. Instead, it is attached to the shaft by means of a spline. A spline is like an internal- and external-gear set. The outside splines are cut on the shaft, while the internal splines are cut in the mating hollow section of the universal joint. The splines are cut long enough to permit the shaft to change its length, as required by the spring action, without coming out of mesh and stopping the rotating action. One end of the drive shaft, usually the transmission end, is always equipped with a slip-joint type of universal.

21-11 INSTALLATION ANGLES

The transmission and the rear-axle housing are installed in the car at a definite angle in relation to the car's frame. The transmission is rigidly attached to the frame, and its angular change is limited by the engine and transmission-mount deflection. However, the rear-axle housing installation angle is constantly changing because of the up-and-down

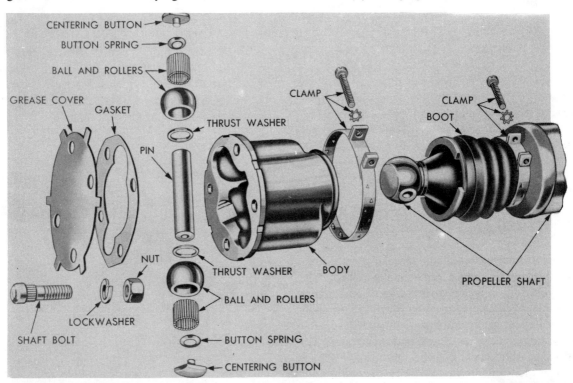

Fig. 21-9   Ball-and-Trunnion Universal Joint

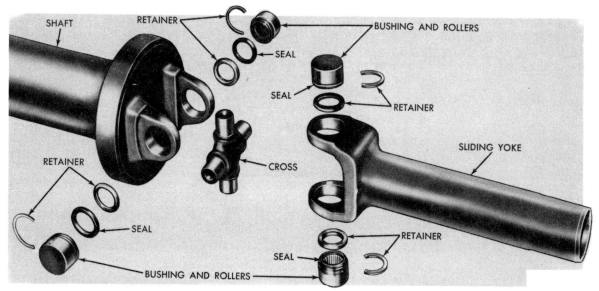

(A) EXPLODED VIEW

Fig. 21-10   Typical Sliding-Yoke Type Universal Joint

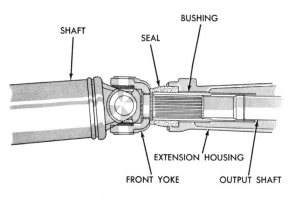

(B) ASSEMBLED VIEW

spring action and the axle-housing rotation which is caused by acceleration and braking. The rear-axle inclination angle is specified when the car is standing still and at curb weight.

The *transmission installation angle* is the angle formed by the centre line of the transmission output shaft crossing the frame line. The angle can be measured by placing a spirit-level protractor on the machined surface of the transmission. The variation from the vertical or horizontal is the installation angle.

The *rear-axle installation angle* is the angle formed by the drive-shaft pinion centre line intersecting the frame line. This angle can be measured by placing a spirit-level protractor on the machined surfaces of the differential carrier housing or the drive-pinion flange.

The *drive-shaft angle* is measured by placing a spirit-level protractor on the drive-shaft tube. The

universal-joint angle is the angle formed by the crossing of the centre lines of the two components which are coupled by the universal joint. This angle is referred to as the *included angle*; it cannot be measured directly but must be calculated from the installation angles of the two components connected by the joint.

To calculate the angle, find the difference between the installation angles when the components are tilted in the same direction. Or find the sum of the installation angles if the components are tilted in opposite directions.

The size of the universal-joint operating angles is very important because the universal joints in many drive lines are of the nonconstant-velocity type.

21-12 VARYING SHAFT SPEEDS

When one conventional universal joint is driven at an angle and at a constant speed, the speed of the driven shaft will not be constant. It will rotate the same number of rpm's, but its speed will fluctuate. The driven-shaft speed will rise and fall two times for each revolution. This is because the angle of the drive is not equally divided between the two shafts.

When two universal joints are used, one at each end of the shaft, the disturbing shaft-speed fluctuations can be eliminated if both universal-joint yokes

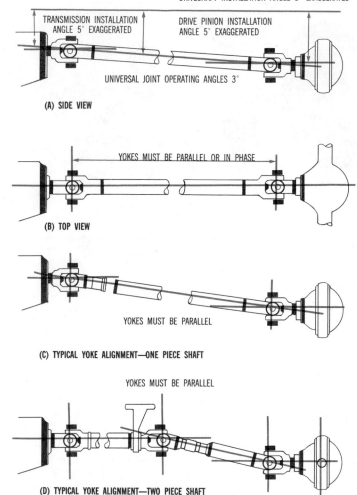

DRIVESHAFT INSTALLATION ANGLE 8° EXAGGERATED

TRANSMISSION INSTALLATION
ANGLE 5° EXAGGERATED

DRIVE PINION INSTALLATION
ANGLE 5° EXAGGERATED

UNIVERSAL JOINT OPERATING ANGLES 3°

(A) SIDE VIEW

YOKES MUST BE PARALLEL OR IN PHASE

(B) TOP VIEW

YOKES MUST BE PARALLEL

(C) TYPICAL YOKE ALIGNMENT—ONE PIECE SHAFT

YOKES MUST BE PARALLEL

(D) TYPICAL YOKE ALIGNMENT—TWO PIECE SHAFT

Fig. 21-11   Drive Shaft Angles and Yoke Alignment

are in the same plane. This is sometimes referred to as in line or *in phase*. With two universal joints in phase, the speed of the transmission shaft and the differential pinion shaft will be constant and the same if the angles of both shafts are uniform. The speed of the connecting propeller shaft will rise and fall, but this is unimportant as long as the speed of the driving and driven shafts are uniform.

21-13 CONSTANT-VELOCITY JOINTS

A constant-velocity joint is a joint designed to produce even transfer of torque without speed fluctuations.

One type of constant-velocity joint consists of two individual yoke-and-cross universal joints connected by a ball and socket. The ball and socket bisect the angle of the two drive shafts between the two universal joints. Since the two joints are now operating at the same angle, the acceleration of one is cancelled out by the de-acceleration of the other.

A second type of constant-velocity joint uses rolling balls in curved grooves. The balls, which are the driving contact, move laterally as the joint rotates. This allows the point of driving contact between the two halves of the joint to remain in a plane which splits the angle between the two shafts, thus eliminating the speed fluctuations.

21-14 DRIVE-SHAFT BALANCE

The constantly fluctuating speeds of a drive shaft have a tendency to produce vibration. This vibration can be greatly magnified if the drive shaft is not properly balanced.

To illustrate the magnitude of an unbalanced

(A) ADJUSTING GAUGE ON ENGINE (FRONT JOINT ANGLE REFERENCE)

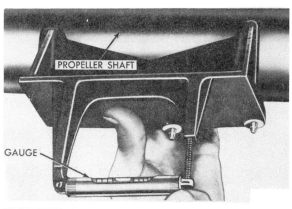

(B) MEASURING FRONT UNIVERSAL JOINT ANGLE

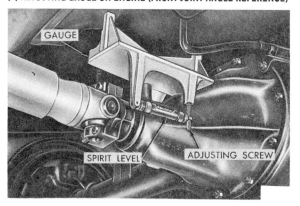

(C) ADJUSTING GAUGE ON DIFFERENTIAL (REAR JOINT ANGLE)

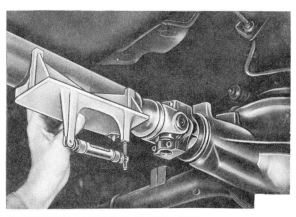

(D) MEASURING REAR UNIVERSAL JOINT ANGLE

UNIVERSAL JOINT	ANGULARITY MEASUREMENT AND CORRECTION CHART	
	FRONT JOINT ANGLE	REAR JOINT ANGLE
CAR TYPE AND WHEELBASE	ADJUST POSITION OF BUBBLE WITH GAUGE AT ENGINE OIL PAN FLANGE	ADJUST POSITION OF BUBBLE WITH GAUGE ON DIFFERENTIAL CARRIER
	← FRONT OF CAR	← FRONT OF CAR
FINAL READING ON PROPELLER SHAFT (ALL MODELS)	ACCEPTABLE REGION — ANGLE LOW / ANGLE HIGH — ← FRONT OF CAR	ACCEPTABLE REGION — ANGLE LOW / ANGLE HIGH — ← FRONT OF CAR
CORRECTION PROCEDURE	ADD SHIMS AT ENGINE REAR MOUNT (⅛″ FOR EACH GAUGE DIVISION) TO REDUCE FRONT JOINT ANGLE. CORRECT LOW ANGLES ONLY IF FLOOR PAN INTERFERENCE IS ENCOUNTERED.	ADD SHIMS AT REAR AXLE HOUSING SPRING SEATS. 1° WEDGE SHIM MOVES BUBBLE 3 TO 4 GAUGE DIVISIONS. TO REDUCE ANGLE, INSTALL THICK END OF WEDGE TO FRONT OF CAR.

(E) UNIVERSAL JOINT ANGULARITY REFERENCE CHART

Chrysler Canada Ltd.

Fig. 21-12   Measuring Universal Joint Angularity

condition, assume that a drive shaft is rotating at 3,750 rpm. If a 2-oz weight were placed 2″ from the centre of the shaft, the magnitude of the centrifugal force produced would be equal to 50 lbs. This 50-lb force would be exerted in opposite directions 62½ times per second.

Drive-shaft misalignment can also produce vibration. Transmission and differential flanges and splines must be machined true. A drive shaft weighing 25 lb mounted .005″ off centre will develop a centrifugal force of 50 lb at 3,750 rpm.

An unbalanced condition can result from using mounting bolts, washers and nuts which do not have the same weight, from worn joint crosses and

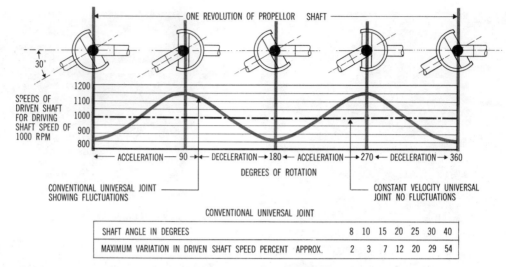

CONVENTIONAL UNIVERSAL JOINT							
SHAFT ANGLE IN DEGREES	8	10	15	20	25	30	40
MAXIMUM VARIATION IN DRIVEN SHAFT SPEED PERCENT APPROX.	2	3	7	12	20	29	54

Fig. 21-13   Conventional Universal Joint Speed Fluctuation Chart

bearings, from worn splines, from looseness in the mounting bolts, or from a belt-driven shaft.

21-15 DRIVE SHAFT SERVICE

Drive shaft service consists of periodic inspection and lubrication. During inspection, excessive wear in the universal joints or the centre support bearing can be ascertained by shaking the drive shaft up and down while noting the play in the joints or support bearing.

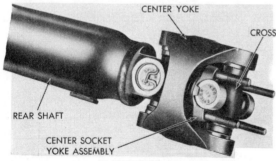

(A) ASSEMBLED

(B) EXPLODED

Chrysler Canada Ltd.
Fig. 21-14   Constant-Velocity Type Universal Joint

On many vehicles the drive shaft and the universal joints are carefully balanced and marked during assembly. The marking is done to ensure correct reassembly when worn parts are replaced. Unmarked drive shafts should be marked before disassembly.

If a drive shaft has been disassembled without being marked, the shaft yokes must be assembled in line with each other.

REVIEW QUESTIONS

1. What is the purpose of a drive shaft?
2. Define the term "rear-end torque."
3. What absorbs rear-end torque when the following types of drive shafts are used: (a) torque-tube type (b) Hotchkiss type with leaf-spring suspension (c) Hotchkiss type with coil-spring suspension?
4. Why are two-piece type drive shafts used?
5. What is the purpose of (a) a universal joint (b) a slip joint?
6. Describe the construction of one type of universal joint.
7. Describe the term "installation angles."
8. What factors affect the rear-axle inclination angle?
9. Why is it necessary to make sure that universal joint yokes are "in-line" or "in-phase"?
11. What causes the drive shaft speed to fluctuate during each revolution of the shaft?
12. Explain how a constant velocity joint eliminates drive shaft speed fluctuations.
13. Why must drive shafts be in balance?
14. Why should a drive shaft be checked for markings or be marked before disassembly?

going around a turn. To prevent this condition, a differential is installed between the two rear-axle shafts. The differential allows the wheels to rotate at different speeds when turns are made.

22-1 CONVENTIONAL TYPE DIFFERENTIALS

22-2 DIFFERENTIAL TYPES
There are two methods of differential construction: the *Removable-Carrier Type* and the *Integral-Carrier Type*. In the removable-carrier type, the differential assembly is located in a differential carrier housing which is bolted to the rear axle housing.

In the integral-carrier type the carrier housing is included as part of the rear axle housing assembly. In this case the differential unit is assembled within the axle housing instead of being assembled as a separate unit and attached to the axle housing.

22-3 DIFFERENTIAL CONSTRUCTION
Differential Bearings. In both types of differential

Chapter 22
DIFFERENTIALS

If a vehicle were to be driven in a straight line without having to make turns, no differential would be necessary. However, when a vehicle makes a turn, the outer wheel must travel farther than the inner wheel. If the drive shaft were geared rigidly to both rear wheels so that they had to rotate together, one wheel would have to skid when the vehicle was

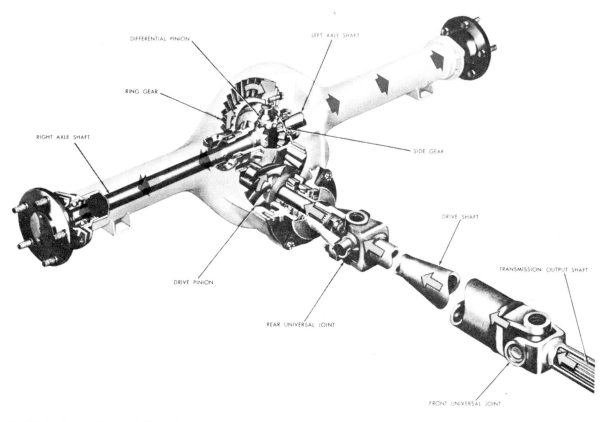

Fig. 22-1   Drive Line and Rear Axle

Ford of Canada

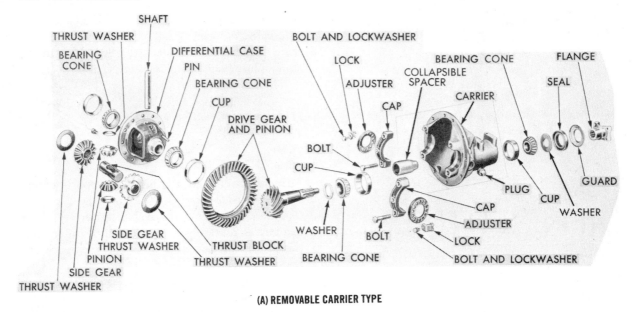

Fig. 22-2 Typical Differential Assemblies

(A) Chrysler Canala Ltd.

(B) Ford of Canada

construction the carrier housing portion is fitted with four tapered roller bearings. Two of these bearings are called pinion bearings and support the pinion drive gear; the other two, called carrier bear-

ings, support the differential case. These bearings allow the unit to rotate freely within the carrier housing and maintain proper ring-gear and pinion-gear mesh. When the drive pinion is driving the ring gear, two resultant forces are acting—an end thrust and a radial load.

The Drive Pinion Gear. The drive pinion gear and shaft assembly is supported by the pinion bearings in the differential housing. The forward end of the shaft is splined to accept a companion flange which is part of the universal joint. As the drive shaft rotates, so does the pinion gear. The pinion gear meshes with the ring gear.

The drive pinion may be either straddle mounted or overhung mounted. The two types of pinion mounting refer to the location of the pinion-shaft bearings in relation to the pinion gear.

A straddle-mounted pinion—has bearings installed on both sides of the pinion gear. Two tapered roller bearings, which absorb all of the thrust load and some of the radial load, are placed close together on the drive-shaft side of the pinion gear. A pilot bearing, usually an annular-type ball bearing, is mounted in the housing in back of the pinion-gear support at the rear end of the pinion shaft. This bearing absorbs the radial load only.

In the overhung mounting—the two tapered roller

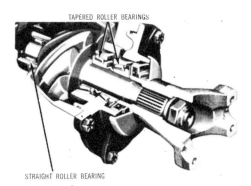

TAPERED ROLLER BEARINGS

STRAIGHT ROLLER BEARING

(A) STRADDLE MOUNTED

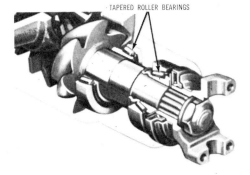

TAPERED ROLLER BEARINGS

(B) OVERHUNG MOUNTED

Ford of Canada

Fig. 22-3   Types of Drive Pinion Mounting

bearings are spaced farther apart so that the front bearing has a longer lever arm to absorb the radial load. Both bearings are placed on the drive-shaft side of the pinion gear.

The Ring Gear. The ring gear is bolted to a flange which is part of the differential case and is meshed with the drive pinion gear. The ring gear and differential case always rotate as a unit in the carrier bearings.

Drive Pinion and Ring Gear Sets. Different types of pinion-drive and ring-gear sets are used.

Most modern automobiles use *hypoid-type* gears; older automobiles and some trucks use *spiral-bevel gears*. Some heavy "off-the-road" vehicles, which require a large gear ratio in the differential, use a worm-and-gear wheel type of drive.

The hypoid-type of gear set—has the advantage over the spiral-bevel type because it allows the drive pinion to mesh with the ring gear below the horizontal centre line of the ring gear. This enables the engineers to lower the centre of gravity of the vehicle without having a deep drive-shaft tunnel in the rear of the passenger compartment. Hypoid gears also produce an end-wise sliding action between the teeth, along with a rolling action. This sliding action permits the lapping of the ring and pinion-gear teeth. The lapping results in a more perfect match, smoother action, and quieter operation.

Ring and pinion-gear sets may be classified as *hunting, nonhunting,* or *partial nonhunting.* Each type has its own requirement for a satisfactory gear-tooth contact pattern.

A hunting-gear set—is one in which the number of teeth on the pinion cannot be divided into the number of teeth on the ring gear evenly. As a result any one tooth of the pinion will come into contact with all the teeth of the ring gear. For example, if a pinion has 9 teeth and the ring gear has 32 teeth, and number 1 tooth of the pinion were meshed with number 1 tooth of the ring gear, during the first revolution of the ring gear number 1 tooth of the pinion will contact ring-gear teeth numbers 1, 10, 19, 28. On the second revolution of the ring gear, number 1 pinion tooth will contact numbers 5, 14, 23, 32—on the third revolution, numbers 9, 18, 27, etc., until on the ninth revolution it contacts ring-gear teeth numbers 6, 15, 24, and 1 again.

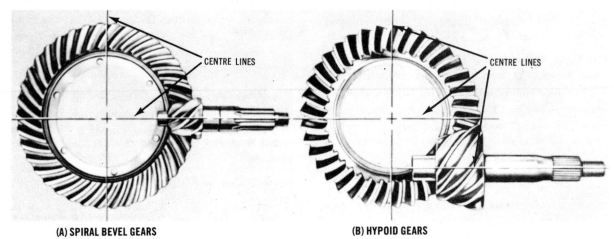

(A) SPIRAL BEVEL GEARS   (B) HYPOID GEARS

Ford of Canada

Fig. 22-4 Hypoid Gears

A nonhunting-gear set—is one in which the pinion-gear teeth will divide into the ring-gear teeth evenly, such as 10 and 30 or 13 and 39. In this type any one pinion tooth will contact only a few ring-gear teeth, and all possible gear-tooth combinations will be produced in one revolution of the ring gear.

A partial nonhunting-gear set—is one in which any one pinion tooth will come in contact with only some of the ring gear teeth, but it takes more than one revolution of the ring gear to bring out all possible gear tooth combinations. An example is a pinion with 10 teeth and a ring gear with 35 teeth.

Both partial- and nonhunting-gear sets have a marked "timing" tooth on both the pinion and the ring gear. Should the pinion and ring gears be assembled out of time, then gear teeth will be mating together which have not been lapped together. This will result in increased gear noise and roughness.

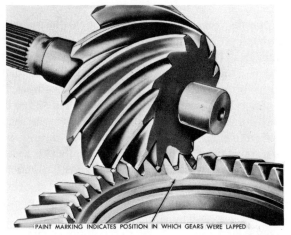

PAINT MARKING INDICATES POSITION IN WHICH GEARS WERE LAPPED

Ford of Canada

Fig. 22-5 Gear Set Timing Marks

Differential Case. The differential case or carrier provides a flange to which the ring gear is bolted and surrounds the differential pinion or spider gears and the axle-bevel or side gears. The case keeps the spider and axle gears in constant mesh. The ring gear, case, spider, and axle gears always rotate as a unit in the carrier bearings.

Differential or Axle Side Gears. These gears are small bevelled gears that are mounted inside the differential case and are splined to the inner ends of the two axle shafts. The axle side gears face each other and are meshed with the differential pinion or spider gears.

Differential Pinion or Spider Gears. These gears are small bevelled gears that are free to rotate on a shaft which is mounted in the differential case. These gears are in constant mesh with the axle side gears. When the case is rotated, the spider gears and their shaft rotate with the case and transmit the drive to the axle side gears and axle shafts.

Lubrication. The differential gears and bearings are lubricated by filling the differential housing and a portion of the rear-axle housing with gear lubricant. In the case of the worm-and-gear wheel or the spiral-bevel type of gear sets, ordinary gear lubricant is used. When a hypoid-gear set is used, special hypoid-type lubricant is required.

A filler plug in the housing is used to fill the differential and to check the lubricant level. Most differential housings or axle housings are equipped with a breather to allow air pressure, caused by heat generated through normal operation, to escape. This pressure could cause the lubricant to be forced out past the oil seals.

Oil seals, mounted in the differential case around

the pinion-drive gear shaft and in the axle housing around the axle shafts, prevent leakage.

22-4 DIFFERENTIAL OPERATION

When the vehicle is being driven in a straight line, the ring gear, driven by its pinion, rotates the differential case. The rotation of the differential case carries the spider or pinion-gear shaft with it. This movement of the spider makes the two side gears rotate about their axis, rotating the axles and wheels at equal speeds and in the same direction as the rotation of the differential case. The power from the ring gear is equally divided between the two axle shafts. When the vehicle is being driven in a straight line, the spider gears act only as a connection between the two rear axles.

When the vehicle goes around a corner, one wheel must rotate faster than the other. Therefore, the side gears must rotate at different speeds. Since the differential case is rotated by the ring gear, and the spider gears no longer act as a solid connection between the two axle shafts, the spider gears must start to walk about the slower axle side gear and therefore rotate on their own axis. The other axle is forced to rotate at a speed equal to the sum of the speeds of the differential case and the spider gears. The action of the gears provides the difference in speed. The power delivered to each wheel is the same, but the inner wheel receives greater torque.

The difference in speed between the two wheels is in direct proportion to the sharpness of the turn being made. The outer wheel gains speed in direct proportion to the inner wheel's loss of speed, while the speed of the ring gear and case remain the same. For example, if a vehicle is travelling straight ahead and the ring gear and case are rotating at 75 rpm, each side gear, axle shaft, and wheel will rotate at 75 rpm. If the vehicle rounds a curve, while retaining the same ring gear and case speed of 75 rpm, the inner wheel might slow down 5 to

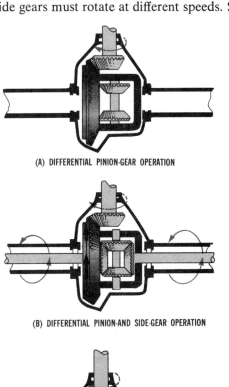

(A) DIFFERENTIAL PINION-GEAR OPERATION

(B) DIFFERENTIAL PINION-AND-SIDE-GEAR OPERATION

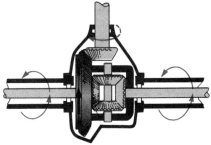

(C) DIFFERENTIAL POWER FLOW DURING STRAIGHT-AHEAD TRAVEL

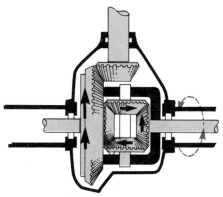

(D) DIFFERENTIAL POWER FLOW WITH ONE WHEEL STATIONARY

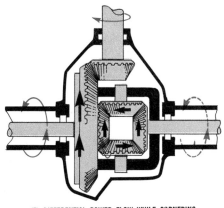

(E) DIFFERENTIAL POWER FLOW WHILE CORNERING

Fig. 22-6   Differential Operation

70 rpm. The outer wheel must increase its rpm by 5 to 80 rpm.

The sum of the speeds of the two axle shafts divided by 2 must always equal the speed of the ring gear and case. For example, the inner wheel at 70 rpm, plus the outer wheel at 80 rpm, equals 150 rpm, divided by 2 equals 75 rpm—or the speed of the ring gear and case.

The action of the differential is controlled by the relative resistance of the two rear wheels, and only comes into action when the wheel resistance is different. This should occur only when the vehicle rounds a curve or when one wheel encounters unevenness in the road. Unfortunately, when the resistance between the rear wheels is different, because of one wheel being on ice while the other is on dry pavement, the wheel with the lesser resistanc spins around; the other wheel remains stationary, and the vehicle does not move.

22-5 NONSLIP TYPE DIFFERENTIALS

To avoid the loss of driving force that occurs when one wheel begins to slip, nonslip differentials are used. The nonslip differential is designed to automatically transfer driving torque to the wheel that is not slipping; thus the vehicle is able to continue its forward motion. Two types of nonslip differentials are used, the *two-pinion* and the *four-pinion* types.

22-6 TWO-PINION TYPE NONSLIP DIFFERENTIALS

The power flow through the two-pinion type nonslip differential is the same as a conventional differential, except that the differential action is partially controlled by clutches of either a multiple-disc type, or a cone type.

When multiple-disc type clutches are used, each clutch consists of a series of dog-ear steel clutch

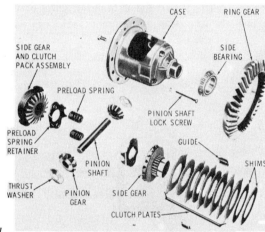

(A) MULTIPLE-DISC CLUTCH TYPE

Fig. 22-7   Two-Pinion Nonslip Differential

(B) CONE CLUTCH TYPE

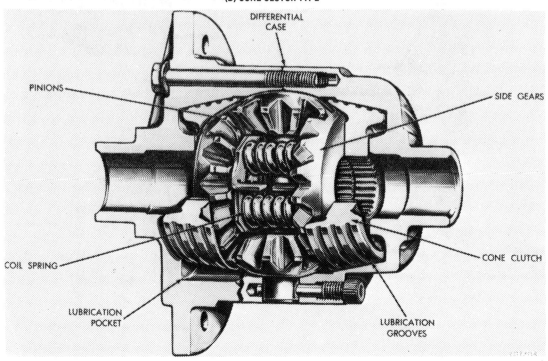

plates which are locked into the differential case, and a series of bronze-bonded clutch plates which are splined to the clutch hubs. The clutch hubs are splined to the axle shafts. A series of coil springs mounted between the two clutches maintain a constant pressure on the bonded and steel clutch plates so that the clutch is always engaged. This clutch action opposes the differential action at all times.

When cone type clutches are used, the cone of each clutch is splined to the axle shafts. The tapered surface of one cone locks up into the flange half of the differential case, and the tapered surface of the other cone locks up in the cap half of the differential case. A series of coil springs is placed between the cone clutches to maintain a constant pressure on the cones, forcing them into tight engagement with both sections of the differential case. The clutch action opposes the differential at all times.

When the vehicle rounds a corner, the clutches slip, allowing the differential to operate in a normal manner to vary the speeds of the inner and outer wheels. If one or both wheels are on a low-traction surface, such as ice, snow, or mud, the clutch transmits a portion of the usable torque to the wheel with the most traction. The wheel that is on the low-traction surface will not spin but will have a tendency to operate with the wheel having the most traction, in a combined driving effort.

22-7 FOUR-PINION NONSLIP DIFFERENTIAL

The four-pinion nonslip differential is basically a standard differential plus two extra spider gears and two multiple-disc clutches.

The side gears are driven by four spider gears. Two separate spider-gear shafts are required. The two spider-gear shafts cross but are free to move independently of each other. The ends of these shafts are machined with two flat surfaces that form a shallow V. The ramp-like V surfaces engage a similar ramp cut in the differential case. One pair of ramps face the ring gear; the other pair face away from the ring gear.

A multiple-disc clutch assembly is inserted on each side of the differential between the axle side-gear thrust members and the differential case. Three of the clutch discs are splined to the differential case; the other two are splined to the side-gear thrust member. The thrust member in turn is splined to the axle shaft.

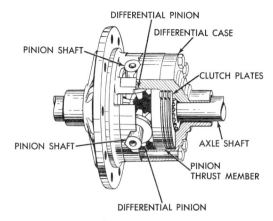

(A) SCHEMATIC

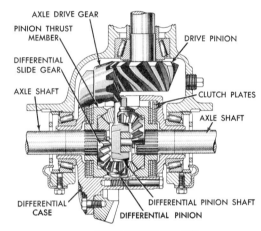

(B) CROSS-SECTION VIEW

Chrysler Canada Ltd.

Fig. 22-8   Four-Pinion Type Nonslip Differential

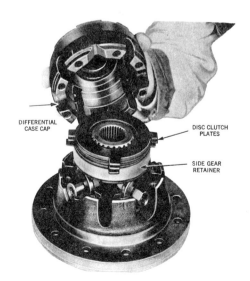

Chrysler Canada Ltd.

Fig. 22-9   Differential Clutch Unit

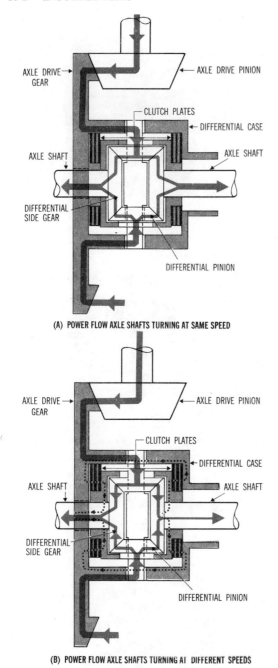

(A) POWER FLOW AXLE SHAFTS TURNING AT SAME SPEED

(B) POWER FLOW AXLE SHAFTS TURNING AT DIFFERENT SPEEDS

Fig. 22-10   Four-Pinion Type Nonslip Differential Operation

When the vehicle is being driven straight ahead, the spider gears encounter resistance when they attempt to turn the axle side gears. This resistance is transferred to the spider-gear shafts. Since both ends of the spider-gear shafts are seated in the V ramps, and have some "play" at this point, the spider-gear shaft is forced to slide up the ramp surfaces. This sliding motion moves both spider-gear shafts and their gears in an outward direction. This outward motion of the spider gears presses against the side-gear thrust members forcing them to lock up the clutches. Some of the clutch discs are splined to the differential case and others to the thrust member; the thrust member is in turn splined to the axle shaft. Locking the clutch discs together causes the differential case, the clutch thrust members, and the axle shafts to rotate as a unit.

When the vehicle rounds a curve, the inner axle shaft slows down. The spider gears start to rotate on their axes as they walk around the slower axle side gear and, in doing so, they increase the speed of the other axle shaft. This action is similar to the action on a standard differential. However, as the outer axle shaft starts to rotate faster than the differential case, the outer spider-gear shaft will start to slide down its ramp. As it slides down the ramp, it releases the pressure on the outer clutch discs, so that now the power is transferred through the axle side gears, instead of through the clutch and thrust member, to the axle shaft.

After completing the curve, the inner wheel again speeds up, the spider gears no longer rotate on their axes, and the spider-gear shaft climbs its ramp to relock the clutch.

By the simple expedient of the wedging action of the V ramps at the ends of the spider-gear shafts, the nonslip differential works just the opposite to the conventional type. The nonslip type applies more pressure instead of less to the wheel that is harder to turn.

NOTE: On a vehicle equipped with either type of limited-slip differential, both rear wheels will always be driving. If, while the vehicle is being serviced, only one wheel is raised off the floor and the other wheel is being driven by the engine, the wheel on the floor will move the vehicle, causing it to fall off the jack or stand.

22-8 TWO-SPEED TYPE DIFFERENTIALS

Two basic types of two-speed differential assemblies are in general use: the *double-reduction gear type*, and the *planetary-gear type*.

22-9 DOUBLE-REDUCTION GEAR TYPE

The double-reduction gear type uses a spiral-bevel gear meshed with a comparatively small ring gear

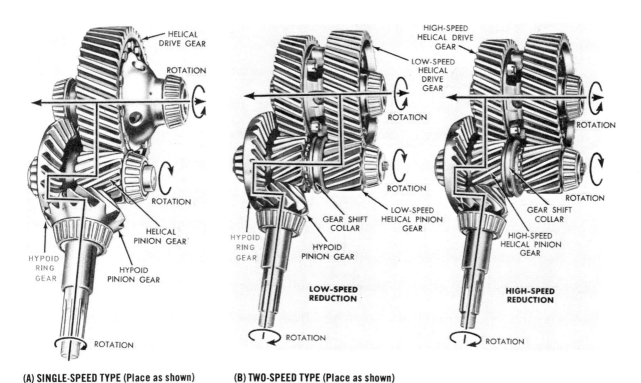

(A) SINGLE-SPEED TYPE (Place as shown)   (B) TWO-SPEED TYPE (Place as shown)

Fig. 22-11   Power Flow in Double-Reduction Type Differentials

Ford of Canada

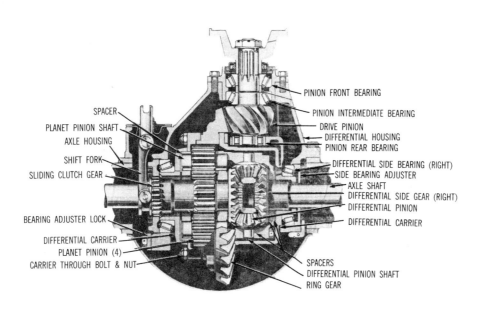

Chrysler Canada Ltd.

Fig. 22-12 A   Assembly—Planetary-Gear Type Differential

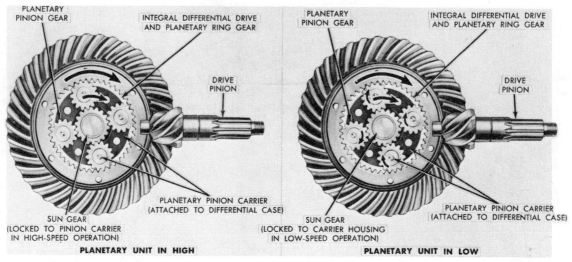

Fig. 22-12 B   Power Flow—Planetary-Gear Type Differential

Chrysler Canada Ltd.

for the primary reduction. The ring gear is assembled to a straight shaft on which there is a reduction-gear set that provides either one or two choices of secondary reduction. The reduction-gear set consists of two pair of helical gears of different gear ratios, separated by a shifting device, to lock either driving gear to the ring-gear shaft. The large driven gear of the helical-gear set is connected to a conventional type of differential case. The drive and the differential action between the differential case and the axle shaft is the same as a conventional differential.

The driver, by operating the shifter mechanism, can move the driven helical gears in and out of mesh to select the desired high-speed or low-speed gear ratio.

22-10 THE PLANETARY-GEAR TYPE

The planetary-gear type uses a planetary-gear set. The internal gear of the planetary-gear set is attached to and driven by the differential ring gear. The planetary carrier drives the differential case. The sun gear has been extended so that it can be shifted back and forth by the driver. When the sun gear is placed in one position, it is locked to the differential housing to produce an overdrive gear ratio. When it is moved to the other position, the sun gear is meshed to lock up the planetary-gear set and produce direct drive. The axle side gears and spider gears are mounted in the usual way and the differential action and drive is the same as in a conventional differential.

22-11 SHIFT CONTROL SYSTEMS

Electrical Shift Control. An electric shift control is sometimes used in conjunction with the two-speed differential.

The electric shift control system is composed of the *control switch*, the *speedometer adaptor*, the *axle shift unit*, the *circuit breaker*, and the *wiring harness*.

The control switch, usually mounted on the gearshift lever, has two positions — up for high axle range and down for low axle range. When the switch is in either of these positions, a slide-contact, attached to the control switch shaft, completes the circuit between the battery and the motor in the axle shaft unit.

The axle shaft unit is mounted on the differential carrier. This unit contains a reversible electric motor which, when energized, shifts the axle into the desired range through the mechanism contained in the unit.

The speedometer adapter is installed between the transmission and the speedometer, and compensates for variations in the speed of the drive shaft between the high and low ranges of the axle. The adapter is held in the high range by a spring and in low range by an electromagnet.

Air Shift Control. The air-shift type control is composed of the *control switch*, the *speedometer adapter*, a *solenoid-operated air-control valve*, the *axle shift unit*, a *circuit breaker*, and the necessary *wiring* and *hose connections*.

The control switch, usually mounted on the gearshift lever, has two positions — up for high axle range and down for low axle range. When the switch is in either of these positions, a slide-contact attached to the control switch shaft completes the electric circuit between the battery and the solenoid of the air control valve, and to the speedometer adapter.

When the control switch is placed in the high range position, the solenoid is energized and it opens the control valve permitting air pressure to enter the shift unit mounted on the differential carrier. As the supply of air enters the shift-control

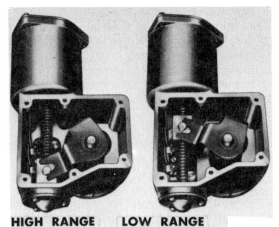

(A) CONTROL SWITCH GEAR SHIFT LEVER

(B) AXLE SHIFT CONTROL POSITIONS

(C) TYPICAL AXLE SHIFT UNIT INSTALLATION

Ford of Canada

Fig. 22-13   Electric-Type Differential Shift Control

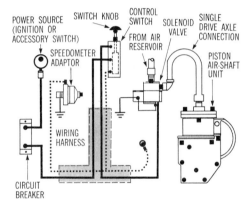

(A) SCHEMATIC OF SYSTEM

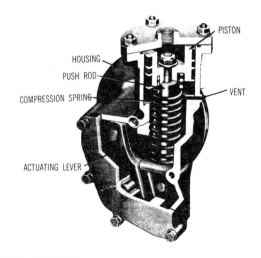

(B) AIR-SHIFT UNIT

Courtesy of General Motors

Fig. 22-14   Air-Shift Type Differential Shift Control

unit cylinder it causes the piston to travel downward against a compression spring, transferring motion through the push rod and actuating lever to the shift fork, shifting the axle into high range. When the control switch is in low range position the air pressure is exhausted from the air shift cylinder, permitting the piston and return spring to return the axle gearing to the low ratio.

The speedometer adapter is installed between the transmission and the speedometer, and compensates for variations in the speed of the driver shaft between the high and low speed ranges of the differential. The adapter is held in high range by a spring and in low range by an electromagnet.

REVIEW QUESTIONS

1. What is the purpose of a differential?
2. State the purpose of the four tapered roller bearings installed in the differential carrier housing.
3. Describe (a) a straddle-mounted (b) an overhung-mounted type of drive pinion.
4. Why are hypoid-type gear sets the most commonly used type today?
5. Explain the ring and pinion-gear set terms (a) hunting (b) nonhunting (c) partial nonhunting.
6. Describe the operation of the differential assembly as the vehicle travels (a) in a straight line (b) round a curve.
7. Explain why the difference in speed between the two rear wheels is in direct proportion to the sharpness of the curve.
8. What is the purpose of a non-slip differential?
9. Explain the operation of (a) the two-pinion types (b) a four-pinion type of nonslip differential.
10. Describe the basic difference in operating principle between the two-pinion and four-pinion types of nonslip differential.
11. Describe briefly a planetary type two-speed differential.
12. Describe one type of differential shift control.

Chapter 23
DIFFERENTIAL SERVICE

23-1 DIFFERENTIAL TERMS

Before discussing the servicing of differentials, several terms must be discussed. The term *drive* indicates that the engine power is driving the car. In the differential it means that the pinion is driving through the ring gear and differential case to the rear wheels. The pinion-shaft end thrust is in a forward direction.

The term *coast*, or *overrun*, indicates that the car's momentum is driving the engine. In the differential it means that the rear wheels are driving the differential case, ring gear, and pinion. The pinion-shaft end thrust is rearward.

The term *float* indicates that the rear-wheel drive and engine drive are equal. Under this driving condition, there is no pinion-shaft end thrust.

The term *bearing-preload* means that the bearing cones are actually forced against the rollers or balls, which in turn are forced against the bearing cups to ensure zero end play at all times. This is accomplished by tightening the pinion-shaft nut or carrier-bearing adjusting nuts to a prescribed tightness, as outlined in the manufacturers' service manual.

In some cases a special spacer is placed between the pinion-shaft bearings. As the pinion nut is torqued, the spacer is squeezed, or crushed, to a shorter length. As the spacer gets shorter, the bearing cones are pulled closer together. When the pinion-bearing nut has been tightened to the torque required to turn the shaft, the bearings have been properly preloaded. As the sleeve is compressed, the pinion-gear shaft also is put under tension. This tension tends to keep the bearing rollers seated under all operating conditions.

Bearing preload is necessary to ensure that the ring and pinion gears are held exactly in proper mesh. There must not be any end play in the pinion or carrier bearings. Zero end play in a shaft supported on two opposed tapered roller or cup and cone bearings means that there must be zero clearance between the cones, cups and the rollers or balls of the bearing.

The term *radial run-out* refers to the amount of sideways motion or wobble a rotating gear may have.

Chrysler Canada Ltd.

Fig. 23-1   Checking for Runout and Zero End Play

To check radial run-out, attach a dial indicator gauge to the gear housing in such a manner that the plunger of the indicator rests against the gear. Observe the readings of the dial indicator gauge as the gear is rotated 360°. The differential gear run-out should not exceed .003".

23-2 GEAR TOOTH NOMENCLATURE

Toe — is the narrow part of a gear tooth

Heel — is the wide part of a gear tooth

Pitch line — is an imaginary line along the side of the tooth at the mid-position

Flank — is the portion of the contact side of the gear tooth below the pitch line

Face — is the portion of the contact side of the gear tooth above the pitch line

Clearance — is the distance between the top of one gear tooth and the bottom of the groove between the teeth of the meshing gear

Backlash — is the space between the pitch line of the contacting faces of two meshing gears

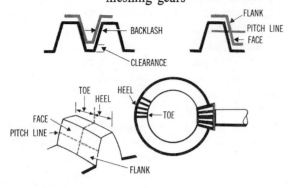

Fig. 23-2   *Gear Tooth Nomenclature*

Chrysler Canada Ltd.

Fig. 23-3   *Measuring Backlash Between Drive Gear and Pinion*

23-3 TROUBLE SHOOTING DIFFERENTIAL NOISES

The most common differential complaint is noise. The differential should not be disassembled until a thorough diagnosis is made of the trouble and the symptoms observed during the operation of the vehicle. Care must be exercised to determine if the noise originates in the differential or if it is caused by the engine, tires, transmission, wheel bearings, or some other part of the vehicle. Some clues as to the cause of the trouble may be obtained by noting whether the noise is produced while the vehicle is being driven straight ahead or on turns only; whether the vehicle is on drive, coast, or float. Gear noises change in pitch and volume as the vehicle speed changes. Backlash may be checked by driving

on a smooth road at about 25 mph and lightly pressing and releasing the accelerator pedal. The backlash is indicated by the slapping noise made each time the accelerator is moved. If the differential has been operated for long periods in an out-of-adjustment condition, permanent damage will result; adjustment will **not** correct noise.

A steady noise on the drive is usually caused by loss of or improper lubricant, or the improper mesh of the crown gear and pinion. This indicates the gears have too heavy a heel contact and corrections may be made by adjusting the ring gear nearer to the drive pinion.

A steady noise on the coast is usually caused by badly scored gear teeth, caused by excessive end play in the pinion bearings, or because of too heavy a toe contact on the gear teeth. Heavy toe contact can be corrected by adjusting the ring gear away from the drive pinion.

A humming noise on both drive and coast is usually caused by worn, chipped, cracked, or scored pinion or carrier bearings. A sharp, metallic thumping sound may be caused by a broken or nicked gear tooth. If the noise is only noticeable while rounding a curve, the trouble is usually because of defective differential case components, such as axle side gear or spider gears.

Do not mistake tire or axle noises for differential noises. Tire noises change as the type of road surface changes; differential noises do not. Axle-bearing noise may be determined by applying the brakes during the road test. This action will take some of the load off the axle bearings. A decrease in noise indicates a defective axle bearing.

23-4 TWO-PINION TYPE

Nonslip differentials can be checked for proper operation by jacking up one rear wheel and attach-

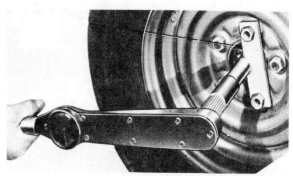

Ford of Canada

Fig. 23-4   *Checking Nonslip Differential Operation*

ing the proper adapter to the end of the axle shaft. Use a torque wrench of at least 200 foot-pound capacity to rotate the axle shaft. Check the torque required to continuously rotate the shaft, and compare the torque required with the manufacturer's specifications. The initial breakaway torque may be higher than the continuous turning torque, but this is normal. The torque required to turn the axle continuously should be even. Any increase or decrease in the amount of torque required indicates slipping or binding of the differential clutches.

Lubricant leakage is another common differential problem. Leakage can be caused by too high a lubricant level, plugged rear-axle vent, worn pinion oil seal, or damaged gaskets.

23-5 DIFFERENTIAL REPAIRS

If, after proper diagnosing of the problem the differential requires disassembly for repairs, it is most important to mark all mating parts so that they may be correctly reassembled. For example, the two halves of the differential case, the pairs of bearing caps, and the adjustors must all be marked. Many of the gears, bearings, etc., are press fits. Therefore, a press or puller should be used to prevent chipping of the hardened parts or distortion of others.

After disassembly clean all parts and carefully inspect for wear, cracks, warpage, etc. Bearing surfaces must be carefully checked and the cup and cone must fit snugly on the shaft or in the housing.

Thoroughly clean the housing of all grease and oil to ensure that no metal chips or abrasive material are left to be circulated by the new lubricant.

During reassembly follow manufacturer's specifications concerning bearing preload, the method of adjusting the gear-tooth contact, run-out, etc.

23-6 GEAR-TOOTH CONTACT

The correct gear-tooth contact is of paramount importance, particularly on hypoid-type gears. Often hypoid gears can be ruined even though they haven't made any noise to indicate trouble. Because of the wiping action between the teeth of this type of gear, they can overheat and pit the contact surface very quickly.

To check gear-tooth contact, paint the gear teeth with a suitable marking compound, such as a paste of red lead and oil. Rotate the drive pinion back and forth until a clear tooth pattern is obtained. Certain types of tooth patterns indicate incorrect adjustment. The type of pattern will depend upon the type of gear set used. The hunting-, non-hunting-, and partial nonhunting-gear sets produce different contact patterns. Generally speaking, a contact drive pattern should be fairly well centered on the tooth face. The coast pattern should also be centered or may show up slightly toward the toe. There should be some clearance between the pattern and the top of the tooth, and there should be no hard lines where pressure is high.

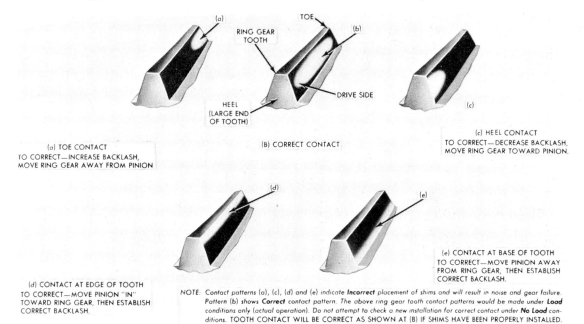

Fig. 23-5   Typical Gear Tooth Contact Patterns

Ford of Canada

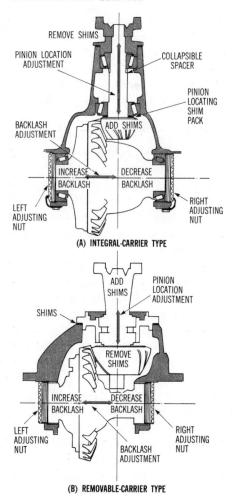

(A) INTEGRAL-CARRIER TYPE

(B) REMOVABLE-CARRIER TYPE

Fig. 23-6   Pinion and Ring Gear Tooth Contact Adjustment

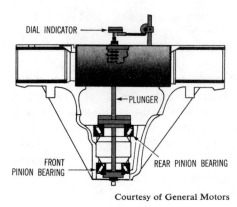

Courtesy of General Motors

Fig. 23-7   Measuring Pinion Depth

Pinion depth is frequently checked by a special depth gauge. Pinion gears used by some manufacturers are marked to indicate the thickness of the shims required for proper depth settings.

Ring-gear adjustments are usually made by backing off one carrier-bearing adjusting nut and tightening the other a similar amount.

The proper backlash setting is also obtained by loosening one carrier-bearing adjusting nut and tightening the other the same amount. Care must be exercised when moving the ring gear during tooth contact or backlash adjustment to maintain the **proper carrier-bearing preload.** It is necessary also to recheck the backlash after **any** pinion adjustment.

Both the drive pinion and the ring gear may be adjusted to give correct gear-tooth patterns. If the pattern shows too much heel contact, adjust the ring gear closer to the pinion gear. Move the ring gear away from the pinion if there is heavy toe contact. Heavy flank contact indicates the pinion must be adjusted away from the ring gear, and heavy face contact means the pinion gear must be moved closer to the ring gear.

Pinion adjustments are usually made by installing or removing shims between the pinion gear and its bearing, or between the housing and the pinion-shaft end plate.

REVIEW QUESTIONS

1. Explain briefly the following differential terms: (a) drive (b) overrun (c) float (d) **bearing preload (e) radial run-out.**
2. Make a sketch to indicate the gear tooth terms: toe, heel, pitch line, face, and flank.
3. State two methods of obtaining bearing preload.
4. List three types of differential noise and give a possible cause of each noise.
5. How can the operation of a nonslip differential be checked?
6. **Why is proper gear-tooth contact important?**
7. Make a sketch of a gear tooth and shade in an area to show proper gear-tooth contact.
8. **How can heavy flank gear-tooth contact be corrected?**
9. How can the proper backlash setting be obtained?

Chapter 24
REAR AXLES

The rear axle must perform several important functions. First, the axle shaft must hold the two rear wheels. Second, it must support the weight of the vehicle. Third, it must transmit driving torque to the wheels. Fourth, it must absorb the side thrust when the vehicle rounds a curve. Fifth, it must absorb the tendency of the wheels to toe-out which results from the vehicle drive — that is, when the wheel traction is applied back to the vehicle to propel it. These forces must be transmitted to the housing either through the axle shaft or directly from the wheel to the housing, depending upon the type of assembly used.

24-1 REAR-AXLE CONSTRUCTION

The rear-axle assembly is made up of several major sections: *housing*, *axle shafts*, and the *differential*.

The axle housing is usually made of stamped steel parts welded together. Some manufacturers use a centre section of cast steel to which are welded the stamped steel side sections.

Two basic types of housing are used: the *banjo type*, a one-piece unit so named because of its resemblance to the musical instrument in appearance; and the *split-housing type*, consisting of one or more pieces, a centre section and two side sections which are bolted together.

Two steel axle shafts are used. These are placed inside the axle housing. The inner ends are supported and driven by splines which fit into the differential axle side gears. The outer ends are supported in the housing by ball or roller axle-shaft bearings. The outer ends of the axle shafts protrude past the end of the housing and form a base to which the wheel hubs are attached.

Two methods of attaching the wheel hubs to the axle shaft are used. In one method a flange is formed as part of the axle shaft and the wheel and brake drum are bolted to this flange. In the other method the end of the axle shaft has been tapered and has had a key-way cut in the taper. The wheel hub is drawn onto the tapered axle end. A key,

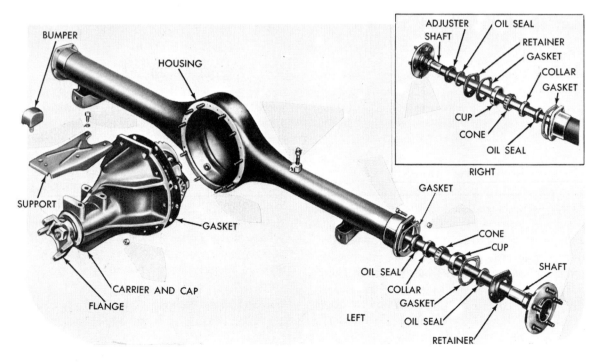

Fig. 24-1 Rear Axle Assembly

Chrysler Canada Ltd.

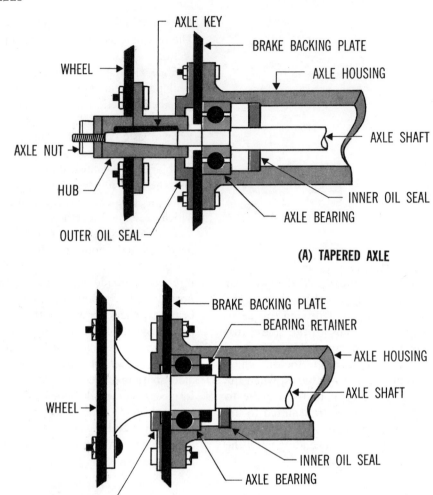

AXLE KEY

WHEEL →

BRAKE BACKING PLATE

AXLE HOUSING

AXLE NUT →

AXLE SHAFT

HUB →

INNER OIL SEAL

AXLE BEARING

OUTER OIL SEAL

(A) TAPERED AXLE

BRAKE BACKING PLATE

BEARING RETAINER

AXLE HOUSING

WHEEL →

AXLE SHAFT

INNER OIL SEAL

AXLE BEARING

OUTER OIL SEAL

Fig. 24-2   Methods of Attaching Wheels and Hubs

(B) FLANGED AXLE

placed between the axle shaft and the hub, prevents the hub from turning. The wheel is bolted to the hub.

24-2 TYPES OF REAR AXLES

Axles may be divided into two types: the *dead axle*, in which the axle is stationary and the wheel rotates; and the *live axle*, in which both the axle shaft and the wheel rotate as a unit. The front wheels of an automobile are mounted on dead axles, while the rear wheels are mounted on live axles. There are three types of live axles: the *semi-floating*, *three-quarter floating*, and the *full-floating*. Each type is identified by the manner in which the outer end of the axle is supported in the axle housing. The inner ends of all axles are attached to the differential or side gears by means of a spline.

Semi-Floating Axle. This type is used in most automobiles. The outer or wheel end of the axle is supported in the axle housing by a single bearing mounted about six inches from the outer end of the axle. With this type of axle the axle shaft not only transmits the driving torque, but resists the bending movements caused by the forward motion of the car and the side thrusts imposed when the vehicle makes a turn. It must carry the entire weight of the vehicle. As a result, a great stress is set up in the axle shaft of the semi-floating rear axle.

Three-Quarter Floating Axle. This type of axle is used on three-quarter and one-ton trucks. In this type of axle the single bearing used to support the outer end of the axle shaft is placed between the outside of the axle housing and the wheel hub. In

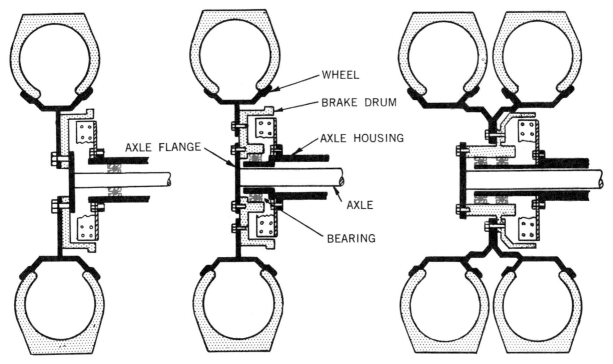

Fig. 24-3   Types of Rear Axles

this location approximately 75% of the vehicle's weight goes directly from the axle housing to the wheel. Therefore the axle shaft only supports about 25% of the vehicle's weight. However, it must still resist the bending movements of the vehicle's forward movement and the side thrust when turns are made and transmit the driving torque. Since the shaft has been relieved of some of the vehicle's weight, heavier loads may be carried without the danger of axle breakage.

Full-Floating Axle. The full-floating axle is used in all large trucks. In this type two tapered roller bearings are used to support the outer end of the axle. These bearings are placed between the outside of the axle housing and the wheel hub, one on the inner and one on the outer edge of the hub. The wheel is mounted on the axle housing in a similar manner to the mounting of a wheel on a dead axle. The weight of the vehicle, the bending movement of the forward motion, and all side thrusts are transferred from the wheel directly to the axle housing through the tapered roller-bearings. The axle shaft has only to transmit the driving torque to the wheels. Only on this type of axle arrangement may the axle shaft be removed without first jacking up the vehicle and removing the wheel. This is a convenient feature for the truck operator.

24-3 REAR AXLE OIL SEALS

In all except the full-floating type of rear axle, the brake backing plate is used to secure the ball or roller axle bearing in the axle housing. The backing plate must be removed before the axle shaft can be removed. The bearings are pressed onto the axle shafts.

Two oil seals, an inner one placed inside the end of the axle housing and an outer one placed on the outside of the brake backing plate, prevent the differential lubricant from leaking.

In the full-floating type axle, a seal mounted on the inner end of the wheel hub prevents leakage of the wheel bearing grease, and a seal around the shaft inside the axle housing prevents differential lubricant leakage.

24-4 INDEPENDENTLY SUSPENDED REAR WHEELS

When the rear wheels are independently suspended, a solid axle housing is not used. Instead the wheels are mounted on swing axles, or axle shafts using two universal joints.

The swing-type axles are usually used in conjunction with rear engine vehicles. The outer end of each axle is supported by the axle bearing which is mounted in a housing attached to the lower control arm. The inner end of each axle shaft is

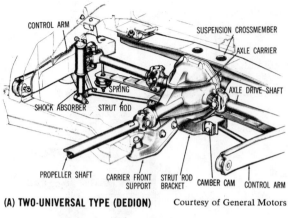

(A) TWO-UNIVERSAL TYPE (DEDION)   Courtesy of General Motors

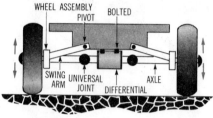

(B) SWING—AXLE TYPE

Fig. 24-4   Independently Suspended Rear Wheel Drive Assemblies

connected to the differential through a slip-type universal joint. This single universal joint accommodates both the up-and-down movement of the wheel and the changes in axle shaft length as the wheel moves up and down. With this type of drive the tread measurement of the rear wheels varies as the wheels move up or down. Also, depending on the angles of the axle supporting members, the rear wheels may require a small amount of either toe-in or toe-out to prevent excessive tire wear.

When two universal joints are used on each drive axle (the *DeDion system*) the differential is attached to a frame crossmember and connected to the front-mounted engine by a conventional type of drive shaft. The short outer axle shaft is supported by two tapered roller bearings in a housing attached to the lower control arm. The wheel flange is attached to the outer end of this short axle and a universal joint is attached to the other end. An axle drive shaft joins this universal joint to the universal joint at the differential. With this type of drive the tread measurement of the rear wheels does not change as the wheels go up and down.

24-5 FRONT-WHEEL DRIVE

Some vehicles are driven by the front wheels instead of the rear, thereby utilizing the weight of the engine to improve traction properties, and at the same time eliminating the drive shaft tunnel from the passenger compartment.

When front-wheel drive is used, the transmission is sometimes placed to one side of the engine instead of behind it and is connected directly to the final drive or differential unit. This places the differential unit in an offset position but above the front wheels. The left drive axle is therefore much shorter than the right. The drive axle is similar in construction to the two universal-joint type used with independently suspended rear wheel drive units. The outer universal joint not only helps compensate for the up-and-down movement of the wheel, but also permits pivoting of the wheel for steering purposes.

Constant velocity-type universal joints are frequently used. The inner joint of each axle has complete flexibility, plus inward and outward movement, to compensate for changes in drive axle length as the wheel moves up and down over bumps; the outer joint has complete flexibility only. The longer right drive axle has a torsional damper mounted midway along its length.

The front driving wheels are mounted on their spindles in a similar manner to the rear wheels in a full-floating rear axle, except that the drive flange is splined to the drive axle shaft instead of being forged as a part of the shaft.

24-6 FOUR-WHEEL DRIVE

The primary purpose of four-wheel drive is to provide additional tractional effort in order to overcome obstacles such as sand, deep mud or snow, or steep grades.

The four-wheel drive vehicle is essentially a conventional vehicle which has been modified to include a driving front-axle assembly, a transfer case to distribute power equally to the front and rear axles, and the required propeller shafts and controls.

The driving front-axle assembly includes an axle housing, the outer ends of which are equipped with steering knuckles and either a conventional type or nonslip type of differential unit. To permit the front

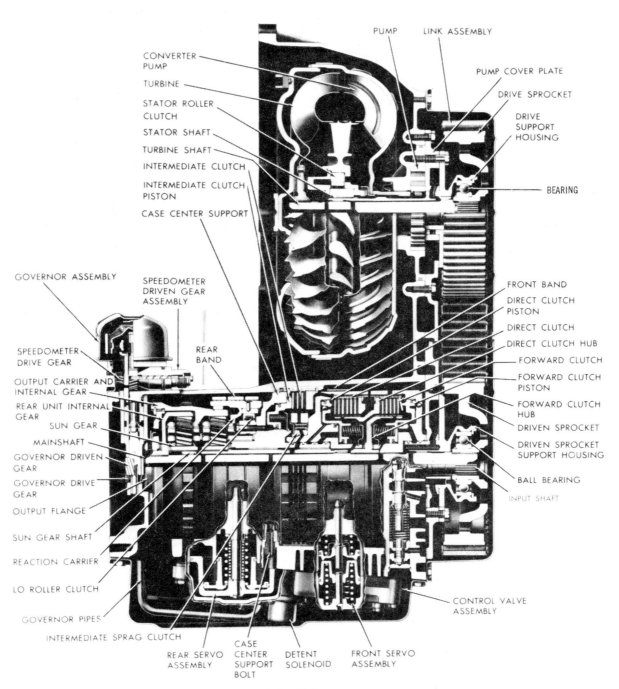

CONVERTER PUMP
TURBINE
STATOR ROLLER CLUTCH
STATOR SHAFT
TURBINE SHAFT
INTERMEDIATE CLUTCH
INTERMEDIATE CLUTCH PISTON
CASE CENTER SUPPORT

PUMP
LINK ASSEMBLY
PUMP COVER PLATE
DRIVE SPROCKET
DRIVE SUPPORT HOUSING
BEARING

GOVERNOR ASSEMBLY
SPEEDOMETER DRIVEN GEAR ASSEMBLY
REAR BAND
SPEEDOMETER DRIVE GEAR
OUTPUT CARRIER AND INTERNAL GEAR
REAR UNIT INTERNAL GEAR
SUN GEAR
MAINSHAFT
GOVERNOR DRIVEN GEAR
GOVERNOR DRIVE GEAR
OUTPUT FLANGE
SUN GEAR SHAFT
REACTION CARRIER
LO ROLLER CLUTCH
GOVERNOR PIPES
INTERMEDIATE SPRAG CLUTCH
REAR SERVO ASSEMBLY
CASE CENTER SUPPORT BOLT
DETENT SOLENOID
FRONT SERVO ASSEMBLY

FRONT BAND
DIRECT CLUTCH PISTON
DIRECT CLUTCH
DIRECT CLUTCH HUB
FORWARD CLUTCH
FORWARD CLUTCH PISTON
FORWARD CLUTCH HUB
DRIVEN SPROCKET
DRIVEN SPROCKET SUPPORT HOUSING
BALL BEARING
INPUT SHAFT
CONTROL VALVE ASSEMBLY

Fig. 24-5   Front-Wheel Drive Automatic Transmission Unit

Courtesy of General Motors

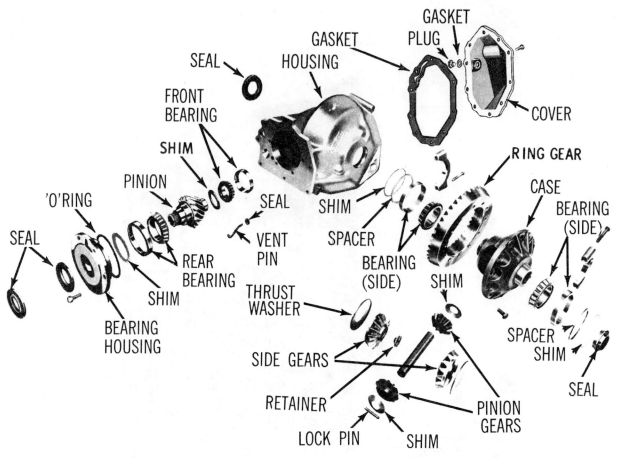

Fig. 24-6   Final Drive and Differential Assembly

Courtesy of General Motors

wheels to be driven as well as steered, the axle **shafts** are **equipped with** yoke-and-trunnion type universal joints between the inner and outer axle. The outer axle is mounted in the steering knuckle. The front wheel hubs are of the full-floating type and the method of attaching the outer axle to the wheel hub is similar to that used in full-floating type rear axles.

Some front driving hubs include a free wheeling device which, when operated manually at each wheel, disengages the front wheels from the axle shafts. This reducing the friction and wear on the axle assembly, differential, and drive line when the vehicle is being operated under normal road conditions.

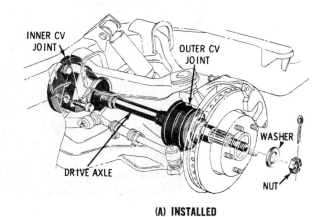

(A) INSTALLED

(B) ASSEMBLY

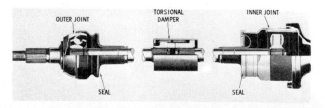

Courtesy of General Motors

Fig. 24-7   Front-Wheel Drive Axle Shafts

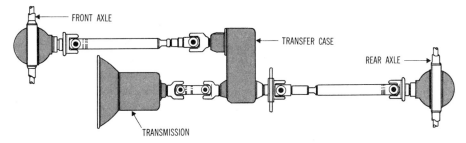

Fig. 24-8   Four-Wheel Drive Line Assembly

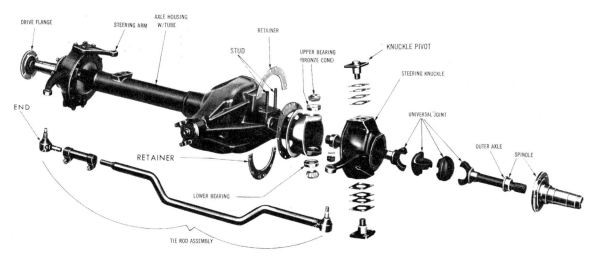

Fig. 24-9   Front Driving Axle Assembly

Chrysler Canada Ltd.

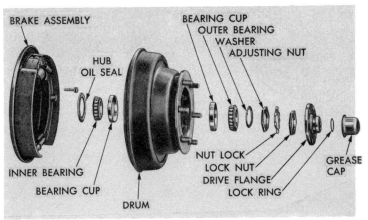

Chrysler Canada Ltd.

Fig. 24-10   Front Drive Hub and Drum Assembly

24-7 REAR-AXLE SERVICE

Rear axles themselves give very little trouble except for defective axle bearings and leaking oil seals or gaskets. However, the axle shafts must be removed to facilitate repairs to the differential unit.

Noise is usually the first indication of rear-axle trouble. Do not mistake axle noise for differential noise, tire, or other noises. Tire noise changes as the type of road surface changes. Differential noise is usually on the drive or coast or when cornering. Axle-bearing noise can usually be determined when applying the brakes during a road test. Applying the brakes will take some of the load off the axle bearings, causing a decrease or change in the noise.

Grabbing brakes are sometimes an indication that the axle oil seals are defective. Any liquid thrown on the inside of the tire could indicate leaking of the axle-shaft seals, too high a lubrication level in the differential, or leaking brake wheel cylinders.

Semi-floating axle-shaft bearings must be replaced by using a press. They should never be hammered into place as this could cause damage to the bearing.

Full-floating rear-axle bearings are packed with grease and adjusted in a similar manner to front-wheel bearings. Two bearing nuts, separated by a lock plate which is bent over the flats of both the inner and outer nuts, are used to lock them in position. The nuts are used to provide the proper wheel bearing adjustment.

REVIEW QUESTIONS

1. List the five important functions of the rear axle.
2. Describe the two basic types of rear-axle housings.
3. What are the two methods of attaching the wheel hubs to the axle shaft?
4. State the path followed by the vehicle's weight as it is transferred from the rear spring to the rear wheel in (a) a semi-floating (b) full-floating type of rear-axle assembly.
5. Describe briefly one type of rear-axle assembly used in conjunction with (a) independent rear-wheel suspension (b) front-wheel drive.
6. **State two common rear-axle problems and give one cause for each.**

UNIT FOUR
The
Engine

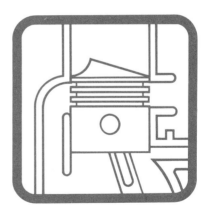

Chapter 25
PRINCIPLES OF ENGINE OPERATION

An engine is composed of a group of related parts assembled in a specific order which will convert energy given off by a fuel into a useful form of mechanical energy or power. This power may be used to propel a vehicle.

Before discussing engine fundamentals, it is necessary to review a few basic scientific definitions.

25-1 DEFINITIONS

Atoms. All substances are made up of atoms. Each atom, regardless of how complex it is, is composed of three basic particles: electrons which have a negative electric charge (indicated by a — sign), protons which have a positive electric charge (indicated by a + sign), and neutrons which have no electric charge. The electrons orbit around the centre, or nucleus, which is made up of protons and neutrons. The electrons are held in orbit around

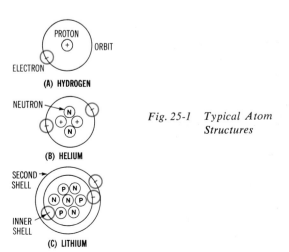

(A) HYDROGEN

(B) HELIUM

(C) LITHIUM

Fig. 25-1 Typical Atom Structures

the proton by the attraction of the opposing electric charges (positive and negative). Most atoms have the same number of electrons as protons. Because of this equality in the number of positive and negative charges, atoms are considered to be electrically neutral.

Elements. Each type of atom in quantity is called an element. The element of Hydrogen (H) is made up of 1 proton in the nucleus and 1 electron orbiting around it; Carbon (C) is made up of 6 protons and 6 neutrons in the nucleus with 6 electrons in orbit; Oxygen (O) is composed of 8 protons and 8 neutrons in the nucleus with 8 electrons in orbit around it. The electrons may orbit around the nucleus in 1, 2, 3 or more shells or rings, each shell or ring being farther away from the nucleus. The number of shells varies according to the type of element. Elements may be catalogued, and they are usually listed in the following manner: the element name such as hydrogen, carbon, and oxygen; its chemical symbol; its atomic number, which is the number of protons in the nucleus; the atomic weight, which is the weight of the element compared to hydrogen, and usually equal to the number of protons plus the number of electrons plus the number of neutrons; and the electron arrangement, which is given in a manner so as to indicate the number of electrons in each shell or ring.

Some elements are highly reactive; others are chemically inert. A reactive element is one that has less than the maximum number of electrons in any shell (2 in the inner, 8 in the second, 18 in the third and 32 in the fourth). An inert element is one that has the maximum electrons in its shell. Oxygen is a reactive element since it has 2 electrons (maximum) in the inner shell but has only 6 electrons (maximum 8) in the outer shell. Helium is an inert element because it has the maximum of 2 electrons in its shell.

Elements frequently combine their atoms to form larger particles called molecules.

Molecule. A molecule is the smallest portion that matter may be divided into and still retain all of the properties of the original matter. A molecule of water, for example, is made up of 2 atoms of hydrogen and 1 atom of oxygen. Its chemical symbol is H_2O. The uniting of the atoms to form molecules is called a *chemical reaction*.

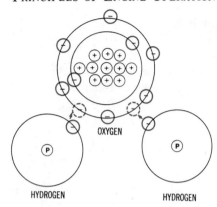

Fig. 25-2   Formation of a Molecule of Water

Heat and Temperature. Heat is the total amount of heat energy contained in a body. Scientifically, it is the rapid motion of the atoms or molecules of a substance. The more rapid the motion, the greater the heat.

Temperature is the word used to represent the degree of hotness or coldness of a body. The intensity of the heat in a body is measured by its temperature.

Combustion. Combustion is a chemical reaction in which oxygen combines with other elements such as hydrogen or carbon. During combustion the rapid movement of the elements during the chemical reaction creates heat. The combustion that takes place within the cylinder of an automobile engine results from the uniting of the oxygen in the air with the hydrogen and carbon of the gasoline to form water and carbon dioxide.

Expansion of Gases. All matter, whether a solid, a liquid, or a gas is made up of molecules which are moving and colliding at high speed. When the molecules collide, they bounce apart and cause the matter to expand. Increasing the temperature of the molecules increases their speed, causing more collisions and expansion — if there is room for expansion. If this expansion is confined, pressure will develop.

When a proper mixture of gasoline vapour and air is confined under pressure within a cylinder, the pressure will generate heat. This heat will cause the mixture to expand and exert a much greater pressure within the cylinder. If this mixture is ignited, instant combustion occurs. As a result, heat, pressure, and the tendency to expand are multiplied many times, thus creating the force which drives the automobile engine.

25-2 LAWS OF GASES

Gas pressure, temperature and volume are related in specific ways as outlined in the various gas laws.
Boyle's Law — states that as long as the temperature of a gas remains the same, the volume of a specific mass of gas is inversely proportional to the pressure.
Charles' Law — states that at constant pressure, the volume of a given mass of gas increases a specific amount for each degree Centigrade of temperature. The specific amount is $\dfrac{1}{273.16}$ of its volume at 0°C.

Heat Flow. It is a basic law of nature that heat flows from hot areas to cold areas. Molecularly, the faster moving molecules of hot areas gradually lose velocity to the slower moving molecules of the cold areas until all are moving at the same speed and both areas are at the same temperature.

Specific Heat. Specific heat refers to the amount of heat required to raise the temperature of a substance a specific number of degrees. Each substance has a different heat or thermal capacity. For example: to raise the temperature of water from 15°C to 16°C it requires one calorie of heat per gram of water; or expressed in British Thermal Units (BTU) it requires one BTU of heat to raise one pound of water from 60°F to 61°F. Water has been given the specific heat rating of 1.000. Gasoline has a specific heat of 0.53.

25-3 ATMOSPHERIC PRESSURE

The layer of air which surrounds the earth is a mixture of gases known as the *atmosphere*. The atmosphere extends all around us and thins gradually into outer space. This means that there are, in effect, many thousands of cubic feet of air piled on top of each other. Each cubic foot of air weighs about .08 of a pound, or 1.25 ounces. The total weight of a column of atmosphere is equal to about 14.7 pounds per square inch (psi) at sea level. The higher the altitude, the less the pressure. For example, on a mountain 10,000 feet above sea level, the pressure is only 12.2 psi.

Since atmospheric pressure surrounds us at all times, it goes unnoticed. All pressure-recording instruments are set to read zero under normal atmospheric pressure. An increase in pressure is recorded as the number of pounds of pressure above 14.7 psi.

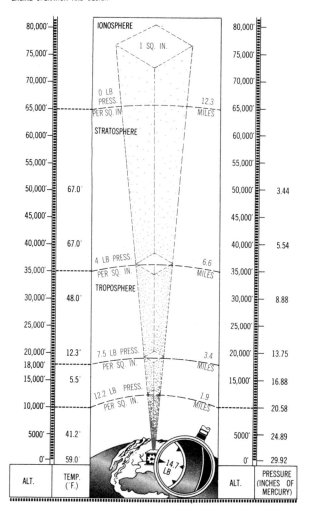

ALT.	TEMP. (°F.)		ALT.	PRESSURE (INCHES OF MERCURY)
80,000'		IONOSPHERE 1 SQ. IN.	80,000'	
75,000'			75,000'	
70,000'		0 LB PRESS. PER SQ. IN.	70,000'	
65,000'		12.3 MILES	65,000'	
60,000'		STRATOSPHERE	60,000'	
55,000'			55,000'	
50,000'	67.0°		50,000'	3.44
45,000'			45,000'	
40,000'	67.0°		40,000'	5.54
35,000'		4 LB PRESS. PER SQ. IN. 6.6 MILES TROPOSPHERE	35,000'	
30,000'	48.0°		30,000'	8.88
25,000'			25,000'	
20,000'	12.3°	7.5 LB PRESS. PER SQ. IN. 3.4 MILES	20,000'	13.75
18,000'				
15,000'	5.5°		15,000'	16.88
10,000'		12.2 LB PRESS. PER SQ. IN. 1.9 MILES	10,000'	20.58
5000'	41.2°		5000'	24.89
0'	59.0°	14.7 LB	0'	29.92

Fig. 25-3   Atmospheric Pressure

Vacuum. When the pressure is less than atmospheric pressure, 14.7 psi, it is called a *partial vacuum*. Vacuum is the absence of air or other matter and is recorded in inches of vacuum. Atmospheric pressure at 14.7 psi is therefore 0 pounds pressure or 0 inches of vacuum. Each pound of pressure less than 14.7 psi is equal to about 2 inches of vacuum.

When the pressure in a sealed container, such as an engine cylinder, is less than atmospheric pressure, a partial vacuum exists in the cylinder. If an opening is made in the container, atmospheric pressure will force air to rush into the container until the pressure inside the container is equal to the atmospheric pressure.

The creation of partial vacuum and pressure differences is the basic scientific principle which contributes to the operation of the engine, fuel pump, carburetor, and other units.

25-4 TRANSFORMING ENERGY

Energy is the capacity or ability to do work. There is a great deal of energy stored in liquid gasoline. This energy is called *potential energy* because it has the ability to do work. In order to do work the potential energy must be released by converting the liquid gasoline to a gas. This gas is compressed and burned, thereby releasing the energy so that it can do work. This working energy, called *kinetic energy*, forces the piston to move downward in the cylinder. The downward motion of the piston can be classified as *mechanical energy*, which can easily be put to useful work.

25-5 ENGINES

There are two popular methods of producing power for land transportation: one is the *internal-combustion* engine which uses gasoline or diesel fuel; and the other is the *external-combustion* engine which burns fuel such as coal or wood to produce steam.

In a steam engine, steam is produced by heating a boiler. It is then forced under great pressure into a cylinder. The pressure of the steam forces a piston to move in the cylinder, causing the engine to operate. The fuel to produce the steam, by heating a boiler, is burned outside the engine. Hence the name external-combustion engine. This type of engine is not used in automobile production today.

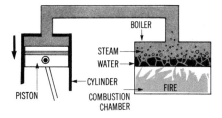

(A) EXTERNAL

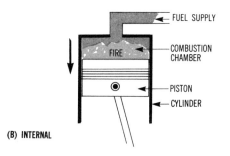

(B) INTERNAL

Fig. 25-4   Types of Combustion Engines

The internal-combustion engine has affected the rapid progress of modern transportation more than any other kind of engine. The development of this engine has been responsible for the widespread use of the bus, automobile, truck, tractor, and airplane. Its popularity is primarily because of the fact it is a self-contained unit, capable of operating for a prolonged period on a relatively small amount of fuel.

25-6 THE INTERNAL COMBUSTION ENGINE

The internal-combustion engine utilizes what is known as a *constant-volume cycle.* A constant volume cycle is one in which the cylinder is filled with fuel and air at atmospheric pressure and then is compressed, without heat being added or subtracted. Heat is then added (combustion of the fuel) at a constant volume to cause a pressure increase which is followed by expansion, again without the addition or subtraction of heat until the charge is exhausted to the atmosphere at a constant volume. Therefore, the operation of an internal-combustion engine depends upon the fact that a gas expands when heated. If the expansion of a heated gas is confined, pressure will develop. The energy required is generated by the fuel — the most popular fuel is gasoline. The potential energy contained in gasoline must be released and converted into another form of energy before it can be applied mechanically.

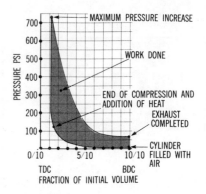

Fig. 25-5   *Typical Pressure-Volume Diagram*

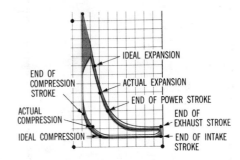

Fig. 25-6   *Comparison of Ideal and Actual Pressure-Volume Diagrams*

When a proper mixture of fuel enters a cylinder and is ignited, instant combustion occurs. The great heat of combustion causes an expansion of the gases in the cylinder which forces the piston to move downward in the cylinder. The downward motion

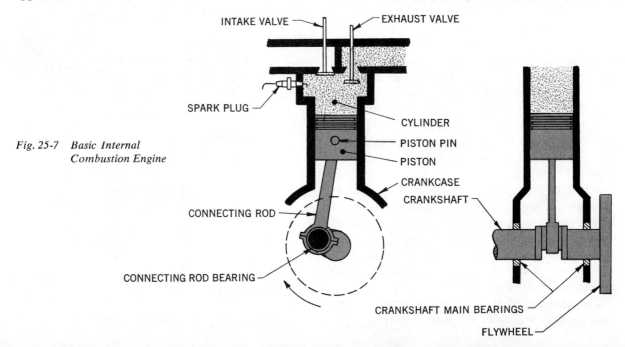

Fig. 25-7   *Basic Internal Combustion Engine*

of the piston can be classified as mechanical energy which can easily be put to useful work.

Internal-combustion engines have many parts, but only the more necessary ones will be considered here. A one-cylinder gasoline engine can be used as an example. The cylinder is open only at the lower end and is fitted with a piston having a solid top, or head. The piston is free to travel up and down in the cylinder but must fit well enough to provide a gas-tight seal. The seal is provided by the *piston rings*. Below the cylinder is the *crankcase* which houses a pair of bearings, called *main bearings*, that support the crankshaft. A *connecting rod*, connecting the piston to the crankshaft, is attached to the piston by a *piston pin*, and to the *crankshaft crank* by a *crankpin*. The connecting rod is free to oscillate or move back and forth on the piston pin, and the crankpin is free to turn in the *connecting-rod bearing*. The *flywheel* is mounted at one end of the crankshaft.

If a charge of gasoline is placed in the chamber at the top of the cylinder and is ignited, the expanding gases formed force the piston down in the cylinder. The action of the piston is referred to as *reciprocating* (up-and-down) action and must be converted into rotary motion to supply a practical form of power. The crankshaft and connecting rod accomplish this conversion of power. The downward motion of the piston causes the connecting rod to turn the crankshaft and flywheel in the main bearings. The momentum attained by the rotating crankshaft and flywheel serves to carry the piston back to its original position if the pressure in the cylinder is released.

25-7 AIR PRESSURE IN ENGINE

In order to produce power from the burning of fuel, it is necessary to (a) secure fuel for combustion (b) prepare the fuel for combustion (c) ignite and burn the fuel to develop the power and (d) remove the burnt and waste products of combustion. In the internal-combustion engine these four operations are accomplished by the changing of the air pressure inside the cylinder.

To understand the operation of the internal-combustion engine it is necessary to make a comparison of the pressures inside the cylinder on each stroke.

Pressure During the Securing of Fuel or Intake Stroke. When the piston on the intake stroke moves

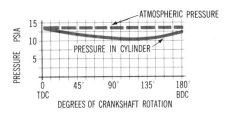

Fig. 25-8   Pressure in Cylinder During Intake Stroke

from Top Dead Centre (TDC) to Bottom Dead Centre (BDC), the volume of the cylinder chamber is enlarged. This enlargement of the cylinder chamber causes a decrease in air pressure which creates a partial vacuum inside the cylinder. Since the movement of air is always from a high-pressure area (atmospheric pressure in this case) to a low-pressure area (partial vacuum in this case), it is possible for atmospheric pressure to force the necessary charge of fuel for combustion into the cylinder.

Pressure during the Preparation or Compression Stroke

As the piston moves from BDC to TDC during the compression stroke, it can readily be seen that the volume of the cylinder decreases. Since the fuel mixture has no means of escape, it is squeezed into a smaller space. This increases the pressure above atmospheric pressure. The name given to this pressure in the automotive-service trade is *compression pressure* and depending on the type of engine, it usually ranges between 120 and 140 psi.

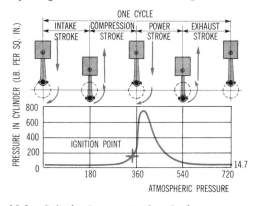

Fig. 25-9   Cylinder Pressure in One Cycle

Pressure during the Combustion or Power Stroke

When the compressed fuel and air mixture is ignited and combustion follows, the burning gases expand rapidly and a much greater pressure is created inside the cylinder. This pressure increase is approximately five times greater than the compression pressure and therefore is between 600 and 700 psi. It is this pressure that pushes the piston down from TDC to BDC in the cylinder and creates the mechanical effort necessary to operate the engine.

Pressure during the Cleaning or Exhaust Stroke

It is necessary to rid the cylinder of the burnt or waste gases. This is accomplished by creating a pressure higher than atmospheric pressure in order to force the waste gases out into the atmosphere. During the exhaust stroke the piston moves from BDC to TDC and the volume of the cylinder is again decreased thus increasing the pressure. This increase in pressure forces the burnt gases out of the cylinder through an exhaust opening.

25-8 THE FOUR-STROKE-CYCLE PRINCIPLE

It has been shown that four operations are required to complete one cycle, namely: the collection of the fuel, the preparation of the fuel, the burning of the fuel, and the disposing of the burnt fuel. Since each of these operations requires one stroke, the internal-combustion engine is said to operate on the *four-stroke-cycle principle*. In the trade the four

strokes are known as the *intake, compression, power*, and *exhaust* strokes.

In order to accomplish these strokes, it is necessary to open and close small openings called *ports* in the upper cylinder chamber. When these ports are open, they allow either fuel to enter the cylinder or burnt gases to escape. To open or close these ports, a *valve* is used. In order to have the ports open at the right time, a valve-operating mechanism is necessary which opens the intake valve only during the intake stroke and opens the exhaust valve only during the exhaust stroke.

The four-stroke-cycle principle can be described as follows:

1. During the intake stroke, the piston travels downward in the cylinder from TDC to BDC, creating a partial vacuum in the cylinder. Atmospheric pressure forces air through the carburetor where it mixes with gasoline and enters the cylinder through the intake manifold and the open intake valve. The exhaust valve remains closed during this stroke and the crankshaft turns through half a revolution.

2. The intake valve closes, the piston moves up from BDC to TDC, and the gas in the cylinder is compressed in the combustion chamber.

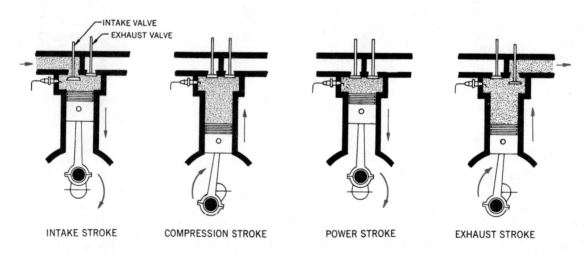

STROKE	DIRECTION	INTAKE VALVE	EXHAUST VALVE	GAS
Intake	Down	Open	Closed	Enters
Compression	Up	Closed	Closed	Compressed
Power	Down	Closed	Closed	Burnt
Exhaust	Up	Closed	Open	Expelled

Fig. 25-10   Four-Stroke-Cycle Principle

This stroke is called the compression stroke. Both valves remain closed throughout this stroke. The crankshaft has now completed one revolution.

3. The fuel is now ready to be ignited. This is accomplished by an electric spark at the spark plug. Combustion immediately takes place and the gas, as it burns, heats and expands instantly. The rapid expansion of the gas greatly increases the pressure in the cylinder and forces the piston down from TDC to BDC, causing the crankshaft to turn. This is known as the power stroke. Both valves remain closed during this stroke.

4. The crankshaft has now rotated one and one-half revolutions, and the cylinder is now filled with burnt gases which must be removed. The exhaust valve opens and the piston moves from BDC to TDC, forcing the burnt gases out of the cylinder. This is known as the exhaust stroke. During this stroke the intake valve remains closed. The crankshaft has completed two revolutions. The piston is at top dead centre and the engine is ready to repeat the cycle of operation.

Since one stroke is equal to one-half a revolution of the crankshaft, two revolutions of the crankshaft are required to complete one four-stroke cycle. In order to keep the engine in continuous operation, the momentum of the flywheel is used to carry the engine through the exhaust, intake, and compression stroke.

Applying the expansion-of-gases principle to the four-stroke cycle, we find that during the compression stroke the molecules that compose the fuel and air mixture have been pushed together. This causes them to bump into the piston and cylinder walls more frequently and results in an increase in pressure. The molecules also collide with each other more frequently. This, in turn, sets them in more rapid motion and increases the temperature. Therefore, when the fuel-air mixture is compressed, both the pressure and the temperature of the mixture increases.

When the compressed fuel-air mixture is ignited, it burns very rapidly. During combustion the hydrocarbon molecules of the gasoline are violently split apart into hydrogen and carbon atoms. The hydrogen and carbon atoms unite with the oxygen in the air. This activity sets the molecules in very rapid motion, increases the temperature to as high as 4500 degrees, and the pressure to 600 psi or more. This pressure of 600 psi or more is applied to each square inch of the piston head. On a 3-inch diameter piston this results in a downward push on the connecting rod of over two tons.

25-9 TWO-STROKE-CYCLE ENGINES

Small two-stroke-cycle engines are used as the power plant for lawn mowers, snow blowers, small garden tractors, and as marine outboard engines. These engines may be *air cooled* (lawn mowers, etc.) or *liquid cooled* (outboards). They are lubricated by mixing the lubricating oil with the gasoline, and have *magneto-type* ignition systems.

The most common type of large two-stroke-cycle engine is the diesel engine, although some large two-stroke-cycle gasoline engines are manufactured for special applications.

In a two-stroke-cycle engine, only two strokes of the piston (one revolution of the crankshaft) are required to complete one cycle. To accomplish the four operations (intake, compression, power, and exhaust) with only two strokes of the piston, both the top and bottom sides of the piston are utilized. The underside of the piston is used to create the low pressure in the crankcase which is required to bring the fuel and air mixture in through the carburetor, and to partially compress this fuel and air mixture in the crankcase just before the piston uncovers the intake port.

Several types of two-stroke-cycle engines have been produced: the two-port type, the three-port type, and the exhaust-valve type, all of which require sealed crankcases; and a type which uses a blower or supercharger to produce the initial pressure to force the fuel and air, or air only (diesels) into the cylinder. The latter type does not require a sealed crankcase.

25-10 CONSTRUCTION

Crankcase. In order to utilize the underside of the piston, the two-stroke-cycle engine must have an enclosed and air-tight crankcase with separate sealed compartments for each cylinder.

The two-port-type engine requires a *reed* or *flapper* type valve mounted between the carburetor and the crankcase. This valve opens to permit the entrance of fuel and air into the crankcase when the pressure in the crankcase is less than atmospheric pressure and closes when the crankcase pressure is above atmospheric pressure.

In the three-port-type engine, the carburetor to crankcase passageway is located at the bottom of the cylinder. The piston skirt acts as a valve which uncovers and covers the port that admits the fuel-air mixture into the crankcase. This occurs when the crankcase pressure is lower than atmospheric pressure.

Provision for the main bearing supports in the crankcase is similar to that of the four-stroke-cycle engine.

Cylinder Block, Cylinder Head, Piston and Rod Assembly. The cylinder block may be cast separately or may be an integral part of the cylinder head. It may consist of a steel cylinder assembly and a separate cast head. The assembly may be made of cast iron, aluminum, or die cast alloys, and is designed to include the cooling fins

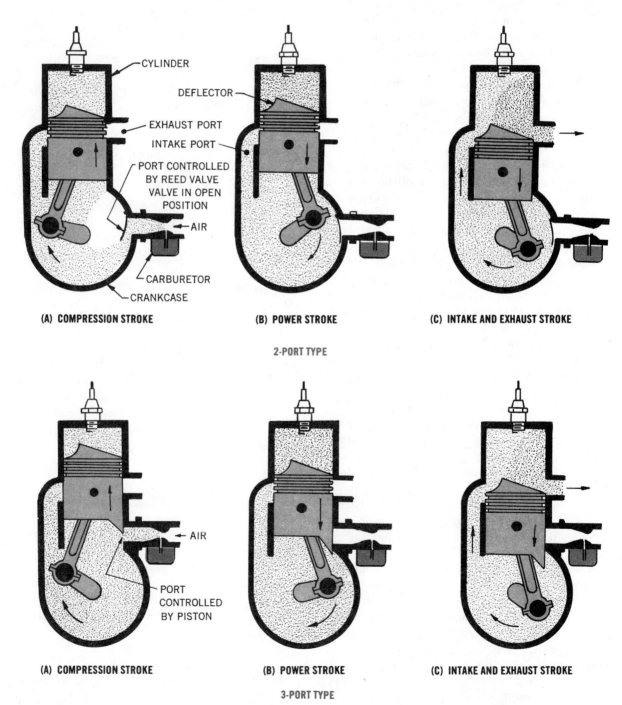

Fig. 25-11   *Two-Stroke-Cycle Principle*

or water jackets and the inlet transfer passageway.

Instead of using valves to control the entry of the fuel-air mixtures into the cylinder, or the exhaust gases from leaving the cylinder, most two-stroke-cycle engines use *ports* (holes in the cylinder walls). The ports are covered and uncovered as the piston travels up and down in the cylinder and are located on opposite sides of the cylinder just above BDC of the piston travel. The exhaust port is located higher up in the cylinder than the intake port so that it will be uncovered first on the exhaust stroke.

When exhaust ports are used, a *deflector*, formed on the inlet side of the piston head, diverts the fresh fuel-air mixture up into the cylinder while the exhaust gases are leaving the cylinder on the opposite side.

Some two-stroke-cycle engines use one or two exhaust valves located in the cylinder head, instead of the cylinder wall port. This valve is operated and timed by a camshaft and timing gears.

The piston, piston rings, piston pins, and connecting rods are similar to those used in four-stroke-cycle engines.

Crankshaft. The crankshaft is similar in design to the four-stroke-cycle type except that it must include machined surfaces for the crankcase seals. These seals are placed around the crankshaft between each cylinder and at each end and form an air-tight seal for each crankcase compartment.

The magneto cam is mounted on one end of the shaft, and the drive pulley or coupling on the other.

25-11 OPERATING CYCLE (TWO-PORT TYPE)

Crankcase Action. As the piston is moved from BDC to TDC it creates a partial vacuum in the

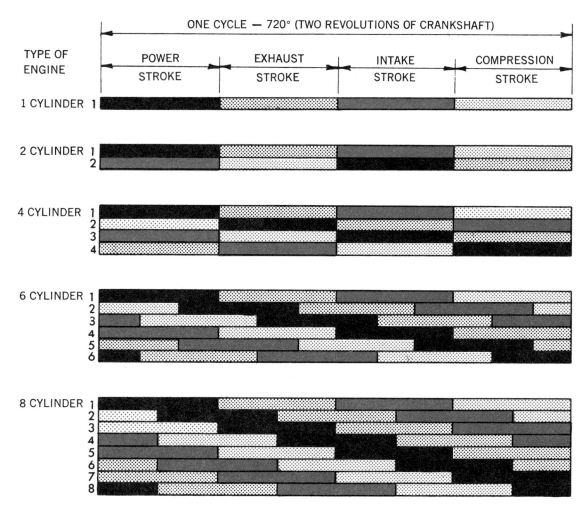

Fig. 25-12   Power Stroke Chart

crankcase, causing the crankcase to carburetor valve to open and admit a charge of fuel-air mixture. When the piston travels from TDC to BDC, the fuel-air mixture in the crankcase is slightly compressed. Near the end of the stroke, the upper edge of the piston uncovers the intake port, and the compressed fuel-air mixture in the cylinder passes through the passageway into the cylinder.

Cylinder Action. As the piston is moved from BDC to TDC, first the inlet port, then the exhaust are covered by the piston, and the fuel-air mixture is compressed. Near the end of the compression stroke, the mixture is ignited, causing combustion. The resulting pressure forces the piston from TDC to BDC to turn the crankshaft and develop power. Near the end of the power stroke, the piston uncovers the exhaust port and the burnt gases escape. As the piston moves further down in the cylinder, it uncovers the inlet port to admit the next charge of fuel-air mixture.

Since the actions above and below the piston are simultaneous, the four operations of intake, compression, power, and exhaust are completed in one revolution of the crankshaft.

25-12 MULTICYLINDER ENGINES

The simple one-cylinder engine that has been described would not be satisfactory for operation of the modern motor vehicle. Nowadays most motor vehicles use either a four-cylinder, six-cylinder, or eight-cylinder engine. The power strokes or multicylinder engines are so timed that they occur at intervals of 180° of crankshaft rotation in a four-cylinder, 120° in a six-cylinder, and 90° in an eight-cylinder engine.

The greater the number of cylinders an engine has, the shorter the interval between the power strokes. In six-cylinder and eight-cylinder engines the second power stroke starts before the first power stroke finishes. This overlap of power strokes is known as *power lap*.

Regardless of the number of cylinders in an engine, each cylinder operates as a single self-contained unit, following the basic four-stroke-cycle principle. Each unit is connected to a common crankshaft and uses a common fuel supply, exhaust and ignition system.

REVIEW QUESTIONS

1. What is the difference between an atom and a molecule?
2. How is pressure developed because of the expansion of gases?
3. Why is atmospheric pressure at sea level approximately 14.7 psi?
4. If a vacuum gauge read 12″ of vacuum, what would the equivalent pressure be in psi?
5. Explain each of the following terms: (a) energy (b) potential energy (c) kinetic energy.
6. State the scientific law upon which the operation of the internal combustion engine depends.
7. Make a sketch of a simple one-cylinder engine and label the important parts.
8. State the four operations necessary in order to produce power from the burning of fuel.
9. How are the four operations mentioned in question 8 accomplished?
10. Describe in detail each stroke of the four-stroke cycle principle. Include the purpose of the stroke, the cylinder pressure during the stroke, direction of movement of the piston, and the valve action for each stroke.
11. How many degrees and revolutions does the crankshaft make during (a) one cycle (b) one stroke?
12. Describe the actions that take place (a) above (b) below the piston as the piston moves downward in a two-port two-stroke-cycle engine.
13. **How many degrees of crankshaft rotation is required for one cycle of a two-stroke-cycle engine?**
14. Why must a two-port two-cycle engine have a sealed crankcase?
15. What are reed valves? Why are they necessary?
16. State the number of degrees of crankshaft rotation between the power strokes of (a) four-cylinder (b) six-cylinder (c) eight-cylinder engines.

Chapter 26
ENGINE DEFINITIONS, MEASUREMENTS, AND PERFORMANCE

In order to understand the operation of an internal-combustion engine, it is necessary to become familiar with a number of terms which describe its mechanical, operational, and power features.

26-1 DEFINITIONS

Top Dead Centre (TDC) is the farthest point of upward travel of the piston in its cylinder.

Bottom Dead Centre (BDC) is the lowest point of downward travel of the piston in the cylinder.

Stroke is the distance in inches travelled by the piston in its movement from top to bottom dead centres. The piston makes a stroke while travelling downward and another stroke while travelling upwards. One downward plus one upward stroke of the piston equals one revolution of the crankshaft.

Bore is the inside diameter of the cylinder, usually measured in inches.

Relationship of Bore and Stroke. Early automotive engines were designed with a small bore and a long stroke. This type of construction had high friction losses because of the length of the stroke, and greater inertia and centrifugal loads on the crankshaft bearings.

In the modern automobile engine the bore is usually larger than the stroke and it is referred to as an "oversquare" engine. A "square" engine is one in which the bore and stroke measurements are the same. The oversquare engine not only reduces frictional losses and reduces inertia and centrifugal forces; it also permits lower engine hood body design.

Throw is the distance in inches from the centre of the crankshaft main bearing to the centre of the crankpin, or connecting-rod bearing. The length of the throw is equal to one-half of the stroke.

26-2 MEASUREMENTS

Revolutions Per Minute (rpm) is the unit of measurement used to determine the speed of rotating parts. For example, if an engine is operating at 2,000 rpm, it means that the crankshaft is rotating 2,000 times in each minute of engine operation.

Clearance Volume (CV) for one cylinder is the

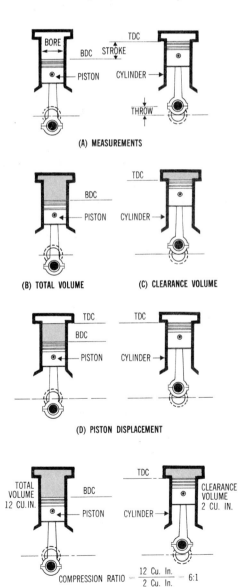

(A) MEASUREMENTS

(B) TOTAL VOLUME

(C) CLEARANCE VOLUME

(D) PISTON DISPLACEMENT

COMPRESSION RATIO $= \dfrac{12 \text{ Cu. In.}}{2 \text{ Cu. In.}} = 6:1$

(E) COMPRESSION RATIO

Fig. 26-1   Engine Terms

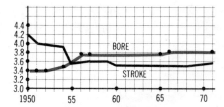

Fig. 26-2   Comparison of Bore and Stroke Measurements

volume of the combustion chamber above the piston when the piston is at TDC.

Piston Displacement (PD) for one cylinder refers to the volume that the piston displaces as it travels from BDC to TDC and is expressed in cubic inches or cubic centimeters. To calculate PD for one cylinder, the following formula is used:

$$PD = \pi \times r^2 \times stroke$$

where r = one half of the bore diameter.
Total Piston Displacement for an engine = PD for one cylinder × number of cylinders.

Total Volume (TV) of a cylinder is the volume above the piston when the piston is at BDC and is equal to Clearance Volume plus Piston Displacement.

Compression Ratio (CR) for a cylinder is the ratio of the Total Volume of a cylinder to the Clearance Volume. It is calculated by dividing the Total Volume by the Clearance Volume and is expressed as a ratio (i.e., 10 to 1).

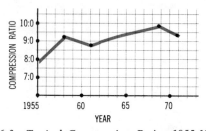

Fig. 26-3   Typical Compression Ratios 1955-1970

Volumetric Efficiency (VE) is the ratio between the amount of fuel-air mixture that enters the cylinder on the intake stroke and the amount required to completely fill the cylinder to atmospheric pressure. It is expressed as a percentage (e.g., 80%). A volumetric efficiency of 80% is considered good for an engine running at high speeds.

Work is said to be done when a force, overcoming a resistance, moves through a distance. The unit of work is the *foot-pound* (ft lb) and is the amount of work done when a force overcomes a resistance

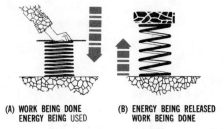

(A) WORK BEING DONE
ENERGY BEING USED

(B) ENERGY BEING RELEASED
WORK BEING DONE

Fig. 26-4   Work and Energy

of one pound, while moving through a distance of one foot.

Energy is the capacity or ability to do work. The unit of energy is the *foot-pound*. There are many kinds of energy, such as mechanical, heat, chemical, and electrical.

Mechanical energy may also be subdivided into (a) *potential* energy; energy of position (b) *kinetic* energy; energy of motion.

Inertia is the property of matter by which it will remain at rest, or in uniform motion in the same straight line or direction unless acted upon by some external force.

Torque is turning or twisting effort that may or may not result in motion. Torque is measured in pound-feet, (lb ft) and calculated by multiplying the force applied by the distance between the centre and the point of force application.

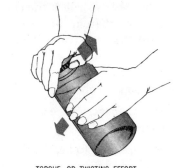

TORQUE, OR TWISTING EFFORT

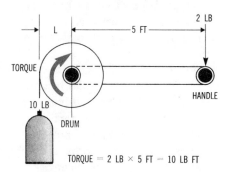

TORQUE = 2 LB × 5 FT = 10 LB FT

Fig. 26-5   Torque

Friction is the resistance to relative motion between two bodies in contact. There are several types of friction:

(a) *Dry friction* is the relative resistance to movement of two dry objects, such as when the brake shoes are pressed against the brake drum, or when the clutch pressure plate forces the clutch friction disc against the flywheel.

(b) *Greasy friction* is the friction between two objects separated by a thin layer of lubricant. This thin layer of lubricant is not sufficient to prevent resistance and wear.

(c) *Viscous friction* is the friction or resistance to relative motion between adjacent layers of a liquid. The thicker the liquid, the greater the viscous friction.

Power is the rate of doing work. The unit of measurement is foot-pounds per minute or foot-pounds per second.

Horsepower (hp) is the unit of power equal to the lifting of 33,000 pounds one foot in one minute.

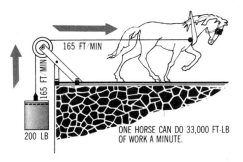

Fig. 26-6 Horsepower

Indicated Horsepower (ihp) is a theoretical power rating based on the pressure produced in the cylinder by combustion. Ihp does not take into consideration the power lost in overcoming engine friction. Therefore, ihp is always greater than bhp (brake horsepower).

To calculate ihp, it is necessary to use an oscilloscope (a special indicating device) to determine the pressures in the cylinder during the entire cycle. (See Fig. 41-48.) The *Mean effective Pressure* (MEP) is calculated by determining the average pressure during the power stroke and subtracting from it the average pressure during the other three strokes. The MEP is the pressure that in effect forces the piston down on the power stroke. To determine ihp the following formula is used:

$$ihp = \frac{PLANK}{33,000}$$

where P = mean effective pressure in psi
L = length of stroke in feet
A = area of cylinder in square inches
N = number of power strokes per minute (rpm ÷ 2)
K = number of cylinders

Friction Horsepower (fhp) is the amount of horsepower required to overcome the friction created by the engine moving parts. Fhp can only be determined by driving the engine by an electric motor at various speeds. During the test the engine must be at normal operating temperatures, with no fuel in the carburetor, and the throttle wide open.

A typical fhp curve is illustrated in Fig. 26-7. The higher the engine rpm, the greater the losses. About 75% of fhp is created between the piston rings and the cylinder walls; the other 25% is created between all other moving parts.

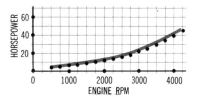

Fig. 26-7 Typical Frictional Horsepower Diagram

Brake Horsepower (bhp) of an engine is the horsepower delivered to the flywheel and is measured by either a *Prony Brake* or a *Dynamometer*. The Prony Brake is an adjustable friction braking device mounted on the flywheel with a lever that rests on the platform of a scale. As the braking device is tightened and the throttle valve is open at the same time to maintain engine speed, the lever produces a greater pressure on the scale. When the throttle valve is wide open, maximum engine power is being developed.

The Brake Horsepower may be determined by using the following formula:

$$Brake\ hp = \frac{2\pi \times r \times w \times rpm}{33,000}$$

where: r = length of arm in feet
w = load on the scale in pounds
rpm = engine speed

When a Dynamometer is used to measure brake horsepower, the engine drives a generator, and the amount of electric energy produced can be calculated to determine the Brake Horsepower of the engine.

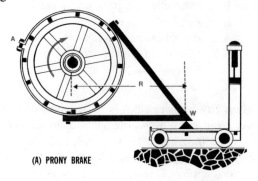

(A) PRONY BRAKE

DYNAMOMETER WITH HIGH AND LOW INERTIA CAPABILITY

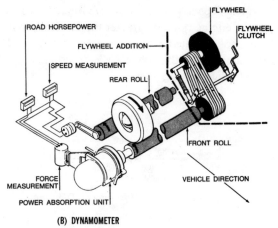

(B) DYNAMOMETER

Fig. 26-8   Horsepower Measuring Devices

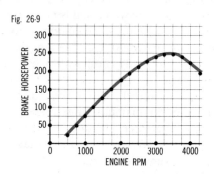

Fig. 26-9   Typical Brake Horsepower Diagram

26-3 PERFORMANCE

Relating bhp, ihp, and fhp

Indicated Horsepower (the theoretical power produced by the engine) minus Friction Horsepower (the engine power required to overcome the friction of the engine moving parts) equals Brake Horsepower. Brake Horsepower is the net horse-

power delivered by the engine that is available to do work.

SAE Horsepower, or *Taxable Horsepower*, which is the **Society of Automotive Engineers' rating** of engines, is used to compare engines according to the number and diameter of the cylinders. The following formula is used to compute SAE Horsepower:

$$\text{SAE hp} = \frac{(\text{bore of cylinder})^2 \times \text{number of cylinders}}{2.5}$$

Engine Torque is the measurement of the turning effort of the engine. The torque is produced by the combustion and expanding of the gases pushing down on the piston and connecting rod to the throw of the crankshaft. The higher the combustion pressures, the greater the engine torque. Engine torque is affected by compression ratio and volumetric efficiency. Engine torque is usually measured along with brake horsepower on a Dynamometer.

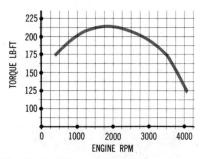

Fig. 26-10   Typical Torque Diagram

Brake Horsepower Versus Torque. The torque an engine develops is affected by two factors: volumetric efficiency and compression ratio. At low and intermediate engine speeds, the cylinders have time to fill up with fuel-and-air mixture. At higher engine speeds, there is not enough time for the cylinder to fill with fuel-and-air mixture; therefore, the volumetric efficiency decreases. A reduction in volumetric efficiency results in a proportional reduction in compression pressure, combustion pressure, and pressure applied to the throw of the crankshaft. Thus, engine torque is reduced.

Increasing or decreasing the compression ratio of an engine causes proportional changes in compression, combustion and crank-throw pressures, thereby increasing or decreasing engine torque.

Bhp, on the other hand, increases proportionately as engine speed increases. Even though, as

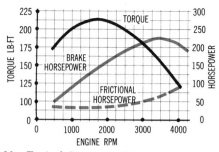

Fig. 26-11   *Typical Composite Diagram*

speed increases, the pressure produced by each power stroke decreases, the increase in the number of power strokes per minute more than compensates for the pressure loss and results in an increase in brake horsepower. However, at very high engine rpm the increase in the number of power strokes per minute is not sufficient to overcome the loss in pressure, because of decreased volumetric efficiency and the increase in fhp. As a result bhp also drops off.

Engine Efficiency is the relationship between the potential energy supplied and the amount of work done. Gasoline contains a certain amount of potential energy, or ability to do work. The amount of work to be done is the movement of the vehicle along the road. During each step of the process of converting gasoline to mechanical energy to rotate the wheels of the vehicle, energy is lost. These losses occur in many ways, such as: mechanical, thermal, engine accessories, drive-line friction, rolling resistance, air resistance, and acceleration.

Mechanical losses can be calculated by dividing bhp by ihp to find mechanical efficiency. The loss is the amount of potential energy used to overcome the friction of the engine (fhp).

Thermal losses are heat losses. Since it is heat that creates the pressure of the power stroke, any loss of heat results in a decrease in power. Gasoline contains a quantity of heat. If all of this heat were used to produce pressure, the thermal efficiency of the engine would be 100%. However, some of the

heat produced by combustion is carried away by the cooling system. More heat is lost with the exhaust gases, since they are still hot when they leave the engine. The remaining heat is the heat that causes the gases to expand to produce the pressure which develops the power. About 35% of the heat is lost in cooling the water and oil, and approximately another 35% of the heat is lost in the exhaust gases. The remaining 30% is all of the potential heat energy that is used to develop power.

The *brake thermal efficiency* may be computed by using the following formula:

$$\text{Brake Thermal Efficiency} = \frac{\text{bhp} \times 33,000}{778 \times \dfrac{\text{fuel heat}}{\text{value}} \times \dfrac{\text{weight of fuel}}{\text{burned per minute}}}$$

778 is Joule's equivalent; the fuel heat (calorific) value is based on the British Thermal Units (Btu's per pound.)

Engine accessories that are necessary for the continuous operation of the engine, such as the fuel pump, fan, generator, or alternator, water pump, and oil pump absorb some of the power from the engine and can reduce its efficiency.

Drive-line friction and automatic-transmission components absorb some engine power, thereby reducing the efficiency.

Rolling resistance between the tires and the road reduces the efficiency. Oversized, overloaded, and underinflated tires, plus irregularities in the road affect rolling resistance.

Air resistance, the resistance air offers to the passage of objects through it, reduces the efficiency. As a vehicle's speed increases so does its air resistance. The top speed of a vehicle is limited by the engine's ability to overcome the air resistance. The more streamlined the vehicle's body, the higher the top speed, with a given engine power.

During acceleration, more power is required to increase the vehicle's speed than is required to maintain a constant speed. The more frequent or faster the vehicle is accelerated, the less the efficiency.

As a result of all the various losses in efficiency, only about 15% of the potential energy in a gallon of gasoline is used to drive the vehicle along the road.

The poorer the mechanical condition of the engine, its accessories, and other mechanical com-

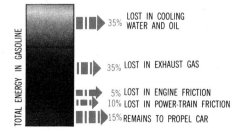

Fig. 26-12   *Typical Energy Losses*

ponents of the vehicle, the lower the overall efficiency. It is the job of the automotive service man to maintain the mechanical condition of the vehicle in order to obtain as high an overall efficiency as possible.

26-4 METHODS OF ENGINE HORSEPOWER RATING

An engine's horsepower may be rated three ways: gross or brake horsepower, net horsepower, or road horsepower.

Gross or Brake Horsepower. For many years gross or brake horsepower has been the method generally used by manufacturers to rate their various engines. This method of rating was not realistic but was the most favourable power figure for the engine and was used in advertising.

Gross or brake horsepower ratings are taken when the engine is mounted on a test stand in a laboratory. The engine has had all of the accessories removed except those actually needed to make it run, such as flywheel, fuel and oil pumps, etc. Coolant and electrical energy are generally provided from an outside source.

A sample engine rated under this system could have 350 horsepower.

Net Horsepower. This is a more realistic method of rating engine horsepower. According to the new SAE-245 standard, the engine must be tested in the form that it is used in the vehicle. Net horsepower ratings of the engine are taken with the engine mounted on a test stand. The engine is complete with operating accessories such as carburetor air cleaner, radiator, fan, water pump, alternator, starter, full exhaust system, and exhaust-emission components. The engine is under considerable load from these engine driven accessories but still has a fairly high horsepower rating.

The 350 horsepower engine tested under brake horsepower ratings could be rated as a 250 horsepower engine under the net horsepower rating system.

Road Horsepower. This is the most realistic method of rating an engine's power. Road horsepower is the amount of horsepower available at the driving wheels, either front or rear, after the engine has been installed in the vehicle. The horsepower produced by the engine is dissipated by many friction areas such as the transmission, differential, drive shaft, rear axle, tires and wheels. The weight of the vehicle also contributes to a loss of horsepower at the point where the tires meet the road.

Power accessories such as the air conditioning compressor, the power steering pump, etc., reduce the available horsepower still further.

The 350 brake horsepower engine with a net horsepower rating of 250 horsepower could have only a road horsepower rating of 150 horsepower.

It should be noted that engine torque ratings are frequently considered as a more accurate indicator of an engine's performance potential. Vehicle acceleration in any gear closely parallels the torque curve of the engine and is a more consistent power indicator than horsepower ratings.

REVIEW QUESTIONS

1. By means of sketches, illustrate the following engine terms: (a) TDC (b) BDC (c) stroke (d) throw (e) bore.
2. Calculate the piston displacement for a six-cylinder engine with a bore of 3″ and a stroke of 3.5″.
3. Calculate the compression ratio of an engine with a bore of 4 in., a stroke of 4 in., and a clearance volume of 6 cu. in.
4. Using a compression ratio of 10 to 1, calculate the compression pressure in a cylinder having the following volumetric efficiency: (a) 100% (b) 80% (c) 60% (d) 40%.
5. Define the following terms: (a) work (b) torque. State the unit of measurement in each case.
6. Explain each of the following horsepower ratings: (a) indicated horsepower (b) brake horsepower (c) SAE horsepower.
7. Calculate the friction horsepower of an engine that when tested for brake horsepower gave the following readings: 90 lb ft of torque on the end of a 4 ft arm at a speed of 5,500 rpm. The indicated horsepower information for the engine is: mean effective pressure 330 psi, bore 4 in., stroke 4 in., number of cylinders 8, engine speed 3,000 rpm.
8. What two factors affect engine torque?
9. Explain why only 15% of the potential energy contained in a gallon of gasoline is all the energy that is used to move the vehicle along the road.
10. Name and give a brief description of the most realistic method of rating engine power.

Chapter 27
TYPES OF ENGINES

The popular motor vehicle engine may be classified in many different ways:

1. By the number of cylinders—2, 4, 6 or 8
2. By the arrangement of cylinders—in line, V, horizontal, or radial
3. By the types of valve arrangement—I, L, T, or F (the I arrangement being the most common today)
4. By the type of cooling system—air or liquid
5. By the type of cycle—2 or 4 strokes
6. By the type of fuel used—gasoline or diesel

Before discussing the design of the various types of engines the term *firing order* should be defined.

Firing Order is the order in which the cylinders deliver their power. Firing orders are given from front and rear. The cylinders must not fire in sequence (1, 2, 3, 4, etc.) as this would set up a rocking action within the engine similar to a small boat riding over waves. The firing order distributes the power strokes, alternating from one end of the crankshaft to the other. Each type of cylinder arrangement has a different firing order. Some of the common firing orders will be given for each type of engine discussed.

27-1 NUMBER AND ARRANGEMENT OF CYLINDERS

27-2 CYLINDER NUMBERING
The numbering of the cylinders varies, depending on the manufacturer. See Fig. 27-1.

27-3 TWO-CYLINDER ENGINES
Some small imported vehicles use a two-cylinder, horizontally opposed, I-head engine. The crankshaft and camshaft are placed in the crankcase which is between the two cylinders.

27-4 FOUR-CYLINDER IN-LINE ENGINES
Four-cylinder in-line engines have the cylinders cast vertically in a single row in the engine block. The crankshaft is supported by three or four main bearings, and the throws are set 180° apart, with the throws for 1 and 4 cylinders in one position and the throws for 2 and 3 cylinders in the other. The camshaft is designed to produce a firing order of either 1, 3, 4, 2, or 1, 2, 4, 3. Either I-head or L-head valve arrangements may be used.

27-5 SIX-CYLINDER IN-LINE ENGINES
Six-cylinder in-line engines have the cylinders cast in the engine block in a single row. The cylinders are placed either vertically or at an angle of 30° from the vertical (slant). The crankshaft, supported by three or more main bearings, has the throws

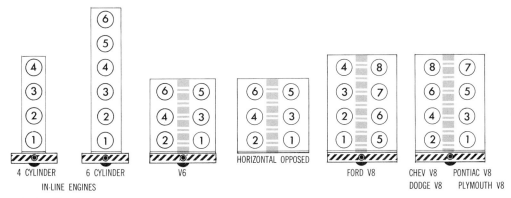

Fig. 27-1   Cylinder Numbering

225

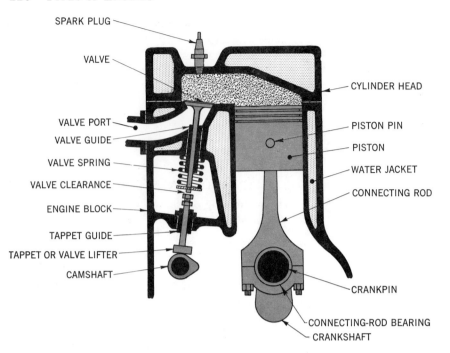

SPARK PLUG

VALVE

CYLINDER HEAD

VALVE PORT
VALVE GUIDE

PISTON PIN
PISTON

VALVE SPRING

WATER JACKET

VALVE CLEARANCE

CONNECTING ROD

ENGINE BLOCK

TAPPET GUIDE

TAPPET OR VALVE LIFTER

CAMSHAFT

CRANKPIN

CONNECTING-ROD BEARING
CRANKSHAFT

Fig. 27-2   L-Head Engine

placed 120° apart, with the throws for 1 and 6 cylinders in one position, 2 and 5 in the second position, and 3 and 4 in the third position. The camshaft is designed to produce a firing order, the most common being 1, 5, 3, 6, 2, 4. Either L-head or I-head valve arrangements may be used.

27-6 FOUR- AND SIX-CYLINDER HORIZONTALLY OPPOSED ENGINES (PANCAKE)

Four- and six-cylinder horizontally opposed engines have the cylinders in two rows, 180° apart. The cylinders are individual cast-iron sleeves and are attached in groups of two or three to an aluminum cylinder head. The heads contain integral valve ports, combustion chambers, and valves for each cylinder. The cylinders are attached to each side of the aluminum crankcase, which can be split into halves. The crankcase supports the camshaft and the crankshaft, the latter being mounted on four main bearings. The crankshaft throws and the camshaft are arranged to give a firing order of 1, 4, 3, 2 for the four-cylinder engine and 1, 4, 5, 2, 3, 6 for the six-cylinder engine.

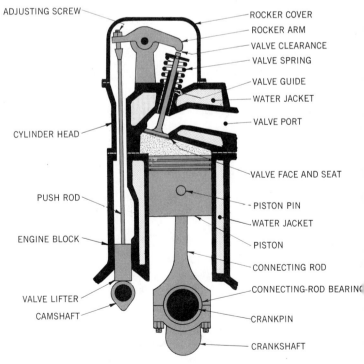

ADJUSTING SCREW

ROCKER COVER
ROCKER ARM
VALVE CLEARANCE
VALVE SPRING
VALVE GUIDE
WATER JACKET
VALVE PORT

CYLINDER HEAD

VALVE FACE AND SEAT

PUSH ROD

PISTON PIN
WATER JACKET

ENGINE BLOCK

PISTON

CONNECTING ROD

CONNECTING-ROD BEARING

VALVE LIFTER

CAMSHAFT

CRANKPIN

CRANKSHAFT

Fig. 27-3   I-Head Engine

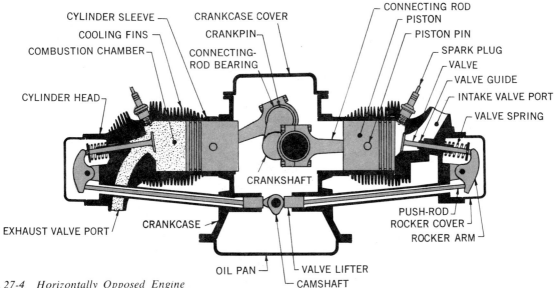

CYLINDER SLEEVE
COOLING FINS
COMBUSTION CHAMBER
CYLINDER HEAD
CRANKCASE COVER
CRANKPIN
CONNECTING-ROD BEARING
CONNECTING ROD
PISTON
PISTON PIN
SPARK PLUG
VALVE
VALVE GUIDE
INTAKE VALVE PORT
VALVE SPRING
CRANKSHAFT
EXHAUST VALVE PORT
CRANKCASE
PUSH-ROD
ROCKER COVER
ROCKER ARM
OIL PAN
VALVE LIFTER
CAMSHAFT

Fig. 27-4   Horizontally Opposed Engine

27-7 V6 CYLINDER ENGINES

V6 cylinder engines have two banks of three cylinders set at an angle of 60° to each other. The crankshaft has four main bearings. The crankshaft throws and the camshaft are arranged to give a firing order of 1, 6, 5, 4, 3, 2. The valve arrangement is of the overhead valve type. These engines are sometimes coupled together to form a V12 engine for heavy trucks.

27-8 V8 CYLINDER ENGINES

V8 cylinder engines have two banks of four cylinders each, usually set at an angle of 90° to each other. The crankshaft is supported by five main bearings. The connecting rods are attached in pairs, one from each bank, to the crankpins. Late model V8 engine are of the I-head type, although the L-head type has been used. Because of the wide variety of cylinder-numbering systems used, the firing orders vary greatly.

27-9 OTHER CYLINDER ARRANGEMENTS

Engines have been made with as many as 12 to 16 cylinders and arranged in various ways such as the V, horizontally opposed, in three banks to form a W, or in four banks to form an X. The W- and X-type engines are used for industrial applications. The radial-type engine has the cylinders radiating from a common centre like the spokes of a wheel. The crankshaft has only one throw to which all connecting rods are attached through a master rod.

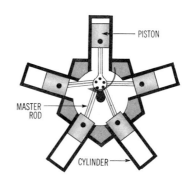

PISTON
MASTER ROD
CYLINDER

Fig. 27-5   Radial-Type Engine

Radial engines have an odd number of cylinders, such as 3, 5, 7, 9, etc., and use a cam ring or plate instead of a camshaft. The firing order uses this pattern—1, 3, 5, 2, 4, etc., depending on the number of cylinders.

27-10 V-TYPE ENGINES VERSUS IN-LINE ENGINES

The eight-cylinder in-line engine is no longer used in automobiles because of its long length, its tendency to flex or bend, and its tendency to produce torsional vibrations unless the crankshaft and block are extremely heavy. The V8 engine, on the other hand, is short in length, the engine block is very rigid, and it uses a short but heavy crankshaft.

The more rigid V8 engine permits higher compression ratios, combustion pressures, and running speeds with less flexing of the crankshaft and engine

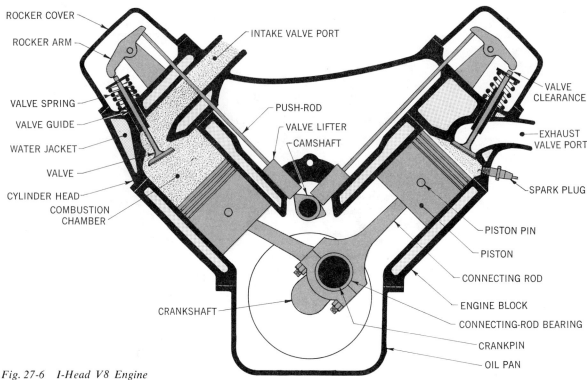

Fig. 27-6 I-Head V8 Engine

block. The shorter V8 block permits larger passenger compartments or shorter wheel-base vehicles without reducing the passenger-compartment size. Since the carburetor and other engine parts are placed between the two cylinder banks, the hood-line can be lower.

27-11 OVERHEAD CAMSHAFT TYPE ENGINES

Some engines have the camshaft mounted on the cylinder head above the valves. The valves are opened and closed by the cam of the camshaft acting through a type of rocker arm which is pivoted at one end on a hydraulic lash adjustor; the other end of the rocker arm rests upon the end of the valve stem with the cam riding in between. The hydraulic lash adjustor is similar in construction and operation to a hydraulic valve lifter and maintains zero clearance between the camshaft and the valve.

Some manufacturers use separate intake and exhaust camshafts, while others use a single common shaft. The camshaft may be driven by a chain or cogged belt which can be adjusted to proper tightness in a similar manner to fan or alternator drive belts.

The advantage of the overhead camshaft design is the elimination of the added weight of the rocker arms and push rods that could cause the valves to "float" at high speeds.

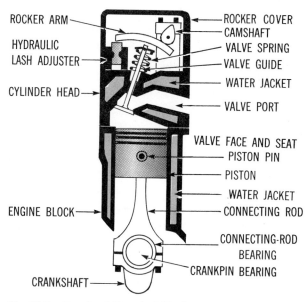

Fig. 27-7 Overhead Camshaft Engine

27-12 CLASSIFICATION BY VALVE ARRANGEMENTS AND COMBUSTION-CHAMBER DESIGN

Four types of valve arrangements have been used in automobile engines, the T, F, I, and L. Each derived its name because of its similarity to the different letters. For many years, up to the mid 1950s, the L-head engine was the most popular type, but it lost its popularity because its larger combustion chamber made it very difficult to produce the high compression ratios which are required for today's powerful engines. Today most engines are of the I-head type.

27-13 I-HEAD VALVE ARRANGEMENT

In the I-head-type valve arrangement, sometimes known as the *valve-in-head* or *overhead valve arrangement*, the valves are located side by side in the cylinder head. A series of rocker arms are mounted on top of the cylinder head and are operated by push rods. These rods are located beside the cylinders in an in-line engine or between the banks of a V6 or V8 engine. In both cases only one camshaft is used.

The valve operation is as follows: as the high point of the cam passes under the valve lifter, the lifter is raised. This, in turn, raises the push rod, which lifts one end of the rocker arm, causing the rocker arm to pivot around its axis. Since the rocker arm is a first-class lever, when one end moves up, the other end moves down. This downward motion is applied to the valve stem, which opens the valve and compresses the valve spring between the cylinder head and the retaining washer. The retaining washer is locked to the valve stem by the valve keeper. As the high point of the cam moves away from the lifter, the valve spring expands, closing the valve.

In many high performance I-head engines an overhead camshaft is used. The overhead camshaft eliminates the need for push rods and rocker arms to operate the valves, resulting in quicker valve response. The camshaft is driven by the crankshaft through a chain and sprocket drive. On V-type engines two camshafts are required. Some in-line engines use a separate camshaft for the intake and exhaust valves.

27-14 L-HEAD VALVE ARRANGEMENT

In an L-head valve arrangement, sometimes referred to as *valve-in-block* or *flat head*, the cylinders and combustion chamber form an inverted L. The intake and exhaust valves of each cylinder are located side by side in the engine block beside the cylinder. In L-head engines the valves are located between the two banks. Only one camshaft is required in both cases.

The valve operation is as follows: as the high point of the cam passes under the valve lifter, or tappet, the lifter is raised, which in turn raises the valve. As the valve is raised, the valve spring is compressed between the engine block and the retaining washer, the latter being locked to the valve stem by the valve lock, or keeper. As the high point of the cam moves away from the lifter, the valve spring expands, closing the valve.

27-15 F-HEAD VALVE ARRANGEMENT

The F-head valve arrangement places the intake valve in the head and the exhaust valve in the block. Both valves are driven by a common camshaft. The operation of the valves is similar to the I- or L-head valve operation.

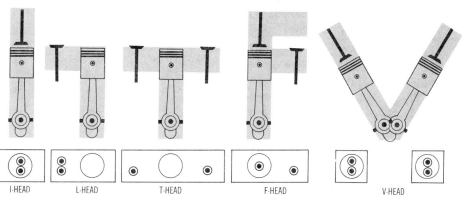

I-HEAD   L-HEAD   T-HEAD   F-HEAD   V-HEAD

Fig. 27-8   Valve Arrangements

27-16 T-VALVE ARRANGEMENT

The T-valve arrangement places both valves in the block. The intake valves are on one side, the exhaust valves are on the opposite side of the cylinder. There are separate camshafts for each side. The valve operation is the same as the L-head type. Although this type of engine is not in production today, it is frequently used for clarity in illustrating engine operation.

27-17 COMBUSTION CHAMBER DESIGN

The size, shape, and design of the combustion chamber depends on the type of valve arrangement and the compression ratio desired. The L-head engine combustion chamber usually uses the *Recardo Principle*, while I-head engines may use either the *hemispherical* or *wedge-shape* designs.

In using the Recardo Principle, the combustion chamber is located over the valves. This allows the piston to come very close to the head. As the piston travels upward on the compression stroke, the fuel-air mixture is forced into the area over the valves. As the piston reaches TDC, the remaining mixture is rapidly compressed, causing it to shoot into the combustion chamber with considerable force and create turbulence in the combustion chamber. The turbulence results in a smoother flame travel through the compressed mixture and allows higher compression ratios to be used without detonation (the uneven burning of the fuel).

The most common combustion chamber for I-head engines is the wedge-shape type. This type is easily machined and when properly designed is very efficient.

The cylinder-head portion of the combustion chamber is machined at an angle of about 10°. This creates a wedge-shaped area between the piston head and the underside of the cylinder head. The spark plug is located at the thick end of the wedge to provide a smooth flame travel. When the fuel is first ignited, the pressure presses only on a portion of the piston, starting the piston down smoothly. As the piston has moved downward slightly, the flame travel spreads across the entire piston head to apply full pressure. Since the combustion chamber slants downward away from the spark plug, the compression pressure does not decrease as rapidly before combustion as it would if the combustion chamber were not wedge shaped.

Compression pressures may be further increased

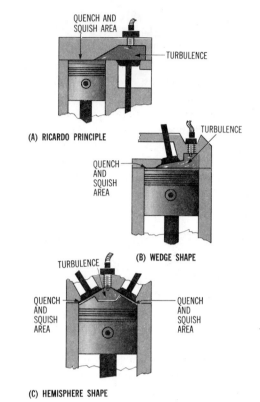

(A) RICARDO PRINCIPLE

(B) WEDGE SHAPE

(C) HEMISPHERE SHAPE

Fig. 27-9   Combustion Chamber Design

by using a matching wedge shape on the piston head.

Many high performance type engines use the Hemispherical or "Hemi"-type combustion chamber. The Hemispherical combustion chamber is compact and produces a high compression ratio with very little detonation. This type of combustion chamber permits the use of larger diameter valves resulting in improved engine breathing and higher volumetric efficiency. The valve stem axes are about 90° apart. The intake valves are on one side of the hemisphere, the exhaust valves on the opposite side. They are operated by push rods from a common camshaft. The spark plug is located in the highest point of the hemisphere between the two valves. To increase compression ratios, a dome type of piston is frequently used. In some engines it is necessary to have indentations in the head of the piston to clear the valve head when the valves are open between the intake and exhaust strokes.

27-18 CLASSIFICATION BY COOLING

Two general types of cooling systems are used, liquid cooling and air cooling. The former system is the most popular. A complete discussion of the construction and operation of the cooling system will be found in Chapter 34.

27-19 CLASSIFICATION BY CYCLE

Internal-combustion engines may be of the two-stroke-cycle or the four-stroke-cycle design. Most motor vehicles and many fhp engines using gasoline for fuel are of the four-stroke-cycle design. Some small, imported gasoline-powered vehicles, most outboard boat engines, and some fhp engines are of two-stroke-cycle design. Most diesel engines are of the two-stroke type, although the four-stroke-cycle type may be used. For a complete description of the two types of cycles see Chapter 25.

27-20 CLASSIFICATION BY FUEL

Internal combustion engines may be designed to use gasoline, diesel fuel oil, or LPG (Liquid Petroleum Gas). These fuels will be discussed in detail in Chapter 36.

27-21 OTHER ENGINES

The gasoline internal-combustion engine is not the only engine that can provide power for motor vehicles. The diesel engine has proved very successful in trucks, tractors, and for stationary engine applications. The search for better, more efficient, and less costly engines is never ending. Many designs have been tried and adopted; others have failed. The turbine and Wankel engines are at the present time being tested in motor vehicles. Other types of engines, such as the free piston type and the Wankel and Sterling engines, are in the experimental or developmental stages.

27-22 DIESEL ENGINES

Diesel engines are similar in construction to gasoline engines, except that they are generally heavier in construction in order to withstand the higher pressures resulting from the higher compression ratios used. These compression ratios may be as high as about 20 to 1 in a full diesel engine, slightly lower in a semi-diesel engine. Diesel engines may be either two or four cycle, air or liquid cooled.

A full diesel engine is one in which the compression ratio raises the heat of compression high enough (1,000 to 1,200° F) to ignite the fuel without the assistance of an electric spark.

A semi-diesel engine is one which uses a lower compression ratio and, therefore, does not develop

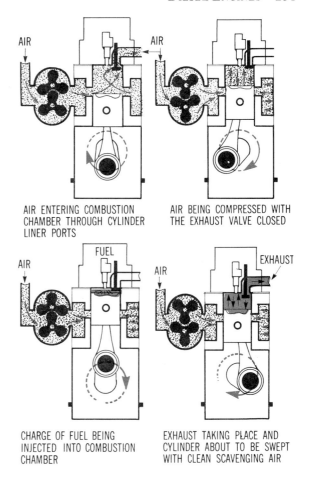

AIR ENTERING COMBUSTION CHAMBER THROUGH CYLINDER LINER PORTS

AIR BEING COMPRESSED WITH THE EXHAUST VALVE CLOSED

CHARGE OF FUEL BEING INJECTED INTO COMBUSTION CHAMBER

EXHAUST TAKING PLACE AND CYLINDER ABOUT TO BE SWEPT WITH CLEAN SCAVENGING AIR

Fig. 27-10   Typical Diesel Engine Cycle

the heat of compression that is necessary to ignite the fuel. Instead, it usually uses spark plugs for ignition purposes.

A diesel engine has no carburetor. Only air enters the cylinder on the intake stroke and only air is compressed on the compression stroke. At the proper time, fuel is sprayed into the heated air under pressure. The heat of compression ignites the fuel, and the fuel-air mixture then burns the same as it does in a gasoline engine, to produce power. The injection of fuel into the cylinder must be "timed" in accordance with engine speed and load in the same way as the spark at the spark plug of a gasoline engine must be "timed."

Since diesel fuel is less volatile than gasoline, it does not vaporize readily. Therefore, it must be broken up, or atomized, and sprayed into the cylinder in the form of a mist. The mist is produced by forcing the fuel through a nozzle or series of fine holes located at the discharge end of the injector.

Four-cycle diesel engines follow the same cycle as a gasoline engine and use both intake and exhaust valves. In a two-cycle diesel, the air enters through a port in the cylinder wall and the burnt gases leave the cylinder through an exhaust valve located in the engine cylinder head. Unlike the small gasoline two-cycle engine, the diesel engine does not use crankcase compression to move fuel and exhaust gases through a cylinder. Instead, the air is forced into the cylinder, and the exhaust gases are forced out by a superchanger, or "blower," or a rotary-type pump.

27-23 TRUCK ENGINES

There are three general types of truck engines: the light duty truck, the heavy duty truck, and the diesel.

Engines for light duty trucks are very similar or the same as passenger car engines. Any changes that are made are to compensate for the difference in operating conditions. Generally speaking, truck engines are required to move heavier loads than passenger car engines. Truck rear-axle gear ratios are usually lower than passenger car units. As a result the engine must run at higher rpm to attain the same road speed. Truck engines are frequently required to run at full power for prolonged periods of time.

Truck operating conditions result in higher combustion temperatures. These higher temperatures necessitate the use of valves and valve seats made of special heat-resistant materials and, in some cases, special sodium-filled valves. The clearance between the piston and piston rings and the cylinder walls must be large enough to compensate for the greater heat expansion of these parts. In many cases larger cooling system components are used to help dissipate the excess heat.

Heavy duty trucks usually have specially designed engines. These engines may be of either the gasoline or diesel type. In order to withstand the heavier loads, reinforced crankcases and heavier and larger diameter crankshafts, supported by larger bearings made of different materials, are used. The piston displacement is usually increased and the engine speed decreased in order to produce the same amount of power as a passenger car engine. Increased capacities of the cooling and lubricating systems are required to maintain normal operation.

27-24 TRACTOR AND INDUSTRIAL ENGINES

Small tractor and industrial engines, although usually specially designed, follow closely the design, construction, and service procedures of a passenger-car engine. The major difference is in operating conditions. Whereas the passenger-car engine is always changing speed to meet traffic conditions, the tractor or industrial engine operates at

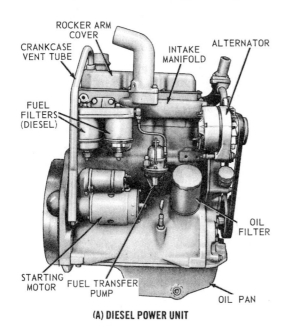

(A) DIESEL POWER UNIT

(B) GASOLINE POWER UNIT

Fig. 27-11   Typical Tractor Engines

John Deere Ltd.

Fig. 27-12   Typical Power Generator Unit

Courtesy of General Motors

a constant governed speed. The governed speed is set near the peak of the torque curve established for the engine. The engine is free to accelerate or de-accelerate freely up to the governed speed depending on the load requirements. Most tractor and industrial engines are designed with large piston displacements and are intended to operate at lower engine speeds.

Large tractor, bulldozer, crane, earth moving, and industrial equipment use mainly diesel engines of a heavier type than the heavy-duty truck. Usually they are operated at governor speed. Many of these engines are so large and heavy that the normal electrical starting system must be replaced by a small auxiliary gasoline engine. This engine is connected by a clutch to the heavy engine in order to crank the large engine for starting purposes. Maintenance operations are not determined by mileage, but in accordance with the number of hours of engine operation. Many firms require the operator to record, in a log book, the number of hours of engine operation each day.

27-25 MARINE ENGINES

Inboard marine engines are similar to tractor engines since they are designed for constant speed operation. Governors are frequently used—not to limit the speed of the boat, but to prevent the

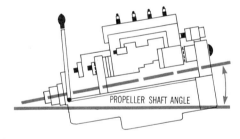

Fig. 27-13   Typical Mounting of Marine Inboard Engine

PROPELLER SHAFT ANGLE

engine from over-revving should the propeller come out of the water during rough weather, or if the propeller shears its drive pin.

A radiator and fan are not required since water is readily available. The water is picked up by a scoop, circulated through the engine by the water pump, and discharged through the exhaust system. Thermostats are used to regulate the engine operating temperature. In order to line up with the propeller shaft, most marine engines are mounted on an angle with the front of the engine much higher than the rear. This necessitates a specially designed oil pan in order to maintain the proper oil level.

Outboard marine engines are usually of the two-cycle type, and are available in single and multi-cylinder designs producing a range of horsepower from as low as 3 hp to over 100 hp. Lightness is an important factor in design since the smaller models in particular must be portable. Although some of the smaller types are air cooled, most use liquid cooling systems of a similar design to inboard engines. Since they are two-cycle engines, lubrication is accomplished by mixing the required amount of oil with the gasoline.

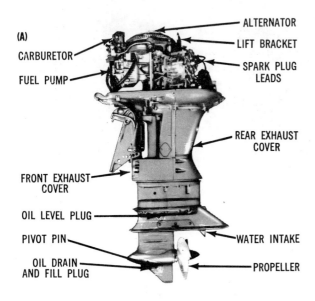

(A)

CARBURETOR
FUEL PUMP
ALTERNATOR
LIFT BRACKET
SPARK PLUG LEADS
REAR EXHAUST COVER
FRONT EXHAUST COVER
OIL LEVEL PLUG
PIVOT PIN
OIL DRAIN AND FILL PLUG
WATER INTAKE
PROPELLER

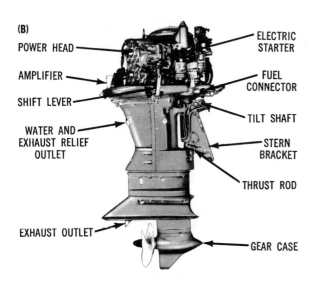

(B)

POWER HEAD
AMPLIFIER
SHIFT LEVER
WATER AND EXHAUST RELIEF OUTLET
EXHAUST OUTLET
ELECTRIC STARTER
FUEL CONNECTOR
TILT SHAFT
STERN BRACKET
THRUST ROD
GEAR CASE

Outboard Marine Corp. of Canada Ltd.

Fig. 27-14 Typical Outboard Engine

27-26 SMALL OR FRACTIONAL HORSEPOWER ENGINES

Many lawn mowers, chain saws, garden equipment, and snow blowers are equipped with two- or four-cycle engines producing 1 to 10 hp. These engines

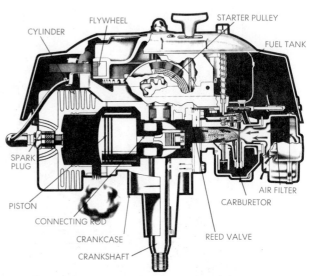

CYLINDER
FLYWHEEL
STARTER PULLEY
FUEL TANK
SPARK PLUG
PISTON
CONNECTING ROD
CRANKCASE
CRANKSHAFT
AIR FILTER
CARBURETOR
REED VALVE

Outboard Marine Corp. of Canada Ltd.

Fig. 27-15 Cut-away Lawn Mower Engine

are air cooled and are designed to operate at fairly high, but constant, speed. The major difference is in the ignition system. Since very few of these units contain a battery, the spark for ignition purposes is produced by a magneto.

27-27 RACING ENGINES

Racing engines are designed to produce the maximum power and rpm regardless of anything else. Quietness of operation is of minor importance.

In order to use a standard automobile engine as a racing engine, it must undergo many modifications. The engine is disassembled, the parts checked for possible signs of defects, accurately measured to establish proper fits and clearances, and, in many cases, carefully weighed in order to maintain perfect balance and to reduce vibration at high rpm. The valve action is changed to include very large headed valves. A very high lifting type of camshaft is installed to open the valves faster, wider, keep them open longer, and close them faster. The valve action changes improve the volumetric efficiency of the engine at higher engine speed, but result in a noisier, poorer idling engine.

The combustion chamber is also changed to increase the compression ratio. The cylinder size (bore and stroke) is sometimes enlarged to meet the specified racing classifications. Greater clearances are used between the moving parts to accommodate the extra expansion of the metal because of higher operating temperatures.

Special accessories such as super chargers, modified manifolds, and exhaust systems, extra or four-barrel carburetors are frequently used to further improve the volumetric efficiency at the higher speeds.

27-28 AIRPLANE ENGINES

Gasoline *reciprocating* engines are a popular source of power for small to medium sized aircraft; while *turbine* and *jet* engines power most medium to large type planes. Air-cooled reciprocating engines are the most popular, although the liquid type has been used.

Aero engines are designed for sustained operation at a cruising speed that is close to the full-power speed of the engine. As a result, the engine frequently sounds noisy and sloppy because of the larger clearances between the moving parts which are necessary for higher operating temperatures. The fuel system must be specially designed to incorporate devices which will compensate for the differences in atmospheric pressure at various altitudes, and to maintain satisfactory engine operation should the plane be flown upside-down, in a steep climb, or dive during aerobatics.

27-29 JET ENGINES

A jet engine depends upon air, fuel, and ignition to make it operate. Air enters the front end of a jet engine and is compressed. Burning fuel heats the air and causes it to expand, forcing a jet of hot gases out of the rear of the engine at very high speed. The action of a jet engine is similar to that of a toy balloon. When a toy balloon is inflated, the air inside the balloon is under pressure and is pushing out in all directions trying to expand. Since the force is pushing equally in all directions, there is no pressure difference to cause the balloon to move. If the stem of the balloon is released, air rushes out of the stem, and the balloon will shoot away in the opposite direction to the stem. This is because there is less force pushing on that side of the balloon than on the other. The larger force causes the balloon to move, not the jet of compressed air pushing against the free air.

In a jet engine all the work is done inside the engine in the same way in which the forces caused the balloon to move. To provide continuous high pressure inside the jet engine the exhaust gases pass through a turbine which is used to drive the compressor. The compressor, in turn, draws in the required amount of air for combustion. Because of the extremely high velocity of the air entering the engine and the very high temperature of the escaping gases, jet engines are, as yet, not suitable for use in motor vehicles.

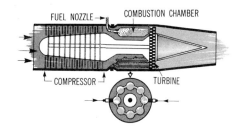

Fig. 27-16   Basic Jet Engine

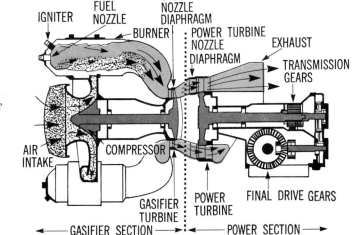

Fig. 27-17   Basic Turbine Engine

27-30 TURBINE ENGINES

The force produced by a jet-type engine can be exerted against a turbine to produce rotary motion. A basic turbine consists of a series of inclined planes attached to a rotating shaft which is placed in a liquid or air force. Turbines of the liquid type are used as components of automatic transmissions; the air type is used to produce motive power.

Turbine engines consist of two basic sections: the first stage, or gasifier section, produces the thrust similar to a jet engine and includes the com-pressor, combustion chambers, and the turbine; the second stage, or power section, contains one or more turbines and whatever transmission and final drive gears are necessary. The first section provides a supply of hot compressed gases, and the second section extracts and converts the hot exhaust gases to energy necessary for rotating motion. The two sections are entirely separate mechanically. Since most of the energy in the hot gases is harnessed by the power turbines, very little energy is left to produce jet thrust, and the temperature of the exhaust gases are reduced to reasonably safe

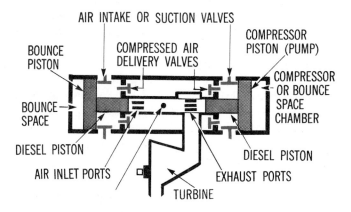

(A) CONSTRUCTION

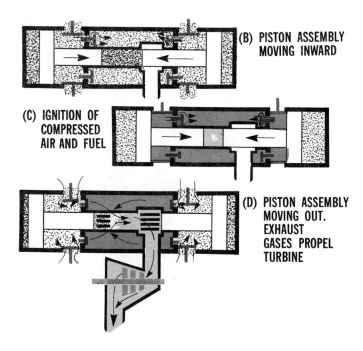

(B) PISTON ASSEMBLY MOVING INWARD

(C) IGNITION OF COMPRESSED AIR AND FUEL

(D) PISTON ASSEMBLY MOVING OUT. EXHAUST GASES PROPEL TURBINE

Fig. 27-18   Basic Free Piston Engine

limits. The turbine engine is being used in experimental motor vehicles.

27-31 FREE PISTON ENGINES

A free piston engine is a substitute for the gasifier section of a jet or turbine engine. The free piston engine is not a complete power unit. Instead, it is a means of producing high-pressure gas to drive a turbine.

A free piston engine contains a pair of piston assemblies that oppose each other in a cylinder. Attached to one end of this assembly is a small *power* or *diesel piston*; at the other end is a large *bounce piston*.

When the pistons are driven or bounced inward, the air between the two power pistons is compressed. Near the end of the inward travel of the power pistons, fuel is injected into the combustion chamber between the pistons. The heat of compression is sufficient to ignite the fuel, and combustion takes place. The pressure created by the expanding gases forces the pistons outward. As the power pistons move outwards, they uncover the exhaust ports; the escaping exhaust gases drive a turbine and produce rotary motion. Further outward travel of the power pistons uncovers the inlet ports to admit a fresh charge of air.

While the power piston has been moving outward, the air between the bounce pistons has been compressed in the bounce cylinder. This pressure drives the piston assemblies inward again, thus completing the cycle.

To provide fresh air under pressure for the power cylinder, the power-piston side of the bounce cylinder is used to draw in fresh air as the bounce piston moves outward, and to partially compress this fresh air in the manifold leading to the intake port of the power cylinder. Spring-loaded valves are located in the compression cylinder to control the air flow.

27-32 WANKEL ENGINES

The original Wankel or rotary engine sketches were made in 1924 by Dr. Felix Wankel, a German mechanical inventor. The first successful rotary engine was completed in 1957.

The rotary or Wankel engine is about half the size and weight of a comparable reciprocating engine. It runs quieter and has a better horsepower-to-weight ratio. The engine breathes easier because it has no angles to restrict the incoming gases, it is

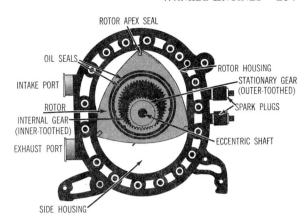

Fig. 27-19 *Cross Section of a Wankel Engine*

less complicated in design, and has only three moving parts which wear less under rotary motion only. Pollution emission control of a Wankel engine can be accomplished easier and cheaper with less loss of efficiency than would be the case with an equivalent reciprocating engine.

27-33 CONSTRUCTION

The Wankel engine consists of a triangular rotor mounted off centre, that rotates or floats eccentrically in an oval shaped chamber. The rotor is geared through a set of internal-external gears which turn the main shaft, which corresponds to the crankshaft of the reciprocating engine. The changing relationship between the three corners of the rotor and the chamber walls forms three pockets that become larger or smaller as the rotor turns. The changes in size of the pockets produces similar conditions to that found in the internal combustion engine four-stroke-cycle principle.

The intake and exhaust ports are fixed in the chamber wall, constituting fixed port type valving thus eliminating the complicated valve mechanisms required by most internal combustion engines. The chamber assembly of a Wankel engine corresponds to the cylinder block of a piston type engine and the spinning rotor inside performs similar functions to the piston of the reciprocating engine.

The fuel system of the Wankel engine uses a fairly conventional type carburetor or in some cases fuel injection. The fuel-air ratio is approximately the same as that used in piston-type engines. Some models of the engine are built with two fixed intake ports per chamber for better volumetric efficiency, combustion, and smoother low and high speed performance. The type of fuel used can be lead-free,

70 octane gasoline. The compression ratio of the engine is in the same range as that of conventional-type engines.

The engine electrical system includes a 12-volt battery, starter, alternator, voltage regulator, ignition coil, distributor and spark plug. Early type Wankel engines used only one spark plug per chamber; most new models use a dual ignition system consisting of two spark plugs per chamber each with its own distributor and ignition coil. The lower plug in the chamber is referred to as the leading plug and the upper plug as the trailing plug. The dual ignition system results in more complete combustion, reduced pollution emissions, and greater reliability. Since each revolution of the rotor produces three power strokes, the failure of the spark plug would be equal to the loss of three cylinders of an internal combustion engine. Therefore, with dual ignition should one spark plug fail the engine would continue to operate, but at part power.

The lubrication system of the Wankel engine is a pressurized system similar to the type used in conventional piston engines. The oil is pumped through a full-flow type oil filter to the main oil gallery located in the engine housing. Drilled passageways in the housing provide the oil required to lubricate both front and rear main bearings of the main shaft. Oil is circulated through an oil feed hole in the eccentric shaft and is circulated inside the rotor where it is used as a cooling agent.

To lubricate the chamber walls and rotor surfaces, a separate small metered oil pump is used. This pump circulates oil on these surfaces in an amount proportionate to acceleration, load, and speed. This system improves the anticorrosion and gas-sealing functions of the lubricating oil.

To dissipate the heat picked up by the lubricating oil, the system includes an integral oil cooler and a thermostat to control oil flow. A sizeable oil pan serves as the oil reservoir.

The cooling system of a Wankel engine is similar to that of the piston type engine. The engine housing contains ribbed water jackets for maximum heat dissipation. The coolant is circulated through the water jackets and the sealed type radiator by a conventional belt-driven water pump. A thermostat maintains the efficient engine operating temperature.

To provide a seal between the rotor tips, rotor sides, and the chamber surfaces various types of rotor tipped and side seals are used. One common type is made from a combination of aluminum and carbon.

27-34 OPERATION

The operating cycle includes the familiar phases of intake, compression, power, and exhaust. These phases go on simultaneously around the rotor, the complete cycle being completed during one revolution of the rotor. The cycle of operations is as follows: (use Fig. 27-20 as a guide)

A. Intake stroke starts between lobes 1 and 3 and continues as the space between the rotor and the chamber wall enlarges. When the rotor has rotated approximately 90°, lobe 3 has passed by the intake port, sealing off the fuel air mixture in the chamber.

B. During the next approximate 90° of rotation, the space between lobes 1 and 3 and the chamber wall decreases, thus compressing the fuel-air mixture.

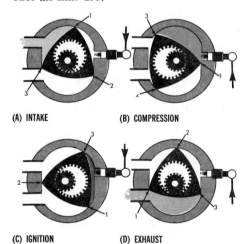

(A) INTAKE   **(B) COMPRESSION**

(C) IGNITION   **(D) EXHAUST**

Fig. 27-20 *Four Stage-Cycle of a Wankel Engine*

C. Near the end of the compression stroke, a spark occurs at the spark plug, igniting the fuel-air mixture which causes combustion and rapid expansion of the burning mixture, thus producing power. This pressure forces the rotor to rotate through the next approximately 90° until lobe 1 uncovers the exhaust port.

D. During the next approximate 90° the burnt gases are allowed to escape, until lobe 3 covers the exhaust port and lobe 1 again uncovers the intake port.

The rotor has made one revolution and is in position to begin the cycle all over again. Since the lobes on the rotor are approximately 120° apart, each space between them is capable of producing its own cycle. Therefore, it is possible to produce 3 power phases in each revolution of the rotor, resulting in an almost continuous delivery of power.

REVIEW QUESTIONS

1. State five ways in which the automobile internal combustion engine may be classified.
2. What is meant by the term "firing order"?
3. Describe three types of cylinder arrangements.
4. By means of sketches, illustrate the cylinder numbering systems used by (a) Chevrolet six cylinder (b) Ford eight cylinder (c) Plymouth eight cylinder.
5. Sketch four different types of valve arrangements.
6. Explain why the "wedge shape" combustion chamber is very efficient.
7. Give three advantages of the "Hemi"-type combustion chamber.
8. Explain why the compression ratio of a diesel engine must be approximately 20 to 1.
9. How does the fuel enter the air in a diesel engine?
10. Why are sealed crankcases not required on two-stroke cycle diesel engine?
11. Why are heavy duty truck engines designed differently than light duty truck engines?
12. What is the purpose of an industrial engine log book?
13. How are most marine engines cooled?
14. List four modifications performed on standard passenger car engines to convert them to racing engines. List the advantage of each modification.
15. Explain briefly the operating principle of a jet type engine.
16. Describe briefly the construction of a turbine type engine.
17. Describe the operating principle of a Wankel type engine.

Chapter 28
VALVES AND VALVE-TRAIN CONSTRUCTION

28-1 CYLINDER HEADS

The cylinder head encloses the top of the cylinders and forms the combustion chambers in which the combustion of the fuel-air mixture takes place. The cylinder head is bolted to the top of the cylinder block and can be readily moved in order to give access to the valves and cylinders when repairs are required.

28-2 CYLINDER HEAD CONSTRUCTION

The cylinder head is usually cast in one piece from grey cast iron or from aluminum. To make a casting, the molten cast iron or aluminum is poured into a mould made of sand. A core is placed within the mould to form the hollows and passageways within the head, such as combustion chambers, valve ports, water jackets, etc. After the casting has cooled, it is removed from the mould and the sand core is dissolved and washed out. The rough casting is then tested for possible defects, such as cracks and sand holes, and machined as required.

There are three types of cylinder heads: the *L-head*, the *I-head*, and the *air-cooled*.

L-Head. The L-head is the simplest of the three types. It is most frequently made of cast aluminum which has the advantage of combining lightness with high heat conductivity. The head contains the water jackets for cooling, which are connected through openings to the cylinder-block water jackets, the spark-plug holes, the combustion chamber, and pockets into which the valves move as they open. A pocket connected to the water jackets is frequently provided in the top of the head to accommodate the cooling-system thermo-

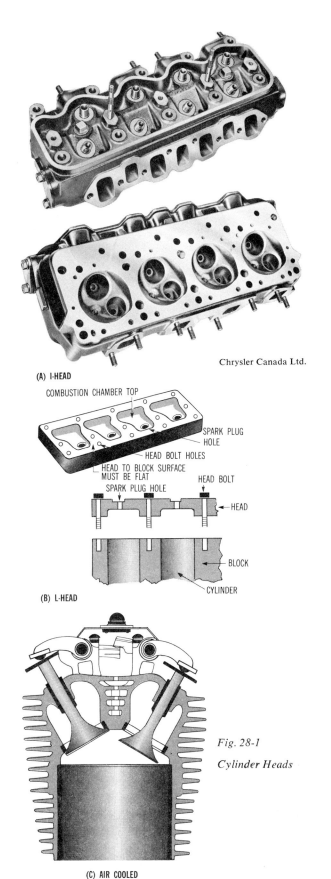

Chrysler Canada Ltd.

(A) I-HEAD

(B) L-HEAD

(C) AIR COOLED

Fig. 28-1

Cylinder Heads

241

stat and water-outlet connection. Other openings are provided for passenger-compartment heater connections and the temperature-gauge sending unit.

I-Head. The I-head is more complex than the L-head since it must include all the items noted for the L-head, plus the valve ports, valve guides, valve seats, and supports for the valve operating mechanism. An I-head is usually much thicker than an L-head and is most frequently made of cast iron instead of aluminum. Larger water jackets are required to compensate for cast iron's poorer heat conductivity.

There are two basic types of intake and exhaust port arrangements which can be cast into the I-type cylinder head, the *siamesed* ported, and the *individual* ported. In the siamesed type one port serves two adjacent cylinders. When the exhaust ports are siamesed the exhaust valves run hotter because there is less space for the coolant to circulate around the exhaust valve area. The individual-port type is easier to cool but requires a more complex valve train mechanism.

Both I- and L-heads are frequently provided with frost or expansion plugs which help prevent the head from cracking should the coolant freeze.

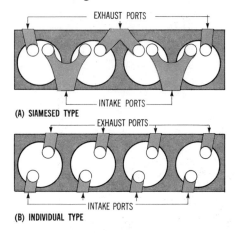

Fig. 28-2 Valve Port Arrangements

Air-Cooled Head. Air-cooled engines generally have individually mounted cylinders. The heads may be individual or cast in groups. They may be of either the L- or I-type, depending upon the design of the engine. On some engines the cylinder head and cylinder may be removed as a unit; on others they may be removed separately. Air-cooled heads are usually made of aluminum. They have no

water jackets and rely on fins, cast as part of the outer portions of the head, to dissipate the heat to the circulating air. The intake manifold is sometimes cast integrally with air-cooled cylinder heads.

28-3 VALVES AND VALVE OPERATING MECHANISMS

The valves and valve operating mechanisms control the admission of the fuel-air mixture into the cylinder, seal the cylinder to permit compression and combustion of the mixture and allow the ejection of the burnt gases from the cylinder after combustion. The valves operate under extreme conditions of heat and pressure. For example: while driving at 40 mph for one hour, the 16 valves of an 8-cylinder engine will open and close 840,000 times. In doing so, they will travel up and down in their guides approximately ¼ mile for each mile of automobile travel on the road. The valves move up and down at a high rate of speed, as it takes only $\frac{1}{25}$ second to complete the four strokes of the cycle at a moderate speed.

The exhaust valves and seats are exposed momentarily to combustion temperatures as high as 4000 F, or more, and normally operate at a cherry-red heat, while maintaining hardness and form. Each valve weighs only about 6 oz. yet must make a seal against pressures ranging from 600 to 800 psi.

The opening and closing of the valves in their port openings is controlled by the operating mechanism to coincide with the position of the piston and the stroke of the cycle. The operating mechanism consists of a camshaft, valve lifters, push rods, rocker arms, valve springs and retainers, and the valves. The valves are opened by cams on the camshaft and closed by pressure exerted by the valve spring. Regardless of the type of valve arrangement used, they all contain parts which perform similar functions.

28-4 VALVE CONSTRUCTION

Various types of valves have been used: rotary, sliding, and mushroom, or poppet. The poppet-type valve is used universally today. This type are noisy and difficult to cool; nevertheless, they are simple and do provide an effective seal under operating conditions.

The poppet valve consists of a valve head and a valve stem. The valve head has a face machined

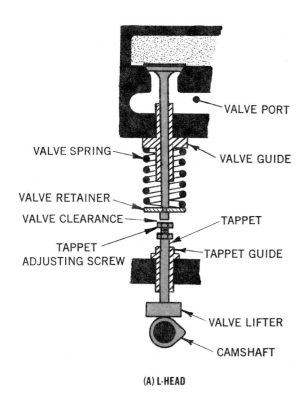

(A) L-HEAD

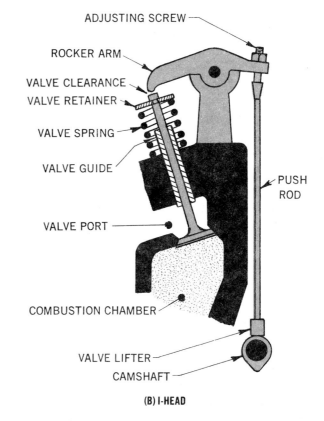

(B) I-HEAD

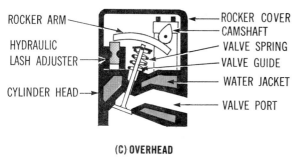

(C) OVERHEAD

Fig. 28-3   Valve Train Mechanisms

on its outer edge at an angle of between 30° and 47°. This face closes against the valve seat which is machined in the block or cylinder head. The valve stem has a retainer groove machined near the lower end to receive the *split locks* which hold the valve spring retainer and valve spring in place. The valve stem is machined to a given size to provide a clearance fit between the stem and the valve guide. The valve guide, in turn, is pressed into the cylinder block or head. The valve guide holds the valve in proper position and alignment with the valve seat.

The edge of the valve head between the valve face and the top of the head is called the *valve margin.*

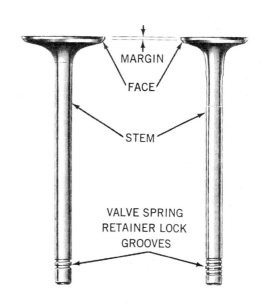

Fig. 28-4   Valves

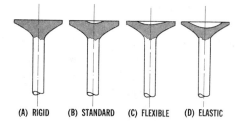

(A) RIGID   (B) STANDARD   (C) FLEXIBLE   (D) ELASTIC

Fig. 28-5   Valve Head Shapes

Valves can be made of one piece of special alloy steel (the most common practice), or of two pieces, consisting of an alloy steel head electrically welded to a steel stem. A chromium-nickel alloy is often used for intake valves; a special heat-resistant alloy type of steel is used for the exhaust valves because of the extremely high temperatures they must withstand. On some engines, the intake and exhaust valves are made of the same material.

The valves must be light in weight to keep the inertia forces low, yet have sufficient metal to dissipate the excess heat.

28-5 VALVE TEMPERATURE AND COOLING

The intake valve operates at relatively cool temperatures since it passes only fuel-air mixture which is at, or even below, atmospheric temperature. The exhaust valve operates at very high temperatures since it must pass the hot exhaust gases. The temperature around the seating surface of the exhaust valve is frequently between 1000 to 1200° F. The central portion of the valve head will even be hotter at 1200 to 1400° F. The stem adjacent to the head will run slightly cooler at 800 to 1000° F. The exhaust valve runs at a cherry-red heat under normal conditions. A leaking valve or defective cooling system could increase these temperatures to the point where the valve could melt, or a small section of the head could burn away.

Valves cannot be cooled directly by the liquid of

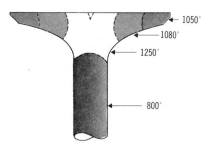

— 1050°
— 1080°
— 1250°
— 800°

Fig. 28-6   Exhaust Valve Head Temperatures

the cooling system. The only cooling comes from the contact of the valve stem with the valve guide and the short intervals of contact between the valve face and seat. As a result, most of the heat must travel from the head of the valve down the valve stem, transfer to the valve guide, to the engine cylinder block or head, then transfer to the coolant in the water jackets. Some heat flows from the valve face to the seat, through the cylinder head or block, to the coolant. The paths followed by the heat emphasize the importance of proper valve stem-to-guide fits and proper valve seating. The transfer of heat from the valve to the cooling system can be restricted by any one of the following: improper mating of the valve face and seat, too narrow a face and seat contact area, rough or worn valve face or seat, or excessive valve stem-to-guide clearance.

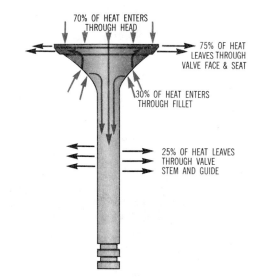

70% OF HEAT ENTERS THROUGH HEAD
75% OF HEAT LEAVES THROUGH VALVE FACE & SEAT
30% OF HEAT ENTERS THROUGH FILLET
25% OF HEAT LEAVES THROUGH VALVE STEM AND GUIDE

Fig. 28-7   Valve Heat Path

The valve and seat may be round and true when the engine is cold, but out of round and untrue (warped) when the engine reaches normal operating temperature. Warping can be caused by hot spots in the cylinder block or head, by unequal tightening of the cylinder head bolts, by variations in volume or velocity of the exhaust gases passing by one portion of the valve rim, or by the valve margin being too thin or uneven.

In addition to the changes in valve and valve-seat shape, the diameter of both may change. The higher operating temperature of the valve head, as compared to the valve seat, will cause the head to expand more than the seat. This causes the valve to rise and reduce the contact area and seal between the mating surfaces. The valve stem also expands in length more than the surrounding parts. Therefore, if proper valve stem-to-lifter clearance is not maintained, the contact area and the seal between the face and seat will be reduced. Failure of the face and seat to make a perfect seal allows the hot gases to escape during the combustion period and therefore increases the valve face and seat temperatures in some spots.

All of the conditions mentioned can increase the valve operating temperature by several hundred degrees above normal, with local hot spots at even higher temperatures. The hotter the operating temperature, the shorter the life of the valve.

To assist in dissipating the heat from the valve head, some valves have a hollow stem which is partially filled with metallic sodium. Metallic sodium melts at 208° F and is therefore a liquid at normal operating temperatures. As the valve moves up and down, the liquid sodium bounces back and forth between the head and the stem. The sodium absorbs heat from the head and transfers the heat to the cooler stem. A sodium-cooled valve will run up to 200° F cooler than a solid-stem type of valve.

Caution: Do not try to cut the stem of a sodium-cooled valve as the stem may explode as the cut reaches the inner sodium-filled chamber.

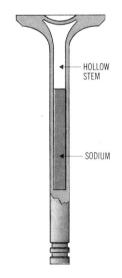

Fig. 28-8   Sodium-Cooled Valves

28-6 VALVE SEATS

A valve seat is the machined surface in the cylinder head or block which mates with the valve face to form a seal. Valve seats may be cut in the cast-

iron cylinder block or head, or may be made of special heat-resistant steel inserts pressed, shrunk, or screwed into a counterbore cut in the casting. Intake seats frequently are a machined surface of the casting, while the exhaust seats are usually of the insert type. The special alloys used in exhaust seat inserts are more serviceable than the block and head materials. Also, when they do become worn or burnt beyond repair, they are easily replaced.

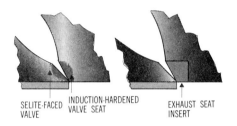

Fig. 28-9   Valve Face and Seat Materials

The common valve seat and face angles are 30° and 45°, 45° being the most common. Some manufacturers machine a ¼ to 1° difference in the angles of the face and seat. This is known as "valve interference angle." The seat may be 44°, the face 45°, or vice versa.

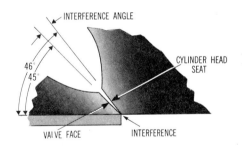

Fig. 28-10   Valve Interference Angle

Valve interference angle is helpful in cutting through deposits that may form on the contact surfaces. It produces greater pressure at the upper edge of the valve seat; therefore, this edge has a tendency to cut through the deposits to form a better seal.

28-7 VALVE GUIDES

The valve guide may be machined as part of the cylinder block or head, or may be made as a separate cast-iron unit and pressed into a hole in the block or head. In either case, the valve stem passes through a hole reamed to give the proper stem clearance. Extreme accuracy is important as the guide maintains the proper position and alignment between the valve face and seat. The fit of the guide also plays an important part in valve heat dissipation.

When separate type valve guides become worn, they may be easily replaced. When the guide is machined directly into the block or head, the guide hole must be reamed to a larger size, and a valve with an oversized stem must be used.

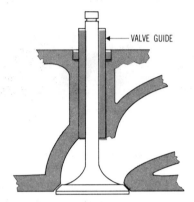

Fig. 28-11   Typical Replacement Valve Guide

28-8 VALVE SPRINGS

Valve springs are used to close the valves. They are wound spirally of high grade spring-steel wire, and are ground flat at each end to ensure an even distribution of pressure. Most engines use one spring per valve, although some may use two or three, one placed inside the other. Multiple springs are used to ensure a more even distribution of pressure.

Valve springs are held in position by a retainer which, in turn, is held in position on the valve stem by split-type *wedge collars.*

The pressure the spring exerts on the valve must be sufficient to ensure that the valve and lifter follow the cam and close tightly. If this pressure is not sufficient, the valve will not close tightly at higher engine speeds but will bounce or flutter, causing a high-speed engine miss. A decrease in spring pressure can be caused by weak valve springs or by excessive refacing of the valve face and seat. When valves and seats are refaced, the valve sits lower in the block or head, and the stem protrudes a greater distance. Therefore, it is not necessary to compress the valve spring as far to insert the valve retainer locks, and spring tension is reduced. Special *valve-spring tension washers* are available to compensate for this condition.

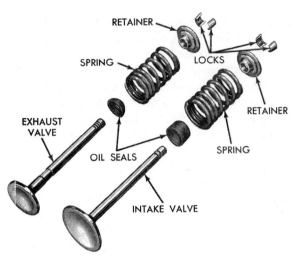

Fig. 28-12   Valve Assembly   Chrysler Canada Ltd.

Valve spring vibration can develop at various engine speeds. This vibration can cause poor engine performance and spring breakage. Through spring design, engineers try to have this vibration take place at infrequently used speeds. The use of special spring dampeners and cups, or springs with coils wound closer together at one end than the other, reduces this vibration. When unevenly wound springs are used, the end with the closely spaced coils must be placed against the head or block.

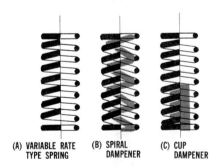

Fig. 28-13   Method of Valve Spring Dampening

Unequal or cocked valve springs will upset valve face-to-seat alignment, producing a poor seal. Too much spring tension will cause the valve stem and/ or neck to stretch. Excessive stretching will result in valve breakage, warpage, or excessive face and seat wear.

28-9 VALVE ROTATORS

When a valve opens and closes and the mating surfaces contact in the same spot time after time, a carbon buildup may develop on the surface. This could cause the valve to remain open and produce a hot spot which will burn the valve. If the valve could be made to turn a few degrees each time it opened, the wiping action between the surfaces of the face and seat would help reduce the carbon buildup. The turning will also prevent localized hot spots by rotating the valve away from the hottest areas. To accomplish this turning, there are two basic types of valve rotators: the *free type* and the *positive type*.

Free-Type Valve Rotators—use a type of mechanism which removes the spring tension from the valve when the valve is open. Engine vibration induces rotation on the free valve. In order to reduce spring pressure from the valve, the regular valve spring-retainer lock is replaced by a *split-washer lock* and a *tip cup*. The upper edge of the tip cup compresses the valve spring, through the split lock and retainer. Because the valve stem rests in the tip cut, it is also raised. But, since only the valve's weight rests on the stem, engine vibration causes the valve to rotate.

Positive Valve Rotators—do not rely on engine vibration to turn the valve. Instead, the mechanism rotates the valve a few degrees each time the valve opens. The mechanism consists of: a seating collar upon which the valve spring rests; a flexible washer placed between the seating collar and the inclined ball race; a series of balls and return springs; and a base plate called a *spring retainer* which also surrounds the valve stem locks.

When the valve is raised by the cam and lifter, the valve-spring pressure presses down on the seating collar and flattens the flexible washer. The flexible washer presses down on the balls causing them to roll downward on the inclined planes of the race and to compress the return spring. The rolling action of the balls causes the spring retainer and the valve to rotate a few degrees.

When the valve closes, the pressure on the seating collar is released. The flexible washer releases the pressure from the balls, and the ball-return springs push the balls up the inclines of the race, ready for the next valve-lifter action.

28-10 VALVE LIFTERS

The valve lifters or cam followers are the units placed between the end of the valve stem (L-head

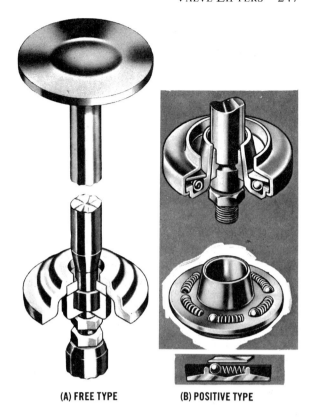

(A) FREE TYPE   **(B) POSITIVE TYPE**

Thompson Products
A Division of TRW Canada Ltd.

Fig. 28-14   Valve Rotators

engines), or the push rod (I-head engines), and the camshaft. The lifter rides on the cam of the camshaft and, when the lobe of the cam passes under the lifter, it moves the lifter upward. Valve lifters may be of the *solid mechanical* or *hydraulic* type.

Mechanical Lifters—or solid lifters, are usually made of cast iron and are hollow in order to reduce weight. The bottom surface that contacts the cam is usually case-hardened in order to reduce wear. L-head solid lifters usually have a valve-clearance adjusting screw in the top. In an I-head engine, the adjusting screw is part of the rocker-arm mechanism, not part of the lifter.

Hydraulic Lifters—consist of a hollow lifter body, an inner plunger which fits snugly inside the body, an inner plunger spring, a push check-valve assembly, and a plunger cap which includes a valve stem or push-rod seat.

Hydraulic valve lifters are silent and self adjusting. The hydraulic unit itself automatically maintains zero valve clearance; requires no adjustment

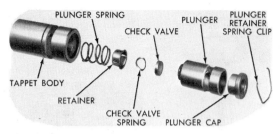

Chrysler Canada Ltd.

Fig. 28-15 Hydraulic Valve Lifter Construction

after its initial setting; and compensates for variations in valve stem length, because of temperature changes, hydraulically.

Hydraulic valve lifters operate in this manner: when the valve is closed, engine oil under pressure enters the lifter body and plunger from an oil gallery that runs the length of the engine block. This oil forces the ball or disc of the push check valve from its seat and passes into a cavity beneath the plunger. The oil raises the plunger until it contacts the valve stem or push rod. The oil pressure is not high enough to open the valve but takes up any clearance in the valve operating mechanism.

When the cam lobe raises the lifter, valve-spring pressure is applied to the plunger. This produces a sudden increase in pressure on the oil in the cavity beneath the plunger. This pressure closes the push check valve, trapping the oil in the cavity. Since a liquid cannot be compressed, the lifter acts as a simple one-piece lifter.

As the cam lobe lowers the lifter and the valve closes, the pressure on the plunger is released.

When the valve is off its seat, the load is carried by the oil. During this period, pressure on the plunger will cause a slight leakage of oil between the plunger and the lifter body. This leakage is necessary to compensate for the expansion of the valve stem because of heat and to ensure proper seating of the valve. This "leak down," as it is called, is not sufficient to hamper the normal opening and closing of the valve. Any excess clearance which may develop is taken up by the plunger spring pushing up against the valve stem or push rod when the valve is closed. Oil from the engine oil pump will open the push check valve and refill the cavity again.

When the engine is stopped, certain valves remain in the open position. Their valve-spring pressure causes the lifter to leak down. The lifter may be noisy until the engine oil pump fills up the cavity.

28-11 PUSH RODS AND ROCKER ARMS

I-head engines require push rods and rocker arms to transfer the lifter action to the valves. Two push rods and rocker arms are required for each cylinder.

Push Rods—may be solid or tubular. They are usually made with ball-shaped ends to fit the ball-and-socket joints of the valve lifter and rocker arm. Some push rods have a ball-shaped lower end and socket-shaped upper end. The socket accommodates the ball end of the adjusting screw in the rocker arm.

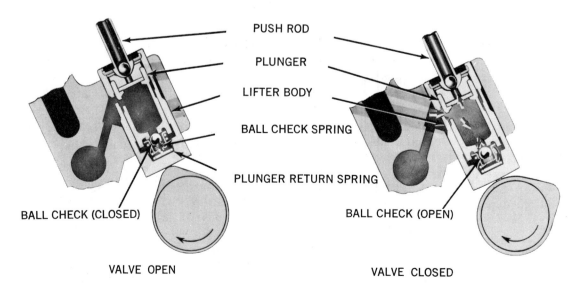

Fig. 28-16 Hydraulic Valve Lifter Operation

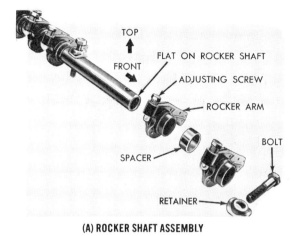

(A) ROCKER SHAFT ASSEMBLY

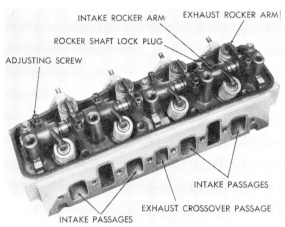

(B) ROCKER ARM ASSEMBLIES INSTALLED

Chrysler Canada Ltd.

Fig. 28-17   Shaft Mounted Valve Rocker Arms

Rocker Arms—are used to reverse the direction of the valve-lifter action. The upward motion of the lifter, as the cam passes under it, is transmitted to one end of the rocker arm by the push rod. Since the rocker arm is pivoted in the centre, one end goes up when the other goes down. The other end of the rocker arm contacts the valve stem. As the valve lifter moves up, the valve moves down to open.

On some engines the rocker arms are supported by a hollow rocker-arm shaft which is attached by supports to the engine head. Bushings in the rocker arms help to reduce wear. On other engines the rocker arms are attached to the cylinder head and pivoted on a rocker-arm stud. The rocker arm is held in place on the stud by a ball and adjusting nut.

To lubricate the rocker arms, oil is supplied through the hollow rocker-arm shaft to the rocker-

arm bushings and via drilled passageways in the rocker arms to the ball sockets. The oil is delivered to the rocker-arm shaft through special oil lines or through drilled passageways in the cylinder block and head. On engines using the individual rocker-arm studs, the oil is usually supplied through the hollow push rods.

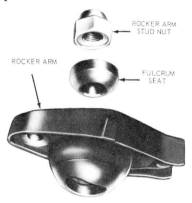

(A) VALVE ROCKER ARM ASSEMBLY

(B) ROCKERS ASSEMBLED

Ford of Canada

Fig. 28-18   Ball- and Stud-Type Valve Rocker Arms

28-12 CAMSHAFT, CAMSHAFT DRIVES, AND VALVE TIMING

28-13 CAMSHAFTS

The camshaft is a drop forging or casting made of either alloy steels or chilled cast iron, heat treated to resist wear. It may be located in the crankcase to one side and above the crankshaft in L-head and I-head engines; between the two banks of cylinders and directly above the crankshaft on V8 engines; or attached to the top side of the cylinder head in overhead camshaft-type I-head engines.

The camshaft is used to open and close the valves. It holds the valves open for the correct

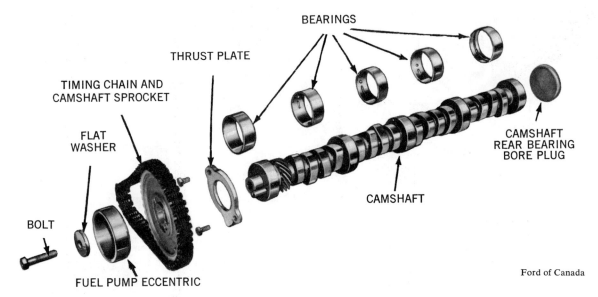

Ford of Canada

Fig. 28-19   Camshaft and Related Parts

length of time during the stroke of the piston. Each valve of the engine has a cam which is a device that changes rotary motion into linear or straight line motion. A cam consists of an opening ramp, a high spot, called the lobe or nose, a closing ramp, and a heel. The shape or profile of the cams are very carefully determined so that they open the valves at the proper speed and lift without imposing excessive strains on the moving parts, and with a minimum amount of noise. Various designs of cams are used, one-half, three-quarter, and full race. The full-race cams are used in high performance engines. These cams are designed to open the valves wider and to open and close them faster with little regard for the extra noise that develops. The increase in volumetric efficiency that is obtained more than offsets the extra noise.

The arrangement of the cams on the camshaft and the design of the crankshaft determines the firing order of the engine.

A spiral gear located on the camshaft is used to drive the oil pump and distributor at the same speed as the camshaft. An extra cam is usually included in camshaft design and is used to operate the fuel pump.

The camshaft has three or four bearing journals along its length which support the shaft in sleeve-type *babbett bearings* in the crankcase. The journals are usually larger in diameter than the cam so that the shaft may be installed by sliding it through the bearings in the crankcase. The camshaft is kept

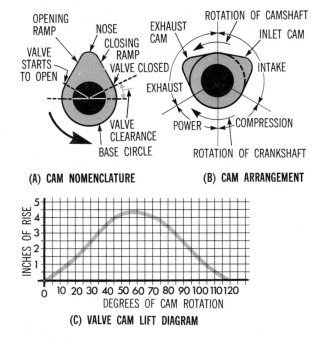

Fig. 28-20   Cams

in place by a thrust washer placed behind the timing gear and bolted to the front of the crankcase.

28-14 CAMSHAFT DRIVES

The camshaft is driven by the crankshaft by means of *timing gears* or a *timing chain* and *sprockets*. In four-cycle engines, the camshaft gear or sprocket is twice the diameter of the crankshaft gear or sprocket and, therefore, operates at one-half the crankshaft speed. The use of gears or a chain and

(A) SPROCKET AND CHAIN

(B) GEAR

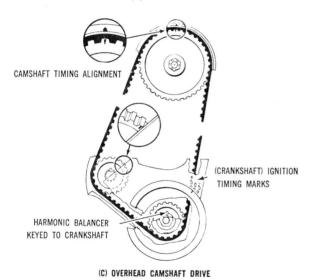

CAMSHAFT TIMING ALIGNMENT

(CRANKSHAFT) IGNITION
TIMING MARKS

HARMONIC BALANCER
KEYED TO CRANKSHAFT

(C) OVERHEAD CAMSHAFT DRIVE

Courtesy of General Motors

Fig. 28-21   Camshaft Drives

sprockets maintains a definite relationship or "timing" between the two shafts. The timing gears or chain are usually located at the front of the engine and enclosed with a timing-gear case cover. The crankshaft protrudes through the cover, and an oil seal is mounted around the shaft and in the cover to prevent oil leakage.

Timing Gears—are usually helical-type gears. The two gears are rarely made of the same material. Combinations of fibre, steel, or aluminum are used to achieve quiet operation and longest wear. Gear-driven camshafts rotate in the opposite direction to the crankshaft.

The crankshaft gear is pressed on the crankshaft and is prevented from turning on the shaft by means of a *key*. The camshaft gear may be secured by a series of unevenly spaced capscrews to a *flange*, which is forged as part of the camshaft. Or it may be pressed on the shaft and secured in position by a key and a lock nut. It is important that each gear be assembled to its shaft in the correct position with reference to the timing-gear marking.

The timing-gear markings will, when aligned according to manufacturer's specifications, show the proper point of mesh. With the gears mounted on the shafts correctly, they will ensure the proper opening and closing of the valves in relationship to the position of the piston in the cylinder.

The crankshaft gear generally has a gear tooth marked with an "O," or a punch mark. The camshaft gear has a similar mark placed in the space between two teeth. During assembly, the marked tooth of the crankshaft gear is placed so that it will mesh in the marked space of the camshaft gear.

Chain Drives. In the chain-type drive, sprockets replace the timing gears, and the camshaft rotates in the same direction as the crankshaft. The camshaft sprocket has twice the number of teeth as the crankshaft sprocket in order to maintain the one-half speed ratio. These sprockets are attached to their shafts in a manner similar to timing gear. The sprockets are properly marked with the necessary timing marks. The relative position of these marks in relationship to each other and to the chain is given in the manufacturer's specification. The timing chain meshing continuously with the teeth of the sprockets maintains the proper relationship between the two shafts while driving the camshaft.

The chain is kept from sliding off the sprockets by means of guides, one on each side of the chain, or by a single guide in the centre of the chain. The centre guide runs in a groove cut in the sprockets.

When timing chains become loose and worn, they may "jump" one or more teeth or become extremely noisy. Some manufacturers provide a means of adjusting timing-chain tension, but in most cases the worn chain must be replaced.

28-15 OVERHEAD CAMSHAFT DRIVES

Some overhead camshafts are driven by two pair of bevel gears mounted on the ends of a vertical shaft. One pair of bevel gears drives the shaft from the crankshaft; the other pair drives the camshaft.

Most overhead camshafts are driven by sprockets and a chain or by a clogged belt. Additional idler sprockets are used to keep the chain tight and prevent "whipping."

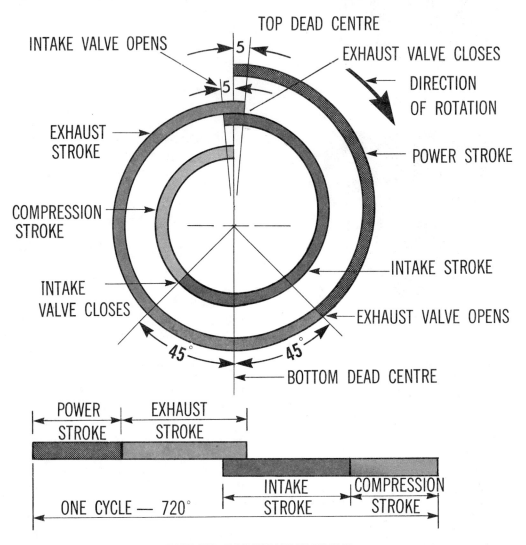

INTAKE AND EXHAUST VALVE TIMING

STROKE	THEORETICAL LENGTH	START OF STROKE	END OF STROKE	ACTUAL LENGTH
Power	180°	TDC	45° before BDC	135°
Exhaust	180°	45° before BDC	5° after TDC	230°
Intake	180°	5° before TDC	45° after BDC	230°
Compression	180°	45° after BDC	TDC	135°
One Cycle	720°			730°

Fig. 28-22   Relationship Between Theoretical and Actual Strokes

28-16 VALVE TIMING

During the discussions of the four-stroke-cycle principle, it was assumed that the valves opened and closed at TDC or BDC and that a cycle was 720° in length. In practice, the valves do not open and close on the dead centres, but open before or close after dead centre is reached.

The changing of the stroke length increases volumetric efficiency and engine power. This may seem odd at first, as the power stroke is shortened by 45°. However, by the time the power stroke reaches 45° before BDC, the pressure in the cylinder has dropped considerably, and the crankshaft throw is not in a position to effectively produce turning effort. It is more advantageous, therefore, to open the exhaust valve earlier and allow the remaining pressure to force the exhaust gases through the exhaust system. Leaving the exhaust valve open for 5° after TDC takes advantage of inertia of the moving gases to further "scavenge" (remove burnt gases) from the cylinder.

As the exhaust gases rush past the area of the intake valve, they create a low pressure in that area. Opening the intake valve 5° before TDC of the intake stroke utilizes this low pressure to start the fuel-air mixture flowing into the cylinder. Leaving the intake valve open for 45° after BDC also makes use of the inertia of the moving gases to fill the cylinder more completely. The more fuel-air mixture that enters the cylinder on the intake stroke, the higher the volumetric efficiency and the more power produced.

The opening of a valve before either TDC or BDC is called *valve lead*. The closing of a valve after TDC or BDC is called *valve lag*. When the valves are open at the same time between the exhaust and intake strokes, it is called *valve lap*.

28-17 POWER LAP

The simple one-cylinder engine would not be satisfactory for the operation of the modern motor vehicle. Nowadays, most motor vehicles use either a four-cylinder, six-cylinder, or eight-cylinder engine. The power strokes of multicylindered engines are so timed that they occur at intervals of 180° of crankshaft rotation in a four-cylinder, 120° in a six-cylinder, and 90° in an eight-cylinder engine.

The greater the number of cylinders an engine has, the shorter the interval between the power strokes. In the six-cylinder and eight-cylinder engines, the second power stroke starts before the first power stroke finishes. This overlap of power strokes is known as "power lap."

REVIEW QUESTIONS

1. Describe the method of cylinder head construction.
2. What is the disadvantage of siamesed valve ports?
3. What is the basic requirement of good valve design?
4. How are valves (a) opened (b) closed?
5. Describe the construction of a valve.
6. How is heat dissipated from a valve?
7. Name three ways heat dissipation for a valve can be reduced.
8. What causes a valve to warp?
9. How does the sodium help dissipate valve heat?
10. What are the advantages of valve seat inserts?
11. Explain the term "valve interference angle."
12. What are the advantages of valve interference angle?
13. What is the important function of valve guides?
14. How can valve-spring pressure be decreased?
15. Name two methods of decreasing valve-spring vibration.
16. What will result if valve-spring tension is too great?
17. What is the purpose of valve rotation?
18. Describe the operation of a positive-type valve rotator.
19. What is the advantage of hydraulic valve lifters?
20. Explain how a hydraulic valve lifter maintains zero valve clearance.
21. Describe two methods of mounting rocker arms.
22. Describe the methods of lubricating each type of rocker arm mounting.
23. What are the basic requirements of cam design?
24. What are (a) the advantages (b) the disadvantages of a full race cam?
25. What is meant by the term "valve timing"?
26. Why must the camshaft operate at one-half crankshaft speed?
27. Explain how volumetric efficiency can be increased by changing the point at which the intake valve opens and closes.
28. Why is the exhaust valve timed to open before the piston reaches BDC of the power stroke?
29. Explain the valve terms (a) lead (b) lap (c) lag (d) margin.
30. What is meant by the term "power lap"?

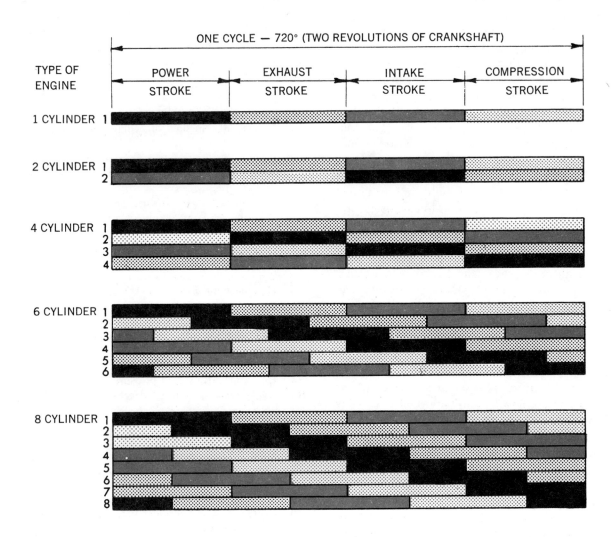

Fig. 28-23   Power Lap Chart

Chapter 29
VALVE AND VALVE-TRAIN SERVICE

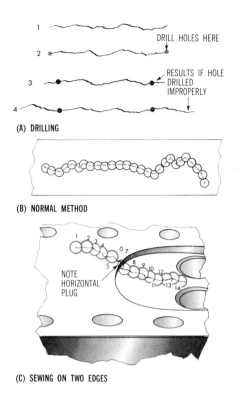

(A) DRILLING

(B) NORMAL METHOD

(C) SEWING ON TWO EDGES

Fig. 29-1   Sewing a Crack

29-1 CYLINDER HEADS

Before removing the cylinder head, check the manufacturer's manual for proper instructions. Once the head has been removed, it should be disassembled as completely as possible to permit thorough cleaning, inspection, and repair. Remove water-outlet and thermostat connections to permit inspection of the water jackets and testing of the thermostat. On I-heads, remove the valve assemblies and place in their proper order so they may be reinstalled in the same location.

Remove the carbon from the combustion chambers and the valve ports by using a power-driven wire brush or by a hand carbon scraper. Carbon deposits in the valve guides may be removed with a valve-guide cleaning tool. Grease and dirt may be removed by using a suitable solvent.

After cleaning, inspect the head for cracks, warpage, or rough gasket surfaces. Cracks are usually caused by overheating or freezing. To check for cracks, moisten the surface with kerosene, tap the head with a hammer, wipe the surface, and tap the head again. If the head is cracked, lines of kerosene will reappear along the cracks. Cracked cylinder heads are usually replaced. However, cracks may be repaired if desired. Small cracks may be sealed by peening them shut with a power peening hammer. Larger cracks may be repaired by what is known as "sewing." To sew a crack, drill and tap small holes at each end of the crack. Insert threaded plugs or screws into the holes. Drill another hole and tap partially into the existing plug and partially into the casting along the crack. Insert

a second plug or screw. Additional holes are drilled, tapped, and have plugs or screws inserted in them until the other end of the crack is reached. The repaired surface then must be machined true.

Castings may be welded provided they are properly preheated to prevent new cracks forming because of the difference in temperature and metal expansion of one part of the casting compared to another.

Cylinder-head warpage is usually caused by improper tightening of the cylinder bolts or nuts. Overtightening of the head studs or bolts can also cause the mating surface on the cylinder block to warp. The mating surfaces of both the cylinder head and the block should be flat and true to within .010″. A .010″ feeler gauge should not be able to pass between a straight-edge and the surface when the straight-edge is placed in the centre and diagonally from each corner. If the surface is warped more than .010″, it may be ground or milled true and flat by special equipment made for this purpose. When an I-head or V8-cylinder head or cylinder-block mating surface is refinished, the relative positions of the cylinder-head intake-port openings are changed. Therefore, the mating surface of the intake manifold must also be resurfaced

255

proportionately so that the port openings of the manifold and cylinder head will align properly.

Spark-plug and water-temperature threaded holes should also be checked for damaged threads and repaired as required.

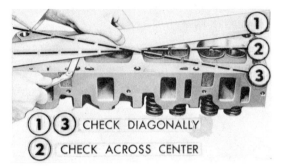

Ford of Canada

Fig. 29-2   Checking Cylinder Head for Warping

When replacing the cylinder head, follow the step by step procedure as outlined by the manufacturer. Pay particular attention to: cleanliness of the mating surfaces, cleanliness of the cylinder-head bolt holes, use of guide or pilot pins, torque specifications, tightening sequence, and retightening after complete assembly.

Generally speaking, cast-iron cylinder heads are retightened when the engine is at operating temperature. Aluminum heads are retightened after they have reached normal operating temperature and then have been allowed to cool.

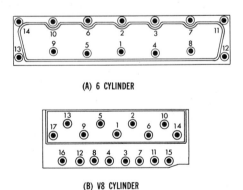

Fig. 29-3   Typical Cylinder Head Tightening Sequences

29-2 VALVE TROUBLES

The valve assembly in the modern engine represents the latest developments in metallurgy and the highest skill in precision manufacturing. The improvements in valve mechanisms, however, have been absorbed in higher compression ratios and higher engine speeds. Today the valve assembly needs inspection and servicing more than ever before. With faulty valve action, the value of high compression, power, and economy is lost. Carbon, corrosion, wear, and misalignment are inevitable products of normal engine operation. Valve troubles include sticking, burning, formation of deposits, wear, and leakage.

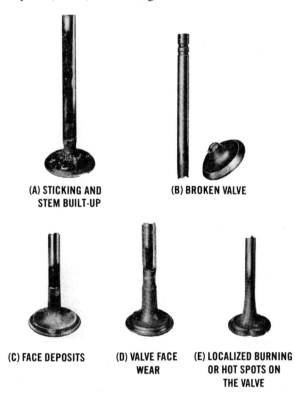

Thompson Products
A Division of TRW Canada Ltd.

Fig. 29-4   Typical Valve Damage

Valve sticking—can be caused as a result of unburned carbon-residue gums forming on the valve stems and guides. Worn valve stems and/or guides will speed up the formation of gum deposits. Sometimes the addition of certain additives to the fuel or oil will dissolve the gum formations and relieve the condition.

Valve sticking also can be caused by warped valve stems. The warping is a result of excessive heat, cocked valve spring or retainer, misalignment between the valve guide and the seat, or insufficient lubrication.

Valve burning—can be caused by any condition that prevents normal exhaust valve face-to-seat contact, poor valve heat dissipation, overloading or overheating of the engine, lean carburetor fuel-air mixtures, weak or cocked valve springs, and distortion caused by improper tightening of the cylinder head.

Formation of deposits and carbon—particularly on the intake valve, is a result of excessively rich fuel-air mixtures, defective ignition and combustion, engine operating below normal operating temperature, excessive amounts of gum in the fuel, or oil passing between the valve guide and stem.

Wear—on the valve face or seat can be caused by impact seating because of too strong a valve spring, dirt or carbon, insufficient valve clearance, warpage, or misalignment. Stem wear can be caused by dirt and carbon or insufficient lubrication.

Valve stretching or breakage—the valve stem can be stretched because of overheating or too heavy valve-spring tension. Excessive valve clearance results in heavy impact seating. Any misalignment between the valve face and seat causes a sideways movement of the valve head each time the valve closes. This results in metal fatigue and valve-stem breakage. A small scratch, put on the stem when cleaning, could be the starting point of a crack and valve-stem breakage.

29-3 VALVE SERVICE

Before the valves can be removed, the cylinder head must be taken off, and the carbon removed from the head and block. As the valves are removed, the valve spring, retainer, and lock must be kept together as an assembly and be replaced in the same valve port from which it was removed. A similar procedure should be followed for valve lifters, push rods, and rocker arms.

When the valves have been removed, they are thoroughly cleaned in order to remove carbon and varnish deposits. This may be done with a wire brush or buffing wheel. Clean the valve stem with fine abrasive cloth. After cleaning, inspect the valves carefully. Discard valves with cracks, burns, deep pits, excessive wear, and bent stems. The remaining valves are then placed, temporarily, in their valve guides to check for excessive valve-guide clearance. If the guides are worn excessively, replace or ream out to a larger size and install valves with oversized stems. Check valve lock grooves for wear. Discard valves with worn lock grooves.

Place the valves which have passed the visual and guide inspections in a special valve-refacing machine. The chuck of the valve refacer must be set at the proper angle to give the correct angle to the face of the valve. The first cut should be a light one. If this cut does not remove metal from the entire face of the valve, the valve may not be centered in the chuck properly, or the valve stem may be bent or the head warped. Replace the valve if the stem is bent or the head warped. Succeeding cuts should not be heavy; only enough material should be removed to clean up the face. If the

(A) VALVE FACE

(B) VALVE STEM

Black and Decker

Fig. 29-6   Machining Valves

Courtesy of General Motors

Fig. 29-5   Cleaning Combustion Chamber

amount of material that must be removed reduces the valve margin to less than 1/32″, replace the valve. During the refacing operation the grinding stone must be inspected and trued to maintain a true valve face.

The valve-stem tip usually requires refacing to remove roughness, unevenness, and pitting. This is done by grinding the stem lightly in the special attachment which is part of the valve-refacing machine.

29-4 VALVE-SEAT SERVICE

After the cylinder head or block has been thoroughly cleaned, carefully inspect the valve seat for cracks, burns, wear, or to determine if there is sufficient metal remaining for another grind. If the seat does not pass the visual inspection, it should be replaced, or the cylinder head or block counterbored to accept a seat insert.

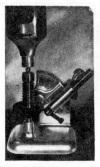

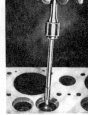

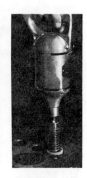

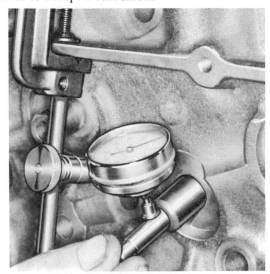

(A) DIAL INDICATOR METHOD

Courtesy of General Motors

SMALL HOLE
GAUGE
VALVE
GUIDE
MICROMETER

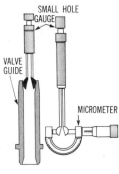

(B) HOLE GAUGE AND MICROMETER METHOD

Fig. 29-7 Measuring Valve Guide Wear

(A) DRESSING STONE (B) INSTALLING PILOT (C) GRINDING SEAT

Black and Decker

Fig. 29-8 Refacing Valve Seats

Since the grinding-stone pilot is locked into the valve guide, the valve guide must be cleaned and be of the proper size. Guides that are excessively worn, worn out-of-round, or bell mouthed will not position the guide properly so that the stone will grind the seat concentric with the guide, or at the proper angle. Replace worn guides prior to valve-seat refacing.

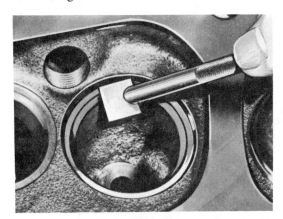

(A) CHECKING

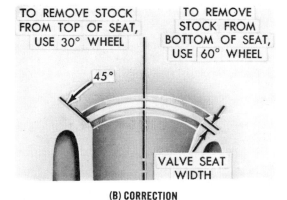

TO REMOVE STOCK
FROM TOP OF SEAT,
USE 30° WHEEL
TO REMOVE
STOCK FROM
BOTTOM OF SEAT,
USE 60° WHEEL
45°
VALVE SEAT
WIDTH

(B) CORRECTION

Ford of Canada

Fig. 29-9 Valve Seat Width

Valve-seat refacing stones must be of the proper angle and trued frequently to ensure a perfect seating surface. After refacing, the valve seat may be too wide or too narrow. Too wide a seat will encourage carbon flakes to adhere to the seat; too narrow a seat will not dissipate heat from the valve head properly. A valve seat should be about $\frac{1}{16}''$ wide. Seat width may be reduced by grinding the top of the seat with a $20°$ stone and/or the bottom of the seat with a $60°$ stone. After the seat has been narrowed, reface it again with the proper angle stone.

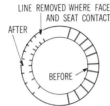

(A) PENCIL METHOD

(B) WITH BLUEING

Black and Decker

Fig. 29-10   Checking Valve Face and Seat Contact

After refacing, the valve seat may be so enlarged that the valve head sinks deeply into the seat. In this case a valve-seat insert is required.

Special gauges are available to check the valve seats for concentricity and width. Valve face-and-seat contact may be checked by marking around the valve face with lead pencil marks spaced about $\frac{1}{4}''$ apart. Place the valve in its seat and rotate it about a half a turn each way. The portions of the pencil marks which are removed indicate the contact area. Prussian blue may also be used. Coat the valve seat lightly with blueing, insert the valve, and turn it lightly. The area of the valve face that is coated with blueing indicates the contact area. In both cases the contact area should be approximately the centre third of the valve face.

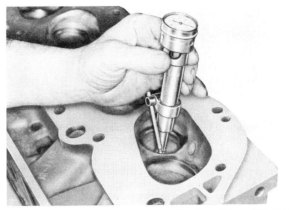

Courtesy of General Motors

Fig. 29-11   Measuring Valve Seat Concentricity

29-5 VALVE-SEAT INSERT SERVICE

Screw-in type inserts are easily replaced by screwing out the old one and screwing in the new. Pressed-in or shrunk-in inserts are usually held in position by peening or rolling the metal around the edge of the insert. They may be pulled out with a special puller or broken into halves with a cold chisel to facilitate removal. The counterbore must be then cleaned and checked for roundness, trueness, and size. If the new insert does not bottom, or fit tightly, there will be poor heat transfer.

Most new inserts have an "interference fit," that is, they are about .002″ larger than the counterbore. This necessitates shrinking the insert by placing it in dry ice for about 15 minutes. When frozen, the insert must be handled carefully and quickly since it is now quite brittle and will crack or break easily.

Both types of inserts require refacing to the proper angle after installation.

29-6 VALVE-GUIDE SERVICE

Clean and check valve guides for wear before the valve seats are refaced. The valve guide must be thoroughly cleaned of carbon; special tools and brushes are available for this purpose. After cleaning, carefully check the guide for wear. Guides may wear in such a way as to produce too much clearance, or wear *bellmouth*. Bellmouth wear is when the guide has worn to a larger diameter at each end than in the centre. A comparison between the manufacturer's specifications and the guide and valve-stem sizes will determine if the wear has taken place on the guide or the valve stem. Proper clearance between the two is important to proper valve-face and seat alignment and valve heat dissipation.

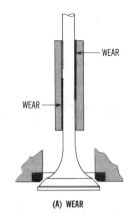

(A) WEAR

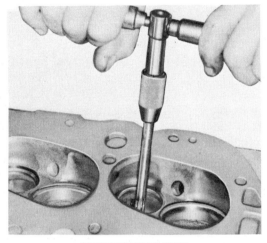

(B) REAMING VALVE GUIDE

Courtesy of General Motors

Fig. 29-12   Valve Guide Service

Valve-guide service procedures differ depending on whether the *replaceable* insert or the *integral* type is used.

Valve guides of the replaceable type may be removed in a press by a special puller, or by driving them out with a hammer and a special drift punch. Before removing old guides, carefully measure the distance that the guide protrudes into the port so that the new guide can be installed properly. Some manufacturers make available special valve-guide drivers to ensure proper positioning.

Install new valve guides by using the special driver to ensure against damage. After installation, new guides require reaming to size. This usually is done in two steps: a rough ream and a finish ream. The guide-to-valve seat concentricity should be checked and corrected by regrinding the seat as required.

Valve guides of the integral type must be reamed to an oversize to correct all types of wear. To ream the guides, use a special aligning jig or pilot to keep the reamed hole in alignment. Long aligning bushings are used with a tapered arbor to keep the reamer in alignment with the jig. The guide hole is reamed true to provide the proper clearance for valves with .003″, .005″, .015″ and .030″ oversized valve stems. After the reaming operation, check the guide-to-valve seat concentricity and correct as required.

29-7 VALVE-SPRING SERVICE

Clean valve springs thoroughly and check for *etching*. Etching is a chemical reaction caused by poor valve-chamber ventilation. Corrosive vapours, steam, or moisture create flecks of rust on the spring which eat away the material, thereby weakening the spring.

Valve springs should be square on each end or they will have a tendency to pull the valve to one side and cause undue wear on the valve stem and guide.

Compare valve-spring free length and the pressure in pounds that the spring should exert when compressed to a given length to the manufacturer's specification. Discard springs that are not within the minimum or maximum allowable tolerances. Weak springs can cause a high-speed miss, while too strong a spring can damage the valve seat and face, or stretch the valve stem and cause breakage. Special tools are available to test valve-spring tension.

29-8 ROCKER-ARM AND SHAFT SERVICING

When disassembling rocker-arm assemblies, keep all the units in their proper order and reassemble them in their original positions. After removal clean and inspect rocker arms for grooves and pits in the contact faces. On some rocker arms, the valve end can be refinished to provide a flat surface by dressing the surface on the valve-refacing machine. Remove excessively grooved or pitted rocker arms. Rocker arms with bushings can be rebushed if the old bushing is worn.

Inspect rocker-arm shafts for wear and replace as required. Clear the oil passageway. When assembling the rocker-arm assembly to the cylinder head, make sure the oil holes in the shaft line up

Black and Decker

Fig. 29-14   Refacing Rocker Arm

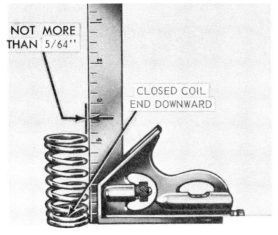

(A) VALVE SPRING SQUARENESS

(B) VALVE SPRING MEASURE

(A) REMOVING

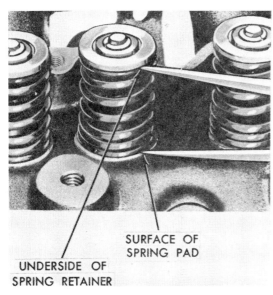

(C) VALVE SPRING ASSEMBLED HEIGHT

Ford of Canada

Fig. 29-13   Checking Valve Springs

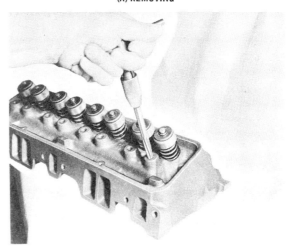

(B) REAMING

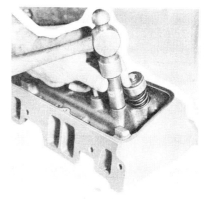

(C) REPLACING

Courtesy of General Motors

Fig. 29-15   Rocker Stud Servicing

with the oil supply holes in the cylinder head or mounting brackets.

On engines with independently mounted ball pivoted-type rocker arms, inspect the push-rod socket, stem-contact surface, the ball-pivot contact area and the ball pivot for wear. Replace as required. It is not advisable to dress the contact surfaces of this type of rocker arm.

Check the rocker-arm studs for wear or damage, or looseness in the head. On most models, the studs are a press fit in the head and must be removed by using a special puller. If the cylinder head is worn, ream it to accommodate an oversized stud. Install new studs to the proper depth by using a special driver tool and measuring gauge. Some rocker-arm studs are threaded into the cylinder head.

29-9 PUSH-ROD SERVICE

As push rods are removed, they should be kept in their proper order and reinstalled in their original positions. Clean and inspect them for straightness and tip wear. Discard damaged rods.

On some engines, special short length push rods are used to maintain proper valve-train length. These shorter push rods compensate for the longer valve-stem length after valve face and seat regrinding. Other manufacturers recommend grinding the end of the valve stem to maintain proper valve-train length. Too long or too short push rods will prevent the normal operation of the hydraulic valve lifters.

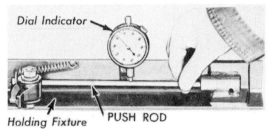

Ford of Canada

Fig. 29-16   Checking Push Rod Run Out

29-10 VALVE-LIFTER SERVICE

Solid valve lifters—should be kept in their proper order and reinstalled in their original position. After cleaning, inspect the adjusting screw face (if used), push-rod socket, and cam face for wear and replace as required. Dress adjusting screw faces on a valve-refacing machine. On some engines, if the lifter bores become worn, they may be reamed oversize and oversized lifters installed.

Ford of Canada

Fig. 29-17   Testing Hydraulic Valve Lifters

Hydraulic valve lifters—must be kept in their proper order and the components of each lifter must be kept separate and reassembled in their original positions. Before disassembly, test the lifter for wear by performing a "leak-down" test. During this test the lifter is placed under a uniform pressure, and the time that is required to force the lifter to bottom is accurately measured. If the time

(A) ROCKER SHAFT TYPE

(B) ROCKER STUD TYPE

Ford of Canada

Fig. 29-18   Adjusting Valve Clearance

is too short, the lifter is worn and must be replaced.

If the lifter passes the leak-down test, disassemble it and clean it in solvent. On reassembly, fill the lifter with light engine oil and retest; then refill before installation.

29-11 VALVE-TAPPET CLEARANCE

Valve-tappet clearance is necessary to ensure that the valve will seat properly during all running temperatures. The method of checking and setting this clearance varies with each make and model of engine. On engines with solid lifters, the checking is done by using a thickness gauge. Adjusting screws are located in the lifter (L-head) or in the rocker arm (I-head). Engines equipped with hydraulic lifters usually require only a basic setting after installation. Others may be readjusted during service. In all cases, follow the procedures in the manufacturers manuals.

29-12 CAMSHAFT SERVICE

Since camshafts only revolve at one-half of engine crankshaft speed, the amount of wear that takes place on the journals of the camshaft and the bearing shells is considerably less. New, improved materials and heat treating processes have reduced cam-lobe wear. However, the forces imposed on the camshaft as it opens and closes the valve does wear the lobes, journals, and bearings.

Inspect the camshaft and replace it if it shows scored or damaged cams, or worn, scored, or discoloured bearing journals. Check the cams for wear. Camshafts with worn lobe faces must be replaced.

Check the cam-lobe lift with the camshaft in the engine by placing a dial indicator in the end of the push rod. Rotate the camshaft and note the maximum and minimum dial readings. The difference between the readings is the amount of lobe lift. The height of the lobe can also be measured with a micrometer when the camshaft is removed from the engine.

The forces imposed on the camshaft journals and bearings tend to wear the shaft out-of-round. This may be checked with a micrometer by measuring each journal in two places which are at right angles to each other. The amount of variation in the two readings indicates the out-of-round wear.

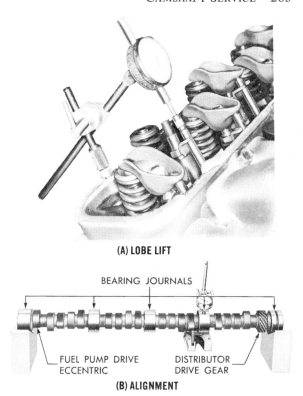

(A) LOBE LIFT

(B) ALIGNMENT

Courtesy of General Motors

Fig. 29-19   Checking Camshaft

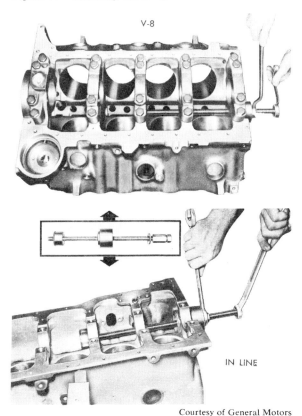

Courtesy of General Motors

Fig. 29-20   Replacing Camshaft Bearings

Measure the camshaft bearings at several points with a telescoping gauge and a micrometer. A comparison between the shaft and bearing measurements indicates the clearance. Excessive camshaft-bearing clearance can cause excessive oil consumption. Replace worn, pitted, or scored bearings.

Camshaft end play must be checked. This may be accomplished by either measuring the clearance between the thrust plate and the timing gear spacer with a thickness gauge, or by attaching a dial indicator against the camshaft gear and moving the camshaft in and out.

Check the camshaft for alignment. This may be done by placing the camshaft in V blocks, and using a dial indicator to check eccentricity. Bent shafts may sometimes be straightened in a press.

To replace worn camshaft bearings, use a puller to draw the shell out evenly. A special tool equipped with a pilot is used to install new bearings. When installing new bearings, clean the oil holes in the cylinder block, and exercise care to ensure that the oil hole in the bearing lines up with the oil hole in the block. Some manufacturers provide prefinished undersize cam bearings, while others only supply semifinished bearings which must be line-reamed to provide the proper clearance.

29-13 TIMING-GEAR SERVICE

Worn timing gears become noisy and produce a humming or knocking sound. This sound results where there is too much clearance between the gear teeth. Camshaft-bearing clearance is a factor that must be considered when determining gear-tooth clearance. Excessive camshaft-bearing clearances change the distance between the centre line of the camshaft and the crankshaft and, therefore, can influence gear-tooth clearance.

Replace the gears if they are visibly worn, broken, or have chipped teeth. Replace the camshaft gear if the gear-tooth clearance is .010″ or more. After the new camshaft gear is installed, and the clearance still exceeds .005″, the crankshaft gear should be replaced.

The method of camshaft-gear replacement depends upon the method of installation; some are bolted, others are pressed on and positioned by a key. Crankshaft gears are usually positioned by a key and are removed by a gear puller or by using an arbor press. They are usually replaced by using an arbor press.

(A) CAMSHAFT END PLAY

(B) GEAR RUN OUT

(C) GEAR BACKLASH

Courtesy of General Motors

Fig. 29-21   Checking Timing Gears

REFERENCE POINT   RIGHT SIDE OF CHAIN

TAKE UP SLACK ON LEFT SIDE, ESTABLISH
REFERENCE POINT. MEASURE DISTANCE **A**.
TAKE UP SLACK ON RIGHT SIDE. FORCE
LEFT SIDE OUT. MEASURE DISTANCE **B**.
DEFLECTION IS **A** MINUS **B**.

Ford of Canada

Fig. 29-22   Typical Timing Chain Deflection

29-14 TIMING-SPROCKETS AND CHAIN SERVICE

Before a timing chain is removed, check it for stretch. This may be done by pushing the chain toward the sprockets to draw the opposite side of the chain tight. Then move the slack portion away from the sprockets. If the chain can be moved away from the sprockets 1″ or more, it should be replaced. Replace the sprockets if the teeth are worn or chipped. On engines equipped with automatic chain adjustors, replace the chain when the adjustor is at the end of its travel.

To remove the chain, the camshaft sprocket must be removed. When replacing the chain, the timing marks must be properly aligned.

29-15 SERVICING TIMING GEAR-COVER OIL SEAL

Whenever the timing gear cover is removed, inspect the oil seal and replace if it shows wear or leakage. To remove the old seal, place the cover on a flat surface and drive out the seal with a punch and hammer.

To install the new seal, place the seal in the recess with the free end of the leather or composition toward the inside of the cover. Using a seal driver or a piece of flat metal slightly larger than the seal, tap the seal into place with a hammer. Make sure the seal bottoms in the recess.

Before installing many types of oil seals, it is necessary to soak the seal in oil for an hour. Before installing, see manufacturer's instructions.

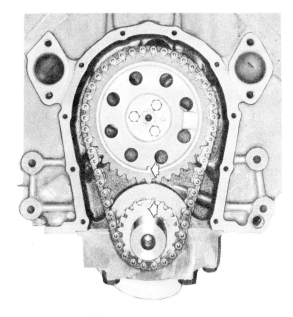

Courtesy of General Motors

Fig. 29-23   Setting Valve Timing

REVIEW QUESTIONS

1. Describe briefly how small cracks in cylinder heads may be repaired.
2. What causes cylinder heads to warp?
3. Why must the intake manifold-to-cylinder head mating surfaces also be machined when V8 cylinder heads are remachined?
4. When are (a) aluminum (b) cast-iron cylinder heads retightened?
5. List four common valve troubles and give one cause for each.
6. State four reasons for discarding a valve.
7. What is the approximate minimum valve margin thickness?
8. List four points to be checked during the visible inspection of valve seats.
9. Why must worn valve guides be replaced before

regrinding the valve seats?

10. Describe two methods of checking valve face and seat contact area.

11. How are new valve-seat inserts installed?

12. Describe two methods of determining valve-guide wear.

13. What causes valve-spring etching?

14. What effect would (a) bent (b) weak valve springs have on valve operation?

15. What effect would excessive grinding of the valve face and seat have on valve-spring tension? Why?

16. How are push rods modified to maintain proper valve train length?

17. Describe a hydraulic valve lifter "leak down" test.

18. Why is valve clearance necessary on engines using solid valve lifters?

19. How can cam-lobe wear be checked?

20. How can camshaft-bearing clearance be checked?

21. What effect will worn camshaft bearings have on timing-gear clearance? Why?

22. How may timing-chain stretch be checked?

23. Describe the procedure of installing an oil seal.

Chapter 30
CYLINDER BLOCKS, CRANKSHAFTS, AND BEARINGS

30-1 CYLINDER BLOCKS

The cylinder block and crankcase form the main body of the engine. They house the reciprocating and revolving engine parts and provide for the cooling of the engine. The design and construction of the cylinders and cylinder blocks depend upon several factors: the number and arrangement of the cylinders (in-line, slant, or V); the bore, stroke, and compression ratio; the valve arrangement; the method of cooling; the materials used, and the methods of casting and machining.

30-2 MATERIALS

Most cylinder blocks and crankcases are made of cast grey iron; some are made of die-cast aluminum. Cast grey iron is popular because of its low cost. It

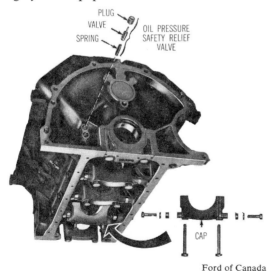

Fig. 30-1   Typical V8 Cylinder Block Details

PLUG
VALVE
SPRING
OIL PRESSURE
SAFETY RELIEF
VALVE
CAP
Ford of Canada

will not warp under high temperatures and pressures. For its strength, it is not exceptionally heavy. It is soft enough to be machined easily, yet it can be finished to a smooth surface that wears well, absorbs vibrations, and is corrosion resistant. It can be easily cast, using the sand mould process, into the intrical shapes required to form the water jackets, valve ports, etc. Frequently, small quantities of nickel, molybdenum, or chromium are added to the cast grey iron to improve the strength (nickel) and hardness (molybdenum and chromium) of the casting without decreasing the machinability.

Some engines use a cast iron block attached to a cast aluminum crankcase, while others use a cast aluminum block and crankcase assembly. Aluminum castings reduce the weight and increase the heat dissipation. Since aluminum wears more rapidly than cast iron, the cylinder bores are lined with grey cast iron or steel sleeves.

30-3 CASTING

There are two basic methods of casting cylinder block and crankcase assemblies: the *en bloc* method, usually used for liquid-cooled engines; and the individual cylinder casting used on air-cooled engines. Casting the cylinders as a complete unit results in a shorter, more compact, more rigid, and less expensive unit. When the assembly is made of cast aluminum, nonreplaceable cast grey iron or steel cylinder sleeves are placed in the mould before the block assembly is cast.

Individual aluminum cylinder castings are usually used in air-cooled engines because of aluminum's higher heat dissipating properties. The cylinders are cast around the cylinder sleeve, and the cooling fins are an integral part of the casting. The individual cylinder castings are bolted to an aluminum or cast grey iron crankcase.

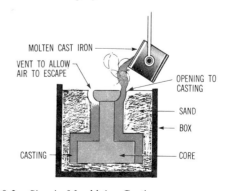

MOLTEN CAST IRON
VENT TO ALLOW
AIR TO ESCAPE
OPENING TO
CASTING
SAND
BOX
CASTING
CORE

Fig. 30-2   Simple Mould for Casting

30-4 MACHINING

When a casting is removed from the mould, internal strains caused by the uneven cooling between the thin and thick sections of the casting are present. These internal strains could cause the casting to warp or change its shape slightly if it were immediately completely machined. Two methods are used to prevent this warpage. One method is to partially machine the casting in order to remove the hard surface layer of iron, and then allow the casting to season by storing it in the open for a period of time. The other method uses special heat-treating operations which relieve the strains and reduce the time required for seasoning.

The machining processes include boring, grinding and/or honing (in that order) to finish the cylinders to a standard size which allows for proper piston clearance. The out-of-round and taper tolerances rarely exceed .0005″. The cylinder bores must be at right angles to the crankshaft and to the cylinder-head and pan surfaces. The head and pan surfaces are ground flat and true. The camshaft-bearing shell bores and crankshaft-bearing bores are line-bored accurately. All cylinder head, oil pan, manifold, etc., attaching capscrew and stud holes are accurately located, drilled and tapped. All of the machine operations are frequently completed on one large, automatic machine that accepts a raw casting at one end and turns out a completely machined assembly at the other.

30-5 CYLINDER SLEEVES

When wear takes place on engines with nonreplaceable cylinder sleeves, remachine the cylinders by boring to a maximum of .040″ oversize. Then the cylinder block must be specially machined to install cylinder sleeves or be scrapped. Many truck, tractor, and large gasoline or diesel engine cylinder blocks are made with replaceable cylinder sleeves.

These cylinder sleeves make possible the rapid and economical replacement of the cylinder bores, when required. The sleeves are made of either cast grey iron, steel or other alloys and are frequently heat-treated to improve wearing qualities. Two types of sleeves are used, the dry type and the wet type.

Dry-type cylinder sleeves—do not contact the engine coolant. They are accurately machined on

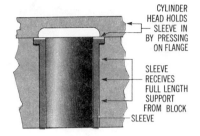

(A) "DRY" SLEEVE IN PLACE

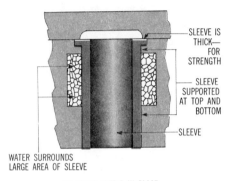

(B) "WET" SLEEVE IN PLACE

Fig. 30-3   Cylinder Sleeves

both inner and outer surfaces and are pressed or driven into the cylinder block to form the finished cylinder surface.

This type of sleeve is frequently used to recondition passenger-car cylinder blocks in which the cylinder bores have worn more than .040″, or have been badly scored or damaged. To accommodate the sleeve the damaged block is bored to the proper diameter to accept the cylinder sleeve. Then the sleeve is pressed into position.

Wet-type sleeves—are the most popular type for truck and tractor application. This type of sleeve contacts the coolant and forms the cylinder wall and water-jacket wall between the water jackets and the cylinder. This results in better heat dissipation from the sleeve. The sleeve is pressed into the cylinder block. Special sealing rings and gaskets between the sleeve and block prevent cooling-system leaks.

Many fleet operators stock cylinder sleeves fitted with piston and rings which are ready to be quickly placed in the cylinder block. This reduces the time the vehicle is off the road.

30-6 OTHER FEATURES

The cylinder block usually includes special drilled or cast-in oil-line passageways. These passageways

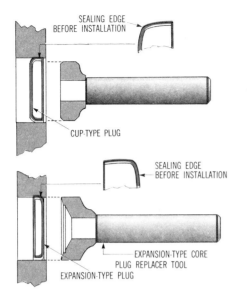

Fig. 30-4   Expansion Plugs

direct the lubricating oil to the crankshaft main bearings, the camshaft bearings, etc.

Round openings in the sides of the block are often cast or machined to accept expansion plugs. These plugs provide a means of cleaning rust and scale from the water jackets, or reduce the possibility of the cylinder block cracking should the coolant freeze.

30-7 MOTOR MOUNTS

To support the engine in the automobile frame, motor mounts consisting of resilient rubber pads or washers are placed between the support lugs on the engine and the brackets on the frame. These rubber pads or washers prevent metal-to-metal contact. They insulate the engine vibrations and noise and prevent their transfer to the body. Motor mounts also absorb and ease the torque or twisting strain loading of the drive line.

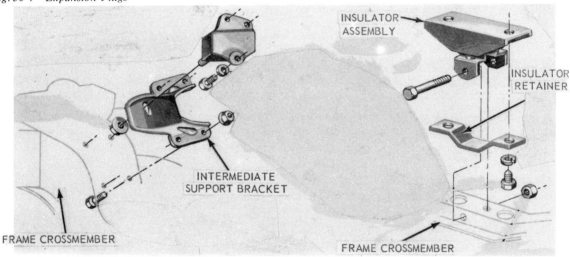

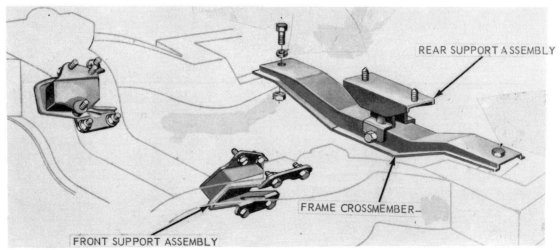

Fig. 30-5   Typical Engine Mounts

Ford of Canada

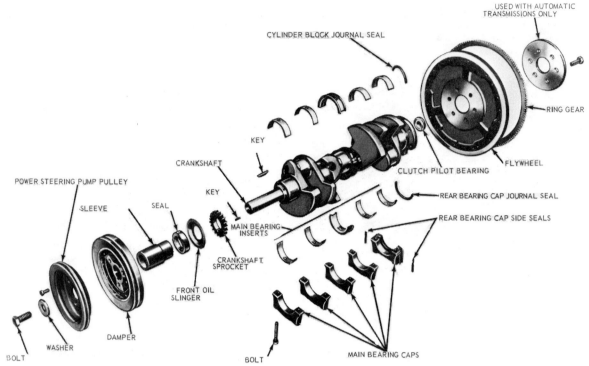

Fig. 30-6 Typical Crankshaft and Related Parts

Ford of Canada

The "three-point" type of suspension is the most popular today. Two types of three-point suspension are used. In one type, one mount is placed on either side near the front of the engine and one mount usually is placed under the rear of the transmission. In the other type one mount is placed on either side of the engine near the rear and one mount under the front centre of the engine. Usually the side mounts are placed somewhat up on the sides of the engine, in order to minimize torque deflections when a load is placed on the engine.

30-8 CRANKSHAFTS

The crankshaft receives power from the piston and connecting rod and converts this power in the recip-

rocating motion of the piston and connecting rod into rotary motion of the flywheel. This conversion of motion is accomplished by the use of offset crankarms, or throws, on the crankshaft. The connecting rod is attached to the crankpin which is located between the crank throws. The number, grouping, and spacing of the crank throws and crankpins depends upon the number of cylinders and the design of the engine.

Crankshafts are made by either the drop-forged process or are cast of steel alloys. They are especially heat-treated to resist wear, bending, and twisting. After the crankshaft has been forged or cast to its approximate size and heat treated, the main and connecting-rod bearing surfaces, called

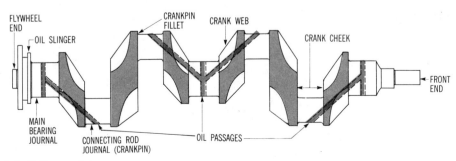

Fig. 30-7 Crankshaft Nomenclature

journals, are accurately finished to size by turning and grinding.

Some crankshafts have hollow crankpins to reduce the weight and the rotating force that is developed.

In order to balance the rotating force of the crankarm, crankpin, and connecting rod, counterweights are attached to the crank throws opposite the crankpin. These counterweights may be forged or cast as an integral part of the crankshaft, or may be bolted to the crankshaft. A crankshaft must be properly balanced; that is, no unbalancing force develops when the shaft is rotating. These forces tend to twist, bend, and distort the shaft, causing vibration and high main-bearing pressures. The shaft must be in both *static* and *dynamic balance*.

Static balance is balance at rest. A statically balanced crankshaft will remain at rest regardless of its position. A statically unbalanced crankshaft will revolve as gravity pulls the heavy side downward. Holes are usually drilled in the counterweights to remove sufficient metal to obtain the proper balance.

Dynamic balance is balance of motion. A crankshaft is in dynamic balance when it is rotated at various speeds without developing vibration. If vibration develops, special meters indicate the area of the shaft that is out of balance. Drilling is used to remove the necessary metal to obtain proper balance.

The crankshaft is usually balanced with the flywheel attached, since the flywheel is part of the revolving mechanism.

Although manufacturers exercise extreme care in balancing crankshafts to eliminate vibration, there are other variable factors which cause engine vibration. These factors are: the inertia forces that are developed; the starting and stopping of the piston each time it reaches top or bottom dead centre; and the load deflections induced by the power strokes which produce a tortional or twisting effect. As a result, crankshafts have one or more critical speeds at which vibration will develop. By careful design and balance, the manufacturer locates the critical vibration periods at infrequently used speeds or out of the normal speed range entirely.

Flywheels and vibration dampers are attached to the crankshaft to assist in the reduction of engine crankshaft vibration.

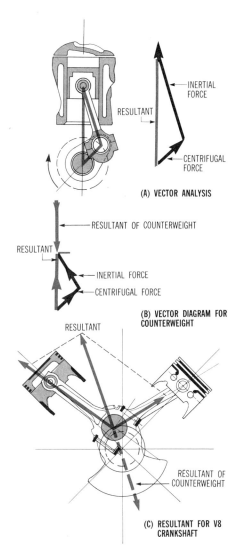

Fig. 30-8 *Crankshaft Inertial and Centrifugal Forces*

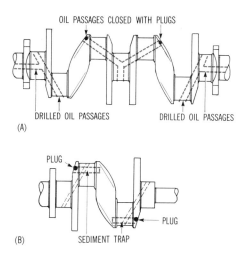

Fig. 30-9 *Crankshaft Oil Passageways*

Most modern crankshafts have oil passageways drilled from the main-bearing journals to the crankpins to provide the necessary lubrication to the connecting-rod bearings. On some crankshafts, a plug closes one end of the drilled passageway. These plugs may be removed during engine overhaul to facilitate cleaning of the passageways.

The crankshaft main-bearing journals rotate in the main bearings located in the engine crankcase, and must be strongly supported in the crankcase. To provide this support, place a main bearing at each end of the crankshaft and one or more additional main bearings between the crankpins.

As the crankshaft rotates, a tendency to move endwise, called *end thrust*, is produced. In order to limit this end play, one crankshaft main-bearing journal has thrust cheeks machined at both ends of the journal. The main bearing also has thrust-bearing surfaces to take the end thrust that is imposed upon the crankshaft.

30-9 TYPES OF CRANKSHAFTS

A number of factors enter into the design of the crankshaft. The length, number, and arrangement

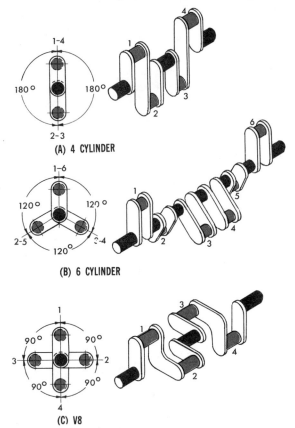

(A) 4 CYLINDER

(B) 6 CYLINDER

(C) V8

Fig. 30-10   Typical Crank Throw Arrangements

of crank throws around the crankshaft is determined by the number of cylinders and the arrangement of cylinders (in-line, V, horizontally opposed, etc.). The firing order of an engine is determined by the arrangement of the crank throws and the design of the camshaft.

Six-cylinder in-line crankshafts may be classified as right- or left-hand crankshafts. This refers to the location of crank throws 3 and 4 as compared to throws 1 and 6. When 1 and 6 are vertical, a right-hand crankshaft has 3 and 4 throws to the right of 1 and 6 when viewed from the front of the engine; a left-hand crankshaft has 3 and 4 throws to the left of 1 and 6.

Four-cylinder engines usually have three main bearings, six-cylinder engines have either 3, 4, or 7 main bearings, eight-cylinder engines have either 3 or 5 main bearings.

On four-cylinder engines, the crank throws are **arranged in one plane; the two end throws are** spaced 180° from the two centre throws. In a six-cylinder in-line engine, the crank throws are spaced 120° apart—throws 1 and 6 in one position, 2 and 5 120° away, and 3 and 4 another 120°. In six-cylinder V-type engines, each throw accommodates a connecting rod from each cylinder bank; therefore, only three throws are required, spaced 120° apart. Six-cylinder opposed engines use a crankshaft similar to the six-cylinder in-line engines. V8 crankshafts have only four throws, as each throw accommodates a connecting rod from each cylinder bank. One type of V8 crankshaft has all throws in one plane and spaces them 180° apart, similar to a four-cylinder crankshaft. The other type has each crankpin in a separate plane spaced 90° apart. This type provides better engine balance and smoother operation.

30-10 ENGINE BEARINGS

The simple appearance of a main, connecting-rod, or camshaft bearing is deceiving for it is complex in structure and has a very difficult job to do. A main or connecting-rod bearing consists of two semicylindrical pieces, usually referred to as a pair. Camshaft bearings are usually circular. Each type usually consists of a steel or bronze backing. Any one of a number of alloys, called bearing alloys, is adhered on the inside surface of the bearing. The special alloy is called the *bearing lining material.*

Each type of bearing lining material must pass certain desired requirements. These requirements

FULL ROUND BUSHINGS, BEARINGS AND HALF-BEARINGS

Fig. 30-11   Typical Engine Bearings   Federal-Mogul Corp.

are: compatibility, fatigue strength or load-carrying capacities, conformability, embedability, and physical requirements.

Compatability—is the ability of a bearing to "get along with" a rotating shaft in the presence of a good lubricant without aggravation or undue friction. Most dissimilar metals are compatible; similar metals are not.

Fatigue strength or load-carrying capacity—a bearing metal must have the ability to support a rotating shaft while the shaft is under heavy load or pressure without the bearing breaking down from fatigue or from wiping.

Conformability—Not all bearing journals are totally round or straight laterally, nor are the

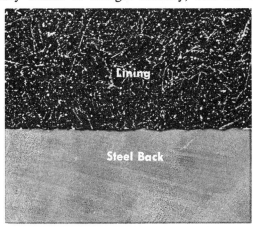

(A) A POPULAR TIN BASE BABBITT LINING AND PHOTOMICROGRAPH

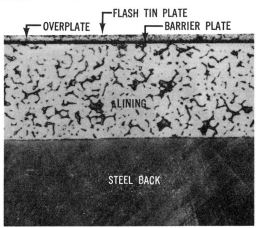

(B) HEAVY DUTY, LOW CONTENT COPPER ALLOY LINING AND PHOTOMICROGRAPH

Fig. 30-12   Typical Bearing Materials   Federal-Mogul Corp.

crankcase and connecting-rod bores always round and true. Therefore, a bearing metal should possess some softness or ability to change slightly, to even the load distribution over the entire bearing area.

Embedability—is the ability of the bearing metal to totally absorb or completely pass off foreign abrasive materials that may be circulated by the lubricant. A bearing material should be such that these foreign particles will either become completely embedded in the lining or passed off. If they become semi-embedded and protrude from the bearing lining, they act as a cutter, thus damaging the shaft.

Physical requirements—are the requirements that are dictated by either performance or manufacturing. The bearing material must have a high temperature-strength ratio; it must not weaken when being operated at normal or above normal engine temperatures. The bearing material should not contain materials that will act as an abrasive and score the shaft. It should be capable of operating against a soft, nonheat-treated shaft. The material should not be affected by the compounds formed in the lubricant because of condensation, blow-by, heat, or cold. The material must also have good thermal conductivity to dissipate the heat that is produced because of load and rotation. It must be capable of being bonded to another type of material such as steel or bronze.

30-11 BEARING MATERIALS

There is no universal type of bearing material and construction that will do the job better than any other type. Bearing liners may be made from tin-base babbitts, lead-base babbitts, copper alloys, aluminum alloys, multilayer bearings in copper alloys, and in aluminum alloys and silver combinations.

Tin-Base Babbitt—according to SAE specification No. 12, contains 3¼% copper, 7¾% antimony, and 89% tin. This type of babbitt is regarded as an all round good bearing material. It will operate well under slight handicaps of poor oiling and some misalignments, but will not withstand the highest loads and temperatures.

Lead-base Babbitt—according to SAE specification No. 15, contains 1% tin, 15% antimony, 1% arsenic, and 83% lead. This is a popular bear-

ing alloy. The load-carrying abilities of lead-base babbitts are as good as, if not slightly better than, tin-base babbitts and, at the same time, have better conformance and embedment properties.

Multilayer Bearing—A bearing may be made up of three or more layers, counting the steel liner as one, the lining material as the second, and a dissimilar layer of material placed on top of the lining. This third layer may be placed on the initial lining by either mechanical or electronic means. If it is applied mechanically, it is classed as a three-layer bearing and usually has a shiny inside finished surface. If it is applied electronically or by plating, it is classed as an overplated bearing and usually has a dull satin-finish inside surface. Various types of materials are applied to the steel backing in a multilayer bearing: a bronze inner layer with a lead or tin overlay; a silver inner layer with a lead overplate; or an aluminum-alloy lining with a lead-alloy overplate and a flash of tin plate over the entire bearing. This type of bearing has excellent wear resistance and also resists the high loadings of **heavy-duty service.**

30-12 BEARING NOMENCLATURE

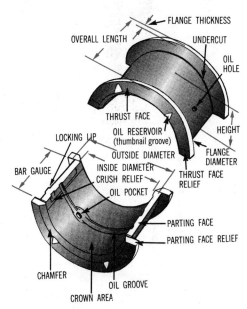

Fig. 30-13   Bearing Nomenclature

30-13 BEARING DESIGN

Bearings are designed to include some means of retention, bearing spread, bearing crush, oil holes, and grooving.

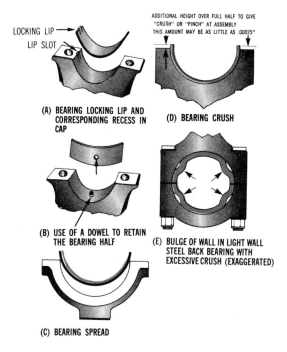

(A) BEARING LOCKING LIP AND CORRESPONDING RECESS IN CAP

(D) BEARING CRUSH

ADDITIONAL HEIGHT OVER FULL HALF TO GIVE "CRUSH" OR "PINCH" AT ASSEMBLY THIS AMOUNT MAY BE AS LITTLE AS .00025"

LOCKING LIP
LIP SLOT

(B) USE OF A DOWEL TO RETAIN THE BEARING HALF

(E) BULGE OF WALL IN LIGHT WALL STEEL BACK BEARING WITH EXCESSIVE CRUSH (EXAGGERATED)

(C) BEARING SPREAD

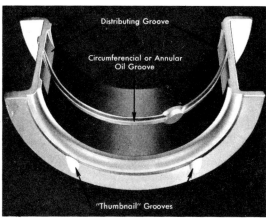

Distributing Groove

Circumferencial or Annular Oil Groove

"Thumbnail" Grooves

(F) SOME TYPICAL GROOVES IN ENGINE BEARINGS

Federal-Mogul Corp.

Fig. 30-14 Bearing Design Features

Bearing retention—provides a suitable means of locking the bearing to keep it from rotating or shifting endwise in its housing. Bearings may be held in position through the use of a projection at the parting face or edge, called a *locking lip* or *tang*. This lip fits into an accurately machined groove in the housing. The lip prevents endwise motion and the bearing cannot rotate because, after assembly, the locking lip butts against the finished surface of the housing mating half. Another method of bearing retention is through the use of a *dowel*. This dowel may be a part of the housing which fits into a hole in the bearing or may be formed as part of the

bearing and fits into a hole in the housing. In either case, the dowel prevents both endwise and rotary motion of the bearing.

Bearing spread—is the extra distance across the parting faces of a bearing half, in excess of the actual diameter of the housing bore. This distance ranges between .005″ and .030″ depending on the thickness, size, and structural stiffness of the bearing. Spread requires the bearing to be snapped or forced lightly into its place. The purpose of spread is to ensure a definite fitting of the bearing against its seat and to keep the bearing in position during assembly.

Bearing crush—creates a radial pressure which holds the bearing tightly in the housing after assembly. It ensures full contact between the bearing and the housing and assists in good heat dissipation. Crush is accomplished by making the length of the bearing shell slightly longer than the circumference of the housing half. When the two bearing halves come together during assembly, they are squeezed or pressed tightly into the housing bore by the slight interference of one half against the other at the parting faces.

Crush is carefully calculated by the bearing manufacturer for a given type of bearing; too much or too little crush will lead to bearing trouble.

Bearing oil holes and grooves—All bearings need not have oil holes, but when oil holes or grooves are required to lubricate the bearing or adjacent parts, the holes or grooves must be of the right size and properly located. The holes must be in line or register with the supply holes drilled in the crankcase.

Frequently, oil grooves are necessary to help distribute the oil and maintain an oil film over the bearing surface under the operating conditions of speed and load. Speed assists the forming of this film, while pressure hinders it. Oil grooves frequently are necessary to maintain the oil film in the high-pressure areas of the bearing.

Oil grooves are also used, particularly in main bearings, as oil carriers or feeders to convey oil to other parts, or to carry excess oil back to the oil pan.

"Thumb nail" grooves are placed in select locations on flange-bearing faces to help distribute the oil evenly over the thrust faces.

30-14 TYPES OF ENGINE BEARINGS

Direct-babbitted bearings or poured bearings—are formed by pouring or spinning the bearing metal, usually tin-base babbitt or lead-base babbitt, directly into the bearing bores. The bores are first tinned, and the bearing metal adheres permanently until melted out. After pouring, the bearings are line-reamed or bored to the correct dimensions and finish.

Frequently, direct-babbitted bearings are designed to incorporate several shims between each bearing cap and base to permit the adjustment of the bearing when the clearance becomes excessive.

Precision-type insert bearings—As previously pointed out, insert bearings have thin layers of bearing material placed on steel liners. Precision inserts are manufactured to such exactness that no boring, scraping, or other fitting is required. These bearings are so accurately manufactured that tampering of any kind usually results in a poorer fit and premature bearing failure. When precision inserts wear, they are not adjustable and therefore must be replaced.

Since the precision insert is manufactured so accurately and since it may only have a thin (.002 to .005″) layer of bearing material, it is imperative that both the bore and the shaft be exact and round within specified limits. The amount of oil clearance becomes automatic when the shaft is a standard size, or has been ground to a standard undersize, the bearing bore is round and to size, and the proper insert is installed.

Since some wear takes place on the shaft, replacing worn bearings with new standard size inserts may not result in proper oil clearance. The amount of wear that has taken place on the shaft may be calculated by measuring the bearing journals and comparing with standard size. Special .001″ and .002″ undersize bearing shells are available to compensate for this wear and maintain proper oil clearances.

30-15 PRECISION-TYPE CAMSHAFT BEARINGS

Precision-type camshaft bearings are as accurately manufactured as insert bearing halves. Full, round camshaft bearings have a relatively thin wall and a steel back with a suitable babbitt lining and are produced of seamless tube or flat strip rolled to form a straight seam. When these bearings are pressed into their respective housings, the correct oil clearance is automatically obtained because of the design, provided the crankcase bores are within the close limits set by the engine manufacturer.

To compensate for camshaft wear, the shaft may be reconditioned by grinding to a standard undersize, and undersized bearings installed. As in standard sizes, no fitting is required. Special semi-finished bearings are available. These bearings require align-boring to establish proper fit.

30-16 PISTON-PIN BUSHING

Bushings are made of solid bronze strip rolled up with a straight or V-seam, or with a steel back and a bronze lining. They are made to a precise outside diameter that is greater than the hole into which they are to be pressed. This ensures that the bushing will remain in its proper place and have good heat dissipation. Additional material is provided on the inside so that the bushing may be fitted to the piston pin.

30-17 OIL OR BEARING CLEARANCE

In order to produce long bearing life, lubrication is necessary to absorb shock, reduce friction, and dissipate heat. To accomplish this, oil must be permitted to flow through a space between the shaft and the bearing. This space is called *oil* or *bearing clearance* and is provided by making the inside diameter of the bearing slightly larger than the shaft, and is expressed as the difference between the two diameters.

Under ideal conditions of constant speed and load, the provision of a predetermined oil clearance and a constant supply of oil allow a continuous film to slide under the loaded area between the shaft and the bearing. Thus the shaft never touches the bearing, even though the shaft is not revolving on the same centre as the centre line of the bearing. The crescent formed by the shaft in an eccentric position, with respect to the bearing diameter, fills with oil from the oil pump. The thick part of the crescent formed in the oil clearance acts as a reservoir for the oil. As the shaft rotates, it actually slides oil under the loaded area so that it is lifted away from the bearing area to permit the passage of oil. This is called the *oil-wedge effect*. This process lifts the shaft so that oil supports the weight, or load. The shaft is supported or floats on layers of oil, and there is not metal-to-metal contact.

This wedging effect is brought about by the

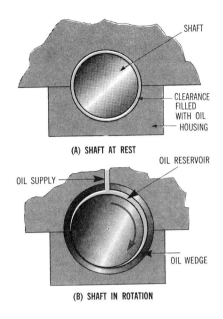

Fig. 30-15   Bearing Oil Wedge

tendency of the oil molecules to form into laminar layers. One layer tends to cling to the shaft and to some degree rotate with it; another layer clings to the bearing surface and tends to remain stationary. The other layers are in various states of speed and slippage. Those closest to the shaft layer are moving faster than those near the bearing layer. The resistance to slippage of these molecules is known as *viscous* or *fluid friction*.

The reciprocating engine speed and load are not constant; therefore, a different set of conditions exist. Under these conditions the shaft operates on

a film of oil for only part of the operating cycle. At other times the oil becomes squeezed to the extent that the shaft and bearing surfaces are only wetted, and the oil film is thin enough to permit the surfaces to protrude through the film. This is known as *boundary lubrication* and is defined as a condition where the oil film is not thin enough to cause engine seizure, nor thick enough to have a full film of oil between the shaft and the bearing.

Examination of used bearings will indicate that there has been actual contact between the shaft and the bearing during engine operation.

The amount of bearing or oil clearance determines the amount of oil which will pass through the bearing and escape at the ends. The greater the clearance, the greater the throw off. For example, .0015″ is proper clearance, then throw off is normal; plus .003″ clearance, the throw off is 5 times normal; plus .006″ clearance, the throw off is 25 times normal. Thus, badly worn bearings increase throw off and results in a reduction of the wedge effect. This increases bearing wear and increases the task of the pistons and piston rings in preventing the excess oil from working up into the combustion chamber and being burnt.

30-18 FLYWHEELS

The flywheel is a heavy, carefully machined, perfectly balanced wheel, usually bolted to a flange on the rear end of the crankshaft. Two or more dowels on the crankshaft position the flywheel.

When a heavy wheel is turned, there is a force produced known as *momentum* which tends to keep

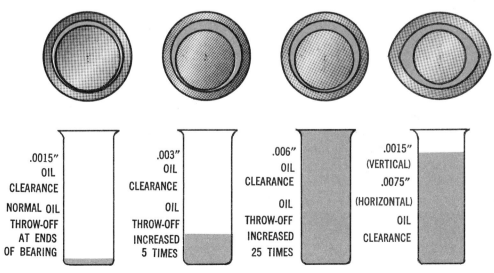

Fig. 30-16   Effect of Oil Clearance on Actual Amount of Oil Throw-Off

it turning. Because of this momentum, the flywheel tends to keep the crankshaft and the moving parts of the engine moving or turning between the power strokes. An engine with many cylinders does not need as heavy a flywheel as an engine with fewer cylinders because of power lap.

The flexibility and pick-up of an engine are dependent to some extent upon the flywheel design. A light flywheel tends to permit rapid acceleration; while a heavy flywheel gives smoother low-speed operation.

Valve and ignition timing marks, or a ignition timing ball, are stamped on the front face of the flywheel in some engines; other engines have these markings on the rim of the vibration damper.

When the flywheel is used with a friction clutch, it is made of grey cast iron (special aluminum flywheels are available for sport or racing engines) and has a steel ring gear shrunk onto its outer diameter. The starter drive pinion meshes with the ring gear to crank the engine for starting purposes. The rear face of the flywheel is accurately machined and acts as one of the clutch pressure surfaces.

When a fluid coupling, or torque converter, is used, it provides the weight to produce the necessary momentum. Therefore, a light, sometimes spoked, flywheel is used. The coupling or converter is bolted to the flywheel. The ring gear may be bolted or welded to the perimeter of the flywheel or to the coupling or converter outer case.

30-19 VIBRATION DAMPERS

Vibration dampers or harmonic balancers are attached to the front end of the crankshaft and are used to damp out torsional vibration.

Torsional vibration is the twisting of the crankshaft caused by the sudden application of power. This twisting results because the mass of the flywheel resists sudden changes in speed. Therefore, when the power impulse occurs in one of the cylinders, the force on the crankpin twists the crankshaft between the cylinder and the flywheel. As the force of the power impulse decreases, the crankshaft unwinds. Thus, the crankshaft tends to twist back and forth with each power impulse. The amount and speed of the twisting action depend on the stiffness of the crankshaft and the spacing of the power impulses.

Crankshafts usually have several speeds at which torsional vibration occurs. The shorter the crank-

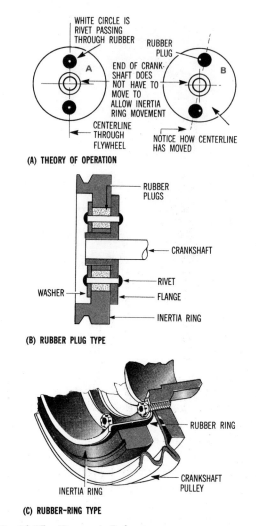

Fig. 30-17   Harmonic Balancers

shaft, the less the tendency to develop torsional vibration.

Vibration dampers are combined with the crankshaft fan drive pulley and frequently have ignition and valve timing marks stamped on the rim of the balancer weight.

Rubber-type vibration damper—has a flywheel or balancer weight connected to the drive hub through rubber mountings. The rubber mountings permit the balancer weight to float on the hub with a slight back-and-forth movement. Since the balancing weight floats on the hub, any sudden increase or decrease in crankshaft speed because of twisting must be transferred to the balancer weight through the hub and rubber mounts. The weight of the balancer is sufficient to resist such sudden changes in speed. The balancer weight exerts a force on the crankshaft in the opposite direction to the twist, thus reducing the amount of twist and the torsional vibration.

Friction-type damper—consists of a balancer weight enclosed in a metal housing. The weight is driven by spring-loaded friction faces between the weight and the housing. The damper weight resists sudden changes in speed and damps out the vibration through the slipping action of the weight. The slipping action of the weight develops a force which opposes the twist of the crankshaft, thus reducing the torsional vibration of the crankshaft.

Fluid-type vibration damper—consists of a metal inertia ring which floats in oil enclosed in a dampener housing. The housing is keyed to the crankshaft. Since the inertia ring is driven by the floating oil, it resists the sudden changes in motion. The dampening action is transferred to the crankshaft through the oil and housing.

REVIEW QUESTIONS

1. Why is grey iron the most popular material used for cylinder blocks?
2. What are the (a) advantages (b) disadvantages of aluminum cylinder blocks?
3. What type of material is used for cylinder blocks of most air-cooled type engines? Why?
4. State two methods of relieving the internal strains in a casting.
5. When are (a) replaceable (b) nonreplaceable sleeves used?
6. What is the advantage of a wet-type cylinder sleeve?
7. State two reasons why expansion plugs are used.
8. Why are the side engine mounts placed somewhat up the sides of the cylinder block?
9. How are crankshafts made?
10. What forces must a crankshaft absorb?
11. What is the purpose of crankshaft main bearings?
12. State the factors that enter into crankshaft design.
13. Why are V8 type crankshaft throws usually placed 90° apart instead of 180°?
14. List four bearing material requirements and state one reason for each.
15. Select the best type of bearing material and give reasons for your selection.
16. Give one reason for each of the following bearing design features: (a) retention (b) spread (c) crush.
17. Why are bearing thumb nail grooves used?
18. Why is it not usually good policy to replace worn bearings with new standard size bearings?
19. Describe in detail the oil wedge effect.
20. Explain the action of each of the laminar layers of oil.
21. **Explain why (a) oil pressure decreases (b) oil throwoff increases, when bearing clearance is increased.**
22. What is the purpose of a flywheel?
23. **Explain how a harmonic balancer damps out crankshaft torsional vibration.**

Chapter 31
CYLINDER-BLOCK, CRANKSHAFT, AND BEARING SERVICE

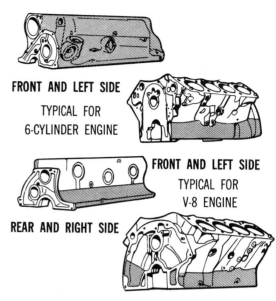

FRONT AND LEFT SIDE
TYPICAL FOR
6-CYLINDER ENGINE

FRONT AND LEFT SIDE
TYPICAL FOR
V-8 ENGINE

REAR AND RIGHT SIDE

REAR AND RIGHT SIDE
Ford of Canada

Fig. 31-1   Location of Cylinder Block Repair Areas

Practically all engine parts are fitted to the cylinder block and crankcase. If they are cracked, warped, worn, or otherwise damaged, it will affect the operation of the crankshaft, pistons, piston rings, bearings, camshaft, cooling, lubrication, etc. The extent of the damage will determine whether repairs or replacement is required.

31-1 CLEANING

The first step in cylinder-block service is dismantling and cleaning. The block must be cleaned down to the bare metal to facilitate inspection and accurate measurement. Before cleaning, remove all old gasket material; remove all oil-line plugs and the oil relief valve. Run a small diameter rod or a stiff bristle brush through the oil passageways to loosen any carbon or sludge. Remove the water-jacket expansion plugs to facilitate the removal of rust and lime deposits.

The assembly may be cleaned with petroleum solvents and a stiff brush, steam, emulsified cleaners, or by placing the assembly in a special cleaning tank. During the cleaning operation, flush the oil passageways and blow out with compressed air.

When the block is thoroughly cleaned, replace the water-jacket expansion plugs, oil line plugs, and oil relief valve.
NOTE: Aluminum cylinder-block assemblies require a special cleaning solution which will not cause damage to the aluminum.

31-2 INSPECTION

The cylinder block should be inspected both visu-ally and with precision instruments. The visual inspection determines whether the block is clean and whether water jackets are free of rust and lime deposits. Check gasket surfaces for burrs and nicks, and make repairs as required. Inspect all threaded holes for cleanliness, repair damaged or pulled threads.

Inspect the cylinder walls, the top of the block, the water jackets, the valve seats, ports, etc., of L-head engines, and the main bearing bores and the engine mounting brackets for cracks. Minute cracks will show up if the suspected area is first coated with a mixture of kerosene and oil, and then wiped with zinc oxide dissolved in wood alcohol.

The method of repair depends on the location of the crack and the type of casting. External cracks may, in some cases, be repaired with metallic **plastic. Internal cracks may be sewn (see section 29-1, Cylinder Head Service) cracked cylinder walls may require the installation of a cylinder sleeve (see** section re sleeving cylinders), or the block may require replacing. When a cracked block is suspected but the crack cannot be found, it may be necessary to pressure-test the block. This is accomplished by plugging all water-jacket, oil-line, and threaded holes, placing the block in a tank of hot water (approximate engine operating temperature), and connecting a compressed air line to the water jacket passageways. Bubbles of escaping air indicate the location of the crack. Special magnetic

281

flux machines sometimes are used to locate small cracks in castings.

31-3 PRECISION MEASUREMENT

Cylinder Head. Check the cylinder-head mating surface for warpage by laying a straight edge against the surface. If warpage beyond the manufacturer's specifications is indicated, the surface must be re-machined.

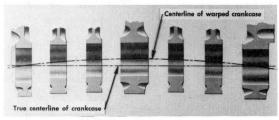

(A) WEAR

(B) ARBOR METHOD

(C) STRAIGHT EDGE METHOD

Federal-Mogul Corp.

Fig. 31-2   Main Bearing Bore Alignment

Main-Bearing Bore Checks—If, on disassembly, uneven main-bearing wear was noticed, with some bearings showing more wear than others, out-of-round bearing bores or a warped block could be the cause.

To check out-of-round bores or bore alignment, remove the bearing shells and place a special, properly ground arbor (about .001″ less in diameter than the smallest bore specification and as long as the crankcase) in the main-bearing bores. The bearing caps are installed in correct relationship to the front of the engine, and the cap bolts are tightened to the proper torque specifications. If the arbor can be turned with a 12″ handle, the main-bearing bores are round and in alignment.

If the special arbor is not available, place a metal straight-edge in three alternate, but parallel, positions in the bores. Using a feeler gauge of one-half the maximum specified oil clearance, try to slide the feeler under the straight-edge. If this can be done, the bores are at least that much out of alignment.

Out-of-round bores also may be checked by bolting up the caps and checking the bores with an out-of-roundness indicator.

Out-of-round or out-of-alignment bores must be corrected by using special automotive machine-shop equipment.

31-3 CYLINDER CHECKS

After the cylinder ridge has been removed, the piston pulled, and the cylinder bore thoroughly cleaned, the size of the cylinder and the amount of wear can be accurately measured with a telescoping gauge and a micrometer.

The wear that takes place in the cylinders is caused by the side thrust of the pistons and the pressure of the piston rings against the cylinder

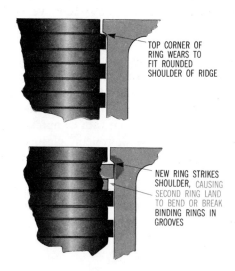

TOP CORNER OF RING WEARS TO FIT ROUNDED SHOULDER OF RIDGE

NEW RING STRIKES SHOULDER, CAUSING SECOND RING LAND TO BEND OR BREAK BINDING RINGS IN GROOVES

Fig. 31-3   Cylinder Ridge

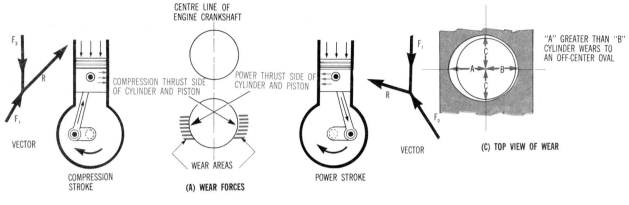

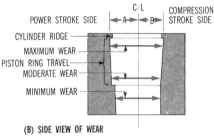

Fig. 31-4 Cylinder Wear

walls. This wear results in the cylinder becoming out-of-round and tapered.

The side thrust of the pistons against the cylinder wall is a result of the angular relationship between the crankshaft, the connecting rod, and the piston, plus the pressures developed in the cylinder during the compression and power strokes. Since the pressure on the piston is much greater on the power stroke than on the compression stroke, a greater side thrust is produced as the piston moves downward. Therefore, the cylinder wears more on the power-thrust side than on the compression-thrust side. Since both power and compression pressures are greatest when the piston is near TDC and decrease as the piston moves downward, a larger amount of wear takes place near the top of the cylinder than near the bottom.

The pressure exerted by the piston rings against the cylinder walls also cause the walls to wear. This wear extends from just below the top of the cylinder to the bottom of the piston-ring travel, which is about 2 to 3″ above the bottom of the cylinder. Lack of lubrication in the upper portions of the cylinder walls, because of the scraping effect of the piston rings, and the high temperatures of combustion, which tends to burn off the lubricating oil, also increase the wear near the top of the cylinder.

This wear creates a ridge, or shoulder, around the top of the cylinder. This cylinder ridge must be removed by a special ridge reamer tool before attempting to remove the piston, or serious damage to the piston could result. Also, if the ridge is not removed before new rings are installed, the shape of the corner of the new ring will knock against the ridge, producing a knocking sound. The ridge may break the ring and ring land, which binds the ring, and prevent the effective operation of the ring in the cylinder.

Excessive out-of-round or taper in the cylinder

Courtesy of General Motors

Fig. 31-5 Measuring Cylinder Bore

reduces the efficiency of the rings and piston, which produces a tight seal to maintain proper compression and power pressures.

To determine the amount of cylinder wear, use a special cylinder gauge. Measurements are taken both laterally and longitudinally across each cylinder at points just below the ridge near the bottom and at the mid-position; there are six measurements in each cylinder. To determine the maximum amount of wear, compare the top and bottom lateral measurements. The difference indicates the amount of taper. Determine out-of-roundness by calculating the greatest difference between any pair of lateral and longitudinal measurements.

The maximum amount of taper should not exceed .010″; out-of-round should not exceed .005″. Cylinders that equal or exceed these amounts should be reconditioned by honing or boring to the next standard oversize. Cylinders are usually reconditioned to fit standard oversized pistons of .005, .010, .015, .020, .030, .040, and .060″ oversize.

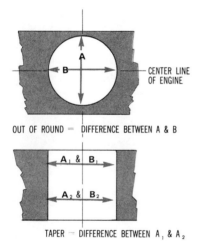

OUT OF ROUND = DIFFERENCE BETWEEN A & B

TAPER = DIFFERENCE BETWEEN A_1 & A_2

Fig. 31-6   Calculating Cylinder Wear

Since a greater amount of wear has taken place on the power-thrust side, the cylinder is worn off-centre. In order to return the cylinder to its proper centre line, the cylinder must be enlarged to approximately twice the maximum amount of taper or out-of-round wear, whichever is the largest, plus whatever additional amount is necessary to obtain the next largest standard oversize.

Cylinders that are worn less than the maximum limits are overhauled without reconditioning the cylinder bores, except for the removal of the cylinder ridge and deglazing of the high polish of the cylinder walls.

31-4 RECONDITIONING CYLINDERS

Removing Cylinder Ridge. Adjustable ridge reamers fit various sized cylinders and usually have only one cutting blade. The reamer is firmly supported in the cylinder and is adjusted to size. Care must be exercised to cut no more than $\frac{1}{64}$ inch below the bottom of the ridge.

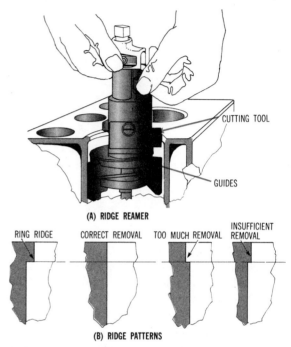

(A) RIDGE REAMER

RING RIDGE | CORRECT REMOVAL | TOO MUCH REMOVAL | INSUFFICIENT REMOVAL

(B) RIDGE PATTERNS

Fig. 31-7   Removing Cylinder Ridge

Deglazing Cylinders. A high polish, or glaze, is formed on the cylinder walls by the action of the piston rings. In order to ensure the proper seating of new piston rings in a cylinder that is within the maximum taper and out-of-round limits, some manufacturers recommend the removal of this glaze. To remove the glaze, a cylinder hone driven by an electric drill is adjusted to light pressure against the cylinder walls and moved rapidly up and down while being rotated. This action leaves a cross-hatched pattern on the cylinder walls. After overhaul always clean the cylinder walls and the engine thoroughly to remove abrasive materials and cuttings in order to prevent damage to the engine.

Honing is used when the removal of .001 to .002″ will clean up a cylinder bore so that the surface is sufficiently improved without enlarging the cylinder too much. Honing more than .002″ necessitates

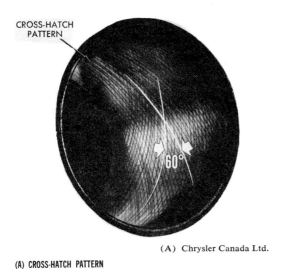

(A) Chrysler Canada Ltd.

(A) CROSS-HATCH PATTERN

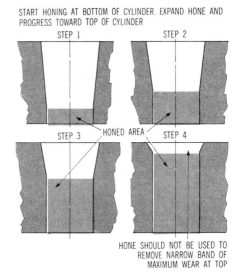

START HONING AT BOTTOM OF CYLINDER. EXPAND HONE AND PROGRESS TOWARD TOP OF CYLINDER

Fig. 31-10   Honing a Cylinder

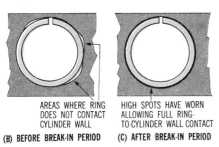

Fig. 31-8   Cylinder Honing and Ring Seating

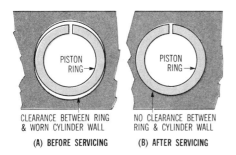

Fig. 31-9   Servicing Cylinders

the expanding of the piston to ensure a proper fit.

To hone a cylinder, follow the hone manufacturer's instructions to ensure good results without damaging the cylinder block or honing equipment. Always clean the cylinder thoroughly to remove abrasive materials and cuttings.

Reboring of a cylinder is required when the cylinder taper or out-of-round is greater than .005 inch. A boring bar is a machine that attaches to the cylinder head and cuts metal from the cylinder walls to resize the cylinder true and on the proper centre line. All cylinders are resized to the standard oversize required for the most worn cylinder.

Before attaching the boring bar, lightly file the top of the cylinder to remove any burrs, which would cause misalignment of the boring bar. Main-bearing caps should be in place and properly torqued to prevent distortion of the main-bearing bores.

Follow manufacturer's instructions for proper use of the boring bar.

After boring, remove the final .002″ required to reach the proper oversize by honing to ensure a satisfactory cylinder-wall seating surface.

Clean the cylinder bores thoroughly by scrubbing the cylinder walls with soap and water until the suds stay white. Dry the cylinders and apply a light coat of oil to prevent rusting.

Resleeving Cylinders. Some engines are designed with either wet or dry cylinder sleeves. These

(A) CUTTING

(B) CENTREING

(C) BORING BAR

Rottler Boring Bar Co.

Fig. 31-11   Reboring Cylinders

(A) REMOVING CYLINDER LINING

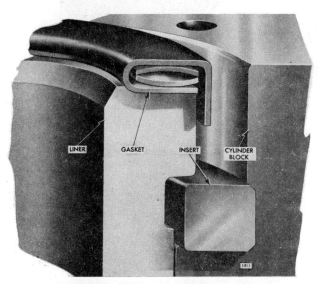

(B) CYLINDER LINER MOUNTING IN BLOCK

Courtesy of General Motors

Fig. 31-12   Cylinder Liners (Diesel)

sleeves may be removed and replaced by using special pullers and replacing tools.

Frequently, a dry sleeve is installed in an engine when the cylinder or cylinders are worn beyond the maximum rebore size, or when a cylinder has been badly scored or cracked. The cylinder block is rebored to accommodate the sleeve which is pressed or shrunk into place. This method makes it possible to obtain additional service from a cylinder block that would otherwise be scrapped.

31-5 CRANKSHAFT AND BEARING WEAR

The main bearing journals, crankpins, and their bearings are subject to wear during engine operation. The pressures imposed on the journals and crankpins, the misalignment of parts, excessive engine vibration, variations in the quantity of oil reaching the bearings, variations in bearing operating temperatures because of their location in the engine, and the abrasive materials in the oil cause the journals, crankpins, and their bearings to become scored, grooved, worn out-of-round, tapered, or worn undersize. All of these conditions increase bearing oil clearance.

Out-of-Round Wear—of the crankshaft is caused by the greater pressure imposed on the journals and

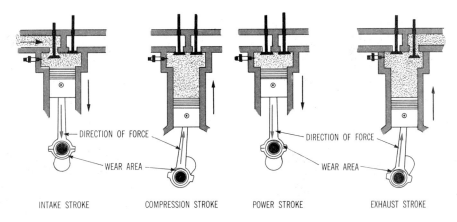

INTAKE STROKE   COMPRESSION STROKE   POWER STROKE   EXHAUST STROKE

Fig. 31-13   Crankshaft Out-of-Round Wear

crankpins during the power stroke as compared to the other strokes. The power-stroke pressure is always applied at the same spot on the journals and crankpins, thus tending to cause a flat spot at that point.

Taper Wear—of the main-bearing journals is usually caused by warpage of the bearing caps, or crankcase main-bearing support webs. Crankpin taper wear may be caused by a bent connecting rod, a misaligned piston pin, or abrasive materials in the oil.

If the crankshaft has drilled oil passageways, the abrasive materials in the oil will tend to wear one side of the crankpin more than the other. This is because of the angle of the drilled hole in the crankcase which causes the oil and abrasive material to flow more readily to one side of the crankpin in the direction of the flow.

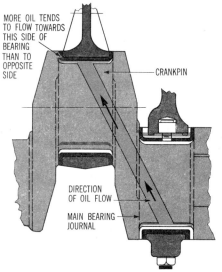

Fig. 31-14   Crankshaft Taper Wear

Straightness. The forces imposed on the crankshaft may cause it to spring or bend at some point between the front and rear main-bearing journals. If the shaft is sprung or bent it has a tendency to whip as it revolves. This whipping action imposes greater than normal loads on the main bearings, causing excessive wear. (See Fig. 31-2A.)

31-6 ENGINE-BEARING WEAR

When engine-bearing wear is excessive, it is advisable to determine the cause so that steps may be taken to prevent its recurrence.

The following table illustrates the major causes of excessive bearing wear:

Dirt	43%
Insufficient Lubrication	15%
Misassembly	13%
Misalignment	10%
Overloading	9%
Corrosion	5%
Intermediate and other causes	5%

Note that dirt far exceeds all other causes of excessive bearing wear.

Dirt—can include: iron and steel machinings or particles worn off engine parts; grinding wheel, honing, or emery grit; sand or road dirt; or carbon. The most common are iron, steel, and grit from machining operations that were not thoroughly cleaned before reassembly. Dirt produced by normal wear can usually be removed by the normal preventative maintenance practice of regular oil and filter changes.

The embedability of the bearing metal enables the bearing to protect itself by allowing small particles of dirt to embed in such a way that they will

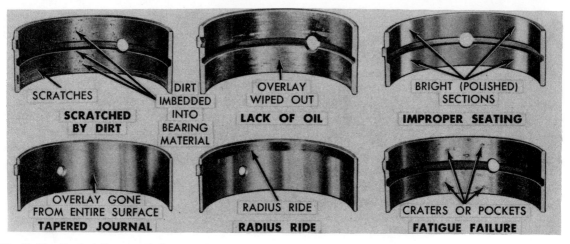

Fig. 31-15   Typical Bearing Failures

Ford of Canada

not scratch the bearing journal or crankpin. The larger particles may partially embed and push the bearing metal up around the particle, thus reducing the oil clearance in that area. Sometimes the bearing metal will flow outward enough to restore adequate oil clearance. Large particles will not completely embed in the thin layer of bearing material. The bearing material then acts as a tool holder and the particle scores the shaft. This often creates localized heating and melting out of the surrounding bearing metal. Dirt particles between the shell and housing cause bearing distortion, improper seating, and poor heat dissipation which reduce oil clearance. All of these conditions could cause bearing failure.

Insufficient lubrication means that there is not sufficient oil reaching the bearings to prevent metal-to-metal contact, thus creating heat. This heat results in a wiping action—where some of the bearing lining material is picked up and circumferentially redeposited in another area of the same bearing. Insufficient lubrication may affect all of the bearings or only one, possibly only the main bearings, or only the connecting-rod bearings.

Oil starvation of a bearing can be caused by clogged oil lines, a defective oil pump or oil relief valve, insufficient oil in the crankcase, oil dilution, or improper oil clearance. The oil clearance between all engine bearings should be the same. Bearings with excessive clearances may pass most of the oil from the oil pump so that other bearings will starve and thus fail.

Another cause of wiping or seizure during early engine running is a dry start, that is, a condition under which the lubricating system has not been primed with oil before starting the first time after an engine overhaul. With only oil in the oil pan and a smear of oil on the bearings, there will be a short period of time after the engine is started before oil under pressure will be delivered to the bearings. This period could be sufficient to cause wiping of the bearings.

Misassembly can be caused by: bearing shells installed in the reverse position, thereby blocking oil passages; poor seating caused by distortion; out-of-round or enlarged bores resulting in inadequate crush fit; bearing caps mixed or reversed; failure to mark bearing caps on disassembly resulting in mismating of the caps, thus causing distorted bores; marking or nicking of the journals and crankpins by bolts and studs during assembly, causing premature failure.

Misalignment of the main bearing bores or warped crankshaft causes heavy false loads in one direction on the main bearings. Excessive torsional vibration, out-of-balance crankshaft, flywheel, or clutch assembly produce a similar type of bearing wear.

Overloading driving conditions are frequent causes of bearing failure by creating bearing fatigue. Repeated application of loads causes the fatigue. As a result the bearing material starts to crack and flake out creating craters or pockets in the bearing.

The larger the craters, the harder the remaining bearing material must work; therefore, the faster the fatigue rate.

An out-of-round journal causes a small area of the bearing to be overloaded, thus creating fatigue.

Excessive idling or low speed operation places most of the load on the centre part of the upper half of the connecting-rod bearing, causing fatigue in that area. Heavy lugging, pre-ignition or detonation of the engine causes fatigue in the crown of the upper half of the connecting-rod bearing and/or in the lower half of the main bearing. Overspeeding creates fatigue in one or both halves of the connecting-rod or main bearings.

Corrosion occurs when the bearing alloys are attacked by organic acids formed in the lubricating oils. These acids can reduce the lead to a soap, which can be washed out of the bearing. Lack of proper crankcase ventilation, stop and start type of driving, incompatible oils, and excessive blowby are common causes of acid formation.

Intermediate or Other Causes. Bearing failure can be caused by radii ride. This usually occurs after a crankshaft has been reground undersize, and the radii were not sufficiently relieved.

Failure to remove the ridge that has formed on the crankpin or journal adjacent to an oil groove can result in bearing failure. The new bearing may not conform to the ridge, causing bearing failure. A tapered journal or crankpin places all of the load on one side of the bearing. This side will overheat and wipe, ruining the bearing.

31-7 CLEANING CRANKSHAFT

Thoroughly clean the crankshaft, crankshaft bearings, flywheel, and vibration damper. Clean out the oil passageways and sediment traps (if used) with a rifle brush, a wire, or solvent. In some cases

Federal-Mogul Corp.

Fig. 31-16 Checking Crankshaft with Dial Indicator for Alignment

plugs in the ends of the drilled passageways must be removed to facilitate cleaning.

Inspection
Check the crankshaft for straightness in V-blocks, or place it between the centres of a lathe and a dial indicator used to check the runout of the main-bearing journal. The shaft should run true within .003 inch. Any bend in excess of this amount can usually be corrected by straightening the shaft in an arbor press.

31-8 INSPECTING CRANKSHAFT JOURNALS AND CRANKPINS

If the journals, crankpins, or the thrust collars are grooved or scored, remachine the crankshaft to a standard undersize, or oversize in the case of thrust collars.

Journals that appear satisfactory should be measured to determine the amount of wear, out-of-round, and taper. Each bearing surface should be measured in four places. Measure each surface at both ends to determine the amount of taper. Take two measurements at right angles to each other at each end of the surface to determine the amount of out-of-round. Bearing surfaces that are .0015″ out-of-round or tapered more than .001″ require remachining.

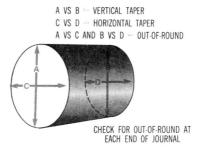

A VS B = VERTICAL TAPER
C VS D = HORIZONTAL TAPER
A VS C AND B VS D = OUT-OF-ROUND

CHECK FOR OUT-OF-ROUND AT EACH END OF JOURNAL

Fig. 31-17 Crankshaft Journal Measurement

Bearing surfaces need not be remachined if they are worn evenly, are within out-of-round and taper limits, and if proper oil clearance can be obtained through the use of new, standard or undersize inserts.

31-9 CHECKING BEARINGS

Inspect and measure the crankshaft bearings with precision instruments to determine their condition and the amount of oil clearance. The inspection will indicate if the insert-type bearing is serviceable or should be replaced; or whether a shimmed-type bearing is satisfactory for adjustment to obtain proper oil clearance.

Replace bearings that are worn, scored, pitted, cracked or show signs of corrosion.

If it is necessary to remove the crankshaft, check the main-bearing bores for warped or out-of-round condition (see section 31-2). Damaged main-bearing bolts, studs or nuts must be replaced.

31-10 CHECKING BEARING CLEARANCES

Determine bearing clearance by calculating the difference between the outside diameter of the crankshaft journals or crankpins and the inside diameter of their bearing shells, or through the use of plastigage.

Measuring Methods. Measure the diameter of the main bearing journals or crankpins at several points with a micrometer and record the readings. Measure the inside bearing diameters with a telescoping gauge and a micrometer. Before measuring the bearings, reassemble the bearings and caps on the crankcase or connecting rods in their proper order and tighten to specified torque. Take measurements at several points in each bearing to determine the largest diameter.

The difference between the largest bearing diameter and the largest journal diameter equals the bearing clearance.

Plastigage Method. Plastigage is a plastic thread of a calibrated size which flattens when placed between the journal or crankpin and the bearing.

To use plastigage, wipe the bearing cap and journal or crankpin clean of oil, since oil dissolves the plastigage. In the case of main bearings, place paper shims in the lower halves of adjacent main bearings to raise the crankshaft in the bearing being checked; crankpins should be turned to a position approximately 30° before BDC. Then place a strip

(A) MEASURING CRANKSHAFT

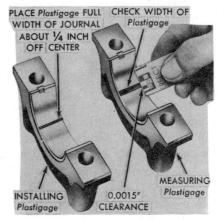

(A) ON BEARING CAPS

(B) MEASURING BEARING

Federal-Mogul Corp.

Fig. 31-18   Checking Bearing Clearance by Measurement

(B) ON CRANKSHAFT   Ford of Canada

Fig. 31-19   Checking Bearing Clearance by Plastigage Method

of plastigage in the bearing cap, tighten the cap to the proper torque specification, and then remove the cap.

The amount the plastigage has flattened indicates the amount of bearing clearance. If the plastigage is flattened only a little, then the oil clearance is large. If it is flattened considerably, the oil clearance is small. Actual clearance is determined by comparing the flattened material with a special gauge supplied with the plastigage.

Do not turn the crankshaft when plastigage is in place, as this would further flatten the material and throw off the clearance measurement.

Checking Crankshaft End-play. Measure crankshaft end-play with the crankshaft in place and all bearing caps tightened to torque specifications. Measure the end-play on one side of the thrust

(A) DIAL INDICATOR METHOD

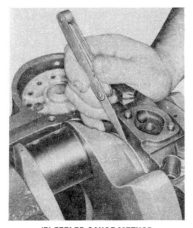

(B) FEELER GAUGE METHOD

(A) Ford of Canada
(B) Courtesy of General Motors

Fig. 31-20   Checking Crankshaft End-Play

bearing between the thrust-bearing face and the crankshaft thrust collar. Pry the crankshaft to the extreme front or rear position and measure the clearance with a thickness gauge.

The amount of end-play may also be measured by attaching a dial indicator to the engine block so that the gauge plunger bears against the end of the crankshaft. As the crankshaft is pried from its extreme rear to extreme forward position, the dial indicator will indicate the number of thousandths of an inch of end-play.

If the crankshaft end-play exceeds the manufacturer's specifications, replace the thrust bearing and fit a new bearing to specification.

31-11 ADJUSTING BEARINGS

The method of adjusting bearings to restore oil clearance depends on whether the bearings are of the precision-insert type or the cast type with shims for adjustment.

Precision-Insert Type. Bearings are available in standard, in .001, .002, .010, .020, .030, and .060″ undersize, and in semifinished bearings. Semifinished bearings can be bored to the correct undersize when the proper oil clearance cannot be obtained by using standard available undersized bearings.

To determine the correct size of insert required, assuming that the bearing journal or crankpin is within wear limits, compare the greatest journal or crankpin diameter with the original standard diameter. The difference between these two measurements is the amount that the bearing surface has worn and is the size of the undersized bearing that should be installed. A bearing surface that measures .002″ smaller than the original would require a .002″ undersized bearing to establish proper oil clearance.

Standard size bearings should be installed if the bearing surface is worn less than .001″. Wear of more than .001″ requires a standard undersized bearing of the correct size to establish proper oil clearance.

If proper crankshaft end-play cannot be obtained through the use of thrust bearings of standard width, semifinished thrust bearings should be used. The bearing must be bored and refaced to establish the proper oil clearance and end-play.

Shim Type. Bearings can be adjusted provided the journals or crankpins are within the allowable limits of wear and there are sufficient shims on each bearing to secure adjustment.

If the wear on the bearing surfaces exceeds the allowable limits, or there are insufficient shims for adjustment, regrind the crankshaft to a standard undersize, and recast and line bore the bearings to the correct diameter to establish proper oil clearance.

To adjust bearing clearances, loosen all bearing caps to permit the shaft to turn freely. Remove one bearing cap and remove one shim from each side. Replace and tighten the cap to proper torque. Rotate the shaft to determine the amount of drag. If it does not drag, remove additional shims in pairs, checking each time until a slight drag is felt. Then replace one shim on each side, tighten the cap, and rotate the shaft. If the shaft rotates freely, the bearing is properly adjusted. Loosen the cap and repeat operation for each bearing. Finally, when all bearings have been adjusted, tighten all caps to proper torque and rotate the crankshaft. If it drags, recheck and readjust bearings.

Federal-Mogul Corp.

Fig. 31-21   Grinding Crankshafts

31-12 RECONDITIONING CRANKSHAFTS

If the crankshaft journals or crankpins are worn, out-of-round, or tapered beyond limits, or if the bearing surfaces are rough, pitted, scored, or damaged in any way, they must be ground undersize. Special crankshaft grinders or lathes are available for this purpose.

Sometimes only one, or possibly all, of the crankpins are damaged. In this case a special grinding machine is available to refinish the crankpins without removing the crankshaft from the engine.

Worn or damaged crankshafts may also be metalized. In this case the journals and crankpins are rough turned in a lathe; then a high temperature flame is used to spray liquid metal on to the bearing surfaces. When cool, this new metal adheres to the surfaces and can be ground to the proper standard size.

31-13 FLYWHEEL SERVICE

Through normal use, the clutch surface of a cast-iron flywheel may become scored, grooved, or roughened by heat cracks. If these conditions exist, reface the surface in a lathe or special facing machine.

Inspect the ring gear for cracks, or worn or chipped teeth. If damaged, replace the ring gear.

31-14 VIBRATION DAMPER SERVICE

Vibration damper parts are not serviced separately. The entire unit must be replaced if the fan drive pulley is damaged or if the rubber mountings or friction inserts have become softened or worn. Leaking fluid type dampers must be replaced.

REVIEW QUESTIONS

1. Give three reasons why the cylinder block must be thoroughly cleaned before it is measured or inspected.
2. State three methods of locating small cracks in a cylinder block.
3. How are cylinder heads checked for warping?
4. Describe two methods of checking crankshaft main-bearing bores.
5. Explain why a cylinder wears out-of-round.
6. Describe the method of measuring a cylinder for wear.
7. Calculate the smallest standard oversize required for a cylinder that has worn to .008″ taper and .004″ out-of-round.
8. Why is it necessary to deglaze cylinders?
9. Under what type of cylinder conditions should (a) honing (b) reboring (c) resleeving be recommended?
10. Explain why a crankshaft wears (a) out-of-round (b) tapered.
11. **What effect does a bent crankshaft have on** engine bearing wear? Why?
12. Explain why dirt is the largest single cause of **engine-bearing wear.**
13. How does embedability of bearing materials help protect against wear caused by dirt?
14. Why should the oil clearance between all engine bearings be the same?

15. State three causes of bearing corrosion.
16. Describe the procedure of checking a crankshaft for wear.
17. What factors determine that a used crankshaft may be reinstalled without machining the bearing surfaces?
18. Why should bearing caps not be mixed up or reversed?
19. Describe the procedure of checking a crankshaft for wear.
20. Describe two methods of determining crankshaft bearing clearance.
21. Explain how crankshaft end-play is checked.
22. Describe the method of obtaining the proper oil clearance when precision-insert type bearings are used.

Chapter 32
CONNECTING RODS, PISTONS, AND PISTON RINGS

32-1 CONNECTING RODS

The connecting rod is used to carry the power thrusts from the piston to the crankpin. The piston end of the connecting rod is attached to the piston by means of a piston pin. The crankpin end of the rod is attached to the crankpin by the rod cap and bolts. A split-type bearing is placed between the crankpin and the rod and rod cap.

The upper end (small end) of the rod oscillates, while the lower end (big end) rotates. Since there is little bearing movement at the upper end, the bearing surface can be small. However, a large bearing area is required for the rotating lower end.

Connecting rods must be strong and rigid, and also be as light as possible to minimize the inertia force. They are generally made of alloy steel, drop forged to an I-beam shape. After forging, they are machined to close limits of size and weight to ensure interchangeability and balance.

To ensure good engine balance, connecting rods and caps are carefully matched and marked in sets. All rods for an engine must be of equal weight to prevent vibration which could result in premature bearing failure.

32-2 TYPES OF CONNECTING RODS

Connecting rods may be solid, may have an oil hole drilled the entire length of the connecting rod, or may have an oil spray hole drilled in the saddle of the upper half of the connecting rod.

The connecting rod cap may be split at 90° to the rod shank, or at an angle of 30 or 45°. The angular split rods are used in some V-type engines to permit easier disassembly and assembly, and to permit the passage of the rod through the cylinder bore.

Offset rods have the large end of the connecting rod and bearing offset to one side of the rod shank.

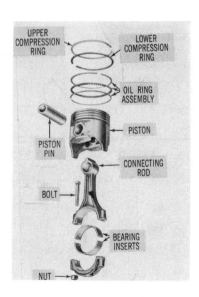

Ford of Canada

Fig. 32-1   Piston, Connecting Rod and Related Parts

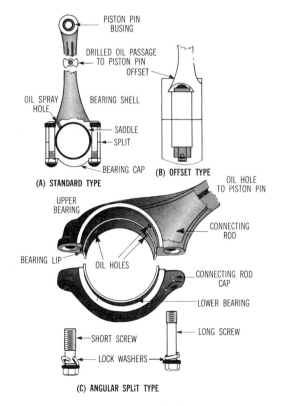

Fig. 32-2   Types of Connecting Rods

The offset may be slight or quite noticeable. It may be to the front or the rear of the engine. Offset rods are necessary when the design of the engine is such that the cylinders are not directly over the crankpins.

Rod Bushings. The small end of the connecting rod is equipped with a bronze bushing if the rod is free to oscillate on the piston pin. If the rod does not move on the pin, no bushing is installed.

Rod Bearings. The large end of the connecting rod is fitted with either a cast or precision bearing insert. For information read Engine Bearings, Chapter 30.

32-3 PISTON PINS

The piston pin, wrist pin, or Gudgeon pin attaches the piston to the connecting rod. It passes through one piston boss, the small end of the connecting rod, and then the other piston boss.

Piston pins are made of alloy steel and are case hardened, ground, and lapped, to provide a smooth durable wearing surface. Case hardening is a process that hardens the surface of the steel but leaves the inner part fairly soft and tough to prevent brittleness. Case hardening penetrates to a variable depth of from .004″ to any depth desired.

Piston pins are made hollow to reduce weight and the inertia forces that are developed at the end of each stroke.

32-4 BUSHINGS

Bearing surfaces for the piston pin are provided in the piston, or in the connecting rod, or both, depending upon the type of piston-pin locking. Cast-iron pistons may or may not have bushings in the pin bosses, depending upon the types of lock. The aluminum has satisfactory bearing properties; therefore, bushings are rarely used in aluminum pistons. A bushing may or may not be installed in the small end of the connecting rod, depending on the type of lock used.

32-5 PISTON-PIN LOCKING

Piston pins may be free floating or oscillating. The oscillating type may be locked in various ways to either the piston or the connecting rod.

Free Floating. This type of pin requires bearing surfaces in both the piston bosses and the small end of the connecting rod, as the pin is free to rotate in both the piston and the connecting rod.

The pin is prevented from moving out and scoring the cylinder walls by lock rings that fit into undercuts in the piston.

Centre Lock requires bearing surfaces in the piston only since the pin is locked to the connecting rod by a clamp screw adjacent to the small end. The screw passes through a centering groove in the pin to ensure proper pin location.

Fig. 32-3   Piston Pin Locking Devices

SET SCREW ANCHORS PISTON PIN TO PISTON

HALF-SLOT ANCHORS PISTON PIN TO UPPER END OF CONNECTING ROD

SNAP RINGS LOCK PISTON PIN IN PISTON

HOLE FOR SET SCREW

SET SCREW

CLAMP SCREW

BUSHING

(A) SEMIFLOATING TYES OF PISTON

(B) FULL FLOATING

End Lock. This type requires a bearing surface in the connecting rod only. The pin is locked by a set screw threaded into one of the piston bosses. To position the pin, the set screw enters a drilled hole in the pin.

Press Fit requires bearing surfaces in the pin bosses. The pin is locked into position by being pressed into the connecting rod to a specified depth. The press fit is tight enough to prevent the pin from moving out of position.

32-6 PISTONS

A piston is a sliding plunger that moves up and down in a cylinder. Automotive pistons must be strong enough to withstand the high temperatures and pressures produced by combustion. They must be as light as possible to reduce the inertia forces created by the starting and stopping of the piston at each end of its stroke. Pistons must be made within close limits of weight and size so that they are interchangeable, well balanced, and free from vibration.

Materials. Pistons may be made of cast grey iron, semisteel (a combination of iron and steel), or aluminum alloys. Pistons are frequently electroplated with soft materials such as tin. This plating acts as a lubricant and shortens the break-in period.

Cast-iron and semisteel pistons are capable of withstanding the stresses imposed; have a melting point above the cylinder operating temperature; they expand at the same rate as the cast iron cylinders; and do not generate excessive friction when properly lubricated. Their main disadvantage is excess weight. This disadvantage has increased in importance as engine speeds have been increased.

Aluminum-alloy pistons have high heat-dissipating properties and therefore operate at lower temperatures, thus making possible higher compression ratio. However, aluminum's strength decreases rapidly as the temperature increases, and it becomes soft and plastic when overheated. To prevent this and to increase its strength, materials such as copper, magnesium, nickel, or silicon are added. Aluminum has a high coefficient of expansion and would ordinarily require greater clearance between the piston and the cylinder wall. However, various piston designs have been developed to permit this higher rate of expansion without materially changing the piston clearances.

The main advantage of using aluminum-alloy pistons is their light weight. Lighter weight results in a reduction of inertia forces, a decrease in bearing loads, and less side thrust on the cylinder walls.

Aluminum alloy pistons are frequently heat treated and given an electronic treatment that produces an aluminum oxide coating that is quite hard, yet slightly porous. This coating resists water and will retain oil in its pores; it thus helps to protect the piston during periods of sparse lubrication, such as starting.

32-7 CONSTRUCTION

Piston Head or "crown" is the top surface of the piston against which the combustion forces are applied. The head may be flat, concave, or convex. The shape of the head is designed to promote turbulence or to help control combustion. The heads of some pistons have indentations to provide for valve-head clearance.

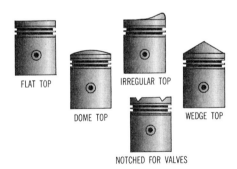

Fig. 32-5 Piston Head Design

Piston Ribs are used often to reinforce the underside of the piston head and to assist in transferring the heat from the head to the piston rings and skirt, where it may be dissipated into the cylinder walls and cooling system. Ribs, around the inside of the piston skirt, are used for balancing purposes. Material may be removed from this rib in order to balance the piston within specified weight limits. Other ribs strengthen the piston between the head and the piston-pin boss.

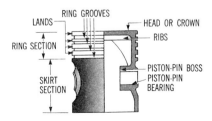

Fig. 32-4 Piston Nomenclature

Piston Boss provides the support and the bearing surface for the piston pin. The pin bosses are usually placed in the exact middle of the piston, but may be offset as much as $\frac{1}{16}''$ to either side. This offset has a tendency to reduce the slap or rock of the piston in the cylinder.

The piston wall area around the piston-pin boss is usually relieved or undercut to reduce the weight of the piston and to provide an allowance for the boss expansion caused by heat.

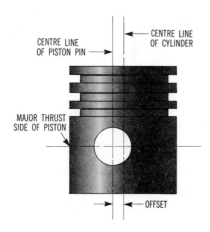

Fig. 32-6 Piston Pin Offset

Ring Grooves and Lands. Ring grooves are provided at the top of the piston to accommodate the piston rings. The lower groove, or grooves, usually has holes or slots in the bottom of the groove to permit the oil to drain from behind the oil rings.

The land is the part of the piston between the ring grooves. It provides a seating surface for the sides of the piston rings.

Piston Skirt forms the main section of the piston. It provides the bearing area between the piston and the cylinder wall and takes the thrust, both the power (major) and compression (minor), that is produced by the actions of the crankshaft, connecting-rod, piston and combustion-chamber pressures.

Several piston-skirt designs are used to permit skirt expansion without excessively increasing the diameter across the thrust faces. The piston head and skirt are usually tapered, being .020 to .030″ larger at the bottom of the skirt than at the head. Since the head of the piston may operate at a temperature 200 or more degrees hotter than the skirt, additional room for expansion is required.

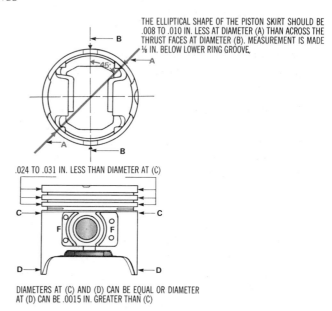

Fig. 32-7 Piston Measurements

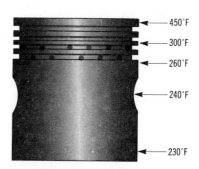

Fig. 32-8 Typical Piston Operating Temperatures

Piston Skirt Design. In order to control the expansion of the piston, various designs have been used. The cam ground, solid skirt, split skirt, T-slot, U-slot, slipper, and steel strut are examples.

Cam-ground solid skirt pistons are made of either cast iron, semisteel, or aluminum. The piston, instead of being round, is ground so that it is elliptical, or egg shaped. The thrust side diameter is larger than the diameter along the line of the piston-pin bosses. The thrust diameter clearance is only sufficient to provide for the necessary lubricating oil film. This reduces piston slap noise when the engine is cold. As the piston heats up, it does not expand much in the thrust diameter, but will expand along the line of the pin bosses. This will cause the piston to become round when fully heated.

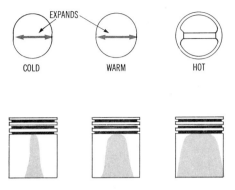

Fig. 32-9   Cam Ground Piston Heat Expansion

Split skirt has a diagonal slot cut in the compression thrust side of the piston skirt. The slot may or may not extend the full length of the piston skirt. The thrust surfaces of the piston skirt are separated from the head by horizontal slots. These slots force the heat to travel through the pin bosses to reach the skirt. When the piston warms and begins to expand, it cannot bind in the cylinder, as the skirt merely closes the slots.

T-slot and U-slot pistons are usually cam-ground pistons with a T-slot cut in the compression thrust side of the skirt and a horizontal slot cut in the power thrust side just below the bottom ring groove

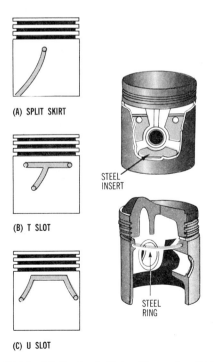

Fig. 32-10   Methods of Piston Expansion Control

and above the piston pin. The inverted U of a U-slot type piston has a slot cut in the compression thrust side only. The combination of the cam-ground piston and the slots permits the piston to expand when heated with a minimum reduction in operating clearances.

Slipper—or partial skirt piston, is a cam-ground piston with a large area of the nonthrust sides of the skirt removed. This reduces piston weight and allows the use of shorter connecting rods without interference between the skirt and crankshaft counterweights. Since the nonthrust sides of the piston do not carry much of a load, their removal is not detrimental to piston operation.

Steel strut—piston has special alloy steel struts or rings cast into aluminum pistons. Since the alloy steel does not expand with temperature increase as much as aluminum, the steel struts or rings tend to control or minimize the piston expansion.

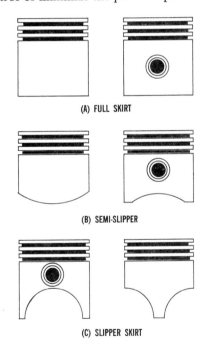

Fig. 32-11   Types of Piston Skirts

32-8 PISTON RINGS

Piston rings serve three purposes: they seal the space between the piston and the cylinder wall, preventing the escape of the burning gases from the combustion chamber; they control the flow of oil over the cylinder walls to permit proper lubrication of the cylinder; and they assist in dissipating heat from the pistons to the cylinder walls.

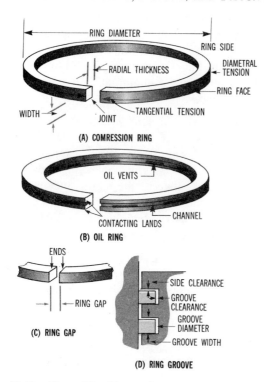

Fig. 32-12   Piston Ring Nomenclature

Materials. Grey cast iron is the most common material used to manufacture piston rings, although alloy steels are used to manufacture some types. Both cast-iron and alloy steels have excellent wearing properties, are capable of withstanding the high temperatures imposed upon them, and will retain much of their elasticity after being exposed to considerable heat and use.

Piston rings are frequently plated with cadmium, tin, or chrome or have a coating of black magnetic oxide or phosphate placed on all surfaces of the ring. This plating or coating tends to prevent scuffing or scoring of the piston rings during the break-in period.

Design. Piston rings vary in circumference, joint construction, anchoring, cross-section, and ring pressure.

Ring Joints. Piston rings are split at one point on their circumference to permit installation of the ring in the ring groove. The split allows the ring to be compressed for installation into the cylinder and must have sufficient end clearance at the split or gap to allow for expansion as the ring temperature increases. Insufficient end-gap clearance will cause the ring to break up into several pieces.

Several types of gaps or joints are used; the butt,

miter, and step joints. Automotive engines usually use butt-joint rings; heavy duty engines use the miter or step-joint types.

Anchoring. Some piston rings are anchored into position by small dowel pins, located in the bottom of the ring grooves. This practice is more common on small engines than in automobile engines.

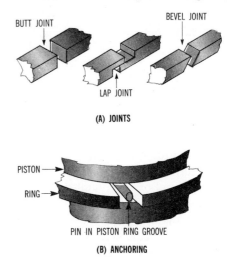

Fig. 32-13   Piston Ring Joints and Anchoring

Cross Section. Most piston rings have a rectangular cross-section. Some, however, are tapered in cross-section: that is, the back of the ring is thinner than the front. The ring groove is also tapered to match the ring taper. Rings of this type are usually used in engines where freedom from ring sticking is a prime factor.

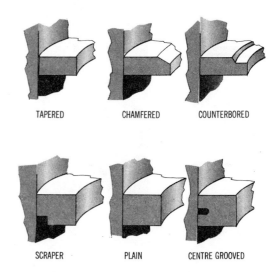

Fig. 32-14   Compression Ring Cross Sections

Other rings have cross-section areas that include bevelled inside corners, recessed corners, or tapered outer faces. Rings of the bevelled inside corner cross-section are designed to allow the ring to twist in the ring groove, so that the lower edge of the face presses more tightly against the cylinder wall. The recessed or bevelled face rings are designed to increase unit pressure.

Ring Pressure. Piston rings must exert a certain pressure to maintain a gas-tight seal between the piston and the cylinder wall. The total pressure exerted by the rings is usually between 7 and 12 lb. High ring pressures will cause excessive drag and cylinder wall wear, and are frequently responsible for scuffing or scoring the ring face.

The unit pressure (pressure per square inch) that

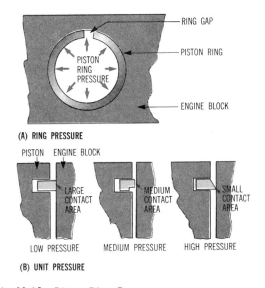

(A) RING PRESSURE

(B) UNIT PRESSURE

Fig. 32-15   Piston Ring Pressures

a piston ring exerts on a cylinder wall is in direct relationship with the amount of ring face that contacts the cylinder wall. Rectangular cross-section rings exert less unit pressure on the cylinder walls than rings with recessed or bevelled corners, because of the reduced contact area. As the face of the piston ring is made narrower, its pressure per unit of face area increases. Piston rings are designed with faces of different widths in order to maintain compression and to control oil consumption.

32-9 TYPES OF PISTON RINGS

The number, type, and arrangement of piston rings varies with each type of engine. Three- and four-ring pistons are the most common. There are three general classifications of piston rings: compression rings, oil control rings, and combination or compression scraper rings.

Compression Rings are located in the first (top) and second ring grooves. Their purpose is to prevent leakage (blow-by) of the combustion pressure from the combustion chamber and to assist in controlling the amount of oil on the cylinder wall. Compression rings are usually one-piece rings and may be rectangular, or with a groove or bevel in the upper inner or lower outer corners, or have a tapered face.

The internal forces which exert an outward pressure tend to become unbalanced in the grooved or bevelled type of ring. This unbalanced condition tips or twists the ring in its groove. On the intake stroke, the ring tips in such a manner that the bottom edge of the ring scrapes off most of the oil left by the oil ring, leaving only a thin film of oil on the cylinder wall. On the compression and power

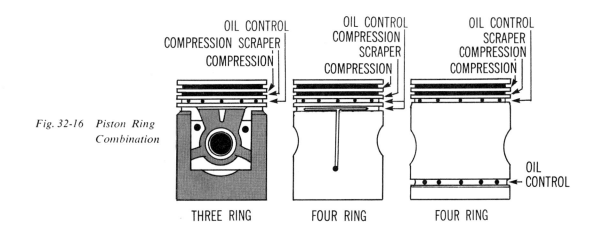

Fig. 32-16   Piston Ring Combination

strokes, pressures in the combustion chamber overcome the twisting force in the ring, causing it to flatten out in the groove. The full face of the ring now contacts the cylinder wall, producing a more effective seal. On the exhaust stroke, the ring is again tipped. But since the ring is moving upward, it slides over the cylinder wall without scraping the oil upward.

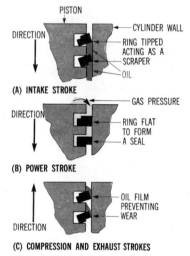

Fig. 32-17   Compression Ring Action

Tapered Face. Rings of this type are about .001″ wider at the bottom than the top, resulting in the face of the ring being tapered away from the cylinder wall. On the intake and power strokes, the sharp lower edge of the ring tends to scrape off the excess oil, leaving only a thin film of oil on the cylinder walls. On the compression and power strokes, the ring has a tendency to "skate" over the oil without scraping it upward. Tapered rings seat themselves rapidly and give efficient service in the break-in period.

Tapered and grooved rings must be installed right side up and are usually marked "top" on the side to be installed on the top. Tapered-face compression rings are usually installed in the top and second ring grooves. Compression rings with the groove or bevel on the top inside corner usually are installed in the top ring groove, and compression rings grooved or bevelled on the lower outside edge usually are placed in the second groove.

The top ring normally has a wider face than the ring in the second groove. The wider face results in lower unit pressure against the cylinder wall and helps to decrease the wear near the top of the cylinder wall.

Oil Rings are located in the third ring groove and the fourth ring groove, if provided. They are used to prevent excessive amounts of oil from working up into the combustion chamber. Under most engine operating circumstances, far more oil is thrown onto the cylinder walls than is required for lubrication. This excess oil must be scraped off and returned to the oil pan. The excess oil helps carry away carbon particles and dust, and provides some cooling effect. Sufficient oil must be left on the cylinder walls to provide the necessary lubricating and sealing functions.

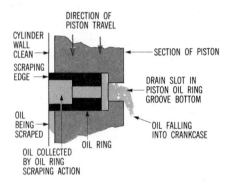

Fig. 32-18   Oil Ring Operation

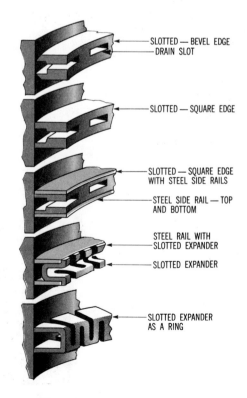

Fig. 32-19   Oil Ring Cross Sections

As engine speed increases, the amount of oil thrown onto the cylinder walls increases. As engine operating temperature increases, the oil becomes thinner. Thus, the oil rings have a harder job to do at higher engine speeds and have less time to do it.

Oil rings may be of the one-piece ventilated type, or two-, three-, or four-piece spring expander type.

One-piece Ventilated-Type Oil Rings have a continuous channel cut in the face of the ring and have slots cut through the ring at equal intervals around the channel. The ring faces above and below the channel bear against the cylinder walls and collect the excess oil in the channel and slots. The excess oil drains back into the crankcase through holes drilled in the bottom of the ring groove. The narrower the ring faces, the greater the unit pressure and the more effective the scraping action of the ring.

Spring-expander Type Oil Rings have a special spring expander or inner ring placed in the groove behind the outer ring. Spring expanders are made of spring steel with a number of humps or crimps equally spaced around its circumference. When expanders are used, the outer ring usually exerts about 50% of the pressure normally exerted by one-piece rings. The expander exerts the balance of the pressure against the cylinder wall. Expanders used with oil rings are slotted to permit the oil drainage.

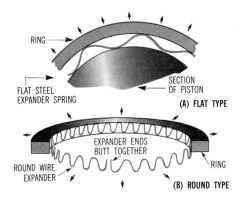

Fig. 32-20 Piston Ring Spring Expanders

It should be noted that the use of expanders is not confined to oil rings, but they are frequently placed behind compression rings when the cylinders have an excessive amount of taper and out-of-round. Expanders tend to support the piston centrally in the cylinder, thus tending to reduce piston slap.

Two-piece Expander-Type Oil Rings consist of a ventilated oil ring with a spring expander and are available in different ring-face widths to provide effective oil control.

Three-piece Expander-Type Oil Rings consist of a cast-iron ventilated ring upper segment, a spiral steel coil made of two turns of flat steel, and a ring expander. The design of this ring is such that during the break-in period the expander does not touch the spiral-steel insert until the cast-iron segment has worn a few thousandths of an inch. This produces high unit pressure on the two faces of the cast-iron segment during the break-in period, and reduced unit pressure on the four contact faces after break-in.

Four-piece Expander-Type Oil Rings consist of a cast iron or spring-steel centre section, upper and lower single turn steel side rails, and a spring expander ring. The expander ring may apply pressure to the side rails only, or to the rails and the centre section. The highest unit pressure and most effective scraping is obtained when the expander pressure is applied to the steel side rings only.

Spring-steel centre sections are used in pistons with slightly worn ring grooves. The centre spring tends to hold the side rails snugly against the sides of the ring grooves, thus preventing up and down motion of the ring.

Combination or Compression Scraper Rings are usually installed in the second ring groove and are one-piece cast-iron rings with a groove machined in the lower corner of the ring. The sharp lower corner assists the oil ring in scraping excess oil from the cylinder wall, while the ring face assists in sealing combustion pressures.

32-10 REPLACEMENT RINGS

The type of replacement rings selected depends upon the condition of the cylinder walls. If the cylinder walls have been reconditioned, then less unit pressure on the face of the ring is required to seal combustion chamber pressures and to control the oil film. The more the cylinders are worn, out-of-round, and tapered, the higher the ring face unit pressure required. Ring sets are manufactured in amounts of unit pressure for different cylinder wall wear conditions. The selection of the proper type of ring set is important for proper engine operation and long engine life.

REVIEW QUESTIONS

1. What is the purpose of the connecting rod?
2. Why must the connecting rod be as light as possible?
3. Why must connecting rods be matched and marked in sets?
4. Why are some connecting rods split on an angle of 30° or 45°?
5. What are offset connecting rods? Why are they used?
6. Why are piston pins case hardened?
7. Describe three methods of securing the piston pin in the piston.
8. State three important features of good piston design.
9. Name three types of materials from which pistons are made. List the advantages and disadvantages of each type of material.
10. Why are some pistons electroplated with soft materials?
11. Why are different types of piston heads used?
12. State three purposes of piston ribs.
13. Why is the piston head usually .020 to .030″ smaller in diameter than the piston skirt?
14. Why is piston skirt design of vital importance?
15. Describe the principle of cam-ground piston design and operation.
16. Why are slipper-type pistons used?
17. Explain why cast iron is an excellent piston ring material.
18. Give three reasons why piston rings are split on one point of their circumference.
19. Sketch three types of piston ring cross section.
20. What results from (a) too little (b) too much piston ring pressure?
21. Explain the term "unit pressure," and state how it can be increased or decreased.
22. Name and state the purpose of the three basic types of piston rings.
23. Explain in detail the action of a compression-type piston ring as the piston moves (a) upward (b) downward in the cylinder.
24. Describe the operation of an oil control ring.
25. Why is it more difficult to control oil consumption at higher engine speeds and temperatures?
26. What is the purpose of piston ring expanders? When are they used?
27. What factors determine the selection of replacement piston rings?

Chapter 33

CONNECTING-RODS, PISTONS, AND PISTON-RING SERVICE

Connecting rod, piston, and piston-ring service is required because of wear, which usually results in noise, loss of compression, and oil consumption. The individual parts must be inspected to determine their condition and if repairs are required.

33-1 REMOVING AND REPLACING PISTON AND ROD ASSEMBLIES

Before removing any piston and rod assembly, examine the connecting rod and cap for identifying marks. If unmarked, mark them with metal numbering dies, centre punch, or file marks. These marks are necessary to ensure that the parts are properly matched and returned to the proper cylinder.

INDENT-ASSEMBLY
TOWARDS
FRONT OF
ENGINE

OIL HOLE-ASSEMBLE
TOWARDS (RIGHT SIDE)
OF ENGINE

Chrysler Canada Ltd.

Fig. 33-1   Piston and Connecting Rod Markings

Exercise care during removal to prevent scratching of the crankpins by the rod bolt threads. Use thread protectors if specified. Before reinstalling piston and rod assemblies, make sure they are properly matched and are being installed in the proper cylinder.

(A) REMOVING

(B) REPLACING

Courtesy of General Motors

*Fig. 33-2   Removing and Replacing Piston and
Connecting Rod Assembly*

The piston rings must be properly spaced around the cylinder, except when rings are anchored in position. The assembly should be dipped in heavy motor oil or castor oil to provide initial lubrication. Castor oil is preferred since it has greater film strength and is not as easily diluted. A ring compressor is required to compress the piston rings in their grooves while the piston is being installed in the cylinder. Use connecting-rod bolt thread protectors, if specified, to prevent scratching of the

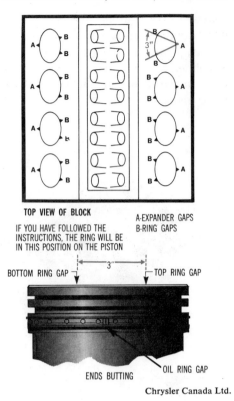

TOP VIEW OF BLOCK

IF YOU HAVE FOLLOWED THE
INSTRUCTIONS, THE RING WILL BE
IN THIS POSITION ON THE PISTON

A-EXPANDER GAPS
B-RING GAPS

BOTTOM RING GAP   TOP RING GAP

ENDS BUTTING   OIL RING GAP

Chrysler Canada Ltd.

Fig. 33-3   Proper Piston Ring Gap Positioning

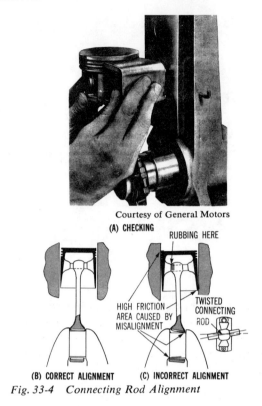

Courtesy of General Motors
(A) CHECKING

RUBBING HERE

HIGH FRICTION
AREA CAUSED BY
MISALIGNMENT

TWISTED
CONNECTING
ROD

(B) CORRECT ALIGNMENT   **(C) INCORRECT ALIGNMENT**

Fig. 33-4   Connecting Rod Alignment

crankpins. Check bearing clearances and tighten the rod cap properly to torque specification.

33-2 CONNECTING RODS

After disassembly, check connecting rods for proper alignment, piston-pin bore, and connecting-rod bore wear. Inspect connecting rod cast type or bearing inserts and note their condition. (See engine bearing Chapter 30.)

Connecting-Rod alignment may be checked by placing the piston and rod assembly on the arbor of a special rod alignment fixture. Some misaligned rods may be straightened by using a straightening rod inserted in the piston pin hole. Many misaligned rods must be replaced, as experience has shown that these rods, if bent, take on a permanent set. When realigned, they tend to drift back to the permanent set or bent condition.

Connecting-rod bearings are subject to wear and failure as described in Chapter 30 on engine bearings and should be inspected, checked and measured as outlined in that chapter. Out-of-round, tapered, or worn connecting-rod bores may be resized to original size by a special process that grinds the parting faces of the rod, and rebores the bore to correct size, roundness, straightness, and finish.

(A) ROUNDNESS   **(B) STRAIGHTNESS**

(C) SURFACE FINISH   **(D) BORE SIZE**

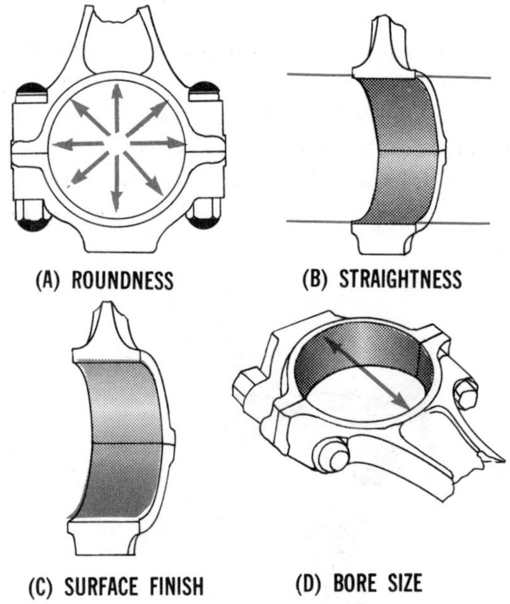

Fig. 33-5   Connecting Rod Bore Requirements

Piston Pins and Bushings. Check pins and their bearing surfaces for condition, wear, and oil clearance. The connecting rod and pin boss bores should be round, straight, have correct surface finish, and be in alignment. Oil clearances can be calculated by comparing the outer diameter of the pin and the diameter of the bearing surface. The differences in the expansion rates between the aluminum piston and the steel piston pin requires extreme care and precision when fitting piston pins.

Each manufacturer's method of fitting piston pins to connecting rods and pistons is described in the manufacturer's service manual.

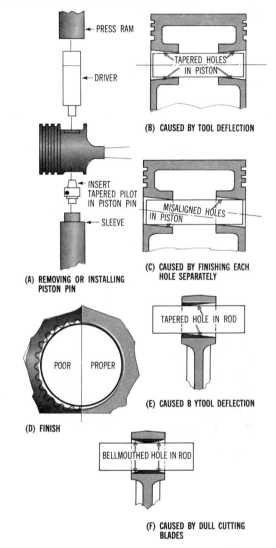

Fig. 33-6   Piston Pin Service

33-3 PISTONS

Piston wear causes excessive clearances which increase oil consumption and noise.

Inspection. After a thorough cleaning, pistons should be inspected for scuffing or scoring, collapsed skirts, worn ring grooves, bent or broken ring lands, cracks in the skirt or head, burned spots, and fit in the cylinder bore. Badly worn, cracked, scored or burnt pistons must be replaced. Others may be repaired and reconditioned.

(A) BY PRE-IGNITION   (B) BY DETONATION

(C) BY SCUFFING AND SCORING   (D) BY MISALIGNED CONNECTING ROD

Perfect Circle Piston Ring Co.

Fig. 33-7   Damaged Pistons

Scuffed or Scored Pistons. Scuffing or scoring is the abrading of a surface caused by insufficient lubrication, heating, or dirt. Piston scuffing is usually apparent on the thrust faces of the piston skirt. Minor cases of scuffing can be usually corrected by polishing and resizing of the piston.

Worn Ring Grooves. The top ring groove of aluminum pistons wears quite rapidly because of the high temperatures and abrasives in the top ring-groove area. This wear increases the top ring-groove side clearance and causes increased blow-by and oil consumption. Worn ring grooves allow the ring to tip. This tipping reduces the sealing area between the ring face and the cylinder wall, and between the sides of the ring and the ring groove, thus increasing blow-by. The tipping action also forces the upper corner of the ring face to contact the cylinder wall, causing the oil to be wiped up into the combustion chamber instead of down into the crankcase, thereby increasing oil consumption. In addition, continued deflections of the ring will cause ring fatigue and breakage.

Determine the ring-groove clearance by placing a new ring in the groove and measuring the clearance

(A) CLEANING

(B) CHECKING

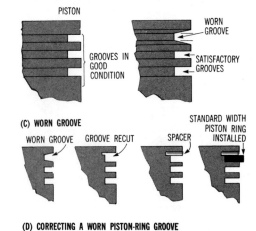

(C) WORN GROOVE

(D) CORRECTING A WORN PISTON-RING GROOVE

Fig. 33-8   Piston Ring Groove Service

Piston skirt collapse occurs along the thrust surfaces of the piston. The amount of piston collapse can be determined by comparing the diameter of the piston immediately below the ring grooves and at the bottom of the skirt.

NOTE: New pistons are generally .0015″ smaller at the top than at the bottom.

33-4 PISTON AND CYLINDER CLEARANCE

The amount of clearance between the piston and cylinder walls should be within manufacturer's specifications. Too little clearance will cause the piston to scuff or seize in the cylinder. Too much ring clearance reduces ring-face unit pressure and results in excessive blow-by, noise, and oil consumption.

To check piston-to-cylinder clearance consult the manufacturer's service manual for procedure.

Chrysler Canada Ltd.

Fig. 33-9   Checking Piston to Cylinder Clearance

with a thickness gauge, or use special ring-groove wear gauges. Clearances of .006″ or more are excessive and unsatisfactory.

Correct excessive ring groove clearance by machining the groove with a special regroover to accommodate a new, standard size ring, plus a special steel ring-groove spacer. Always install the steel spacer above the new top ring.

Collapsed Skirt. Worn or collapsed piston skirts allow the piston to rock in the cylinder. This rocking action not only produces piston slap noises, but also causes the piston ring face to wear oval, causing blow-by and high oil consumption.

33-5 RESIZING PISTONS

Various methods are available to correct a collapsed piston skirt or to reduce piston-to-cylinder wall clearance. Before the pistons are serviced, the cylinder walls must be trued up in order to determine the amount of piston correction required. The pistons may be expanded by means of piston-skirt expanders or piston expanding processes.

Piston-skirt expanders are made of heavy spring steel and fit inside the piston skirt. The pressure of the expander forces the skirt outward, thus restoring the skirt to nearly the correct shape and reducing piston-to-cylinder wall clearance.

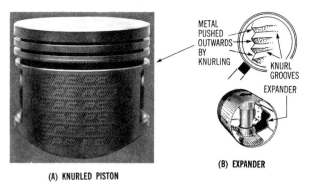

(A) KNURLED PISTON

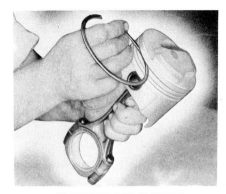

(B) EXPANDER

(A) Perfect Circle Piston Ring Co.

Fig. 33-10 Resizing Pistons

(A) CHECKING RING IN GROOVE

Shot blasting is a process which expands the piston skirt by directing a blast of compressed air and steel shot against the inner surface of the thrust sides of the piston skirt. The hammering force of the steel balls increases the density and hardness of the inner surfaces and imparts an expansive force to the metal, thereby expanding the piston. The amount of expansion can be controlled by varying the force impact of the shot and the length of time the process is applied.

Knurlizing is a process where each thrust side of the piston is placed between a pair of knurling rollers that roll under pressure. These rollers squeeze and raise the metal in a lined or diamond-shaped pattern. The metal is permanently displaced and the amount of roller pressure controls the amount of expansion. The interrupted expanded surface has a high load-carrying capacity and can be fitted within close limits with minimum danger of scuffing or scoring.

33-6 NEW PISTONS

New pistons are supplied in either standard, finished oversizes, or semifinished.

Standard or finished oversize pistons are ready to install and usually have a special coating or finish that should not be removed. Resizing this type of piston removes this finish and could cause rapid piston wear.

Any resizing that is required to obtain proper piston-to-cylinder wall clearance must be done by honing the cylinder wall. Finished oversize pistons usually have the same weight as standard size pistons. Therefore, it is not necessary to replace all pistons when only one or two are badly worn or damaged, in order to maintain proper balance.

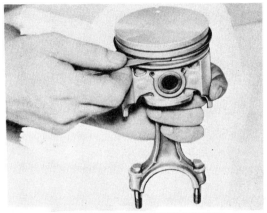

(B) MEASURING RING GROOVE CLEARANCE

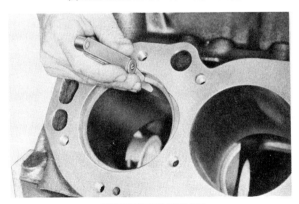

(C) MEASURING RING GAP

Courtesy of General Motors

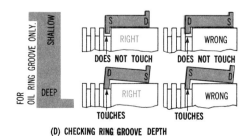

(D) CHECKING RING GROOVE DEPTH

Fig. 33-11 Fitting Piston Rings

Semifinished pistons are oversize and must be machined and finished down to the proper size to fit the cylinder. Semifinished pistons do not necessarily weigh the same as standard pistons. Therefore, if only a partial set of semifinished pistons is to be installed, the new pistons must be balanced to the old pistons to prevent vibration.

33-7 PISTON-RING SERVICE

When an engine is being overhauled, new piston rings are installed. The new piston rings should be of the correct size and of the type best suited to the condition of the cylinder walls. New piston-ring sets are available in different ranges of unit pressure (from standard sets for new or rebored cylinders, to severe sets for cylinders with high taper and out-of-round wear) and in sizes of standard, and .010, .020, .030, .040, and .060″ oversize.

Before installing new piston rings, check for side clearance and depth in the ring grooves, and for end gap in the cylinders.

Measuring Side Clearance. Side clearance can be determined by first rolling the new ring around the groove in which it is to be installed. It should roll freely and not bind. Binding is usually caused by nicks and carbon on the face of the ring lands. The nicks or carbon can usually be removed by additional scraping or by using a small file.

Check the clearance by placing a thickness gauge in the groove beside the ring as the ring is rolled around. The clearance should neither be more or less than manufacturer's specifications.

Measuring End-Gap Clearances. End gap clearance is necessary to provide for heat expansion of the ring.

To measure clearance, place the ring in the cylinder and press down in the cylinder by inverting the piston to a depth of about 1″ for a rebored cylinder, and to the lower limit of the ring travel in worn or tapered cylinders. The ring gap, the space between the ends of the ring, may now be measured with a thickness gauge. If the gap is less than specifications, then try a smaller ring. It is no longer considered good practice to file the ends of the ring with a fine file to increase the end gap.

Ring Depth. Many piston-ring manufacturers provide a special temporary depth gauge with each ring set. The gauge should be used as specified to determine proper ring groove depth. The main cause of insufficient depth is improper ring-groove cleaning.

REVIEW QUESTIONS

1. Why must the piston, connecting rod and cap be matched and returned to the proper cylinder upon the assembly?
2. Why should connecting-rod-bolt thread protectors be used?
3. Why must piston-ring gaps be properly spaced around the piston?
4. List all the areas of excessive wear which result from the use of misaligned connecting rods.
5. State three causes of poor piston pin-to-piston fit.
6. Explain why blow-by and oil consumption increase if the top piston ring groove is worn.
7. Explain how knurling increases piston diameter.
8. How is scuffing and scoring of the piston reduced through the use of knurling?
9. Why should finished oversize pistons not be resized?
10. What are the common oversizes of piston ring sets?
11. Describe the tests necessary to assure the proper fit of a piston ring.

Chapter 34
THE COOLING SYSTEM: PRINCIPLES, CONSTRUCTION, AND SERVICE

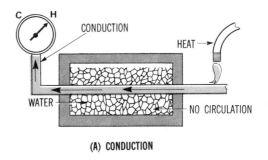

(A) CONDUCTION

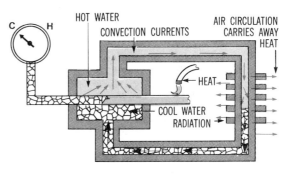

(B) CONVECTION CURRENTS AND RADIATION

Fig. 34-1   Conduction, Convection and Radiation

An engine's cooling system is designed to conduct heat away from the metal surrounding the combustion chamber. The heat developed by combustion may be as high as 4500° and the operating flame temperature around 2000°F. About one-third of this heat is carried away through the exhaust system and the remainder is absorbed by the cylinder head, pistons, valves, cylinder walls, etc. If this heat is not quickly dissipated, the metal parts would expand, and the lubricating oil would be burnt off. Either condition would cause the pistons and cylinders to score, finally resulting in seizure of the engine.

Heat may be transferred from one medium to another in one of three ways: radiation, convection, or conduction.

Conduction. The excess heat of combustion is conducted through the metal of the cylinder head and the cylinder walls to the liquid of the cooling system. The liquid acts as a transferring agent to carry the heat to the radiator.

Convection. As the liquid in the cooling system becomes heated it expands and becomes lighter, and has a tendency to rise. The cooler, heavier liquid has a tendency to fall. The location of the hoses and the radiator inlet and outlet connections are designed to take advantage of the convection currents developed by the heating and cooling of the liquid. These convection currents assist the centrifugal-type water circulating pump.

Radiation. The heated liquid in the cooling system transfers its heat by conduction through the metal walls of the tubes to the fins of the radiator. The fins of the radiator radiate the heat to the surrounding air which carries away or dissipates the heat.

Although the dissipation of heat is the primary job of the cooling system, the system must perform several other important functions:

1. Maintain a minimum operating temperature of approximately 180°F under all operating conditions because the engine does not operate efficiently when cold.
2. It must reach this operating temperature as quickly as possible.
3. Provide a convenient means of heating the passenger compartment in cold weather.

34-1 TYPES OF COOLING SYSTEMS
Two general types of cooling systems are used, the *liquid-cooling* and the *air-cooling*, the former system being the more popular.

Air-cooled engines usually have separately cast cylinders so that the cooling air can be circulated around each cylinder to remove the heat. The cylinders and cylinder heads are finned to increase the heat-dissipating area.

311

In the liquid-cooled system, the cooling liquid is circulated around the hottest parts to remove the excess heat. The liquid acts as a transferring agent to convey the heat from the metal parts of the engine to the radiator where the heat is radiated to the cooling medium, the air.

34-2 AIR-COOLED ENGINES

In an air-cooled engine many thin, heat-radiating fins are attached to the outside of the cylinder head and walls. Heat from the burning fuel is transferred to the fins. A constant stream of cooled air passes over the fins, absorbing the excess heat and carrying it away.

(A) CROSS SECTION

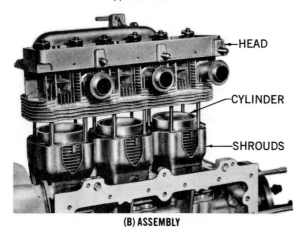

—HEAD

—CYLINDER

—SHROUDS

(B) ASSEMBLY

Courtesy of General Motors

Fig. 34-2   Typical Air-Cooled Cylinders

This air is directed around each cylinder and cylinder head by sheet-metal forms, called *shrouds,* which encase the engine (Fig. 34-2). The amount of air circulated is controlled by a blower and a thermostatically controlled valve. The blower is a centrifugal type fan, belt-driven from a pulley attached to the crankshaft. The thermostat that operates the air-regulator valve is of the bellows type. As the engine reaches its normal operating temperature, the bellows expand, operating a mechanical linkage that opens the valve. The valve is located near the top of the engine; as the valve

opens, it allows the fan to circulate more air past the fins of the cylinders and cylinder heads. The air picks up the excess heat and carries it away through an opening in the lower rear portion of the shrouds.

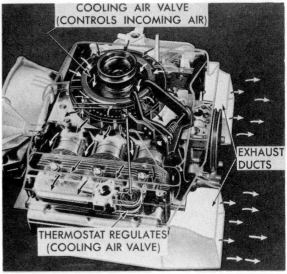

Courtesy of General Motors

Fig. 34-3   Engine Air-Cooling System

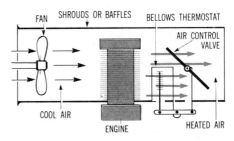

Fig. 34-4   Temperature Control on Air-Cooled Engines

34-3 LIQUID-COOLING SYSTEMS

Liquid-cooling systems may be of the *thermo-syphon* or the *pump* type, the latter being the most common.

Thermo-Syphon Type. The thermo-syphon or natural-circulation type of cooling system is used on some small stationary engines. The system depends upon gravity to circulate the coolant. As pointed out previously, a liquid when heated expands, becomes less dense, and therefore rises and the cooler liquid takes its place. In this type of system the liquid in the water jackets surrounding the cylinders becomes heated and rises. The heated water passes through the upper hose connection into the top of the radiator. The liquid is cooled by

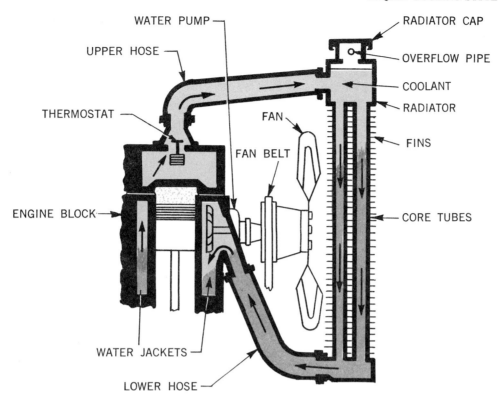

Fig. 34-5   Basic Liquid Cooling System

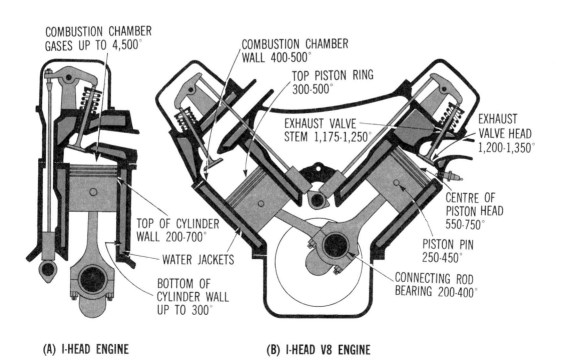

(A) I-HEAD ENGINE

(B) I-HEAD V8 ENGINE

Fig. 34-6   Typical Engine Operating Temperatures

the air passing through the radiator and increases in density and weight. Gravity carries the cooler liquid to the bottom of the radiator, through the lower hose connection to the bottom of the water jacket. The coolant continues this cycle as long as the engine block is warm.

Pump Type. The pump or forced-circulation type of cooling system uses a centrifugal-type pump to circulate the coolant through the engine and radiator. The pump draws cool liquid from the bottom tank of the radiator, forces it through the water jackets of the cylinder block and cylinder head where the liquid picks up the excess heat. The liquid is then forced through the top hose to the top tank of the radiator. The heat is dissipated as the liquid passes through the radiator. The cool liquid in the lower tank is ready to repeat the cycle.

34-4 UNITS OF THE LIQUID-COOLING SYSTEM

Water Jackets. Water jackets are cast as an integral part of the cylinder block and cylinder head. They provide passageways around the cylinders and valves for the circulation of the coolant.

Most engine blocks have full-length water jackets that extend the entire length of the cylinder. An opening at the front of the engine block connects the water jackets and the water pump. Matching openings between the cylinder block and the cylinder head allow the liquid to circulate between each unit. An outlet opening in the top of the cylinder head allows the liquid to pass out of the water jackets to the radiator. One or two drain holes are usually provided in the lower portion of the jackets so they may be drained when required.

Water Pump. To circulate water through the cooling system, a water pump is used. Usually mounted at the front end of the cylinder block between the block and the radiator, the pump is driven by a belt connected to the drive pulley which is attached to the front end of the engine crankshaft.

Most water pumps are of the impeller type, consisting of a housing with coolant inlet and outlet, and an impeller, a series of curved blades or vanes attached to one end of a sealed pump shaft. As the impeller rotates, the coolant between the blades is thrown outward by centrifugal force, and forced through the pump outlet into the cylinder block. Coolant from the bottom of the radiator is drawn into the pump through a hose connected to the

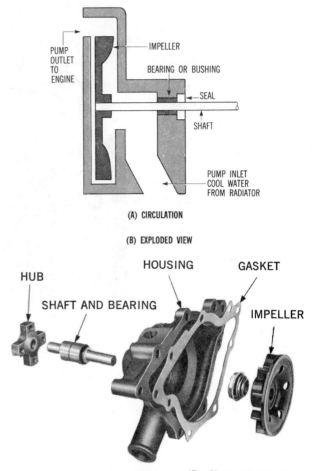

(A) CIRCULATION

(B) EXPLODED VIEW

Fig. 34-7   Typical Water Pump

(B) Chrysler Canada Ltd.

water-pump inlet. The impeller shaft is supported by one or more bearings and a seal is used to prevent the coolant from leaking out around the bearing.

Radiator. The radiator is made up of three assembled units: the top tank, the bottom tank, and the centre or cooling section called the core. The tubular type of core is the most widely used. It consists of many, small tubes placed in rows, running from the top to the bottom tank. They are held in position by a horizontal series of thin metal strips called fins, which are spaced about one-eighth inch apart. The fins help to transfer heat from the coolant to the air. As the hot coolant leaves the top tank and enters the tubes, it is divided into many small streams; while the coolant is passing through the tubes, its heat is transferred to the tubes. This heat is rapidly conducted to the fins and is carried away by the air passing through the radiator core.

An overflow pipe, which serves as an outlet for

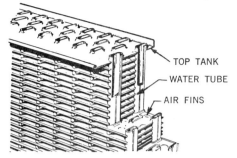

(A) RADIATOR CORE CONSTRUCTION

TOP TANK
WATER TUBE
AIR FINS

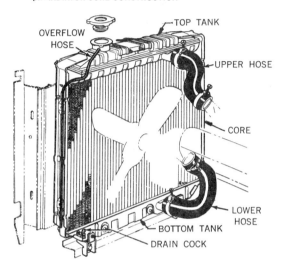

(B) RADIATOR AND CONNECTIONS

OVERFLOW HOSE
TOP TANK
UPPER HOSE
CORE
LOWER HOSE
BOTTOM TANK
DRAIN COCK

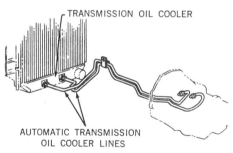

(C) COOLING THE AUTOMATIC TRANSMISSION

TRANSMISSION OIL COOLER
AUTOMATIC TRANSMISSION OIL COOLER LINES

Ford of Canada

(D) DOWN-FLOW RADIATOR

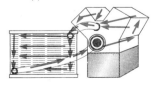

(E) CROSS-FLOW RADIATOR

Fig. 34-8   Radiators

steam and surplus coolant, is attached to the filler neck on the top tank of the radiator. This pipe leads to the bottom of the radiator. The lower end is open to the atmosphere.

A drain cock, fitted in the bottom of the lower tanks, permits draining of the coolant from most cooling systems. Some systems have additional drain cocks mounted in the engine block.

Radiators may have a baffle plate soldered inside the top tank above the radiator inlet to direct the liquid toward the radiator core.

Not all radiators have a vertical liquid flow through the core; some have a horizontal flow. These are called cross flow radiators. The top and bottom tanks are called headers and are mounted on each side of the radiator core. A cross flow radiator requires a separate supply tank. This tank which includes the radiator filler neck and cap is mounted between the upper hose connection and the radiator inlet. The tank serves as an expansion chamber and a supply reservoir. The overflow pipe is connected to this tank.

Tubular-type radiator cores consist of a series of round or flattened tubes, the ends of which are soldered into the top and bottom tanks or headers. The cooling fins are soldered to the tubes.

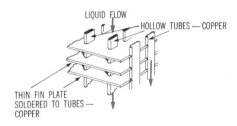

LIQUID FLOW
HOLLOW TUBES — COPPER
THIN FIN PLATE SOLDERED TO TUBES — COPPER

(A) FLAT TUBE AND FIN

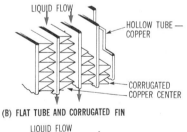

LIQUID FLOW
HOLLOW TUBE — COPPER
CORRUGATED COPPER CENTER

(B) FLAT TUBE AND CORRUGATED FIN

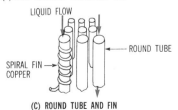

LIQUID FLOW
ROUND TUBE
SPIRAL FIN COPPER

(C) ROUND TUBE AND FIN

Fig. 34-9   Radiator Core Construction

Cellular-type radiator cores consist of pressed metal sections forming straight narrow passageways through the core between the two tanks or headers. The cooling fins are soldered to the pressed steel sections.

On many vehicles equipped with automatic transmissions, the bottom radiator tank houses an oil cooler to cool the transmission fluid.

Radiator Hoses. Radiator hoses are used to transfer the coolant between the engine and the radiator. The upper or outlet hose connects the water outlet housing on top of the engine to the top radiator tank, and the lower or inlet hose connects the bottom tank of the radiator to the water pump. These hoses are made of rubber which is able to withstand the vibration between the engine and the radiator.

Three types of hoses are used. The common straight hose is made of rubber with one or two plies of fabric to provide the necessary strength. This type of hose cannot be bent without collapsing and restricting the flow of the fluid. The moulded or shaped type of hose is made of rubber with one or two plies for strength and has all the necessary bends moulded during its manufacture. This hose will not collapse when bent. The accordion-type hose is also made of rubber and plies similar to the other two, but has a flexible accordion centre section. This section may be bent as required and will not collapse.

All three types of hose may use a special wire in their construction. The wire can be moulded as part of the hose or may be inserted later. This wire is commonly used in lower radiator hoses to prevent the hose from collapsing because of the low pressure created by the water pump.

To calculate the size of radiator hose used, measure either the inside diameter of the hose or the outside diameter of the connection.

Hose clamps of the spring tension, screw, or worm-tightened band type are used to secure the hose to the connection and to prevent leakage.

Fan. When the engine is running, the fan forces air through the radiator core, cooling the liquid in the radiator. The fan may have two, three, four or more blades. The blades may be evenly or unevenly spaced. Unevenly spaced fan blades are used where, because of the harmonic principle, evenly spaced blades have proven noisy. Most fans draw air through the radiator, although on some rear engine vehicles the air circulation is in the opposite direction. This type of fan is called a *pusher fan* since the air is pushed through the radiator.

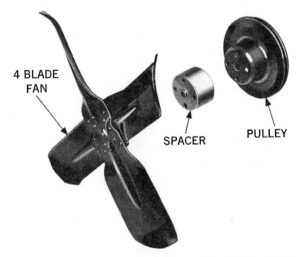

4 BLADE FAN   SPACER   PULLEY

Chrysler Canada Ltd.

Fig. 34-11   Standard Fan Drive

Fans are usually mounted on the water pump pulley, but may be mounted on a separate shaft and bracket, or attached directly to the crankshaft pulley.

The cooling action of the air caused by the fan is most important while the engine is idling or being operated at city driving speeds. At highway driving speeds, the fan is not as important because the forward motion of the vehicle is sufficient to force the required amount of air through the radiator for cooling purposes. However, several horsepower is required to drive the fan as the speed of the engine increases.

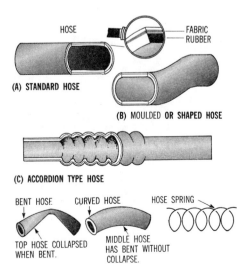

HOSE   FABRIC   RUBBER

(A) STANDARD HOSE

(B) MOULDED OR SHAPED HOSE

(C) ACCORDION TYPE HOSE

BENT HOSE   CURVED HOSE   HOSE SPRING

TOP HOSE COLLAPSED WHEN BENT.   MIDDLE HOSE HAS BENT WITHOUT COLLAPSE.

Fig. 34-10   Various Types of Radiator Hose

(A) TYPICAL FAN DRIVE CLUTCH INSTALLATION

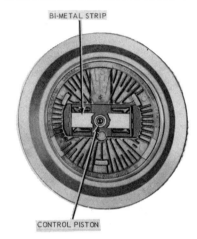

(B) FAN DRIVE CLUTCH WITH FLAT BIMETAL SPRING

(C) FAN DRIVE CLUTCH WITH FLAT COIL BIMETAL SPRING

Ford of Canada

Fig. 34-12   Variable Speed Fans

Variable-speed fans are used to reduce the power required to drive the fan at higher road speeds when the movement of the vehicle through the air reduces the need of the fan's action.

The variable-speed fan consists of a fluid clutch assembly attached to the water pump pulley. The

fluid clutch is equipped with a temperature sensing coil. This coil controls the flow of a silicone oil through the clutch. When the air discharge temperature is high, the more silicone oil in the clutch, the greater the fan speed. When the air discharge temperature is low, the less oil in the clutch and the lower the fan speed.

Fan Drives. A fan belt is necessary to drive the water pump, fan assembly, generator, and other accessories. Most fan belts are made in a V or wedge shape. The wedge of the belt fits firmly into the pulley grooves, so that belt slippage is eliminated by the extra friction.

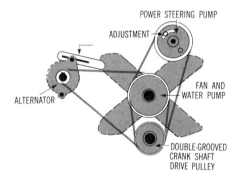

Fig. 34-13   Typical Fan, Water Pump and Power Steering Belt Drive

Engine Baffles. Engine baffles are sheet-metal parts which are used to direct the air to provide the most efficient cooling. They are used between the grill and the radiator to assure that all the air entering the grill passes through the radiator core. The hood

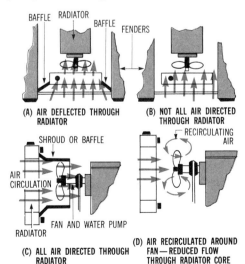

Fig. 34-14   Effect of Air Baffles and Shrouds on Air Circulation

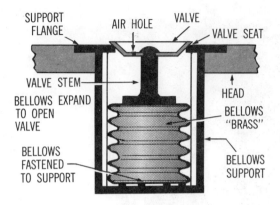

(A) BELLOWS TYPE

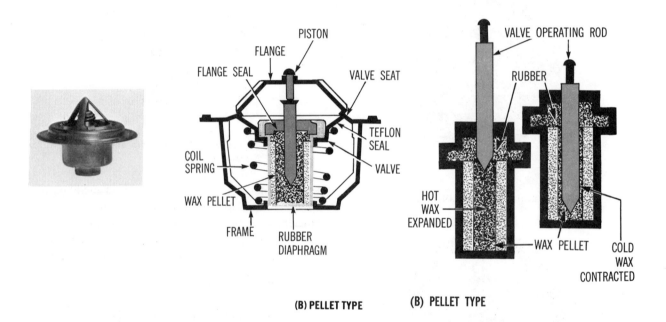

(B) PELLET TYPE   **(B) PELLET TYPE**

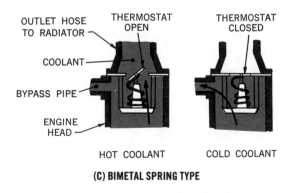

HOT COOLANT   COLD COOLANT

(C) BIMETAL SPRING TYPE

Fig. 34-15   Thermostats

J. C. Adam Company Limited

and inner fenders are used as baffles in the engine compartment to direct the air over the surface of the engine to pick up heat. On some engines a baffle or shroud is attached to the back of the radiator to assure that the fan draws the air through the total area of the radiator core instead of just from in front of the fan. This is of prime importance during low vehicle speeds.

Thermostats. The thermostat is a heat-operated valve that controls the flow of the coolant to the radiator. It maintains the proper engine operating temperature, which is usually between 160 and 180°F in hot climates and between 177 and 190°F in cold climates, when permanent-type antifreeze is used. The thermostat is usually located inside the water-outlet housing near the top front section of the engine block or cylinder head. The older type of thermostat was of the *bellows* or *bimetal spring* type. Both work on the basic scientific principle that materials and gases expand when heated.

Pellet-type thermostats are used in most modern automobiles. This type of thermostat contains a copper impregnated wax pellet that expands when heated and contracts when cooled. The pellet is connected to the thermostat control valve through a piston. As the pellet is heated, it expands and moves the piston which opens the valve. Cooling the pellet reverses the action to close the valve. The pellet-type thermostat is not pressure sensitive and works well in pressurized cooling systems.

The cooling system is designed to provide the

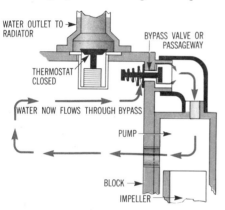

(A) BYPASS SYSTEM

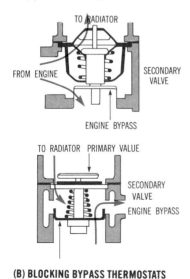

(B) BLOCKING BYPASS THERMOSTATS

Fig. 34-16   Cooling System Bypass Principle

necessary cooling for high-speed operation in hot weather. This amount of cooling is not required for light driving or for cool weather. Under the latter conditions, the thermostat valve controlling the flow of water to the radiator remains nearly closed, and the water pump either recirculates the coolant through the engine water jackets by means of a by-pass pipe, or the water stops circulating completely. As the engine warms up, the thermostat valve-operating mechanism expands and opens the valve. Hot coolant now flows from the water jacket to the radiator to be cooled before it returns to the water jackets.

Since the water pump is trying to circulate the coolant as long as the engine is running, various methods are used to provide for partial circulation during the warm-up period. One method uses a spring-loaded bypass valve that opens and allows the water to re-enter the pump. The bypass valve spring is weaker than the thermostat so that the valve will open whenever the thermostat is closed. Another method is to attach a fixed type of bypass between the cylinder head and the pump. This allows continuous recirculation of a small amount of coolant regardless of the temperature of the coolant. Some engines have three-stage cooling systems. When an engine equipped with a three-stage cooling system is started, the coolant only circulates around the cylinder head. As the coolant warms up, a thermostat opens to permit circulation around the cylinder block. When the coolant reaches normal operating temperature, it is then circulated through the radiator.

Thermostats are designed to open at specific

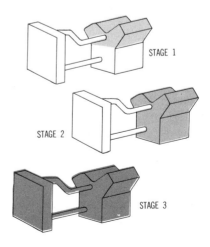

Fig. 34-17   The Three Stages as Engine Reaches Normal Operating Temperature

temperatures. A thermostat marked 170° should start to open between 166 and 174° and should be fully opened at 194°.

Radiator Pressure Cap. The radiator pressure cap is a device which permits higher operating temperatures, increased cooling efficiency, and reduced evaporation and surge losses.

Water at atmospheric pressure (14.7 psi) boils at 212°F. If the air pressure is increased, the boiling point of water is raised about 3° for every pound of pressure added. Therefore, the water in a system designed to operate under a pressure of 7 lbs would not boil until it reached a temperature of 233°. In this way water can be circulated through the cooling system without boiling at 212°. Because the temperature of the coolant is above 212°, the difference between air and coolant temperatures is greater. This causes the heat to be transferred more quickly to the air, resulting in improved coolant efficiency.

(A) VACUUM VALVE OPEN   (B) PRESSURE VALVE OPEN

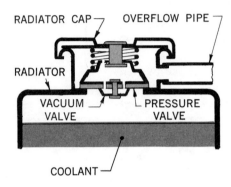

Fig. 34-19   Radiator Pressure Cap

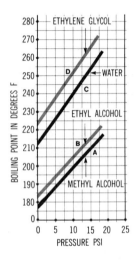

Fig. 34-18   Effect of Pressure on the Boiling Points of Various Coolant Solutions

Two valves are included in the pressure tap. One valve prevents excess pressures in the cooling system by allowing the excess pressure to escape through the overflow pipe. The other valve prevents a vacuum from forming in the cooling system after the engine has been shut off and the coolant begins to cool.

Water-distribution Tubes. In order to prevent "hot spots" around such parts as the exhaust-valve seats, a portion of the coolant from the water pump is directed through a water-distribution tube. This is a long tube which fits in the water jackets and has

holes or nozzles in it to direct the water to the hot spots. Without the tubes, damage would occur at the hot spots.

34-5 SEALED AND CLOSED TYPE COOLING SYSTEMS

The sealed and closed types of cooling systems are similar to the conventional cooling system except that they include a separate expansion tank or reservoir either in place of or in conjunction with the radiator overflow pipe. This tank is usually made of translucent plastic which is marked to indicate when the system is at operating level or requires additional coolant. The tank is used in place of the expansion space usually provided in the top radiator tank. In a sealed or closed system the radiator is filled to capacity. In both types the tank accommodates the increased volume of the coolant as the coolant temperature is increased. The tank prevents the loss of coolant as the temperature increases.

The expansion tank or reservoir usually includes a removable cap to permit the addition of coolant if required or the testing of the freezing point of the solution.

Sealed Type of Cooling System. In this type of system the expansion tank is connected directly to the top tank of the radiator. The radiator does not use

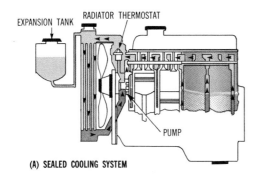

(A) SEALED COOLING SYSTEM

EXPANSION TANK
RADIATOR THERMOSTAT
PUMP

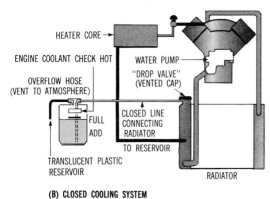

(B) CLOSED COOLING SYSTEM

HEATER CORE
ENGINE COOLANT CHECK HOT
OVERFLOW HOSE (VENT TO ATMOSPHERE)
WATER PUMP
"DROP VALVE" (VENTED CAP)
FULL
ADD
CLOSED LINE CONNECTING RADIATOR TO RESERVOIR
TRANSLUCENT PLASTIC RESERVOIR
RADIATOR

Fig. 34-20   Sealed and Closed Cooling Systems

a pressure-type radiator cap. However, the expansion tank is equipped with a combination pressure-vacuum valve which is similar in operation to the valves in a pressure-type radiator cap.

During normal engine operation the level of the liquid in the tank is constantly changing as the temperature of the coolant increases or decreases. The normal expansion of the coolant is absorbed by the cushion of air in the tank. As the cushion of air is compressed, it provides the pressure increase required to raise the boiling point of the coolant during high temperature operation. The pressure valve opens when the cooling system pressure, caused by the expanding coolant, reaches a predetermined value. The vacuum valve opens when the coolant cools and contracts, therefore lowering the system pressure below that of atmospheric pressure.

The Closed-Type Cooling System. This system has the reservoir attached to the overflow outlet of the radiator filler neck. The system uses a type of pressure radiator cap which is referred to as a "drop valve vented cap." The valve in the cap is temperature operated and is in the open position until the coolant approaches the boiling point, at

which time it closes, sealing off the reservoir from the cooling system. The reservoir is vented to the atmosphere so that the system can operate at atmospheric pressure when the engine is comparatively cool.

As the engine warms up, the coolant expands and the excess coolant is forced into the reservoir. Should the coolant reach near the boiling point the temperature-controlled drop valve closes, preventing the coolant from reaching the reservoir and the engine cooling system operates as a normal pressurized cooling system. When the engine cools, the drop valve opens to permit the coolant to flow back from the reservoir into the top tank of the radiator.

34-6 ANTIFREEZE SOLUTIONS

In winter weather, plain water in the radiator and water jackets would freeze. This would result in serious damage to the cooling system parts as the expansion, because of freezing, would burst these parts. Various mixtures known as antifreeze solutions are used to prevent freezing. Some of the substances used in antifreeze solutions are ethylene glycol, ethyl alcohol, and mentol alcohol. The most popular is ethylene glycol.

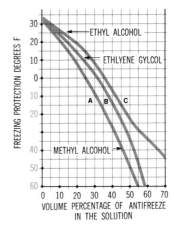

Fig. 34-21   Freezing Protection Chart

Ethylene glycol is sold as an antifreeze under various trade names. It is a by-product in the manufacture of certain gases. In concentrated solution it has a boiling point of 330° F. Undiluted ethylene glycol will slush up at relatively high temperatures. The maximum possible protection against freezing, a temperature of −75° F, is obtained with a mixture of 68% ethylene glycol and 32% water. Ethylene glycol does not evaporate, has no odour, and will not injure the finish of an automobile.

The mixing of an antifreeze with water forms a solution which has a lower freezing point than water. The amount that the freezing point of the solution is lowered is proportional to the amount of antifreeze in the solution.

The following table indicates the proportions of ethylene glycol and water per gallon which are necessary to withstand various temperatures without freezing.

QUANTITY OF WATER	QUANTITY OF ETHYLENE GLYCOL	FREEZING POINT
6 pt	2 pt	10° F
5½ pt	2½ pt	0° F
5 pt	3 pt	−10° F
4½ pt	3½ pt	−20° F
4 pt	4 pt	−30° F

Antifreeze solutions expand more than water when heated.

A temperature rise of 140° F will cause water to expand approximately ¼ pt per gallon. Under the same temperature rise, a solution of ethylene glycol and water good for −20° F protection will expand approximately ⅓ pt per gallon. Therefore, to avoid the loss of antifreeze solution because of expansion the cooling system must not be filled completely.

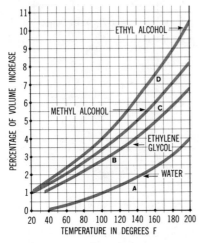

Fig. 34-22   Heat Expansion of Coolants

Since ethylene glycol has a higher boiling point than water, the greater the percentage of ethylene glycol in an antifreeze solution the higher the boiling point of the solution. A solution of ethylene glycol and water with a freezing temperature of −20° F will not boil until the temperature reaches 223° F. With the combination of ethylene glycol

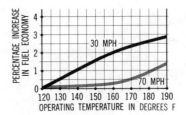

(A) EFFECT ON FUEL ECONOMY

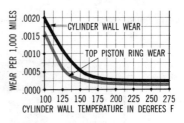

(B) EFFECT ON ENGINE WEAR

Fig. 34-23   Effect of Engine Operating Temperatures

and water solution in a sealed pressurized cooling system, it is possible to raise the boiling point of the coolant to 250° F or more, for more efficient operation of the cooling system.

Most ethylene glycol based permanent-type antifreeze solution contains a rust inhibitor to help prevent corrosion of the cooling system. This type of antifreeze solution is usually left in the cooling system for year round operation.

34-7 COOLING SYSTEM SERVICE

Cooling system trouble is usually first indicated by the engine overheating or by the appearance of leakage. (While overheating is a common cooling system complaint, it also can be caused by troubles in the engine, inadequate lubrication, or unusual driving conditions such as prolonged high speed, lugging, or driving at high altitudes.) Once it is established that the trouble lies in the cooling system, the trouble should be repaired to prevent permanent damage to the engine.

34-8 COOLING SYSTEM TROUBLES

The most common cause of cooling system trouble is the accumulation of rust, scale, and grease or oil in the water jackets and the radiator. This accumulation will clog up the water passageways in the cylinder block, head, and the radiator, thereby reducing the efficiency of the cooling system.

Water scale results from the continuous heating of water that contains minerals such as calcium or

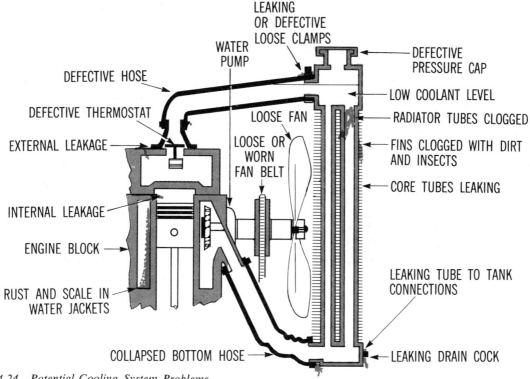

Fig. 34-24 *Potential Cooling System Problems*

magnesium salts. These salts leave the water to form what is known as *water scale*. The scale forms an insulating barrier between the metal parts and the coolant.

Oil films are formed because of the seepage of water-pump lubricants into the coolant. The oil film clings to the metal and traps dirt and sediment and prevents effective cooling.

Rust is the result of the water's oxygen combining chemically with iron and steel to form an oxide called rust. Air in the cooling system increases the speed at which the rust will form. Rust is not soluble in water.

Exhaust Gas Leaks. Exhaust gas leaks are another cause of corrosion. These gases contain strong acids which when heated attack the metal and form insulators which will not conduct heat.

Restricted Air Flow. Restricted air flow can be caused by the accumulation of dirt and insects in the radiator air passages. This cuts down on the flow of air through the radiator which is necessary to dissipate the heat.

Thermostats. Thermostats can cause overheating by failing to open at the proper temperature.

Radiator Caps. Failure of the pressure cap to seal

(A) Courtesy of General Motors

(A) REPLACING THERMOSTAT

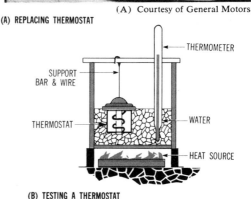

(B) TESTING A THERMOSTAT

Fig. 34-25 *Thermostats*

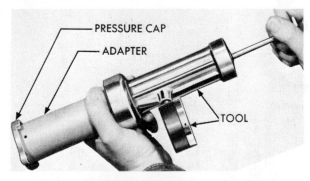

(A) TESTING RADIATOR CAP

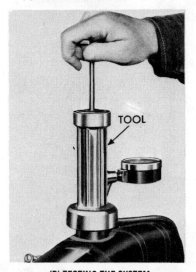

(B) TESTING THE SYSTEM

Chrysler Canada Ltd.

Fig. 34-26   Pressure Testing the Cooling System

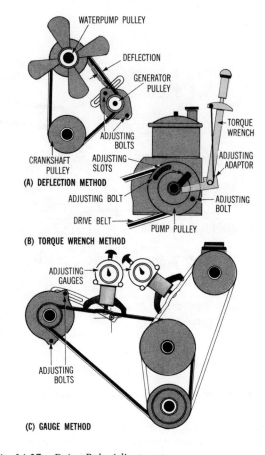

Fig. 34-27   Drive Belt Adjustments

the system and allow the pressure to build up can cause the coolant to overheat.

Fan Belts. Loose fan belts can cause a reduction in both air and coolant circulation, either of which can cause overheating.

Fan-belt Tension. Fan-bent tension is adjusted by moving the generator or alternator away from the engine block. This adjustment varies according to the type of generator or alternator mounting. A general rule to be followed when adjusting the fan-belt tension is to tighten the belt so that when a light thumb pressure is applied at a point midway between the drive and one of the driven pulleys the belt will sag approximately its own width.

Belt tension may also be tested and adjusted by using a special adjusting adaptor and a torque wrench. With the adjusting bolts loosened, the adaptor attached to the accessory and to the torque wrench, the specified torque is applied and retained until the adjusting bolts are retightened.

Belt tension can also be determined by measuring the torque applied to the pulley nut of the accessory until the pulley slips on the belt.

Another method of testing belt tension requires a special belt strand tension gauge and bracket assembly. This gauge deflects the belt and, in doing so, indicates the belt tension on a dial.

34-9 REVERSE FLUSHING THE RADIATOR AND CYLINDER BLOCK

Reverse flushing of the cooling system forces water through the system in the opposite direction to its normal flow. The reversal of the flow loosens the particles that may be jammed into openings or built up in a gradual slope in the direction of normal coolant flow.

To reverse flush the radiator, the water enters the bottom or outlet tank, flows through the core and out the top or inlet tank, or through the filler

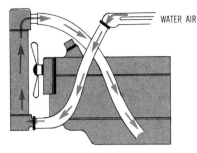

(A) RADIATOR

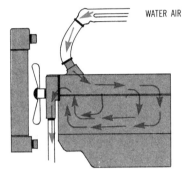

(B) CYLINDER BLOCK

Fig. 34-28 Reverse Flushing Cooling System

neck. To reverse flush the engine block, the thermostat is removed to permit the water to enter the cylinder block through the water outlet housing. The water flows through the water jackets in a reverse direction and out through the water pump inlet connection.

Additional agitation during reverse flushing can be obtained through the use of special compressed air-water nozzles. The air pressure must not exceed 20 psi, to prevent rupture of the radiator.

REVIEW QUESTIONS

1. Name and describe three methods by which heat may be transferred from one medium to another.
2. Explain how each of the methods of heat transfer are used in the automotive cooling system.
3. State the three purposes of the cooling system.
4. Explain how the air is used as the cooling medium of both the air-cooled and liquid-cooled systems.
5. Why is it important to maintain an efficient operating temperature?
6. Explain how the efficient operating temperature is maintained in (a) air-cooled (b) liquid-cooled engines.
7. Describe the operation of a thermo-syphon type cooling system.
8. What are the advantages of a forced-circulation type cooling system?
9. Describe the operation of a water pump.
10. Describe the construction of a radiator core.
11. What causes the lower radiator hose to collapse? How can this collapse be prevented?
12. When is the air circulation of the fan most important? Why?
13. What is the advantage of a variable speed fan?
14. Why is the use of air baffles and shrouds important?
15. What type of thermostat is most satisfactory for use in pressurized cooling systems? Why?
16. Describe the operation of a three-stage cooling system.
17. What are the advantages of a pressurized cooling system?
18. Calculate the boiling point of water in a cooling system operating under pressure of 14 psi.
19. Describe the difference between a sealed cooling system and a closed cooling system.
20. State three advantages of an ethylene-glycol base antifreeze.
21. What is the amount of ethylene-glycol type antifreeze required for a 16-quart capacity cooling system to give protection against freezing at $-20°F$?
22. The ethylene-glycol antifreeze solution in a 14-quart capacity cooling system is tested and found to give protection to $-10°F$. How much additional antifreeze is required to give protection to $-30°F$?
23. What effect does cylinder wall temperature have on cylinder wall wear?
24. How is water scale formed?
25. State how (a) scale (b) oil film (c) rust reduce the efficiency of the cooling system.
26. Why is proper drive belt tension important?

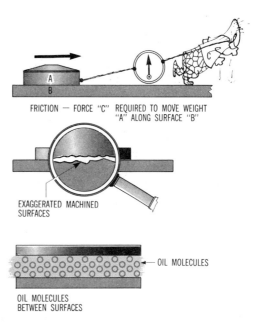

FRICTION — FORCE "C" REQUIRED TO MOVE WEIGHT "A" ALONG SURFACE "B"

EXAGGERATED MACHINED SURFACES

OIL MOLECULES

OIL MOLECULES BETWEEN SURFACES

Fig. 35-1   Friction

Chapter 35
THE LUBRICATION SYSTEM

35-1 LUBRICATION

In the automobile there are a great many parts that rotate or slide against another part. This motion creates what is known as *friction*. Friction can be described as resistance to motion, caused by the contact of the surfaces of the bodies and exists in various degrees between all moving parts. The speed, load, type of material, and finish are the main factors affecting friction. Even highly polished surfaces have small projections and irregularities which set up a resisting force (friction) which is converted into heat. The heat can cause abnormal expansion of the parts and ultimately could cause the part to bind or seize.

There are several types of friction: dry friction, greasy friction, and viscous friction.

Dry or solid friction is when two bearing surfaces are allowed to rub against each other without lubrication.

Greasy friction is the friction between two surfaces that are thinly coated with oil or grease. The lubrication between the surfaces where greasy friction exists is not sufficient to prevent wear.

Viscous or fluid friction is the term used to refer to the tendency of liquids, such as oil, to resist flowing. Viscous friction is the friction, or resistance to motion, between the layers of a liquid.

Lubrication helps to reduce friction by placing a film of oil or grease between the moving surfaces. The molecules of a lubricant are very small, flexible, and slippery, yet will stick to most surfaces. The lubricating film acts like a layer of small balls

which prevents the actual contact of the two metal surfaces. A good lubricant must have adhesive and cohesive properties.

Adhesion is the property of the lubricant to stay between the surfaces it is to lubricate.

Cohesion refers to the force of attraction of the light particles of the lubricant and is expressed as viscosity or body.

Fluidity—lubricating oils must also have fluidity, the property which allows oil to flow through oil lines and then to spread evenly over all the bearing surfaces.

Wedging Action of Oil.   When a shaft is rotating within a bearing, it is lubricated by an oil film created and maintained by the wedging action of the oil. The oil molecules that adhere to the shaft are carried along with the shaft as it rotates. This layer of molecules drags along adjacent layers of oil molecules. The weight and load conditions of the shaft tend to force the shaft into the oil. This causes the shaft to assume an eccentric position in the bearing. The rotation of the shaft and the cohesion between the molecules of the oil cause some of the layers of oil to be forced under the shaft. This wedging action lifts the shaft and places a film of oil between the shaft and the bearing. The wedging action creates high and low pressure areas on the bearing surfaces. The new oil from the oil pump enters the bearing at the low pressure area.

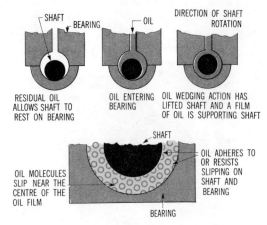

SHAFT
BEARING
OIL
DIRECTION OF SHAFT ROTATION

RESIDUAL OIL ALLOWS SHAFT TO REST ON BEARING

OIL ENTERING BEARING

OIL WEDGING ACTION HAS LIFTED SHAFT AND A FILM OF OIL IS SUPPORTING SHAFT

SHAFT

OIL MOLECULES SLIP NEAR THE CENTRE OF THE OIL FILM

OIL ADHERES TO OR RESISTS SLIPPING ON SHAFT AND BEARING

BEARING

Fig. 35-2   Action of Oil on Bearing Surfaces

Lubricants are used in the automobile for five main reasons. First, they form a film between the moving parts, thereby reducing friction which causes loss of power. Second, lubricants help to carry away heat from such parts as pistons and valves, in the same way that water does when it is splashed on a hot surface. Third, lubricating oil helps to seal the space around the pistons and piston rings, thereby preventing loss of compression. Fourth, it acts as a cushion to protect the parts and fifth, it acts as a cleaning agent.

35-2 REFINING CRUDE OIL

Crude oil, as it comes from the ground, contains many petroleum products. Refining is the name given to the processes necessary to separate crude oil into gasoline, motor oil, greases, etc. The first step in the process is called *fractionation.*

Fractionation, like distillation, depends upon the vaporization and subsequent condensing of a liquid and is used to separate liquids having different boiling points. The crude oil is heated in the bottom of a tall, vertical tower containing a series of trays. Since the temperature in the tower is lower at the top than at the bottom, the portion of the crude oil having the highest boiling point condenses on the lowest trays, while the portion with the lowest boiling point keeps rising in the form of vapour and condenses on the trays nearest the top of the tower.

Fractionation does not release enough gasoline from crude oil to satisfy today's demands. To

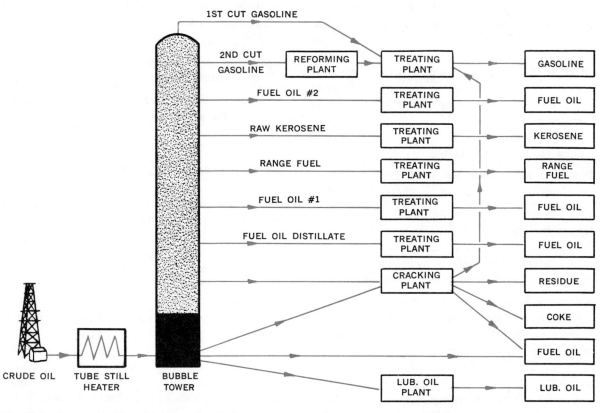

1ST CUT GASOLINE

2ND CUT GASOLINE — REFORMING PLANT — TREATING PLANT — GASOLINE

FUEL OIL #2 — TREATING PLANT — FUEL OIL

RAW KEROSENE — TREATING PLANT — KEROSENE

RANGE FUEL — TREATING PLANT — RANGE FUEL

FUEL OIL #1 — TREATING PLANT — FUEL OIL

FUEL OIL DISTILLATE — TREATING PLANT — FUEL OIL

CRACKING PLANT — RESIDUE

COKE

FUEL OIL

CRUDE OIL   TUBE STILL HEATER   BUBBLE TOWER   LUB. OIL PLANT — LUB. OIL

Fig. 35-3   Composite Flow Diagram of a Modern Refinery

obtain sufficient gasoline a process called *cracking* is used.

Cracking is the process of breaking down the original structure of oil, or breaking the molecules apart so that they can be re-formed in a different structure. This process makes it possible to produce large amounts of gasoline from low-grade materials.

After cracking, the manufacturing is divided into three sections: gasoline, lubricating oil, and gear lubricants and greases. During the manufacture of gasoline, a product known as tetraethyl lead is added to give the gasoline a high antiknock rating. This reduces the pinging noise that is technically referred to as *detonation*.

Engine lubricating oils are manufactured by blending stocks called neutrals (light oils) and bright stocks (heavy oils) in the correct proportions to produce oils of a given viscosity, such as SAE 10, SAE 20, and SAE 30. Other chemicals called *additives* are used to produce detergent (heavy duty) motor oils.

Gear lubricants and greases are manufactured by adding certain chemicals and soaps, which increase the clinging properties of oil. In this category we find transmission and differential oils, and chassis, cup, wheel-bearing, and special greases.

35-3 ENGINE OILS

An engine oil must be able to withstand crankcase temperatures as high as 250° F without breaking down and permitting metal-to-metal contact. It must not thicken at low temperatures or it would not circulate through the oil passages of an engine to provide the necessary lubrication; it must not contain the lighter, more volatile molecules which evaporate at normal crankcase temperatures; and finally, its tendency to form carbon at normal temperatures must be held to a minimum.

During the refining process, the dissolved solids and substances such as acids, tar, and paraffin which create corrosion and gum deposits must be carefully removed.

Many tests to determine and rate the properties of lubricants have been developed. Some will be discussed here.

Viscosity. The term viscosity refers to the tendency of a liquid such as oil to resist flowing. It may be measured by determining the speed at which a given amount of oil will flow through a given hole at a given temperature. When oil is hot, it has a lower viscosity and will flow faster than when cold. An oil of high viscosity may be termed a heavy oil; an oil of low viscosity, a light oil.

Cold Test. The cold test is used to determine the temperature at which oil congeals and ceases to flow. The *cloud point* of an oil is the temperature at which the solids in the oil begin to crystalize or separate out from the solution.

Flash Point Test. The flash point test is used to determine the temperature at which the lubricant has vaporized sufficiently so that when an open flame is passed over its surface, a small flash of short duration will occur.

Carbon Residue Test. The carbon residue test is to determine the amount of carbon that is left after a given quantity of oil has been evaporated.

Volatility Test. The volatility test is used to determine the temperature at which the lubricant will evaporate.

35-4 SAE SYSTEM OF OIL CLASSIFICATION

In order to have a convenient and widely understood method of labelling oils according to their viscosity, the Society of Automotive Engineers adopted the system described as the SAE Recommended Practice for Lubricant Viscosity Numbers. With this rating system, the lower the rating number, the lower the viscosity of the oil. The numbers do not indicate proportionate increases in the viscosity according to the increase in the number; an SAE 20 oil, for example, is not necessarily twice as heavy at a given temperature as an SAE 10 oil. The SAE rating does not indicate in any way the quality of the motor oil.

The petroleum industry has developed oils that have a low viscosity for winter starting temperatures. These oils are modifications of the SAE 10 and SAE 20 grades. They are known as 10W and 20W, because they will meet both winter viscosity specifications and the standard SAE specification.

Refiners have added a further oil classification, namely SAE 10W-30 oil, which has a viscosity rating when cold equal to SAE 10W oil and when hot a viscosity rating equal to SAE 30 oil. In other words, as the temperature rises the oil does not become as thin as a number 10W oil would normally be, but retains a viscosity comparable to SAE 30 oil.

Oil thickens in cold weather and makes the engine difficult to start because the oil does not flow readily through the small spaces between the moving parts. If the oil is too thick, the engine loses much of its power in turning over and many of the parts will not be properly lubricated. If the oil is too thin, it will be squeezed from between the surfaces of the moving parts too quickly, causing increased friction and wear. Oil with the correct viscosity should be used in accordance with the temperature and the season of the year.

35-5 SAE OILS AND THEIR USES

SAE 40—Used in heavy engines in very hot weather.

SAE 30—Used in almost all automobile engines during summer months.

SAE 20—Used during spring and fall months down to freezing temperatures, or to break in new engines during summer months.

SAE 10—Used during winter months below freezing temperatures.

During normal engine operation, carbon and other harmful impurities tend to form deposits on working parts. Engine efficiency is thus decreased. To help overcome this problem, heavy duty oils, which contain detergent additives, have been developed. Detergent oil holds the impurities in suspension, preventing the buildup of deposits.

35-6 API SERVICE RATINGS OF OIL

In addition to the SAE system of oil classification which determines the grade of oil, another method of oil classification is used. It is called the API (American Petroleum Institute) *service-ratings system*. The service ratings classify oil as to the type of driving conditions for which the oil is best suited. Under the system, oils are divided into six groups: MS, MM, and ML for gasoline-powered engines, and DG, DM, and DS for diesel-power engines.

MS oil is designed for severe service, such as stop-and-start city driving, prolonged high-speed highway operation, or heavy-load operation, such as highway truck-transport work.

The MM type is designed for medium service, such as short-run, high-speed highway operation, long-trip operation at moderate speeds, and average cold-weather operation in moderate highway and city driving.

ML oil is designed for light service where most trips are no longer than 10 miles, at average speeds, under average climatic conditions.

DS oil is designed for use in diesel engines operated under severe conditions.

DM oil is designed for use in diesel engines operated under medium conditions.

The DG type is designed for use in diesel engines under light operating conditions.

35-7 ASTM SERVICE RATINGS OF OIL

Due to the more severe demands made upon crankcase lubricants and to the insistance of less crankcase emissions, the original 1952 API service-rating system was changed in 1968. At that time the American Petroleum Institute, the American Society for Testing Materials, and the Society of Automotive Engineers joined forces to present new service classifications. Under the new system, oils are divided into eight groups: SA, SB, SC, for gasoline-powered engines, and CA, CB, CC, and CD, for diesel-powered engines.

SA—typical of engines operated in such a manner that straight mineral oils are satisfactory.

SB—typical of engines operated in such a manner that oils designed for this service provide only antiscuff capability and resistance to oil oxidation and bearing corrosion.

SC—typical of gasoline engines in 1964-through-1967 model vehicles. Oil design for this service provides detergent-dispersive characteristics as well as protection against wear, rust, and corrosion.

SD—typical of gasoline engines beginning with 1968 model vehicles and operating under engine manufacturing warranties. Oils for this service provide more protection from high- and low-temperature deposits, wear, rust, and corrosion.

CA—typical of diesel engines operating in mild to moderate duty with high quality fuels. These oils provide protection from bearing corrosion and high-temperature deposits.

CB—typical of engines operated as at CA but using lower quality level (high sulphur) fuels.

CC—typical of lightly super-charged diesel engines in moderate to severe duty. The oils provide protection from high-temperature deposits.

CD—typical of super-charged diesel engines in high-speed, high-output duty, requiring highly effective control of wear and deposits.

API/ASTM/SAE MOTOR OIL CLASSIFICATION	
New Service Classification	Old Service Classification
SD	MS
SD-CC	MS-DM
	MS
CC-SC	DM-MM

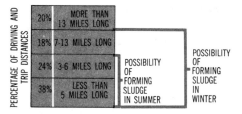

Fig. 35-4   Sludge Formation Possibilities

35-8 FACTORS DETERMINING THE TYPE OF OIL TO BE USED

Proper engine lubrication requires the use of the thinnest oil that will remain between the bearing surfaces and retain an oil film under operating loads. However, the oil must not be so thin that it causes excessive oil consumption.

The selection of the proper grade of oil is determined by: the rubbing or surface speed of the bearing, the bearing clearance, the load imposed on the bearing, the heat of the bearing, and the operating temperature of the lubricant.

The greater the shaft speed, the less the bearing clearance, and the greater the adhesive properties required in the oil. The greater the bearing load, the greater the cohesive properties required in the oil. The adhesive properties of oil are considered in the service ratings of oil and the cohesive properties in the SAE system of oil classification.

In order to obtain the best results from the lubricating oil, the operation of the vehicle must be considered under both the SAE system and the service-ratings system. Then the proper oil can be selected to suit the type of operating conditions under which the vehicle will be used.

35-9 OIL CONTAMINATION

When engine oil is put into the oil pan, it is clear and clean. When it is removed, it is usually black and dirty. The oil becomes dirty during the operation of the engine when harmful impurities such as carbon, gasoline, water, oxidation, metal particles, and dust and dirt mix with the oil to form sludge.

Sludge—This is a black, brown, or grey deposit having the consistency of soft mud. It clogs oil-pump screens and oil lines, thus reducing the oil supply which can result in bearing damage and failure. Sludge causes rings and valves to stick and increases oil consumption. The formation of sludge is a result of engine operation, particularly at low engine temperatures during starting, warm up, and idling speeds.

Carbon—As fuel is burned in the cylinders, carbon is formed. Most of this is blown out through the exhaust system, but some settles on the cylinder walls. The movement of the pistons and piston rings scrapes this carbon from the cylinder walls, mixing it with oil, making the oil black and gritty.

Gasoline—When an engine is started, especially in cold weather, it is necessary to use the choke. This prevents most of the air from entering the carburetor and allows the engine to draw a very rich gasoline mixture into the cylinders. If the choke is used too much, not all of the gasoline burns; some seeps down past the pistons and rings, mixing with and diluting the oil. This thinning of the oil causes scored or scratched pistons.

Water—During combustion, the oxygen in the air combines with the hydrocarbons of the fuel to form water vapour. Most of this vapour passes out the exhaust system. During cold engine operation some of this vapour condenses on the cylinder walls. It may find its way into the crankcase by the scraping action of the piston and piston rings or as a result of blow-by past the piston rings.

Differences in temperature between the inside and outside of the oil pan, especially in winter, causes water vapour to condense on the inside walls of the oil pan. This water runs to the bottom of the oil pan and freezes, thereby preventing the flow of oil into the oil pump. Condensation of water in the oil pan is greater in engines which run for a short time and then are allowed to cool off again.

Water in the oil also forms acids which attack the metal parts.

Oxidization—Oxidization is the result of a molecule of oxygen attaching itself to an oil molecule to form a more complex compound. The higher the oil temperature, the greater the possibility of oxidation. Oxidation forms acids, which attack the metal parts, and creates a varnish-like coating which causes sticking valves and piston rings.

Metal Particles—Because the moving parts are constantly wearing, small particles of metal which are worn away mix with the oil and help make the oil gritty.

Dust and Dirt—These contaminants enter the crankcase through the carburetor air intake and the crankcase ventilating system. They increase the amount of grit in the oil and cause additional wear of the engine parts.

Until recently, most manufacturers recommended that engine lubricating oils be changed every 1,000 miles in summer and every 500 miles in winter. Now, most manufacturers suggest longer periods between oil changes, ranging from a low of 1,000 miles for vehicles used mainly for stop-and-start driving, to a high of 6,000 miles for vehicles used mainly for highway driving.

35-10 ENGINE LUBRICATION

Two types of engine lubrication systems are used in internal-combustion engines: the *splash system* and the *pressure-feed system*. The pressure-feed system, with small modifications, is the more popular for the modern automobile engine. The splash system is used on most fractional horsepower and outboard engines.

Pressure-Feed System. In the pressure-feed system, oil is forced by the oil pump through oil lines and drilled passageways. The oil, passing through the drilled passageways under pressure, supplies the necessary lubrication for the crankshaft main bearings, the connecting-rod bearings, piston-pin bushings, camshaft bearings, valve lifters, valve push rods, and rocker studs. Oil passing through the oil lines is directed to the timing gears and valve rocker shafts in order to lubricate these parts. The cylinder walls are lubricated by oil thrown off the connecting-rod and piston-pin bearings. Some engines have oil-spit holes in the connecting rods that line up with drilled holes in the crankpin during each revolution, and throw or spit a stream of oil onto the cylinder walls.

To enable the oil to pass the drilled passageways in the engine block to the rotating crankshaft, the main bearings must have oil-feed holes or grooves that line up with the drilled holes in the crankshaft each time the crankshaft rotates. The same is true in the case of the connecting-rod bearings and the drilled passageways in the connecting rods. Since the oil in the passageways is under pressure, each

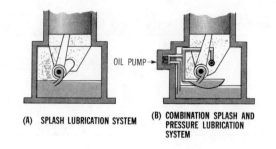

(A) SPLASH LUBRICATION SYSTEM   (B) COMBINATION SPLASH AND PRESSURE LUBRICATION SYSTEM

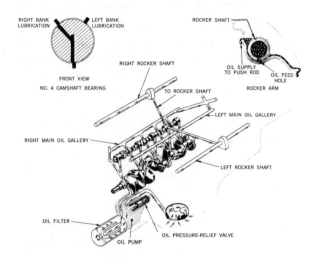

(C) FULL PRESSURE LUBRICATING SYSTEMS

Fig. 35-5   Engine Lubrication Systems

time the drilled holes in the crankshaft and connecting rod line up with the holes in the bearings, the pressure forces the oil through these drilled passages into the crankshaft and connecting rod, lubricating their respective bearings.

After the oil has been forced to the area requiring lubrication, it falls back down into the oil pan ready to be picked up again and returned through the system. As the oil falls, it is frequently splashed by the moving parts onto some other part requiring lubrication.

The Splash System. The splash system is used only on small four-stroke-cycle engines such as lawnmower engines. As the engine is operating, dippers on the ends of the connecting rods enter the oil supply, pick up sufficient oil to lubricate the connecting-rod bearing, and splash oil to the upper parts of the engine. The oil is thrown up as droplets, or fine spray, which lubricates the cylinder walls, piston pins, and valve mechanism. Frequently, small oil cups are used to catch the splashed oil in order to lubricate certain parts of the engine such as the crankshaft main bearings.

In two-cycle engines used on some lawnmowers and outboard engines, the proper amount of lubricating oil is added to the gasoline. The oil is atomized as it enters the air stream in the carburetor, forming a fine mist which circulates through the crankcase to provide the necessary lubrication. Sometimes, small oil cups or troughs are used to catch the condensed oil and direct it to particular points requiring lubrication.

35-11 UNITS OF THE ENGINE LUBRICATING SYSTEM

Oil Supply. The oil supply is carried in the oil pan or lower half of the crankcase. It is poured into the case through the oil filler, and the amount is indicated by reading the graduated oil-gauge rod or dip stick.

Since the oil absorbs some of the heat from the engine, this heat must be dissipated. The heat is conducted from the oil to the oil pan which is exposed to the air stream under the car. The moving air picks up the heat and carries it away.

Oil Pump. An oil pump is used to produce the pressure necessary to circulate the oil through the lubricating system. The oil pump may be mounted on the engine above the oil supply, but it is customary for it to be submerged in the oil supply, thus eliminating any need of priming. The pump is driven by a shaft which is usually geared to the camshaft. Two types of oil pump are used—the gear pump and the rotor pump.

The gear pump depends upon a pair of meshing gears enclosed in a housing. As the gears rotate and unmesh, a partial vacuum is created. Atmospheric pressure on the oil in the oil pan forces the oil to enter the pump and fill the spaces between the gear teeth. As the teeth mesh again, the oil is forced out of the spaces between the teeth, through the pump outlet, and to the various parts of the engine.

The rotor pump uses an inner and outer rotor. The inner rotor is attached to the oil-pump drive shaft, which is mounted off-centre in the housing. The inner rotor drives the outer rotor. As the two units turn, the spaces between the inner and outer rotors are first filled with oil. After one-half a revolution, the lobes of the inner rotor move into the spaces of the outer rotor, forcing the oil out of the spaces, through the pump outlet, and to the various parts of the engine.

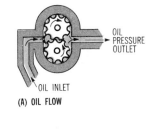

(A) OIL FLOW

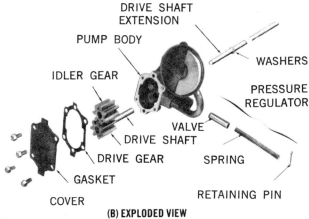

(B) EXPLODED VIEW

Fig. 35-6   Gear-Type Oil Pump

Oil Regulator and Relief Valve. The pressure built up by the oil pump increases with the speed of the engine. To relieve any excess pressure caused by high engine speed, a relief valve is included in the system. The valve consists of either a ball and spring, or a plunger and spring, and is mounted in the housing on the outlet side of the oil pump. When the pressure produced by the pump is greater than the pressure of the oil relief-valve spring, this greater pressure causes the ball or plunger to move, compressing the spring and opening the port. The opening of the port permits the oil to flow back to the oil pan, thus reducing the pressure in the system.

Oil Galleries and Lines. In order to transfer the oil under pressure from the oil pump to the parts requiring lubrication, oil lines or galleries are used. The lines are made up of steel tubing and connectors. Oil galleries are drilled or cast holes in the engine block. The main oil gallery runs lengthwise in the cylinder block and most other lines connect to it. Many engines have plugs at each end of the gallery which are removed to facilitate cleaning of the gallery. Other holes are drilled in the cylinder block to connect the gallery to the main-bearing bores, the camshaft bearings, hydraulic valve lifters, and other engine parts.

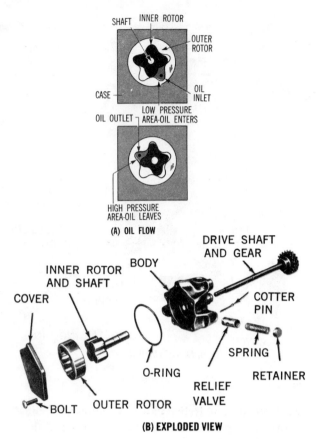

SHAFT   INNER ROTOR

OUTER ROTOR

CASE

OIL INLET

OIL OUTLET   LOW PRESSURE AREA-OIL ENTERS

HIGH PRESSURE AREA-OIL LEAVES

(A) OIL FLOW

COVER

INNER ROTOR AND SHAFT

BODY

DRIVE SHAFT AND GEAR

COTTER PIN

SPRING

RETAINER

O-RING

RELIEF VALVE

BOLT   OUTER ROTOR

(B) EXPLODED VIEW

Fig. 35-7   Rotor-Type Oil Pump   Chrysler Canada Ltd.

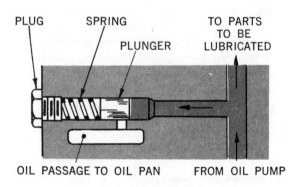

PLUG   SPRING

PLUNGER

TO PARTS TO BE LUBRICATED

OIL PASSAGE TO OIL PAN   FROM OIL PUMP

(A) NORMAL OIL PRESSURE-VALVE CLOSED

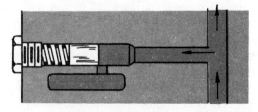

(B) NORMAL OIL PRESSURE-VALVE OPEN

Fig. 35-8   Oil Relief Valve

The crankshaft is drilled to carry oil from the main bearings to the crankpins to lubricate the connecting-rod bearings. The connecting rod may be drilled from the rod-bearing bore to the piston-pin bore to lubricate these bearings. The connecting rod may include spit holes that line up with the crankpin hole to spit oil onto the cylinder wall. To lubricate the rocker-arm mechanism, oil may be delivered by tubing, by the valve push rods, or drilled holes in the engine block and rocker-arm supports.

Oil Pressure Gauges. Motor vehicles are equipped with a gauge which indicates the oil pressure in pounds per square inch, or with a warning light which comes on when the oil pressure drops below the safe limit. Engine oil pressure is usually between 30 and 50 pounds per square inch.

Strainer. A wire gauze strainer or screen is placed in the oil pan around the oil-pump inlet. This strainer or screen prevents any small, solid matter, such as broken cotter pins, from entering the oil pump. In some engines the strainer floats near the top of the oil in the oil pan. Since dirt and metal particles are heavier than oil, they sink to the bottom, leaving the cleanest oil at the top.

Oil Filters. Carbon particles, dust, and dirt become mixed with the lubricating oil during the operation of the engine. The heavier particles usually drop to the bottom of the oil pan, but some of the smaller particles may travel through the oil lines to the bearing surfaces, causing damage to the bearings and journals. To reduce the possibility of damage by these particles, many lubrication systems filter part or all of the oil. The filtering material traps the particles of foreign material but permits the oil to pass through. All modern oil filters use the replaceable cartridge. The cartridge may be made of cloth, paper, or felt. The oil enters around the outside of the filter cartridge, flows through holes in the outer shell of the cartridge, through the filtering material, and exits through the centre collector tube and the outlet fitting. The filter cartridge collects the foreign matter until it becomes clogged; then it must be replaced.

Filters are of two types, those that filter part of the oil from the pump, called *bypass filters*, and those that filter all of the oil in circulation, called *full-flow filters*. As the filter cartridges become clogged with foreign particles and impurities, their efficiency decreases.

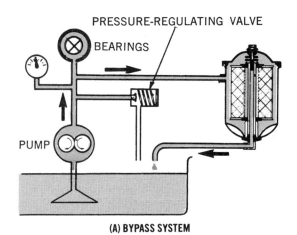

BYPASS

(A) BYPASS SYSTEM

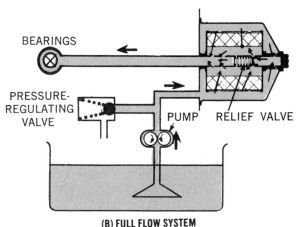

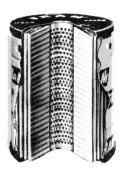

FULL FLOW

Fram-Canada Limited

Fig. 35-10   Typical Oil Filter Cartridges

(B) FULL FLOW SYSTEM

Fram-Canada Limited

Fig. 35-9   Oil Filter Systems

In the bypass filter, as the cartridge becomes clogged, less and less oil passes through the filter, until finally the filter is practically inoperative. Before this happens, the filter cartridge or element should be replaced or cleaned, depending on the type of filter.

In the full-flow filter, the oil needed to lubricate the engine must pass through the filtering media. The cartridge must have a flow rate ten to fifteen times as great as in the bypass-type filter. Therefore, all full-flow filters use coarser filtering media than the bypass type.

A filter relief valve that opens at a relatively low pressure must be provided around the filter. Otherwise, if the cartridge were to become plugged, the engine would be ruined through lack of lubrication. In cold weather, or after the cartridge has become partially plugged, a large part of the oil bypasses the filter, thus reducing its efficiency.

Since the full-flow filter filters all of the engine oil before it reaches the first part to be lubricated,

the filter is located between the oil pump and the main oil gallery. Bypass filters may be mounted on any convenient part of the engine and connected to the oil gallery by flexible oil lines.

35-12 CRANKCASE VENTILATION

The crankcase must be ventilated for several reasons. There is always a certain amount of pressurized gases leaking from the combustion chamber past the rings and into the crankcase. If this pressure was allowed to build up, it would force oil to escape past the oil seals. It is also important to eliminate these gases as they form moisture and deposit sulphuric acid in the oil. A certain amount of raw gasoline will also escape past the piston rings and enter the oil. As the oil becomes heated, the water and gasoline evaporate, forming gases which must be eliminated.

The crankcase ventilating system provides for a constant stream of fresh air to pass through the valve chamber and crankcase. This relieves the excess gas pressure and carries away the gasoline, water vapours, and oil fumes.

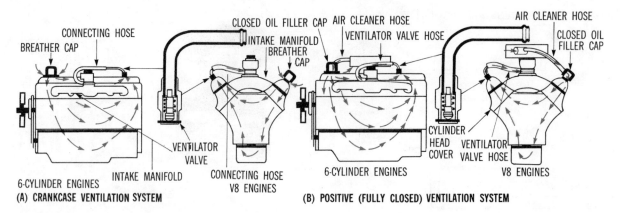

Fig. 35-11   Crankcase Ventilation

Chrysler Canada Ltd.

The air usually enters through the combination oil filler and breather cap, which is normally located near the top front part of the engine and contains a filter of oil-soaked metal wool to prevent the entrance of dirt. The air passes through the valve chamber, down the push-rod openings, through openings in the valve-lifter section and into the crankcase. The rotating engine parts create an air disturbance within the engine which circulates the air to all parts of the crankcase. An outlet pipe which runs down below the engine is used to draw air through the engine. When the vehicle is in motion, a partial vacuum is formed at the end of the pipe, causing the air to enter the breather cap and circulate through the engine.

All late-model vehicles must be equipped with positive crankcase ventilating systems to assist in smog control. With this system, the crankcase fumes and vapours are burnt in the cylinders instead of being deposited in the atmosphere.

To operate this system, a vacuum line from the intake manifold is attached to the crankcase ventilating-system outlet breather. A second line is attached between the carburetor air cleaner and the ventilating-system inlet. When the engine is started, engine vacuum pulls filtered air through the engine and the fumes are burnt in the cylinder. The residue is expelled through the exhaust system.

A special crankcase ventilating valve, called a *positive crankcase valve* (PCV), is inserted in the vacuum line to maintain proper engine operating vacuum.

The purpose of the PCV is to prevent excessive air flow during idling. When engine vacuum is high, the vacuum overcomes the tension of the valve spring and moves the valve to the low-flow position where there is a minimum of ventilation. When the engine vacuum decreases, the spring moves the valve to the high-flow position and ventilation is increased. A defective PCV valve can prevent any ventilation of the crankcase from taking place, therefore increased formation of acids, sludge and oil dilution can take place.

35-13 CHASSIS LUBRICATION

Other parts of the vehicle such as the suspension system, transmission, drive line, differential, and rear axle also require lubrication. However, these units do not usually require the pressurized type of lubrication that is required by the engine. They are lubricated by splashing gear oils onto the parts or by applying grease periodically by a pressure grease gun. Nevertheless, the proper lubricant must be used. The vehicle and petroleum manufacturers provide lubrication charts which specify the type, grade, location, and frequency for all parts of the

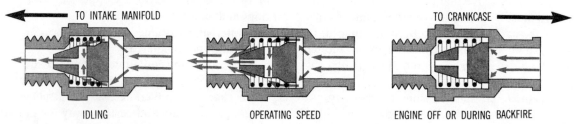

Fig. 35-12   PCV Valve Operation

vehicle that require lubrication. Strict adherence to these recommendations is advised if satisfactory results are to be obtained.

35-14 LUBRICATING GREASES

Grease is basically mineral oil thickened with metallic soap. The primary purpose of the soap is to make the oil adhere at the point of application. Thus the soap is the medium that traps the mineral oil within its mass; but the actual lubrication job is performed by the mineral oil in the grease. Greases are made in many varieties to suit different purposes. In automobile-lubrication work, chassis grease and wheel-bearing grease are the most frequently used, although some older models require water-pump and cup grease.

Chassis Grease. Chassis grease is used in all pressure-gun fittings of the automobile. It is relatively soft in consistency and varies in tackiness. It is important that it be insoluble in water, so that it will not wash off when exposed to rain. Chassis grease should not dry out or oxidize.

With the addition of extended relubrication periods, such as 30,000 miles, in many late-model automobiles special chassis greases are required. These greases contain lithium-lead soap and molybdenum disulphide. The addition of these chemicals produces a chassis grease having the following advantages: a high melting point; better protection against rust and corrosion; improved load-carrying ability and shock resistance; better adhesion; and higher resistance to water washing. Special grease guns and adapters are required for this type of lubrication.

Wheel-bearing Grease. Since the automobile uses four-wheel brakes there is a considerable amount of heat generated during brake application, and the proximity of the wheel-bearing lubricant to the braking mechanism makes it necessary to use only greases having a high melting point. Wheel-bearing greases generally have a sodium base, as sodium soaps impart high melting-point properties to the grease.

Special Greases. There are many other greases prepared for special applications. One such compound, used on rubber spring shackles, is made by blending an oil with a talc and asbestos fibre. Other compounds or grease and graphite are used on rubber body mountings and door-lock assemblies.

35-14 GEAR LUBRICANTS

The correct application of gear lubricants is so vital to any lubrication program that refiners have developed several types of gear lubricants to meet different gear lubrication problems. These types may be classified as straight mineral oils, compounded mineral oils, extreme pressure oils, all-purpose or universal-type oils, and automatic-transmission fluids.

Straight Mineral Oils. Straight mineral oils of highly treated, carefully refined materials are used for standard gear designs operating under normal conditions.

Compounded Mineral Oils. Compounded gear oils are blends of mineral oils and fatty oils or soaps with a sodium or lead base. Compounded gear lubricants are used principally in worm-gear units.

Extreme-Pressure Oils. In ordinary straight-tooth gear design, one gear tooth rolls across the surface of the other. This simple rolling action is comparatively easy to lubricate. However, since the drive shaft of the modern automobile has been lowered, it is no longer possible to use the straight-cut spur-gear contact. Instead, hypoid gears are used. Hypoid gear teeth are cut on a curve and not only have a rolling action but also a wiping action, which creates high pressures. These pressures can exceed 100,000 pounds per square inch and the wiping action or slip often reaches a speed of 1,500 feet per minute. This pressure and sliding action could be described as a welding action in which tiny irregularities on the surface of one gear tooth becomes so hot that they actually weld themselves to the opposing gear tooth. Under these conditions ordinary gear lubricants would either be wiped off the surfaces of the gear teeth because of the high pressure and sliding action, or be burned off because of the high temperatures present. To meet these conditions certain chemical compounds, such as chlorine and sulphur, have been added to prevent the lubricant from being removed from between the teeth.

All-Purpose or Universal-Type Oils. All-purpose or universal-type oils combine all the desirable features of straight mineral oils, compounded gear oils, and extreme-pressure oils. These lubricants are ideal because they are noncorrosive, stable, inexpensive, yet capable of meeting the lubrication requirements of most automotive applications. As a

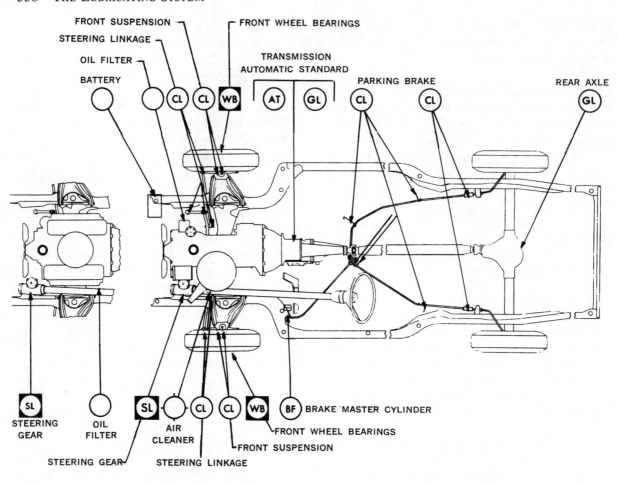

FRONT SUSPENSION
STEERING LINKAGE
OIL FILTER
BATTERY
FRONT WHEEL BEARINGS
TRANSMISSION
AUTOMATIC STANDARD
PARKING BRAKE
REAR AXLE

CL   CL   WB   AT   GL   CL   CL   GL

SL
STEERING
GEAR

OIL
FILTER

SL
STEERING GEAR

AIR
CLEANER

CL   CL   WB

STEERING LINKAGE

BF   BRAKE MASTER CYLINDER
FRONT WHEEL BEARINGS
FRONT SUSPENSION

○   LUBRICATE OR SERVICE EVERY 6000 MILES

○   REPLACE EVERY 24000 MILES

◻   LUBRICATE EVERY 36000 MILES

AT — Automatic Transmission Fluid
BF — Hydraulic Brake Fluid
SL — Steering Gear Lubricant
GL — Multi-purpose Gear Lubricant
WB — Wheel Bearing Lubricant
CL — Chassis Lubricant

Fig. 35-13   Typical Lubrication Chart   Courtesy of General Motors

result, the all-purpose gear lubricants are the most popular.

Automatic-Transmission Oils or Fluids. Automatic-transmission fluids are combinations of high-quality base oils with special oxidization inhibitors, antiwear additives, antifoam agents, and detergent compound.

An automatic-transmission fluid must perform a variety of functions. In the fluid coupling or torque converter, it is the means of transmitting power and thus it is exposed to very high temperatures. In the transmission it serves as a gear and bearing lubricant; controls the friction characteristics of the clutches and bands that provide the various gear ratios; transfers the pressures required to operate the clutches and bands; maintains cleanliness in the close fitting control valve; and prevents the drying out of the seals used in the transmission. This fluid is also used in power-steering units.

35-15 OIL-SYSTEM SERVICE

Oil-system service is required when there is evidence of a steady consumption of oil, a loss of oil pressure, or when the oil becomes dirty, diluted, or indicates the formation of sludge within the engine.

High oil consumption—may be because of the oil being burnt in the cylinders, or from leakage. High consumption because of burning is usually indicated by the presence of light blueish coloured exhaust emissions. It is usually caused by worn crankshaft main- and connecting-rod bearings, piston rings, or valve guides. Leakage is indicated by external signs of oil on the engine, engine compartment, or chassis parts.

Low oil pressure—can be caused by worn engine bearings, worn oil pump, broken or cracked oil lines, weak oil relief-valve spring, insufficient or excessively thin oil, obstructions in the oil lines, or a defective oil-pressure indicator.

Oil contamination—can be corrected by changing the oil and the filter cartridge. Under favourable operating conditions vehicle manufacturers suggest oil changes every two months or between 4,000 and 6,000 miles, whichever occurs first. However, the oil should be changed more frequently under the following driving conditions: stop-and-start, cold-weather, low-mileage, or dusty driving conditions. Most manufacturers suggest that the filter cartridge be changed every time the engine oil is changed.

Chassis lubrication periods—vary depending upon the vehicle, its use, and the type of lubricant required. Consult the manufacturer's service manual for complete information.

Positive crankcase ventilator (PCV) Systems—require periodic service. It is widely recommended that the PCV valve be replaced after one year's service. Should the valve become clogged, it will cause the engine to idle poorly. Most modern PCV valves cannot be serviced but must be replaced. Various types of testers are available to check PCV-system operation.

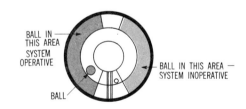

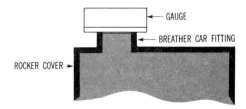

Fig. 35-14   Checking PCV System

REVIEW QUESTIONS

1. Define friction.
2. List the three factors that affect friction.
3. Name and describe three types of friction.
4. How does lubrication reduce friction?
5. Describe three properties of a lubricant.
6. Explain the wedging action of oil.
7. Give five purposes of the engine lubrication system.
8. Explain the process of fractionation.
9. After the cracking and fractionation processes, the manufacture of fuels and lubricants is divided into three classifications. Explain each classification.
10. Name and describe three methods of determining and rating lubricants.
11. There are three methods of classifying engine oils. Name and state the purpose of each classification.
12. What effect does (a) grade of oil (b) shaft speed (c) bearing load have on the selection of engine oils?
13. Name four substances which contaminate motor oils and state how each gets into the oil and how it affects the oil.
14. Describe briefly two types of engine lubricating systems.
15. Name and describe the operation of six engine lubrication-system components.
16. Why is the full-flow type oil filter the most common type used on modern automobile engines?
17. Why must the crankcase be ventilated?
18. Describe the operation of the Positive Crankcase Ventilating System.
19. Why are metallic soaps used?
20. What are the essential characteristics of a chassis grease?

21. What effect does the addition of lithium-lead soap and molybdenum-disulphide have on chassis greases?

22. What type of gear lubricant must be used in hypoid type differentials? Why?

23. List the purposes of automatic-transmission fluids.

24. When should engine oil be changed?

25. How does a defective PCV valve affect engine operation?

UNIT FIVE
Fuel

Chapter 36
FUELS

Many fuels can be used to operate the internal combustion engine. These include methanol, benzol, alcohol, alcohol-gasoline blends, liquid petroleum gas, and the most popular fuel, gasoline. Gasoline is a hydrocarbon compound in the form of a colourless liquid and is obtained from crude oil by a complicated distillation, fractionation, and cracking process.

36-1 FUEL MANUFACTURING PROCESSES

Fractionation. Fractionation, like distillation, depends upon the vaporization and subsequent condensing of a liquid and is used to separate liquids having different boiling points. The different boiling points of hydrocarbons such as gasoline, LPG and natural gas are shown in Fig. 36-1. The lighter hydrocarbons, such as those in the gasoline range, have quite low boiling points. The heavier elements of crude oil that are used in the manufacture of lubricating oils, etc., have higher boiling points.

The straight run gasoline that is obtained by the fractionation process is of insufficient quantity and of too low an antiknock quality to satisfy today's needs. Therefore, several other manufacturing processes are used to increase the quantity and quality of gasoline obtained from crude oil. These processes are thermal cracking, catalyst cracking, thermal reforming and catalytic reforming, and polymerization.

Thermal Cracking. Thermal cracking is the process of breaking down the original structure of oil or breaking the molecules apart so that they can be re-formed in a different structure.

The thermal cracking process uses the oil remaining from the distillation process and through the use of high temperatures and high pressures, it causes a series of chemical changes which results in the production of various petroleum products.

Catalytic Cracking. Catalytic cracking uses a catalyst (a catalyst is a material that has the ability to cause a chemical change to take place without the catalyst being changed or consumed during the process) along with heat and pressure to break down and reform the molecular structure of the remaining oil from distillation.

Catalytic cracking produces gasoline with a

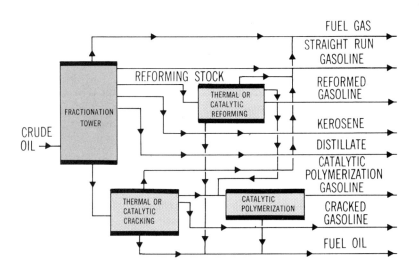

Fig. 36-1 Refining of Fuels

higher octane rating than that produced by thermal cracking.

Thermal Reforming. Thermal reforming is a similar process to thermal cracking but it is used to rearrange the molecular structure of straight run gasoline, thereby improving its antiknock qualities.

Catalytic Reforming. Catalytic reforming uses a catalyst to rearrange the molecular structure of straight cut gasolines to improve their antiknock qualities.

Polymerization. Polymerization produces gasoline from the large quantities of gases created during the cracking and re-forming operations. The process uses heat and pressure or a catalyst to create the reaction necessary to produce the liquid fuel.

36-2 GASOLINE

Gasoline is a blend of various types and proportions of the fuels obtained by the various manufacturing processes. Fuel chemists prepare the best product for all-round performance by compounding the various different types of gasoline. The compounds are changed to meet the temperature conditions found during the different seasons of the year and to match temperature conditions in various regions of the country.

Several characteristics are considered in the compounding procedure, among which are volatility, antiknock value, and freedom from harmful chemicals and gum formations.

Volatility. Volatility refers to the ease with which gasoline or other liquids vaporize. For example, since alcohol vaporizes at a lower temperature than water, it is said to be volatile. Gasoline is compounded of many kinds of hydrocarbons each having a different volatility. These hydrocarbons have boiling points ranging from approximately 100° to 400°F. (See Fig. 36-2.) The volatility of gasoline affects the ease of starting, length of warming-up period, and engine performance during normal operation.

For easy starting of a cold engine the gasoline must be highly volatile. Gasoline blended during the winter months is more volatile than that blended during the summer months. If the fuel is too volatile during the summer months, the fuel vaporizes and forms a vapour lock or a vapour bubble in the fuel line or fuel pump. This bubble expands or contracts according to the pressure or vacuum pro-

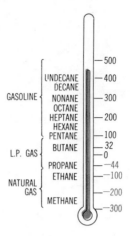

Fig. 36-2   Boiling Points of Hydrocarbons (Degrees F)

duced by the fuel pump and therefore can prevent the delivery of the fuel to the carburetor fuel bowl.

During the warming-up period, a less volatile gasoline is required. For maximum power and economy of operation, fuel with a lower volatility but higher heat content is required. Therefore the volatility of the fuel must be such that the fuel will remain in liquid form until it reaches the air stream in the carburetor. Then it must vaporize quickly and mix uniformly with the correct proportions of air for the driving and temperature conditions.

Antiknock Value. Various chemicals and manufacturing processes were employed by fuel chemists in developing higher octane gasolines that would permit the use of higher-compression engines. These chemicals and processes improved the gasoline by reducing the rate of flame travel during combustion that resulted in the prevention of excessive pressures which cause detonation or knocking.

When a substance burns, it is actually uniting in rapid chemical reaction with oxygen. The molecules of the substance and oxygen are set into very rapid motion that produces heat. If the molecules are confined, such as in the combustion chamber of an engine, they strike the sides of the chamber, producing pressure. The more rapid the movement, the greater the pressure.

Combustion takes place in three stages. These stages are called the *nucleus* or formation of flame, the *hatching-out*, and *propagation*.

The nucleus is a small ball of blue flame that develops around the spark-plug gap when the spark occurs. The nucleus grows slowly with very little increase in temperature or pressure. As the nucleus grows it begins to hatch-out. During this stage the

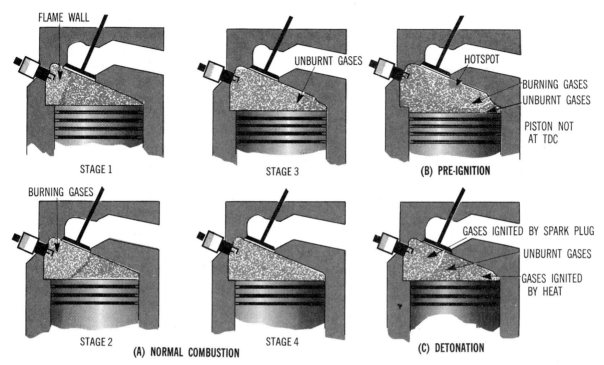

Fig. 36-3 Fuel Combustion Patterns

nucleus sends fingers of flame outward into the unburnt mixture. This creates a moderate increase in temperature and pressure. Finally, propagation takes place. During propagation a flame wall sweeps across the chamber, burning rapidly and creating great heat and pressure. As long as the fuel-air mixture burns evenly in these stages, maximum power without detonation will be produced. However, if during the third stage of combustion the combination of the heat of combustion plus the heat generated by the further compression of the unburnt fuel is sufficient to ignite the unburnt gases before the flame wall reaches them, detonation will occur.

Detonation. The knocking or pinging sound of detonation is produced when the secondary flame front produced by the uncontrolled burning collides with the normal flame front.

Detonation is harmful to an engine as it tends to damage the pistons, connecting-rod and main bearings, and the spark plugs. It results in the engine overheating, high fuel consumption, and loss of power.

Detonation knocks are usually regular in character and occur when the engine is being accelerated under heavy load or climbing a hill. It occurs when the accelerator is wide open and the engine is taking in a full charge of fuel-air mixture on the intake stroke. This increases the compression pressure and the heat of compression and can cause the fuel to ignite before the flame wall reaches the unburnt fuel.

Pre-ignition. Pre-ignition is an irregular knock that occurs when the fuel-air mixture is ignited by any means other than the spark at the spark plug. Ignition is usually caused by hot spots of carbon that form on the piston or combustion chamber or by an overheated exhaust valve or spark plug.

Pre-ignition is referred to as wild knocking and can occur any time after the intake valve has opened to admit a fresh charge of fuel-air mixture.

36-3 OCTANE RATING

In order to identify the antiknock qualities of gasoline, an octane rating system is used. This rating can be determined by two methods: the *motor method*, and the *research method*.

The motor method correlates better with the ratings of car-fuel combinations at high road speeds, while the research method correlates with ratings made in cars that knock at low road speeds. The research method is considered to be "mild", while the motor method is considered to be more severe. Most oil companies prefer the research method ratings since they consider them a better

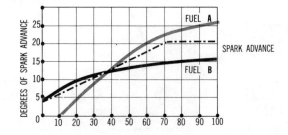

Fig. 36-4   Fuel Borderline Knock Curves

criterion of a gasoline's antiknock quality. The differences in the ratings given by the two tests is referred to as fuel sensitivity.

Fuel sensitivity is controlled by the fuel's chemical composition which is directly related to the type of crude used and the refining process to which it is subjected. Cracked gasolines are quite sensitive. A sensitivity range of 15 octane points is not uncommon, but the average range is between 6 and 8 octane points.

The octane rating of a fuel is determined by using a special test engine. This engine is especially designed so that the compression ratio can be varied while the engine is running. It is also equipped with a small diaphragm in the combustion chamber. This diaphragm actuates a bouncing pin to record electrically on a "knock meter" to determine the severity of the detonation.

The gasoline to be tested is used to operate the test engine and the results are recorded. Then the engine is operated on a mixture of special fuels. These fuels are iso-octane, a member of the gasoline family which has been given an octane rating of 100, and heptane, which can be obtained from crude oil or from the sap of the Jeffery Pine tree, and has been given the octane rating of zero. The octane rating of the gasoline is determined by the amount of iso-octane in the iso-octane-heptane mixture that gives the same results as the gasoline being tested. In other words, if the iso-octane-heptane mixture requires 90% iso-octane and 10% heptane to match the performance of the gasoline tested, that gasoline would be given a 90 octane rating.

It should be noted that the tendency of a fuel to detonate varies in different engines and in similar engines operating under different conditions. For example: a rise of 20°F in air temperature increases the octane requirement by about three numbers. A 10% increase in humidity at 85°F reduces the octane requirements by one number, hence an engine does run somewhat better and quieter in wet weather. Engine combustion-chamber deposits increase the compression ratio and therefore increase the octane requirements of the fuel. Octane requirements can also be increased by advancing the spark timing or leaning the fuel-air ratio. The higher the altitude in which the engine operates, the lower the octane requirements.

As a result of the variation in octane requirements, most gasolines are blended according to the seasons of the year and the altitudes of the location in which the fuel is to be used.

36-4 CHEMICAL CONTROL OF DETONATION

Detonation may be controlled by adding chemicals, the most popular of which is tetraethyl lead (ethyl), to the gasoline. These chemicals tend to increase the reaction time of the fuel by breaking down into metals and oxides, and interfering with the normal combustion chemical reaction. This interference gives the flame wall time to reach all the fuel in the cylinder so that instead of the fuel exploding, normal combustion can take place.

To prevent lead deposits from forming in the combustion chamber, other compounds such as ethylene dibromide and ethylene dichloride are also added to change the lead compounds into a form which will vaporize and leave the cylinder with the exhaust gases.

36-5 COMBUSTION-CHAMBER DESIGN AND DETONATION

The shape of the combustion chamber determines the turbulance, squish and quench effects of the fuel-air mixture in the cylinder.

Turbulance—is the name given to the swirling action of the fuel-air mixture as it enters the cylinder. It is produced by the design of the combustion chamber and is used to improve the mixing of the fuel-air mixture. The greater the turbulance of the fuel-air mixture entering the cylinder, the more uniform the mixture; therefore, the more uniform the combustion. Also, the greater the turbulance, the less time is required for the flame wall to ignite all the fuel in the cylinder.

Squish—refers to the manner in which the fuel-and-air mixture is pushed out of one area of the

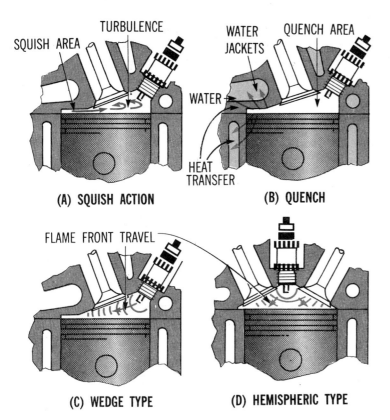

(A) SQUISH ACTION

(B) QUENCH

(C) WEDGE TYPE

(D) HEMISPHERIC TYPE

Fig. 36-5   Combustion Chamber Design and Detonation

combustion chamber near the end of the compression stroke. The combustion chamber and piston head are designed so as to push the fuel-air mixture into the main area of the combustion chamber with great turbulence, thus improving the uniformity of the mixture and combustion.

Quench—refers to the cooling of the unburnt fuel-air mixture in the combustion chamber. It helps to prevent the mixture from igniting because of the high temperatures in the combustion chamber before the mixture can be ignited by the flame wall. The squish area of the combustion chamber is also the quench area. These areas are very close to the water jackets; they are relatively cool and extract heat from the unburnt mixture.

Spark plug location—determines the distance the flame wall must travel in order to ignite all of the fuel-air mixture. In a hemispheric-type combustion chamber the spark plug is located near the centre of the dome. After ignition the flame wall can travel in all directions with an increasing circular pattern. With this design the flame wall travels a short distance and there are no distant pockets of the fuel-air mixture to detonate. Therefore, no squish or quench areas are required and little if any turbulance is produced.

When the spark plug is located to one side of the combustion chamber, as in the wedge shaped combustion chamber, the flame wall must travel across the diameter of the combustion chamber. Squish and quench areas are required along with turbulence in order to have complete combustion without detonation.

Heat of compression—is increased as the compression ratio increases. Therefore, detonation can occur if the compression ratio is high enough so that the combined temperatures of the heat of compression and the heat of combustion will ignite the fuel-air mixture ahead of the flame wall.

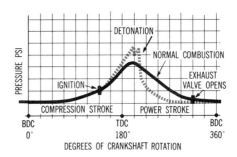

Fig. 36-6   Typical Pressure Curve of Normal Combustion and Detonation

36-6 FUEL ADDITIVES

Gasoline often contains additives or chemicals to improve its operating qualities. Tetraethyl lead is the most popular compound added to gasoline to improve the octane rating. Dyes are added to identify the different grades of gasoline. Metal deactivators are added to prevent the gasoline from reacting with certain metals. Phosphorus compounds are added to prevent metallic deposits from the gasoline combining with combustion-chamber deposits to form a composition which retains heat and could cause pre-ignition. Anti-oxidant inhibitors are added to prevent the formation of resins and gum. Anti-icing chemicals are added to prevent carburetor icing.

36-7 DIESEL FUEL

The type of fuel available for use in diesel engines varies from the volatile type of jet engine fuels, to kerosene, and to heavier furnace oils. The properties of the diesel fuels depend upon the nature of the crude used and the type of refining process. Diesel fuels are produced with a boiling range of between 300° and 750°F.

Diesel fuels are graded as D1, D2, and D4. A D1 fuel is one that has a range from kerosene to intermediate distillates and has a low boiling point. A D2 fuel is heavier and has a higher boiling point; D4 fuel is even heavier and has higher boiling points. D2 and D4 fuels contain more impurities.

While refining removes the impurities and produces higher grade fuels, it also lowers the heat value of the fuel. Therefore, a given quantity of high-grade fuel will produce slightly less power than an equal amount of low-grade fuel.

Cetane Rating. Gasolines are classified by octane ratings; diesel fuels are classified by cetane ratings. This rating system classifies diesel fuel according to the time lag or delay between the time the fuel is injected into the combustion chamber and the time it is ignited by the heat of compression. The shorter the time lag, the more volatile the fuel, and the higher the cetane rating. The longer the lag, the lower the rating. Most engines require fuels with a cetane rating of between 30 to 60. For starting engines in cold weather, fuels with ratings of 85 to 95 are frequently used.

In addition to the cetane ratings, the boiling point of diesel fuel is an important consideration. Since the fuel must be completely vaporized in order to burn completely, the boiling range of the fuel should be low enough to permit complete vaporization at normal engine operating temperatures. Engines operating at low speed and light load or in cold weather require fuels with lower boiling points in order to give satisfactory operation.

36-8 OTHER FUELS

Liquid Petroleum Gas. Liquid petroleum gas (LPG) is a mixture of gaseous petroleum compounds, such as butane and propane, which are surplus material in the oil fields. LPG is a very volatile fuel with a boiling point of minus 44°F. It has an excellent octane rating of approximately 96, is a dry gas, and does not create carbon in the engine. LPG engines are easily started in cold weather and have less objectionable exhaust odours.

For storage and transportation, LPG is compressed and cooled to a liquid state. Approximately 250 gallons of gas are compressed into one gallon of liquid and stored in strong tanks.

Alcohol. Alcohol, a distillate of wood or grain, has a high octane rating and is sometimes blended with benzol to be used as a fuel for racing engines. Alcohol is also frequently used as an additive to gasoline to absorb water which is formed in the fuel system because of condensation. The water causes corrosion of the metal parts or could freeze and block the passage of fuel. Water will not pass through the fuel filters of the pump and carburetor; instead it is collected there and eventually prevents the passage of gasoline. The alcohol additive absorbs the water, thus permitting it to pass through the filters, carburetor jets, and into the combustion chamber, where it is converted into steam and passes out through the exhaust system.

Benzol. Benzol is a hydrocarbon obtained from the refinement of coal tar. It is highly volatile and has a high octane rating. It may be blended with gasoline to increase the octane rating of the fuel or be mixed with alcohol to be used as a fuel for racing engines.

36-9 COMBUSTION AND HEAT

Combustion is the rapid combination of a fuel with oxygen to produce heat. When gasoline is used as the fuel, it is the combining or oxidation of the carbon and the hydrogen that produces the chemical change that results in heat. The chemical equation for the combustion of gasoline is:

$$C_8H_{18} \ 12.5 \ O_2 = 8CO_2 \ 9H_2O$$

When C_8H_{18} represents the chemical formula for gasoline, and 12.5 O_2 is the oxygen required to burn one part of gasoline, this produces 8 parts of carbon dioxide (CO_2) plus 9 parts of water (H_2O). For each gallon of gasoline burned, over a gallon of water is produced.

However, air is a mixture of approximately one part of oxygen and **3.5** parts nitrogen; therefore, nitrogen must be considered as a part of combustion. Since it requires **12.5** parts of oxygen for combustion of one part of gasoline, combustion must also include 43.75 parts of nitrogen. Therefore, the chemical formula now reads:

$$C_8H_{18} \ 12.5 \ O_2 \ 43.75N_2 = 8CO_2 \ 9H_2O \ 43.75N_2$$

The burning of the fuel in the combustion chamber is rarely complete. Not all of the carbon in the gasoline is converted into carbon dioxide. When there is a shortage of oxygen, free carbon and carbon monoxide are formed. Twice as much oxygen is required in the formation of carbon dioxide as in carbon monoxide. The more carbon monoxide an engine produces, the less power it produces. Therefore, an ample supply of oxygen is required for maximum power.

The power produced from any fuel is determined by its heat value which is measured in British Thermal Units (Btu). A Btu is the amount of heat required to raise one pound of water from 39 to 40 degrees Fahrenheit, and is equal to 778.6 foot-pounds. The amount of heat derived from the burning of one pound of octane is approximately 20,500 Btu.

The temperatures produced in the combustion chamber vary widely. The compression ratio, the combustion-chamber design, the cooling system, the fuel-air ratio, and the amount of burnt gases left in the cylinder at the end of the exhaust stroke all affect combustion-chamber temperatures.

At the end of the compression stroke the temperature could rise to approximately 1500°F in an engine with a 9 to 1 compression ratio. After ignition this temperature will rise rapidly to as high as 5500°F.

REVIEW QUESTIONS

1. What is fractionation?
2. What is the purpose of thermal cracking?
3. Describe the refining processes used to increase the antiknock qualities of fuels.
4. What is a catalyst?
5. Why is volatility an important characteristic of automotive fuels?
6. Describe the normal combustion pattern of gasoline.
7. Explain the difference between detonation and pre-ignition.
8. What is meant by the term "fuel sensitivity"?
9. Describe the motor method of establishing an antiknock rating of a fuel.
10. Explain how tetraethyl lead controls detonation.
11. How does turbulence improve combustion?
12. Explain how quench reduces the possibility of detonation.
13. Name and state the purpose of three fuel additives.
14. List three reasons why an engine would require gasolines with different octane ratings.
15. What determines the grade of diesel fuel?
16. Why is the boiling point of diesel fuel important?
17. Why is a mixture of alcohol and benzol a good fuel for racing engines?
18. Describe the chemical reaction that takes place during the combustion of gasoline.
19. Define the term "British Thermal Unit."
20. Give three reasons why the combustion chamber temperatures vary widely.

Chapter 37
THE FUEL SYSTEM

The fuel system is used to provide the supply of gasoline to the engine so that it may operate for prolonged periods of time. On engines used in lawnmowers, small outboard engines, etc., and many heavy industrial engines, fuel is supplied to the carburetor by gravity. Many older outboard engines used a pressurized fuel tank to supply gasoline to the carburetor. On motor vehicles, either a mechanical or an electrical fuel pump supplies the fuel to the carburetor. The fuel system must also prepare the fuel for combustion in the cylinders and carry away the exhaust gases.

The units of the fuel system include: the fuel tank, filters, lines, fuel pump, carburetor, air cleaner, intake manifold, and the exhaust system.

37-1 FUEL TANK, FILTERS, AND LINES

Fuel Tank. The fuel tank may be located at the rear of the chassis on front-engine automobiles, at the front of the vehicle in rear-engine cars, under the seats or attached to the sides of the frames of trucks. Passenger-car and light truck fuel tanks are made of thin sheet steel and protected by rust-resistant plating, and have a capacity of between 12 to 25 gallons. Large truck-frame mounted tanks are made of heavy gauge steel and have a much larger capacity. All fuel tanks have internal *baffles* which are arranged to prevent sloshing of the gasoline. A filler neck is placed in a convenient location and is either built as part of the tank or is connected by a neoprene hose to the tank. The tank must be vented to the atmosphere to assist in rapid filling, to compensate for the expansion and contraction of the fuel because of temperature changes, and to maintain a constant pressure in the tank regardless of the fuel level. Atmospheric pressure acts in conjunction with the vacuum produced in the fuel pump to deliver fuel.

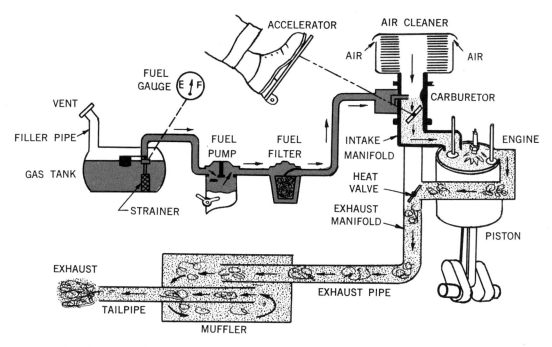

Fig. 37-1   The Fuel System

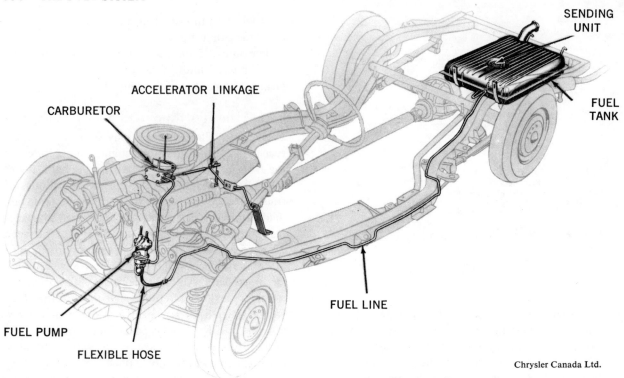

SENDING UNIT

FUEL TANK

ACCELERATOR LINKAGE

CARBURETOR

FUEL LINE

FUEL PUMP

FLEXIBLE HOSE

Chrysler Canada Ltd.

Fig. 37-2   Typical Fuel System Installation

Fuel Pick-Up Pipe. A pipe the same diameter as the fuel line enters the tank to draw off the fuel required for the engine. This pipe is usually incorporated as part of the fuel-gauge tank unit. The end of the pipe is generally located about one-half inch from the tank bottom. This location allows some water and sediment to form in the bottom of the tank without either being drawn into the pipe.

Some vehicles have a filter made of a plastic screen or sintered (oclite) bronze (small particles of bronze that have been pressed into a porous mass)

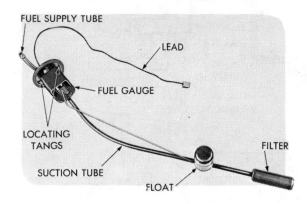

FUEL SUPPLY TUBE

LEAD

FUEL GAUGE

LOCATING TANGS

FILTER

SUCTION TUBE

FLOAT

Chrysler Canada Limited

Fig. 37-3   Fuel Pick-up Pipe and Gasoline Gauge Tank Unit

attached to the end of the pick-up pipe. These filters are designed to filter out sediment and water without the filter clogging.

The water forms because of condensation when the tank is partially full; and, since water is heavier than gasoline, the water sinks to the bottom of the tank. The sediment is a natural formation accompanied by dust and dirt picked up during the handling of the fuel between the refinery and the vehicle tank.

Fuel Filters. Fuel filters may be located at the inner end of the pick-up pipe in the fuel tank, in the fuel pump, in the carburetor, or in the fuel lines. Many types of materials have been used as the filtering media: fine screen, ceramic (a porous clay substance which is hardened by baking), sintered bronze, and treated paper to name a few. The filtering media must be porous enough to pass all the fuel required by the engine, yet not pass water or sediment.

All filters require periodic cleaning. Some, however, cannot be cleaned and must be replaced.

Fuel Lines. Steel tubing, positioned along the frame and held in place by clips, is used to transfer the fuel from the fuel tank to the fuel pump, and from the pump to the carburetor. This tubing is connected to the various units by either flexible neoprene hose and clamps or by tubing connectors. The tubing is

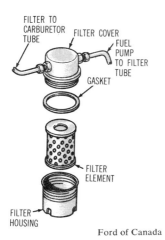

FILTER TO CARBURETOR TUBE
FILTER COVER
FUEL PUMP TO FILTER TUBE
GASKET
FILTER ELEMENT
FILTER HOUSING

Ford of Canada

Fig. 37-4   Typical In-line Fuel Filter

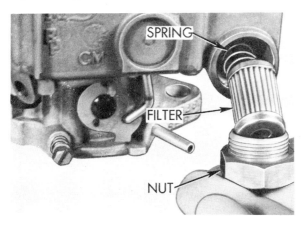

SPRING
FILTER
NUT

(A) PAPER TYPE

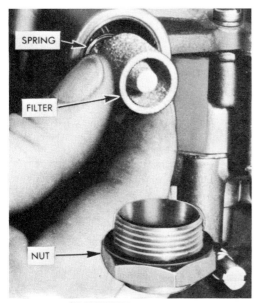

SPRING
FILTER
NUT

(B) BRONZE TYPE

Chrysler Canada Ltd.

Fig. 37-5   Carburetor Inlet Fuel Filters

usually located so that it is afforded the maximum protection against flying stones, where vibration is least likely to work-harden it, and away from the exhaust system to minimize the possibility of creating a vapour lock.

Vehicles equipped with air-conditioning units frequently have a fuel vapour-return line running from the fuel pump to the fuel tank. This line is necessary because of the higher under-the-hood temperatures created by the heat dissipation of the air-conditioning condensor unit. These higher temperatures and the vacuum created in the fuel pump (*note*: liquids boil at lower temperatures when the pressure upon them is reduced; water boils at $212°$ at 14.7 psi but boils at $198°$ when the pressure is reduced to 10 psi) can cause the fuel to vaporize in the fuel pump. This creates what is known as a vapour lock, a condition that prevents the fuel pump from delivering fuel to the carburetor.

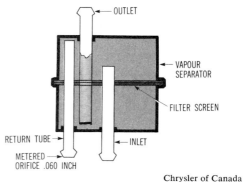

OUTLET
VAPOUR SEPARATOR
FILTER SCREEN
RETURN TUBE
INLET
METERED ORIFICE .060 INCH

Chrysler of Canada

Fig. 37-6   Fuel Vapour Separator

The vapour-return line is connected to a special outlet on the fuel pump and is used to return the fuel vapours to the fuel tank. It also permits the excess fuel that is being pumped by the fuel pump to return to the fuel tank instead of remaining in the fuel pump. This results in a constant circulation of the fuel which helps to keep the fuel pump cool, thus reducing the possibility of a vapour lock forming.

Some vehicles have a vapour-separator unit installed in the fuel line between the fuel pump and the carburetor. Should the fuel in the fuel pump vaporize, the vapour will enter the separator in the form of bubbles along with the fuel. These bubbles of vapour will rise to the top of the separator. Fuel-pump pressure forces the vapour out of the separator through a metered orifice to the return line, through the return line to the fuel tank, where the vapour can condense into a liquid.

37-2 THE FUEL PUMP

Mechanical Fuel Pump. The mechanical fuel pump is operated by means of a cam on the camshaft of the engine. The pump is of the diaphragm type, and is actuated by a rocker arm through a link and pull rod from the cam. A rocker-arm spring keeps the rocker arm against the cam at all times.

The majority of mechanical fuel pumps operate in the following manner. As the highest part of the special fuel-pump-operating cam on the camshaft comes around, it pushes on the rocker arm which, through linkage, pulls the diaphragm down. As the diaphragm moves down, it creates a vacuum in the fuel chamber, which opens the inlet valve and closes the outlet valve. Gasoline is forced into the chamber by atmospheric pressure on the fuel in the storage tank. As the lowest part of the cam on the camshaft comes around, the diaphragm return spring forces the diaphragm up, creating a pressure on the gasoline in the chamber. This closes the intake valve and opens the outlet valve, forcing the gasoline up to the carburetor.

The needle valve in the float bowl of the carburetor maintains a constant level of fuel in the carburetor bowl. When this valve is closed, fuel cannot enter the bowl and pressure is built up in the fuel line between the carburetor and the fuel-pump chamber. As the pressure increases in the fuel-pump chamber, it resists the action of the diaphragm return spring and prevents the diaphragm from taking a complete stroke, thus reducing the flow of fuel. When the needle valve in the carburetor is open, the pressure in the line and chamber is reduced and gasoline is needed in the carburetor bowl. This reduced pressure allows the diaphragm to take longer strokes which increases the flow of fuel.

Fuel pumps frequently have a built-in air dome with a diaphragm to dampen out pulsations in the fuel stream. The air dome and diaphragm provide a pocket in which the fuel under pressure can compress a certain volume of air. When the pump diaphragm is on its downward (vacuum) stroke, the pocket of compressed air pushes on the pulsa-

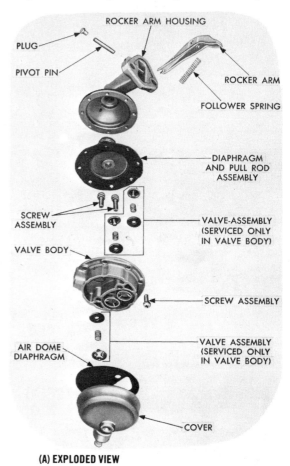

(A) EXPLODED VIEW

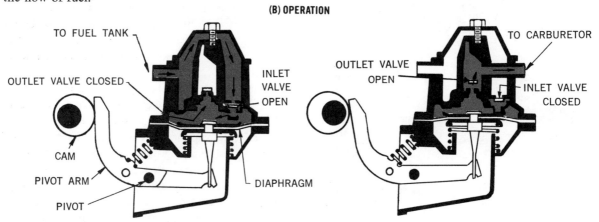

(B) OPERATION

tion diaphragm to force the fuel in the chamber out of the pump under pressure.

Most fuel pumps include a fuel strainer or filter which removes from the gasoline any solid particles of foreign material before they can damage either the pump or the carburetor. Some filtering elements are also capable of preventing water, which may be in the gasoline, from entering the pump or carburetor.

Electric Fuel Pump. There are two basic types of electric fuel pumps: the diaphragm or bellows type which are similar to the mechanical fuel pump, and the pusher type of pump which are electric motor-driven impellor-type pumps mounted in the bottom of the fuel storage tank.

The diaphragm- and bellows-type pumps—are mounted on the engine side of the fire wall or any other relatively cool location in the engine compartment and consequently have a lesser tendency to become vapour locked. Racing engines frequently have more than one electric fuel pump in order to provide the necessary volume of fuel and to keep the engine running should one pump fail.

Both bellows and diaphragm-type pumps are operated by a *solenoid* which is connected into the ignition circuit. When the ignition circuit is completed, the solenoid is energized. The magnetic field produced in the solenoid attracts the bellows or diaphragm armature, pulling the bellows or diaphragm down, compressing the drive spring. This creates an area of low pressure in the pump chamber. Fuel enters through the inlet valve. The downward motion of the armature breaks the electrical circuit to the solenoid, thus collapsing the magnetic field. The drive spring pushes the bellows or diaphragm up, closing the contact points and creating pressure in the pump chamber. This cycle is repeated until the carburetor fuel bowl is filled to the proper level and the needle valve closes. The pressure now builds up in the fuel line and pump chamber to balance the drive spring pressure thus stopping the pumping action. The opening and closing of the contact points control the speed of

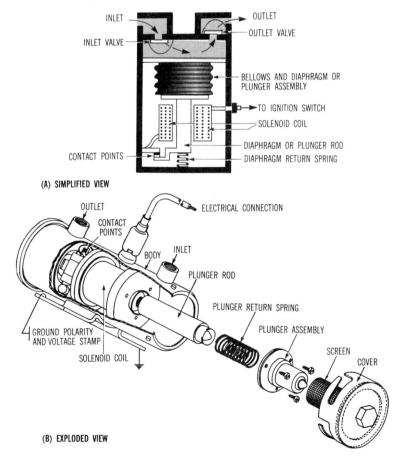

(A) SIMPLIFIED VIEW

(B) EXPLODED VIEW

Fig. 37-8 Typical Electric-Type Fuel Pump   Chrysler of Canada

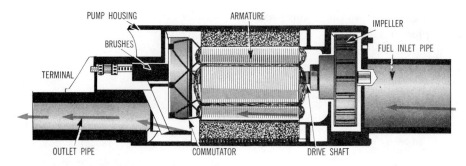

Fig. 37-9   Typical Pusher-Type Fuel Pump   Courtesy of General Motors

the pump. Pump operating pressures range between 3 to 5 psi.

Pusher-type pumps—are operated by small electric motors which drive an impeller. The rotating impeller creates centrifugal force which throws the fuel outward into a voluted casting creating sufficient pressure (2.5 to 4 psi) to force the fuel up to the carburetor.

When the proper fuel level in the carburetor bowl closes the needle valve, the pump continues to operate but just circulates the fuel through the pump and returns it to the tank.

Combination Fuel and Vacuum Pump. This type of pump is used on vehicles equipped with vacuum operated windshield-wiper motors. It is used to provide a constant supply of vacuum regardless of engine load. The fuel-pump portion operates in a similar manner to the conventional mechanical fuel pump. The vacuum portion of the pump is also similar in construction and operation to the fuel-pump portion. However, it pumps air instead of fuel and, in doing so, provides a constant source of vacuum.

37-3 CARBURATION

The carburetor is a device which automatically atomizes, vaporizes, and mixes the gasoline and air in the proper proportions necessary for starting, idling, low speed, high speed, acceleration, and power at various speeds.

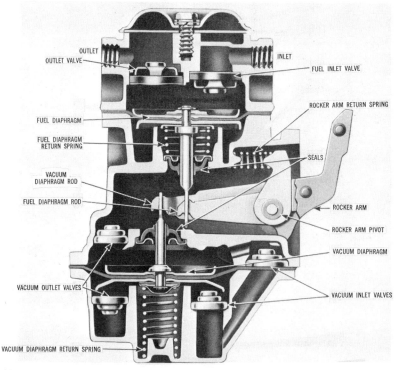

Fig. 37-10   Typical Combination Fuel and Vacuum Pump   Courtesy of General Motors

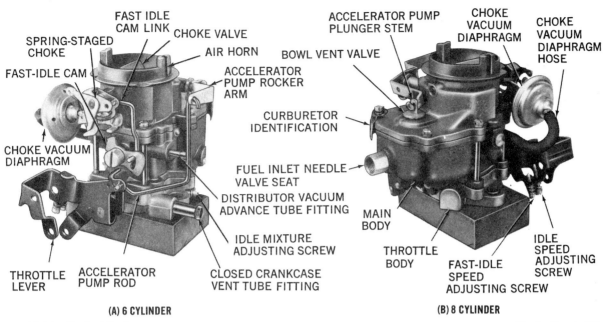

Fig. 37-11   Typical Carburetors

(A) 6 CYLINDER

(B) 8 CYLINDER

Chrysler Canada Ltd.

Principles of Carburation. Gasoline in its raw liquid form will not burn satisfactorily to operate an internal-combustion engine. It must first be broken up into tiny particles, or atomized. After being atomized the gasoline is vaporized and thoroughly mixed with air in proper proportions for combustion. While these proportions vary slightly for different makes of engines, one part of gasoline to fifteen parts of air by weight is the average mixture used. By volume that would amount to about 10,000 gallons of air for each gallon of gasoline.

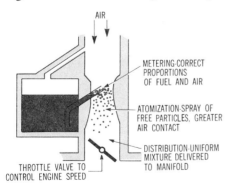

Fig. 37-12   Purpose of Carburetor

A mixture with more than 15 parts of air to 1 part of gasoline is said to be lean, and a mixture of less than 15 parts of air to 1 part of gasoline is said to be rich. The various engine operating conditions require the carburetor to provide a variety of fuel-air mixtures. When the engine is cold, is

being accelerated, or is under load, it requires a richer mixture, which may contain only 12 parts of air to 1 of gasoline. When the engine is at normal operating temperature and runs at medium speeds and under light loads, the fuel-air ratio can be as high as 17 parts of air to 1 part of gasoline.

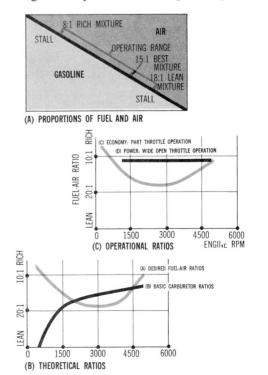

(A) PROPORTIONS OF FUEL AND AIR

(C) OPERATIONAL RATIOS

(B) THEORETICAL RATIOS

Fig. 37-13   Fuel-Air Ratios

At idling speeds a richer mixture is required than that required for cruising speeds.

The fuel-air ratio is controlled by the various jets, valves, and air bleeds contained in the various carburetor circuits.

Jets.—A jet contains a calibrated-size hole. The size and design of the hole determines the amount of gasoline which can flow through the jet. The jet may be integral with the casting or a separate part fitted into a passageway in the casting. Each carburetor circuit has one or more jets to control the flow of the fuel.

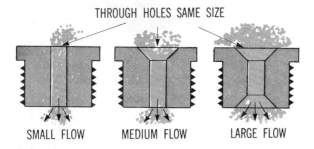

THROUGH HOLES SAME SIZE

SMALL FLOW MEDIUM FLOW LARGE FLOW

Fig. 37-14   Jet Design and Flow Characteristics

Air Bleeds.—Air bleeds are small openings that conduct air from the air horn to the various carburetor circuits. By mixing air with the fuel, the fuel is partially atomized before it reaches the discharge point.

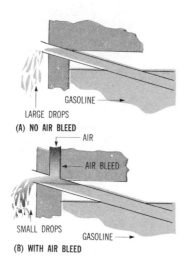

GASOLINE
LARGE DROPS
(A) NO AIR BLEED
AIR
AIR BLEED
SMALL DROPS
GASOLINE
(B) WITH AIR BLEED

Fig. 37-15   Air Bleed Principle

Valves.—Valves of various types are used to control the flow of fuel and air. Needle or plunger type valves usually control the fuel and butterfly type valves control the air.

The Venturi Effect.—The venturi is a narrowed section of the carburetor air passage (throat). Its purpose is to create a partial vacuum in the air passage. When the same amount of air moves through the venturi as through the rest of the passage, the velocity of the air will be greatest at the narrowest point; as a result the greater the velocity, the less the pressure. The low pressure draws fuel through the discharge nozzle which is mounted in the narrowest part of the venturi. The faster the air passes through the venturi, the more fuel will be drawn out of the nozzle. Frequently dual and triple venturies are used to produce the low pressure in a desired place in the passageway.

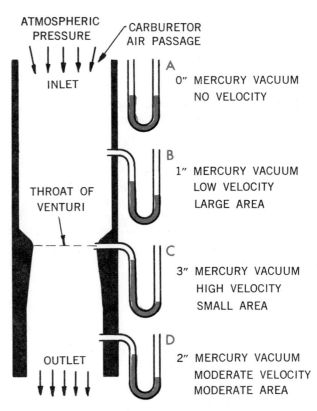

ATMOSPHERIC PRESSURE   CARBURETOR AIR PASSAGE

INLET

A   0" MERCURY VACUUM
NO VELOCITY

B   1" MERCURY VACUUM
LOW VELOCITY
LARGE AREA

THROAT OF VENTURI

C   3" MERCURY VACUUM
HIGH VELOCITY
SMALL AREA

D   2" MERCURY VACUUM
MODERATE VELOCITY
MODERATE AREA

OUTLET

Fig. 37-16   Operation of the Venturi

Atomization.—Atomization is the breaking up of a solid stream of liquid into a fine spray or droplets. Each droplet is exposed to the air on all sides so that it will evaporate quickly.

Evaporation.—Evaporation is the process of changing a liquid into a vapour. The greater the area exposed to the air, the more rapid the vaporization

Vaporization.—Vaporization is the name given to the process during which a liquid is changed into its gaseous state.

37-4 CARBURETOR CONSTRUCTION

The carburetor usually consists of three separate castings: the upper, called the *air horn*; the centre called the *main body* and *fuel bowl*; and the lower, called the *throttle body*. The passageway through which the air passes is called the *throat*.

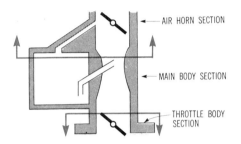

Fig. 37-17   Carburetor Sections

The air horn, to which the air cleaner is attached and where the air enters the carburetor, includes the choke assembly. The main body includes the venturi and most of the carburetor circuits. The throttle body includes the throttle valve, idle mixture and speed screws, and facilities to attach the carburetor to the manifold.

Carburetors are classified according to the location of the fuel bowl. If the fuel bowl is off to one side of the throat, the carburetor is classed as eccentric. If the bowl surrounds the throat, then the carburetor is classed as concentric.

If the carburetor is mounted below the manifold, it is classed as an up-draft carburetor. A down-draft carburetor is mounted above the intake manifold. A carburetor mounted in-line and to the side of the manifold is classed as a side-draft carburetor.

Carburetors may have one, two, or four throats, frequently referred to as barrels. Multiple-barrel carburetors have certain circuits duplicated in the additional barrel and use other circuits that are common to all barrels.

Carburetors may be classified as balanced or unbalanced. Since the fuel bowl must have a hole (vent) to allow air to enter or leave as the fuel level changes, the location of this vent determines the class. In a balanced carburetor the vent passageway leads into the air horn. The advantage of this type of venting is that should the air cleaner become restricted, the vacuum in the venturi would increase proportionately. The pressure on the fuel in the fuel bowl would also decrease proportionately, and therefore the pressure difference between the venturi and the bowl would remain the same, resulting in a more normal flow of fuel from the discharge nozzle. This pressure difference would not remain constant under similar conditions in a carburetor that is vented directly to the atmosphere. The venturi vacuum would increase while atmospheric pressure would remain the same, thus producing a greater pressure difference between the two areas. The greater pressure difference would increase the flow of fuel resulting in a richer fuel-air mixture. This type of carburetor would be classified as unbalanced.

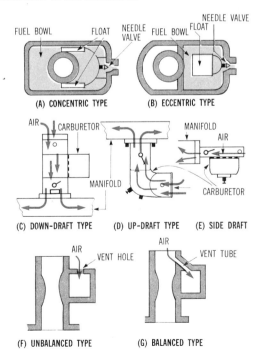

Fig. 37-18   Types of Carburetors

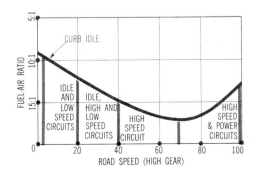

Fig. 37-19   Periods of Circuit Operation

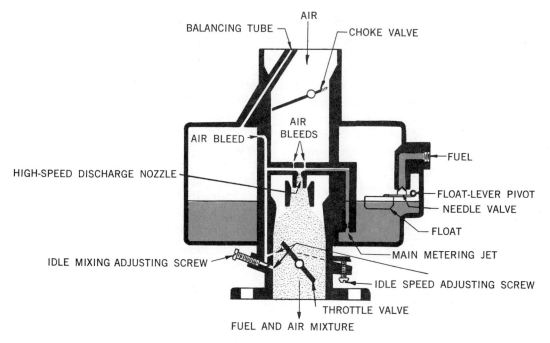

(A) ROCHESTER TYPE

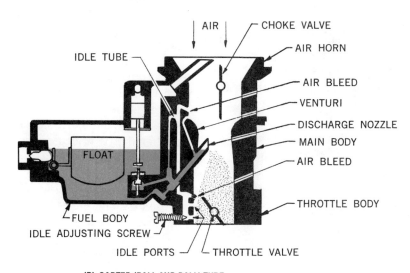

(B) CARTER (BALL AND BALL) TYPE

Fig. 37-20 Basic Carburetors

37-5 CARBURETOR CIRCUITS

In order for the carburetor to automatically vaporize and mix the gasoline and air in the proper proportions for starting, idling, acceleration, and power at various speeds, many different carburetor circuits are required.

Throttle. The throttle is a butterfly or disc-type valve, mounted on a shaft in the throttle body and connected by linkage to the accelerator pedal. It is a device for varying the amount of fuel-air mixture that enters the intake manifold. The valve can be tilted to various angles, thereby allowing more or less fuel-air mixture to flow through the throat of the carburetor.

Float Circuit. The float circuit is the most important circuit because it controls the height of the

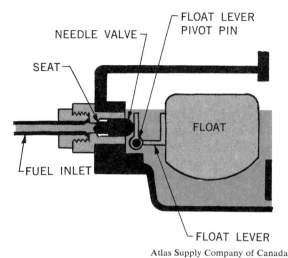

Atlas Supply Company of Canada

Fig. 37-21   Typical Float Circuit

gasoline level in the bowl and nozzle. A gasoline level too high or too low will cause trouble in the other circuits and make complaints difficult to trace. The float bowl acts as a reservoir to hold a supply of gasoline throughout the entire range of engine performance. Gasoline is available at a fairly constant pressure from the fuel pump, and when the needle valve is off its seat, gasoline will flow into the float bowl. If gasoline enters more rapidly than it leaves, the bowl will tend to fill up, causing the float to rise. The float is connected to a lever and a pivot, and as the float rises, the lever bears against the lower end of the needle valve, causing it to be moved into the needle-valve seat. This closes the inlet, preventing further delivery of gasoline into the float bowl until some of the gasoline is withdrawn through the carburetor circuits. When this happens, the float drops and releases the needle valve from its seat so that additional gasoline will be delivered into the bowl from the fuel pump. In actual operation, the gasoline is maintained at a practically constant level in the bowl, the float tending to hold the needle valve partly closed so that the incoming gasoline just balances the gasoline being drawn through the fuel passages in the carburetor.

Idle Circuit. The idle circuit completely controls the supply of gasoline to the engine during idle and low speeds up to approximately 20 mph, and partially controls the supply of gasoline for no-load speeds between approximately 20 and 30 mph.

When the throttle valve is almost closed (idling speeds) there will be very little air flowing through the venturi. Therefore, very little vacuum will be produced in the venturi area. However, on the manifold side of the throttle valve, engine vacuum will be very high. The idle circuit uses this engine vacuum to draw fuel through the circuit and into the air stream.

The idle discharge port is located directly below the closed position of the throttle valve. The idle port is made in a variety of slotted or round shapes so that, as the throttle valve is opened, it will not only allow more air to come past it, but will also uncover more of the idle port or ports. This allows a greater quantity of gasoline and air mixture to enter the carburetor throat from the idle-mixture passage. The idle position of the throttle is such that an idling speed of approximately 10 mph leaves enough of the slotted port covered to act as a reserve to supply the necessary mixture for the time when the carburetor changes from the idle to the high-speed circuit.

During idle operation of the engine, the gasoline flows from the float bowl, through the idle-speed jet, to a point where it is combined with a stream of air coming in from the carburetor throat through the upper air bleed. The combining of the stream of air with the stream of gasoline tends to atomize or break up the gasoline. This mixture of air and gasoline continues through the passage until it begins to pass the point where it is combined with a

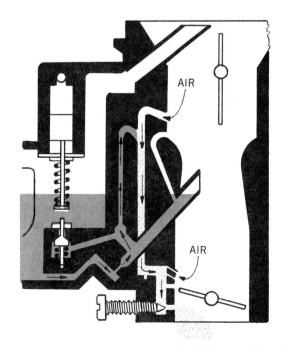

Atlas Supply Company of Canada

Fig. 37-22   Typical Idle Circuit

stream of air coming in through the lower air bleed. This further breaks up the gasoline particles. The gasoline and air mixture that flows downward into the passage from the lower air bleed is still richer than required, but when it mixes with the air which has come past the throttle valve, it forms a combustible mixture.

An adjustable needle valve is located in the discharge port so that the amount of fuel being discharged can be varied to provide the proper fuel-air mixture for idling speeds.

The upper-idle air bleed serves a secondary purpose, that of preventing a syphoning action from continuing to discharge fuel out of the idle discharge port when the high-speed circuit is in full operation or when the engine is stopped.

Exhaust emission control carburetors provide for leaner idling mixtures. In some cases finer pitch threads on the idle-mixture screws provide more accurate fuel-air ratio adjustment. Some carburetors have an idle-limiter device which sets a limit on the enrichment of the idle mixture. Other carburetors incorporate a preset fixed mixture restriction in the idle fuel passages which limits the maximum amount of fuel available during idling.

The idle speed on engines equipped with exhaust emission-control carburetors is slightly higher than normal and must be accurately set to specifications.

Low-Speed Circuit. As the throttle valve is opened, it uncovers the lower air bleed. This air-bleed hole that was in the high-pressure area above the throttle is now in the low-pressure area below the throttle valve and therefore supplies the additional fuel required for off-idle speeds.

As the throttle is opened sufficiently for a no-load speed of approximately 20 mph, the velocity of the air flowing down through the carburetor throat creates a pressure difference between the end of the nozzle and the float chamber. Since the gasoline in the float bowl is acted upon by atmospheric pressure, the difference in pressure between the two points causes the fuel to flow from the fuel bowl, out of the main nozzle, into the throat of the

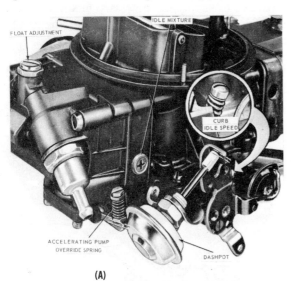

(A)

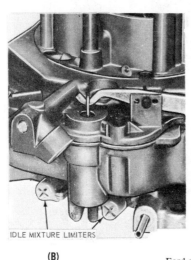

(B)

Ford of Canada

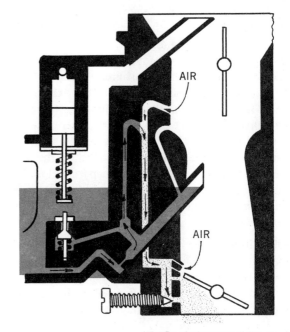

Atlas Supply Company of Canada

Fig. 37-23   Idle Mixture Limiters

Fig. 37-24   Typical Low-Speed Circuit

carburetor. As the speed increases, the high-speed system continues to cut in more and more while the idle or low-speed system continues to cut out until the car reaches a speed of approximately 30 mph. At this point the high-speed system is carrying the entire load, and the idle and low-speed systems cease to operate.

The idle or low-speed circuit ceases to function completely because the throttle valve has moved past the idle port openings. Now there is little or no difference in pressure between the upper and lower parts of the carburetor.

High-Speed Circuit. The high speed circuit consists of the main discharge nozzle which is located in the venturi, and the main metering jet located in the fuel bowl. The high-speed circuit supplies fuel from partially open to fully open throttle-valve positions. However, as the rate of flow of air through the venturi increases, the rate of flow of fuel increases, but at a faster rate. This is because of the fact that the density of the air becomes less while the density of the fuel remains the same. As a result, the fuel-air ratio will not remain constant but will become progressively richer as the engine speed increases. Several methods are used to maintain proper fuel-air ratios for all throttle positions.

Main metering jet—controls the size of the stream of fuel that can pass through the high-speed system. The speed at which the stream flows is controlled by the pressure difference between the venturi and the fuel bowl. Main metering jets are made in various sizes to suit different engines. Standard size jets are intended for use in engines operating in altitudes up to 5,000′ above sea level. Smaller than standard size jets are used in altitudes above 5,000′ because of the lower atmospheric pressure.

Metering rods—Some main metering jets are designed to include the insertion of a two-step metering rod in the jet opening. The position of the rod in the jet is determined by engine vacuum or throttle position. Thus the rod can control the amount of fuel flowing through the jet in accordance with engine load or throttle position.

Mechanically controlled metering rods are actuated by a linkage connected to the throttle. As the throttle is opened the rod is raised. The linkage is

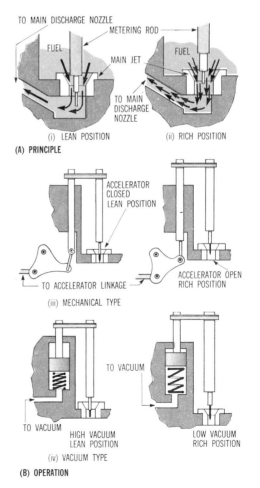

37-25   High-Speed System

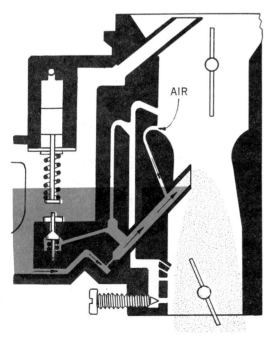

Fig. 37-26   Metering Rods

designed to have the proper step of the metering rod in the jet according to throttle opening. A mechanically controlled metering rod is satisfactory for providing the proper fuel-air ratio according to engine speed, but makes no allowance for engine load.

Vacuum-controlled metering rod—is attached to a vacuum piston or to a diaphragm. A return spring keeps the rod in a certain position. When engine vacuum is applied to one side of the diaphragm or piston, it overcomes the return-spring pressure and moves the rod in accordance to the amount of vacuum provided. High vacuum places the larger step of the metering rod in the jet opening; low vacuum the smallest. Therefore, the flow of fuel through the jet is controlled by engine vacuum. A cruising engine provides high vacuum resulting in less fuel flowing and a lean fuel-air ratio. An engine under load has low engine vacuum and requires a rich mixture.

Both mechanical and vacuum-operated metering rods provide a means of maintaining proper fuel-air ratios according to speed and load conditions.

Air-bleed principle—The air-bleed type of main discharge nozzle consists of inner and outer sections with a small space between each section. The inner or main nozzle has a series of small bleed holes at various points below the gasoline level in the nozzle and the fuel bowl. They provide communication between the inner and outer nozzle. The lower end of the outer nozzle is closed off from the fuel bowl; the upper end is closed off from the carburetor throat, but is open to the atmosphere by way of the high-speed air bleed. Gasoline from the fuel bowl is fed through the main metering jets into the main nozzle, and through the bleed holes into the outer nozzle.

When the high-speed circuit is in operation, the pressure difference between the venturi and the fuel bowl causes the fuel to flow through the high-speed nozzle. As engine speed increases, gasoline flows out of the discharge nozzle faster than it can flow into the nozzle through the main metering jet. This results in a lowering of the fuel level in the main nozzle. Gasoline from the outer nozzle then enters the main nozzle through the bleeder holes. Further lowering of the fuel level allows air from the high-speed air bleed to enter the main nozzle, thus offsetting the tendency of the high-speed circuit to deliver too rich a mixture at high engine speeds. The faster the engine is operated, the lower the fuel level in the main nozzle becomes. This results in more bleed holes being uncovered which admit additional air from the high-speed air bleed to lean out the mixture. The air entering from the high-speed air bleed helps break up the stream of fuel to provide for easier atomization of the fuel, and also increases the air ratio in the mixture. Air from the high-speed air bleed also increases the pressure at the tip of the main nozzle, thus reducing the pressure difference between the venturi and the fuel bowl. This decreases the rate of flow of fuel through the main metering jet. The use of the air-bleed principle maintains a uniform fuel-air mixture regardless of engine speed.

Accelerator Circuit. When the throttle is opened suddenly, it causes the engine vacuum to drop. Without sufficient vacuum in the throat of the carburetor, the gasoline flow through the high-

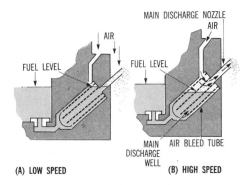

(A) LOW SPEED   (B) HIGH SPEED

Fig. 37-27   Air-Bleed Principle

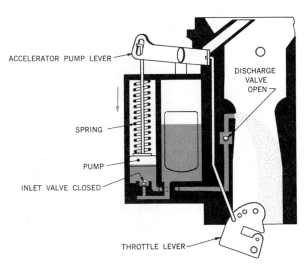

Atlas Supply Company of Canada

Fig. 37-28   Typical Accelerator Pump Circuit

speed circuit decreases. The result is a lean mixture reaching the cylinders and causing a drop in engine power. To prevent this, a plunger-type pump, operated by the throttle linkage, discharges a stream of gasoline into the air stream as the throttle is opened. The pump discharge maintains the proper fuel-air ratio during the initial acceleration period.

The pump consists of a piston, or diaphragm, an inlet and an outlet valve, and a discharge jet. When the throttle is closed, the linkage lifts the pump piston, creating an area of low pressure beneath it. Fuel from the carburetor bowl enters by way of the inlet valve. When the throttle is opened, the piston is forced down, creating a pressure on the fuel beneath it. This pressure opens the outlet valve and forces the fuel out through the discharge jet.

In order to facilitate quick movement of the accelerator pedal, the accelerator pump or diaphragm is spring-operated. When the throttle is opened, this spring is compressed. The expansion

of the spring creates the pressure required to force the fuel out of the pump discharge jet. This prolongs the discharge time to provide the necessary fuel until the high-speed circuit can deliver sufficient fuel for the increased engine speed.

Power Circuit. Since a richer mixture is required for high-speed or heavy-load conditions, it is necessary to vary the fuel-air ratio automatically to meet these conditions. This is the job of the power circuit. The power circuit is controlled by engine vacuum. When engine vacuum is high, then the power circuit is closed. When engine vacuum drops below a specified amount, the power valve starts to open to allow additional fuel to enter the high-speed circuit to richen the mixture, in accordance with engine load or speed. This system provides for power when needed and economy at other times.

Various valving arrangements are used in the power circuit. The vacuum piston rod may contact a spring-loaded power-valve ball check. Low

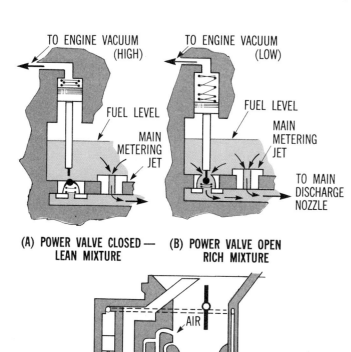

(A) POWER VALVE CLOSED — LEAN MIXTURE   (B) POWER VALVE OPEN RICH MIXTURE

(C) TYPICAL POWER CIRCUIT

Fig. 37-29   The Power Circuit

engine vacuum causes the rod to push the ball away from its seat to open the fuel passageway. A spring-loaded disc check valve or a needle-type check valve is sometimes used in place of the ball type.

The step-type metering rod discussed previously is also another form of the power circuit.

It should be noted that the power circuit is sometimes referred to as the *economizer circuit*. When this reference is used the carburetor is designed for a continuous full power mixture that is reduced to a leaner mixture for cruising speeds and economy. The operation of this circuit is similar to the power circuit since it is controlled by engine vacuum. When engine vacuum is high, the fuel-air mixture is leaned out.

Choke Circuit. The choke is used to provide the rich mixture needed for starting a cold engine. The choke valve controls the amount of air entering the air horn. It may be operated manually or automatically.

The rich starting mixture is required because the gasoline vapours condense when they contact the cold engine parts and because the engine produces a low vacuum at cranking speeds.

When the choke valve is closed, the throttle valve partly opened, and the engine cranked, engine vacuum produces a low-pressure area in the entire carburetor throat. This low pressure causes fuel to flow out of the idle, low-speed and high-speed circuits to provide the necessary rich mixture for starting.

When the engine starts, the choke must be partially opened to prevent flooding. As the engine warms up, a leaner mixture is required. Therefore the choke must be gradually opened to its full extent at normal engine-operating temperatures to maintain the proper fuel-air ratio.

Manual choke—Positioning is controlled by the driver through a choke cable attached to a button mounted on the dash. A spring relief valve is mounted in the choke valve. To prevent flooding of the engine if the choke valve is not opened immediately the engine starts. This relief valve is a small circular disc held in position over a hole in the choke valve by a light spring. As soon as the engine starts, the vacuum in the carburetor is sufficient to allow atmospheric pressure above the choke to overcome the spring and open the relief valve to admit sufficient air to keep the engine running.

The choke valve is also offset on its shaft so that as the engine speed increases, the air flow pressures are unequal on each side of the valve shaft, causing the valve to open an additional amount to prevent high-speed flooding.

Automatic choke—In an automatic choke the various stages of choke-value positioning are controlled by the combination of a temperature-operated thermostatic spring, the engine vacuum, and the air flow through the throat of the carburetor.

When the engine is stopped and cold, the choke valve is closed by the winding action of the thermos-

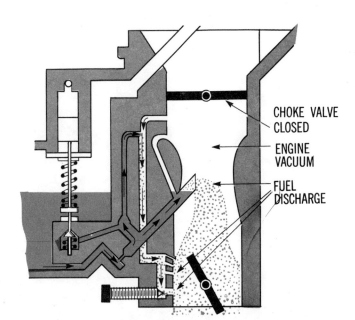

CHOKE VALVE CLOSED

ENGINE VACUUM

FUEL DISCHARGE

Atlas Supply Company of Canada

Fig. 37-30   Fuel Discharge When Choke Valve Closed

tatic spring as the accelerator pedal is depressed. The instant the engine is started, engine vacuum is applied to a piston which is connected to the choke valve. As engine vacuum moves the piston, the choke valve is opened sufficiently to prevent flooding. In order to maintain the proper fuel-air ratio at higher engine speeds during the warm-up period, the choke valve is offset on its shaft. As the engine speed increases, the uneven pressures on the valve, because of one side being larger than the other, allows the air flow to open the choke valve an additional amount to prevent high-speed flooding. When a heavy load is placed on the engine, the engine vacuum drops and its effect on the choke piston decreases. This closes the choke valve, resulting in an enrichment in the fuel-air ratio. As the engine warms up to its normal operating temperature, the thermostatic spring expands because of the temperature change and opens the choke valve to its maximum position.

The thermostatic spring may be mounted directly on the end of the choke-valve shaft, or mounted on the exhaust manifold and connected to the choke shaft by a connecting link. When the spring is mounted on the carburetor, engine vacuum from the choke piston is used to draw warm air through a tube from a stove mounted on the exhaust manifold. Sometimes the tube is wrapped in asbestos to prevent a heat loss between the manifold and the thermostatic-spring housing.

Fast-Idling Devices. A fast-idling device is incorporated in both types of choke mechanisms. This device increases the throttle-valve opening in proportion to the position of the choke valve. The device provides a stepped plate which is used as a stop for the idle-speed adjusting screw. The higher steps provide for proportionately higher idling speeds according to choke position during the warm-up period to prevent stalling.

Unloader Devices. Unloader devices are incorporated as part of the automatic-choke mechanism. When the choke valve is closed, prolonged cranking will result in the engine becoming flooded. To overcome this condition, linkage is provided as part of the automatic choke mechanism which, when the accelerator is pushed to the floor, will open the choke valve. Then, as the engine is cranked, only air will enter the cylinders to clear the excessive gasoline and produce a combustible mixture.

Antipercolator Devices. During hot weather, prolonged periods of idling, or when the engine has been shut off for a short period when it is hot, heat rises up past the carburetor. This heat can become sufficient to vaporize the gasoline and build up pressure in the fuel bowl and carburetor circuit. The pressure buildup forces fuel out of the discharge jets and causes a flooded condition. The antipercolator device opens a valve on the top of the carburetor fuel bowl when the throttle valve is closed. This valve releases any vapours which may develop.

Antistall Dash Pot. In order to prevent hesitation or stalling when the throttle is closed quickly on vehicles equipped with automatic transmissions, an antistall dash pot is sometimes used. An antistall

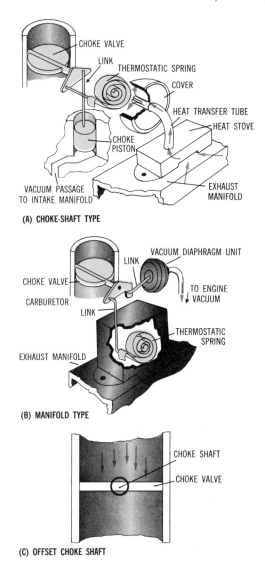

(A) CHOKE-SHAFT TYPE

(B) MANIFOLD TYPE

(C) OFFSET CHOKE SHAFT

Fig. 37-31   Automatic Choke Types

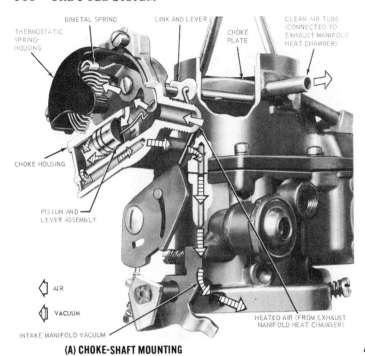

(A) CHOKE-SHAFT MOUNTING

Fig. 37-32   Automatic Chokes

Courtesy of General Motors

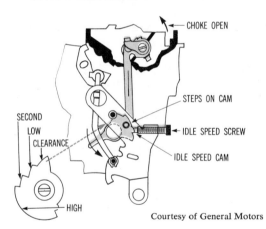

Courtesy of General Motors

Fig. 37-33   Fast-Idling Device

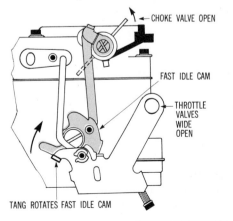

Courtesy of General Motors

Fig. 37-34   Choke Unloader Devices

dash pot usually consists of a spring-loaded diaphragm which traps air, or sometimes fuel, behind it when the throttle is opened. The shaft and adjusting screw are moved forward by the spring tension when the throttle is opened. When the throttle is closed, the air or fuel trapped behind the diaphragm can only escape through a small opening, and also the return spring pressure must be overcome. This results in slower final closing of the throttle and prevents the possibility of stalling. The device only operates during the final few degrees of throttle closing and has no effect in the normal operating speed ranges.

Anti-Icing Passages. As gasoline enters the air stream and turns into a vapour, it takes heat from the surrounding air and metal. Under certain humidity and temperature conditions, it is possible for the moisture in the air to condense and freeze in the carburetor throat. Sufficient ice can form to cause the engine to stall. Many carburetors have passageways for hot exhaust gases to pass through the throttle body near the idle ports and throttle valve. The exhaust gases add sufficient heat to the

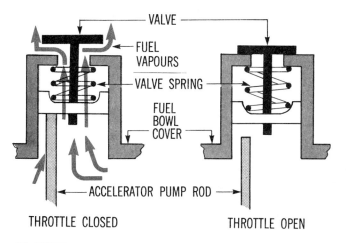

(A) SCREW-VALVE TYPE

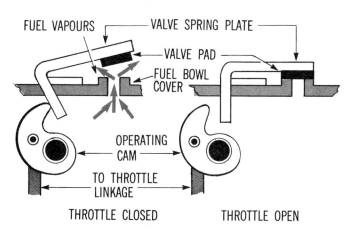

(B) SAXAPHONE-VALVE TYPE

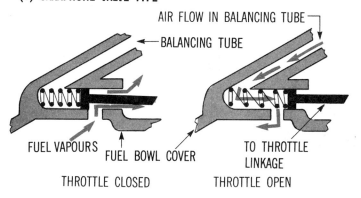

(C) PISTON TYPE

Fig. 37-35   Types of Antipercolating Devices

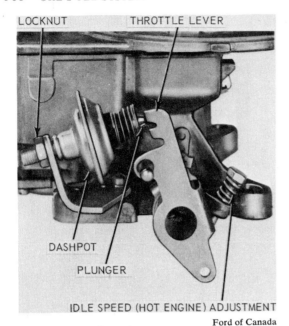

Fig. 37-36   *Typical Dash Pot*

Ford of Canada

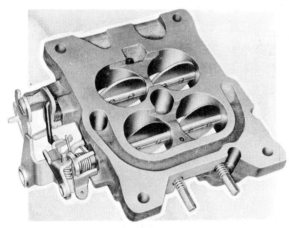

(A) EXHAUST-HEAT TYPE

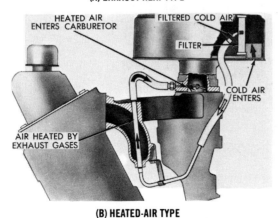

(B) HEATED-AIR TYPE

(A) Chrysler Canada Limited
(B) Courtesy of General Motors

Fig. 37-37   Anti-Icing Devices

metal to prevent the formation of ice. Some carburetors have water passages in the throttle body to provide the heat necessary to prevent the ice from forming.

Spark-Control Devices. Some carburetors include a spark-control system. The carburetor is calibrated to provide the required vacuum to operate the distributor advance mechanism. This vacuum is produced as a result of an inter-reaction of venturi vacuum and manifold vacuum. Venturi vacuum is obtained through a pick-up tube mounted in the venturi. This vacuum is supplied to the distributor only when it is greater than engine vacuum, and is controlled by the spark valve mounted on the carburetor. When the engine is accelerated, manifold vacuum drops, the spark valve closes, and venturi vacuum is directed to the spark advance mechanism to provide the proper amount of spark advance.

Idle-Stop Solenoids. Since exhaust emission-control carburetors idle at higher speeds, plus higher operating temperatures and slightly retarded spark, a condition known as *dieseling* (the engine continuing to run after the ignition has been shut off— ignition continues because of combustion chamber temperature) may develop. The idle-stop solenoid eliminates the possibility of dieseling by closing the throttle valve completely when the engine is turned off.

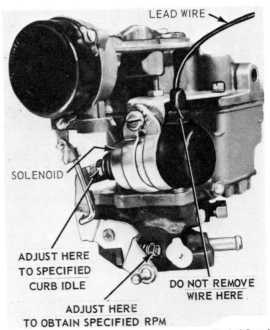

Ford of Canada

Fig. 37-38   Idle-Stop Solenoid

37-6A SINGLE-BARREL CARBURETOR

A single barrel carburetor has one throat and one opening to the intake manifold. It contains all of the carburetor circuits and devices required to operate the engine under all operating conditions. Single-barrel carburetors are standard equipment on most engines of six cylinders or less.

37-6B TWO-BARREL CARBURETOR

A two-barrel carburetor is essentially two carburetors in one. It has a single air horn, single float circuit, and single accelerator pump circuit with two discharge ports. It may have one or two choke valves, depending upon the design. Two-barrel carburetors have two throats each containing a venturi, two idle circuits, two low-speed circuits, two high-speed circuits, two throttle valves, and two outlets into the intake manifold. Only single carburetor devices, such as automatic choke, anti-percolating device, etc., are required.

When used on a V8 engine, each throat of the carburetor supplies all the fuel requirements for two cylinders on each bank. The selection of cylinders depends upon the design of the manifold.

37-6C FOUR-BARREL CARBURETOR

In most four-barrel carburetors, half of the carburetor, the primary side, operates as a two-barrel caburetor during light load and cruising speeds. The second half of the carburetor, the secondary side, is used as a supplementary carburetor that operates only during heavy load or high-speed conditions. A four-barrel carburetor consists of a common air horn, two float circuits (which are interconnected to prevent the fuel in the secondary float chamber from forming gum and resins because of prolonged periods between usage), primary and secondary idle circuits, four high-speed circuits, four throttle valves, and four outlet ports to the intake manifold. Single carburetor devices, such as automatic choke, dash pot, etc., are used.

When a four-barrel carburetor is designed so that the primary side provides fuel during all engine operating conditions, then some provision must be made to control the secondary throttle valves. These valves remain closed during light load and speed operation, but start to open when the primary throttle valves have opened approximately 50°.

The opening of the secondary throttle valves may be controlled manually by a mechanical mechanism incorporated in the throttle linkage or automatically by a velocity vacuum-operated diaphragm. The vacuum required to operate the diaphragm is created in the primary venturi.

Primary and secondary barrels form pairs to supply two cylinders of each bank of a V8 engine.

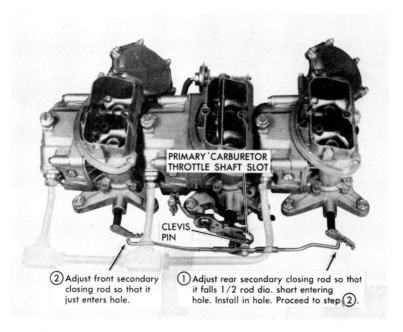

Fig. 37-39   Multiple Carburetors   Courtesy of General Motors

370

Fig. 37-40
SINGLE-BARREL CARBURETOR

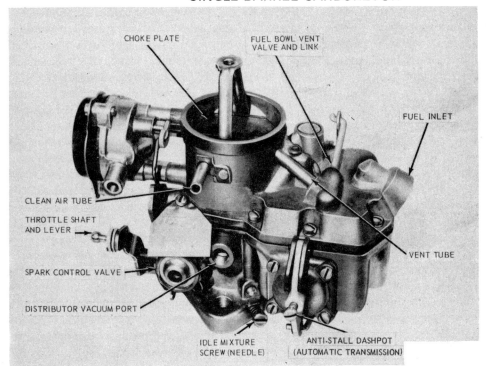

(A) CARBURETOR

Ford of Canada

(B) FLOAT CIRCUIT

Ford of Canada

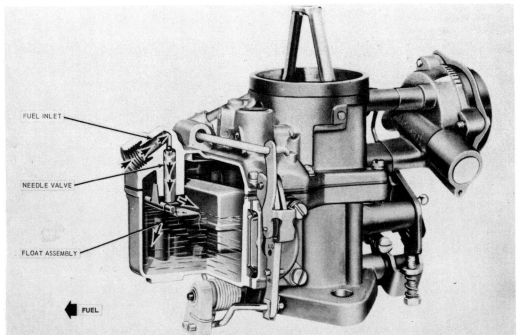

Fig. 37-40

SINGLE-BARREL CARBURETOR

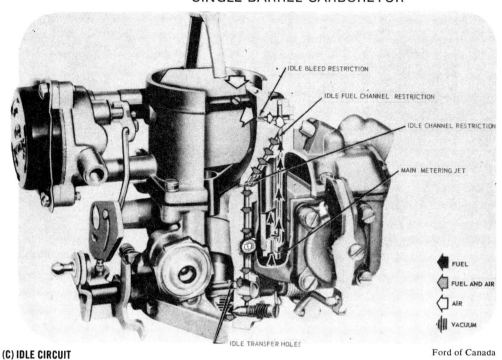

IDLE BLEED RESTRICTION

IDLE FUEL CHANNEL RESTRICTION

IDLE CHANNEL RESTRICTION

MAIN METERING JET

FUEL

FUEL AND AIR

AIR

VACUUM

IDLE TRANSFER HOLES

(C) IDLE CIRCUIT

Ford of Canada

Ford of Canada

(D) HIGH SPEED CIRCUIT

BOOSTER VENTURI

HIGH SPEED AIR BLEED

ANTI-SIPHON AND FUEL/AIR MIXING HOLE

MAIN WELL TUBE

MAIN WELL

FUEL/AIR MIXING HOLES

FUEL

FUEL AND AIR

AIR

VACUUM

MAIN METERING JET   MAIN VENTURI

MAIN FUEL DISCHARGE TUBE

Fig. 37-40

SINGLE-BARREL CARBURETOR

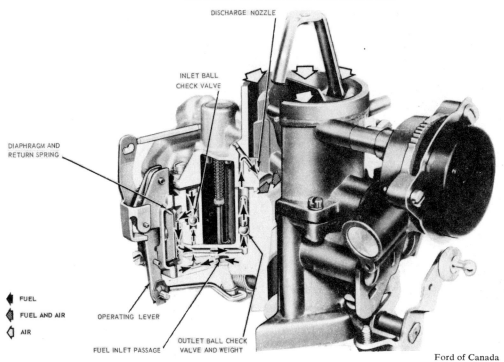

DISCHARGE NOZZLE

INLET BALL
CHECK VALVE

DIAPHRAGM AND
RETURN SPRING

FUEL

FUEL AND AIR

AIR

OPERATING LEVER

FUEL INLET PASSAGE

OUTLET BALL CHECK
VALVE AND WEIGHT

Ford of Canada

(E) ACCELERATING CIRCUIT

(F) POWER CIRCUIT

Ford of Canada

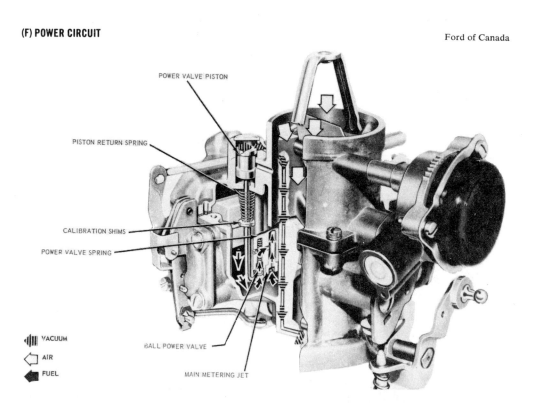

POWER VALVE PISTON

PISTON RETURN SPRING

CALIBRATION SHIMS

POWER VALVE SPRING

VACUUM

AIR

FUEL

BALL POWER VALVE

MAIN METERING JET

Fig. 37-41
TWO-BARREL CARBURETOR

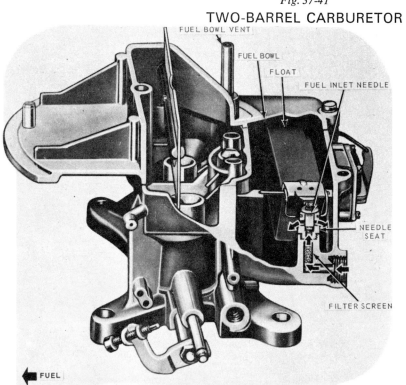

(A) CARBURETOR

Ford of Canada

(B) FLOAT CIRCUIT

Ford of Canada

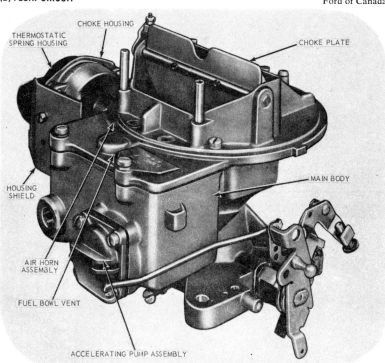

374

Fig. 37-41

TWO-BARREL CARBURETOR

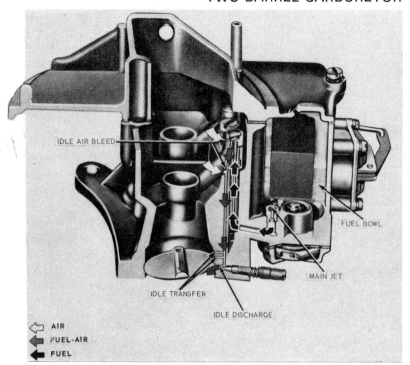

IDLE AIR BLEED

FUEL BOWL

IDLE TRANSFER

MAIN JET

IDLE DISCHARGE

AIR
FUEL-AIR
FUEL

(C) IDLE CIRCUIT

Ford of Canada

(D) HIGH-SPEED CIRCUIT

Ford of Canada

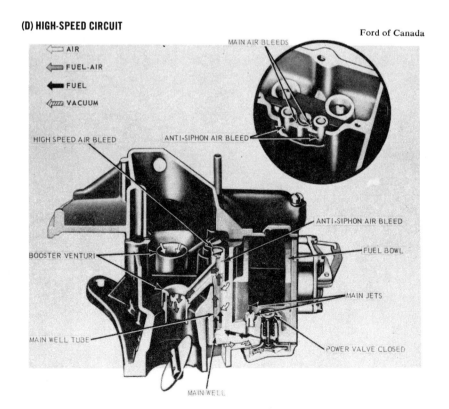

AIR
FUEL-AIR
FUEL
VACUUM

MAIN AIR BLEEDS

HIGH SPEED AIR BLEED

ANTI-SIPHON AIR BLEED

ANTI-SIPHON AIR BLEED

FUEL BOWL

BOOSTER VENTURI

MAIN JETS

MAIN WELL TUBE

POWER VALVE CLOSED

MAIN WELL

Fig. 37-41

TWO-BARREL CARBURETOR

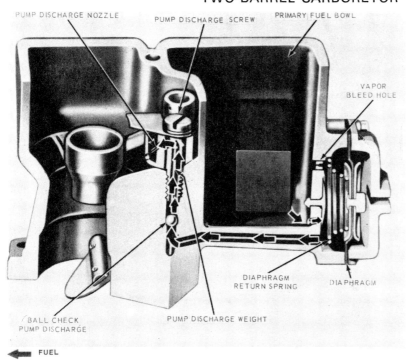

PUMP DISCHARGE NOZZLE

PUMP DISCHARGE SCREW

PRIMARY FUEL BOWL

VAPOR BLEED HOLE

DIAPHRAGM RETURN SPRING

DIAPHRAGM

BALL CHECK PUMP DISCHARGE

PUMP DISCHARGE WEIGHT

FUEL

(E) ACCELERATOR CIRCUIT

Ford of Canada

(F) POWER CIRCUIT

Ford of Canada

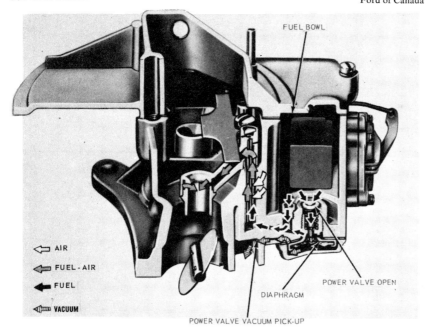

FUEL BOWL

AIR

FUEL - AIR

FUEL

VACUUM

POWER VALVE OPEN

DIAPHRAGM

POWER VALVE VACUUM PICK-UP

Fig. 37-42
FOUR-BARREL CARBURETOR

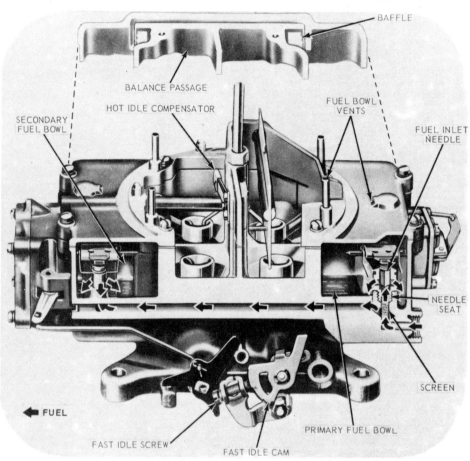

BAFFLE

BALANCE PASSAGE

HOT IDLE COMPENSATOR

FUEL BOWL VENTS

SECONDARY FUEL BOWL

FUEL INLET NEEDLE

NEEDLE SEAT

SCREEN

FUEL

PRIMARY FUEL BOWL

FAST IDLE SCREW

FAST IDLE CAM

(A) FLOAT CIRCUIT

Ford of Canada

(B) IDLE CIRCUIT

Ford of Canada

IDLE AIR BLEED

IDLE AIR BLEED

PRIMARY FUEL BOWL

SECONDARY FUEL BOWL

MAIN JET

FUEL

FUEL-AIR

VACUUM

IDLE DISCHARGE

SECONDARY TRANSFER

IDLE TRANSFER

IDLE DISCHARGE SCREW (NEEDLE)

Fig. 37-42

FOUR-BARREL CARBURETOR

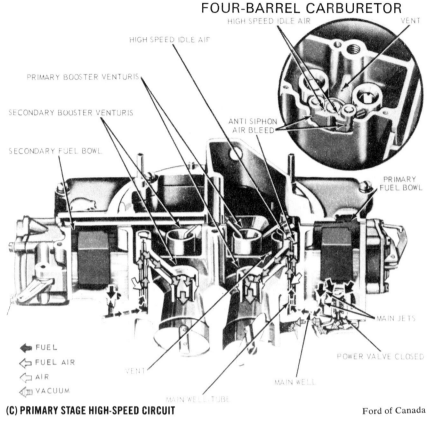

(C) PRIMARY STAGE HIGH-SPEED CIRCUIT — Ford of Canada

(D) SECONDARY STAGE HIGH-SPEED CIRCUIT — Ford of Canada

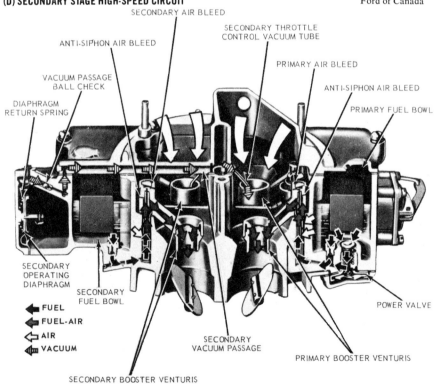

Fig. 37-42
FOUR-BARREL CARBURETOR

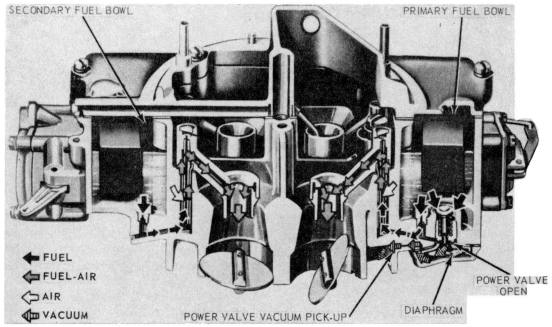

SECONDARY FUEL BOWL

PRIMARY FUEL BOWL

POWER VALVE OPEN

DIAPHRAGM

POWER VALVE VACUUM PICK-UP

◀ FUEL
◀ FUEL-AIR
◁ AIR
◀ VACUUM

(E) ACCELERATOR PUMP CIRCUIT

Ford of Canada

(F) POWER CIRCUIT

Ford of Canada

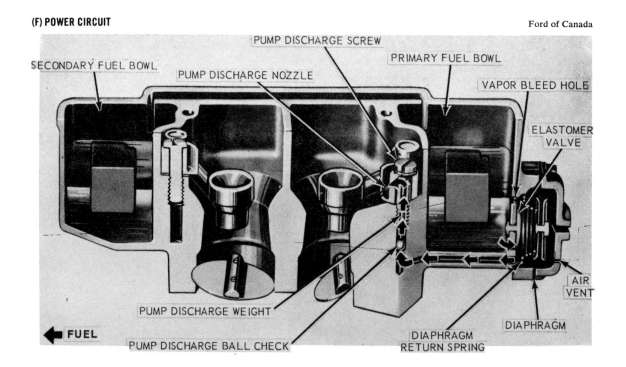

PUMP DISCHARGE SCREW

SECONDARY FUEL BOWL

PUMP DISCHARGE NOZZLE

PRIMARY FUEL BOWL

VAPOR BLEED HOLE

ELASTOMER VALVE

AIR VENT

DIAPHRAGM

PUMP DISCHARGE WEIGHT

PUMP DISCHARGE BALL CHECK

DIAPHRAGM RETURN SPRING

◀ FUEL

37-7 MULTIPLE CARBURETORS

High performance engines frequently use more than one carburetor. Two and three carburetor combinations are used. The use of the multiple carburetor provides better distribution of large quantities of fuel-air mixture. When three carburetors are used, the centre unit usually provides all of the fuel-air mixture required until its throttle valves are opened approximately half way; then the other units assist in providing the fuel-air mixture for higher engine speeds. (See Fig. 37-39, page 369.)

37-8 AIR RAM

Air ram or ram jet is the name given to the principle of using the forward motion of the vehicle to increase the amount of air entering the carburetor. The ram effect is in a way a degree of supercharging. The effect is produced by using forward-facing air scoops in the hood or in the grille that are connected by flexible tubing to the air cleaner.

During normal engine operation, the air enters the air cleaner through the conventional air duct and valve assembly. However, when heavy engine loading or wide open throttle operation causes the intake manifold vacuum to drop to approximately 4″ Hg (hydrargyrum mercury), the air-ram valve is opened by a vacuum-operated motor. The opening of the air-ram valve permits air to be forced into the air cleaner directly from the hood air scoop. The faster the vehicle is driven, the greater the ram effect. Basically, ram air increases the volumetric efficiency of the engine at higher speeds.

37-9 SUPERCHARGER

Another method of increasing the volumetric efficiency of an engine is to place a supercharger either at the air inlet to the carburetor or between the carburetor and the intake manifold. Superchargers are designed to produce from 4 to 20 psi (boost). Two types are in use: *rootes type* and the *centrifugal type*.

The rootes type consists of two rotors with two or more lobes each. In the two rotor type each rotor resembles a figure 8. The action of the rotors is similar to that of a gear-type pump. During operation, air enters the housing by the action of the rotors, and passes between the lobes of the rotors and the housing. The air is then forced out through the outlet opening. The speed of the rotors is about twice engine speed.

The centrifugal-type supercharger consists of an impeller rotating at high speed inside a housing.

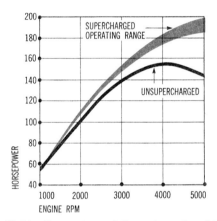

Fig. 37-44   Comparison of Supercharged and Unsupercharged Horsepower Curves

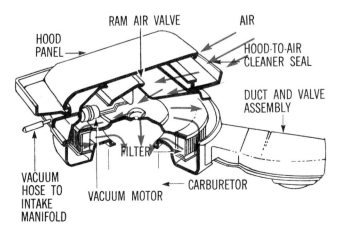

Fig. 37-43   Air-ram Type Air Cleaner

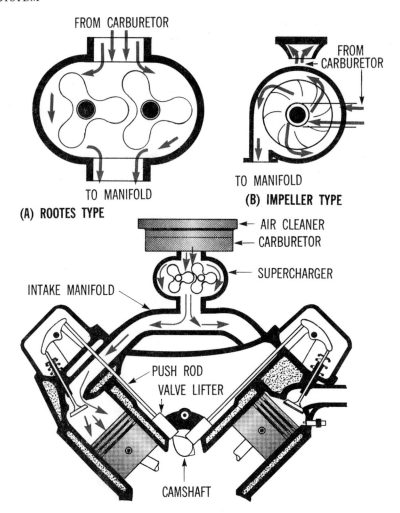

FROM CARBURETOR

TO MANIFOLD

(A) ROOTES TYPE

FROM CARBURETOR

TO MANIFOLD

(B) IMPELLER TYPE

AIR CLEANER
CARBURETOR
SUPERCHARGER
INTAKE MANIFOLD
PUSH ROD
VALVE LIFTER
CAMSHAFT

Fig. 37-45   Superchargers

The impeller produces centrifugal force which increases the pressure in the intake manifold. The impeller speed is approximately five times the engine speed.

37-10 FUEL INJECTION

A fuel-injection system sprays fuel either directly into the cylinder (diesel) or into the intake manifold (gasoline).

When a fuel-injection system is used on a gasoline engine, it consists of an air-intake and air-meter assembly, a conventional fuel pump, a high-pressure fuel pump, a fuel meter, and an intake manifold with an injector nozzle for each cylinder of the engine. The fuel is injected into the intake manifold in high-pressure spurts. The spurts are timed to coincide with the intake stroke of the cylinder.

The engine speed is controlled by a throttle valve in the air-intake assembly. This valve is connected by linkage to the accelerator pedal and operates in a similar manner to the throttle valve of a carburetor except that it admits only air instead of fuel-air mixture. The amount of fuel reaching the injector is controlled by the fuel meter. The correct fuel-air mixture for engine speed and load conditions is provided for by interconnecting the fuel meter and the air control.

In one type of system the fuel requirements are determined by a number of sensors: the intake-manifold pressure sensor, the cylinder-head temperature sensor, and a crankcase sensor. These sensors send electrical signals to a transistorized control unit which determines the amount of fuel to be injected into the air stream according to engine speed and load.

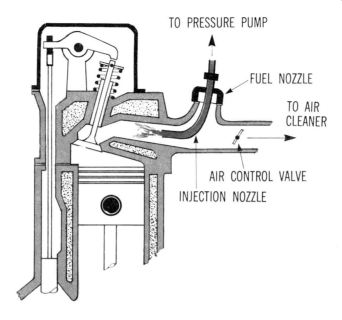

Fig. 37-46   Fuel-Injection Gasoline

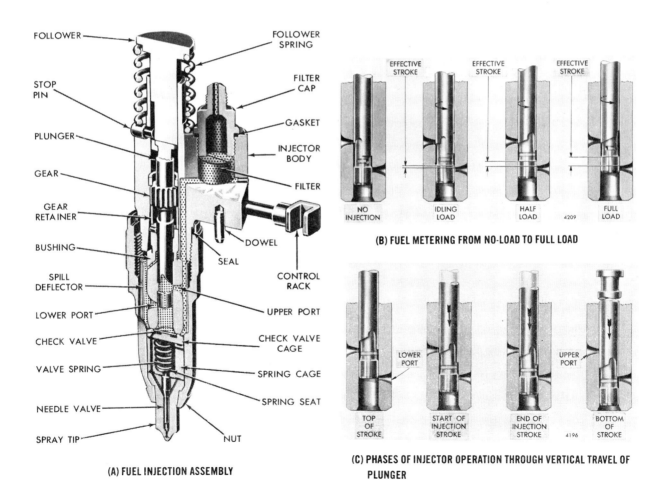

(A) FUEL INJECTION ASSEMBLY

(B) FUEL METERING FROM NO-LOAD TO FULL LOAD

(C) PHASES OF INJECTOR OPERATION THROUGH VERTICAL TRAVEL OF PLUNGER

Fig. 37-47   Diesel Fuel Injectors

Courtesy of General Motors

When fuel injection is used on a diesel engine, the fuel is sprayed directly into the cylinder. In a true diesel engine no spark plug is used. Instead, the fuel is ignited by the heat of compression. The amount of fuel and the exact time of injection is determined by engine speed and load conditions and is controlled by the accelerator. The accelerator controls the amount of air entering the cylinder

(A) OIL-BATH TYPE

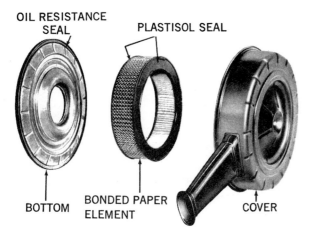

BOTTOM OIL RESISTANCE SEAL — PLASTISOL SEAL — BONDED PAPER ELEMENT — COVER

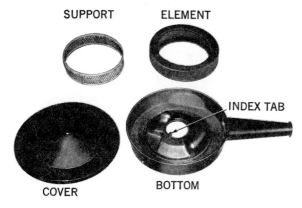

SUPPORT   ELEMENT

INDEX TAB

COVER   BOTTOM

(B) DRY TYPE

(A) Chrysler Canada Limited
(B) Courtesy of General Motors

Fig. 37-48   Carburetor Air Cleaners

and is also connected to an actuating mechanism that controls the high pressure pump output.

37-11 AIR CLEANERS

The air cleaner is mounted on the air horn of the carburetor and does three jobs: it removes dust particles from the air before they enter the carburetor; it muffles the noise of the air rushing into the engine; and it acts as a flame arrester, should the engine backfire through the carburetor.

Two types of air cleaners are used, the *oil-bath type* and the replaceable or washable cellulose *fibre-element dry type.*

In the oil-bath cleaner the air passing through the air cleaner is made to reverse its direction directly above a small pool of oil. Since the dust particles do not change direction as easily as air, many of the dust particles fall into the pool of oil instead of continuing in the air stream. The air then passes through a copper mesh or similar filtering element to remove any remaining dust particles. Silencing pads, usually made of felt, muffle the hissing sound of the rushing air.

In the dry-air cleaner the dust particles are trapped by a filtering element as the air passes through it. Silencing pads, usually made of felt, muffle the hissing sound of the rushing air.

The paper-type filtering element consists of a special paper which has been formed into an accordion-pleated ring and sealed at the top and bottom by plastic rings.

The polyurethane-type filtering element consists of a cellulose element supported by a perforated metal ring. In both types the air particles are trapped in the element as the air passes through.

37-12 THERMOSTATICALLY CONTROLLED AIR CLEANERS

This type of air cleaner is designed to improve carburetor operation and engine warm-up characteristics. It accomplishes this by maintaining the temperature of the air entering the carburetor between a minimum of 85 to 105°. The thermostatically controlled valve selects warmed air from a heat stove attached to the exhaust manifold and/or cooler air from the engine compartment.

The system includes a temperature sensor, a vacuum motor, and control damper (all of which are mounted in the air cleaner), a manifold heat stove, and the necessary vacuum and heat hoses.

When the temperature of the air entering the

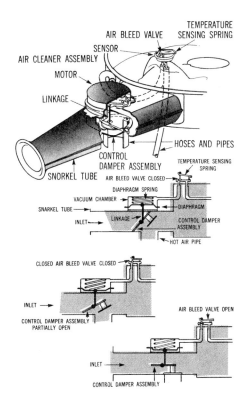

Fig. 37-49   Thermostatically Controlled Air Cleaner

carburetor throat is below 105°, the sensor control admits engine vacuum to the vacuum motor. The motor moves the control damper to the position which permits only the air which has been warmed by passing through the heat stove to enter the carburetor. When the temperature of the air reaches approximately 100°, the sensor control reduces the amount of vacuum reaching the vacuum motor. Then the damper is moved to regulate the flow of under-the-hood air and the warm air from the exhaust-manifold heat stove, maintaining the minimum temperature required. Eventually, the temperature of the under-the-hood air will be high enough so that the sensor will close, stopping the vacuum from reaching the vacuum motor; the damper will be in a position to admit only air from under the hood.

37-13 MANIFOLDS

A manifold is essentially a tube or series of tubes designed to efficiently convey fuel-air mixture from the carburetor to the intake-valve ports or move exhaust gases away from the exhaust-valve ports to the exhaust pipe. Manifolds for passenger cars and commercial vehicles are usually made of cast iron or aluminum.

37-14 MANIFOLD DESIGN

The basic concept of manifold design is to supply each cylinder with the same quality and quantity of fuel-air mixture. Since gasoline is a mixture of hydrocarbons of various weights and vaporizing temperatures, it is difficult to maintain a balance in quality and quantity. Regardless of how well mixed and vaporized the fuel mixture is as it leaves the carburetor, its characteristics will change as it passes through the intake manifold. There are several reasons for this: fuel characteristics, directional changes, and temperature.

Since the fuel is made up of heavy and light particles, the heavier particles will have greater inertia and therefore will resist directional changes. They will tend to continue in a straight line and move past a branch line in the manifold. Condensation of the fuel vapour will take place as the vapour touches the cold metal. As a result, all cylinders may not receive equal and balanced amounts of the mixture. Some cylinders may not receive the required amount of the heavier particles but receive an excess of the lighter particles, or vice versa. Obviously, the cylinders receiving an abundance of the lighter particles and/or the least amount of tetraethyl lead will have a greater tendency to knock.

A variation in the quantity of the fuel and air mixture reaching a cylinder greatly effects the volumetric efficiency of that cylinder and, therefore, overall engine performance. For example: it has been found that cylinders 3 and 4 of a six-cylinder only produce approximately 125 psi combustion pressures, while 1 and 2 cylinders produce approximately 280 psi and 5 and 6 cylinders produce approximately 310 psi. Enriching the fuel-air ratio to improve the combustion pressure in cylinders 3 and 4 results in an extremely over-rich mixture in cylinders 1 and 2, and consequently a reduction in their combustion pressures.

Engineers are constantly striving to improve manifold design. The more direct the path, or the longer and more sweeping the curves leading from the base of the carburetor to the intake-valve ports, the better the balance in volumetric efficiency, and consequently an improvement in engine performance.

To assist in maintaining the necessary balance in quality, heat is applied to assist vaporization. Since heat expands air, the heating of the mixture has a tendency to reduce the volumetric efficiency

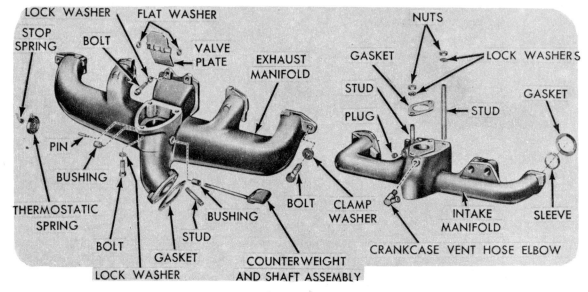

(A) SIX CYLINDER IN-LINE

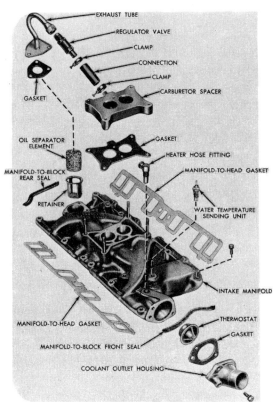

(B) V8

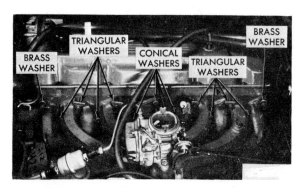

(C) SIX CYLINDER SLANT

(A) and (B) Ford of Canada
(C) Chrysler Canada Limited

Fig. 37-50   Typical Manifolds

manifold depends on the type of engine. On six cylinder in-line engines, the intake manifold is usually placed directly above the exhaust manifold. The centre section of the intake manifold, directly below the carburetor, is usually surrounded by a heat jacket. During the warm-up period the hot exhaust gases are directed through this heat jacket by a thermostatically controlled heat-riser valve.

In V8 engines, when the intake manifold is located between the two cylinder banks and away from the exhaust manifold, a special exhaust passageway, known as the *exhaust crossover*, is usually included as part of the intake manifold. This passageway directs the hot exhaust gases, during the warm-up period, very close to the intake passageways, thus providing the necessary heat.

and therefore the engine power. The heat applied to the intake manifold must be carefully controlled.

37-15 MANIFOLD HEAT

The method of transferring the heat to the intake

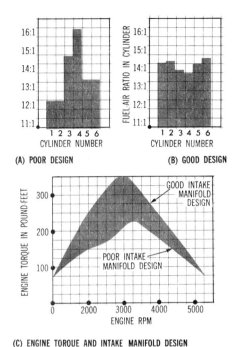

(C) ENGINE TORQUE AND INTAKE MANIFOLD DESIGN

Fig. 37-51   Effects of Good Intake Manifold Design

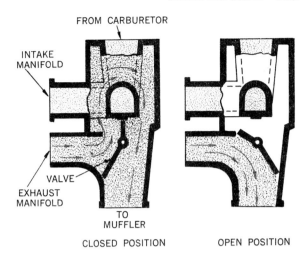

(A) MANIFOLD HEAT CONTROL VALVE FOR 6-CYLINDER ENGINES

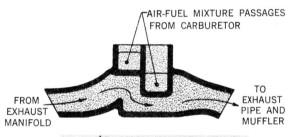

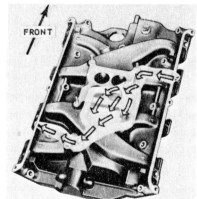

(B) EXHAUST FLOW THROUGH INTAKE MANIFOLD IN V8 ENGINES

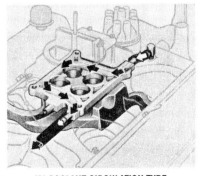

(C) COOLANT CIRCULATION TYPE

Again, the direction of the exhaust gases is controlled by a thermostatically controlled heat-riser valve.

This thermostatically controlled valve is operated by a compound bar or bi-metal spring. It consists of a coil made of two strips of different metals, steel and brass for example, fused together. When heat is applied to the coil, one metal expands faster than the other. If the faster expanding metal, for example brass, is on the outside of the strip the coil will tend to coil up tighter; if the brass is on the inside, the strip will tend to unwind. This principle is a convenient way of converting the heat of the exhaust manifold to mechanical energy. This conversion is used to operate the manifold heat-control valve and some types of carburetor automatic chokes. The bimetal spring mechanically positions the two valves according to the temperature of the exhaust manifold.

When the manifold is cold, the coil positions the heat-riser valve to direct the hot exhaust gases into the heat jacket of a six-cylinder manifold or through the special exhaust passageways in a V8 manifold. As the exhaust manifold temperature increases, the coil gradually changes the position of the heat-riser valve so as to direct the hot exhaust gases away from the heat jacket or special passageways and directly out the exhaust pipe. As a result,

Fig. 37-52   Manifold Heat   Ford of Canada

heat is made available to assist in maintaining the proper balance and quality of fuel and air when the engine is cold, and the heat is removed when the engine is at normal operating temperature so as to not reduce the volumetric efficiency of the engine.

In some engines hot coolant instead of exhaust gases are used to provide intake-manifold heat. Hot coolant from the water-pump bypass outlet is circulated through passageways in the intake manifold. When the engine reaches normal operating temperature and the coolant thermostat is open, no coolant circulates through the water-pump bypass. Therefore, heat is only applied to the intake manifold during the warm-up period.

37-16 MANIFOLD CONSTRUCTION

The number of outlets to the manifold depends upon the number of cylinders, the type of carburetion, and the valve arrangement. Each cylinder may have its individual intake or exhaust port, or some of the parts may serve two cylinders.

Common six cylinder in-line engine manifolds are designed as follows:

(a) single exhaust, two-port intake, two-port exhaust, two-port intake, two-port exhaust, two-port intake and single exhaust.

(b) single exhaust, two-port intake, single exhaust, single intake, two-port exhaust, single intake, single exhaust, two-port intake and single exhaust.

V8 manifolds for two-bore carburetors have the intake manifold designed so that each throat of the carburetor will supply the two end cylinders of one bank and the two centre cylinders of the other.

In a slant six engines, each cylinder has its own long, sweeping, curved manifold arm. The purpose

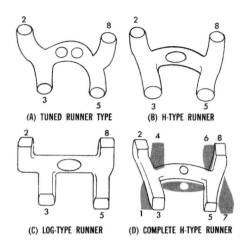

Fig. 37-54   V8-Type Intake Manifolds

of this design is to provide a more equal distribution of the fuel-air mixture into each cylinder.

37-17 EXHAUST SYSTEMS

The exhaust gases come out of the exhaust port with considerable noise. These gases are also poisonous. Therefore, they must be silenced and conveyed away from the passenger compartment to the rear of the vehicle. These functions are accomplished by the exhaust system, which consists of the *exhaust manifold, exhaust pipe, muffler,* and *tailpipe.*

The exhaust manifold, made of cast iron, is bolted over the exhaust ports of the engine and provides heat to the intake manifold, as discussed previously.

The exhaust pipe is the pipe leading from the exhaust manifold to the muffler, which reduces the noise of the exhaust. It does this by slowing down the speed of the escaping gases, and passing these gases through different passages before allowing them to escape through the tailpipe to the rear of the vehicle.

Muffler. The muffler is designed in such a way that the exhaust gases are slowly expanded and cooled before they are discharged into the atmosphere. The muffler must also be designed so that there is a minimum of back pressure developed. Back pressure prevents the free flow of exhaust gases out of the cylinders. The unexpelled exhaust gases dilute the incoming fuel-air mixture and cause a reduction in engine power.

As the speed of the engine increases, back pressure increases proportionally. The power output of the engine decreases very rapidly while fuel

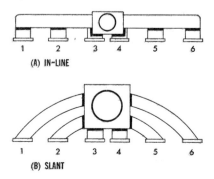

Fig. 37-53   *Typical Six-Cylinder Intake Manifolds*

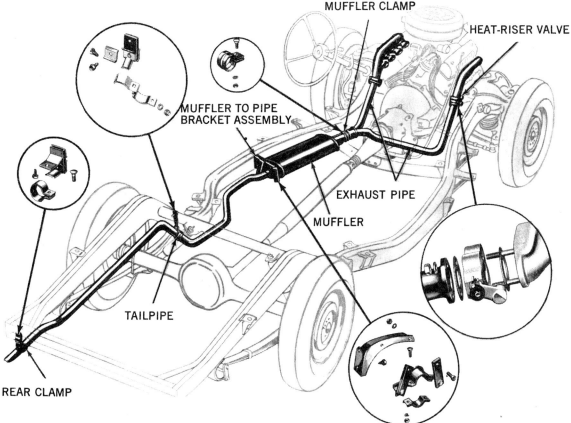

MUFFLER CLAMP

HEAT-RISER VALVE

MUFFLER TO PIPE
BRACKET ASSEMBLY

EXHAUST PIPE

MUFFLER

TAILPIPE

REAR CLAMP

Fig. 37-55   Single Exhaust System

Ford of Canada

consumption increases as back pressure increases.

Some expansion and cooling of the exhaust gases is provided for in the design of the exhaust manifold and exhaust pipe. These units are designed to accommodate between two and four times the quantity of gases that are expelled from a single cylinder.

The muffler may be designed to reverse the flow of the gases or designed with straight-through passageways. The outer shell of the muffler is three to four times the diameter of the exhaust pipe in order to provide the necessary expansion space. The inlet and outlet tubes and the muffler baffles, if used, are perforated to slow down the speed of the gases. Some mufflers are lined with heat-resistant, sound-deadening materials to further deaden the sound.

In order to further reduce the exhaust noise on vehicles equipped with high performance engines and long exhaust pipes, two mufflers in each exhaust line are used. The second, and usually the smaller, unit is referred to as a *resonator*.

Units of the exhaust system corrode very rapidly. The corrosion that takes place on the outside is

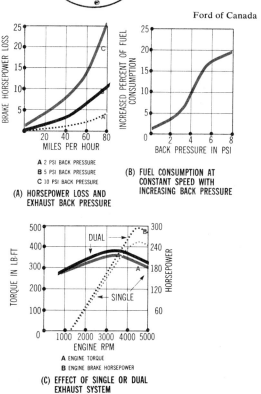

A 2 PSI BACK PRESSURE
B 5 PSI BACK PRESSURE
C 10 PSI BACK PRESSURE

(A) HORSEPOWER LOSS AND
EXHAUST BACK PRESSURE

(B) FUEL CONSUMPTION AT
CONSTANT SPEED WITH
INCREASING BACK PRESSURE

A ENGINE TORQUE
B ENGINE BRAKE HORSEPOWER

(C) EFFECT OF SINGLE OR DUAL
EXHAUST SYSTEM

Fig. 37-56   Exhaust System Design

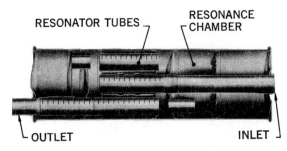

Fig. 37-57   Muffler Cross Section

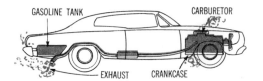

Fig. 37-58   Sources of Motor Vehicle Air Pollution

because of rain, snow, and humidity. The inner corrosion occurs because for every gallon of gasoline burnt, approximately one gallon of water is formed. This water, mixed with the acids formed during combustion, must pass through the system. When the exhaust system is cold, this moisture condenses in the system. The exhaust system is usually operated at a temperature that is at or above the boiling point of water so that the moisture won't condense in the system. The exhaust system on vehicles used for stop-and-start operation will not reach this temperature and will corrode faster than vehicles driven greater distances between stops. To increase exhaust-system life many units are treated with rust-resisting coating, made of special metal alloys, or are coated with ceramic materials.

37-18 AIR POLLUTION EMISSION CONTROL

There are many factors contributing to air pollution. The modern automobile is responsible in part for this pollution. The automobile engine and fuel system release into the atmosphere a variety of gaseous compounds such as: unburnt hydrocarbons, carbon monoxide, nitrogen oxides, and unburnt particulates.

Hydrocarbons (HC) result from unburned fossil fuel, due primarily to incomplete combustion of the fuel-air mixture.

Carbon monoxide (CO) is a toxic gas usually resulting from too rich a fuel-air mixture and incomplete combustion.

Oxides of Nitrogen (No_x) is produced whenever air comprised of oxygen and nitrogen is heated to temperatures which normally exist in the combustion chambers. When combined with hydrocarbons and acted upon by sunlight, they are instrumental in the forming of photochemical smog.

Exhaust particulates consist of solid matter comprised of oxidized lead salts, carbon, rust, dirt and

other matter. Exhaust particulates represent only a small part of automotive air pollution. Hence, most of the research and design effort is concentrated on finding ways to effectively reduce and, hopefully, eventually eliminate the other three causes of exhaust pollution.

The major problem facing the pollution systems design engineers is that while each of these four types of pollutants can effectively be controlled individually by content or volume, the development of a system to reduce all four without sacrificing engine performance or fuel economy is more difficult.

Starting in 1963 a definite program for the control of motor vehicle emissions was begun. The hydrocarbons were required to be reduced by 21% in 1963, 62% by 1968, 83% by 1973, 95% by 1975, and 97% by 1980. Carbon monoxide emissions must be reduced by 54% in 1968, 70% by 1973, 80% by 1975, and 94% by 1980. Nitrogen oxides must be reduced by 54% by 1973, 83% by 1975, and 93% by 1980. The exhaust particulates must be reduced by 67% by 1975 and 90% by 1980.

There are four possible sources of polluting substances in the automobile: the crankcase, carburetor, gasoline tank, and the exhaust system.

To meet the reduction requirements, crankcase ventilating systems were redesigned; alterations to the combustion chambers, to the fuel system, to the exhaust system, and to the ignition system are being made.

37-19 POSITIVE CRANKCASE VENTILATING SYSTEMS

The positive crankcase ventilating system is a closed ventilating system. With this system the crankcase fumes and vapours are burned in the cylinders instead of being deposited in the atmosphere.

To operate the system a vacuum line from the intake manifold is attached to the crankcase ventilating-system outlet breather. A second line is

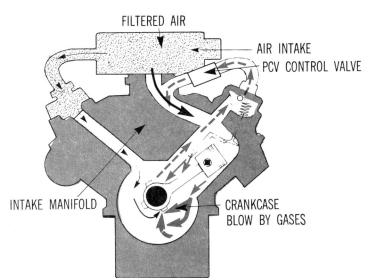

Fig. 37-59 Positive Crankcase Ventilating System

attached between the carburetor air cleaner and the ventilating-system inlet. When the engine is started, vacuum pulls filtered air through the engine and the fumes and vapours are burnt in the cylinders. The residue is exhausted through the exhaust system. A special crankcase ventilating valve called the Positive Crankcase Valve (PCV) is inserted in the vacuum line to maintain proper engine operating vacuum.

37-20 EXHAUST EMISSION SYSTEMS

In the past, exhaust gases contained about 1% of unburned hydrocarbons. Most of the unburned hydrocarbons resulted from unburned fuel along the walls of the combustion chamber. When the flame wall of the burning fuel approaches the relatively cool cylinder walls, a quenching action occurs and the flame wall is snuffed out. This leaves a very small quantity of partially burned fuel-air mixture which contains the unburned hydrocarbons that are discharged into the exhaust system.

In order to reduce the hydrocarbons and carbon monoxide that comes from the exhaust pipe, two different types of systems were designed. One type was designed to reduce or eliminate the formation of the pollutants in the cylinder by raising the combustion efficiency. The other type was designed to destroy or alter the pollutants after they had been formed.

37-21 RAISING COMBUSTION EFFICIENCY

Combustion Chambers—have been redesigned to reduce the area of the cold surfaces that tend to

quench the flame wall before all the fuel-air mixture is burned. By reducing these cold areas, the flame wall burns all the fuel and reduces the hydrocarbons expelled into the exhaust system.

Cooling System—Higher engine operating temperatures increase the temperature of the metal in the combustion chamber to help reduce quenching of the flame wall before all the fuel-air mixture is burnt. Many cooling systems are now equipped with thermostats which open at temperatures up to 200° F.

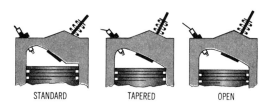

(A) COMBUSTION CHAMBER QUENCH AREAS

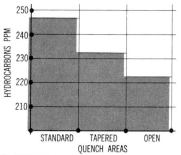

(B) RELATIONSHIP BETWEEN COMBUSTION CHAMBER AND HYDROCARBONS PPM

Fig. 37-60 Combustion Chamber Design and Exhaust Emissions

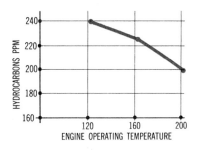

Fig. 37-61   Relationship Between Engine Operating Temperature and Exhaust Emissions

The Carburetor—Changes include higher idling speeds and methods of preventing mechanics from adjusting the idle mixture too rich. To prevent rich idle mixtures some idle screws have their travel restricted by a lock screw; others have the taper of the adjusting needle extended so that part of it remains in the idle port until the screw is completely removed from the throttle body; others have the idle discharge port so reduced in size that the mixture will not be too rich even though the adjusting screw is completely removed.

Climatic-controlled air cleaners are used on some vehicles to increase the temperature of the air entering the engine to a minimum of approximately 100° F. This helps to reduce quenching.

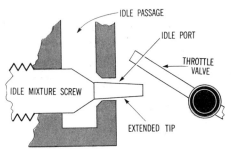

(A) EXTENDED TIP TYPE IDLE MIXTURE ADJUSTING SCREW

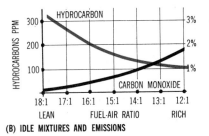

(B) IDLE MIXTURES AND EMISSIONS

Fig. 37-62   Idle Mixtures and Exhaust Emissions

Ignition Timing—has been retarded at idling speeds to improve complete combustion. Mechanical advance curves have been modified to provide greater advance so that the timing is most efficient at normal speed. Special sensing valves have been designed to provide additional spark advance during periods of deceleration so as to allow as much time as possible for complete combustion.

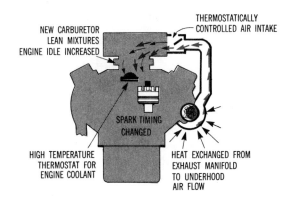

Fig. 37-63   The Effect of Spark Timing on Exhaust Emissions at Idle

37-22 COMMON EMISSION CONTROL SYSTEMS

Various combinations of the previously mentioned factors are used by various motor vehicle manufacturers and classified under various trade names such as: CAS, Cleaner Air System (Chrysler); CCS, Combustion Control System (General Motors); CCC, Climatic Combustion Control (General Motors); IMCO, Improved Combustion Exhaust Emission Control System (Ford); EMS, Engine Mod System (American Motors). A general description of the various systems follows. For specific applications consult the manufacturers' service manual.

Controlled Combustion System. This method of controlling exhaust emissions is designed to reduce pollutants in the exhaust gases by improving the combustion process. The system consists of a combination of design feature changes including a thermostatically controlled air cleaner (see air cleaners 37-11) which thermostatically controls heated air admitted into the carburetor air horn, a specially calibrated carburetor and distributor, along with a modified combustion chamber design.

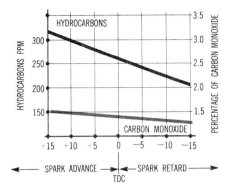

Fig. 37-64   Controlled Combustion System

Air Injector System. This type of system is designed to reduce air pollution by oxidizing (burning) the hydrocarbons and carbon oxides after they leave the combustion chamber.

The air injector system pumps a constant supply of air into each exhaust port near the exhaust valve. The oxygen in this air mixes with the unburned hydrocarbons to form a combustible mixture. The temperature of the mixture is sufficient to ignite it and burn up the balance of the hydrocarbons.

The system consists of an engine driven pump that draws air from the air cleaner, and forces it through a check valve into the air manifolds, then through stainless steel nozzles located in each exhaust port. A check valve prevents the reverse flow of exhaust gases into the pump should the exhaust gas pressure become greater than pump pressure.

To prevent backfire, because of rich mixtures in the exhaust manifold during deceleration, a diverter or antibackfire valve and a check valve are included in the system. These valves are controlled by engine vacuum. When engine vacuum is exceptionally high, such as when on deceleration, these valves are moved to the open position. In the open position the diverter valve directs fresh air into the intake manifold to lean out the mixture, thus reducing the hydrocarbons in the mixture and preventing backfire. The check valve cuts off the supply of air to the exhaust nozzles and redirects it up to the air cleaner. Since no air from the pump is directed into the intake manifold or the exhaust manifold, no explosive mixture is present to produce a backfire.

The system also includes a specially calibrated carburetor and distributor.

Exhaust Gas Recirculation System. This type of system is designed primarily to control the formation of oxides of nitrogen. The system consists of a metering valve located in the exhaust manifold which directs a metered amount of exhaust gases into the intake manifold. The exhaust gases mix with and dilute the fuel-air mixture in the intake manifold thus lowering the combustion temperature and reducing the formation of oxides of nitrogen.

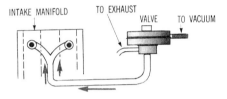

Fig. 37-65   Exhaust Gas Recirculation System

Transmission-Controlled Spark and Speed-Controlled Spark Systems. The transmission-controlled spark system permits the distributor vacuum advance unit to advance the ignition spark during high gear operation only, while the speed-controlled spark system permits vacuum spark advance only above certain driving speeds. Each system is designed to provide the advantage of spark advance timing when it is most needed.

The systems include a solenoid-controlled valve mounted in the carburetor-to-distributor vacuum line. The solenoid valve controls the vacuum to the distributor vacuum advance unit in response to a signal from a linkage-operated switch in the transmission-controlled spark system or a speed-sensitive control switch in the speed-controlled spark system.

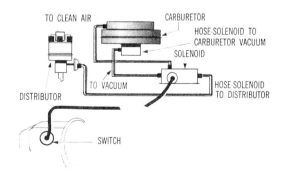

Fig. 37-66   Transmission-Controlled or Speed-Controlled Spark System

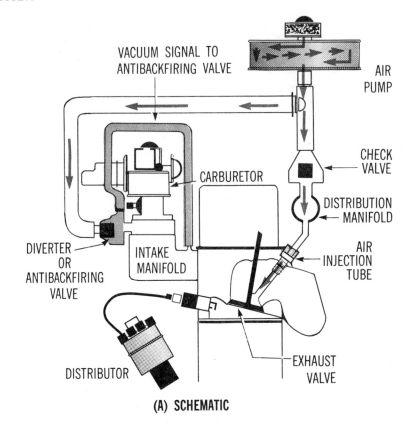

(A) SCHEMATIC

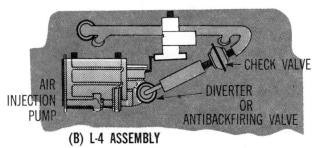

(B) L-4 ASSEMBLY

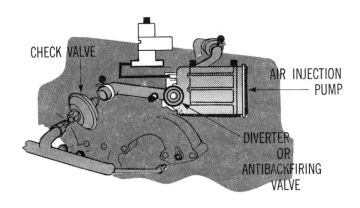

(C) V8 ASSEMBLY

Fig. 37-67   Air Injection System

37-23 DESTROYING POLLUTANTS AFTER THEY HAVE BEEN FORMED

Two methods are used to burn the discharged hydrocarbons after they leave the combustion chamber: the *after-burner*, and the *thermal reactor*.

37-24 AFTER-BURNERS

After-burners may be placed in the exhaust manifold or just ahead of the muffler. There are two types used; the *catalytic* or the *open-flame type*.

Catalytic-type after-burners, sometimes referred to as catalytic mufflers, use a chemical reaction to consume hydrocarbons. The unit is a muffler-like canister installed in the exhaust system, but it does not replace the conventional system muffler. The unit contains chemically coated plastic pellets arranged so that the heat of the exhaust gases activates the pellets, promoting oxidization of the unburnt hydrocarbons. A minimum temperature of 400° F is required to activate the pellets. The resulting chemical action converts the unburnt hydrocarbons into harmless water vapour and carbon dioxide. Any carbon buildup on the pellets is prevented by the flow of exhaust gases agitating the pellets. Unfortunately, the catalytic material is expensive and deteriorates rapidly in reaction with the lead in gasoline.

Fig. 37-68   Catalytic-Type After-Burner

Flame-type after-burners use an open flame to consume the unburned hydrocarbons. The exhaust gases must contain a controlled amount of unburned gases to maintain the flame. Too little unburned gases causes the burner to "flame out," too much unburned gases increases the temperature causing the unit to burn out because of excessive heat.

37-25 THERMAL REACTORS OR EXHAUST MANIFOLD REACTORS

These reactors are, in effect, an extension of the present air-injector reactor system, with exhaust gases from each bank of cylinders fed into its separate reactor. Here, combined with oxygen supplied by air pumps, an after-burner effect takes place to produce more complete combustion. A metering valve in the exhaust gas recirculating system recirculates some gases back into the combustion chambers for improved internal burning of the fuel mixture under certain engine load conditions.

The reactor system allows greater latitude of fuel mixtures than the present air-injector reactor system. With a rich mixture they reduce nitrogen oxides, with a leaner mixture hydrocarbons and carbon monoxide are reduced.

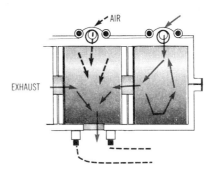

Fig. 37-69   Thermal Reactor

37-26 EVAPORATION LOSSES

Evaporation losses from the gasoline tank and carburetor account for 10 to 15% of the hydrocarbons discharged into the atmosphere. To reduce this amount, gasoline tanks and carburetors are no longer vented to the atmosphere. Two types of systems are used to recapture the hydrocarbons: the *vapour-recovering system* and the *absorption-regenerating system*.

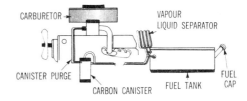

Fig. 37-70   Evaporation Control System

The Vapour-recovering system vents the fuel tank and carburetor to the crankcase ventilating system where the vapours will be drawn into the intake manifold for burning in the combustion chamber.

The system includes a special fuel tank and filler cap, liquid-vapour separator, carbon canister, canister purge hoses, and carburetor modifications.

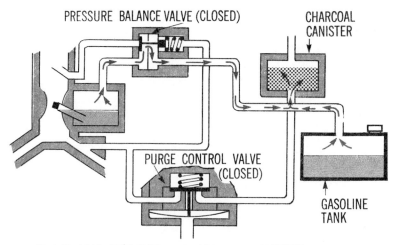

(A) HOT SOAK CONDITION VAPOURS ENTER CANISTER

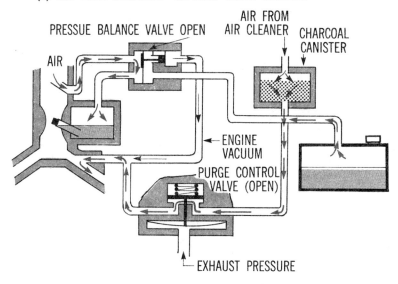

(B) PURGING CONDITION VAPOURS LEAVE CANISTER

Fig. 37-71   Fuel Vapour Absorption Regeneration System Esso Research and Engineering

Fuel vapours which would otherwise escape to the atmosphere are directed into the carbon canister. The carbon absorbs the vapours and stores them. The vapour is removed from the canister during periods of engine operation as manifold vacuum draws the vapours into the engine and burns them.

The Absorption-regeneration system has the vapours from the fuel tank and carburetor held in a canister filled with activated charcoal until they can be fed into the intake manifold for burning. The absorption-regeneration system requires two valves; a pressure balance valve and a purge control valve.

The pressure balance valve opens and closes the carburetor vents. The vents are open to the atmosphere during normal engine operation periods to maintain the proper pressure relationship between the fuel bowl and the venturi. The vents are closed when the engine is stopped. The pressure balance valve then directs the hydrocarbon vapours from the fuel bowl to the charcoal canister.

The purge control valve directs a flow of fresh air through the canister to pick up the hydrocarbons that have been trapped in the charcoal. These vapours are then fed into the intake manifold and burned in the combustion chamber at times when the richer mixture will not affect engine operation.

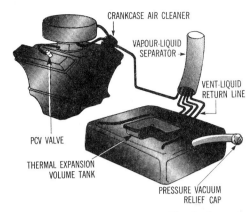

CRANKCASE AIR CLEANER

VAPOUR-LIQUID SEPARATOR

VENT-LIQUID RETURN LINE

PCV VALVE

THERMAL EXPANSION VOLUME TANK

PRESSURE VACUUM RELIEF CAP

Chrysler Canada Ltd.

Fig. 37-72   Vapour Saving System

REVIEW QUESTIONS

1. List three general purposes of the fuel system.
2. Give tnree reasons why the fuel tank must be vented.
3. Why is the end of the fuel pick-up pipe placed about a half inch above the bottom of the fuel tank?
4. How does sediment form in a fuel tank?
5. How are (a) ceramic (b) sintered bronze filters made?
6. What is a vapour lock?
7. How are (a) vapour-return lines (b) vapour separators used to dissipate vapour locks?
8. Why is the possibility of a vapour lock more common in a vehicle equipped with an air-conditioning unit?
9. Explain how a fuel pump regulates the delivery of fuel to the carburetor according to the carburetor's requirements.
10. Explain how the fuel-pump pulsation diaphragm reduces fuel-pump pulsations.
11. State two advantages of electric fuel pumps.
12. When are combination fuel and vacuum pumps used?
13. List three general purposes of a carburetor.
14. What is meant by the term fuel-air ratio?
15. Give three fuel-air ratios and state the driving conditions for each.
16. Define (a) jets (b) air bleeds (c) venturi effect.
17. By means of a sketch, show how the flow of fuel through a given size jet may be increased.
18. Explain the terms (a) atomization (b) evaporation and (c) vaporization.
19. Describe briefly the three main sections of a carburetor.
20. Describe briefly the ways in which carburetors may be classified.

21. What is the advantage of a balanced carburetor?
22. Explain how the speed of an engine is controlled by the throttle valve.
23. How does the float circuit maintain a constant level of fuel in the carburetor bowl?
24. Why will there be no fuel flow from the high-speed nozzle when the engine is at idling speed?
25. How is the vacuum required for idle-circuit operation produced?
26. Give two reasons why air bleeds are required in the idle circuit.
27. How is a leaner idling mixture obtained on exhaust emission-control carburetors?
28. Explain the operation of the low-speed circuit.
29. Explain how the venturi effect controls the amount of fuel delivered from the main discharge nozzle.
30. What is the purpose of the main metering jet?
31. Explain how a metering rod controls the amount of fuel flowing through the main metering jet.
32. Describe two methods of controlling metering-rod operation.
33. Explain how the air-bleed principle is used to change the fuel-air ratios at higher engine speeds.
34. Why is there not sufficient fuel flowing from the idle-low speed and high-speed circuits to supply the engine demands during acceleration periods?
35. How is the accelerator pump discharge prolonged? Give two reasons why this is necessary.
36. Why is a power circuit necessary?
37. What effect would low-engine operating vacuum have on fuel consumption? Why?
38. Why is the fuel discharged from both the idle-low speed circuits and the high-speed circuit during choking?
39. State the purpose of each of the three principles of automatic-choke operation.
40. Why are (a) fast-idle devices (b) unloader devices required when a carburetor is equipped with an automatic choke?
41. Why are carburetor antipercolating devices required?
42. What is the purpose of a dash pot?
43. Why is venturi vacuum used in some cases to control ignition spark advance?
44. Why are idle-stop solenoids used?
45. Make a chart to show the numbers of each carburetor circuit required in a single, two-barrel, and four-barrel carburetor.
46. Describe two methods of controlling the operation of the secondary throttle valves in a four-barrel carburetor.
47. Explain how (a) the air-ram principle (b) supercharging can be used to increase the volumetric efficiency of an engine.

48. Describe briefly the construction and operation of a fuel-injection system when it is used on (a) gasoline- (b) diesel-powered engines.
49. Why does a thermostatically controlled air cleaner improve engine operation during the warm-up period and also reduce exhaust emissions.
50. What effect does a poorly designed manifold have on the fuel-air ratio reaching each cylinder? Why?
51. List three design features of a good intake manifold.
52. Why does the application of heat improve the balance and quality of the fuel-air mixture reaching the cylinders?
53. Explain two methods of applying heat to the intake manifold.
54. From Fig. 37-54, select the best type of intake-manifold design and give reasons for your selection.
55. State the purposes of the exhaust system.
56. Explain why exhaust back pressure decreases engine horsepower and torque.
57. How does a muffler reduce engine-exhaust noise?
58. How can exhaust-system corrosion be reduced?
59. List four sources of automotive air pollution.
60. Name the gaseous compounds given off by the motor vehicle.
61. How does the PCV system reduce hydrocarbon emission?
62. Two general methods of reducing motor vehicle exhaust emissions have been developed. Explain each method.
63. Describe four design changes which have reduced exhaust emissions and explain how each accomplished its purpose.
64. From manufacturers' service manuals, determine what design changes have been used in each of the following emission-control systems (a) CAS cleaner air system (Chrysler) (b) CCS combustion control system (General Motors) (c) IMCO improved combustion exhaust emission-control system (Ford).
65. Explain how the air-injector reactor system reduces exhaust emissions.
66. Explain how the hydrocarbon emissions from evaporation losses are reduced.

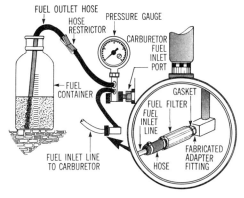

Ford of Canada

Fig. 38-1   Typical Fuel Pump Capacity and Pressure Tests

Chapter 38
FUEL-SYSTEM SERVICE

Fuel-system service is frequently required when the engine shows signs of poor acceleration, poor gas mileage, hard starting, stalling, etc. Of course, other units of the engine can cause similar problems. It is suggested that an engine with the symptoms listed above should be given an engine tune-up before proceeding with major fuel-system work.

When performing fuel-system service, cleanliness is of the utmost importance. A particle of dirt in any unit of the fuel system can cause malfunction of that unit. Gasoline vapours are very explosive; therefore, extreme care in fire prevention is required.

38-1 FUEL-PUMP SERVICE

Fuel-pump problems can be divided into the following categories: low pump pressure, low pump vacuum, low volume of fuel, high pump pressure, leakage, or noise.

The ability of the fuel pump to deliver fuel can be determined by using a pressure-vacuum gauge or a flow-meter type fuel-pump testing gauge. The pressure gauge or the flow meter are connected into the pressure side of the pump, the vacuum gauge is connected to the inlet side of the pump, the engine is cranked, and the readings recorded and compared to specifications.

Low fuel-pump pressure causes fuel starvation and poor engine performance. Low-pump pressure can be caused by worn or damaged pump diaphragm, or worn pump linkage, or weak diaphragm return spring. To overcome the problem the pump must be repaired or replaced.

High-fuel pump pressure causes poor gas mileage and flooding. It raises the level in the fuel bowl by forcing the needle valve off its seat. This condition rarely develops in service; it usually occurs because of faulty assembly of the pump, or the installation of the wrong type of pump.

Low vacuum readings are caused by air leakage into the pump, worn linkage, or damaged diaphragm, or valves. Readings below specifications require that the pump be repaired or replaced.

Frequently fuel-pump readings will be within the specified range but the volume of fuel delivered is too small. Then the fuel lines and filters should be checked for leakage or for being clogged. Either condition reduces the amount of fuel the pump can deliver.

Fuel pump noises are usually caused by worn linkage or weak or broken linkage return springs. Repair or replacement of the pump is necessary.

38-2 CARBURETOR SERVICE

Carburetor service can be divided into three categories: quick checks to determine the availability of fuel and, in general, the condition of the carburetor circuits; minor service adjustments; and carburetor overhaul.

38-3 CARBURETOR QUICK CHECKS

Float level—With the engine idling, observe the high speed discharge jet. If the tip of this jet is wet and fuel is dripping from the jet, then the float level is probably too high or the fuel-pump pressure too great.

Idle and low-speed circuits—A rough or uneven idling condition that cannot be corrected by minor adjustment of the mixture or speed screws indicates problems in the idle or low-speed circuits. Rough operation at the off-idle speeds indicates problems in the low-speed circuit. (Remember both conditions can be caused by other engine problems which can be determined by performing a complete engine tune-up.)

High-speed circuits—with the engine running at a medium speed, slowly cover part of the air horn with a piece of stiff cardboard. If the engine incretases its speed slightly, then the system is working properly. If the speed remains the same or slows down, then the system requires service.

Accelerator circuit—a small amount of fuel should spray from the accelerator discharge jet each time the throttle valve is opened. The discharge should continue for a few seconds after the movement of the throttle has been stopped. Failure of either condition indicates repairs are required.

38-4 MINOR SERVICE ADJUSTMENTS

Adjustments to the carburetor mixture or speed-adjustment screws are often required to compensate for the slight changes that take place because of normal wear of ignition and carburetor components, and changes in fuel chemistry. Provided the changes are minor, usually no further service is required.

38-5 CARBURETOR OVERHAUL

Major carburetor repair work is required when trouble in any circuit is indicated from the results of the quick checks, or when minor adjustments do not bring about the desired results.

Carburetor overhaul includes the complete disassembly of the unit, cleaning in a suitable cleaner, the testing and replacement of worn or defective parts, and the re-assembly and accurate setting of the specified adjustments according to the manufacturers' specifications.

38-6 AUTOMATIC-CHOKE SERVICE

Automatic-choke service can be divided into the following areas: failure of the choke to close; failure of the choke to open in proportion to engine temperature; failure of the choke to respond to engine load conditions during the warm-up period; or failure of the choke to open in the unload position.

Failure of the choke to close—can be caused by a defective thermostatic spring, improper adjustment

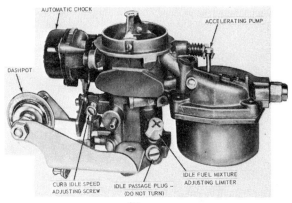

(A)

(B)

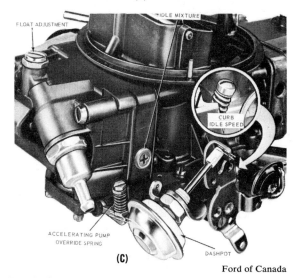

(C)

Ford of Canada

Fig. 38-2   Typical Minor Carburetor Adjustments

of the spring (when the spring is mounted directly on the choke-valve shaft), or connecting link (when the spring is mounted on the manifold), or improper setting of the fast-idle device.

Failure of the choke valve to open—is caused by improper adjustment of the thermostatic spring or linkage, or lack of heat transfer to the spring because of lack of engine vacuum, clogged heat transfer pipe or heat losses in the transfer pipe when the spring is attached directly to the choke shaft.

Failure to respond to engine load conditions during the warm-up period—can be caused by lack of engine vacuum or defective or sticking vacuum piston or linkage.

Failure to open in the unload position—is caused by improper adjustment or defective linkage.

38-7 AIR-CLEANER SERVICE

Air cleaners should be removed periodically, and the filter elements cleaned or replaced as specified.

Paper-Element Filters—may be cleaned by holding a compressed air nozzle about 2″ away from the inside screen and blowing from the centre of the element outward. After cleaning, inspect the element for punctures. Any small puncture necessitates the replacement of the element.

Polyurethane-Type Elements—may be washed in kerosene, gently squeezed to remove the excess cleaner, and inspected for punctures or rips. Replace the element if it is damaged in any way. If the element is satisfactory for use, dip it in engine oil, squeeze out the excess oil, and re-install.

Oil-Bath Type Cleaners—are cleaned by disposing of the used oil, washing the chamber with kerosene, and refilling it to the proper oil level with engine oil. The gauze element is cleaned in kerosene and dried with compressed air.

Thermostatically Controlled Air Cleaner—elements can be serviced according to their type. The cleaner can be checked for proper operation by using a thermometer to determine the operating temperature range and comparing it to the specified operating range. Deviations from the specified operating range can be caused by a defective sensor, defective vacuum motor, or lack of available engine vacuum.

38-8 MANIFOLD SERVICE

After a manifold has been removed, it should be thoroughly cleaned of all traces of carbon from the passageways. It should be carefully inspected for cracks, and the mating surfaces checked for warpage.

A cracked or warped manifold can upset the quality and balance of the fuel-air mixture reaching a cylinder. It can also cause loss of engine vacuum, and thereby cause malfunction of certain carburetor circuits, the distributor vacuum advance mechanism, and the vacuum-operated control valves in an automatic transmission.

It is particularly important that the manifold heat-control valve be free. Heat, rust, and corrosion cause this valve to seize, usually in the position which directs the exhaust gas out the exhaust pipe. Therefore, proper vaporization of the fuel will not take place during the warm-up period. Should the valve seize and constantly direct hot gases around the intake manifold, vapour lock and reduced volumetric efficiency will result, thereby reducing engine power.

To ensure free operation of the manifold heat-control valve, special oils, usually containing graphite, are used. To release a seized valve, apply a liberal amount of penetrating oil, then tap the valve shaft back and forth with a light hammer. The shaft is free when it can be moved easily by the counterweight or the coil.

REVIEW QUESTIONS

1. List four operating conditions which would indicate possible fuel system trouble.
2. Why should an engine tune-up be performed before proceeding with major fuel system work?
3. When fuel system work is being performed, why is cleanliness of the utmost importance?
4. What affect will too high a fuel-pump pressure have on engine operation? Why?
5. List three causes of slight changes in engine operation at the idle.
6. How will low engine vacuum affect (a) automatic choke operation (b) thermostatically controlled air-cleaner operation?
7. What affect will a heat-riser valve that is stuck in the hot position have on engine operation during (a) the warm-up period (b) normal-temperature operation?

UNIT SIX
The Electrical System

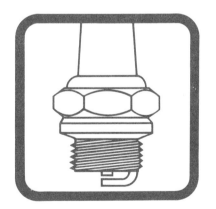

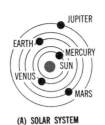

(A) SOLAR SYSTEM

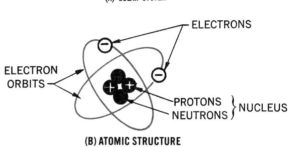

(B) ATOMIC STRUCTURE

Fig. 39-1   The Solar System and Atomic Structure

Chapter 39
ELECTRICAL FUNDAMENTALS

39-1 ELECTRICITY

Men have learned to control electricity, predict its reactions, and harness it in many ways. They have also observed the effects and powers of a force called *magnetism*. In fact, the effects of both forces have been observed for many centuries, and new information in these areas is being discovered and applied every day.

Electricity is known in many forms. One form is *static* electricity. Static may be observed when dry hair is combed, or it may be seen in the form of lightning during a thunderstorm. Another form is *current* electricity, which can be produced by several methods. The two basic sources with which we are concerned are *mechanical* and *chemical*.

Current electricity is the type of electricity used to light our homes and operate our factories and motor vehicles. The electricity used in motor vehicles is produced both mechanically, by the generator or alternator, and chemically, by the battery.

The electrical system of the automobile consists of the *battery* and the *ignition, starting, charging, lighting,* and *accessory circuits.*

39-2 THE ELECTRON THEORY

In spite of the fact that people have experimented with and controlled electricity for many years, no one can explain just what electricity is. Many different theories have been advanced as to the nature of electricity. Early automotive electricians adhered to what is known as the *current flow theory*, which assumed that electric current flowed from the positive terminal to the negative terminal of the source.

Today, the *electron theory* is most widely accepted. By this theory it is assumed that the current flows from the negative to the positive terminal of the source.

The electron theory is based on the concept that all matter may be divided into extremely small particles called *atoms*. An atom is not a solid particle but consists of a miniature "solar system."

The centre of each atom is called its *nucleus*. A nucleus may consist of one or more particles that have positive electrical charges. These particles are called *protons. In addition* to protons, the nucleus also contain particles which have no electrical charge. These are called *neutrons*.

Revolving around the nucleus, in much the same manner as the earth revolves around the sun, are much lighter particles of matter that carry a negative electrical charge. These are *electrons*.

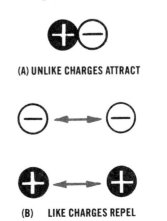

(A) UNLIKE CHARGES ATTRACT

(B)   LIKE CHARGES REPEL

Fig. 39-2   Law of Charges

401

The word charge implies a potential force. Since like charges repel and unlike charges attract, in an atom the positive charge of the proton attracts the negative charge of the electron. Because the positive charge of the proton is equal in magnitude to the negative charge of the electron, the atom is electrically neutral. A properly balanced atom normally has exactly the same number of protons and electrons. Should an atom become deficient in electrons (therefore, have more protons than electrons), it is said to be positively (+) charged and is referred to as a *positive ion*. If the atom acquires additional electrons, it is said to be negatively (−) charged and is referred to as a *negative ion*. The neutrality of an atom can be changed if some means can be used to cause a number of electrons to leave their atoms and congregate in a certain area, leaving behind atoms which are deficient in their normal number of electrons.

39-3 ATOMIC STRUCTURE OF MATERIALS

Atoms of different substances have varying numbers of electrons; hydrogen, for example, has only one electron, whereas carbon has six. Of the approximately 100 natural elements, each having a different atomic structure, the hydrogen atom is the simplest. It has only one proton in its nucleus and one electron in orbit around its nucleus. The uran-

ium atom is one of the most complex, with 92 protons in its nucleus and 92 electrons in orbit around its nucleus. Between these two elements are the remaining natural elements, each having a different number of protons and a matching number of electrons. It is this difference in the number of protons and electrons that causes the approximately 100 elements to be different. Thus, hydrogen, a gas with one proton and one matching electron per atom, is quite different from copper which is a solid containing 29 protons and 29 electrons.

All of the elements can be placed in numerical order according to their atomic number. The atomic number of an element represents the number of protons in the nucleus. Thus, the atomic number of hydrogen is 1, copper is 29, and uranium is 92.

In the complicated atoms, such as copper, iron, or silicon, there are differences in construction which are important in considering electrical properties. The nucleus in most elements is composed of protons and neutrons. This nucleus is surrounded by closely held electrons which never leave the atom. These are said to be "bound" electrons, and where this type of electron predominates in an element or compound, the material is said to be an insulator or nonconductor. Glass and hard rubber are examples of this type of material.

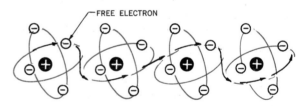

Fig. 39-4 *Movement of Free Electrons*

In some materials, the nucleus is surrounded by another group of electrons which under electrical stress (voltage) can be made to move from one atom to another. Electrons of this type are called "free" electrons. Materials having an abundance of free electrons are called conductors. Silver and copper are examples of this type of material.

In order to understand the electron theory, it is necessary to visualize open spaces in the materials which allow room for the movement of the electrons. According to theory, the ability of electrons to move about is the secret of electric current flow. Visualizing the existence of these open spaces in all materials will help in clearing up the mystery of electric current flow through what appears to be a solid.

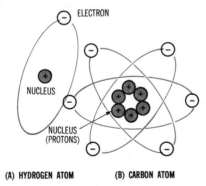

(A) HYDROGEN ATOM   (B) CARBON ATOM

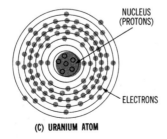

(C) URANIUM ATOM

Fig. 39-3 *Atomic Structure of Materials*

39-4 ATOMIC STRUCTURE OF CONDUCTORS, INSULATORS, SEMICONDUCTORS

It is important to observe that all the electrons do not occupy the same path around the nucleus. Instead, there are a number of paths, rings, or shells which are located at different distances from the nucleus. The hydrogen atom has 1 ring, the copper atom 4 rings, and the uranium atom 7 rings.

It is the number of electrons in the outermost ring that is of special significance, because it is these electrons that determine the electrical characteristics of an element. Therefore, we shall concern ourselves only with the outermost ring, which is often referred to as the *valence ring*.

If the number of electrons in the valence ring is less than 4, the electrons are held to the nucleus rather loosely, and can be made to move from one atom to another atom. This occurs in the element copper, which has only 1 electron in its valence ring. All materials which have fewer than 4 electrons in the valence ring are called *conductors*. The movement of electrons from one atom to another constitutes electric current.

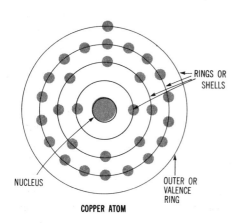

RINGS OR SHELLS

NUCLEUS

OUTER OR VALENCE RING

COPPER ATOM

Fig. 39-5   Atomic Nomenclature

If the number of electrons in the valence ring is greater than 4, the electrons are held to the nucleus rather tightly, and normally cannot be made to leave the atom. Such an element or material is called an *insulator*. In an element, the number of electrons in the valence ring is never greater than 8.

When the valence ring of an element contains just 4 electrons, it is neither a good conductor nor a good insulator. Materials of this type are called *semiconductors*.

39-5 METALLIC CONDUCTORS

In the uncharged state, each atom is neutralized with equal positive and negative charges, and the continuous electron movement is concentrated about each individual nucleus. With some disturbing force, such as an excess of electrons, in any part of a circuit, there is a drift of electrons from one atom to another. This drift is called a *flow of current*, and this is the basis of the electron theory of electricity. When an atom loses an electron it will do the necessary amount of work to pull another electron from the next atom, so as to keep in balance. The ability of atoms to do this is the secret of electric power.

In materials such as copper, the electrons of the valence ring of one atom may gain enough energy to go into orbit in the valence ring of an adjacent atom. If an external force, such as a battery, is connected to a piece of copper wire, some electrons will "drift" from one atom to another. Because electrons each carry a negative charge, they repel each other. Thus, when one electron is repelled from the negative terminal of the battery, it in turn repels another electron, and so on throughout the wire. This movement of electrons constitutes an electric current. The greater the number of electrons flowing, the larger is the current flow. It is necessary to have 6,280,000,000,000,000,000 electrons passing a given point in one second to have one ampere of electric current.

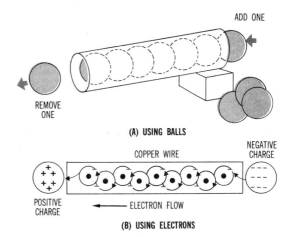

ADD ONE

REMOVE ONE

(A) USING BALLS

COPPER WIRE

NEGATIVE CHARGE

POSITIVE CHARGE

ELECTRON FLOW

(B) USING ELECTRONS

Fig. 39-6   Free Electron Drift in a Conductor

39-6 NONMETALLIC CONDUCTORS

Metals are not the only materials which will function as electrical conductors, nor are free electrons the only possible current carriers. Liquids and gases can also be conductors.

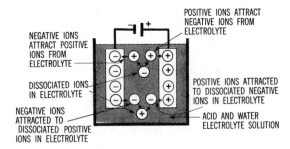

Fig. 39-7   *Current Flow in a Nonmetallic Conductor*

An atom that has either lost or gained electrons does not have the same chemical properties as the neutral atom, and is called an *ion*. When an atom loses an electron, the positive charge of its nucleus predominates, thus forming a positive ion. When an atom gains an electron it is said to become a negative ion. The attraction between the unlike charges of the new atoms binds them together in what is called *ionic bonding*.

When ionic compounds such as acids, bases, and salts are dissolved in water, the ions tend to dissociate, that is, to roam around independently in the solution. A current will pass through the solution because the positive ions tend to be attracted to one terminal and the negative ions to the other. The positive and negative ions are flowing simultaneously in opposite directions through the solution.

There are no free electrons or ions in a vacuum; consequently no current will flow. However, if an ionic-bound gas or vapour is present, a similar reaction as was discussed in reference to liquids takes place, resulting in a current flow.

39-7 SEMICONDUCTORS

Two elements having 4 valance-ring electrons which are widely used in semiconductors are silicon and germanium. If these materials were used in the pure state, they would be relatively inactive, allowing electron flow only upon the application of heat or extremely high voltages. However, inactive semiconductors can be made partially conductive by adding minute quantities of certain impurities. The resultant mixture is said to be "doped." The new material is no longer a very good insulator, and it possesses some unusual electrical properties.

Formation Of "N"-Type Semiconductor Material. When materials such as antimony, arsenic, or phosphorus are added to a semiconductor material in the approximate proportion of 1 part of impurity to

1,000,000 parts of pure semiconductor, the conductivity of the semiconductor is increased 10 times or more.

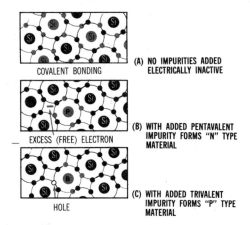

Fig. 39-8   *The Effect of Adding Impurities to Semiconductor Materials*

When the added material contains 5 electrons in its outer ring instead of the 4 electrons found in the pure semiconductor the added material is known as *pentavalent* material. When added, the impurity will find its way into the lattice structure of the normal material as shown in Fig. 39-8.

When the impurity antimony is added to pure germanium or when the impurity phosphorus is added to pure silicon, 4 of the 5 electrons in the outer ring of the antimony or phosphorus will replace the 4 electrons in the outer ring of the germanium or silicon, leaving an unbonded electron which is not part of the normal lattice arrangement. This unbonded electron is much like the free electron in a conductor. This unbonded electron it attracted to its proton in the nucleus of the atom but is not held too tightly to it. With these unbonded free electrons scattered throughout the germanium or silicon there is now a supply of free electrons in the material. For this reason, this type of material is classified as "N" or negative-type material.

Formation Of "P"-Type Semiconductor Material. When materials such as boron, indium, or aluminum (known as *trivalent* materials because they have only 3 electrons in their outer ring), are added to a semiconductor, the lattice would appear as shown in Fig. 39-9.

When a trivalent atom becomes part of the semiconductor lattice structure, an incomplete bond occurs. There is a natural tendency for an incomplete bond to attract an electron. Thus, the in-

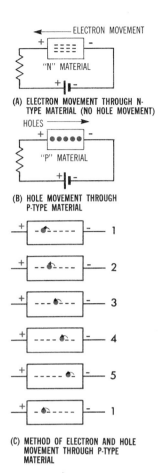

Fig. 39-9 *Semiconductors and Electron Flow*

complete bond, or "hole," acts like a positive charge and is only found in P-type semiconductor material. Since there are no free electrons in P-type material, the hole may capture an electron only by tearing it away from an adjacent covalent bond, thus breaking that bond and creating another hole. The original hole is now filled because a complete bond is formed. The new hole, of course, also acts like a positive charge and attracts electrons, so that we say the hole, or positive current-carrier, has moved. Material in which the current-carriers are holes is called P-type material.

Characteristics Of N- and P-Type Materials. When a battery is connected to a single block of N-type material, the positive side of the battery would attract all of the free electrons present. This would cause a steady flow of electrons through the N-type material from the negative to the positive of the battery.

If the battery were connected to a single block of P-type material, the positive terminal of the battery would attract the electrons out of the near side of the germanium block and at the same time leave vacant holes at this point. As electrons move into the holes, new holes would be formed. In this way, holes move in a continuous stream in the opposite direction to the electrons. The holes move from positive to negative.

39-8 DIODES

N-type and P-type materials are rarely used by themselves. They are usually placed either in pairs to form solid-state diodes, or three or four elements may be arranged end-to-end to form a transistor.

When the PN junction is formed, an electrical action takes place at the contact surfaces of the two materials. At the junction surfaces of the P-type and N-type materials, the unbonded electrons in the N-type material tend to spill over or diffuse into the P-type material near the junction. Since these electrons have left the N-type material, they leave a positive charge in this area. The result of this diffusion of electrons is that a definite electromotive force (emf) is set up internally at the junction. This emf, or voltage, tends to offset any further diffusion of the electrons. When an external voltage, greater than the junction voltage, is applied in the right direction, it can overcome the junction

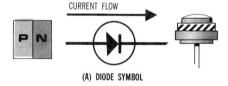

(A) DIODE SYMBOL

ELEMENT	ATOMIC NUMBER	NUMBER OF PROTONS	NUMBER OF ELECTRONS	VALENCE RING ELECTRONS
BORON (B)	5	5	5	3
SILICON (SI)	14	14	14	4
PHOSPHORUS (P)	15	15	15	5

(B) MATERIALS

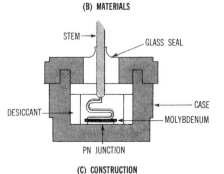

(C) CONSTRUCTION

Fig. 39-10 *Diode Symbols, Material and Construction*

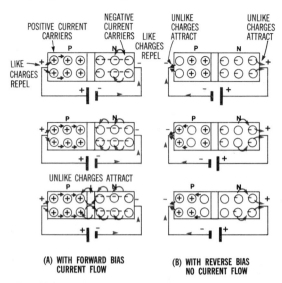

(A) WITH FORWARD BIAS
CURRENT FLOW

(B) WITH REVERSE BIAS
NO CURRENT FLOW

Fig. 39-11   Effect of Current-Carriers in a Diode

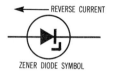

Fig. 39-12   Zener Diode Symbol

voltage and cause the free electrons to flow from the N-type material to the P-type material and the positive carriers to flow in the opposite direction. Therefore, current flows through the entire circuit.

If a reverse voltage is applied, the negative battery voltage would be applied to the P-type material, and the battery's electrons will attract the positive current carriers or holes in the P-type material, while the positive voltage will attract the negative carriers of the N-type material, thereby stabilizing the material. With the material stabilized there is no movement of electrons through the junction; therefore, no current flows through the circuit.

To summarize the operating principles of a diode it can be said that:

1. The diode will allow current to flow when the voltage across the diode causes the electrons and holes to congregate at the junction surfaces. This is called *forward bias.*

2. The diode will not allow current to flow if the voltage across the diode causes the junction area to be void of electrons and holes. This is called *reverse bias.*

A diode, therefore, can control the direction of dc current flow or convert ac current to dc current.

39-9 ZENER DIODE

A zener diode is a specially designed type of diode that will allow current to pass in one way only until a specific voltage is reached. Once this voltage is

reached, the zener diode will then pass current under reverse-bias conditions.

Zener diodes are used to protect a transistor against excessive voltage. Before the transistor voltage reaches a dangerous level, a zener diode will break down and shunt current around the transistor. This is because of the unique operating characteristics of the zener diode. This diode will not conduct current in the reverse direction below a certain predetermined value of reverse-bias voltage. For example, it may not conduct current if the reverse-bias voltage is less than 9 volts, but when the reverse-bias voltage is 9 volts or more the diode will conduct reverse current.

39-10 JUNCTION TRANSISTORS

A three-section solid-state junction transistor consists of either two blocks of N-type material separated by a block of P-type material called an NPN transistor, or two blocks of P-type material separated by a block of N-type material called a PNP transistor. The PNP-type is the most commonly used in automotive electrical systems.

When a three-section transistor is formed, the material at one end is called the *emitter,* the centre section is the *base,* and the other end section is known as the *collector.* The type of material in each section depends upon the type of transistor, NPN or PNP. The most commonly used elements in automotive-type transistors are the P-type material made of germanium doped with indium and the N-type material made of germanium doped with antimony.

Transistors are constructed with a base of exceedingly thin material, measuring only a fraction of a mil in thickness. A metallic ring is attached to the base at its outer circumference, and a circuit connection is made to this ring. This type of construction results in a shorter distance between the emitter and collector than there is between the emitter and the base ring. This accounts for the unusual operating characteristics of a transistor.

When a current from a single source is connected to a transistor, the current will flow through the

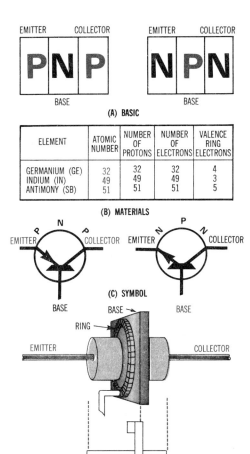

(A) BASIC

ELEMENT	ATOMIC NUMBER	NUMBER OF PROTONS	NUMBER OF ELECTRONS	VALENCE RING ELECTRONS
GERMANIUM (GE)	32	32	32	4
INDIUM (IN)	49	49	49	3
ANTIMONY (SB)	51	51	51	5

(B) MATERIALS

(C) SYMBOL

(D) CONSTRUCTION

Fig. 39-13   Transistors

emitter-base circuit and the emitter-collector circuit simultaneously. The base current will only be a fraction of the collector current in magnitude; yet, the collector current cannot exist without the base current. For example: with the base circuit closed, the collector circuit open, and a 5-ampere current flowing, all the current will pass through the first section of P material and out through the base. The unit would be acting as a simple diode. To explain further—the movement of free electrons from atom to atom constitutes a current flow. Under this definition the electrons in the circuit flow from the negative terminal of the battery, through the base emitter circuit of the transistor, to the positive terminal of the battery. However, in order to understand the operation of a PNP transistor, it is necessary to accept the hole movement as a theory of

current flow and to apply this theory to the PNP transistor.

This theory states that the current flow in a transistor is considered to be a movement of holes through the P material to the N material. The movement of the holes can be considered as current flow.

When the collector circuit is closed, the total current flow through the transistor remains at 5 amperes, but 4.8 amperes will leave the transistor through the collector circuit, and only .2 ampere through the base circuit.

The reason for the difference in current flow in each circuit is as follows: because of the physical arrangement of the emitter, base ring, and collector, with the emitter-collector being closer together than the emitter-base ring, most of the holes that are injected into the base by the emitter travel on into the collector because of their velocity. Also the negative potential at the collector attracts the posiive holes from the base into the collector.

Should the emitter-base circuit be open, no appreciable current will flow; because with the base circuit open, there are no holes being injected into the base from the emitter. Thus, there are no holes in the base which can be attracted by the negative battery potential into the collector. The negative battery potential at the collector attracts the holes in the collector away from the base-collector junction area, thus increasing the resistance in that area and thereby preventing current flow between the emitter and the collector.

An NPN transistor operates in the same manner as a PNP unit, with current flow consisting of a movement of electrons from the emitter to the base and collector.

To operate a transistor, an interruption in the very small current flow in the base circuit results in a corresponding interruption in the very large current flow in the collector circuit. It is said that the base current "triggers" the collector current. A transistor, therefore, can act as a relay with no moving parts.

39-11 DIODE AND TRANSISTOR SYMBOLS

The symbol for a diode is shown, with conventional current flow allowed only in the direction of the arrow. See Fig. 39-12.

The most common symbol for transistors used in circuits is shown in Fig. 39-13. The line with the arrow is the emitter, the heavy line is the base, and the line without an arrowhead is the collector. The arrow points in the direction of conventional current flow.

The zener diode symbol is shown in Fig. 39-12. The heavy arrow indicates the direction of forward current flow; the light arrow indicates the direction of reverse current flow.

39-12 ELECTRICAL TERMS

Amperage—electric current, or electron flow, is measured in amperes of electric current or amperes. An ampere is equal to 6,280,000,000,000,000,000 electrons passing a given point in one second. When only a few electrons flow in an electric circuit, the amperage, or amperes of current, is low. The greater the number of electrons flowing, the greater the amperage and current flow.

A standard international ampere is the amount of current required to deposit 0.001118 grams of silver per second when a current is passed through a standard solution of silver nitrate.

Coulomb—a coulomb is equal to a current flow of one ampere for one second. The total number of electrons in motion when a single ampere flows for one second (one coulomb) is approximately 6,280,000,000,000,000,000. This is read as six quintillion, two hundred and eighty quadrillion, or is frequently expressed as 6.28×10^{18}.

Voltage—voltage is the unit of electrical pressure. The greater the concentration of electrons at any given point, the higher the repulsive force, or pressure, between the electrons; the higher the pressure, the greater the voltage. As the voltage increases, more electrons will flow. A high voltage means a high electrical pressure or a massing of many electrons. This is frequently referred to as *electromotive force* (emf).

Watt and Power—the ability of an electrical device to do work is frequently expressed in the term *wattage*. A watt is equal to the amperage times the voltage required by the electrical appliance. A current of 5 amperes at 12 volts amounts to 60 watts. Wattage can be converted to horsepower by dividing the wattage by 746, or one horsepower equals 746 watts.

Kilo—the prefix kilo means one thousand. For example: A kilowatt is one thousand watts, a kiloampere is one thousand amperes, and a kilovolt is one thousand volts.

Milli—the prefix milli when used in milliamperes or milliamps, millivolts, or milliwatts means that the number is divided by one thousand. Thus a milliamp is .001 amperes.

Micro—means the basic value has been divided by one million. For example, 0.25 microfarad (mf) means 0.25 farad divided by one million or 0.00000025 farad.

Mega or Meg—means that the basic value has been multiplied by one million. For example, two megohms are equal to 2,000,000 ohms or two megacycles are equal to 2,000,000 cycles.

Capacity (The Farad)—the ability of a conductor to accommodate excess free electrons is referred to as its capacity. When no electric current is flowing in a conductor, the free electrons repel each other and arrange themselves as far apart as possible. When a voltage is applied to the conductor, the free electrons are pushed to one end of the conductor. The greater the voltage applied, the closer together the free electrons become, and the greater the number of electrons that can occupy a given space. When the voltage is removed, the electrons again repel each other and try to get as far apart as possible.

The capacity of a material is measured in *farads*. One farad is defined as that capacity which will contain one coulomb (one ampere flowing for one second or approximately 6.28×10^{18} electrons) and show a difference of potential of one volt. Since a farad is a large unit of measurement, microfarads (one millionth of a farad) or fractions of microfarads are most commonly used.

The automotive ignition condenser has a capacity of between 0.20 to 0.35 microfarads.

Ohm—The ohm is the basic unit of electrical resistance. Resistance is the opposition of an electric circuit to the flow of current through that circuit. As the free electrons move through a conductor, they acquire velocity and potential energy. When the free electron collides with one of the metal atoms in the conductor, some of its kinetic energy is converted to heat. The kinetic energy gained by the electron is transferred to the atom with which it collided in the form of heat energy. These many collisions, which constitute an opposition to the flow of the current, produce resistance and its accompanying heat.

Resistance—When current flows through a conductor, the electron drift is relatively slow because of the fact that the free electrons which constitute the current are constantly colliding with the atoms. This opposition to the current flow is called *resistance*. The collisions of the moving electrons create heat. The unit of resistance is called an *ohm* and may be defined as the amount of resistance which will limit the current rate to 1 ampere when 1 volt of pressure is applied.

For example: a 1,000′ length of #10 wire (diameter approximately 0.1″) has a resistance of 1 ohm. A 2,000′ length of a similar wire has a resistance of 2 ohms. Increasing the size of the wire decreases the resistance. A #4 wire (approximate diameter 0.2″ or 4 times the cross-sectional area) reduces the resistance to 0.25 ohms per 1,000′. This is because there are 4 times as many atoms for the electrons to drift between, as well as 4 times as many free electrons in motion. Thus with the same emf, 4 times as much current will flow through a #4 wire then through a #10 wire.

There are four basic factors that affect resistance:

1. Material (some materials offer more resistance than others)
2. Cross-sectional Area (the larger the cross-sectional area, the lower the resistance)
3. Length Of Conductor (the longer the conductor, the greater the resistance)
4. Temperature (the higher the temperature of many materials, the greater the resistance)

39-13 DIRECT AND ALTERNATING CURRENT

Two types of current can be produced: *alternating current* (ac) and *direct current* (dc).

In an alternating current the electrons flow first in one direction, then in the opposite direction. This is called a cycle. A 60-cycle ac current means that the current goes through a complete cycle of changing direction 60 times a second.

In a direct current the electrons flow in one direction only. It is believed that in the automobile battery the electrons flow from the negative post of the battery through the circuit and return to the battery through the positive post.

39-14 AUTOMOTIVE ELECTRICAL SYMBOLS

Figure 39-15 shows the special symbols which the mechanic should be able to recognize in order to do work on automotive electric circuits.

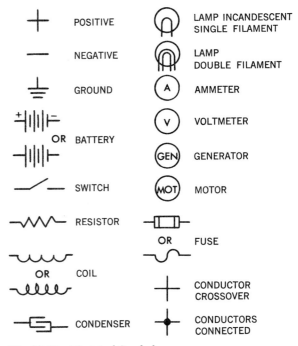

Fig. 39-15   Electrical Symbols

39-15 ELECTRIC CIRCUITS

A circuit is an endless path formed by a conductor from a source of electrical supply to the control, through the load, and back to the source. There are various types of electric circuits used in the modern automobile, among them the series-parallel, and ground-return circuits.

Series Circuit. A series circuit is one in which there is only one path through which the current can flow. Should this path be broken, all of the equipment would cease to function.

Parallel Circuit. A parallel circuit consists of two or more paths through which the current may flow. A breakage in any one path would not interfere with the operation of the remainder of the units in the circuit.

Series-Parallel Circuit. A series-parallel circuit is a circuit in which some of the devices are connected in series while other devices are connected in parallel. For example: the headlights are connected in parallel so that should one burn out the other

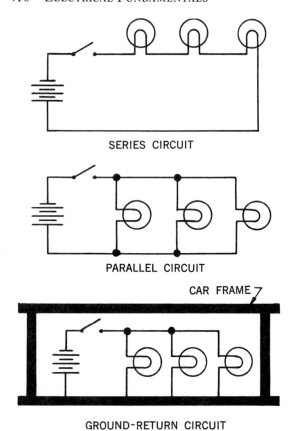

SERIES CIRCUIT

PARALLEL CIRCUIT

CAR FRAME

GROUND-RETURN CIRCUIT

Fig. 39-16   Electric Circuits

will still operate; but they are connected in series to the battery through the switch. Opening or closing the switch operates both lamps.

Ground-Return Circuit. A ground-return circuit uses the metal parts of the automobile as a common conductor for the return of the current to the source of supply. As a result, only one-half as much insulated electrical wire is required.

Short Circuit. A short circuit occurs when the current takes a path of very low resistance back to the source, thereby bypassing the load. For example: faulty insulation that allows a bare wire to touch ground, or faulty insulation between the turns of a coil that reduces the number of turns used in the coil.

Unintentional Ground. The current goes to ground after passing through the load but without following the complete original path.

Open Circuit. There is a break in the complete circuit.

Closed Circuit. A closed circuit is a complete path from source, to control, to load, and back to the source.

39-16 OHM'S LAW

From electrical experiments it has been found that a pressure of 1 volt is required to cause a current of 1 ampere to flow through 1 ohm of resistance. In order for a current to flow in an electric circuit, the voltage or pressure must overcome the resistance in the circuit. It can be summed up by a statement known as Ohm's Law, which is: voltage is equal to amperage times resistance.

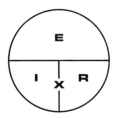

Fig. 39-17   Ohm's Law Wheel

The law can be stated as the mathematical formula:

$$E = I \times R$$
or
$$R = \frac{E}{I}$$
or
$$I = \frac{E}{R}$$

where E = voltage
$\quad\;\; I$ = amperage
$\quad\;\; R$ = ohms

For example: if a voltage of 1 volt was applied to a conductor having a resistance of 1 ohm, then a current of 1 amp would pass through the conductor. Increase the voltage to 2 volts, then a 2-amp current would flow through the conductor. Increase the resistance to 2 ohms, then only ½ an amp would flow through with 1 volt pressure.

Problem 1.
An electric circuit has a resistance of 1 ohm. How much current will flow in the circuit when it is connected to a 12-volt battery?

Solution: Formula $= I = \dfrac{E}{R} = \dfrac{12}{1} = 12$ amps

Problem 2.

An electric circuit has a resistance of 2 ohms. How much voltage is required to cause 6 amps to flow through the circuit?

Solution: Formula $= E = I \times R = 2 \times 6$
$= 12$ volts

Problem 3.

In an electric circuit a voltage of 12 volts causes a current flow of 7.5 amperes. What is the resistance in the circuit?

Solution: Formula $= R = \dfrac{E}{I} = \dfrac{12}{7.5} = 1.6$ ohms

39-17 KIRCHHOFF'S VOLTAGE LAW

This law states that in any complete electric circuit, the algebraic sum of the electromotive forces must equal the algebraic sum of the voltage drops. Therefore, in a series circuit the sum of all the voltage drops across individual resistances must equal the applied electromotive force.

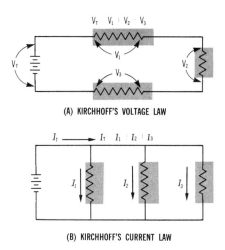

(A) KIRCHHOFF'S VOLTAGE LAW

(B) KIRCHHOFF'S CURRENT LAW

Fig. 39-18 Kirchhoff's Laws

39-18 KIRCHHOFF'S CURRENT LAW

This law states that at any junction point in an electric circuit the algebraic sum of the currents entering the point must equal the algebraic sum of the currents leaving the point. Therefore in a simple parallel circuit the total current is the sum of all the branch currents.

39-19 RESISTANCE IN SERIES AND PARALLEL CIRCUITS

The resistance of a series circuit will be the sum of the resistors in the circuit. The formula used to calculate resistance in series is:

$$R_{\text{Total}} = R_1 + R_2 + R_3 + \text{etc}$$

R_1, R_2, R_3 represent the different resistances.

From Fig. 39-19 the resistance in the circuit equals

$$R_{\text{T}} = 2 + 5 + 4 + 1 \text{ ohm}$$
$$R_{\text{T}} = 12 \text{ ohms}$$

In a parallel circuit there is more than one path for the current to follow; therefore, the resistors are in parallel. Since some current can flow through each path, the resistance for each path affects only that path. The formula used to calculate resistances in parallel is:

$$R_{\text{Total}} = \dfrac{1}{R_1} + \dfrac{1}{R_2} + \dfrac{1}{R_3} + \text{ etc.}$$

R_1, R_2, R_3 represent the different resistances. R_{T} is equal to the total effective resistance.

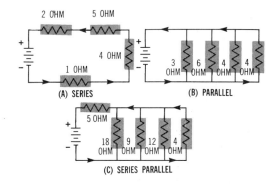

(A) SERIES

(B) PARALLEL

(C) SERIES PARALLEL

Fig. 39-19 Ohm's Law Problems

From Fig. 39-19B the resistance in the circuit equals

$$\dfrac{1}{R_{\text{T}}} = \dfrac{1}{3} + \dfrac{1}{6} + \dfrac{1}{4} + \dfrac{1}{4}$$
$$\dfrac{1}{R_{\text{T}}} = \dfrac{4 + 2 + 3 + 3}{12}$$
$$\dfrac{1}{R_{\text{T}}} = \dfrac{12}{12}$$
$$R_{\text{T}} = 1 \text{ ohm}$$

In a series-parallel circuit the resistance of the parallel portion of the circuit plus the resistance of the series portion of the circuit equals the total resistance of the circuit.

From Fig. 39-19 the resistance equals

(a) R_1, R_2, R_3, and R_4 are resistances in parallel

$$\frac{1}{R_T} = \frac{1}{18} + \frac{1}{9} + \frac{1}{12} + \frac{1}{4}$$

$$\frac{1}{R_T} = \frac{2 + 4 + 3 + 9}{36}$$

$$\frac{1}{R_T} = \frac{18}{36}$$

$$R_T = \frac{36}{18} = 2 \text{ ohms}$$

(b) The total resistance of the circuit is the sum of the effective parallel resistance and R_5.

∴ $R_T = 2$ ohms $+ 3$ ohms $= 5$ ohms.

39-20 VOLTAGE DROP

Ohm's Law can be applied to an electric circuit as a whole, or it can be applied to any part of the circuit. The amperes in the entire circuit equal the voltage across the entire circuit divided by the resistance of the entire circuit. The amperes in a certain section of a circuit equal the voltage across that part, divided by the resistance of that part.

With current flowing, the voltage difference across a resistor, or a piece of electrical equipment, or over a section of live wire, is called the "voltage drop" and is found by a direct application of Ohm's Law, $E = IR$. The total voltage drop in a circuit is always equal to the potential of the source. Voltage drop, in other words, is voltage. The above rules are the law in the electrical field and must be understood before it is possible to trace troubles in automotive circuits.

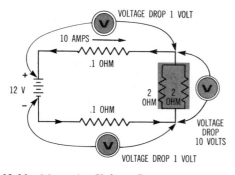

Fig. 39-20   Measuring Voltage Drop

Excessive voltage drop in a headlight circuit results in low voltage at the lamp and consequently dim head lamps. In a charging circuit, excessive voltage drop results in a low charging rate and a discharged battery. Common causes of voltage drop

are: too small a wire, broken wire strands, dirty or loose connections both at the wire ends or in the ground-return circuits, and defective contacts in switches or controls. All of these causes reduce the size of the electron path and therefore reduce the flow of free electrons.

39-21 RESISTANCE HEATING

When an electric current flows through a conductor, the movement of the free electrons creates heat. The greater the movement, the more heat produced. Normally, the heating effect is very small and does no harm. However, if the wire is too small for the amount of current flowing, considerable heating will result. This heat can damage the insulation, even produce a fire. Dirty or loose connections restrict the movement of the free electrons, resulting in excessive heat.

A light bulb uses resistance heat to produce light. When the free electrons flow through the tungsten filament of a light bulb, they produce so much heat that the filament glows brilliantly to produce light.

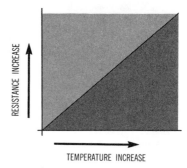

Fig. 39-21   Relationship Between Resistance and Heat

39-22 TEMPERATURE EFFECT
ON RESISTANCE

The higher the temperature of a conductor, the more rapid the movement of the atoms in the material. It is more difficult for the free electrons to move from one orbit to another when the orbits themselves are in rapid motion. Anything that prevents the movement of the free electrons increases the resistance to the flow of an electric current. Thus, temperature changes in or around the conductor affect the resistance of the conductor.

39-23 MAGNETISM

Magnets are of two kinds, natural and artificial. Natural magnets are composed of magnetite, an ore found by the ancients near the town of Magnesia in Asia Minor, which has for iron a particularly strong attractive power called *magnetism*. When a bar of hardened steel is rubbed with a piece of magnetite, it assumes properties of attraction like those of the ore. The steel bar becomes what is termed an *artificial magnet*. When steel or iron, and certain other metals such as nickel and cobalt, are given the power to attract iron, they are said to be *magnetized*.

(A) MAGNETIC EFFECT OF ONE ELECTRON IN ORBIT

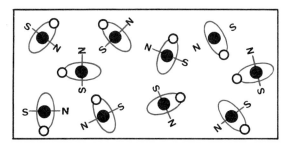

(B) NONMAGNETIZED MATERIAL

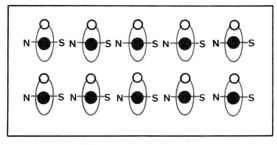

(C) MAGNETIZED MATERIAL

Fig. 39-22   Atoms and Magnetism

Magnetism is an elementary form of energy generated by the motion of electrons. It is believed that the orbiting of the electrons around the nucleus produces the magnetic effect. Each electron thus creates a weak magnetic field. In a piece of unmagnetized matter, the electrons orbit in many directions and each magnetic field created is cancelled out by another. In a piece of magnetized material all of the orbits are arranged in one direction so that instead of the individual magnetic

fields cancelling each other out, they add to each other, creating one strong magnetic field with a north pole at one end and a south pole at the other.

When the orbits are correctly arranged in some types of iron, they remain in that position a long period of time. These are called *permanent magnets*. In other types of iron the orbits will not remain in correct alignment unless some magnetizing force is present. These are called *temporary magnets*.

39-24 PERMANENT MAGNETS

Permanent magnets, if not mistreated, will hold their charges for many years. When they are subjected to sudden jars, or to heat, or stored without first having a piece of iron called a "keeper" placed across the poles, a great deal of magnetic charge may be lost.

Magnetic *permeability* refers to the specific conductivity of a material for a magnetic flux. The magnetic lines of force set up in any given medium, such as air, wrought iron, or steel, by any magnetizing force, vary in density. If a given magnetizing force will set up one line of magnetic force in air under given conditions, it will set up 1,500 lines of force in wrought iron and 1,000 lines of force in steel under the same conditions. These substances are said to differ in their permeability. It is this difference in permeability between air and iron which causes such a loss in strength of a magnet when the keeper is removed.

Materials differ in their behaviour when placed in a magnetic field. Nonmagnetic materials have no effect on the magnitude or direction of the magnetic field. Magnetic materials, such as iron, nickel, cobalt or their alloys, have the property of magnifying or concentrating a magnetic field. Actually magnetic lines of force seem to penetrate all substances and are deflected only by magnetic materials or by another magnetic field. From this we learn that there is no insulator for magnetism or lines of force, but an object can be shielded from magnetic lines of force by using a soft iron to conduct the flux lines away from the object.

Magnetic Lines of Force. A magnetic field is the area around a magnet in which magnetism can be detected, and is made up of magnetic lines of force. These lines of force flow through the magnetic material more readily than they do through air.

Magnetic lines of force converge at the poles of a magnet, where a magnetic field is strongest.

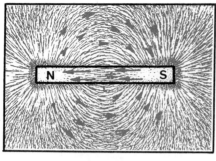

(A) BAR TYPE

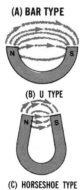

(B) U TYPE

(C) HORSESHOE TYPE

Fig. 39-23 Magnetic Field of Permanent Magnets

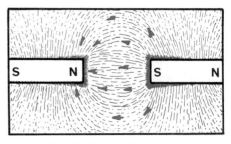

(A) FIELD BETWEEN UNLIKE POLES

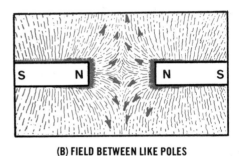

(B) FIELD BETWEEN LIKE POLES

Fig. 39-24 Magnetic Fields Between the Poles of Two Magnets

When a magnet is placed in a box of iron filings, it will attract the small particles of iron. When removed from the box, the iron filings adhere most strongly to the ends of the magnet, where the power of magnetic attraction is the strongest.

The portion of the magnet between the two ends or poles of the magnetized bar is termed the *neutral region* because of the apparent absence of magnetic attraction at that point.

All magnets have both north and south poles; it is impossible to make a magnet with but one pole. If you break a bar magnet into several pieces, you will find that each piece has a north and south pole similar to those of the unbroken magnet. The drawings shown in Fig. 39-23 show the magnetic fields which surround permanent magnets. You will notice that the filings arrange themselves in lines which apparently join the two ends of the horseshoe called the poles.

Magnetism consists of a large number of lines of force which make closed loops as shown in Fig. 39-24. If the keeper is removed, the lines of force must overcome the resistance of the air and hence many of them are lost. Actual tests have shown that the removal of the keeper may cause a loss of as much as 30% of the charge.

When the north pole of a magnet is brought in contact with the south pole of another, the poles attract each other. On the other hand, if two north poles or two south poles are placed together, they will repel each other. In other words, like poles repel, and unlike poles attract one another.

There is a definite relationship between electric current and magnetism: a current passing through a conductor creates a magnetic field around the conductor, and when a conductor is passed through a magnetic field, a flow of electrons is set up in the conductor.

This relationship is the basis of operation for most of the automotive electrical devices such as the starter motor, generator, alternator, and ignition coil.

39-25 ELECTROMAGNETISM

Because there is a relationship between magnetism and electric current, it is possible to produce an electromagnet.

When a current passes through a conductor, there is a small magnetic field set up around the conductor. This magnetic field may be observed by placing the conductor through a piece of cardboard, which is placed in a horizontal position, and sprinkling iron filings on the cardboard around the conductor. When a current passes through the conductor, the iron filings will arrange themselves in a circular pattern around the conductor. The

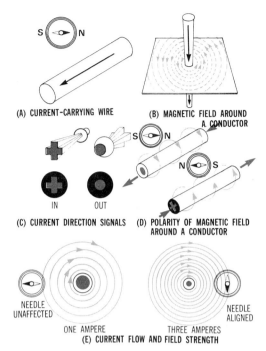

Fig. 39-25   *Magnetic Field and Conductors*
(Electron Theory)

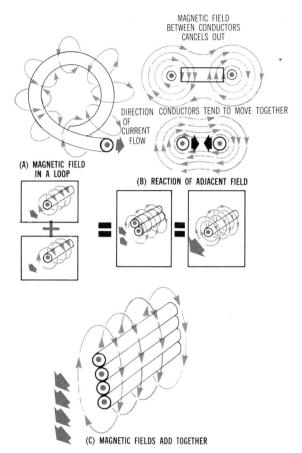

Fig. 39-27   *Electromagnetism Principles*
(Electron Theory)

direction of travel of the magnetic field around the conductor may be determined by the use of a compass or by the left-hand rule for a conductor. This rule states that if the thumb of the left hand points in the direction of current flow, the pointing of the fingers will indicate the direction in which the magnetic field circles the conductor.

Since there is a small magnetic field around every current-carrying conductor, it is only necessary to coil a conductor to unite the magnetic fields of each conductor into a stronger magnetic field. When equal current flows in the same direction through two parallel conductors, each conductor alone

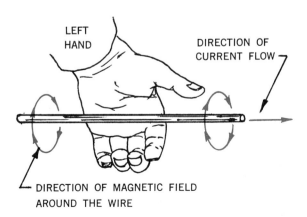

Fig. 39-26   *The Left-Hand Rule for a Conductor*

creates a circular field of force, and the field around each conductor is in the same direction. The lines of force between the two conductors are in opposite direction. The strength of each field being the same, the total magnetic effect between the two conductors is cancelled. The two conductors then act as a single conductor carrying twice the current. With the two conductors combined and acting as a single conductor carrying a current equal to the sum of the two currents, twice the number of lines of force are created as would be produced by either conductor with its original current. The two thereby produce a field pattern which is identical to that obtained with a single conductor carrying twice the current.

When several more current-carrying conductors are placed side by side, the effect as mentioned above with two wires is extended, and the lines of force join and surround all of the conductors. If the same current flow could be maintained in each turn of wire, the strength of the magnetic field would be increased proportionately with each turn of wire. The magnetizing force is therefore in direct proportion to the number of turns of wire as well as to the amount of current flow. The product of amperes-times-turns is thus a means of calculating the magnetizing force created. Thus the total magnetic effect of a coil is proportional to the current flow through it and to the number of turns of wire. Therefore, a common method of expressing magnetic effect is to multiply the current by the number of turns in the coil, producing a product called *ampere-turns*.

The combined field will have a north and south pole. The polarity of the coil may be determined by using a compass or by the left-hand rule for an electromagnet. This rule states that by pointing the fingers of the left hand in the direction of current flow, the thumb will indicate the north pole.

The polarity of an electromagnet can be reversed by reversing the direction of current flow, or by winding the coil either in a clockwise or in a counterclockwise direction.

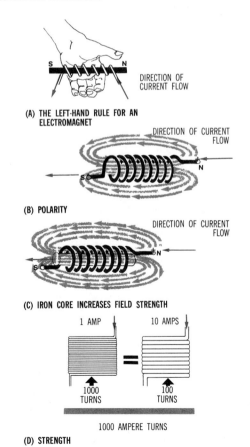

(A) THE LEFT-HAND RULE FOR AN ELECTROMAGNET

(B) POLARITY

(C) IRON CORE INCREASES FIELD STRENGTH

(D) STRENGTH

Fig. 39-28   Electromagnet Polarity and Strength (Electron Theory)

The strength of this field will depend upon the ampere-turns and the type of core on which the coil is wound. Because magnetism acts more easily through magnetic material than through air, winding the coil around a soft iron core concentrates the magnetic field and increases the magnetic strength. As the strength of an electromagnet depends upon the amount of electric current flowing through the coil of wire, and since the electromagnet uses a soft iron core which does not retain magnetism, it is possible to control the strength of the magnetic field by increasing or decreasing the current, or stopping it completely.

Electromagnets to which the current is switched either on or off are used to operate automotive electrical devices such as starter solenoids, horns, and light relays. Electromagnets to which the current is increased or decreased are used to operate the current and voltage units of a voltage regulator or alternator control.

39-26   MAGNETIC INDUCTION

The relationship between electricity and magnetism is also used in another way—to induce a current to flow in a second conductor that is not connected to the first. When a magnetic field is set up, either by a permanent magnet or by an electromagnet, and either an electrical conductor is passed through the field or the field is passed over the conductor, the movement of either induces a voltage in the conductor. When an external circuit is completed, a current will flow.

This induction results because of the tendency of the magnetic lines of force to wrap themselves around the conductor. It has been pointed out that when the current passes through a conductor, a magnetic field is created around the conductor. The reverse is also true; by creating a varying magnetic field around the conductor, a current will result in the conductor.

When a conductor is forced through a magnetic field, lines of force cut or wrap around the conductor on the leading side, as illustrated in Fig. 39-29. This induces a voltage in the conductor which would cause a current to flow in one direction. Should the movement of the conductor be reversed, the lines of force building up on the leading side would induce voltage in the opposite direction, which would cause a current to flow in the opposite direction.

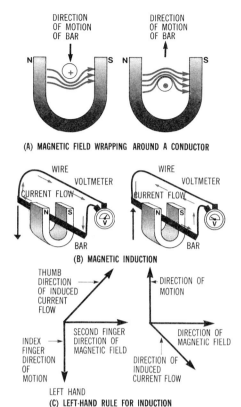

Fig. 39-29 *Inducing an Electromotive Force*

Magnetic Induction. Magnetic induction results when a magnetizable body becomes magnetized when in a magnetic field or flux.

Electromagnetic Induction. Electromagnetic induction results when an electromotive force is produced in a circuit by varying the magnetic field linked with the circuit.

Self-Induction. Self-induction is the inducing of an electromotive force in a circuit by varying the current in the same circuit.

Mutual-Induction. Mutual-induction is the induction produced on two bodies by two adjacent electric circuits.

Inductance. Inductance is that property of an electric circuit by virtue of which a varying current induces an electromotive force in that circuit or in an adjacent circuit. It also refers to the property of an electric circuit which corresponds to inertia of matter. This means that when an electromotive force is imposed, it takes time for the current to rise to its full value. By the same token, when the electromotive force is removed, it takes time for the current to decrease to zero.

Mutual-Inductance. Mutual-inductance is the measure of inductance between two adjacent circuits.

39-27 ELECTRICAL INSTRUMENTATION

Most modern meter movements are of the moving-coil type which consists of a permanent horseshoe or hoop-shaped magnet and a movable coil. Current flowing through the movable coil reacts with the permanent magnetic field, causing the coil to rotate against a light spring tension. The relative movement of the coil is in proportion to the amount of current flowing through the coil windings. A pointer is attached to the coil and moves across a calibrated scale to indicate the amount of current flowing in the coil.

The accuracy of the readings will depend upon the accuracy of the meter used. Voltmeter scales should be calibrated in 0.1 volt divisions, as settings with one-tenth volt variations will be specified. Ammeters may be calibrated in 0.5 ampere divisions. Greater accuracy is desired in the voltmeter than in the ammeter.

Ammeters. Ammeters are connected in series with the circuit in which the current is to be measured. Where necessary, external shunts are provided so

A similar type of electromotive induction would take place if a magnetic field were moved past a stationary conductor. This movement of the magnetic field may be created either by mechanical means or by building up and collapsing the magnetic field of an electromagnet.

To determine the direction the induced current will flow, the left-hand rule for straight conductors may be used. This rule was used to determine the direction of the lines of force created by current flow. Reversing this rule, the direction of the lines of force around a moving conductor may be used as a left-hand rule to determine the direction of current flow induced in a conductor. To expand the rule, it may be said that if the index finger of the left hand indicates the direction of conductor motion, the second finger the direction of the magnetic field, then the thumb indicates the direction of the induced current flow.

The strength of the induced current depends upon:

1. The strength of the magnetic field
2. The speed of the movement
3. The number of conductors in the series

that only a small proportional part of the total current passes through the instrument. Since the current value in a circuit should be the same after the meter is inserted in series as it was before the meter was hooked up, it follows that ammeters must have a low resistance between terminals.

Voltmeters. Voltmeters are connected in parallel with or across the circuit. They must have a very high resistance so that the small amount of current they take will not disturb the circuit.

The voltage of a circuit should be essentially the same after a voltmeter is hooked up across the circuit as it was before. If the voltmeter does not have a sufficiently high resistance, this will not be true.

Meter Shunts. Starting with a basic meter, if a shunt is placed in parallel with the meter, it becomes an ammeter. If a resistance is placed in series with the meter it can be used as a voltmeter.

A typical voltmeter capable of measuring up to 20 volts and requiring 1 milliamp (0.001 ampere) to give full scale deflection would require 20,000 ohms resistance in series. A meter designed to measure only 2 volts and requiring 1 milliamp for full scale deflection would require only 2,000 ohms resistance.

A typical ammeter designed to operate on a 20-volt system and give a maximum amperage reading of 30 amperes with one milliamp flowing through its coil winding for full scale deflection would require approximately a .66-ohm resistor in parallel. A similar meter designed to read a maximum of 300 amperes would require approximately .06 ohm resistance in parallel.

The small amount of current or voltage that is required in the operating winding of a meter indicates the importance of selecting the proper value shunt or resistance before the meter is connected into the circuit, to prevent damage to the windings of the meter.

The same meter movement may be used for either a voltmeter or ammeter. It becomes a voltmeter when connected in series with the proper amount of external resistance. It becomes an ammeter when connected with the proper shunts.

Ohmmeters. An ohmmeter is used to measure electrical resistance. An ohmmeter may be of the moving-type, and contains a resistor and dry cell battery connected internally to the moving coil. When an ohmmeter is connected to a resistor, the

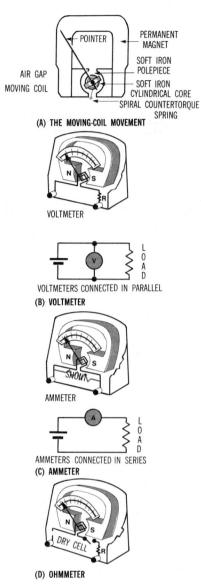

Fig. 39-30 Meters

current flow through the moving coil is directly related to the value of the resistor, and the scale is calibrated accordingly to indicate the resistor value in ohms. Ohmmeters should never be connected to an external source of voltage, as the meter movement may be damaged.

REVIEW QUESTIONS

1. Name and describe two types of electricity.
2. Name and define the three units of an atom.
3. When is an atom electrically neutral?
4. Explain how (a) positive ions (b) negative ions (c) balanced atom are created.
5. Define (a) bound electrons (b) free electrons.

6. What is a valence ring?
7. Explain why the number of electrons in the valence ring determines the ability of the material to conduct a current.
8. Explain the term "electron drift."
9. What will result when an atom loses one electron?
10. Explain in detail how a material such as copper conducts an electric current.
11. Explain in detail how an acid-water solution conducts an electric current.
12. What is a semiconductor?
13. How can an inactive semiconductor material be made partially conductive?
14. Explain how N-type semiconductor materials are formed.
15. Describe the change made in the lattice structure of silicon when the impurity phosphorus is added to it.
16. What is the difference between pentavalent materials and trivalent materials?
17. Describe the change made in the lattice structure of a semiconductor material when a trivalent material is added to it.
18. What are the current carriers in (a) N-type (b) P-type semiconductors?
19. Explain how each of the carriers named in question 18 conducts an electric current through its respective material.
20. Describe the actions that take place when a single block of (a) N-type (b) P-type material is connected to a battery.
21. Explain why a diode will conduct an electric current in one direction only.
22. Define the terms (a) forward bias (b) reverse bias.
23. What is the difference between a diode and a zener diode?
24. Explain the terms NPN and PNP when used in conjunction with transistors.
25. Make a simple sketch of a three-section transistor and label each section.
26. What type of transistor is most commonly used in automotive application?
27. Why is the emitter-base current only a small fraction of the magnitude of the emitter-collector current?
28. Why must there always be a current flowing through the emitter-base circuit in order to have a current flow through the emitter-collector circuit?
29. Explain the statement "the base current triggers the collector current."
30. Make sketches of the symbols for (a) diode (b) zener diode (c) NPN transistor (d) PNP transistor.

31. Define the unit of electric current.
32. Define accurately the unit of electromotive force, the volt.
33. Define the term "wattage."
34. State numerically the following prefix terms: (a) kilo (b) milli (c) micro (d) mega.
35. What is meant by the term "farad"?
36. What is electrical resistance? How is it created?
37. Why does resistance create heat?
38. List the four basic factors that affect resistance.
39. Make sketches to indicate the following electrical symbols: (a) positive (b) ground (c) battery (show polarity) (d) coil (e) condenser (f) conductor crossover (g) conductor connected.
40. Define the term "electric circuit."
41. Make sketches which include the battery, control, and load of (a) a parallel (b) a series (c) a series-parallel circuit.
42. What is the difference between a short circuit and an unintentional ground?
43. What happens to the current flow in a circuit if the resistance is (a) increased (b) decreased, and the voltage remains constant?
44. Calculate the amount of voltage required to cause a 1.34-ampere current to flow in a series circuit which includes the following resistances: 2 ohm, 3 ohm, and 4 ohm.
45. Calculate the amount of current flowing in a 12-volt parallel circuit which includes the following resistances: 2 ohm, 3 ohm, and 4 ohm.
46. Calculate the amount of current flowing in a 12-volt series-parallel circuit which includes a 2-ohm resistor in series with a 3-ohm and 4-ohm parallel resistance.
47. What is meant by the term "voltage drop"?
48. List three common causes of voltage drop.
49. Explain how a light bulb uses resistance to produce light.
50. Explain why temperature affects resistance.
51. Explain the difference between a natural and an artificial magnet.
52. Describe how the motion of electrons is used to produce magnetism.
53. Define in detail magnetic permeability.
54. What are magnetic lines of force?
55. What reaction results when (a) like (b) unlike poles of a magnet are placed together?
56. Describe the relationship between an electric current and magnetism.
57. Explain the difference between an electromagnet and a permanent magnet.
58. State two methods of determining the direction of travel of a magnetic field around a conductor. (Electron flow)
59. Explain why, when equal current flows in the same direction through two or more parallel

conductors, the magnetic lines of force join together to make one large magnetic field.

60. How may a magnetizing force be calculated?

61. State the rule for determining the polarity of an electromagnet. (Electron theory)

62. How may the polarity of an electromagnet be reversed?

63. How can the strength of an electromagnetic field be increased or decreased?

64. What is meant by the term "magnetic induction"?

65. State the principle of magnetic induction.

66. How may the direction of an induced current flow be determined? (Electron theory)

67. State three factors which determine the strength of an induced current.

68. Explain the term "inductance."

69. What is the difference between self-inductance and mutual-inductance?

70. Make sketches to show (a) an ammeter (b) a voltmeter properly connected to an electric circuit.

71. When using either a voltmeter or an ammeter, why is it of the utmost importance to select a meter scale of a higher value than the maximum reading expected?

72. Explain the operation of a basic meter.

Chapter 40
THE BATTERY AND BATTERY SERVICE

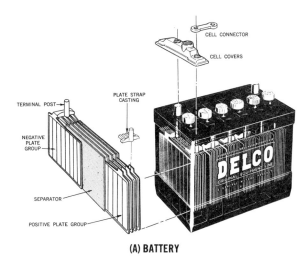

(A) BATTERY

(B) ENERGIZER

Courtesy of General Motors

Fig. 40-1   Section View of Battery and Energizer

The storage battery is an electro-chemical generator and does not store electricity. The energy stored is *chemical* energy, which is transformed into *electric* energy when a circuit is completed across the terminals of the battery.

The most popular type of storage battery is the lead-acid type, whose active ingredients are metal lead and sulphuric acid. There are other types of storage batteries, the nickel-cadmium-alkaline and the nickel-iron-alkaline, to name but two. However, the lead-acid type has been found to be the most practical and economical for automobile use.

40-1 BATTERY CONSTRUCTION

A battery is made up of a number of cells, which are normally enclosed in a hard rubber case. Each cell contains a number of positive and negative plates and is called an *element*.

The element—consists of a number of positive and negative plates grouped together. Each plate is made by applying lead-oxide pastes to a rectangular lattice-like grid moulded from a lead-antimony alloy. The lattice work of the grid holds the pastes in place and helps to distribute the current evenly over the plate. There is usually one more negative plate than positive plate which means there is always a negative plate on each side of the positive plate. This is necessary because more chemical activity takes place at the positive plate than at the negative plate.

For example, a nine-plate cell would have five negative plates and four positive plates.

A plate strap is attached to each negative plate in a cell; while another strap at the opposite end of the cell is attached to each positive plate. The plates are held apart by separators made of either Port Oxford cedar, hard rubber, or glass mesh.

The assembled element is immersed in the electrolyte, a solution of sulphuric acid and distilled water (H_2SO_4) mixed together to form a solution having a specific gravity reading of approximately 1.300.

Since each cell, regardless of the number of plates it contains, is capable of producing only 2.2 volts,

421

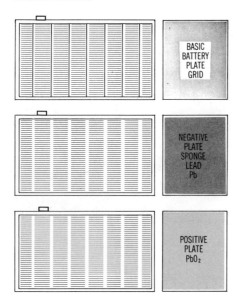

Fig. 40-2   Plate Construction

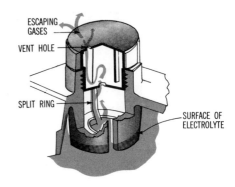

Fig. 40-4   Vent Caps

the plate straps of each cell are connected in series by cell-connecting links. This means that the positive plate strap of the first cell is connected to the negative plate strap of the next cell in order to produce a battery of the required voltage. A 6-volt battery consists of three cells; a 12-volt battery consists of six cells.

When additional plates are added to a cell, it increases the amperage: that is, the amount of current which a battery can produce, or the length of time the battery can produce a given current, or both. Between 9 and 21 plates per cell are used in most automotive batteries.

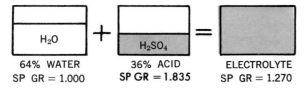

Fig. 40-3   Composition of Electrolyte

To connect the battery to the electrical system of the vehicle, two terminal posts are provided. One post is connected to the positive plate strap, and the other post is connected to the negative plate strap at the opposite end of the battery.

A vent cap screws into a threaded hole located in each cell cover. The cap serves two purposes. First, it closes the opening in the cell cover through which the electrolyte can be checked and water added if necessary and second, it provides a means for the escape of gases formed during charging.

After the battery has been assembled, it is given an initial charge which "forms" the plates. The forming process changes the lead-oxide paste of the positive plate to lead-peroxide (PbO_2) which is a reddish chocolate brown in colour, and the paste of the negative plate to sponge-lead (Pb) which is a grey colour.

40-2 BATTERY OPERATION

When the electrolyte is added to a battery, the sulphuric acid in the electrolyte attacks the active material of the plates. This chemical reaction between the active material on the plates and the electrolyte develops an electrical pressure, or voltage.

The materials used in automotive batteries are such that not only can they produce electricity to flow in one direction, but when an electric current is applied in the opposite direction, the elements can be restored to their original condition, ready to produce more electricity.

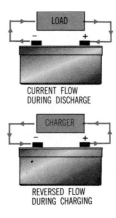

Fig. 40-5   Battery Current Flow

When a battery is connected into a completed electric circuit, current begins to flow from the battery. This current flows because of the pressure difference created by chemical reactions between the active materials in the two kinds of plates and the sulphuric acid in the electrolyte in the battery. The chemical reactions are as follows: the lead peroxide (PbO_2) in the positive plate is a compound of lead (Pb) and oxygen (O_2). Sulphuric acid is a compound of hydrogen (H_2) and the sulphate radical (SO_4). Oxygen in the positive-plate active material combines with hydrogen from the sulphuric acid to form water (H_2O). At the same time the lead in the positive-plate active material combines with the sulphate radical, forming lead sulphate ($PbSO_4$).

A similar reaction takes place at the negative plate where the lead (Pb) of the negative-plate active material combines with the sulphate radical, to form lead sulphate ($PbSO_4$). Thus, lead sulphate

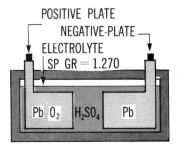

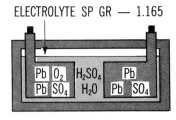

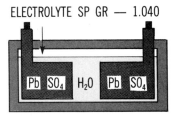

Fig. 40-6   Chemical Changes in Batteries

is formed at both plates as the battery is discharged, while the sulphuric acid in the electrolyte is used up and replaced by water.

The active material in the positive and negative plates becomes chemically similar during the discharging process, as the lead sulphate accumulates. This condition accounts for the loss of cell voltage, since voltage depends upon the difference between the two materials.

As the discharge continues, dilution of the electrolyte and the accumulation of lead sulphate in the plates eventually brings the chemical reactions to a stop. However, the active materials are never completely exhausted during a discharge. At low rates of discharge the reactions are more complete than at high discharge rates. This is because more time is available for the materials to come in contact with each other. When the battery can no longer produce the desired voltage, it is said to be

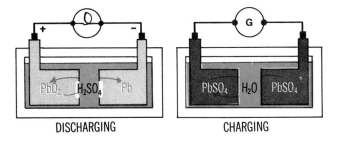

Fig. 40-7   Chemical Action in Batteries

discharged. It must then be recharged by a suitable flow of direct current from some external source before it can be put back in service.

The chemical reactions which take place in a battery cell during charge are essentially the reverse of those which occur during discharge. The lead sulphate on both plates is split up into Pb and SO_4, while water (H_2O) is split up into hydrogen and oxygen. The SO_4 leaves the plates and combines with the hydrogen to form H_2SO_4, or sulphuric acid. At the same time, the oxygen enters into chemical combination with the lead at the positive plate to form lead peroxide (PbO_2). These reactions demonstrate the important fact that water actually takes part in the chemistry of a lead-acid storage battery.

When the battery is idle, the voltage produced chemically is normally a little more than 2 volts per cell. The exact value is determined by several factors, such as the purity of the materials, the state of charge, and strength of the electrolyte. The chemical voltage of a battery while it is idle is usually called *open circuit voltage*.

40-3 MEASUREMENT AND SIGNIFICANCE OF SPECIFIC GRAVITY

The strength or state of charge of a battery may be determined by the condition, strength, specific gravity or density of the electrolyte.

The specific gravity of the electrolyte decreases during discharge for two reasons—sulphuric acid (which is "heavier" than water) is used up and water is formed. Conversely, when the battery is charged, the specific gravity of the electrolyte increases—sulphuric acid is formed and water is used up.

The specific gravity of the electrolyte may be tested by means of a battery hydrometer. Since the

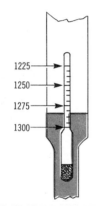

1225
1250
1275
1300

READING FOR FULLY CHARGED BATTERY SHOULD BE BETWEEN 1275 AND 1300

Courtesy of General Motors

Fig. 40-8   Testing the Specific Gravity of a Battery

strength of the electrolyte varies directly with the state of charge of a battery, high or low specific gravity readings of the electrolyte indicate the amount of sulphuric acid in the electrolyte. The higher the reading is, the larger the amount of sulphuric acid in the electrolyte, and therefore the higher the state of charge of the battery. The following specific gravity readings are an approximate guide to the condition of a battery charge.

SPECIFIC GRAVITY READINGS	BATTERY STATE OF CHARGE
1.265 - 1.290	Fully charged
1.250 - 1.265	Three-quarters charged
1.225 - 1.250	One-half charged
1.200 - 1.225	One-quarter charged
1.175 - 1.200	Barely operative

A battery with a specific gravity reading of less than 1.225 is not considered to be in a safe operating condition for the modern automobile.

It should be noted that batteries with specific gravity readings of less than 1.165 will freeze at 0°F.

Temperature also changes the specific gravity of a liquid. As a liquid cools, it becomes thicker and gains specific gravity, but when heated it becomes thinner and loses specific gravity. Therefore, a correction must be made if the temperature varies from standard. During testing of the specific gravity of a battery, this correction involves the adding or subtracting of gravity points according to whether the electrolyte is above or below the 80°F standard. To make the temperature correction, 4 points must be subtracted or added for every 10° below or above 80°F.

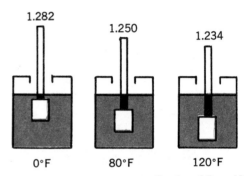

1.282   1.250   1.234

0°F   80°F   120°F

Courtesy of General Motors

Fig. 40-9   Temperature Compensation

Examples: 1.250 at 120°F. Add 0.016 (4 × 0.004). The correct reading is 1.266. 1.230 at 20°F. Subtract 0.024 (6 × 0.004). The correct reading is 1.206.

40-4 SELF-DISCHARGE

Self-discharge results from the additional chemical actions similar to those which produce the flow of current from the battery. These actions continue at varying rates even when the battery is not connected into an electric circuit. Self-discharge causes the battery to run down slowly. The rate of battery self-discharge depends on two things—impurities within the battery, and battery temperature. A battery kept at 0°F temperature will, at the end of 90 days, have lost only a few gravity points. The reason is that at low temperatures the chemical activities are much retarded and very little self-discharge can take place. However, as the battery

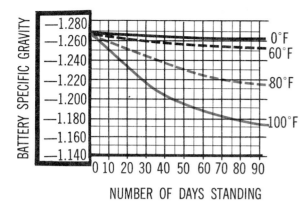

Fig. 40-10 Rate of Self Discharge

temperature is increased, the rate of self-discharge is also increased. A battery charged to 1.270 specific gravity and kept at a temperature of 60°F will, at the end of 90 days, have dropped to about a specific gravity reading 1.255.

At higher temperatures, the rate of self-discharge is even more rapid. A fully charged battery kept at 80°F after 90 days will drop to about 1.220 specific gravity. In other words, a fully charged battery kept at 80°F becomes nearly half discharged in 3 months. A fully charged battery kept at 100°F will at the end of 90 days have self-discharged to about 1.170 specific gravity.

A fully charged battery can be kept successfully in storage by charging it at a very low charging rate. Trickle-type battery chargers have been developed to produce a charging rate measured in milliamperes which is just sufficient to offset the losses due to self-discharge. Do not use these chargers for more than 60 days. Another method used to prevent self-discharge of a battery in storage is to give it a booster charge every 30 days, to bring it back to a fully charged condition. If the storage temperature is high, the battery will require even more frequent boosting. Batteries should be completely charged before being stored.

40-5 DRY CHARGED BATTERIES

A dry charged battery is a battery that has been completely charged but contains no electrolyte until the battery is put into service. The cell elements, composed of positive and negative plates with rubber separators, are given an initial charge in special equipment at the factory. The newly charged positive plates and negative plates, along with the separators, are then thoroughly washed, completely dried, and assembled in the battery cases in a continuous process.

A dry charged battery will retain its full state of charge indefinitely as long as moisture is not permitted to enter the cells. Therefore, it should be stored in a dry place. The negative plates, in the presence of moisture and air, will oxidize and thus lose their charge.

The procedure to activate a dry charged battery is as follows: remove the restrictors from the vents and remove the vent caps. Fill all cells to the proper level with approved electrolyte. The best results are obtained when the battery and the electrolyte are at 60 to 80°F temperature. Some gassing will occur when filling because of the release of carbon dioxide, a product of the drying process, or hydrogen sulphide caused by the presence of some free sulphur. These gases and odours are normal and are no cause for alarm.

Five minutes after adding the electrolyte, check the open circuit voltage of the battery. More than 6 volts or more than 12 volts, depending upon the rated voltage of the battery, indicates that the battery is ready for service. From 5 to 6 volts or from 10 to 12 volts indicates oxidized negative plates in the battery, and the battery should be recharged before use. Less than 5 or less than 10 volts, depending on the rated voltage of the battery, indicates a reverse cell or an open circuit and the battery should be replaced.

As a final precaution, check the specific gravity in all cells. If the specific gravity corrected to 80°F has shown more than a 30-point (.030) drop from the initial filling electrolyte, the battery should be charged before use.

Once a dry charged battery has been filled with electrolyte, its operating and service characteristics are exactly the same as a wet charged battery.

40-6 BATTERY RATINGS

The amount of current that a battery can deliver depends upon the size of each plate, the number of plates, and the amount and strength of the electrolyte. Three common methods of rating the capacity of batteries are the 20 ampere-hour rate, the cold rate, and the watt-hour rate.

The 20 ampere-hour rate—is determined by the amount of electric current or pressure that a battery at 80°F can produce for 20 hours without the cell voltage dropping below 1.125 volts. A battery that

PERFORMANCE RATINGS

SAE MINIMUM COLD TEST (300-amp. discharge at 0° for 6-volt — 150-amp. at 0° for 12-volt)

PLATES	VOLTS	Avg. amp. cap. (20 min.)	SAE avg. amp. hrs. at 20-hr. rate	Watt Hours	COLD TEST 5-sec. volts	Min. to 1-v. per cell
51	6	158	122	732	4.5	4.8
51	6	195	150	900	4.4	5.5
66	12	91	70	840	9.4	6.0
78	12	85	65	780	9.6	5.5
66	12	97	75	900	9.4	6.0

Fig. 40-11   Battery Ratings

could deliver 4 amperes for 20 hours before the cell voltage dropped below 1.75 would be rated as an 80 (4 × 20) ampere-hour battery.

The cold rate—is determined by the number of minutes that a battery at 0°F will deliver 300 amperes before the cell voltage drops below 1.0 volt. This test indicates the battery's ability to crank an engine in cold weather. A 60 ampere-hour, 12-volt battery could supply 300 amperes for 4.4 minutes before the cell voltage drops below 1.0 volt.

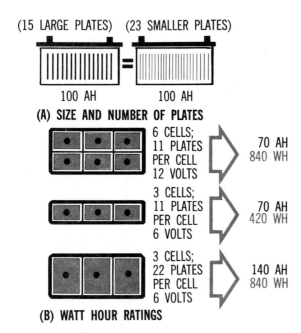

(15 LARGE PLATES)   (23 SMALLER PLATES)

100 AH   100 AH

(A) SIZE AND NUMBER OF PLATES

6 CELLS; 11 PLATES PER CELL 12 VOLTS → 70 AH 840 WH

3 CELLS; 11 PLATES PER CELL 6 VOLTS → 70 AH 420 WH

3 CELLS; 22 PLATES PER CELL 6 VOLTS → 140 AH 840 WH

(B) WATT HOUR RATINGS

Fig. 40-12   Battery Efficiency and Temperature

Cold Cranking Rating. This rating system replaces the old cold rate system. The cold cranking power of a battery is determined at ambient temperature of 0°F.

After determining that a minimum cranking voltage of from 7.0 to 7.5 volts is required to provide adequate cranking speed for the modern engine, the engineers at the Battery Council International (BCI) and the Society of Automotive Engineers (SAE) settled on an arbitrary standard of 7.2 cranking volts as one factor in the cold cranking rate. The other factor is based on the principle that the average internal combustion engine, in an acceptable state of tune, may require up to 30 seconds to start.

Thus the new cold cranking rating is the amperage a fully charged battery can supply at 7.2 volts for 30 seconds. For example, the cold cranking rating of a 42 plate 12 volt battery could be 225 amperes, while a 66 plate 12 volt battery could have a 335 ampere rating.

Battery Reserve Capacity. This rating system replaces the previous 20 ampere hour rating and more accurately represents the electrical load which must be supplied by the battery should the charging system fail.

The BCI and SAE engineers arbitrarily established that at least 25 amperes are required from all sizes of batteries to operate the ignition, lights, wipers, and defrosters when no current is being generated by the charging system.

The reserve capacity is stated as the time required to decrease the battery terminal voltage to below 10.5 volts when a sustained load of 25 amperes is applied and the battery temperature is 80°F.

Watt-Hour Rating. Since power is a product of amperes times volts (amperes $\times$ volts = watts) a fundamental basis for comparing batteries can be established by multiplying ampere-hour ratings by voltage (ampere-hours $\times$ volts = watt-hours). On this basis a 100 ampere-hour 6-volt battery is rated at 600 watt-hour (100 ampere hours $\times$ 6 volts). By comparison, a 70 ampere-hour, 12-volt battery is rated at 840 watt-hours (70 ampere hours $\times$ 12 volts). Consequently, the power rating in watt hours makes possible a direct comparison between the 12-volt battery and the 6-volt battery.

For example: a 12-volt battery that has 11 plates in each of its 6 cells and a rating of 70 ampere-hours. Since ampere-hour capacity depends on the weight of the material, a 6-volt battery with the same number of similar plates in each of its 3 cells would also have a rating of 70 ampere-hours. But, if the total of 66 plates used in the 12-volt battery were divided equally between 3 cells, the unit would theoretically be a "22 plate" 6-volt battery and would produce twice the capacity, or 140 ampere-hours. Thus, the extra "power" available from the 3 additional cells in the 12-volt battery does not show up in the ampere-hour ratings. However, if we consider the effect of voltage on the ampere-hours produced, the extra power becomes evident. Many late model batteries are rated by watt-hours only.

The three tests are frequently used in advertising battery capacity.

40-7 BATTERY EFFICIENCY

Battery efficiency is in proportion to the rate of discharge and the operating temperature. When a battery is being discharged rapidly the chemical activity takes place only on the surface of the plates. The chemical activity does not have time to penetrate the active material under the surface of the plates and utilize it to the fullest extent. The slower the discharge rate, the deeper the penetration, the more efficient the battery.

The lower the temperature of the battery, the more the chemical activity of the electrolyte is reduced. The sulphuric acid solution is more dense and not able to work as actively on the materials in the plates. A battery that is 100% efficient at 80°F is only approximately 30% efficient at 0°F.

The battery terminal voltage will vary considerably according to the rate the battery is being charged or discharged, or as the battery temperature changes.

40-8 BATTERY COUNTER-ELECTROMOTIVE FORCE (CEMF) VARIATIONS

In order to maintain the battery in a useful condition, the electrical energy that has been used must be replaced. This is accomplished by the vehicle's charging circuit. In order to pass the charging current through the battery, the charging circuit must overcome not only the internal resistance (voltage drop) of the battery, but also its chemical voltage. The total of the two opposing voltages is called the battery's counter-voltage or counter-electromotive force (CEMF).

Battery temperature has a tremendous effect on CEMF, since temperature affects the density and thus the resistivity of the electrolyte. Thus, a cold battery requires a much higher charging voltage, for any given charging rate, than a warm or hot battery.

Gassing of a battery while on charge is another source of change in CEMF. When gases form and cling to the surfaces of the plates, CEMF is increased because of two important effects. First, the chemical voltage is increased because the gases (mainly hydrogen at the negative plates) temporarily act as active materials which yield a higher voltage. Second, the internal resistance of the battery is temporarily increased because of the obstructive action of the gas film on the surfaces of the plate. Fortunately, this effect decreases at higher charging rates. Owing to the increased viscosity of the electrolyte and the increased tendency of the battery to gas at low temperatures, gassing usually causes greater increases in CEMF when the battery is cold.

Changes in battery CEMF as a result of improper use or maintenance often are responsible for premature battery failure. A "sulphated" battery is an excellent example. A battery which has been allowed to self-discharge over a long period of time without a booster charge, or which has been discharged and allowed to remain undercharged for a long period of time, will show an increase in internal resistance. A battery in such condition will seldom if ever perform satisfactorily in a vehicle because of its high CEMF.

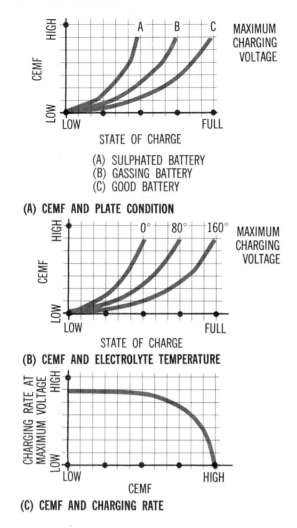

(A) SULPHATED BATTERY
(B) GASSING BATTERY
(C) GOOD BATTERY

(A) CEMF AND PLATE CONDITION

(B) CEMF AND ELECTROLYTE TEMPERATURE

(C) CEMF AND CHARGING RATE

Fig. 40-13   Effects of CEMF

A battery which has been subjected to very high operating temperatures, or to excessively strong electrolyte, offers an opposite example of changed CEMF. Because of the lowering of CEMF which results, such a battery is much more susceptible to overcharging or loss of charging control. Serious losses of electrolyte, by over-filling or leakage, or by spewing out during constant heavy charging, can also cause lowered CEMF.

Failure to maintain the proper liquid level can cause permanent changes in battery CEMF. The plate areas which are allowed to remain exposed for a considerable period of time become very dense and hard, and lose their conductivity. This decreases the active areas of the plates which in turn increases the internal resistance and the CEMF of the battery.

40-9 EFFECTS OF VOLTAGE AND STATE OF CHARGE ON CHARGING RATES

A battery is designed to maintain a definite relationship between the charging voltage and the charging rate under varying conditions. First, the system voltage is controlled mainly by battery characteristics until the charging voltage reaches the limit for which the voltage regulator unit is set. Second, the charging rate, as the battery comes up to full charge, is gradually reduced if the charging voltage is limited. Therefore, as the battery attains a higher state of charge, it requires a higher charging voltage to maintain the same charging rate.

Since the available charging voltage is limited to a predetermined value by the voltage control unit, additional charging voltage is not available. Therefore, the charging rate must necessarily taper off, adjusting itself to the gradual change in the state of charge.

For example, a battery 25% charged will take the maximum output of the generator or alternator and would take even more amperes if the current regulator permitted. When the battery becomes 75% charged, the charging rate will be reduced but is still fairly high. Finally, when the battery attains 100% charge, the charging rate will have reduced to a few amperes. The very rapid change in the charging rate or "taper charge" between 75% charged and 100% charged is a very important characteristic of automotive batteries. Whenever the battery is 75% charged or less, it will accept from approximately one-half to full generator or alternator output. This makes for rapid recovery after a discharge. Also, the sharply tapering effect between 75% and 100% of full charge is an additional factor of safety from damage because of overcharge.

With continued use, a battery tends to operate at lower and lower voltage for any given charging rate or state of charge. Thus, to protect a well-used battery adequately, the voltage-regulator setting must often be reduced somewhat. A battery which has stood idle for a long period of time, or which has been poorly maintained, tends to operate at abnormally high voltage for any given charging rate, or state of charge. Such a battery usually becomes discharged very quickly in normal service when governed by a normal regulator setting. Even the maximum allowable setting of the voltage regulator can be ineffective with such a battery, since the battery tends to heat up excessively when being charged at higher rates. A helpful treatment for a battery in this condition is to charge it at a low rate on a slow-type charger until there is no further rise in gravity for three successive readings taken at hourly intervals. This treatment will often restore battery charging characteristics to normal levels, but will not be effective if the abnormal condition is too far advanced.

Any condition in a battery which affects its voltage will cause a serious deviation from the normal charging characteristics. Common causes are internal short circuits, accumulation of impurities, loss of electrolyte, excessively strong electrolyte, high resistance separators, and excessive sulphation. The presence of such a defect or defects in the battery can upset the charging characteristics completely in an automotive electrical system.

40-10 BATTERY SERVICE

In order to obtain maximum battery life, it is necessary to inspect the battery periodically. These inspections should occur at regular intervals, depending on the number of miles driven, but the period between inspections should never be longer than one month. A great deal of preventive maintenance, which will reduce costly service calls, is part of proper battery service. Excessive water consumption indicates that the battery is being overcharged, and a low specific gravity reading on the hydrometer indicates that the battery is being undercharged. Both conditions indicate that either the generator or alternator, the regulator, or the electric wiring of the vehicle needs attention. The removal of corrosion around the battery terminal promotes longer life of both the terminal and battery cable.

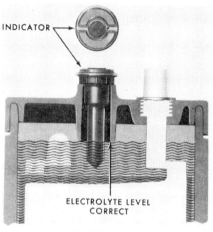

ELECTROLYTE LEVEL
CORRECT

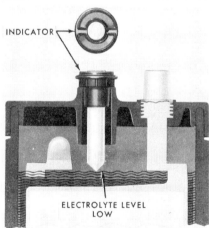

ELECTROLYTE LEVEL
LOW

(A) WITH INDICATOR

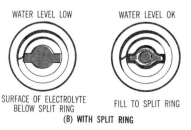

WATER LEVEL LOW

WATER LEVEL OK

SURFACE OF ELECTROLYTE
BELOW SPLIT RING

FILL TO SPLIT RING

(B) WITH SPLIT RING

Courtesy of General Motors

Fig. 40-14   Checking Electrolyte Level

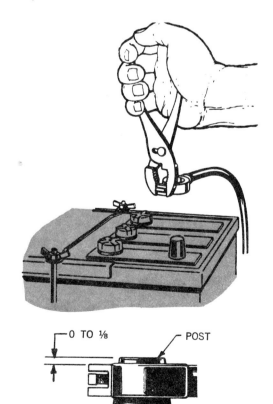

0 TO 1/8   POST

Fig. 40-15   Installing Battery Cables

Batteries that have remained in vehicles for some months may have corroded terminal clamps that are very difficult to loosen. Care must be exercised when these clamps are loosened, as the battery may be damaged. A strong solution of water and bicarbonate of soda may be applied to the terminal and post to eat away the corrosion, after which wrenches may be used to better advantage in removing the nuts from the clamp bolts. Care must be taken not to get the bicarbonate of soda solution in the battery, as this solution could neutralize the electrolyte. The use of a battery puller is recommended to remove the terminal clamp from the battery when a moderate twisting will not loosen it. Inspect the condition of the clamps, bolts, nuts, and cables. Replace badly corroded units. It is possible to solder new clamps to existing cables, but complete replacement is recommended. The placing of a light coat of corrosive inhibitor over the exposed surface of the cable terminals and clamp bolts will reduce the future formation of corrosion.

40-11 TESTING THE BATTERY

The strength of the battery can be determined by the condition or strength of the electrolyte, which may be tested by means of a battery *hydrometer*. This test is significant only when the battery is known to be in good mechanical condition. A second test using an accurate *voltmeter,* when the battery is under load, can determine the mechanical condition of the battery.

Hydrometer Test. A battery hydrometer is a device used to check the specific gravity of the battery electrolyte. It has been calibrated to read accurately within the discharged and charged densities of the electrolyte. Many hydrometers have a thermometer located in the base to give the temperature of the electrolyte being tested.

To use the hydrometer, hold it in a vertical position and draw in sufficient electrolyte to suspend the float. Repeat this several times to bring the float temperature to that of the electrolyte. The float should not touch either the bottom, top, or sides of the float chamber. Allow the gas bubbles, if any, to rise to the surface and any sediment to drop to the bottom. Hold the hydrometer at eye level and note the scale reading at the exact point the float scale emerges from the liquid. Note the temperature of the thermometer in the base of the hydrometer and calculate the necessary temperature corrections.

The state of charge of the battery may be determined by comparing the corrected reading obtained with the chart shown in Fig. 40-18.

A difference of more than 25 points (.025) between individual cell readings indicates that the battery is beginning to deteriorate because of internal shorts, normal use, old age, or loss of acid, etc. Batteries with specific gravity readings below 1,200 should be recharged and then retested.

After completing the hydrometer test, the battery should be given the High-Rate Discharge Test to obtain the most accurate picture of the battery's condition.

High-Rate Discharge Test. A battery's ability to produce current is dependent upon its state of

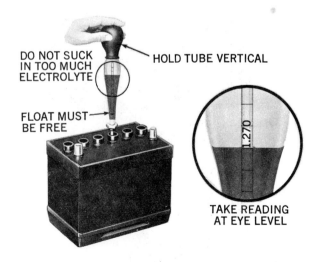

DO NOT SUCK IN TOO MUCH ELECTROLYTE

HOLD TUBE VERTICAL

FLOAT MUST BE FREE

1.270

TAKE READING AT EYE LEVEL

Courtesy of General Motors

Fig. 40-16   Testing the Specific Gravity of a Battery

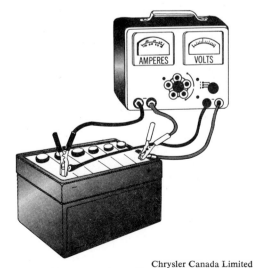

AMPERES   VOLTS

Chrysler Canada Limited

Fig. 40-17   High-Rate Discharge Test

BATTERY CAPACITY TEST

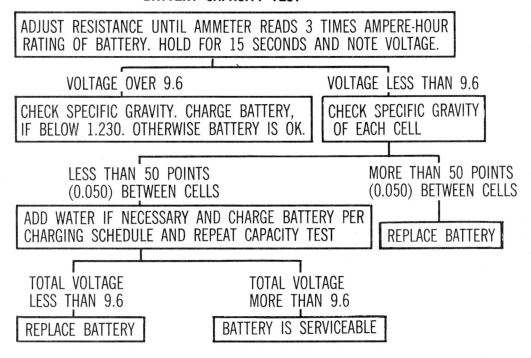

Fig. 40-18 Battery High-Rate Discharge Test Outline   Ford of Canada

charge and the active plate area. The high-rate discharge test indicates the amount of active plate area that is being used. It indicates the battery's ability to produce pressure and current under load without the voltage dropping below a rated amount. Do not perform the test if the specific gravity reading of the battery is below 1.220. If the specific gravity reading is low, the battery should be completely recharged on a slow charger, then retested.

A high-rate discharge tester consists of an ammeter, voltmeter, and a variable carbon load (a device used to place an adjustable electrical load in the circuit).

To perform the test, attach the positive and negative leads of the tester to their respective battery posts. Adjust the carbon pile to place the required load upon the battery.

The proper load may be calculated in the following manner:

6-volt batteries — 2 times the ampere hour rating
12-volt batteries — 3 times the ampere hour rating
watt-hour rated — Divide the watt-hour rating by
   batteries   the voltage of the battery to give the ampere-hour rating. Then multiply as required for a 6- or 12-volt battery.

Keep this load applied for 15 seconds; at the end of this time the voltage reading should not be lower than 9.5 volts for a 12-volt battery or 4.8 volts for a 6-volt battery. Voltage readings below the minimum indicate insufficient usable plate area and the battery should be replaced.

It should be noted here that a starter draw test should be performed in order to compare the current required to crank the engine and the battery's ability to produce the required current. In many cases replacement batteries of too small a capacity have been installed, or the starter's draw is greater than the rated capacity of a standard battery.

Other Battery Tests. Some manufacturers suggest the Open-Circuit (No Load) Test and the Light Load Test. These tests are performed by taking the voltage reading of each individual cell. Since most current-production batteries have a solid plastic top, these tests cannot be used without damaging the cover.

The open-circuit test—is performed on batteries with open cell connectors by placing a low-reading voltmeter across each cell and recording the voltage. Cell voltages below 2.06 volts indicate the need for recharging. Cell differences of 0.5 volt indicate that the high-rate discharge test should be performed to determine the battery condition.

Light load test—to perform this test crank the engine with the starter for 3 seconds, turn on the low-beam headlights for 1 minute, then test individual cells with a low-reading voltmeter. Readings of 1.95 volts or more with cell differences of less than 0.05 volt indicates a battery in good condition. Readings of less than 1.95 volts with variations less than .05 volt indicates recharging is required. Readings of 1.95 volts or more with variations above 0.05 volt indicates a defective battery.

40-12 RECHARGING BATTERIES

When a battery has become discharged to a point where it will no longer guarantee to operate the starting motor, it is necessary to recharge the battery by some means other than the generator or alternator. There are two methods of recharging a dead battery, the *slow-charge* and the *fast-charge* methods.

The slow-charge method—consists of removing the battery from the vehicle and connecting it to a battery charger. If more than one battery is being charged, they are connected in series; that is, the positive post of the first battery is connected to the negative post of the second battery, and so on for the number of batteries being charged. The negative line of the battery charger is connected to the negative post of the first battery, while the positive line of the battery charger is connected to the positive post of the last battery to be charged.

The charging rate for any number of batteries should never exceed 6 amperes and the length of time required to recharge a battery to a state of good condition should never exceed 48 hours. If a longer period is necessary, then the battery is either highly sulphated or has been operated for a considerable period of time without having sufficient electrolyte to cover the plates. If these conditions exist, then the charging rate should be reduced to about 2 amperes.

Batteries which have been exposed to winter weather should not be charged at a high rate until the temperature of the electrolyte is up to 80°F. Excessive temperatures of the electrolyte also indicate a highly sulphated battery and the charging rate should be reduced to about 2 amperes.

As the charging progresses, there will be a tendency for the battery to start gassing, and if charged

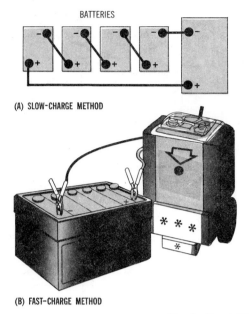

BATTERIES

(A) SLOW-CHARGE METHOD

(B) FAST-CHARGE METHOD

Chrysler Canada Limited

Fig. 40-19   Recharging Batteries

at too high a rate, excessive gassing will be noticed. This gas is highly explosive and, if it is ignited by a spark from the battery charger, it may explode and scatter the battery case and the dangerous sulphuric acid. Never charge batteries with the filler caps in place. These caps must be removed in order to help dissipate the gases as they are formed.

When the battery shows no further rise in specific gravity after being on the charger for a period of 5 hours and being charged at a rate of not exceeding 6 amperes, it will be considered as fully charged. This reading, however, should not be less than 1.265 on the hydometer. If it is less, then the battery is showing signs of sulphation, or the acid has been lost because of spilling or boiling of the battery.

The fast-charge method—does not require the battery to be removed from the vehicle, as most fast chargers are portable. This method is sometimes referred to as a "booster charge," since it very rarely completely charges the battery. Its purpose is to recharge the battery sufficiently to allow the starting motor to start the engine. This is done in a short period of time, usually about 1 hour, and at a very high rate of charge, ranging from 60 to 100 amperes. The remaining recharging of the battery is done by the generator or alternator when the engine is operating.

To operate a fast charger follow the manufacturer's instructions.

When a battery is being fast charged, considerable expansion of the electrolyte takes place. If the electrolyte level is too high, remove the surplus electrolyte and place it in a clean glass. Return the excess electrolyte to the battery after the battery cools down. If the battery electrolyte temperature reaches 125°F, reduce the charging rate at once to prevent damage to the plates.

If the specific gravity readings do not indicate a considerable increase after 1 hour of fast charging, the battery should be removed from the fast charger and given a slow charge.

Trickle charging—a trickle charger passes a very low current, usually measured in milliamperes, through the battery. This type of charger is usually used to compensate for the self-discharge of batteries in storage. Models are available for use on batteries in vehicles.

REVIEW QUESTIONS

1. What type of energy is stored in a storage battery?
2. Name three types of storage batteries.
3. Describe the construction of a battery element.
4. What is the voltage produced by a single wet cell?
5. What determines the amount of amperage and the length of time this amperage can be produced by a fully charged battery?
6. Describe the battery plate forming process.
7. Explain in detail how the chemical process which takes place inside a battery causes an electric current to flow.
8. Why does the battery voltage decrease as a battery becomes discharged?
9. What chemical changes take place during the recharging of a battery?
10. Why does the specific gravity of the electrolyte change as a battery becomes discharged?
11. Why is a battery with a specific gravity reading of less than 1.225 not considered to be in a safe operating condition for the modern automobile?
12. Explain why the specific gravity of a liquid varies as the temperature of the liquid is increased or decreased.
13. Calculate the corrected specific gravity reading for the following tests: (a) 1.250 at 0°F (b) 1.240 at 40°F (c) 1.225 at 120°F.
14. Why does the temperature at which a battery is stored affect the rate of self-discharge?

15. What is the main advantage of dry charged batteries?
16. What tests should be performed on a newly activated dry charged battery before the battery is installed in a vehicle?
17. Explain the following battery rating: (a) 20 ampere-hour rating (b) cold-rating (c) watt-hour rating.
18. Why is the watt-hour rating system considered by some sources as the best method of rating batteries?
19. Explain why battery efficiency decreases as the temperature decreases.
20. How is the cemf of a battery produced?
21. List four ways in which the cemf of a battery may be increased.
22. What causes a sulphated battery?
23. How may the cemf of a battery be reduced?
24. Explain why the charging rate of a battery gradually reduces as the battery nears the full charge, when the charging voltage remains constant.
25. Sometimes it is necessary to change the voltage setting of the regulator in order to prevent undercharging or overcharging of the battery. Explain why this is necessary.
26. Battery condition can indicate problems in the charging circuit. State these conditions and the cause of each.
27. Why do corroded battery terminals frequently result in a low state of charge of the battery?
28. Explain why the specific gravity readings of battery electrolyte can indicate battery condition.
29. State (a) the minimum specific gravity reading (b) the maximum variation of individual cell specific gravity readings of a battery considered satisfactory for vehicle use.
30. Explain why a high-rate discharge test indicates the amount of active plate area that is being used.
31. Calculate the load required for a high-rate discharge test on a 12-volt 720-watt-hour battery.
32. What is the minimum satisfactory voltage for a 12-volt battery being tested by the high-rate discharge method?
33. State the maximum (a) charging rate (b) charging time for batteries being recharged by the slow charge method.
34. Why should extreme care be exercised around batteries that are being recharged?
35. Why is the fast charge method of recharging a battery frequently referred to as a booster charge?
36. Why will the battery plates be damaged if the electrolyte temperature rises above 125°F?
37. When are trickle chargers most frequently used?

Chapter 41
THE IGNITION SYSTEM

The purpose of the ignition system of an internal combustion gasoline engine is to produce high-voltage surges of current and deliver them to the right spark plug at the correct time. There are three types of ignition systems in use today: the *battery* ignition system, the *transistorized* ignition system, and the *magneto* ignition system. The battery ignition system is the most popular.

41-1 BATTERY IGNITION SYSTEMS

The battery ignition system consists of two sections, the low-voltage or *primary circuit* (battery voltage of 6 or 12 volts), and the high-voltage or *secondary circuit* (of 15,000 to 25,000 volts).

The primary circuit consists of the battery, ignition switch, ignition resistor, primary windings of the coil, ignition points, condenser, and the necessary connecting wires. The secondary circuit consists of the secondary windings of the ignition coil, the distributor cap and rotor, the spark plugs, and connecting wires.

When the ignition switch is turned on and the engine started, the ignition points in the distributor are closed by the action of the distributor cam. Current flows through the primary winding of the ignition coil and creates a magnetic field. The rotation of the cam causes the ignition points of the distributor to open. As the ignition points open, the current in the primary winding stops, causing the magnetic field to collapse quickly, and inducing a high voltage in the secondary winding. This high-voltage surge of current passes from the ignition coil through the high-tension lead to the centre of the distributor cap. The current passes from the centre tower of the cap to the distributor rotor. The rotor is opposite the outer terminal, which is connected to the spark plug. The cylinder in which the spark plug is located must be on the proper stroke for the ignition of the fuel. The current passes along this path and jumps across the spark-plug gap between the electrodes of the plug, to ignite the fuel in the cylinder. This series of events takes place very rapidly. At 60 mph, the ignition system of a six-cylinder engine must produce about 9,000 sparks per minute.

41-2 THE IGNITION SWITCH

The ignition switch is an electrical switch that turns the current off or on in the ignition circuit. It is usually located on the instrument panel and is operated by a key, so that only the person who has the key can turn on the switch.

The ignition switch, in addition to completing the ignition circuit, usually has additional terminals which complete the circuits to the instruments or warning lights (fuel, temperature, oil pressure and charging); and to the accessories (heater, radio, etc.); and to the starting motor.

The ignition, instrument, and accessories circuits are completed when the switch is turned to the ignition position. The instruments and the accessories circuits are connected when the switch is turned to the accessories position. Only the starting circuit is connected when the ignition switch is in the start position. A multipurpose switch is used to reduce the drain on the battery.

41-3 IGNITION RESISTOR

Most ignition coils are designed to operate on less than 12 volts. Continuous operation on 12 volts would shorten coil life. Therefore, an ignition resistor which lowers the voltage is placed in the primary circuit between the ignition switch and the coil. Except during starting periods, all the current going to the ignition coil must pass through the ignition resistor, thus reducing the current flow through the primary windings of the coil.

When the key is turned to the start position, the resistor is bypassed and current flows directly from the starting circuit to the ignition coil. Since battery voltage drops during the starting period, the elimination of the resistor from the ignition circuit permits greater current flow through the primary windings of the ignition coil. This produces a better

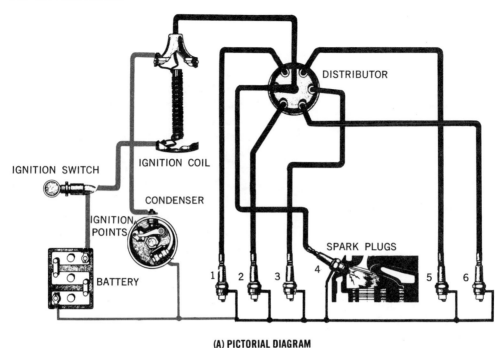

(A) PICTORIAL DIAGRAM

(B) ELEMENTARY DIAGRAM

Fig. 41-1   The Battery Ignition System

spark for starting purposes.

There are two types of ignition resistors used, the *simple* type, and the *ballast* type.

The simple-type ignition resistor—is used to reduce battery voltage reaching the coil and is not temperature-sensitive. This type delivers about the same voltage to the coil regardless of whether or not the coil is cold or at normal operating temperatures. It may include a bimetal spring-type bypass that closes when cold, eliminating the resistor from the circuit.

The ballast-type of ignition resistor—is the most commonly used today. It is a temperature-sensitive variable resistance unit. It is constructed of a special type of wire, the properties of which tend to increase or decrease its resistance in direct proportion to the heat of the wire. This type is used to reduce the voltage available to the coil at low engine speeds, and to increase the voltage at higher engine speeds. Without the resistor the coil would operate efficiently at high engine speeds, but this voltage would cause excessive heating up of the

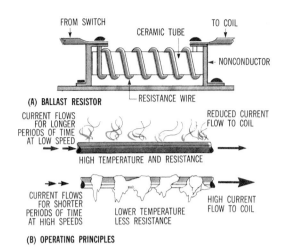

Fig. 41-2 Ballast Resistors

coil at low speed. The high voltage at low speed would also cause oxidation (a blue scale-like deposit) on the ignition-point contact surfaces.

The ballast-type resistor tends to heat up because of the longer duration of current flow through the primary circuit at low engine speeds (when the ignition contact points are closed for a longer period of time). The heating up of the resistor increases its resistance. The higher resistance results in a lower voltage reaching the coil.

At higher engine speeds the ignition contact points are closed for a shorter period of time, thus reducing the time that current flows through the primary circuit. This results in the lowering of the temperature of the resistor. The lower the resistor temperature, the lower its resistance, and the higher the voltage reaching the coil. Thus, as the engine speed increases, the resistor temperature decreases, and the voltage to the coil increases. At high speeds, the coil receives almost all of the battery voltage.

At high engine speeds the coil saturation period (the length of time the ignition points are closed and current flows through the primary windings of the coil) shortens. Therefore, the voltage must increase so that the current flow increases in the primary windings in order to maintain the same build-up of the magnetic field around the windings.

41-4 THE IGNITION COIL

The spark coil, or ignition coil, is a small transformer which operates on the magnetic induction principle to produce a new current with a very high voltage, which is required to jump the space,

or gap, of the spark-plug electrodes. The battery voltage is not strong enough to jump even a space the thickness of paper.

The method used to produce the high voltage may be considered pure electromagnetic induction, as the voltage is not produced by moving parts, but by a change in the magnetic field. All parts remain stationary. The most common application of this principle is the *transformer*. Here two stationary windings, a primary and a secondary, are placed over a common laminated steel core. The primary winding is excited by an alternating current source. Because both windings are linked together magnetically, a change in magnetism produced by the primary winding will induce voltage in the secondary. Transformers with a large number of turns of wire in the secondary are called *step-up transformers* because the output voltage is higher than the input voltage. *Step-down transformers* have more turns of wire in the primary than in the secondary and the output voltage is lower than the input voltage.

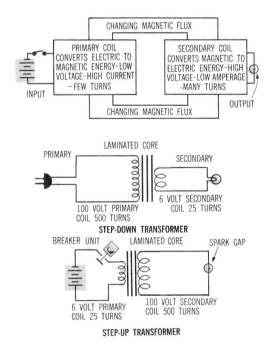

Fig. 41-3 Typical Transformers

The ignition coil operates on this principle. Both the primary and secondary windings are wound around the same core. The magnetic field created by the primary also surrounds the secondary, and the windings are said to be magnetically linked together. Voltage is induced in the secondary, how-

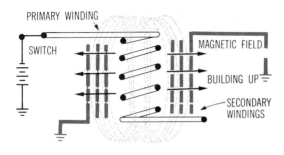

(A) EXPANDING

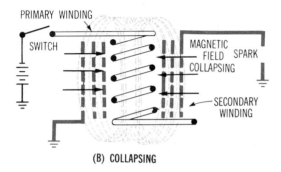

(B) COLLAPSING

Fig. 41-4   Magnetic Induction

ever, only when there is a change in the magnetic field.

When current flows through the primary windings of an ignition coil it creates an expanding magnetic field. This magnetic field produces a magnetizing force proportional to the current in amperes and the number of primary turns. For example: 200 turns × 4 amperes = 800 ampere turns. As the number of turns is fixed, the magnetizing force is proportioned to the strength of the primary current. However, because of the principle of self-induction (the inducing of a voltage in a current-carrying conductor when the current in the conductor is changing), a voltage will be induced in the winding. The polarity of this new induced voltage will be such as to oppose the change in current flow that produced it. As a result of this counter-induced voltage in the primary winding, the current flow in the primary does not reach its maximum value in amperes immediately the primary circuit is completed. Instead, a time lag exists which causes the current to steadily rise to its final value.

Self-induction also takes place when the current flow through the primary winding decreases. This change in current flow induces a voltage in the

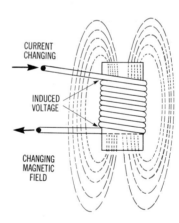

Fig. 41-5   Self-Induction

winding with a polarity that attempts to keep the current flowing in the same direction as the battery current and at its maximum value. This self-induced voltage may rise to 250 volts or more and it is the cause of the arc that appears whenever a switch is opened in an inductive circuit.

Since the secondary winding of an ignition coil is wound around the outside of the primary winding, any changing magnetic flux created by the current flow in the primary winding cuts across the

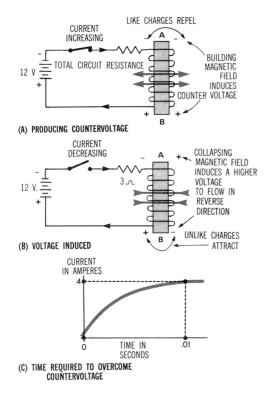

(A) PRODUCING COUNTERVOLTAGE

(B) VOLTAGE INDUCED

(C) TIME REQUIRED TO OVERCOME COUNTERVOLTAGE

Fig. 41-6   Ignition Coil Self-Induction

windings of the secondary coil. This changing magnetic flux will, by the principle of mutual-induction (the inducing of a voltage in one coil because of a changing current flow in another coil) induce a voltage in the secondary winding.

When the primary circuit is completed, the current flow will gradually increase to its maximum value and, in doing so, will induce a voltage in the secondary winding. When the primary circuit is opened, the sudden decrease in current will induce a voltage in the secondary winding. The magnitude of the voltage induced in the secondary winding is determined basically by the ratio between the number of turns of wire in the primary and the number of turns of wire in the secondary, and by the voltage in the primary winding. Therefore, if when the primary circuit is opened a self-induced voltage of 250 volts is created in the primary winding, and if the secondary winding has 100 times more turns of wire than the primary winding, the secondary voltage should be 250 volts $\times$ 100 or 25,000 volts.

It is by the application of this principle that the 12-volt battery voltage can be increased, first by self-induction in the primary winding of the ignition coil to 250 volts, then by mutual-induction to the 25,000 volts that is required to fire the spark plug.

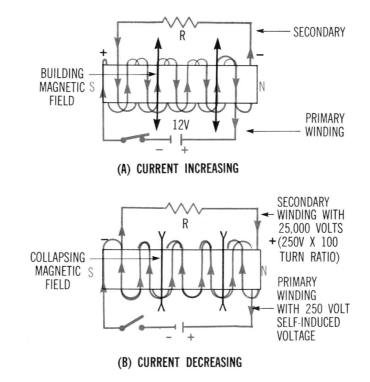

(A) CURRENT INCREASING

(B) CURRENT DECREASING

Fig. 41-7   Ignition Coil Mutual Induction

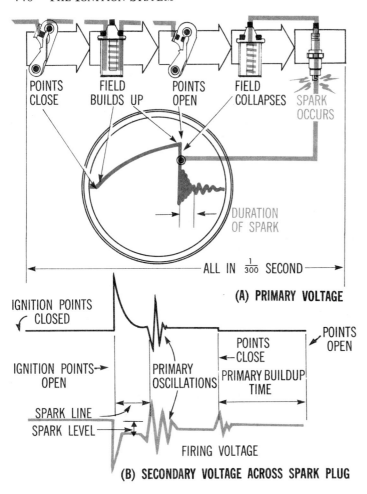

POINTS CLOSE   FIELD BUILDS UP   POINTS OPEN   FIELD COLLAPSES   SPARK OCCURS

DURATION OF SPARK

ALL IN 1/300 SECOND

(A) PRIMARY VOLTAGE

IGNITION POINTS CLOSED

IGNITION POINTS OPEN

SPARK LINE
SPARK LEVEL

PRIMARY OSCILLATIONS

FIRING VOLTAGE

POINTS CLOSE

PRIMARY BUILDUP TIME

POINTS OPEN

(B) SECONDARY VOLTAGE ACROSS SPARK PLUG

Fig. 41-8   Voltages in Primary and Secondary of Ignition Coil During One Spark Cycle

This high voltage is required to first overcome the resistance of the spark-plug gap; then it must maintain the spark. A much smaller voltage is required to maintain the spark for its proper duration period.

41-5 ENERGY INPUT TO THE IGNITION COIL

The voltage output of an ignition coil is in direct proportion to the amount of energy that is stored in the magnetic system in the coil itself and is expressed by the relation $\frac{1}{2}\,LI^2$ (when L is the coil inductance and I is the primary current flowing when the circuit is opened). This equation states that the higher the inductance and the higher the current flow, the greater the amount of energy stored in the coil, and therefore the greater will be the energy available to fire the spark plug.

There are many factors which affect ignition coil input, some of which are: heat, engine speed, igni-

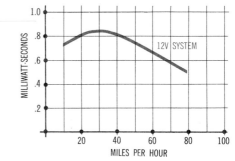

Fig. 41-9   Energy Input to Coil

tion-point spacing, and resistance in the primary circuit.

Heat. Heat plays an important part in ignition-coil operation. After magnetic saturation of the winding core (the point when all the electron orbits are arranged in one direction) has been reached, the energy represented by the current flowing through the primary winding is expended as heat. The power (P) loss through heat is equal to the amount of current flowing squared (I^2), multiplied by the resistance (R) of the copper primary wire. It may be expressed as $P = I^2 \times R$.

As the primary winding heats up, the resistance of the copper wire increases, thus causing a reduction in current flow. This reduces the ampere turns and lowers the magnetic induction obtainable. The lower the magnetic induction, the lower the high voltage output of the ignition coil.

At low engine speeds, the longer duration of current flow through the primary winding produces heat and increases the resistance of the primary winding. At high engine speeds the shorter duration of current flow produces less heat, and therefore less resistance. This feature results in a more even high-voltage output of the ignition coil over a wide range of engine speeds. The cooling oil and the case dissipate the excess heat.

Engine Speed. At low engine speeds, the ignition points remain closed for a long enough period of time for the primary current to reach its maximum value, even though this value is not reached immediately because of self-inductance. At higher engine speeds, the primary current never reaches its maximum value because the ignition points do not remain closed for a long enough period of time for the current to overcome the effects of self-inductance. However, the reduction in resistance, because of the reduced temperature of the primary winding at higher speeds, increases the primary current flow and maintains a more even ignition coil output.

Ignition Point Gap Spacing. Since current only flows through the primary circuit when the ignition points are closed, the smaller the point gap opening the longer the ignition points remain closed. The longer the ignition points are closed, the greater the buildup of the magnetic field around the primary winding. Conversely the wider the ignition point gap spacing, the smaller the magnetic buildup. The designing engineer calculates the proper ignition point gap spacing to provide maximum magnetic field buildup over a wide engine speed range.

Primary Circuit Resistance. Increased resistance results in reduced current flow and any reduction in current flow decreases the magnetic energy of the primary winding, resulting in a reduction of energy available in the secondary windings. Therefore, it is of the utmost importance that the proper voltage be available at the coil at all times.

It should be pointed out that the value of the maximum current flow through the primary circuit is determined from Ohm's Law by the system voltage and the primary-circuit resistance. From this it would appear that by reducing the primary-circuit resistance (thus increasing the current flow and therefore the energy input to the coil), greater secondary output of the coil could be obtained. However, the maximum allowable current flow is limited by the ability of the ignition point contacts to handle the current and still provide an acceptable service life. Each ignition system is designed for maximum voltage output that will allow good ignition point life.

41-6 SECONDARY VOLTAGE REQUIREMENTS

The energy of the secondary circuit of the ignition system appears in the form of a high voltage that charges the capacitances of the secondary circuit and causes the spark plug to fire. The secondary capacity is measured in micro-microfarads, and is determined by: engine compression, fuel-air ratios, spark-plug temperatures, the shape and width of the spark-plug gap, the polarity of the spark plug, the length of the spark-plug leads, and the air gap between the rotor and the distributor cap inserts.

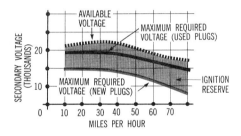

Fig. 41-10   Secondary Voltage Requirements

The maximum energy transferred to the secondary circuit can be calculated by $\dfrac{CE^2}{2}$ when C is the secondary capacity and E is the secondary voltage. From this equation it can be noted that a higher secondary voltage can be obtained by reducing the secondary capacitance.

Misfiring of a spark plug will occur when the voltage required to fire the spark plug is greater than the voltage available from the ignition coil. The margin of voltage which can be obtained from the ignition coil that is above the amount required to fire the spark plug is called the *ignition electrical reserve*. Maintaining this electrical reserve is an important function of ignition service work.

In order to keep spark plug voltage requirements low, it has been found that it is easier for the spark to jump the gap when the electrodes have sharp corners instead of round. During normal service, a spark-plug gap may increase as much as .015 of an inch, and the centre electrode will usually become rounded, losing its sharp edge. These plug conditions increase the voltage required to fire the spark plug by approximately 5,000 volts, and thus reduce the available ignition electrical reserve. Filing off the rounded end of the spark plug centre electrode and readjusting the gap will lower the voltage requirement to approximately that of a new plug.

Also it has been found that electrons flow more readily from a hot surface than a cool one. Since the centre electrode is the hottest part of the spark plug, the spark gap ionizes most readily from this point. Thus a spark plug with a negative polarity at the centre electrode requires approximately 5,000 volts less to fire than one with a positive polarity. For this reason, ignition circuits usually are connected to give negative polarity at the centre electrode of the spark plug. This is accomplished by battery polarity and by phasing the direction of the primary and secondary windings of the ignition coil in such a way as to obtain the desired negative voltage.

Ignition electrical reserve is also improved by installing the ignition coil close to the distributor and by keeping the spark-plug leads as short as possible, thereby reducing the electrostatic capacitance of the distribution system.

High-tension wiring and spark plugs are also points where electrical reserve may be lost. Braided covering on the ignition wiring may form a more conductive path when wet and cause voltage leakage. A wet conductive surface adds capacitance which also will reduce available voltage. The outside surface of a spark plug is also important. Using a rubber boot to cover the spark plug can lower the voltage leakage to 5% as compared to a 50% voltage loss if the spark plug is left unprotected under the same adverse conditions.

Since the high voltage of the ignition coil is not reached instantaneously, but is gradually built up, the voltage will increase until it is sufficient to overcome the resistance offered by the spark-plug air gap. The wider the gap, the greater the voltage required. The specified width of the gap must be such that there is sufficient ignition electrical reserve

to maintain ignition during the normal life of the plug. Should the plug become partly fouled, some current will flow across the coating on the insulator which is acting like a shunt across the air gap. This alternate path reduces the peak voltage that can be built up by the ignition coil. In the case of a badly fouled spark plug, the voltage built up may not be sufficient to allow the current to jump the air gap and the plug does not create a spark to ignite the fuel-air mixture. This causes the engine to miss.

41-7 TYPES OF IGNITION COILS

Can-Type Ignition Coils. The can-type ignition coil is made up of primary and secondary windings, a laminated soft iron core, a protective case, connecting terminals, a bakelite sealing cap, and a cooling oil.

The primary winding consists of about 200 turns of a large wire (No. 20 gauge) capable of carrying the battery current. The secondary winding consists of about 20,000 turns of very fine wire (No. 40 gauge) in which the high-voltage surges of current originate. The windings are wrapped around the core, and the core and windings are positioned and insulated from the bottom of the case by a porcelain insulator. Heavy paper insulation is wrapped around the outside of the primary windings to prevent them from touching the laminated liner placed

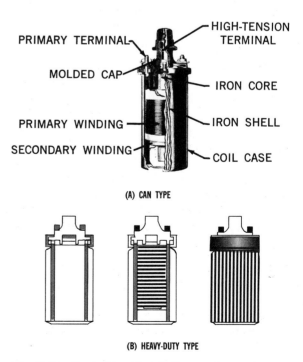

Fig. 41-11 Typical Ignition Coils

inside the case. The core and liner are made of laminated or scored iron to reduce eddy current losses. The ends of the primary winding are attached to their respective primary terminal. One end of the secondary winding is attached to the high-tension terminal, the other end is attached to one of the primary winding terminals. The sealing cap positions the terminals, keeps out moisture, and seals in the oil which is used to help dissipate any heat produced by the primary windings.

The primary current, and to a large extent the secondary voltage characteristics of the coil, will depend upon the primary winding resistance. The normal resistance of this winding in a 12-volt coil is approximately 1.15 ohms.

Heavy-Duty Coils. Heavy-duty ignition coils are built with additional insulation, cast fins on the coil case, oil filling, and other construction features which help to dissipate heat faster and allow this coil to operate with less temperature increase than other coils. The heavy-duty coil can be used in hotter locations, and may be expected to provide long service under difficult operating conditions.

A sealing nipple should be used on the high tension terminal of every ignition coil. Its use prevents the leakage of current to the primary terminal. The accumulation of oil, dirt, and moisture on the coil cap will cause carbonized paths and a breakdown of ignition unless the area surrounding the terminals of the coil are kept clean and dry. Synthetic elastic compounds have proven the best materials for this purpose, as they resist corona effects and oil to a greater extent than rubber.

41-8 THE CONDENSER

When the ignition points separate, and the magnetic field around the primary windings of the ignition coil collapse, a self-induced voltage of 250 volts or more is induced in the windings. The electrons already in motion continue to flow in the same direction and continue to maintain magnetic lines of force. The self-inductance of the coil slows down the collapse of the magnetic field. This induced voltage also causes an arc to form across the ignition-point contacts. In order to bring the primary current to a quick controlled stop, and to reduce the size of the arc and thereby prolong ignition point contact surface life, a condenser (capacitor) is connected across the ignition points. The high voltage induced in the primary windings of the coil causes the condenser plates to become charged

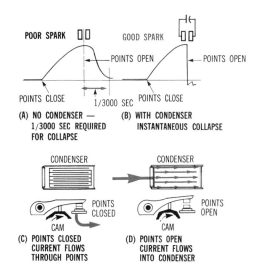

Fig. 41-12   Condenser Action

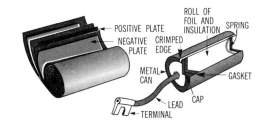

Fig. 41-13   Condenser Construction

when the ignition-point contacts first separate. The condenser acts initially like a short circuit and current flows into the condenser to minimize arcing at the contacts.

The condenser consists of two metallic plates, usually tin foil or aluminum foil, placed in close proximity but separated by a thin layer of insulated paper. The unit is then rolled tightly and placed in a metal container. One layer of the foil is grounded to the container and the other is attached to an insulated terminal.

The principles of condenser action are as follows: when the ignition points open even as small an amount as a millionth of an inch, the current is diverted into and charges the condenser. When the ignition points open, the electrons leaving the battery will congregate on the condenser negative plate. This plate will then have an excess of electrons and be said to be negatively charged. At the same time, electrons will leave the other plate and cause this plate to become positively charged. The electrons flow only through the circuit, not through the insu-

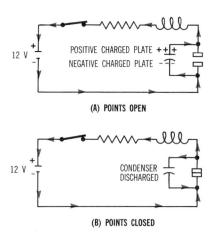

Fig. 41-14   Condenser Principles

lating material separating the condenser plates. As more and more electrons accumulate on the negative plate and leave the positive plate, the voltage across the plates increases until it equals battery voltage, at which time the flow of electrons ceases. However, when the ignition-point contacts separate, the collapsing primary magnetic field induces a high voltage in this primary winding because of self-inductance. This high voltage further charges the condenser plates since the current flows into the condenser, thus minimizing the arcing at the ignition points.

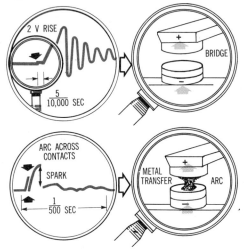

Fig. 41-15   Ignition Point Arc

This charging of the condenser brings about an immediate stop to the flow of current in the primary and results in extremely fast collapse of the primary magnetic field, which in turn produces the high voltage in the secondary winding of the coil.

During the period that the ignition-contact points

are open, the condenser becomes charged to a voltage higher than that of the battery or any other portion of the circuit. This causes a current to flow in a reverse direction to battery current. Since the ignition points are open, this current has no place to go but around the circuit to the opposite plate of the condenser, charging this plate up in the opposite direction. This process continues giving an oscillating current and voltage to the primary which produces an oscillating voltage in the secondary. Because of the dissipating of energy in the spark and the resistance of the primary circuit, the strength of the oscillating current decreases with each cycle or

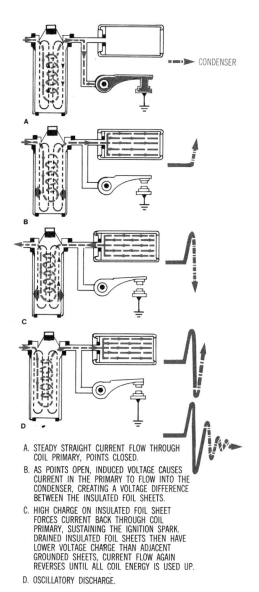

A. STEADY STRAIGHT CURRENT FLOW THROUGH COIL PRIMARY, POINTS CLOSED.

B. AS POINTS OPEN, INDUCED VOLTAGE CAUSES CURRENT IN THE PRIMARY TO FLOW INTO THE CONDENSER, CREATING A VOLTAGE DIFFERENCE BETWEEN THE INSULATED FOIL SHEETS.

C. HIGH CHARGE ON INSULATED FOIL SHEET FORCES CURRENT BACK THROUGH COIL PRIMARY, SUSTAINING THE IGNITION SPARK. DRAINED INSULATED FOIL SHEETS THEN HAVE LOWER VOLTAGE CHARGE THAN ADJACENT GROUNDED SHEETS, CURRENT FLOW AGAIN REVERSES UNTIL ALL COIL ENERGY IS USED UP.

D. OSCILLATORY DISCHARGE.

Fig. 41-16   Condenser Action While Ignition Points Are Open

oscillation. It dies out rather rapidly as the charge of the condenser decreases in voltage, ceasing completely when the voltage drops to battery voltage. The frequency of these oscillations is constant, and a resonant frequency results. This frequency is inversely proportional to the square root of the product of the condenser capacity and the inductance of the coil.

When the ignition points close, the condenser is shorted out and the condenser voltage drops to zero and is completely discharged.

It was once thought that this oscillating current produced by the condenser discharging through the primary windings was responsible for the quick collapse of the primary magnetic field so as to induce the high voltage in the secondary. However, tests have proven that the condenser is still being charged at the instant the spark occurs at the spark plug. Therefore, the discharge of the condenser has no effect on the spark itself. The condenser's only function as far as ignition is concerned is to absorb and hold the current that would otherwise cause arcing across the ignition-point contacts and delay the collapse of the primary magnetic field.

Condenser operation depends upon three factors: *capacity*, *leakage*, and *series resistance* or *power factor*.

Capacity—the capacity of a condenser is dependent upon the ability of the plates of the condenser to store and to discharge electrical energy. When an electrical potential is placed across an uncharged condenser, a charging current starts flowing at a high rate, but then gradually decreases as the plates become charged. The amount of electricity a condenser can store is equal to its capacity multiplied by the voltage applied and is measured in micro farads. Most ignition condensers have a capacity of 0.2 to 0.35 micro farads.

The capacity of the condenser must be large enough to prevent arcing and burning of the ignition-point contact surfaces, yet small enough to reduce the transfer material from one ignition-point contact surface to the other. The exact capacity required depends upon the design of the entire ignition system and also upon the type of operating conditions encountered.

Leakage—because of the limiting factors in condenser construction, a condenser does not represent true capacitance. There is always some leakage resistance because of insulation losses and resistance

in the internal connections. This leakage must be determined in order to evaluate the effectiveness of the condenser.

Series resistance or power factor—refers to the time lag or the time required to fully charge the condenser. Since the condenser is responsible for spark duration, and the current that charges the condenser during this period is an alternating current, the more rapid the oscillations or higher the frequency, the more important the time required to charge the condenser becomes. The power factor of a condenser then takes into account the capacitance, the series resistance, and the number of cycles per second and is usually expressed as a percentage.

Most ignition condensers are mounted inside the distributor housing. The exact location is not important as long as it is close to the ignition points and has a good ground connection and a good insulated lead connection without resistance.

41-9 THE DISTRIBUTOR

The distributor includes units of the primary circuit (points and condenser); units of the secondary circuit (cap and rotor); and the mechanisms required to advance the time the spark occurs at the plug in accordance with engine speed and load conditions.

Distributor Housing and Shaft. The distributor consists of a cast-iron housing into which the distributor shaft and centrifugal weight base assembly are fitted with suitable bearings. These bearings may be of the bronze-bushing type, the ball-bearing type, or the shaft may turn directly in the housing.

The distributor shaft is driven by a gear which meshes with a gear on the camshaft, or by a tongue which fits into the oil pump shaft, which is in turn gear-meshed to the camshaft. In either case the distributor shaft rotates at camshaft speed.

Breaker Points or Ignition Points. Breaker points or ignition points are used to open and close the primary circuit. When the points are closed, current flows through the primary circuit. When they are open, current cannot flow. The breaker-point contact faces are usually made of tungsten. One contact face is on the stationary breaker point. This point is attached to the breaker plate in such a manner that the point gap can be adjusted. It also usually includes a pivot pin for the breaker arm. The other contact face is attached to the breaker arm. This arm includes a fibre or nylon block which

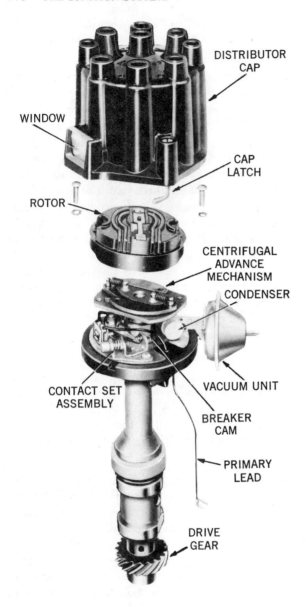

Courtesy of General Motors

Fig. 41-17   Typical Distributor Assembly

contacts the corners or lobes of the breaker cam. A breaker-point spring attached between the breaker arm and the primary distributor terminal conducts the primary current to the points and also returns the points to the closed position after they have been opened by the lobes of the cam. The opening and closing of the ignition points for an 8-cylinder engine takes place 266 times a second to produce the 16,000 sparks required when the engine is running at 4,000 rpm.

The contact breaker arm of a 4- or 6-cylinder engine opens and closes the primary circuit a fewer number of times per second than the arm of an

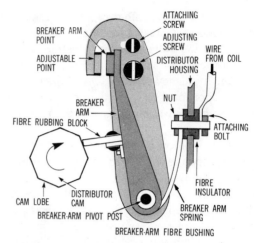

Fig. 41-18   Ignition-Point Construction

8-cylinder engine. Therefore, the 4- or 6-cylinder arm can have somewhat greater mass and perhaps less spring tension than that required for an 8-cylinder engine. An 8-cylinder engine requires the use of a low-inertia or high-speed type of contact arm and requires higher contact-spring tension to assure that the rubbing block will follow the cam contour under high engine speeds.

Contact arm ratio refers to the amount of contact point movement as compared to rubbing block movement. For example: if the arm is pivoted at one end and the rubbing block is placed in the centre of the arm, then the contacts will move twice the distance of the rubbing block. Moving the rubbing block closer to the contact point decreases the contact point movement. Moving the rubbing block closer to the pivot increases the contact point movement.

Rubbing block friction and wear must be balanced against contact point erosion and contact point spring tension. As the rubbing block wears, it decreases contact point spacing and retards the ignition timing. As the contact points erode the contact spacing increases and advances ignition

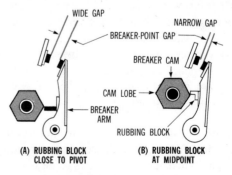

Fig. 41-19   Rubbing Block Location

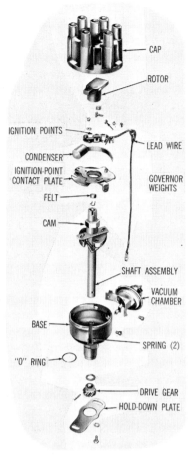

Chrysler Canada Ltd.

Fig. 41-20   Typical 6-Cylinder Distributor
(Exploded View)

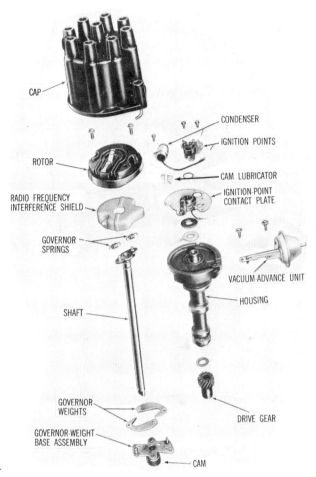

Courtesy of General Motors

Fig. 41-21   Typical V8 Distributor (Exploded View)

timing. It is necessary then to try to balance the rubbing block wear with point erosion to maintain proper contact point spacing throughout the life of the contact. If the rubbing block is properly lubricated with special distributor grease, and proper spring tension is maintained, little rubbing block wear will result.

Too low contact point spring tension does not keep the rubbing block against the cam at high rpm. This prevents the contact points from closing, thus producing what is known as *point bounce*. When the points bounce, they do not close, eliminating one ignition coil cycle and causing the engine to miss.

Oils and greases have deteriorating effects on the contact materials and also create oxides which increase the electrical resistance between the contact point surfaces.

The Breaker Cam. The breaker cam is used to open and close the breaker points. This cam has the same number of lobes as there are cylinders in the engine. The cam is rotated by the distributor shaft, which in turn is geared to and driven by the camshaft. One revolution of the distributor shaft is equal to two revolutions of the crankshaft, or one four-stroke cycle. The distributor drive shaft is so meshed with the camshaft that each time a piston reaches approximately TDC (top dead centre) of the compression stroke, a lobe of the cam is in position to open the breaker points. This is called *ignition timing*.

The design of the breaker cam lobes and the contact point spacing control the buildup of the ignition coil. This is frequently referred to as *cam-dwell angle*. Cam-dwell angle is the number of degrees the distributor drive shaft and cam rotate between the closing of the contact points and when they reopen again.

It should be pointed out that on any given distributor, increasing the cam-dwell angle reduces the contact point spacing and vice versa. When both cam dwell and point spacing specifications are given, the use of the cam-dwell setting is preferred since it can be set more accurately by using a cam-dwell meter. However, a minimum contact point spacing must be maintained. Should the spacing be below the minimum, then a compromise between the two settings is required.

Various means are used in cam design, contact arm ratio, and contact spacing to achieve the proper cam-dwell angle. Many late model distributors are equipped with a special high-rate-of-break cam and a special high speed contact arm which is capable of following the cam shape at high speeds without bouncing. The high-rate-of-break cam separates the contact points faster for each degree of rotation and permits earlier closing of the contact points, thus increasing cam-dwell angle. With the special breaker cam and contact arm combination, it is possible to obtain 34 to 36° of usable cam-dwell angle on an 8-cylinder distributor. On an 8-lobe cam, any further increase of cam-dwell angle may cause loss of engine performance through "overlapping." Overlapping means that the contact points close before the preceding primary surge has collapsed completely, thus making less energy available for the next primary surge.

Distributor Cap. The distributor cap is made of bakelite and fits on top of the distributor housing. Around the perimeter of the cap are terminals for each spark-plug wire, and a central terminal, for the high-tension wire from the ignition coil. On the inside of the cap, the plug terminals have brass fingers extending down past the cap material. The centre terminal has either a spring-loaded or fixed carbon rod which contacts the centre of the rotor brush. The cap is properly positioned on the housing by placing the cap tongue, which is located on the lower edge, into a slot machined in the housing. Spring clips, screw clips, or screws are used to seal the cap tightly to the housing to prevent the entrance of moisture or dirt.

The Rotor. The rotor is used to carry the secondary voltage from the centre terminal of the cap to the plug terminal. It is attached to the top of the shaft and rotates with the shaft. A tongue on the inner surface of the rotor fits into a groove on the shaft to maintain proper relationship between the rotor and the shaft. The outer edge of the rotor has a brass terminal that passes very close to the brass fingers on the plug terminals of the distributor cap. Attached to the rotor terminal is a spring that rubs against the carbon of the centre terminal. When a high-voltage surge from the ignition coil arrives at the centre terminal of the cap, it travels down the carbon rod to the rotor spring, through the spring and rotor terminal, jumps the small gap between

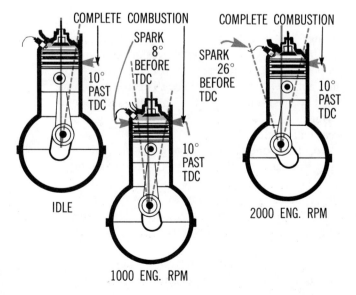

Fig. 41-22   Spark Advance and Engine Speed

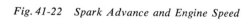

the rotor and the side terminal of the cap, and continues through the high-tension wire to the spark plug. The spark-plug wires are arranged in the distributor cap according to the direction of rotation of the rotor and the firing order of the engine.

41-10 IGNITION ADVANCE MECHANISMS

In order to ensure the application of maximum combustion pressure on the piston, it is necessary to vary the time the spark occurs at the spark plug, according to engine speed and load.

When an engine is idling, the spark is timed to occur in the cylinder just before the piston reaches TDC of the compression stroke. The higher the engine speed, the shorter the interval of time available for the fuel-air mixture to ignite, burn, and give up its power to the piston. The burning time of a normal fuel-air mixture in an automobile engine is approximately .003 of a second. To obtain full power from combustion of this mixture, the maximum pressure must be reached when the piston is between 10° and 20° past TDC. At 1,000 engine rpm, the crankshaft travels through 18° in .003 of a second; at 2,000 rpm the crankshaft travels through 36°. Since the maximum pressure point is fixed, the spark must be produced earlier in the cycle in order to deliver full engine power, as engine speed increases. This is accomplished by the mechanical advance mechanism.

When the engine is operated at part throttle, a high vacuum develops in the intake manifold and a smaller amount of fuel and air is drawn into the cylinder. The mixture is thus leaner and consequently becomes less highly compressed. Under these conditions, additional spark advance (over and above the amount of advance provided by the mechanical advance mechanism) will increase fuel economy. This is because a leaner mixture, at lower compression, burns slower. In order to realize maximum power from lean mixture, ignition must take place still earlier in the cycle. This is accomplished by the vacuum advance mechanism.

Mechanical Advance Mechanism. A centrifugal governor advance mechanism attached to the distributor shaft controls the time at which the spark occurs, according to engine speed. The mechanical advance mechanism consists primarily of two weights, tension springs, and a cam assembly. As engine speed increases, the weights throw out against the spring tension. The motion of the weights turns the cam assembly so that the breaker cam is rotated in the direction of shaft rotation to an advanced position with respect to the distributor drive shaft. The higher the engine speed, the more the weights throw out, and the further the breaker cam is advanced. This revolution of the cam opens the breaker points sooner, thus advancing the spark.

The centrifugal advance required differs considerably among various engines. In order to determine the advance curve for a given engine, the en-

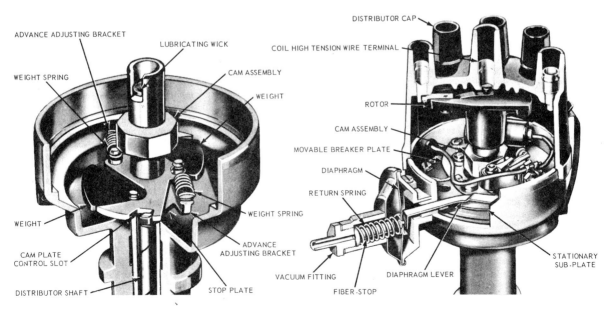

Fig. 41-23 Typical Advance Mechanism

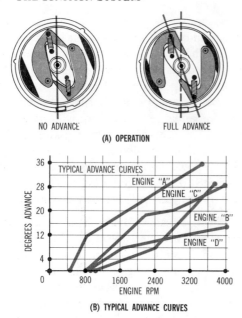

Fig. 41-24   Mechanical Advance Mechanisms

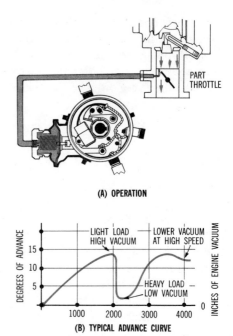

Fig. 41-25   Vacuum Advance Mechanisms

gine is operated on a dynamometer at various speeds with wide-open throttle. Spark advance is varied at each speed until the range of advance that gives the maximum power is found. The cam assembly weights and springs are then selected to give this advance curve. Timing consequently varies from no advance at idle speeds to full advance at high engine speeds, where the weights reach the outer limits of their travel.

Vacuum Advance Mechanisms. Two types of vacuum advance mechanisms are used: the external type which is attached to the distributor housing and rotates the entire distributor in its mounting; and the internal type which rotates the breaker-plate assembly only. The operation of both types is based on intake manifold vacuum conditions. When manifold vacuum is applied to either type, the distributor housing or the breaker plate is rotated. This rotation causes the contact points to be carried around the breaker cam to an advanced position, so that the breaker cam opens and closes the points earlier in the cycle. This provides a spark advance based on the amount of vacuum in the intake manifold. Thus, for varying compressions in the cylinder, the spark advance will vary, permitting greater economy of engine operation. The additional advance provided by the vacuum control is effective in providing additional economy only on part-throttle operation.

At any given engine speed there will be a certain definite amount of spark advance resulting from the operation of the mechanical advance mechanism, plus a possible additional spark advance resulting from the operation of the vacuum-advance mechanism. For example: if a mechanical advance mechanism supplies 15° advance at 40 mph and if the throttle is only partly opened, an additional vacuum advance of up to 15° more may be obtained, making a total of 30° of spark advance. When the throttle is wide open there is no appreciable vacuum in the intake manifold, so this additional vacuum advance will not be obtained. All the spark advance then is based on engine speed alone and is supplied by the mechanical advance mechanism.

The vacuum advance mechanism may be thought of as an economy device which will increase fuel

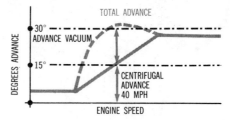

Fig. 41-26   Typical Combination of Mechanical and Vacuum Advance Curves

economy when properly used. Constant wide-open throttle operation, whether in low or high gear, will not obtain this additional advance with its resulting increased fuel economy. Also, since the vacuum advance does not occur at wide-open throttle, it has no affect during rapid acceleration.

External vacuum advance mechanisms — consist of a spring-loaded diaphragm connected by linkage to the distributor housing. The spring-loaded side of the diaphragm is air-tight, and is connected by a vacuum passage to an opening in the carburetor. This opening is on the atmospheric side of the throttle when the throttle is in the idle position. In this position, there is no vacuum in the passage.

As the throttle is partly opened, it swings past the opening of the vacuum passage. Intake-manifold vacuum can then draw air from the air-tight chamber in the vacuum advance mechanism and cause the diaphragm to be moved against the spring. This motion is transmitted by the linkage to the distributor housing, thus rotating the distributor in its mounting. It is important that such distributors move freely in their mountings so that the vacuum advance unit will function properly. The amount of distributor housing rotation is governed by the amount of vacuum in the intake manifold up to the limit imposed by the design of the vacuum-advance mechanism.

Internal vacuum advance mechanisms—contain a spring-loaded diaphragm connected by linkage to the breaker plate. The spring-loaded side of the diaphragm is air-tight and is connected by a vacuum passage to an opening in the carburetor. This opening is on the atmospheric side of the throttle valve when the throttle is in idling position. In this position, there is no vacuum in the passage.

As the throttle is partly opened, it swings past the opening of the vacuum passage. Intake manifold vacuum can then draw air from the air-tight chamber in the vacuum advance mechanism and cause the diaphragm to be moved against the spring. This motion is transmitted by linkage to the distributor breaker plate thus rotating it in its mounting. The breaker plate only rotates with respect to the remainder of the distributor. Several designs have been brought out for this purpose. All have the same action of moving the breaker contact arm against the direction of distributor shaft rotation so that the rubbing block meets the cam earlier in the cycle to provide advanced timing.

Distributors with only vacuum advance units. Some distributors use only a vacuum-advance unit. The vacuum side of this unit is connected to the venturi area of the carburetor instead of to the intake manifold. The linkage of this unit is connected to the breaker-point plate in the usual manner. The amount of spark advance is controlled by the vacuum created by the volume of air rushing through the venturi. The volume of air passing through the venturi is in direct proportion to engine speed and load. Therefore, the vacuum created and applied to the diaphragm of the vacuum advance unit and the resulting movement can be used to advance the spark the correct amount.

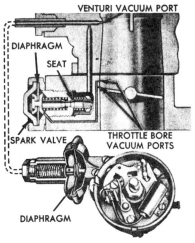

Ford of Canada

Fig. 41-27 Typical Spark Advance Control Using Vacuum Advance Only

41-11 DUAL IGNITION-POINT DISTRIBUTORS

Some high-performance engines are equipped with dual ignition-point distributors in which two complete sets of ignition points are used. The point sets are connected in parallel and are mounted in such a manner that their opening and closing is staggered. That is to say first one set opens, then the other; the first set closes, and then the other. The last set to open is called the *break set* and the first set to close is called the *make set*. With this arrangement it is possible to increase cam-dwell angle.

Dual ignition-point distributor operation is as follows: when the distributor cam is rotated and one cam lobe opens the make set of points, the primary current continues to flow through the break-point set. Further rotation of the cam causes a different lobe of the cam to open the break-point

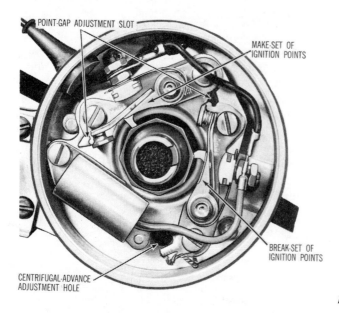

Fig. 41-28   Dual Ignition-Point Distributor

Ford of Canada

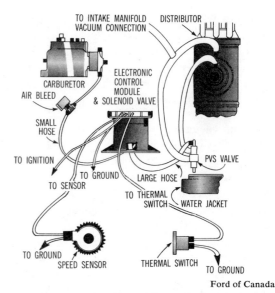

Ford of Canada

Fig. 41-29   Typical Exhaust Emission-Control Ignition System

set (make set is still open), and current stops flowing in the primary windings of the ignition coil, thus inducing a voltage in the secondary. As the distributor cam rotates further, the make set of points will close and current again flows through the primary circuit. As the cam continues to rotate, the break set of points closes. Therefore, the number of degrees that the cam rotates while no current flows in the primary circuit is reduced; thus the build-up time of the primary winding is increased, resulting in more efficient ignition-coil operation at high engine speeds.

41-12 EXHAUST EMISSION-CONTROL IGNITION SYSTEMS

Some ignition systems include a distributor modulator which is a device for reducing engine exhaust emissions by close control of distributor spark advance during specified conditions of acceleration and deceleration. The system contains five major components: a *speed censor*, a *thermal switch*, an *electronic control amplifier*, a *three-way solenoid valve* controlling the vacuum applied to the distributor, and a *dual vacuum chamber distributor*.

The control amplifier and the solenoid valve are usually combined and mounted behind the dash panel. This unit determines the application of vacuum to the two vacuum chambers of the vacuum advance mechanism according to information received from the other units in the system.

The temperature-sensing valve is mounted in the coolant outlet elbow and is used to direct vacuum to the advance mechanism according to engine temperature. For example: should the engine operating temperature rise above normal (such as during periods of prolonged idling), this valve directs engine vacuum to the distributor in a manner so as to advance the spark timing, thereby increasing engine speed. This condition continues until the operating temperature returns to normal.

A thermal switch that is mounted in such a manner so as to be operated by outside air temperature prevents the operation of the modulator system when outside air temperature is below 58°F.

The speed censor is mounted in the speedometer cable and directs engine vacuum to the distributor to prevent spark advance below a specified speed when accelerating, and also prevents spark advance below a specified value on deceleration.

Dual vacuum advance distributors contain a standard type of mechanical advance mechanism and a dual-diaphragm vacuum advance unit. The dual-diaphragm unit consists of two independently operating diaphragms. One unit (the inner) retards the spark the correct amount for idling speeds and during deceleration periods. The other unit (the outer) provides the correct spark advance for acceleration and other types of driving.

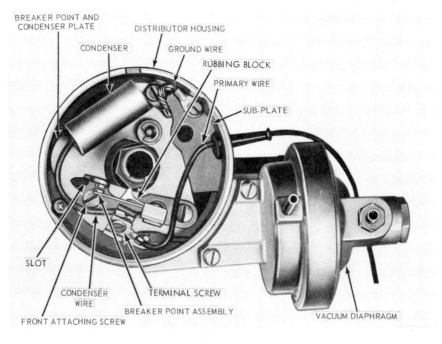

BREAKER POINT AND
CONDENSER PLATE

CONDENSER

DISTRIBUTOR HOUSING

GROUND WIRE

RUBBING BLOCK

PRIMARY WIRE

SUB-PLATE

SLOT

CONDENSER
WIRE

TERMINAL SCREW

BREAKER POINT ASSEMBLY

FRONT ATTACHING SCREW

VACUUM DIAPHRAGM

(A) ASSEMBLY

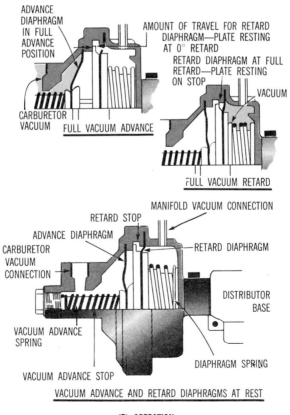

ADVANCE
DIAPHRAGM
IN FULL
ADVANCE
POSITION

AMOUNT OF TRAVEL FOR RETARD
DIAPHRAGM—PLATE RESTING
AT 0° RETARD

RETARD DIAPHRAGM AT FULL
RETARD—PLATE RESTING
ON STOP

VACUUM

CARBURETOR
VACUUM   FULL VACUUM ADVANCE

FULL VACUUM RETARD

MANIFOLD VACUUM CONNECTION

RETARD STOP

ADVANCE DIAPHRAGM

CARBURETOR
VACUUM
CONNECTION

RETARD DIAPHRAGM

DISTRIBUTOR
BASE

VACUUM ADVANCE
SPRING

VACUUM ADVANCE STOP

DIAPHRAGM SPRING

VACUUM ADVANCE AND RETARD DIAPHRAGMS AT REST

(B) OPERATION

Fig. 41-30   Dual-Diaphragm Distributors

Ford of Canada

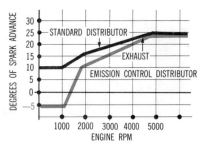

Fig. 41-31   Spark-Advance Curves for Standard and Exhaust Emission-Control Distributors

In this type of advance mechanism, calibrated springs bear against the vacuum sides of the diaphragms of both units. The springs supply resistance to the actuating force of the vacuum. The diaphragm of the outer unit is connected to the breaker-point plate and provides the necessary advance according to engine vacuum and in addition to the mechanical advance.

The diaphragm of the inner unit serves to position a return stop for the outer unit. This stop governs the amount of spark retard when the spark advance vacuum is reduced. In its normal position it gives a spark retard of 6° before TDC for starting purposes. In the other position it gives a spark retard of 12° after TDC which provides a setting more suitable for complete combustion during idling and deceleration periods.

41-13 TRANSISTORIZED IGNITION SYSTEMS

The transistorized ignition system makes use of a solid state electronic transistor that is a low voltage unit with a current-carrying capacity superior to that of the conventional ignition breaker points.

In the conventional ignition system, the ignition breaker points and the ignition coil are in the same circuit and the primary current is limited by the amount of current that the ignition breaker points can withstand. The higher the current flow, the greater the metal transfer between the breaker-point contact surfaces (pitting), and the shorter the ignition point life.

When a transistor is placed in the ignition circuit, the emitter is connected to the ignition switch, the collector to the primary of the ignition coil, and the base circuit to the ignition breaker points. Since only a small amount of current flow through the base circuit will trigger the collector current, only a small amount of current flows through the breaker points, thus prolonging ignition breaker-

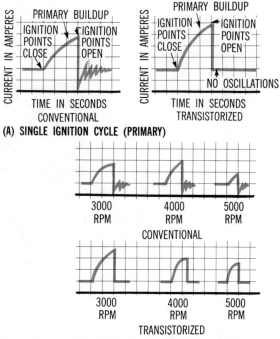

(A) SINGLE IGNITION CYCLE (PRIMARY)

(B) SINGLE IGNITION CYCLE AT VARIOUS ENGINE SPEEDS PRIMARY

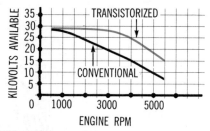

(C) SECONDARY VOLTAGE OUTPUT

Fig. 41-32   Comparison of Ignition Cycles (Conventional and Transistorized)

point life. Also the transistor permits greater current flow to the primary winding of the ignition coil. The transistor also permits the use of an ignition coil in which the current builds up much faster than in the conventional ignition system because of the low coil inductance and the total system resistance ratio. The current buildup in the primary windings in the conventional ignition system is slower and of much less magnitude than in the transistorized system.

With the conventional ignition system, the faster the engine is operated, the shorter the buildup time of the primary, and thus less and less secondary voltage. The transistorized ignition system, however, permits current buildup almost instantaneously so that higher engine speed, with its reduced buildup time interval, has less effect upon the resultant current buildup until a very high engine speed is attained.

At low engine speeds, the magnitude and rapidity of the current buildup of a transistorized ignition system results in only a slight increase in secondary voltage over the conventional system, because the conventional system has sufficient time to become saturated under low-speed conditions. At high engine speeds the lesser inductance is more than compensated for by the higher current flow provided by the transistorized system, so that there is far less drop in available secondary voltage.

41-14 TRANSISTORIZED IGNITION COMPONENTS

The transistorized ignition system includes the following units: the *amplifier* which contains a heat sink, a *condenser*, a *zener diode*, a *torid*, the *transistor*, the *cold-start relay, ballast resistors*, and the *distributor*.

The Amplifier. The amplifier or heat sink is made of cast aluminum and is finned for rapid heat dissipation. This is an important requirement inasmuch as both the transistor and the zener diode have temperature limitations necessitating rapid heat dissipation. The amplifier serves as the housing, or base, in which are mounted the transistor,

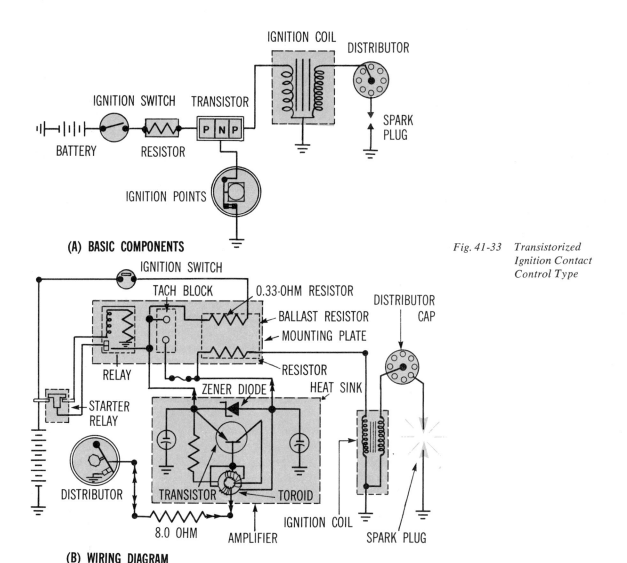

Fig. 41-33 Transistorized Ignition Contact Control Type

the zener diode, the torid, the condenser, a resistor, and capacitor.

The Transistor. The transistor is a continuous duty NPN, germanium-type graded base-type power transistor. It is very rugged in construction and designed to operate satisfactorily within an ambient temperature range of $-40°$ to $160°F$.

Zener Diode. The zener diode is intended for transistor over-voltage protection. It acts as a voltage actuated relay that provides a shunt circuit whenever the voltage to the transistor reaches a predetermined value.

The Torid. The torid is a block and coil assembly. It serves to stop the collector current at the instant the base current is triggered. This is accomplished by the collapse of the magnetic field of the coil which sends a reverse current through the base circuit.

The Condenser. The condenser serves the same purpose as the condenser in the conventional ignition system, that is, the absorption of the high inductive energy during the initial triggering of the base circuit. The condenser is located in the cellector circuit, not in the base circuit.

The Resistor. The resistor is in the base-to-emitter torid circuit and serves as a factor to control the path of the current in the base-emitter circuit.

The Capacitor. The capacitor is a safety device which serves to prevent damage to the transistor because of the opening of the battery circuit with the engine running, or the development of high resistance at the battery terminals.

Cold Start Relay. A cold start relay is connected into the circuit at the starter relay to interrupt the conventional battery-to-coil lead. It is used to furnish additional current to the primary coil windings during the period when the starter draw is excessive.

Ballast Resistors. The collector and emitter resistors are both located in a resistor block which is made of ceramic and provides electrical and thermal insulation. Both resistors serve the same purpose to limit the system current and to control the voltages in their respective circuits.

41-15 THE DISTRIBUTOR AND TRIGGERING DEVICES

The distributor, like the conventional type, is made up of two basic sections: the distributor section, the cap and rotor; and the timing section, including the trigger control device, breaker points or impulse generator, and the necessary advance mechanism. Since all the units other than the trigger control device are the same as the conventional distributor, only the trigger devices will be discussed here. There are several types of trigger control systems used: the *contact-controlled*, the *magnetically controlled*, and the *capacitor-controlled*.

The Contact-Controlled System. The contact-controlled system uses a set of conventional-type ignition breaker points connected into the base circuit. When the points are closed, current flows through the emitter-base and the emitter-collector circuits. When the points open, the base current is interrupted and hence, the collector current. The interruption of the collector current causes the collapse of the primary magnetic field of the ignition coil to produce the high voltage surge in the secondary circuit which is required to fire the spark plug.

Magnetically Controlled System. The magnetically controlled system includes a magnetic pickup or pulse distributor and a pulse amplifier connected between the battery and the ignition-coil primary windings.

The distributor is mounted and driven in the same manner as a conventional distributor. The magnetic pickup or pulse unit is made up of a permanent magnet, a pole piece which has a series of teeth pointing inward, one for each cylinder of the engine, and a coil of many turns of fine wire mounted inside the magnet. This unit is assembled and mounted over the main bearing of the distributor housing. The assembly is not fixed in position, but is free to rotate a given amount. Its rotation is controlled by a vacuum advance unit to provide the proper amount of spark advance in accordance with engine load.

A *timer-core*, made of iron which has the same number of outward pointing teeth as there are cylinders in the engine, is assembled on and rotates with the distributor shaft. The timer-core assembly includes a conventional-type mechanical advance mechanism to provide spark advance according to engine speed. As the distributor shaft rotates, the timer-core and pole-piece teeth align 8 times (for

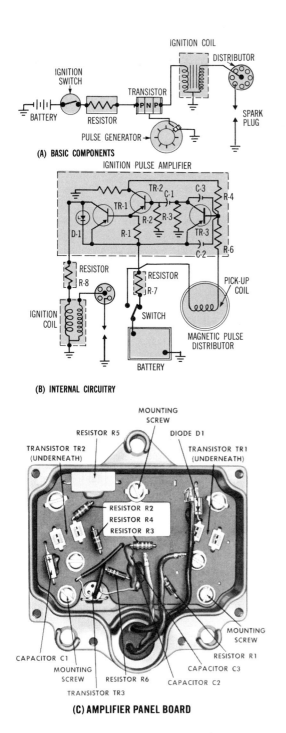

(A) BASIC COMPONENTS

(B) INTERNAL CIRCUITRY

(C) AMPLIFIER PANEL BOARD

Courtesy of General Motors

Fig. 41-34   Transistorized Ignition Pulse Control Type

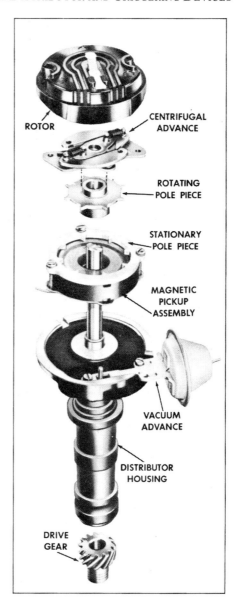

Fig. 41-35   Magnetic Pulse Distributor Components

That is, the magnetic lines of force of the permanent magnet cut through the turns of wire of the pick-up coil, inducing a voltage in the coil. This induced voltage sends a signal or pulse of current to the base circuit of the three-section transistor mounted in the amplifier.

When the current flows through the base of this transistor, battery current flows to ground through the transistor instead of the primary windings of the ignition coil. This causes the collapse of the primary winding magnetic field and induces the voltage in the secondary windings of the ignition coil to fire the spark plug.

an 8-cylinder engine) per revolution of the distributor shaft. This compares with the 8 times (for an 8-cylinder engine) that the ignition breaker points open in a conventional distributor. Every time the timer-core and the pole-piece teeth align, a magnetic path is completed through the pick-up coil.

As the distributor shaft rotates and the teeth of the timer-core and the pole piece are no longer aligned, the magnetic path through the pick-up coil is broken; the surge of current to the base of the transistor ceases. When there is no base current in this transistor, battery current flows to the base of the second transistor mounted in the amplifier. A base current in the second transistor causes battery current to flow through the primary windings of the ignition coil to build up the primary magnetic field.

This series of events occurs each time the distributor shaft rotates far enough to align the teeth of the timer-core and the pole piece.

Capacitor Discharge Controlled Ignition System. A capacitor discharge control, or CD, ignition system utilizes an oscillator (a device which produces electrical fluctuations in a circuit, i.e., produces a flow of electrons alternately in opposite directions) to step up the battery voltage from 12 volts to about 400 volts. This voltage is used to charge a capacitor at the appropriate time and discharge into the primary windings of the ignition coil. The timing of the capacitor charge and discharge may be controlled by ignition breaker points or an impulse generator. When ignition breaker points are used, the circuit requires a silicon control rectifier (SCR); when an impulse generator is used it is connected to the base circuit of a transistor. In either case the charging and discharging of the capacitor provides the necessary current flow to build up and collapse

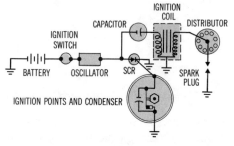

Fig. 41-36   Capacitor Discharge (CD) Ignition

the primary magnetic field to produce the high voltage surge required to fire the spark plug.

41-16 COMPARING THE VARIOUS TYPES OF IGNITION SYSTEMS

The spark-discharge characteristics of each of the ignition systems are decisively different, as shown by the simplified voltage curves in Fig. 41-37. In each case a voltage surge is initiated in the secondary circuit when the breaker points open. The voltage builds up rapidly and continues to rise until the spark plug fires. A conventional ignition system buildup time is usually about 70 microseconds, whereas the transistor system is about 70% slower, or 120 microseconds, and the CD system is about 30% faster, or 50 microseconds. After the spark plug has initially fired, a large amount of electric energy is released and the voltage drops rapidly to a much lower level for the remainder of the spark duration. The spark duration of the conventional system is about 1600 microseconds. A transistor-switched system requires almost twice as long at 3,000 microseconds, and the CD system is much quicker at 300 microseconds.

A comparison of the maximum potential voltage or open-circuit output voltage characteristics of the

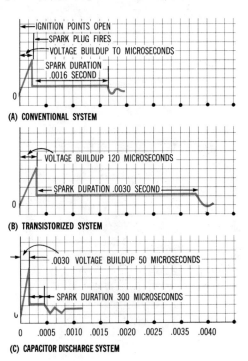

Fig. 41-37   Comparison of Secondary Characteristics

various ignition systems, along with the corresponding current requirements, are shown in Fig. 41-38. The improvements in secondary-output voltage potential gained by electronic switching of the primary circuit at higher currents and voltages is immediately apparent. Voltage potential is shown to be high at cranking speeds to assure positive starts and is uniformly maintained up to very high engine speeds.

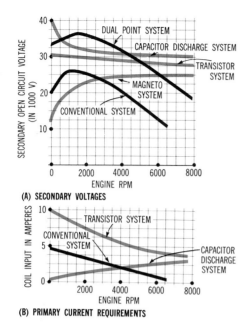

(A) SECONDARY VOLTAGES

(B) PRIMARY CURRENT REQUIREMENTS

Fig. 41-38   Comparison of Primary and Secondary Requirements and Voltages

Tests show very rapid voltage-rise times, such as those encountered on CD ignition systems, are conducive to easy starting and clean-burning spark plugs. Long spark duration, such as that encountered on the transistorized units, has been shown to perform well and can in some cases allow more ignition advance with a more uniform horsepower output at high speeds. The transistor systems, however, because of their extremely long spark duration, cause spark plugs to erode more rapidly and have indicated poor starting characteristics because of the slow voltage-rise time. The CD ignition system, on the other hand, discharges its energy very rapidly, and spark plug erosion is reduced. There is a practical minimum for spark duration, however, for street use. Engine operation at low speed and low power output are poor when spark duration times are below 300 microseconds, particularly with lean fuel-air ratios.

41-17 MAGNETO IGNITION

A magneto is an electrical device which generates, times, and distributes an electrical surge of power to fire a spark plug. A magneto does not require a battery to operate. The magneto ignition system is used on many 2- and 4-cycle engines that power lawnmowers, garden tractors, snowmobiles, or outboard engines.

41-18 MAGNETO CONSTRUCTION

A magneto consists of a primary and secondary circuit. Both circuits have windings which surround the same iron core. Magnets in the flywheel or rotor act on both circuits. Current can be induced by changing the polarity of the magnetism in and around each coil as the flywheel rotates and the magnet is brought into proximity with the coil and core.

The flywheel magnet may be of the ceramic or Alnico type; each type develops very high magnetic strength.

A set of ignition breaker points and a condenser are included in the primary circuit to control the magnetic effect in the primary circuit.

41-19 MAGNETO OPERATION

As first the north pole, then the south pole of the rotating magnet is turned between the laminated coil core-pole shoes. The magnetic field in the core is built up as the north pole passes, collapses as it moves away, and is built up again with opposite polarity as the south pole passes the core-pole shoes. This building, collapsing, and rebuilding with opposite polarity will cause a current to be induced in the coil.

Connecting one end of the primary winding of the coil directly to ground and the other end to ground through the breaker points creates a circuit in which a voltage can be built up when the magnetic field is established. As the magnet is rotated, the field collapses, but the field that has been built up in the primary winding will be retained through electromagnetic action (the tendency of a current to keep flowing). As the magnet continues to turn and the south pole approaches the core-pole pieces, an attempt is made to reestablish the magnetic lines of force, but in the opposite direction. The magnetic field built up around the primary by the current flowing through it will resist the field reversal. Tremendous magnetic stress is therefore set up in the field.

Opening the ignition breaker points at this instant results in the primary field collapsing the lines of force in one direction, and instantly reestablishing them in the opposite direction. This results in two very fast magnetic-force field line changes and is sufficient to induce a high voltage in the secondary circuit.

Each time the magnet passes by the coil, the same series of events produces a high-voltage surge

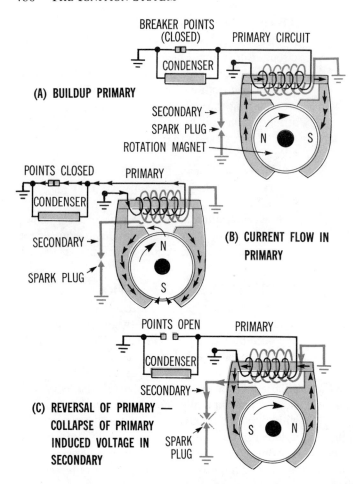

Fig. 41-39   *Magneto Operation*

in the secondary. One or more coils can be placed around the circumference of the flywheel to fire 2 or more cylinders of a 2-cycle engine. In 4-cycle engines the speed of the breaker-point cam must be reduced to one-half crankshaft speed on single cylindered engines to prevent a "Maverick Spark" occurring at the end of the exhaust stroke.

41-20 HIGH-TENSION WIRES

High-tension wires carry the high-voltage surges from the ignition coil to the distributor cap and from the cap to the spark plugs. These wires must be well insulated to prevent the high voltage from escaping to ground before it reaches the spark plug. The insulation, usually rubber, must withstand heat and cold and be impervious to gasoline, oil, and water. The electric conductor may be stranded copper wire, a linen thread impregnated with carbon, or a graphite-saturated fibreglass core. The two latter types, called *resistance wire*, are the most commonly used today as they eliminate radio and television interference. Suitable clips or wire ends

are used to attach the wires to the cap and spark plug.

The capacity of high-tension wiring must be kept as low as possible to have a low capacity reactance. For this reason then, the spark plug wires are kept as short as possible. Corona losses exist at any point in the high-tension wiring where a potential *gradient*, which is a large voltage drop in a short distance, appears. If the potential gradient is sufficient, visable corona may appear. It usually starts at a point where the wire makes a sharp turn, and can be observed along the high-tension wiring in darkness. Corona represents a power loss and causes rapid deterioration of the high-tension wires due to corona cutting.

41-21 SPARK PLUGS

The Spark Plug. The spark plug is threaded into the cylinder head or cylinder block, with its lower end protruding into the combustion chamber. The fuel in the cylinder is ignited by the spark produced by passing a high-voltage surge of current across

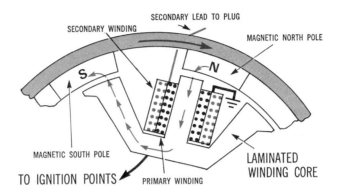

(A) DIRECTION ON MAGNETIC FIELD IN POSITION 1

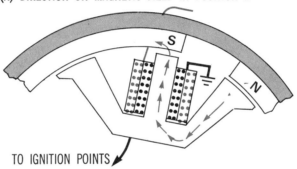

(B) DIRECTION OF MAGNETIC FIELD POSITION 2

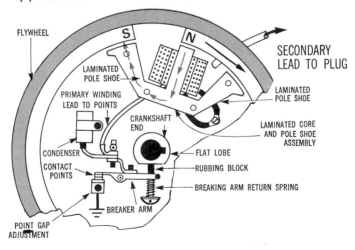

(C) ASSEMBLY

Fig. 41-40   Flywheel Magneto

(A) 6 CYLINDER

FIRING ORDER ①⑤④②⑥③⑦⑧ (EXCEPT SUPER DUTY)
1 5 4 8 6 3 7 2 (SUPER DUTY)

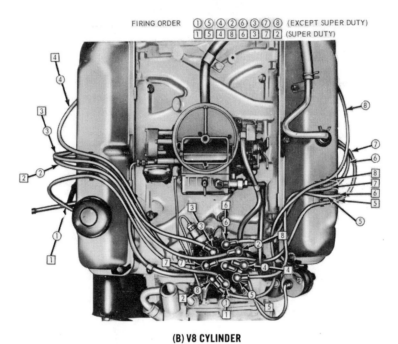

(B) V8 CYLINDER

Fig. 41-41   Secondary Wiring   Ford of Canada

an air gap between two electrodes. The spark plug provides these electrodes in the combustion chamber of the engine; it is built to withstand electric surges of 10,000 to 30,000 volts and pressures up to 800 pounds per square inch.

A spark plug consists of a steel shell threaded on one end so that it may be screwed into the threaded hole in the cylinder block or head. A porcelain insulator that will withstand high temperatures, pressures, and voltages is placed inside the steel shell. A centre electrode is fastened in the insulator with a terminal on top, and extends below the insulator at the bottom. The core and shell are assembled with suitable seals to prevent leakage of the gases in the cylinder and to aid in conducting heat. A ground electrode is welded to the shell. The space between the ends of the two electrodes is called the *air gap*. The air gap varies from .025 to .040″ and can be adjusted by bending the ground electrode.

The designing engineer specifies an air gap that will give the best over-all performance. The amount of gap specified is determined by the voltage required to fire the spark plug.

Spark-Plug Sizes. Spark-plug sizes are determined by the size of the thread and the thread lengths, or reaches. The popular types of threads used are ⅞ inch-18, 18MM and 14MM. The length of the thread or reach depends on the type of cylinder head used and the distance between the spark plug seat in the head and the combustion chamber. The

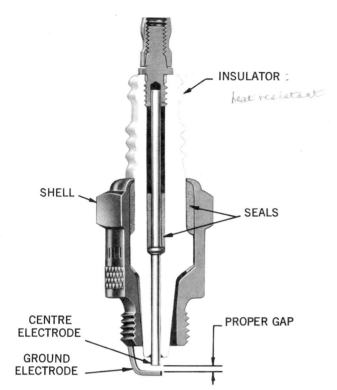

Fig. 41-42 Spark Plug Detail

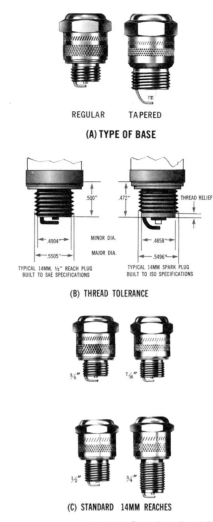

(A) TYPE OF BASE

REGULAR   TAPERED

(B) THREAD TOLERANCE

.500"   .472"   THREAD RELIEF

.4904   MINOR DIA.   .4858"

.5505"   MAJOR DIA.   .5496"

TYPICAL 14MM, ½" REACH PLUG
BUILT TO SAE SPECIFICATIONS

TYPICAL 14MM SPARK PLUG
BUILT TO ISO SPECIFICATIONS

(C) STANDARD 14MM REACHES

⅜"   ⁷⁄₁₆"   ½"   ¾"

Champion Spark Plug Co. of Canada Ltd.

Fig. 41-43 Spark-Plug Sizes

size is usually measured in inches.

Spark plugs may have flat seating surfaces that require a spark-plug gasket to ensure a good seal between the plug and the engine head, or block. Other spark plugs have a tapered seat which provides adequate sealing without the use of gaskets.

Spark-Plug Heat Ranges. The temperature at which the nose of the insulator operates determines the heat range of the spark plug. The temperature of the insulator nose must be high enough to burn off any carbon or other combustion deposits, but not too high so as to cause pre-ignition (igniting of the fuel before the spark occurs at the plug air gap) or deterioration of the insulator or the electrodes. The temperature of the insulator nose varies greatly with different engines and different operating conditions. This temperature depends upon the design of the engine, compression ratios, the cooling system, the fuel-air ratio, and driving conditions.

The nose of the insulator absorbs heat from the burning of the fuel. This heat travels up the insulator to the spark-plug shell, to the cylinder head, and then to the water jackets where it is dissipated.

The longer the length of the insulator, the greater the area that is exposed to the heat of combustion.

The larger the area, the greater the amount of heat of combustion that is absorbed by the insulator. The additional length of the path transversed by the heat in reaching the cooling system, the material of which the insulator is made, and the shape of the insulator all affect its operating temperature.

If the path the heat must follow in order to reach the cooling system is long, then the spark plug will have a higher operating temperature than a plug with a shorter heat path. Spark plugs with long heat paths are known as *hot plugs*. Spark plugs with short heat paths are known as *cold plugs*.

Hot plugs are used when driving conditions or engine wear cause the plugs to become fouled with oil, soft carbon, or other deposits. Hot plugs are better able to burn off or vaporize these accumulations. Where high-speed or heavy-load driving tends to burn the electrodes and insulators, a cold

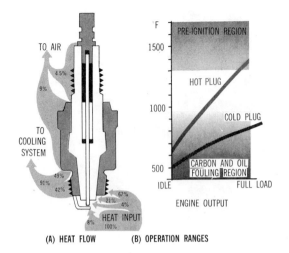

(A) HEAT FLOW   (B) OPERATION RANGES

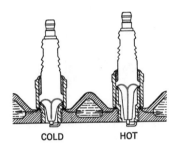

(C) HEAT FLOW PATH (HOT- AND COLD-TYPE PLUGS)

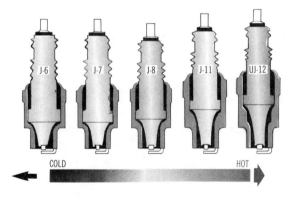

(D) VARIOUS HEAT RANGE PLUGS

Champion Spark Plug Co. of Canada Ltd.

Fig. 41-44   Spark Plug Heat Ranges

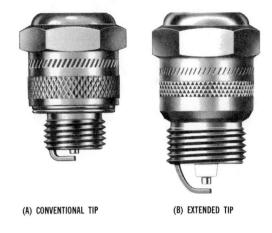

(A) CONVENTIONAL TIP   (B) EXTENDED TIP

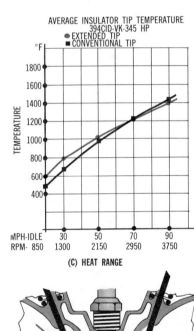

(C) HEAT RANGE

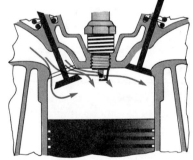

(D) OPERATION

Champion Spark Plug Co. of Canada Ltd.

Fig. 41-45   Extended-Nose Spark Plug

plug gives better service, because it can carry off the heat faster. The engine designer selects a spark plug with a heat range which will give good performance under average driving conditions. Abnormal operating conditions will necessitate the installation of hotter or colder heat-range plugs.

Extended-Nose or Thermal-Tip Spark Plugs. In late-model high-compression engines, where the spark plugs are required to run hotter at low speeds and colder at high speeds, special extended-nose or thermal-tip plugs are used. In this type of plug, the insulator tip extends beyond the lower end of the spark-plug shell. This places the firing tip deeper into the combustion chamber which results in higher firing-tip temperatures at low speed. The higher temperatures, plus the swirling of the exhaust gases around the tip, provide a self-cleaning action which tends to burn away combustion deposits that tend to form during low-speed operation.

At higher speeds, the fuel-air mixture entering the cylinder passes over and around the firing tip, providing additional cooling which results in lower tip temperatures.

Resistor-Type Spark Plugs. Resistor-type spark plugs are used to eliminate radio and TV interference when standard metallic conductor-type spark-plug wires are used. The resistor is placed inside the porcelain between the centre electrode and the spark-plug terminal.

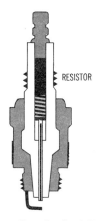

Champion Spark Plug Co. of Canada Ltd.

Fig. 41-46   Resistor-Type Spark Plug

Surface-Gap Spark Plugs. A surface-gap spark plug is one which by design and construction delivers a spark which travels from the centre electrode to the shell across the surface of a ceramic insulator. There is no ground electrode or air gap as on a conventional spark plug. Surface-gap plugs have been designed to operate in specific engines, usually the type with capacity discharge (CD) ignition systems. This type of plug cannot be used indiscriminately in other engines.

The surface-gap spark plug is designed so that the inside diameter of the shell at the firing end is machined to a fixed distance from the centre electrode. The entire end of the shell, therefore, forms one big ground electrode. The spark passes across the ceramic insulator between the shell and the centre electrode to ignite the fuel-air mixture. Usually, each spark occurs at a different location across the surface of the insulator.

In specific applications, surface-gap spark plugs offer the following advantages: they operate cooler, eliminate pre-ignition due to spark plugs, are less

(A) SECTION VIEW

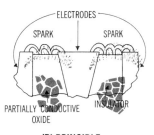

(B) PRINCIPLE

Fig. 41-47   Surface-Gap Spark Plug

susceptible to fouling and require less frequent maintenance and replacement.

41-22 THE OSCILLOSCOPE

The oscilloscope is an electronic ignition testing device which, when connected into the ignition primary or secondary circuits, produces a pattern or wave form of the voltages of either circuit. The device contains a TV-type cathode-ray-oscilloscope

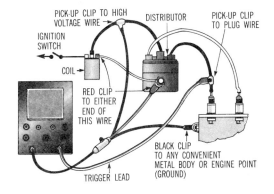

Fig. 41-48   Typical Oscilloscope Connections

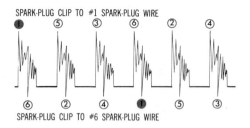

Fig. 41-49 *Typical Oscilloscope Wave Form*

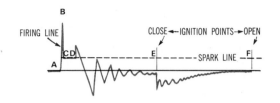

Fig. 41-50 *Typical Secondary Wave Form*

tube. Every voltage surge produced by the ignition coil or condenser is sensed by the pickup device of the tester and a signal is transmitted to the tester. The tester then treats the signal electronically and produces the pattern or wave form of the voltage on the face of the oscilloscope tube. Each part of the wave form represents a specific phase of ignition-system operation. The wave form can be divided into the following sections: the firing, intermediate, and dwell sections for both the primary and secondary circuits.

The pattern or wave-form line (called a *trace*) that is produced by the oscilloscope is a picture of voltage in relationship to time. The vertical movement of the trace represents voltage of one polarity when above the zero line, and a voltage of the opposite polarity when below the zero line. The vertical movement or voltage can be measured by comparing it to the graduations on the scope screen. The scope screen is usually graduated in kilovolts (1,000 volts) to permit accurate reading of the secondary voltages and in 40-volt graduations for the primary circuit comparisons.

The horizontal movement of the trace represents time and is measured by comparing the movement to the cam-dwell scale across the bottom of the screen. Time in this case does not refer to minutes or seconds but to degrees of distributor-shaft rotation. If the scope trace for a 6-cylinder engine is adjusted so that one complete ignition cycle starts at zero and ends at 60° on the dwell scale of the scope screen, then any portion of the trace can be accurately measured in degrees of distributor-shaft rotation.

41-23 WAVE FORM INTERPRETATIONS

41-24 SECONDARY CIRCUIT WAVE FORMS

The Firing Section. It is during this section that the actual firing of the spark plug takes place. This portion of the wave form is composed of only two lines: the firing line, which is a vertical line indicating the voltage required to overcome the spark plug and distributor-rotor gaps; and the spark line, a horizontal line which indicates the voltage required to maintain the spark.

The start of the pattern, point A, represents the instant that the ignition points separate, causing the primary magnetic field to collapse. The resulting high voltage in the secondary circuit is indicated by the vertical rise from point A to point **B**. The height of point B indicates the firing voltage (sometimes referred to as the *ionization* voltage) required to overcome the resistance offered by the rotor and spark-plug gaps. Once this resistance is overcome, there is a noticeable drop in secondary voltage to point C. The voltage remains fairly constant at about one-quarter of the firing voltage until it extinguishes at point D.

The Intermediate Section. This section follows the firing section and is seen as a series of gradually diminishing oscillations that disappear by the time the dwell section starts. Between point D and point E the remaining energy in the ignition coil dissipates itself as an oscillating current. The oscillations are a result of the combined effects of the coil and condenser dissipating the remaining energy.

The Dwell Section. This section represents the period of time that the breaker points are closed and is sometimes referred to as the *coil buildup time*. When the ignition points close at point E, it causes a short downward line, followed by a series of small, rapidly diminishing oscillations, which represent the buildup of the magnetic field around the windings of the ignition coil. The dwell section ends at point F when the ignition breaker points open to start the next wave form. Point F of the first wave form is also point A of the next pattern.

41-25 PRIMARY CIRCUIT WAVE FORMS
The wave forms produced by the primary circuit

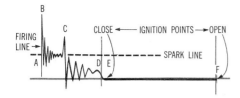

Fig. 41-51   Typical Primary Wave Form

are similar in appearance to those of the secondary circuit, but are indicated on lower voltage scales of either 40 or 400 volts. The lower voltage is because of the ratio of the primary and secondary windings of the coil.

The Intermediate Section. This section is seen as a series of gradually diminishing oscillations that disappear before the dwell section begins. Between point C and point D whatever electric energy remains in the primary circuit dissipates itself as an oscillating current, and is completely dissipated at point D.

The Firing Section. This section produces a pattern that indicates a series of rapid oscillations that take place in the primary circuit while the spark plug is firing. Point A represents the instant at which the ignition breaker points separate. The vertical rise from point A to point B and the diminishing oscillations between point B and point C represent the initial and repeated charging and discharging of the condenser and the induced voltage surges in the primary circuit during the spark-producing period.

The Dwell Section. This section begins at point D when the ignition breaker points close and is indicated by a slight downward line between point D and point E. The dwell section or coil buildup time is represented by the horizontal line between point E and point F. Point F represents the instant the points separate for the start of the next wave form, and would be point A of the following pattern.

41-26 PATTERN SELECTION

Various combinations of patterns may be viewed on an oscilloscope in order to make convenient comparisons between the various cylinders of an engine. These patterns are: *superimposed, raster,* and *display*.

Superimposed. This is the pattern obtained by simultaneously placing the patterns of all cylinders one on top of the other. Superimposed patterns provide a convenient method of comparing each ignition cycle for uniformity.

Raster. This pattern makes use of the vertical height of the scope screen and stacks each cylinder's ignition cycle pattern one above the other so

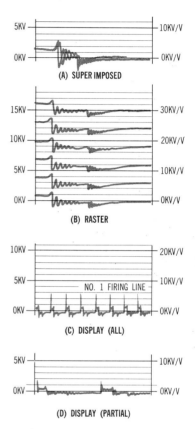

Fig. 41-52   Type of Oscilloscope Patterns

that all of the individual patterns are vertically displayed on the screen. The raster pattern provides detailed, close-up comparison of all ignition cycles simultaneously, and provides easy identification of the variations in the pattern of wave forms that were observed when the patterns were superimposed.

Display. In this pattern the trace moves horizontally from left to right, displaying ignition cycles in the engine's firing order until all cycles are completed. If the pick-up device is connected to number one spark plug it will appear at the extreme left of the screen. The display pattern permits the firing voltages of all cylinders to be measured individually or simultaneously.

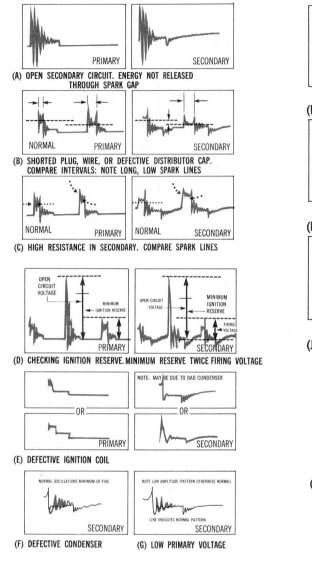

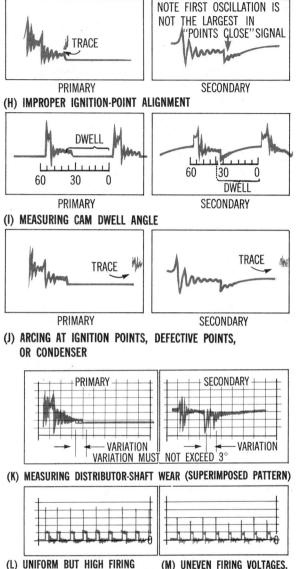

Fig. 41-53   Interpreting Oscilloscope Wave Forms

REVIEW QUESTIONS

1. State the three basic purposes of an ignition system.
2. Name and state the voltage in the two sections of a battery ignition system.
3. List the units of each section of a battery ignition system.
4. Many ignition switches have four positions. State the purpose of each position.
5. Why are multiposition switches used?
6. Why is there a better spark produced for starting purposes when the ignition primary circuit includes an ignition resistance?

7. Explain how a ballast-type ignition resistor helps to maintain a constant voltage to the ignition coil regardless of engine speed.
8. Explain electromagnetic induction.
9. How is the strength of a magnetic field calculated?
10. Explain the term self-induction.
11. What effect does self-induction have on the primary circuit of the ignition coil?
12. How is the self-induced voltage of the primary increased to 250 volts or more?
13. Describe the principle of mutual-induction.
14. Why does the ratio between the number of turns

of wire in the primary and the number of turns of wire in the secondary increase the voltage of the secondary?

15. How is the energy input to the ignition coil determined?

16. What is meant by the term "magnetic saturation"?

17. How is the electric energy flowing through the primary expended after magnetic saturation is reached? What effect does the expending of this energy have on coil operation?

18. How is ignition coil heat dissipated?

19. Why does (a) the primary-current flow not reach its maximum value at high engine speeds? (b) What effect does this have on secondary voltage? Why?

20. What effect does improper ignition point gap spacing have on secondary voltage output?

21. List four factors that determine secondary voltage requirements.

22. Explain the term "ignition electrical reserve."

23. Explain why and how each of the following effects ignition electrical reserve: (a) spark-plug gap, (b) rounded spark-plug electrodes, (c) spark-plug polarity, (d) length of spark-plug leads.

24. Why is the core and liner of an ignition coil made of laminated or scored iron?

25. What are the purposes of an ignition condenser?

26. Explain, using the electron theory, how a condenser becomes charged.

27. Explain how the condenser action prevents arcing at the ignition-point contact surfaces.

28. Describe how the energy that charged the condenser is dissipated while the ignition points are open.

29. When does the condenser become completely discharged?

30. Does the oscillating discharge of the condenser have any effect on the production of the secondary voltage? Why?

31. What is meant by condenser capacity?

32. What factors determine the capacity of a condenser?

33. List the units included in a distributor assembly.

34. How is the distributor shaft driven?

35. List two purposes of the ignition points.

36. What is the basic difference in construction between 4- or 6-cylinder ignition points and 8-cylinder ignition points? Why?

37. Why is it necessary to try to balance rubbing block wear to point erosion?

38. What effect does (a) too little (b) too much point spring tension have on ignition system operation?

39. What is meant by ignition timing?

40. How is the distributor used to produce ignition timing?

41. Explain the term "cam-dwell angle."

42. What effect does cam-dwell angle have on secondary voltage output?

43. What is the relationship between cam-dwell angle and ignition-point gap spacing?

44. Why is the cam-dwell method preferred over the spacing of ignition points by the feeler-gauge method?

45. What are the advantages of a high-rate-of-break cam?

46. Why does ignition overlapping reduce engine performance?

47. Why are ignition advance mechanisms necessary?

48. What is the approximate burning time of a normal fuel-air mixture in a cylinder?

49. How far does the crankshaft rotate during normal combustion when the engine speed is (a) 1,000 rpm (b) 2,000 rpm?

50. What is the most desirable position of the crankshaft when maximum pressure is produced in the cylinder?

51. How can the most desirable position of the crankshaft, when maximum pressure is produced, be maintained over various speed ranges?

52. What effect do various fuel-air ratios have on the time required for complete combustion of the fuel?

53. How can the most desirable position of the crankshaft, when maximum pressure is produced, be maintained as the fuel-air ratio changes?

54. How is centrifugal force used to maintain proper spark timing over various speed ranges?

55. How is engine vacuum used to maintain proper spark timing in accordance with the various fuel-air ratios?

56. How does the operation of the internal and external vacuum-advance units differ?

57. On distributors using only a vacuum-advance unit, how is proper spark timing maintained over the full speed and load ranges?

58. Describe the construction and operation of an exhaust-emission control distributor advance mechanism.

59. What is the main advantage of transistorized ignition?

60. State the manner in which a transistor is connected into the primary circuit.

61. Explain how the transistor controls primary current and at the same time reduces current flow through ignition points.

62. At what speed range is transistorized ignition more efficient? Why?

63. State the purpose of the amplifier in a transistorized ignition system.

64. What is the difference between a zener diode and a standard-type diode?

65. Why is a torid necessary in a transistorized ignition system?

66. Both a condenser and a capacitor are used in a transistorized ignition system. State the purpose of each unit.

67. State the differences in operating principles of the three commonly used triggering devices used in transistorized ignition systems.

68. How is proper spark timing maintained according to speed and load conditions in a transistorized ignition system?

69. Select the ignition system which you consider gives the best overall performance. State the reasons for your selection.

70. Why is the magneto ignition system the most common type of ignition system used on lawn-mower and other small-horsepowered engines?

71. Explain in detail how a magneto produces and times the spark at the spark plug.

72. Explain why the secondary voltage produced by a magneto does not drop appreciably at high engine speeds.

73. What effect will corona have on the ignition system?

74. What is the purpose of the air gap of a spark plug?

75. What effect would improper setting of the spark-plug air gap have on the voltage created in the secondary circuit of the ignition system? Why?

76. Why is the temperature of the spark-plug insulator nose of vital importance?

77. State four factors that affect the nose temperature of a spark plug.

78. What effect does (a) a long nose (b) a short nose have on the nose operating temperature of a spark plug? Why?

79. What are the advantages of extended-nose or thermal-tip spark plugs?

80. What is the difference between a surface-gap spark plug and a conventional-type spark plug?

81. What are the advantages of a surface-gap type of spark plug?

82. What does the wave form or trace produced by an oscilloscope represent?

83. How is this wave form produced?

84. Name and explain each of the four sections of the wave pattern for both the primary and secondary circuits.

85. Various combinations of wave patterns may be viewed on an oscilloscope screen. Name and state the purpose of each combination.

Chapter 42
IGNITION-SYSTEM SERVICE

Ignition-system service can be divided into several sections: the available voltage for the primary, the available voltage from the secondary, timing, distribution, and firing at the spark plug.

42-1 THE AVAILABLE VOLTAGE FOR THE PRIMARY

The effectiveness of the ignition system depends considerably upon the available voltage for the primary windings of the ignition coil. In order to have the proper available voltage, the battery must be fully charged. The battery posts and terminals must be clean, in good condition, and firmly attached. The charging circuit should also be functioning correctly to produce the specified system voltage during operation.

The primary circuit wiring and connections must be in good condition, clean and tight. Should the system develop resistance in the primary circuit above the amount specified by the manufacturer,

CONDITION	CAUSED BY
BURNED	Incorrect voltage regulator setting. Radio condenser installed to the distributor side of the coil.
EXCESSIVE METAL TRANSFER OR PITTING	Incorrect alignment. Incorrect voltage regulator setting. Radio condenser installed to the distributor side of the coil. Ignition condenser of improper capacity. Extended operation of the engine at speeds other than normal.

B1443-C

Ford of Canada

Fig. 42-1   Ignition-Point Inspection

or the available voltage be low, then the primary voltage will be reduced to a point where it can seriously affect the secondary circuit available voltage. The primary voltage at the coil should be tested during both cranking and running periods.

Ignition Breaker Points. Ignition breaker points that are burned, badly eroded, excessively pitted, or show signs of excessive metal transfer create high resistance in the primary circuit. Improperly gapped points or points with worn rubbing blocks change the buildup time of the ignition coil. All of

(A) CORRECT ALIGNMENT

(B) MISALIGNMENT OF CENTRES

(C) MISALIGNMENT OF POINT FACES

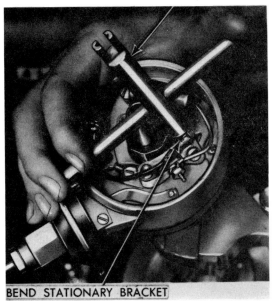

BEND STATIONARY BRACKET

(D) ALIGNING

Ford of Canada

Fig. 42-2   Ignition-Point Alignment

these factors can reduce the available primary voltage.

Ignition points in good condition are a dull, slate grey in colour and show contact in the central area of both contacts.

Ignition Breaker-Point Alignment. If the ignition breaker points are properly aligned, and if the points have flat contact surfaces, they should come together so that the entire surface touches at once. If the contact surfaces are both convex, or if one is convex and the other flat, contact should be in the centre.

If the alignment is not correct, use a suitable tool to bend the stationary point bracket to correct alignment. Never bend the movable arm.

Ignition Breaker-Arm Tension. The breaker-arm tension must be within specified limits to provide proper operation and wear. Too high breaker-arm tension causes excessive rubbing-block wear and reduces the point gap. This will retard the timing and increase the cam-dwell angle. Too little breaker-arm tension will cause the breaker points to float or bounce at high rpm.

To test breaker-arm tension, an ounce-type spring scale is used. Place the scale around the contact of the moveable arm and, with the points closed, pull outwards at right angles to the arm. Read the tension in ounces at the instant the ignition breaker points separate. If the tension is incorrect, it should be adjusted. On point sets with slotted springs, loosen the lock nut and slide the spring toward the pivot pin to decrease spring tension, or away from the pivot pin to increase tension. Tension of nonslotted springs may be decreased by squeezing the spring together, or increased by removing the breaker arm and bending the spring.

Some ignition-point sets are preassembled, the spring tension is set, and the points are properly aligned at the factory. Point sets of this type should be checked upon installation and if they do not meet specifications, adjust where advised or use another new set.

Point Gap and Cam-Dwell Angle. Point gap is the amount of opening between the breaker-point contact surfaces when fully opened by the distributor cam lobe. Cam-dwell angle refers to the distance in degrees of distributor-cam rotation that the cam revolves from the time the breaker points close until they open again. The cam-dwell angle for any given cam is controlled by the point-gap setting so the two must be considered together.

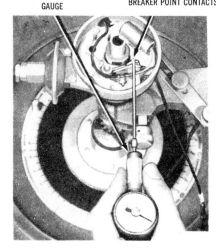

GAUGE   PULL AT RIGHT ANGLE WITH BREAKER POINT CONTACTS

(A) CHECKING

INCREASING TENSION

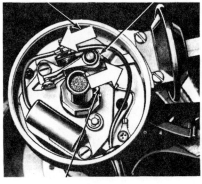

DECREASING TENSION

(B) ADJUSTING

Ford of Canada

Fig. 42-3   Ignition-Point Spring Tension

When the point gap is too small, cam-dwell angle will be too great and the breaker points will arc and burn. Excessive point gap, too little cam-dwell angle, will reduce the ignition coil buildup time and cause missing at high speed.

To check breaker-point gap, turn the distributor cam until the breaker-arm rubbing block is on the highest tip of one of the cam lobes. Measure the distance between the breaker-point contact surfaces with feeler stock. It may also be checked by attaching a dial indicator to the distributor housing, with its operating pin resting against the movable breaker arm. As the distributor cam is rotated, the arm movement will be recorded on the indicator.

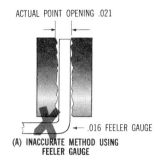

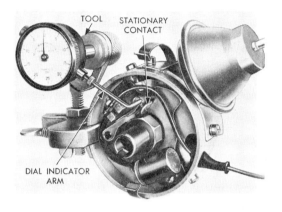

(B) ACCURATE METHOD USING DIAL INDICATOR

(A) Courtesy of General Motors
(B) Chrysler of Canada

Fig. 42-4   Measuring Ignition Point Gap Spacing

Also point gap may be checked by measuring the cam-dwell angle with a cam-dwell meter. The meter method is easy, quick, and accurate and is the most frequently used today.

To adjust point gap, follow the manufacturers' instructions. Generally, new gap specifications are around .003″ larger than those specified for used ignition points. This is to allow for the initial wear-in of the breaker-arm rubbing block.

42-2 THE AVAILABLE VOLTAGE FROM THE SECONDARY

After checking the available primary-circuit voltage, the ignition coil should be checked at normal operating temperature for both primary and secondary resistance and current draw. These tests should be performed both with the engine stopped and at idling speeds.

These tests usually expose any defects in the coil such as internal shorts, grounds, opens, insulation breakdown, and loose or corroded connections. To perform the tests use suitable, reliable test equipment and follow the manufacturers' instructions.

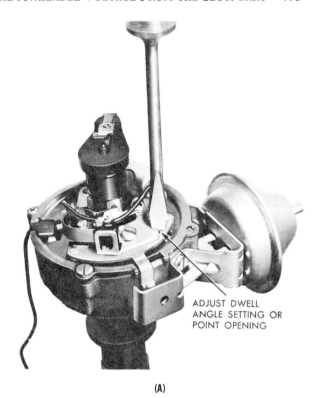

(A)

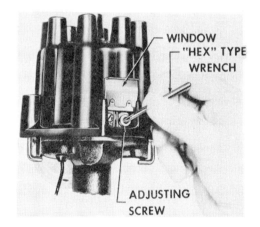

(B)

Courtesy of General Motors

Fig. 42-5   Setting Ignition Point Gap on Cam Dwell Angle

Ignition-Coil Polarity. The ignition coil must be connected into the primary circuit so that the coil polarity matches the battery polarity. If the negative post of the battery is grounded, then the negative-coil terminal must be connected to the distributor where it will be grounded through the ignition breaker points. By connecting the ignition coil in this manner, the centre electrode of the spark plug will assume a negative polarity.

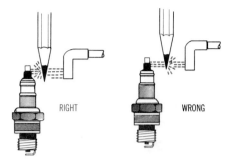

Fig. 42-6   Checking Ignition-Coil Polarity

Engineers have found that it takes considerably less voltage to cause free electrons to move from a hot to a cold surface, than vice versa. Therefore, it is imperative that the secondary current flow from the hot centre electrode to the cooler ground electrode of the spark plug.

Coil polarity may be checked with a voltmeter or by placing a lead pencil between the spark-plug lead and ground and observing the location of the flare. The flare should appear between the lead of the pencil and ground if the coil polarity is correct.

Secondary Wiring. Secondary resistance reduces available voltage at the spark plugs. Many engines use special resistance-type secondary wiring. Use an ohmmeter to check the wiring to determine if the resistance is within specifications.

Crossfiring. The secondary wires should be arranged in such a manner as to prevent crossfiring (one wire imparting enough voltage to an adjacent wire to cause the second wire to fire its spark plug). This can be accomplished by avoiding bunching of the wires and by criss crossing the wires to eliminate long parallel stretches.

The Distributor Cap and Rotor. Inspect the distributor cap and rotor and check for corrosion, burning, or flash-over. Flash-over is an external path to ground created by the secondary current flowing through dirt, moisture, or a small crack.

If the terminal posts or rotor contact are burned or grooved, replace the cap.

Inspect the rotor for excessive burning on the tip, for proper contact spring tension, and the resistance of the resistor if used.

It is considered good policy to replace both the distributor cap and rotor, should either one be found defective.

42-3 FIRING ORDER

Firing order is the numerical order in which the cylinders fire the fuel charge, starting with No. 1 cylinder. No. 1 spark-plug wire tower is marked on some distributor caps. If it is not marked, it should be marked before removing the wires. If No. 1 tower is unknown, it may be determined from the manufacturer's manual, or in the following manner. Remove the distributor cap and spark plugs. Crank the engine over until No. 1 cylinder is coming up on its compression stroke. Continue to crank the engine until the ignition timing mark is aligned with the pointer. The piston is now at approximately TDC of the compression stroke. Mark the outside of the distributor housing directly in line with the rotor tip. Replace the distributor cap, making sure the aligning tang is in place. No. 1 spark-plug wire is placed in the tower adjacent to the mark on the housing. The remaining wires are placed in the towers in their correct firing order, going around the cap according to the direction of rotation of the rotor.

If the distributor has been removed from the engine, the aforementioned method with one additional step may be used to retime the engine. The additional step is as follows: with No. 1 cylinder at TDC of the compression stroke, the distributor housing must be rotated in the opposite direction to rotor rotation until the ignition-point rubbing block just contacts a distributor cam lobe ready to open the ignition points. The distributor is then locked in this position.

42-4 IGNITION TIMING

Ignition timing is the setting of the ignition points so that a spark occurs at the spark plug at the right time to produce maximum power in the cylinder, according to engine speed and load. The initial timing is set most conveniently through the use of a *power stroboscopic timing light*. With this light and a *tachometer* attached as directed by their manufacturers, and following the vehicle manufacturer's instructions, idle the engine at the recommended rpm. Direct the power timing light beam on the timing marks. Loosen and turn the distributor as required to bring the timing marks in line with the pointer. When the mark is exactly in line, tighten the distributor in place and recheck to make certain the timing marks are still properly aligned.

NOTE: Point gap or cam-dwell angle must be properly set before timing is changed, as changing

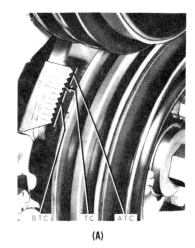

(A)

(B)

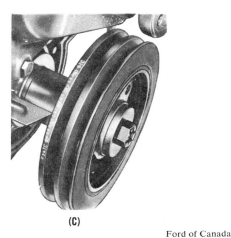

(C)

Ford of Canada

Fig. 42-7 Typical Ignition-Timing Marks

either the cam-dwell angle or point gap will alter the timing.

Testing Advance Mechanisms. Test instruments are available for checking the amount of spark advance produced by either or both the mechanical- or vacuum-advance units. If the checks indicate malfunction of either unit, the distributor should be removed, repaired, and rechecked on a distributor machine.

Overhauling the Distributor. Distributors require overhauling when the shaft, bushings, cam, or gear wear becomes excessive, or when either the vacuum or mechanical-advance mechanisms fail to function correctly.

To remove, repair, and replace the distributor follow the manufacturers' instructions.

42-5 SERVICING TRANSISTORIZED IGNITION SYSTEMS

Transistorized ignition systems can be seriously damaged through the use of conventional methods of ignition system service. Therefore, do not under any circumstances attempt to check, adjust, or repair any transistorized ignition system without the proper instruments and servicing instructions.

42-6 SPARK PLUGS

Spark plug service life varies considerably depending on such factors as engine design, type of service, type of fuel, and driver habits. Some spark plugs may require replacement at 5,000 miles while others may still be serviceable after 10,000 miles. Whether spark plugs should be reserviced or replaced depends upon the cost of the mechanic's time compared to the amount of remaining useful life in the plug. Unless the spark plug is in relatively good condition, it usually pays to install new spark plugs.

After the removal of used spark plugs, a careful study of the plug is helpful in determining engine condition, heat range selection, and trouble resulting from operational conditions. When removing spark plugs it is important to keep the plugs in their proper order so that any particular plug condition can be related to the cylinder from which it was removed.

Normal Spark Plug Appearance. A spark plug operating in an engine of good mechanical condition and of the proper heat range will have some

CARBON FOULED

IDENTIFIED BY BLACK, DRY FLUFFY CARBON DEPOSITS ON INSULATOR TIPS, EXPOSED SHELL SURFACES AND ELECTRODES.
CAUSED BY TOO COLD A PLUG, WEAK IGNITION, DIRTY AIR CLEANER, DEFECTIVE FUEL PUMP, TOO RICH A FUEL MIXTURE, IMPROPERLY OPERATING HEAT RISER OR EXCESSIVE IDLING. CAN BE CLEANED.

OIL FOULED

IDENTIFIED BY WET BLACK DEPOSITS ON THE INSULATOR SHELL BORE ELECTRODES CAUSED BY EXCESSIVE OIL ENTERING COMBUSTION CHAMBER THROUGH WORN RINGS AND PISTONS, EXCESSIVE CLEARANCE BETWEEN VALVE GUIDES AND STEMS, OR WORN OR LOOSE BEARINGS. CAN BE CLEANED IF ENGINE IS NOT REPAIRED, USE A HOTTER PLUG.

GAP BRIDGED

IDENTIFIED BY DEPOSIT BUILD-UP CLOSING GAP BETWEEN ELECTRODES.
CAUSED BY OIL OR CARBON FOULING. IF DEPOSITS ARE NOT EXCESSIVE, THE PLUG CAN BE CLEANED.

LEAD FOULED

IDENTIFIED BY DARK GRAY, BLACK, YELLOW OR TAN DEPOSITS OR A FUSED GLAZED COATING ON THE INSULATOR TIP.
CAUSED BY HIGHLY LEADED GASOLINE. CAN BE CLEANED.

NORMAL

IDENTIFIED BY LIGHT TAN OR GRAY DEPOSITS ON THE FIRING TIP.
CAN BE CLEANED.

WORN

IDENTIFIED BY SEVERELY ERODED OR WORN ELECTRODES. CAUSED BY NORMAL WEAR. SHOULD BE REPLACED.

FUSED SPOT DEPOSIT

IDENTIFIED BY MELTED OR SPOTTY DEPOSITS RESEMBLING BUBBLES OR BLISTERS.
CAUSED BY SUDDEN ACCELERATION. CAN BE CLEANED.

OVERHEATING

IDENTIFIED BY A WHITE OR LIGHT GRAY INSULATOR WITH SMALL BLACK OR GRAY BROWN SPOTS AND WITH BLUISH-BURNT APPEARANCE OF ELECTRODES, CAUSED BY ENGINE OVERHEATING. WRONG TYPE OF FUEL, LOOSE SPARK PLUGS, TOO HOT A PLUG, LOW FUEL PUMP PRESSURE OR INCORRECT IGNITION TIMING. REPLACE THE PLUG.

PRE-IGNITION

IDENTIFIED BY MELTED ELECTRODES AND POSSIBLY BLISTERED INSULATOR. METALLIC DEPOSITS ON INSULATOR INDICATE ENGINE DAMAGE.
CAUSED BY WRONG TYPE OF FUEL, INCORRECT IGNITION TIMING OR ADVANCE, TOO HOT A PLUG, BURNT VALVES OR ENGINE OVERHEATING. REPLACE THE PLUG.

Fig. 42-8   Spark Plug Inspection   Ford of Canada

deposits. The deposit colour will range from tan to grey. The spark-plug gap should have increased about .001 inches per 1,000 miles driven but should show no signs of burning.

Fuel-Fouled Plugs. Fuel-fouled plugs will have dry, fluffy, black fuel carbon deposits. These deposits can be caused from too cold a heat-range plug, improper carburetor float settings (too high), excessive use of the choke, dirty air-cleaner cartridge, or stuck heat-riser valve. If only one or two plugs show signs of fuel fouling, defective spark-plug wires or sticking valves could be the cause.

Oil-Fouled Plugs. Oil-fouled plugs will be covered with a wet, black deposit. This deposit is caused by an excessive amount of oil reaching the combustion chamber, because of worn piston rings, valve guides, etc.

Scavenger-Fouled Plugs. Certain fuels will tend to form heavy white or yellowish deposits around the porcelain and electrodes. For these fuels, this is a normal condition. If the plugs are otherwise sound, they may be serviced and reinstalled.

Overheating. Overheating results in a dull, white or grey blistered insulator. This is the result of too high a heat-range plug for the engine or because of a defective cooling system, advanced ignition timing, or detonation.

Figure 42-8 shows common spark-plug problems. Other spark plug information may be obtained in spark plug manufacturers' pamphlets.

42-7 SERVICING SPARK PLUGS

After studying each spark plug for signs of unusual performance, the plugs may be cleaned externally in a suitable solvent and internally by a spark-plug cleaning machine. Do not overclean the insulator, as excessive blasting by the cleaning machine can cause excessive wear on the insulator or the electrodes.

After cleaning in the machine, the electrodes should be filed. This filing removes the oxidized metal and deposits from the electrodes. The end of the centre electrode should be filed flat and square. This will produce sharp edges which improves spark-plug performance. The plugs should be properly gapped and tested. Discard those spark plugs with weak or intermittent spark.

When installing spark plugs, tighten to the proper torque with a torque wrench. The average tightness for various spark plug sizes are as follows:

18 MM plugs—25-30 ft lb
14 MM plugs—25 ft lb

If a torque wrench is not available, insert the plug until the new gasket just contacts the base, then tighten the plug an additional ½ to ¾ of a turn.

Overtightening spark plugs can change (increase) the gap setting; undertightening can cause the plug to overheat or leak compression and power.

REVIEW QUESTIONS

1. List three possible causes of low primary voltage.
2. Why is ignition contact-point alignment important?
3. What effect will too low ignition point spring tension have on ignition-system operation?
4. Why is cam-dwell angle setting of vital importance?
5. What effect will wrong ignition coil polarity have on secondary voltage requirements? Why?
6. Why is the crisscrossing of spark-plug leads important?
7. Why should the distributor cap be clean and dry?
8. An engine has been cranked over while the distributor was removed. State the procedure to be followed in order to replace the distributor and correctly set the spark timing and the firing order.
9. State the procedure for checking ignition timing.
10. If the point-gap setting was to be reduced after the ignition timing had been set, what effect would this have on ignition timing?
11. When a spark plug is removed from an engine, its condition and appearance can indicate various engine problems. List and state the cause of three of these problems.

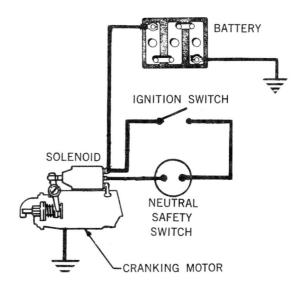

Fig. 43-1 *Cranking Circuit*

Chapter 43
THE STARTING CIRCUIT

The starting circuit consists of the battery, cranking motor, cranking motor drive, solenoid switch, starter switch, and the wiring to connect these various units.

43-1 THE CRANKING MOTOR

All cranking motors are similar in design and operation, differing mainly in the type of drive mechanism used. Basically, they consist of the *drive mechanism*, the *field frame* and *windings*, the *armature* and *brushes,* and suitable *bearings* and *housings*.

All conductors of the cranking motor are made of heavy copper ribbon which has a very low resistance value and thus permits a high current flow. This ribbon is wound and wrapped to form the field coils around the pole shoes. The pole shoes usually have a longer tip on one side of the shoe than the other. They are installed with the long tip pointing in the direction of armature rotation. The long tip produces a better magnetic field and increases cranking motor performance. The pole

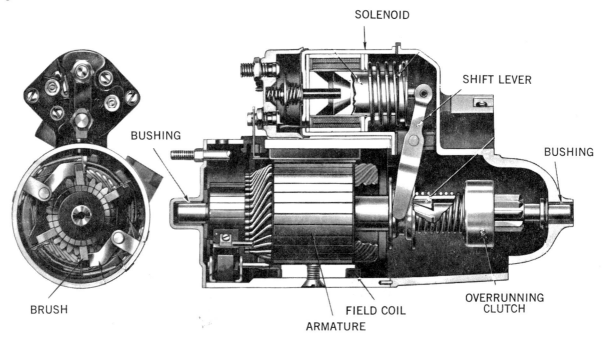

Fig. 43-2 *Cross Section of a Cranking Motor with Overrunning Clutch Drive*

Courtesy of General Motors

pieces must be tightly attached to the field frame to provide the best possible return path for the magnetic field.

The copper-ribbon conductor used in armature construction is placed in the insulated slots of a laminated soft iron core assembled onto the armature shaft. The commutator is made up of a number of copper segments (one pair for each armature winding) assembled together and insulated from each other and from the armature shaft. The conductors are connected to each other and to the commutator in such a way that current flows through all of the conductors when the brushes are placed on the commutator and current is supplied.

The brushes are made of copper compounds for low resistance and long wear and are mounted in spring-loaded holders to provide for proper brush-to-commutator contact. One half of the number of brush holders are insulated; the other half are grounded to the cranking motor frame. Usually all the insulated brushes are joined together by jumper bars or leads, to equalize the voltage at all brushes. The equalizing bars prevent conditions which will cause arcing and burning of the commutator bars, which would result in high resistance between the brush and the commutator.

The armature is supported on bearings or bushings to permit it to rotate freely. The bushings or bearings are mounted in the cranking motor and frames.

The cranking motor is known as a series-wound motor because all of the current that passes through the field coils also travels through the armature. The motor is designed to operate under a great overload and to produce high torque and horsepower for its size. It can do this only for short periods of time, since the high current required creates a considerable amount of heat. The amount of heat produced by prolonged cranking motor operation will cause serious damage to the unit. The motor should not be operated for more than thirty seconds at any one time, and cranking should not be resumed without a pause of at least two minutes to permit cooling.

43-2 CRANKING MOTOR SPEED AND TORQUE CHARACTERISTICS

A series-wound motor produces very high torque. The torque produced varies with the strength of the magnetic field and the current in the armature. As the load on a series-wound motor increases, the

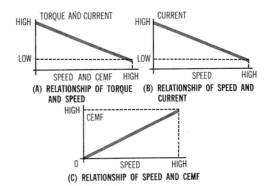

Fig. 43-3　Cranking Motor Speed and Torque Characteristics

current flow through the fields and armature will also increase. As a result, the torque will increase as the load increases. The speed will also vary with the load. The heavier the load, the slower the speed.

Any armature tends to rotate at such a speed that the voltage used in overcoming its resistance, plus the cemf will be equal to the voltage applied to the motor. Under heavy loads, the current and the voltage consumed in overcoming the internal resistance will be large. Therefore, the armature will not have to rotate at very high speed to produce the required counter emf to equal the applied voltage. Under light loads the motor speeds up, inducing higher cemf and decreasing the current flow through the fields and armature windings.

43-3 MOTOR PRINCIPLES

An electric motor operates on the basic electrical theory that when a current-carrying conductor is placed in a magnetic field, movement will result. To illustrate this theory, the magnetic lines of force of a horseshoe-shaped permanent magnet flow from the north pole to the south pole. By using the left hand rule for a conductor, it is possible to determine the direction of the magnetic lines of force surrounding a current-carrying conductor. Now, when the current-carrying conductor is placed in the permanent magnetic field, the circular field around the conductor opposes the permanent magnetic field on one side of the conductor, reducing the field strength. While on the other side of the conductor the two fields unite to form a stronger magnetic field. The conductor then will be forced to move in the direction of the weak field. The greater the current flowing in the conductor, the stronger the force exerted upon it.

When the conductor is bent into a U-shape and placed in a magnetic field, one leg of the U will move in one direction, the other leg in the opposite direction, thus imparting a rotating motion. This rotation will continue until the static neutral point (which is half way between the two poles) is reached. At this point the direction of the current flow through the U-shaped conductor must be reversed if the rotation in the same direction is to continue.

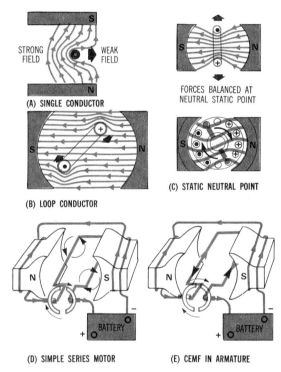

(A) SINGLE CONDUCTOR

(B) LOOP CONDUCTOR

(C) STATIC NEUTRAL POINT

(D) SIMPLE SERIES MOTOR

(E) CEMF IN ARMATURE

Fig. 43-4   Cranking-Motor Principles

In a simple series motor, Fig. 43-4, the current from the battery flows into and around the right-hand field coil, then through the left-hand field coil, coming out to the left-hand brush. This brush conducts the current to the left-hand commutator segment. From the segment the current flows through the armature winding nearest the north pole and returns through the armature winding nearest the south pole to the right-hand segment of the commutator. The current leaves the segment through the right-hand brush and returns to the battery. The magnetic fields built up around the armature windings will be in the direction shown by the circular arrows. As a result of operating on the basic motor principle, the left armature winding will move upwards and the right winding will move downward, imparting a clockwise rotation to the

armature. Since the armature windings and the commutator are assembled together, any rotation of the winding will also cause the commutator to turn.

When the left-hand winding of the armature has swung around toward the south pole, the commutator segments will have reversed their connections with respect to the brushes. The current will now flow in the opposite direction with respect to the winding. However, since the winding has rotated 180°, the force exerted upon it will still tend to rotate the armature in a clockwise direction.

The point half way between the two poles is called the *static neutral point* and is the point where the direction of current flow through the armature windings must be reversed, in order to maintain a turning force in the same direction.

When the current flows through the armature windings, creating the second magnetic field, the first magnetic field produced by the field windings between the poles is distorted. Since it is assumed that magnetic lines of force never cross each other, the neutral point is shifted. Cranking-motor brushes are usually located back of the static neutral point, against the direction of rotation, to prevent excessive arcing at the brushes and to obtain more efficient operation.

It should also be stated that the field frame into which the pole pieces and field windings are assembled forms the return magnetic path for the magnetic lines of force.

Since the wire loop (the armature) is a conductor that is rotating in a magnetic field, it is subjected to self-induction (the inducing of a voltage in a conductor as a result of a change in magnetic field). The voltage induced in the loop and

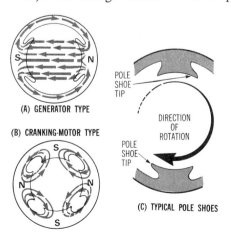

(A) GENERATOR TYPE

(B) CRANKING-MOTOR TYPE

(C) TYPICAL POLE SHOES

Fig. 43-5   Magnetic Flow Produced by Field Windings

the resulting current flow would be in the opposite direction to the battery current flow. This induced voltage is cemf and opposes battery voltage and therefore reduces the amount of current flowing from the battery.

43-4 CRANKING-MOTOR CIRCUITS

Various wiring arrangements are used in cranking-motor construction. There are two-, four- or six-coil types wound in series, series-parallel or series-shunt formation, and lap and wave-wound armatures, to name but a few.

Regardless of the number of field coils or pole shoes used, adjacent pole shoes must be of opposite polarity. For example, in a four-pole unit there is a north, south, north, south, in sequence around the field frame. The magnetic field passes diagonally from one pole to the next and returns through the field frame.

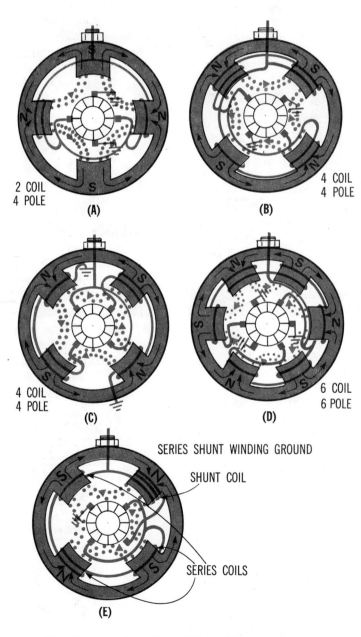

Fig. 43-6   Cranking Motor Wiring Circuits

The Four-Pole Two-Winding Type. This type of starting motor consists of four pole shoes only two of which are surrounded with field windings. In this type both windings produce north poles at their shoe pieces. The lines of force leave the north poles, pass through the armature, and enter the pole shoes without winding and return through the field frame. There are as many lines of force entering the unwound south pole shoe as there are leaving the north wound pole shoe, making the magnetic strength equal for both poles. This type of circuit provides for four-pole action with only two field windings, thus keeping the electrical resistance low.

The Four-Pole Four-Winding Type. This type of starting motor consists of four wound pole shoes, wound in such a manner as to produce the north-south sequence. The field windings are paired off so that half of the current passes through one pair of windings to one of the insulated brushes, while the other half of the current passes through the other pair of field windings to the other insulated brush. The current then passes through the armature, going to ground through the ground brush.

Using four field windings of low resistance, it is possible to create more ampere turns and therefore produce stronger magnetic fields, which result in greater torque output of the cranking motor.

In some four-pole four-winding cranking motors, the current passes through the armature first, then through the field windings. The end of the field winding may be grounded or connected to an insulated terminal. When the field windings are connected to the insulated terminal, it is possible to completely insulate the cranking motor from ground. This type of circuit is used when a 24-volt cranking circuit is used in conjunction with a 12-volt electrical system.

Six-Pole Six-Winding Type. This unit has the field current split three ways, one-third of the current passing through each pair of field windings to one of the three insulated brushes. Splitting the current three ways further increases the ampere turns and therefore cranking motor torque.

Series-Shut Wound Type. This type of winding is used to prevent extremely high top free speed. A shunt-connected coil is used for the purpose of limiting the top free speed. The shunt coil of many turns of comparatively small wire is wound around one or more of the pole shoes in place of the normal field winding. During cranking, the shunt coil

creates a magnetic force similar to the regular field windings and assists in producing cranking motor torque. During free running periods, the strength of the shunt winding remains constant and does not vary with speed. The speed of the armature revolving through this strong magnetic field creates a counter-voltage. This counter-voltage limits the amount of current flow and consequently the top speed of the cranking motor.

43-5 ARMATURE ASSEMBLY

The armature assembly consists of a number of iron laminations placed over a steel shaft, a commutator assembly, and the armature windings. The windings are heavy copper ribbons that are placed in slots in the iron laminations. The winding ends are soldered or welded to the commutator bars which are electrically insulated from each other and from the iron shaft. There are two major types of armature windings: *lap* and *wave*.

Lap- and Wave-Wound Armatures. A lap-wound armature has as many paths for the current to follow as there are poles in the field windings; wave wound armatures have only two paths for the current to follow. A lap-type winding is always used when a low-resistance armature is needed.

In a lap winding the lead ends of a winding element (a complete turn of the conductor) are connected to adjacent commutator bars. The winding

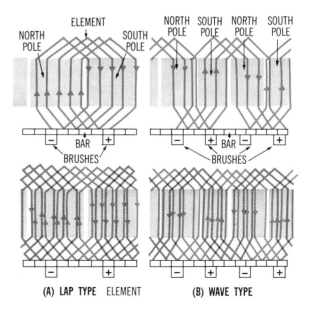

Fig. 43-7 Types of Cranking-Motor Armature Windings

element will span about 90° in a four-pole cranking motor.

In wave-wound armatures there are only two paths for the armature current to flow through; therefore, the conductors must be of a large size. The ends of a wave winding span 180° in a four-pole cranking motor.

The winding elements are effectively shorted out whenever their ends are connected to commutator bars riding under brushes having the same polarity. When in this position, no current flows through this winding. This condition occurs at the neutral static point.

43-6 CRANKING-MOTOR DRIVES

The cranking-motor drive mechanism is a vital part of the cranking motor, since it is through the drive that the power is transmitted to crank the engine. The drive mechanism must transmit the cranking motor torque to the engine flywheel ring gear when the cranking motor is operated. It must disconnect the cranking motor from the flywheel ring gear after the engine starts. The drive mechanism must also provide a gear ratio between the cranking motor and the engine so that there will be sufficient torque to turn the engine over at cranking speeds.

The gear ratio between the cranking-motor drive pinion and the flywheel ring gear is between 15 and 20 to 1. Therefore, to crank the engine over at 100 rpm the cranking motor armature must rotate at between 1,500 and 2,000 rpm.

The cranking-motor drive must disengage quickly after the engine starts. For at an engine speed of 1,000 rpm, if the drive mechanism transmitted its ratio to the armature, the armature would be rotated at between 15,000 and 20,000 rpm. Such high speeds would cause the armature windings to be thrown from the armature slots, and the segments would be thrown from the commutator by the centrifugal force produced.

Several types of drive mechanisms have been developed. Each provides a means of engaging the drive pinion with the engine flywheel ring gear for cranking, and for disengaging the drive pinion from the ring gear as soon as the engine starts.

Bendix-Type Drive. The Bendix-type drive depends upon inertia to provide the meshing of the drive pinion with the flywheel ring gear. The drive consists of a drive pinion, sleeve, spring, and spring fastening screws.

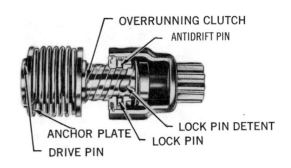

Fig. 43-8   Bendix-Type Starter Drive   Ford of Canada

The drive pinion is unbalanced by a counterbalance on one side and has coarse, square screw threads on its inner bore and is mounted on a hollow sleeve that has screw threads cut on its outer diameter which match the threads of the drive pinion. The sleeve fits loosely on the armature shaft and is connected to the shaft through the Bendix spring and drive head. The drive head is keyed to the armature shaft. The drive pinion and sleeve assembly are free to turn on the armature shaft within the limits permitted by the flexing of the Bendix spring.

When the cranking-motor armature begins to revolve, the rotation is transmitted through the drive head and spring to the sleeve, so that all of these parts pick up speed with the armature. Since the drive pinion is a loose fit on the threads of the sleeve, and because of the increased inertia of the drive pinion because of the unbalanced condition created by the counterbalance, the drive pinion does not rotate and pick up speed along with the sleeve. As a result, the sleeve rotates within the pinion. This forces the drive pinion endwise along the armature shaft to engage with the flywheel ring gear. When the drive pinion reaches the end of its travel, it begins to rotate along with the sleeve and the armature. This rotation is transmitted to the flywheel ring gear. The Bendix spring is used to absorb the shock of the drive pinion meshing with the ring gear.

As soon as the engine starts, engine speed rotates the drive pinion at a higher speed than the speed of the cranking-motor armature. This causes the drive pinion to run back on the threaded sleeve and to back out of mesh with the flywheel ring gear.

The barrel-type Bendix drive—has the same function and operational characteristics of the standard-type Bendix drive. In this type the pinion and barrel assembly operate with a nut on a screw shaft. The pinion is smaller and operates directly on the armature shaft. The smaller size gear permits higher gear ratios which provide more torque to crank the engine.

The Bendix folo-thru-type drive—is a barrel-type unit with the addition of a detent pin which locks the drive in cranking position to prevent disengagement on false starts. The detent pin is thrown out by centrifugal force when the engine runs, and the drive pinion is then disengaged.

The screw shaft is in two pieces connected by a *detent clutch*. This clutch acts as a safety device to prevent overspeeding of the cranking-motor armature. If the engine speed spins the drive pinion faster than the free speed of the armature, the pinion and barrel assembly overruns the armature shaft.

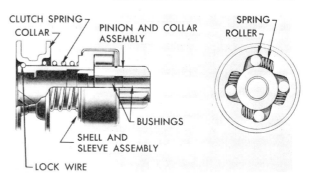

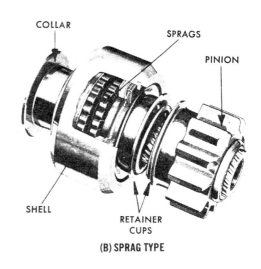

Courtesy of General Motors

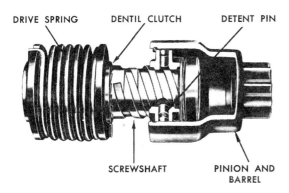

Fig. 43-9   Folo-Thru Type Starter Drive

Fig. 43-10   Overrunning Clutch-Type Starter Drive

The Overrunning Clutch-Type Drive. An overrunning clutch consists of a shell and sleeve assembly which is splined to the armature shaft. A drive pinion and collar assembly fits within the shell. Notches are cut in the shell and a hardened steel roller and spring is assembled into each notch. The notches taper slightly, allowing adequate room for the rollers to operate as a bearing when the clutch is overrunning.

When the unit is required to transmit torque, the rollers tend to rotate between the shell and the drive pinion collar and are forced tightly into the smaller part of the tapered notches. When the rollers jam between the collar and the shell, they force the drive pinion to rotate with the shell. Torque is then transmitted from the shell to the drive pinion and the engine is cranked.

When the engine begins to operate, it spins the drive pinion faster than the armature rotates. This spinning action unlocks the rollers and returns them to the larger portion of the tapered notches where

they act as a bearing, allowing the drive pinion to spin freely with respect to the shell.

Meshing and unmeshing of the drive pinion with the flywheel ring gear is obtained with the overrunning clutch-type drive by moving the clutch and drive pinion endwise along the armature shaft by means of a shift lever. The shift lever may be either manually operated, or operated by a solenoid. In either case the drive pinion is meshed with the ring gear before the cranking motor starts to operate.

On some installations the overrunning-clutch unit is replaced by a *sprag* unit. A sprag is an elliptical shaped roller that rocks slightly to lock up and transmit torque.

The Dyer-Type Drive. The Dyer-type cranking-motor drive combines some of the principles of the Bendix and overrunning-clutch drives and is used on some heavy-duty gasoline and diesel engines.

Like the overrunning-clutch type, the drive pinion is meshed with the flywheel ring gear by a

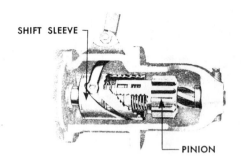

Fig. 43-11   Dyer-Type Starter Drive

shift lever before the lever closes the cranking motor switch. As soon as the cranking motor armature starts to rotate, the shift lever is spun back out of the way. The pinion is held in mesh as long as torque is transmitted from the armature through the pinion to the ring gear.

The instant that the engine starts to operate, it spins the drive pinion faster than the armature is rotating and, as a result, the drive pinion and pinion guide are spun back along the armature shaft out of mesh with the ring gear in a similar manner to the unmeshing of the Bendix-type drive.

When the engine false starts, it is impossible to begin another cranking cycle without completely releasing the shift lever. This is because a milled section in the armature splines holds the pinion in a locked position away from the flywheel ring gear until the shift lever is completely released and operated again.

Reduction-Gear Cranking Motors. A reduction-gear type cranking motor may increase the gear ratio between the armature and the flywheel to as high as 40 to 1 and is used where high cranking torque is required.

The gear-reduction unit consists of a pair of reduction gears in a gear housing located on the drive end of the cranking motor. The smaller driving gear mounts on or is part of the armature shaft, and the larger driven gear mounts on the Bendix or overrunning-clutch drive shaft. The final drive, regardless of the type, operates in its normal manner.

43-7 CRANKING-MOTOR CONTROLS

Basic Circuits. There are two basic types of cranking-motor circuits. The first type uses a motor with a Bendix drive that relies upon inertia to move the drive pinion into mesh with the flywheel ring gear. The second type utilizes cranking motors with drive mechanisms that require a shift lever to either manually or through the use of a solenoid move the drive pinion into mesh with the ring gear.

In a Bendix-type drive cranking motor and magnetic switch circuit, when the starting switch is closed the magnetic switch winding is energized, and the contact disc closes the circuit between the battery and the cranking motor. The cranking cycle then begins and continues until the operator opens the start switch.

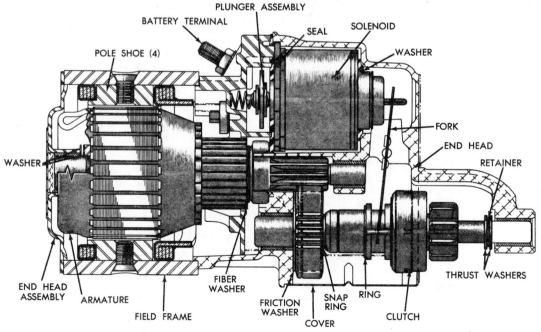

Fig. 43-12   Reduction-Gear Type Starter Drive

Chrysler Canada Limited

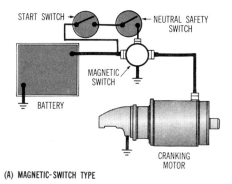

(A) MAGNETIC-SWITCH TYPE

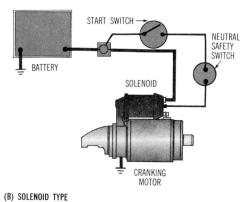

(B) SOLENOID TYPE

Fig. 43-13 Basic Cranking-Motor Control Circuits

A magnetic switch is used to provide a circuit with shorter length and lower resistance between the battery and the cranking motor. Since the cranking motor may draw 100 amperes or more during cranking, heavy cables of short length are needed to reduce the voltage drop in the circuit. The magnetic switch is usually located in close proximity to the battery and the cranking motor in order to reduce battery cable length. If a magnetic switch were not used, and the high cranking motor currents were carried directly through the start switch mounted on the vehicle dash, cables of excessive size would be required to limit the voltage drop to an acceptable value. The use of the magnetic switch means that the long leads connected to the start switch can be of reasonable size since they conduct only the small amount of current drawn by the magnetic switch winding.

The second type of basic circuit uses a cranking motor and a solenoid. The solenoid is used to close the electric circuit to the cranking motor and to shift the drive pinion into mesh with the flywheel ring gear. In this type of circuit, when the start switch is closed the solenoid moves the drive pinion into

mesh and then performs the same function as a magnetic switch to close the circuit to begin the cranking cycle. When the start switch is opened, the cranking cycle ends.

A neutral safety switch is included in all cranking-motor control circuits of vehicles equipped with an automatic transmission. The neutral safety switch is closed only when the transmission shift lever is in the proper position, thereby preventing cranking of the engine with the transmission in gear.

43-8 CRANKING-MOTOR CONTROL SWITCHES

Since cranking motors may draw several hundred amperes of current during the cranking period, special heavy-duty switches with contacts heavy enough to carry this high current without overheating or damage must be used. These switches assume different forms and have several types of controlling devices to open or close them. The most common types used are the *manual*, the *magnetic* switch, and the *solenoid* switch.

The Manual-Type Cranking-Motor Switch. This switch may be hand or foot operated and consists of a plunger-operated contact disc which is forced down against the battery and motor contacts to complete the cranking-motor electric circuit. As soon as the pressure is released, a heavy return spring pulls the contact disc away from the battery and motor contacts to break the circuit. Manually operated switch-control systems require Bendix-type cranking-motor drives

Magnetic Switches. The magnetic switch is a remote-control type of switch that can be mounted conveniently in the cranking-motor circuit and be controlled by a second switch mounted in a convenient place for the operator.

The magnetic switch utilizes the electromagnetic principle, that a flow of current in a winding creates a magnetic field. The winding is wrapped around a hollow core, and a round iron plunger is placed part of the way in the hollow core. When the winding is energized, by closing the remote control switch, the magnetic field created pulls the plunger farther into the core. A contact disc is attached to the plunger. A battery and starting-motor contact are so placed that the plunger movement forces the disc against these contacts to complete the cranking motor circuit. The circuit will remain complete as long as the remote control switch is closed and the winding

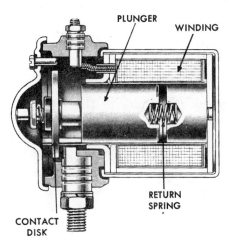

Fig. 43-14   Magnetic Switch

is energized. When the remote control switch is opened, the magnetic field of the winding collapses and a heavy return spring forces the plunger back to break the cranking-motor circuit.

Magnetic switches are only used with Bendix type of cranking-motor drives, since the switch provides no separate means of meshing the cranking-motor drive gear with the flywheel.

Most magnetic switches have only one winding. Others have two, a pull-in winding and a hold-in winding. The operation of the two-winding type is similar to the operation of a solenoid switch and will be discussed under that topic.

Solenoid Switch. A solenoid switch is a variation of the magnetic switch that is designed to do some form of mechanical work, such as operating the cranking-motor drive shift lever, before completing the electric circuit to the cranking motor.

Solenoid switches have two windings wound around a hollow core and a plunger assembly similar to that used in a magnetic switch. One winding is the pull-in winding consisting of a few turns of heavy wire, and the other is a hold-in winding of

many turns of fine wire. The strong magnetic field of the pull-in winding is necessary in order to do the mechanical work. Once the mechanical work is completed, the weaker field of the hold-in winding is sufficient to maintain the solenoid in the closed position.

When the remote control switch is closed, current from the battery flows through both the pull-in and hold-in windings creating one strong magnetic field to pull the plunger into the core, performing the mechanical work first, then closing the switch contact. The current from the hold-in winding goes to ground inside the solenoid itself, while the current from the pull-in winding goes to ground through the cranking motor. This type of circuit is used so that the pull-in winding will be shorted out the moment the contact disc completes the circuit across the switch contacts. Shorting out the pull-in winding in this manner lessens the drain of current on the battery during the cranking period.

When the remote control switch is opened, the current momentarily flows in the reverse direction through the pull-in winding reversing its magnetic polarity. This change is polarity weakens the magnetic field of the hold-in winding, allowing the return spring to push the plunger away from the contacts, and to return the shift lever to the disengaged position.

43-9 IGNITION RESISTOR BYPASS

Many starting-motor circuit magnetic and solenoid control switches include a separate pair of contacts that are used to bypass the ignition-circuit resistor. This resistor is normally in series with the ignition coil and protects the ignition breaker points from excessive current when the engine is running. However, during the cranking period, it is advantageous to have full battery voltage delivered to the ignition coil. This is accomplished through the ignition contact switch operated by the plunger of the magnetic or solenoid switch.

When the plunger closes the ignition contact switch, current from the battery flows from the magnetic or solenoid switch ignition terminal directly to the ignition-coil primary terminal, thus bypassing the ignition circuit resistor and applying full battery voltage to the ignition coil during the cranking period. This improves ignition-coil high-voltage output to assist in easier starting of the engine.

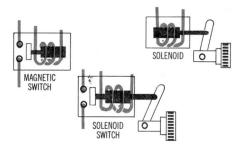

Fig. 43-15   Basic Cranking-Motor Switches

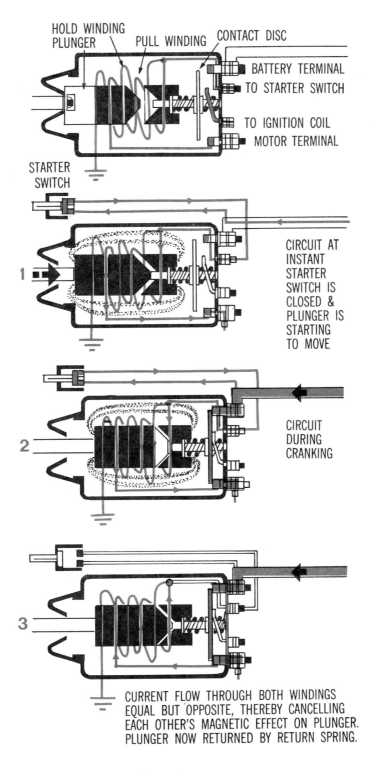

Fig. 43-16   Solenoid Operation

REVIEW QUESTIONS

1. List the units of the starting circuit and state the purpose of each.
2. Why is copper ribbon used as the conductors in a cranking motor?
3. Why must the pole pieces be tightly attached to the field frame?
4. Describe the construction of a cranking-motor armature.
5. Why are most cranking-motor insulating brushes joined by jumper bars or leads?
6. What is meant by the term "series-wound motor"?
7. Why should a cranking motor only be operated for short periods of time?
8. What determines the amount of torque produced by the cranking motor?
9. What effect does cranking-motor load have on cranking speed? Why?
10. State the basic motor principle.
11. What is the static neutral point?
12. State the path of current through a cranking motor.
13. Explain how the magnetic principle of like and unlike poles is used in a cranking motor.
14. Make an elementary drawing of the wiring circuit of (a) a four-pole two-winding (b) a four-pole four-winding cranking motor.
15. What is the advantage of a four-pole four-winding cranking motor over a four-pole two-winding cranking motor? Why?
16. What changes are required to the wiring circuit of a cranking motor when it is used in a 24-volt cranking circuit in a vehicle with a 12-volt electrical system?
17. State the differences between a lap-wound and a wave-wound cranking-motor armature.
18. State the two basic requirements of a cranking-motor drive.
19. What is the approximate gear ratio between the cranking motor and the flywheel ring gear?
20. What damage to the cranking motor would result if the drive mechanism did not disconnect quickly after the engine starts? Why?
21. Explain how a Bendix type of starter drive operates.
22. What is an overrunning clutch?
23. Why does an overrunning clutch make an excellent type of starter drive?
24. What is the advantage of a reduction-gear cranking motor?
25. Describe the difference between a magnetic switch and a solenoid.
26. Why must a Bendix type of cranking-motor drive be used with magnetic switches?
27. Describe the operation of the pull-in and the hold-in windings of a solenoid when the starting circuit is completed.
28. How is the magnetic field of a solenoid collapsed when the starting circuit is opened?
29. Explain why the ignition ballast resistor is by-passed during cranking periods.

Chapter 44
STARTING-SYSTEM SERVICE

Starting-system service can be divided into several sections: the battery, battery cables, terminals and other connections, controls, and the cranking motor.

44-1 HEADLIGHT TEST

To determine the general area of trouble in a starting system, the headlights of the vehicle may be used. Turn on the headlights and then operate or attempt to operate the cranking motor, observing the headlight reaction.

(1) If the headlights are inoperative and no cranking action results when the cranking-motor switch is closed, then the battery is dead or there is an open circuit.

(2) If the headlights go out and there is no cranking action when the starting circuit switch is closed, the possible causes are a dead battery or a loose battery terminal connection.

(3) If the headlights dim slightly with no cranking action when the control switch is closed, the possible causes are a defective cranking motor or control switch.

(4) If the lights dim heavily and no cranking action results, then the possible cause is a low state of charge in the battery.

Some other cranking problems are: if the engine cranks slowly but does not start, then the battery is run down or it is being operated in very cold temperatures. If the engine cranks at a normal speed but does not start, check the ignition and fuel systems for proper operation. If the solenoid plunger chatters, the cause is usually a run-down battery.

Failure of the cranking motor drive to disengage after the engine starts requires checking of the starter-motor drive mechanism.

44-2 THE BATTERY, BATTERY TERMINALS AND CONNECTIONS

Many complaints regarding poor cranking motor performance can be traced to a discharged or defective battery. The battery should be thoroughly tested for state of charge and mechanical condition. (See Chapter 40-10—Battery Service). The starting-circuit wiring should be checked for loose, corroded or burned connections, for frayed, broken or shorted wiring.

The system can be checked for high resistance by performing the voltage drop test using an accurate low reading voltmeter.

To check the insulated side of the circuit, connect the voltmeter (with correct polarity) between the positive battery terminal and the cranking-motor terminal. Crank the engine and observe the voltage reading. If the voltage reading is above specifications, then repeat the test checking each section and unit in the circuit until the defective unit (the one with the greatest voltage drop) is located. A similar test is performed between the cranking-motor housing and the grounded battery post.

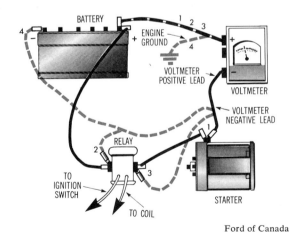

Ford of Canada

Fig. 44-1   Starter Circuit Voltage Drop Tests

44-3 CONTROLS

The controls can be checked for voltage drop by using the low reading voltmeter, or can be eliminated from the circuit by bypassing each unit with a jumper lead.

491

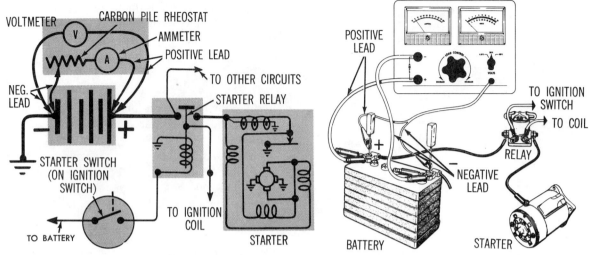

Fig. 44-2   Cranking-Motor Load Test

Ford of Canada

44-4 CRANKING-MOTOR DRAW TEST

This test is performed when the cranking motor is installed on the engine and is used to determine the amount of current required to crank the engine. The equipment used is a voltmeter, an ammeter, and a carbon pile rheostat.

To perform the test, the voltmeter is connected across the battery terminals to determine the open voltage of the battery. Close the starter-motor control switch and, while the engine is being cranked, observe the voltage reading of the battery. This reading will be controlled by the condition of the battery and the amperage draw of the starter motor.

As soon as this reading is obtained, open the starter control. With the ammeter and rheostat connected in series across the battery, adjust the rheostat to obtain the same voltage reading as when the engine was being cranked. The amount of current flowing through the ammeter will equal the amount flowing through the cranking motor when the engine was being cranked. It should be noted that the cranking voltage of the battery should remain above 9.6 volts for a 12-volt battery in order to have sufficient voltage for ignition circuit operation. Failure to maintain this voltage indicates a defective battery or excessive cranking-motor draw.

44-5 CRANKING-MOTOR TESTS

The stall test—is performed to determine the resistance of the starting motor by testing the current draw at a specified voltage with the armature locked.

To perform the test, a locking wedge is placed between the starter housing and the drive gear. With a high current-carrying variable resistance and an ammeter in series with the cranking motor and the battery, and a voltmeter connected across the cranking-motor terminals, close the circuit and adjust the resistor until the proper voltage is obtained at the starter motor. Note the current draw on the ammeter and compare with manufacturer's specifications. Low amperage readings indicate high resistance in the cranking motor and therefore the unit should be overhauled.

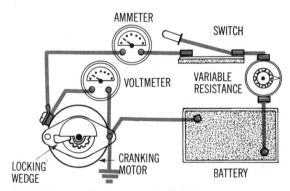

Fig. 44-3   Cranking Motor Stall Test

The no-load test—is performed to determine the armature speed and the amount of current draw at a specified voltage.

To perform the test, attach a tachometer to the end of the armature shaft. With a high current-carrying variable resistance and an ammeter in series with the battery and cranking motor, and a voltmeter across the cranking motor terminal, close the circuit and adjust the resistor to give the speci-

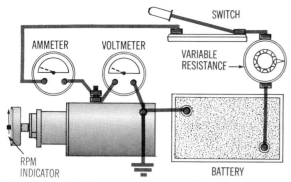

Fig. 44-4 *Cranking Motor No-Load Test*

fied voltage. Note the ammeter and tachometer readings and compare them to the specifications. Any deviation in speed or current draw indicates the need of a cranking-motor overhaul.

44-6 CRANKING-MOTOR OVERHAUL

Cleaning. All parts except the armature, field coils, commutator, and overrunning clutch may be cleaned in a suitable solvent. The armature, field coils, commutator, and the outside of the overrunning clutch may be wiped with a damp solvent-dipped wiper. Never place the overrunning clutch in a solvent as this will destroy the lubricant which was packed in the unit at the factory.

Testing The Armature. Inspect armature for damage to the laminated core caused by worn bearings or bushings allowing the armature to rub on the pole shoes; for signs of missing solder on the commutator-to-commutator segment joints; for signs of burning of the commutator segments that could indicate an open circuit. The commutator should be checked for scoring and run-out. The run-out should not exceed .003 to .005″ If the armature passes the visual inspection, test it electrically.

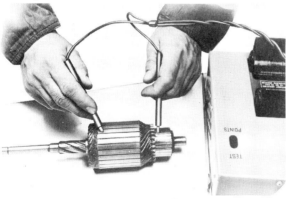

Courtesy of General Motors

Fig. 44-5 *Testing Armature for Shorts*

Testing the armature for short circuits—requires a piece of electrical test equipment called a *growler*. A growler produces an alternating polarity magnetic field from an ac current.

To test the armature, place the armature in the growler and hold a thin steel strip (hacksaw blade) loosely just above the top of the armature, and rotate the armature on the growler. Continue to rotate the armature until the entire core has passed beneath the steel strip. If the steel strip does not vibrate, then the armature is not shorted. If, however, a short circuit exists, the strip will vibrate when the shorted section of the armature passes under it. Do not operate the growler unless an armature is in place. Replace the shorted armatures.

Checking armatures for grounds—most growlers include a pair of 110-volt test prods that are in series with a very small bulb.

To test the armature for grounds, place one test prod on the armature core (not the bearing or bushing surfaces) and touch each one of the commutator segments with the other prod. If the armature is grounded, the test light will light. Discard grounded armature.

Courtesy of General Motors

Fig. 44-6 *Testing Armature for Grounds*

Trueing the commutator—commutators may be cleaned and trued in a lathe or special commutator turning fixture. Remove only sufficient copper from the commutator segments to clean up the scoring, burning, or out-of-round conditions.

Although undercutting of the mica insulation between the commutator segments is not usually done on cranking motors, some manufacturers do recommend it. In such cases, undercut to a depth of $\frac{1}{32}″$, cutting the full width of the mica.

Testing field coils for opens—is performed by using the 110-volt test prods of the growler. Place one test prod on either the field coil terminal stud or on the connector from the solenoid. Place the other test prod on the insulated brush lead. The test lamp will light if the circuit is complete. No light indicates a broken or open field coil circuit. Test each pair of coils in a similar manner.

Chrysler Canada Ltd.

Fig. 44-7   Testing Field Coils for Opens

Testing field coils for grounds—is performed by using the 110-volt test prods of the growler. Place one prod on the field coil terminal stud or on the connector from the solenoid, and place the other prod on the field frame. The light should not light. If it does, then there is a ground between the field windings and the field frame.

Courtesy of General Motors

Fig. 44-8   Testing Field Coils for Grounds

44-7 SERVICING CRANKING-MOTOR DRIVES

The condition of the cranking-motor drive can be established by operating the cranking motor two or three times and noting the action of the drive. On overrunning clutch or Dyer-type drives, operating the cranking motor also serves as a check on the freedom of operation of the drive shift lever.

Bendix Drives. A common damage to the Bendix drive is a wrapped-up Bendix spring or a broken drive end housing. This is caused by the engine backfiring during the cranking period or the operator re-engaging the starter while the engine is rocking backward too soon after a false start. Either condition creates tremendous strain on the parts of the starter drive. This is because of the fact that the cranking motor is attempting to turn the drive pinion in one direction while the engine is trying to turn it in the opposite direction.

Damaged drive pinion and flywheel ring gear teeth are a common cause of Bendix drive troubles. Since the drive pinion is spinning as it meshes with the ring gear, some burring of the teeth is normal. The burred teeth should be relieved so full engagement of the pinion is possible.

Overrunning Clutch Drives. The overrunning clutch drive must never be cleaned by using any high temperature method or any grease dissolving solvent. Use of either method will remove the clutch lubricant originally packed in the clutch assembly during manufacture. Loss of lubricant causes rapid clutch failure.

Overrunning clutch problems are mainly caused by failure of the clutch to lock-up and transmit the

Chrysler of Canada

Fig. 44-9   Checking Starter Drive Pin on Clearance

drive, or failure to overrun when the engine starts to operate. In either case the clutch assembly must be replaced.

On many solenoid switch-operated cranking motors the linkage between the solenoid plunger and the shift lever is adjustable, so that there is clearance between the end of the drive pinion and the housing when the pinion is in operating position. This clearance should be checked according to manufacturers' method and specifications.

REVIEW QUESTIONS

1. Explain how the headlights can be used to determine the general area of trouble in the starting system.
2. Explain how a voltage-drop test can be used to check for high resistance.
3. State how a battery high-rate discharge tester can be used to determine cranking-motor draw.
4. What is the purpose of a cranking-motor no-load test?
5. Describe the procedure for testing cranking-motor armatures for (a) short circuits (b) grounds.
6. Name and describe the tests performed on the field windings of a cranking motor.
7. What causes the teeth of a Bendix-drive gear to become burred?
8. Why are only the teeth in certain areas of the flywheel ring gear damaged by the Bendix-drive gear?
9. Why should overrunning-type clutch drives not be cleaned by high temperature or desolving solvents?

Chapter 45
THE DC CHARGING CIRCUIT

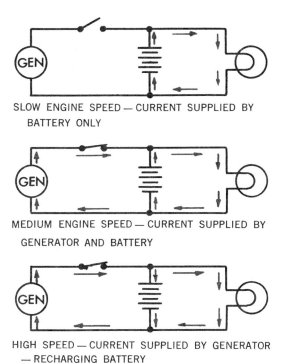

SLOW ENGINE SPEED — CURRENT SUPPLIED BY BATTERY ONLY

MEDIUM ENGINE SPEED — CURRENT SUPPLIED BY GENERATOR AND BATTERY

HIGH SPEED — CURRENT SUPPLIED BY GENERATOR — RECHARGING BATTERY

Fig. 45-2   Current Flow During Engine Operation

The dc charging circuit consists of: a mechanical device, the *generator*, which converts mechanical energy to electric energy; a *control* or *regulator* to regulate the amount of electric energy being produced in accordance with the amount being used and the state of charge of the battery; the *battery*; an *ammeter* or *indicating device* to indicate whether the charging circuit is operating properly; and the *wiring* to connect these various units.

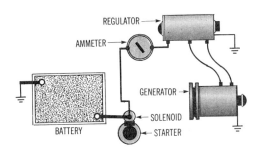

Fig. 45-1   DC Charging Circuit

The purpose of the generator is to convert mechanical energy into electric energy that is required to operate the electrical devices in the automobile and to recharge the battery.

When the engine is cranked by the cranking motor, or operated at very low speeds, the battery is the source of electric energy for all of the electrical units. When the engine is operating at off-idle or faster speeds, the generator supplies part or all of the required electric energy. Any electric energy produced in excess of that required by the electrical units is used to recharge the battery. This recharging compensates the battery for the electric energy used during the cranking or idling periods. The

generator is usually located near the front of the engine, either to one side of or above the engine block. It is driven by a V-belt. In some automobiles, this belt also drives the water pump and fan.

45-1 GENERATOR OPERATING PRINCIPLES

Magnetic Induction. The generator operates on the basic electromagnetic principle that when a conductor, or series of conductors, is moved through a magnetic field, the movement of the conductor will cause a current to be induced to flow in the conductor. This is because as the conductor moves, the magnetic field is distorted and tends to wrap around the conductor. Whenever a magnetic field surrounds a conductor, the field will induce a current to flow in the conductor.

When the conductor moves in one direction, it will induce the current to flow in one direction. This direction of current flow can be determined by the left-hand generator rule. This rule states: that by placing the index finger of the left hand in the direction of the magnetic field movement, the second finger in the direction of the conductor movement, then the thumb will indicate the direction of the induced current flow.

Reversing the direction of conductor movement

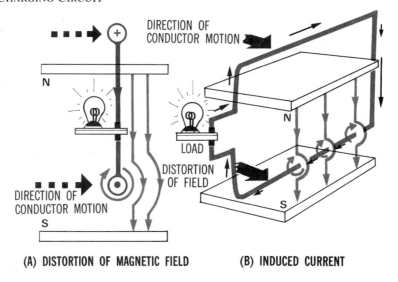

(A) DISTORTION OF MAGNETIC FIELD   **(B) INDUCED CURRENT**

Fig. 45-3   Magnetic Induction

or polarity of the magnetic field reverses the current flow.

The strength of the induced current depends upon: the strength of the magnetic field; the number of turns of wire in the coil or conductor; and the speed with which the conductor passes through the magnetic field. The higher the speed of the conductor, the greater the distortion of the magnetic field; the more the field surrounds the conductor, the greater the induced current.

Since the generator utilizes rotating components, the induced current flows first in one direction and then the other. In the generator the conductor rotates, first passing through the magnetic field in an upward direction and then in a downward direction.

Since the induced current is alternating (ac) in nature it must be rectified (changed) to direction (dc) current before entering the automotive electric circuit. This is accomplished by the commutator of the generator armature.

45-2 GENERATOR CONSTRUCTION

The generator consists of an *armature*, a set of *field coils* mounted in a field frame, a *drive end plate*, and a *commutator end plate* which frequently supports the brush holders. A pulley and cooling fan is attached to the armature shaft and driven by the crankshaft pulley through a V-type belt.

Generator Armature. The armature consists of a shaft mounted through a laminated winding core

and a commutator assembly. The core is wound with coils made up of many turns of wire. Each end of each coil is attached to a commutator segment or bar. The commutator, the coils, the core, and the shaft rotate as one unit.

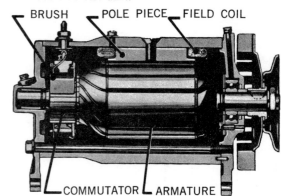

Fig. 45-4   The DC Generator

The armature shaft is supported by bearings or bushings in the end plates. Some armatures are supported by two ball bearings, others use a ball bearing at the drive end and a bushing at the commutator end.

Field Coils. The generator magnetic field is produced by coils of fine wire wrapped around the field pole shoes. The pole shoes are secured by heavy screws to the field frame.

Brush Holders. The commutator brush holders may be of various types such as reaction, swivel, or box, and may be attached to the commutator end frame or to the field frame. One half of the number of holders are insulated from ground, the other half are grounded.

Generator Brushes. The generator brushes are usually of the electrographic type which has high electrical and thermal conductivity. The manufacturing process makes them hard and tough with the ability to withstand high electric loads and high operating temperatures. Most generator brushes have leads called *pig tails* tamped into the brush with silver-plated copper flakes, to form a low resistance connection.

The various types of generator operating conditions necessitate the use of different composition brushes. High-speed high-output generators require hard composition brushes. Low-speed low-output generators require soft composition brushes. Medium composition brushes are used for normal operation.

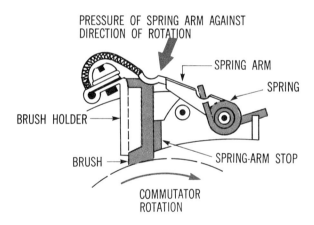

Fig. 45-5   DC Generator Brush and Holder

One factor common to all brushes is the sliding friction between the brush and the segments of the commutator. Normal current flow produces sufficient oxidation to form a copper oxide film on the commutator segments. This oxide film has very little friction, therefore reduces brush wear.

The brushes are held in contact with the commutator by a spring-loaded brush spring arm which is part of the brush holder. Sufficient spring pressure must be applied to the brush to provide good electrical contact, but too high a spring pressure causes rapid brush and commutator wear.

A brush-arm stop is provided to protect the commutator segments from being scored by the brush arm when the brush is worn away. The brush-arm stop also prevents the brush arm from applying pressure on the brush when the brush becomes too short for satisfactory operation.

The components of the generator are held together by long, through bolts which hold the end plates securely against the field frame.

45-3 GENERATOR POLARITY

Generator polarity is the direction of current flow from the generator to the external circuits. The direction of current flow in the conductors depends upon the polarity of the pole shoe pieces. The magnetism of the pole shoe pieces is determined by the direction of current flow through the field coils. The residual magnetism and the polarity of each pole will remain the same as that induced from the magnetism of its field coil the last time current was passed through it. A generator will build up a voltage that will cause a current to flow in either direction depending upon the residual magnetism in the poles. Therefore, a generator must be polarized (see Chapter 46, page 519) to match the polarity of the electrical system of the vehicle in which it is installed.

45-4 DC GENERATOR OPERATING
PRINCIPLES

To illustrate the operating principles of a dc generator, a simple armature with only one coil revolving in the magnetic field of a permanent horseshoe-type magnet will be used. The single coil requires only two segments in the commutator which rotates

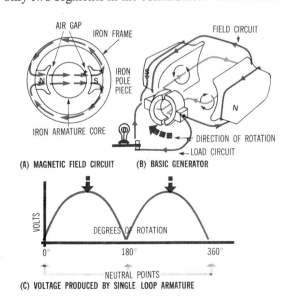

Fig. 45-6   The Basic Principles of a Generator

with the armature. Each segment of the commutator is insulated from the other, and an end of the rotating coil is attached to each commutator segment.

As the commutator revolves with the armature coil, first one segment of the commutator is connected to one brush, then is connected to the other brush. The result is that one brush is always positive, the other negative.

Starting at one neutral point (the neutral point is approximately midway between the poles of the magnet) and as the armature coil is rotated 180°, it passes through the magnetic field. The voltage induced in the coil will reach its maximum after 90° of rotation. At this point the coil is in the strongest area of the magnetic field, which is found when the coil is in line with the poles of the magnet. The induced voltage will decrease as the coil rotates from the 90° to 180° position, reaching zero voltage at the second neutral point at 180°. The voltage induced in the rotating coil will cause a current to flow out of the negative brush and return by way of the positive brush. During the next 180° of coil and commutator rotation, the coil again will cut through the magnetic field in the same direction as it did in the previous 180°. The result is that the current again will flow from the negative brush.

The commutator changes the alternating current that is in the windings of the armature to direct current as it leaves the brushes.

While the current will always flow in one direction, it will rise and fall in value. This rise and fall is known as a *pulsating* current and is as a result of the continuing change of location of the armature winding in the magnetic field. When the coil passes through the maximum density area of the field, the pulse will attain its highest value, and drop to zero where the field is at zero density.

In order to eliminate the two pulses of current per revolution as is obtained with a single core armature, generator armatures are wound with many coils. Each coil end is connected to its individual segment and in series with the other coils. The use of many coils to form an armature results in a number of peaks of voltage that will be equal in number to the number of coils used. Since all the loops are connected in series, any voltage developed in one loop is added to the voltage developed in all the other loops.

In addition to increasing the number of turns of wire in the armature (to increase the generator voltage), the permanent magnet can be replaced with an electromagnet whose strength can be varied to control the amount of voltage produced in ac-

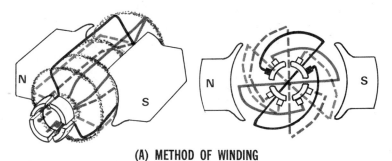

(A) METHOD OF WINDING

Fig. 45-7   Multiloop Armatures

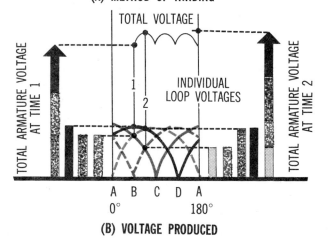

(B) VOLTAGE PRODUCED

cordance with the usage. In addition, the number of field poles and windings can also be increased. The field windings may be connected in series, parallel (shunt), or series parallel with the armature. Automotive generators are usually of the parallel or shunt type.

45-5 ARMATURE REACTION

Armature reaction is the effect that the magnetic field, created by the current-carrying conductors of the armature, has upon the magnetic field created by the field coils. When the armature is rotating, the magnetic field around its conductors will react on and distort the magnetic field set up by the field coils. This distortion changes the location of the neutral points. The new location is called the *load neutral points*.

Two pole generators have two neutral points, one located approximately half way between each of the two poles. Four pole generators have four neutral points which are located between the poles. These basic neutral points are referred to as the *mechanical neutral points*.

Armature reaction has a great bearing on the location of the generator brushes which must be located near the neutral point. Otherwise, the armature loop being connected would be generating voltage and a high current would be short circuited

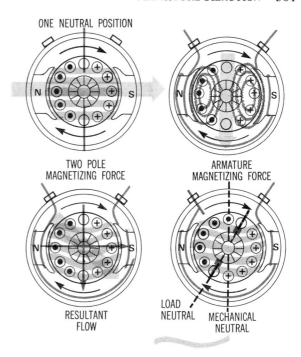

Fig. 45-8   Armature Reaction

between the commutator bars and the brush. This would cause arcing and rapid brush wear.

In a constant-speed and constant-load type of generator operation, the exact location of the load

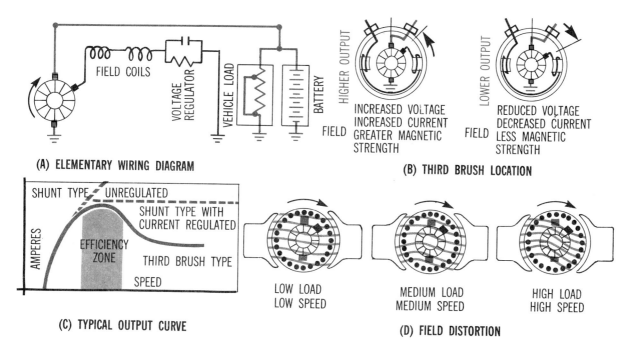

Fig. 45-9   Third Brush Generators

neutral point could be calculated. However, automotive generators do not operate at constant speed or load and, therefore, the designing engineer must select a brush position that will give the minimum of arcing for average operating conditions.

45-6   THIRD-BRUSH GENERATORS

Third-brush generators use the changing of the position of the load neutral point, because of armature reaction, to control the output of the generator.

The two main brushes are located at the neutral points where there is maximum voltage produced. The third brush is connected to the field winding and is placed between the two main brushes where it will pick up less than maximum voltage. As the armature reaction increases, because of generator speed or load, and the magnetic field distorts, the armature windings contacted by the third brush are now in a weak part of the magnetic field. This reduces the amount of voltage generated for use in the fields and reduces the current flow through the fields. The resulting weaker magnetic field reduces generator output.

Moving the third brush in the direction of armature rotation, so that it is closer to the main brush, will increase the maximum output of the generator. Moving the brush in the opposite direction reduces generator output. In this way, the third-brush generator regulates its own current output without an external current regulator. However, some means of controlling the output voltage is frequently used.

45-7   SHUNT-WOUND TYPE GENERATORS

In this type of generator the field windings are connected in parallel or shunted across the armature windings. With this type of field connection, the difference in voltage developed between the two ends of the armature loop when it is rotated through the residual magnetic field causes current to flow through the field coil windings. The additional magnetic field produced strengthens the residual magnetic field of the pole pieces and increases the total field between the two poles. The rotating armature loops cutting through the stronger magnetic field increases the induced voltage in the armature, which in turn increases the flow of current through the field winding. In this manner the voltage of the generator is built up.

The use of the armature current to strengthen the fields places most automotive generators in the

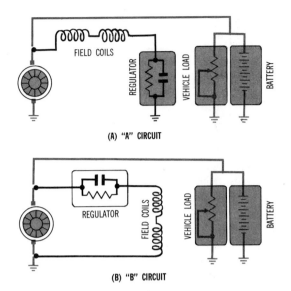

Fig. 45-10   Elementary Wiring of Shunt-Wound DC Generators

classification of self-exciting generators, since no electric current supply is required in order for the generator to produce current.

In order to control the output of a shunt-wound self-exciting generator, a voltage and current control is required. This control is in series with the field circuit. If the field current flows from the fields to the control and then to ground, the generator is classified as having an "A" type circuit. In a "B"-type generator circuit, the field current flows from the control to the fields to ground.

45-8   INTERPOLE GENERATORS

An interpole generator has a narrow pole piece mounted on the field frame between the two regular pole pieces. The interpole is wound with heavy bar copper, since it is connected in series with the armature, and all of the armature current passes through it.

The purpose of the interpole is to reduce the distortion of the field because of the armature reaction. It accomplishes its purpose because it is wound in a direction that produces a magnetic field that will neutralize the magnetic field produced in the armature. Since it is in series with the armature, the amount of current flowing through the interpole and the armature will always be equal. As a result the correct amount of correction is always present. Because of the operation of the interpole coil, the main magnetic field between the poles will remain in a straight line, and the brushes can be located

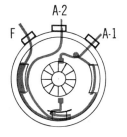

(A) ELEMENTARY WIRING DIAGRAM

(B) NORMAL FIELD DISTORTION

Fig. 45-11   Interpole Type DC Generators

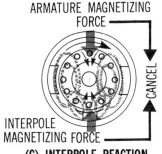

(C) INTERPOLE REACTION

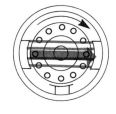

(D) RESULTING MAGNETIC FIELD

exactly on the mechanical neutral point. This reduces brush arcing and increases brush life.

45-9 BUCKING-FIELD GENERATORS

A bucking-field generator has a shunt field coil of high resistance wound on one field coil and connected directly across the armature. The bucking-field coil is wound in such a manner as to produce a magnetic field of opposite polarity to the normal field thus neutralizing the normal field.

At low generator speeds, when the normal field current is large, the neutralizing effect of the bucking field is not large by comparison to that of the main field. At higher generator speeds, when normal field current is reduced by the regulator, the neutralizing effect of the bucking field is greater. This reduces the strength of the main magnetic field and reduces generator output.

45-10 SPLIT-FIELD GENERATORS

A split-field generator is used to produce high output at low speed. The unit has two separate field circuits, thus just about doubling the strength of the magnetic field. This type of generator requires two separate voltage and current control units, one for each field circuit.

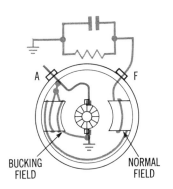

Fig. 45-12   Bucking-Field Type DC Generator

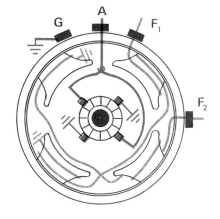

Fig. 45-13   Split-Type DC Generator

45-11 DC GENERATOR REGULATORS OR CONTROLS

The dc generator regulator or control is an electromagnetic device used to control the output of the generator. The type of generator, three-brush or two-brush; the type of generator circuit, "A" or "B" circuits; and the amount of control that the designing engineer deems necessary determines the type of control required. A three-brush generator may only require a one-unit regulator (a cut-out), or may use a two-unit (a cut-out and either a step or vibrating voltage control unit). A two-brush generator requires a three-unit regulator including a cut-out, current control and voltage control units.

Regulators for two-brush generators are grouped in two general classifications called *standard duty* and *heavy duty*. The classification does not necessarily indicate the type of service for which the regulator is designed, but indicates the method of connecting the regulator into the field circuit of the generator. Standard-duty type regulators are used with "A"-type generator circuits and heavy-duty regulators are used with "B"-type generator circuits.

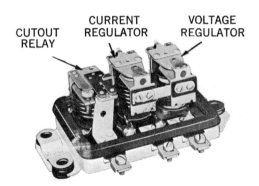

CUTOUT RELAY   CURRENT REGULATOR   VOLTAGE REGULATOR

Fig. 45-14   Generator Regulators

The purpose of the various units of a generator regulator or control are as follows:

1. The cut-out unit is used to connect the generator to the rest of the electrical system when the generator voltage is greater than battery voltage, and to disconnect the generator from the electrical system when the generator voltage is less than battery voltage.
2. The current-control unit is used to prevent the generator from producing more electric energy than the windings of the generator can safely carry.
3. The voltage-control unit is used to protect the battery and other units of the electrical system

by limiting the maximum voltage the generator can produce.

Low-output third-brush generators only require a cut-out relay since the maximum charging rate is determined by the position of the third brush.

High-output third-brush generators require the use of a cut-out plus a device to reduce the charging rate to prevent overcharging of the battery. This device may be a simple manually operated switch which connects or disconnects a resistor into the field circuit to lower the generator output.

A high-output third-brush generator may use a cut-out and what is known as a *step-voltage* control. The step-control unit, operated magnetically, inserts a resistance into the field circuit when a predetermined voltage is reached. It holds the resistance in the field circuit until such time as the voltage drops to another predetermined lower voltage setting. This unit makes possible a high and low charging rate.

A vibrating voltage control and cut-out may also be used with high output third-brush generators. With this type of unit it is possible to limit the charging rate to a given value.

All two-brush generators require the addition of a current-control unit to limit the maximum amount of electric energy the generator can produce.

45-12 THE CUT-OUT RELAY

With any dc generator, a cut-out relay must be used because a dc generator will act as an electric motor if it is not disconnected from the battery when the engine is stopped. The cut-out is a magnetic switch which opens and closes the circuit between the generator and the battery. When the generator is operating at charging speeds, the cut-out relay closes and connects the generator to the battery. When the generator speed decreases or stops, the cut-out relay opens, breaking the circuit and preventing the battery from discharging back through the generator.

Construction of the Cut-out Relay. The cut-out relay consists of two windings assembled on a common core. One is the current or series winding, consisting of a few turns of heavy wire. This winding is connected in series into the charging circuit so that all of the generator output must pass through it. The other winding, called the voltage or shunt winding, is composed of many turns of fine wire. This winding is connected across the generator so that generator voltage is impressed upon it at all

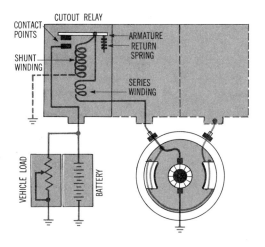

Fig. 45-15   Elementary Wiring Diagram of Cut-Out Unit

times. The shunt winding is the working coil and is responsible mainly for the operation of the relay.

Above the core and winding is a hinged, flat, steel armature, which is held away from the core by spring tension when the unit is not operating. A contact point is mounted on one end of the armature. Directly below, and mating with this contact point, is a stationary contact point which is connected through the vehicle wiring to the battery. The components are mounted on a suitable base and provided with the required electrical connecting tabs.

Cut-Out Relay Operation. When the generator begins to operate, it builds up a voltage which causes current to flow through both the series and shunt windings, both of which produce a magnetic field with common polarity. When the generator voltage reaches the value for which the cut-out relay is set, the magnetism becomes strong enough to overcome the spring tension and the armature is pulled toward the core. The contact point on the armature makes contact with the stationary point, closing the circuit between the generator and the battery. Current then flows from the generator to the battery, passing through the current winding in the proper direction to add to the magnetism holding the points closed.

When the generator slows down sufficiently, generator voltage becomes less than battery voltage and the current begins to flow from the battery back through the generator. This reverses the direction of current flow in the series winding, with the

result that the magnetic field of the series winding is also reversed. The magnetic field of the voltage, or shunt winding, however, remains the same since the same side of the winding is always connected to ground. Therefore, when the magnetic field of the series winding reverses, the magnetic fields of the two windings no longer aid each other, but oppose each other instead. The resultant magnetic field is weakened to such an extent that it no longer can hold the points closed and the armature is pulled away from the winding core by its spring tension. The points are separated, and the circuit is broken between the generator and the battery.

The voltage buildup of the generator that is required to close the contact points is controlled by the tension of the armature spring. Increasing the spring tension increases the voltage required.

45-13 MANUAL GENERATOR-OUTPUT CONTROL

A manually operated switch, mounted in the generator field circuit, can be used to reduce generator output. When the switch is in the closed position, it grounds the generator field directly, permitting full generator output. When the switch is opened, a resistance is inserted into the generator field circuit. This reduces the current flow in the generator field circuit, thus reducing the generator field strength; consequently, a lower generator output results.

This method of control is sometimes used on special applications, such as engines operating air compressors, or arc welding generators, etc.

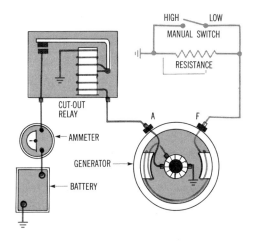

Fig. 45-16   Manual-Type Voltage Control

45-14 STEP-TYPE VOLTAGE-CONTROL UNITS

It is characteristic for the charging voltage of a battery to increase as the battery approaches a full state of charge. Accordingly, in a third-brush generator, which has a high output and which is not controlled, the generator voltage will continue to increase as the battery becomes fully charged. Not only does this cause overcharging of the battery, but it also causes the voltage in the electric system to increase to an excessively high value. To avoid these conditions, a step-type voltage control unit is sometimes used.

The step-type voltage control magnetically operates a switch which inserts, or removes, a resistance from the generator field circuit. This performs magnetically the same function that previously was performed by the manual control switch.

Construction of Step-Type Unit. The step-type voltage control consists of two shunt windings made up of many turns of fine wire, each wound on a separate core. The cores are then mounted side by side and the windings are connected across the generator so that generator voltage is impressed on them at all times. Above the winding cores is a hinged, flat, steel armature held away from the cores by the tension of a spring. With the armature in this position, two contact points, one mounted on the armature and the other on a stationary support, are in contact so that the generator field is grounded directly. This produces a strong magnetic field and high generator output.

Operation of Step-Type Unit. As the battery approaches a charged condition, its cemf increases; therefore, higher voltages are required to maintain the same charging rate. The generator voltage must then also increase in proportion to continue to charge the battery. The increasing generator voltage eventually reaches a value sufficient to operate the voltage-control unit. At this point, the generator voltage is forcing enough current through the voltage-control shunt windings to create a magnetic field strong enough to overcome the armature-spring tension. The armature is pulled toward the winding cores, opening the contact points. When the points open, a resistance is inserted into the generator field circuit, reducing the current flow through the field windings, thus reducing the field strength and generator output.

As long as the battery remains in a charged condition and the system voltage is high, the resistance remains in the generator field circuit and the generator continues to operate at a reduced output. If electrical accessories are turned on, or the battery becomes partly discharged, the system voltage drops below a predetermined value. The lowered voltage becomes too weak to hold the control points open and they close. The generator field circuit is then grounded directly, thus increasing the current flow through the generator fields and thereby increasing generator output.

A wide air gap is used between the armature and the winding cores so that there is a relatively wide step between the opening and closing voltage value.

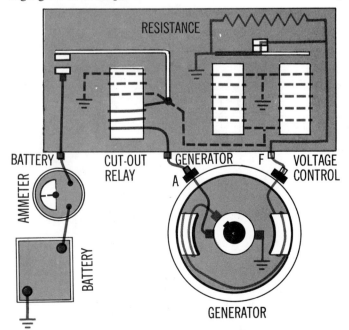

Fig. 45-17   Step-Type Voltage Control

This prevents vibration of the armature, which is very important on this type of voltage control.

With the step-type voltage control there are, in effect, two generators. One is the full-output generator, when the system voltage is low, and the other is the reduced-output generator, when the system voltage is high and a high charging rate is not required. The step-type voltage-control unit is not, therefore, a true voltage regulator. After it comes into operation and inserts the resistance into the generator field, it cannot act to further reduce the generator output. Under certain circumstances it might be possible to obtain battery overcharge and high system voltage, even with the resistance in the generator field circuit. The step-type voltage control, for example, may reduce the output of a generator from 20 amperes maximum to 12 amperes minimum. But, under certain conditions, the 12-ampere charging rate might be excessive, causing battery overcharge and high circuit voltage.

45-15 VIBRATING-TYPE VOLTAGE-CONTROL UNIT

A vibrating-type voltage-control unit is designed to prevent the voltage in the circuit from ever exceeding a predetermined safe value, regardless of generator speed and the state of charge of the battery.

Construction of Vibrating-Type Unit. The vibrating-type voltage-control unit is a magnetic switch, consisting of two windings wound on a common core, a set of contact points, and a resistance. One of the windings is a shunt winding consisting of many turns of fine wire and connected across the generator, so that generator voltage is impressed on the winding at all times. The second winding is a series winding which consists of a few turns of heavy wire. This winding carries the generator field current directly to ground when the regulator points are closed. Mounted above the core is a hinged, flat, steel armature which is held away from the core by spring tension when the unit is not operating. A contact point is attached to the upper side of the armature and, positioned directly above it, is a stationary contact point. Spring tension holds the contact points together when the regulator is not operating.

Operation of Vibrating-Type Unit. Since the cemf of a battery increases as the battery approaches a charged condition, the generator voltage must also increase as required to maintain the charging rate. When the voltage reaches the value for which the voltage regulator is set, the amount of current flowing through the shunt windings produces sufficient magnetism in conjunction with the magnetism of the field series winding, to overcome the armature spring tension. The armature is pulled toward the core and the contact points open.

When the contact points open, the field current

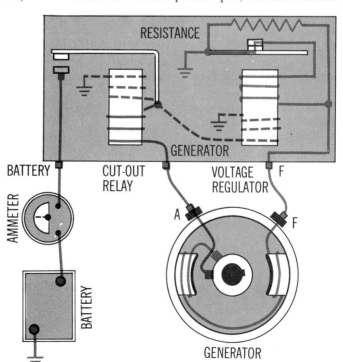

Fig. 45-18   Vibration-Type Voltage Control

must now flow to ground through the resistance. With this resistance inserted into the generator field circuit, the generator voltage and current output drop. However, as soon as the field current stops flowing through the field-series winding of the control unit, the magnetism of this winding collapses. In addition, the reduced voltage in the circuit causes a weakening of the magnetic field of the shunt winding. As a result, the total magnetic field drops to a value too low to retain the armature in the down position. The armature is pulled up by the spring tension, and the contact points again close, thus directing the generator field-circuit current directly to ground. This increases the current flow through the field winding, thereby increasing field strength and the generator voltage and output.

Magnetism again is produced in the control-unit field-current winding and the increasing voltage strengthens the magnetic field of the shunt winding. The total magnetism once again quickly reaches a value sufficient to open the contact points and re-insert the resistance into the generator field circuit. This complete cycle take place 50 to 200 times a second, and the generator voltage is thereby limited to a safe value.

As the battery approaches a full state of charge, the voltage-control unit, by limiting the charging voltage, causes the charging rate to be still further reduced. When the battery reaches a fully charged condition, the voltage regulator will have reduced the charging rate to a few amperes.

The field series winding on the voltage-control unit serves to speed up the rate of armature vibration. Inserting and removing of the resistance in the field circuit at a sufficiently rapid rate allows the control unit to maintain a practically constant voltage. With the generator voltage limited to a fixed value and the battery increasing in cemf as it becomes charged, the difference in voltage between the two units becomes less and less. With less voltage difference, there is less current flow. Thus, by regulating the generator voltage, the generator current output, or charging rate, is also controlled.

The allowable range of voltage adjustment depends upon the condition of the battery, battery operating temperatures, the amount of connected load and operating conditions. It is desirable to have the voltage high enough to keep the battery in a charged condition and yet low enough to prevent battery overcharging or high voltage in the electrical system. This means that the most desirable voltage setting may vary in different sections of the country and with different driving conditions. The most desirable voltage-control unit setting is that which keeps the battery charged with the least amount of battery water evaporation.

45-16 VIBRATING CURRENT-CONTROL UNIT

Since the shunt-wound two-brush generator does not have the current-limiting effect of the third

*Fig. 45-19   Three-State Vibrating
DC Generator Control*

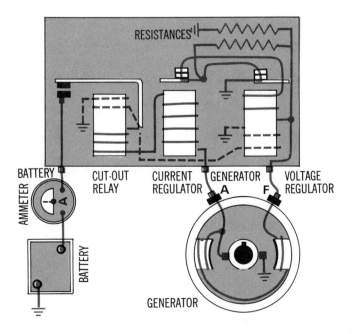

brush, it is necessary to use some other form of current-limiting unit. This device is called the vibrating current-control unit.

Construction of Current-Control Unit. The vibrating current-control unit is assembled on the same base with the voltage-control unit and the cut-out relay. Its job is to limit the amount of electrical energy that the generator can produce, thereby preventing the generator output from exceeding a safe maximum.

The current-control unit has only one winding, a series winding which is current-sensitive and carries the entire generator output. Above the winding and core is a hinged, flat, steel armature with a contact point on top. A stationary contact is positioned directly above the point on the armature. The points are held in a closed position by spring tension which holds the armature up when the current regulator is not operating.

Certain conditions of generator speed, state of charge of the battery and load demands tend to produce excessive generator output. However, when the generator output increases to the value for which the current regulator is set, the magnetism of the series winding is sufficient to overcome the armature spring tension. The armature is pulled toward the winding core so that the points are opened. The generator field current must now flow to ground through two resistors in parallel. These resistances reduce the flow of current through the generator field windings and thereby reduce generator voltage and current output.

The lowered output reduces the strength of the magnetic field in the series winding and the contact points again close, directly grounding the generator field circuit so that the generator output increases. This cycle is repeated 50 to 200 times a second and the action limits the generator output to the value for which the control unit is set.

Two resistances are used on current and voltage regulators. They are connected into the generator field circuit in parallel, when the current-control unit points are open, to give a lower resistance value. When the voltage-control unit points are open, only one resistance is inserted into the generator field circuit. This provides a higher resistance value. This is desirable for the reason that a higher value of resistance is required to reduce the generator output to a few amperes than is required to merely prevent the generator output from increas-

ing beyond the safe maximum of the generator windings.

45-17 WORKING RELATIONSHIP BETWEEN VIBRATING-VOLTAGE AND CURRENT-CONTROL UNITS

When the vibrating-voltage and current-control units are used together, only one of them will operate at any one time; they never operate simultaneously.

If the electrical load requirements are heavy and the state of charge of the battery is low, the system voltage will not be sufficient to cause the voltage-control unit to operate. The generator output consequently will increase until it reaches the value for which the current-control unit is set, at which time the current-control unit will operate to protect the generator from overload.

If the electrical load is reduced, or if the battery begins to come up to full charge, the system voltage will increase to a value sufficient to cause the voltage-control to operate. When this happens, the generator output is reduced below the value required to operate the current-control unit. The current-control unit then stops operating, and all control is dependent on the operation of the voltage-control unit.

The rapid vibration of the contact points of the voltage-control unit and the current-control unit inserts and removes the resistance from the field circuit thus maintaining the resistance in the generator field circuit the correct proportion of time to maintain a constant voltage in the system. When the battery is fully charged and the electrical load is light, the resistance remains in the generator field circuit most of the time because of either the rapid vibration of the points, putting the resistance in the circuit more frequently, or because the points remain open for a longer period of time during each vibrating cycle. Therefore, the resistance remains in the generator field circuit longer. The longer or more frequently the resistance is in the field circuit, the less current that flows through the field winding, the weaker the fields, and the lower the generator output.

If the battery state of charge is low, or the electrical load is heavy, then the resistance is in the circuit a very short period of time, if at all. This increases field current flow and generator output. These conditions are true for both the current- and voltage-control units.

45-18 COMBINED CURRENT AND VOLTAGE-TYPE REGULATORS

This type of regulator was designed for use on farm tractor and stationary-type engines that are operated at constant speeds. The combination current-voltage regulator is a device which, when used in conjunction with a three-brush generator, provides control of the generator output and system voltage simultaneously, so as to meet various battery requirements.

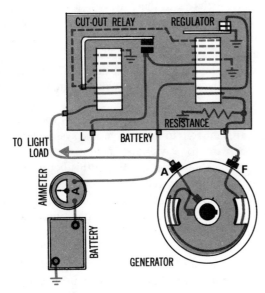

Fig. 45-20 Combined Current- and Voltage-Type Regulator (Third-Brush Generator)

Construction of the Current-Voltage Regulator. The cut-out relay used in this type of regulator is the same in construction and operation as that used in standard-duty regulators.

The regulator unit is made up of three windings wound on a single core. One winding is the series winding, consisting of a few turns of heavy wire which is connected in series with the charging circuit. The second winding is the shunt winding, comprised of many turns of fine wire, and is connected across the generator so that generator voltage is impressed on it at all times. The third winding is the field-series winding, which is made up of a few turns of relatively heavy wire, and is connected in series with the generator field circuit when the contact points are closed. Above the core and windings is a flat, hinged steel armature on

top of which is a contact point. This contact point mates with a stationary contact point above it. The generator field is connected to ground through the points when the regulator is not operating. When the contact points are open, the field circuit is connected to ground through a resistor beneath the regulator base.

Operation of the Current-Voltage Regulator. As the generator begins to operate, the voltage impressed on the shunt winding of the regulator causes some current to flow, creating a magnetic field in the core. Closing of the cut-out relay, as the generator continues to build up output, allows the output current to flow through the heavy series winding of the regulator, creating an additional magnetic field. When these magnetic fields attain sufficient magnetic strength, they pull the armature down and open the contact points. The generator field current is then diverted through the resistor to ground. Placing of the resistance in the field circuit causes the generator output to drop, weakening the magnetic fields of the windings, and the contact points close. This cycle is rapidly and continuously repeated as long as the generator and regulator are in operation, thus limiting the generator output. It is important to note that the regulator unit is sensitive to changes in both current and voltage at the same time.

The field-series winding might be termed an *accelerator* winding since it speeds up both the opening and closing of the contact points. When the contact points are closed, the magnetic field of this winding aids the other two, but when the contact points open, its magnetic field collapses immediately. The sudden loss of this magnetic field greatly reduces the total attraction for the armature. The action of this winding, therefore, accelerates the vibration of the armature in opening and closing the contact points. This results in a more accurate generator control.

The current-voltage regulator has an extra terminal marked "L" which is connected to the lower contact point of the cut-out relay. This extra terminal permits current from the generator to be diverted to the load without passing through the current-voltage regulator. This current has no controlling effect, since the regulator is affected only by current going to or from the battery. Generator output accordingly can increase to a value sufficient to handle the load and still supply a charging current to the battery, provided, of course, that the total load does not exceed the maximum output of the generator. When the generator is not in operation, the electrical load is supplied with current from the battery. The current in this case flows from the battery through the series winding to the "L" terminal and to the load.

It is important that lights, ignition, and other similar loads be attached to the regulator "L" terminal in order not to interfere with regulation.

45-19 TEMPERATURE COMPENSATION IN REGULATORS

Cut-out relays, voltage-control units, and current-control units are usually wound with copper wire and the resistance of these windings changes accord to the temperature of the winding. As the temperature increases, its resistance increases proportionately. A change in the resistance of the winding creates a proportional change in current flow, which in turn changes the magnetic strength of the coil. Change in magnetic strength changes the voltage or current requirements necessary to operate the unit, and therefore it will not function at the proper set voltage or current.

In most designs, the necessary temperature compensation is obtained through the use of a *bimetallic armature hinge*. This bimetallic hinge is made of two thin layers of different metals which are fused together. Each of the metals has a different heat expansion characteristic. A thermostatic action takes place as the temperature of the hinge increases; that is, one metal expands more than the other, causing the hinge to bend.

As the temperature increases and the hinge bends, it reduces the armature spring tension. Reducing the spring tension compensates for the increased resistance because of the temperature increase of the winding, and the regulator will continue to operate at the proper setting.

45-20 REGULATOR POLARITY

Most regulators are designed to operate with a given polarity either positive ground or negative ground, negative ground being the most popular. Using the wrong polarity regulator will cause the regulator contact points to pit badly and shorten point life. Regulators are clearly marked on their base to indicate their polarity.

45-21 REGULATOR AIR GAP

The term *regulator air gap* refers to the distance between armature and the winding core and is usually measured in thousandths of an inch.

The amount of air gap required is determined by two principal factors. One is the ratio of the magnetic pull on the armature to the pull of the spiral spring or springs on the armature. The second factor is in addition to the first and applies on temperature-compensated regulators. This factor is the ratio of the magnetic pull on the armature to the pull of the bimetal hinge on the armature. With temperature-compensated regulators, too wide an air gap will cause overcompensation of the regulator, while too small an air gap will cause undercompensation. This means that a wide air gap will increase the difference between the operating levels when cold and hot. On a voltage-control unit, for instance, the wide air gap will permit a higher regulated voltage when cold and a lower regulated voltage when hot. Or, in the case of the current-control unit, the regulated output in amperes will be high when the unit is cold and low when the unit is hot. With too small an air gap on the voltage-control unit, when the unit is cold the regulated voltage is not quite high enough, and when the unit is hot the voltage is not low enough.

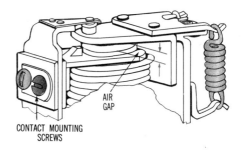

Fig. 45-21   Regulator Air Gap

45-22 DOUBLE-CONTACT VOLTAGE-CONTROL UNITS

The double-contact voltage-control unit gets its name from the dual set of points used on the voltage-control unit. The upper and lower contacts on the movable armature are insulated electrically from each other, and a stationary set of contacts is located between the armature contacts. With this arrangement either the lower set of contacts will be closed, the upper set will be closed, or both sets

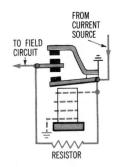

(A) ELEMENTARY WIRING DIAGRAM

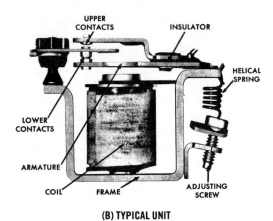

(B) TYPICAL UNIT

Fig. 45-22   Double-Contact Voltage-Control Unit

will be separated at any one time, depending upon the strength of the core magnetic field. An armature spring holds the lower contacts closed when the unit is not operating.

The lower set of contacts is in series with the generator field circuit as in other regulators. The upper set of contacts, when closed, shorts out the generator field circuit.

When the generator speed is low and the electrical load is heavy, the lower set of contacts are in operation. They provide the same means of control by vibrating and placing a resistance in the generator field circuit in the same manner as a standard control unit. However, at high generator speeds and light electrical loads, the generator voltage has a tendency to creep up even with the resistance in the generator field circuit most of the time. When this happens, additional current flows through the core windings and increases the magnetic strength and pulls the armature closer to the core. This action closes the upper contacts, shorting out the generator field circuit by connecting both ends of the generator field circuit into the

charging circuit instead of one end going to ground either directly or through the resistance. When both ends of the generator field circuit are connected into the charging circuit, no current flows through the field windings; hence generator output drops very low. This reduces the magnetic strength of the core windings, causing the upper contacts to open again. Continuing this cycle (vibration) reduces the output of the generator to a very low level.

REVIEW QUESTIONS

1. List the units of a dc charging circuit.
2. What is the purpose of a generator?
3. State the basic operating principle of a generator.
4. Why is the current produced in the armature of a dc generator always ac in nature?
5. State the rule used to determine the direction of flow of the induced current of the generator armature.
6. State three factors which determine the strength of the induced current in a dc generator.
7. Explain how a commutator converts the ac current of the armature to the dc current required by the electrical system.
8. Describe the construction of a generator armature.
9. Why are generator brushes made of different compositions?
10. Why is proper brush spring tension important?
11. What determines the polarity of a generator?
12. Why is generator polarity important?
13. Describe the principle of current induction and commutator action as the armature is rotated 360° through the magnetic field.
14. Why is the voltage output increased as the number of coils in the armature is increased?
15. Explain armature reaction.
16. Define the terms: (a) mechanical neutral point (b) load neutral point.
17. What effect does the neutral point have on the location of the generator brushes? Why?
18. Why does the maximum output of a third-brush type generator decrease when the unit is driven at speeds higher than that required to produce maximum output?
19. How does the source of field current differ between an "A"-type shunt-wound generator and a third-brush type generator?
20. A shunt-wound generator is said to be self-excited. Explain this statement.
21. Why does the output of a shunt-wound generator continue to rise as long as the speed of the armature is increasing?
22. Shunt-wound generators are classified as "A"

type and "B" type. State the difference between the two types.

23. What is the purpose of the interpole coil used in an interpole-type generator?

24. How does the bucking field of a bucking-field type generator help reduce generator output at high speeds?

25. Name and state the purpose of each unit of a three-stage regulator as used on two-brush shunt-wound generators.

26. Why is a current-control unit not required when a three-brush generator is used?

27. Describe the operation of: (a) a step-type (b) a vibrating-type voltage-control unit.

28. Why are two windings required in a cut-out relay?

29. Why is the cemf of the battery an important factor in the operation of a voltage-control unit?

30. Why are two windings required in the coil of a vibrating-type voltage-control unit?

31. List three factors that determine the desirable voltage setting of a vibrating-type voltage control.

32. Why is a current control necessary on a shunt-wound two-brush self-exciting generator and not required on a three-brush generator?

33. Describe the operation of a vibrating-type current control.

34. Why are two resistors in parallel used when the current control is in operation and only one resistor used when the voltage-control unit is in operation?

35. The voltage-control unit and the current-control unit are never in operation at the same time. Why?

36. Explain how a combined current and voltage control unit maintains proper generator output and circuit voltage simultaneously.

37. What effect will (a) too much (b) too little air gap have on regulator unit operation?

38. Why is generator polarity an important factor in regulator service life?

39. What are the advantages of a double-contact type voltage-control unit?

40. Explain the operation of a double-contact type voltage-control unit.

Chapter 46
DC CHARGING-CIRCUIT SERVICE

Charging system troubles can be traced to either the *battery*, *generator*, *regulator*, or the *wiring*. It may be in one unit or, in some cases, all the units.

After a visual inspection of the wiring for breaks and for loose or corroded connections, the generator should be checked for maximum output.

46-1 CHECKING GENERATOR OUTPUT

The generator output test is usually performed with the generator on the vehicle. To perform the test a *voltmeter*, *ammeter*, a *variable resistor*, and a *tachometer* are required.

The generator armature lead is disconnected and the ammeter and resistor are connected in series between the armature terminal and ground. The voltmeter is attached between the armature terminal and ground and the tachometer it attached to the drive end of the armature shaft.

To test "A" circuit generators, the field terminal is grounded to bypass the control and ground the field circuit.

"B" circuit generators require a jumper lead to be connected between the armature and field ter-

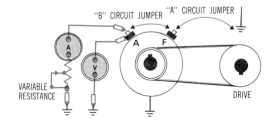

Fig. 46-1   Checking DC Generator Output

minals to bypass the control and supply current to the field circuit.

Drive the generator at a speed slightly below the rated specifications, using the tachometer to record armature speed. Adjust the variable resistance unit to a value that will cause the generator to produce the specified voltage. Increase the generator speed until the current flow through the ammeter and resistance reaches the amount specified. Recheck the voltage to make sure that it is the same as that specified. Adjust the variable resistance and speed, as required, to obtain the correct voltage and amperage.

If the generator is working satisfactorily, the speed of rotation of the armature needed to produce the required voltage and amperage will be that which is specified. If the specified voltage and amperage are obtained at a speed that is lower than that specified, it indicates that the generator is in a satisfactory working condition.

If the armature speed must be greater than that specified in order to obtain the required voltage and amperage, or if there is no output from the generator, this indicates that the generator is in poor or unsatisfactory operating condition. In this case disassemble the generator and check each unit to determine the cause.

46-2 GENERATOR OVERHAUL

Cleaning. All parts of the generator except the armature and field coils may be cleaned in a suitable solvent. Wipe armature and field coils with a damp solvent-dipped wiper.

Testing the Armature. Inspect armature for damage to the laminated core caused by worn bearings or bushings that allow the armature to rub on the pole shoes; for signs of missing solder on the conductor-to-commuter segment joints; for signs of burning of the commutator segments that could indicate an open circuit. Check the commutator for scoring and out-of-round. The run-out should not exceed .003 to .005″. If the armature passes the visual inspection, it should be tested electrically.

Testing the armature for short circuits—requires a piece of electrical test equipment called a *growler*. A growler produces an alternating polarity magnetic field from ac current.

To test the armature, place the armature in the growler and hold a thin steel strip (hacksaw blade) loosely just above the top of the armature and

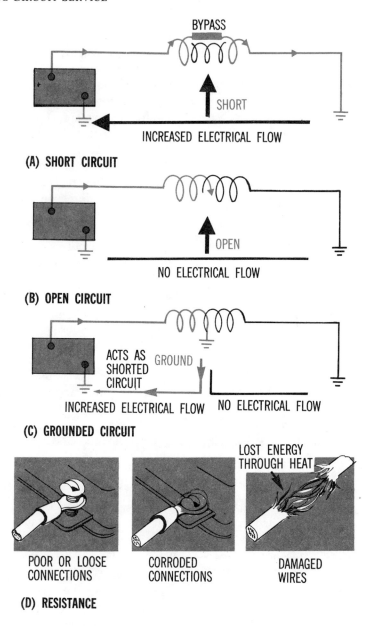

BYPASS

SHORT

INCREASED ELECTRICAL FLOW

(A) SHORT CIRCUIT

OPEN

NO ELECTRICAL FLOW

(B) OPEN CIRCUIT

ACTS AS SHORTED CIRCUIT

GROUND

INCREASED ELECTRICAL FLOW   NO ELECTRICAL FLOW

(C) GROUNDED CIRCUIT

LOST ENERGY THROUGH HEAT

POOR OR LOOSE CONNECTIONS

CORRODED CONNECTIONS

DAMAGED WIRES

(D) RESISTANCE

Fig. 46-2   Basic Generator Electrical Faults

rotate the armature on the growler. Continue to rotate the armature until the entire core has passed beneath the steel strip. If the steel strip does not vibrate then the armature is not shorted. If, however, a short circuit exists, the strip will vibrate when the shorted section of the armature passes under it. Do not operate the growler unless an armature is in place. Shorted armatures must be replaced.

Checking armatures for grounds—Most growlers include a pair of 110-volt test prods that are in series with a very small bulb. To test the armature for ground, place one test prod on the armature core (not the bearing or bushing surfaces) and touch each of the commutator segments with the other prod. If the armature is grounded, the test lamp will light. Discard grounded armatures.

Testing armatures for opens—An open circuited armature is easily identified during the visual inspection of the commutator segments. The trailing edge of the segment attached to the open circuit winding will be badly burned. The severe arcing

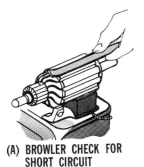

(A) BROWLER CHECK FOR SHORT CIRCUIT

(C) VISUAL INDICATION OF OPEN CIRCUIT IN ARMATURE

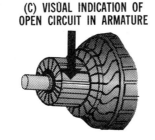

(B) TEST LAMP CHECK FOR GROUND CIRCUIT

(D) GROWLER CHECK FOR OPEN CIRCUIT

Fig. 46-3   Checking and Servicing DC Generator Armatures

(E) TRUEING ARMATURE

(F) UNDERCUTTING ARMATURE

that caused the burning can easily be seen when the generator is operated.

Some growlers include an additional circuit which can be used to locate an open circuit in the armature. To perform this test, follow the manufacturers' instructions.

Turning the commutator—Commutators may be cleaned and trued in a lathe or special commutator turning fixture. Remove only sufficient copper from the commutator segments to clean up scoring, burning, or out-of-round conditions.

After turning the commutator, the mica insulators between each commutator segment should be undercut to a depth equal to the width of the mica. This undercutting is necessary because the mica insulators are harder than the copper commutator segments and, as a result, they do not wear as fast. Mica insulators that are higher than the commutator segments will cause rapid brush wear, bouncing brushes, and arcing.

Testing the field coils for opens—is performed by using the 110-volt test prods of the growler. Before testing the fields of a "B"-circuit type generator, it is necessary to disconnect the grounded end of the field coils. Place one test prod on the field coil terminal and the other prod on the opposite end of the winding. The test lamp will light if the circuit is complete. No light indicates an open field circuit. Test each field coil in the same manner. Discard open field coils.

Testing the field coils for grounds—is performed by using the 110-volt test prods of the growler. After disconnecting the grounded field connection of "B"-circuit generators, both "A"- and "B"-type field coils may be tested by placing one prod on the field-coil terminal stud and the other on the field frame. The lamp should not light; if it does then there is a ground between the field windings and the frame, and the field windings should be replaced.

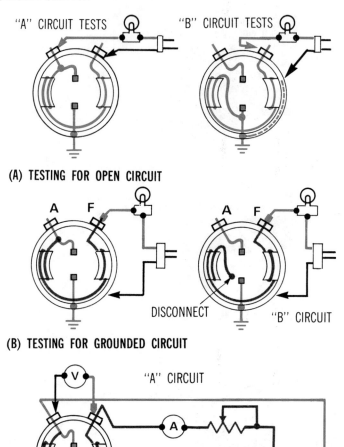

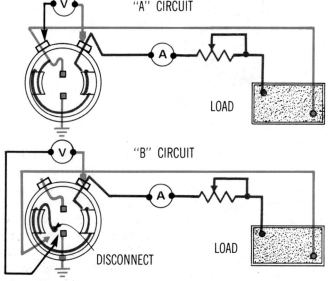

Fig. 46-4   Testing Field Coils

Checking field-current draw—requires a voltmeter, ammeter, a variable resistance, and a proper voltage source. To check "B"-circuit generators, the ground lead must be disconnected, and the field coil temperature for all field coils should be approximately 80°F. Connect the proper voltage source to one end of the field coils through the ammeter and the variable resistance, and connect the other source lead to the opposite end of the field coils. (The two field coils must be connected in series for this test.) Connect the voltmeter in parallel with the field coil. Adjust the variable resistance until the specified voltage is applied to the circuit. The current flow may now be observed on the ammeter. Ammeter readings below those specified indicate high resistance in the field coils.

Current draw readings higher than specified indicate that some of the field winding turns are shorted. In either case the windings must be replaced.

Checking brushes and brush holders—to electrically test brush holders, the 110-volt test prods are used. Place one prod on the grounded brush holder, the other on the field frame. If the brush is grounded properly then the lamp will light. To test the insulated brush holder, one prod is placed on the holder, the other on the field frame. The lamp should not light.

Brush-to-brush holder fit should be checked. The brush should fit snugly in the holder but be free to move toward the commutator without binding. Brush-arm spring tension should be tested by placing a spring scale at a point as close to the middle of the brush as possible and observing the pressure required to lift the brush off the commutator. Compare the pressure required to that specified.

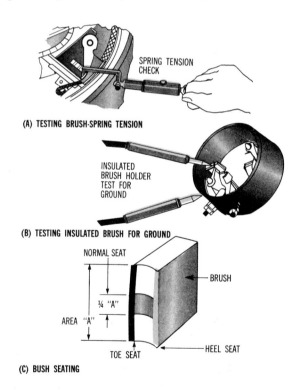

(A) TESTING BRUSH-SPRING TENSION

SPRING TENSION CHECK

INSULATED BRUSH HOLDER TEST FOR GROUND

(B) TESTING INSULATED BRUSH FOR GROUND

NORMAL SEAT

BRUSH

¼ "A"

AREA "A"

TOE SEAT

HEEL SEAT

(C) BUSH SEATING

Fig. 46-5   Checking Brushes and Brush Holders

Weak spring tension will cause the brushes to bounce at high speeds, which will result in arcing and poor commutation. Too high spring tension will cause excessive friction between the brush and the commutator, resulting in short brush life.

When new brushes are installed, a proper brush seating area across the thickness of the brush from front to rear must be obtained. A seating area of 25% of the length of the brush is satisfactory. A seating area of the same size on either the leading or trailing edge of the brush is unsatisfactory, because it would change the mechanical neutral point of the brush and result in excessive arcing and burning of the brush and commutator. Proper brush seating may be obtained through the use of brush seating stones or seating compounds. The abrasive action of these materials produces a perfect seat between the brush and commutator.

46-3 POLARIZING A GENERATOR

After a generator has been disconnected, tested, or repaired, it should be polarized. Polarizing will ensure that the residual magnetism in the pole pieces of the generator will have correct polarity to develop a voltage that will cause a current to flow in the proper direction to the battery in the circuit. Failure to polarize the generator may result in burned cut-out relay points, a discharged battery, or serious damage to the generator. If the direction of current flow from the generator is wrong, the voltages of the generator and battery will be added together to give approximately double voltage across the contact points of the cut-out relay.

For proper polarization, the rule is to pass current through the field coils in a direction that will have the ground side of the field coils connected to the ground side of the vehicle battery.

To polarize an "A"-circuit generator, flash a jumper lead from the insulated or "hot" side of the battery to the armature or "A" terminal of the generator. A convenient place to polarize the generator is at the regulator, by flashing the jumper between the battery and armature terminals of the regulator.

To polarize a "B"-circuit generator, disconnect the field lead from its regulator terminal and flash the lead to the battery terminal of the regulator.

46-4 DC GENERATOR-REGULATOR SERVICE

Dc generator service is usually indicated by one of several complaints: a fully charged battery and a high charging rate; low-charged battery and a low charging rate; no charging rate. Normal operation is represented by a fully charged battery and a low charging rate.

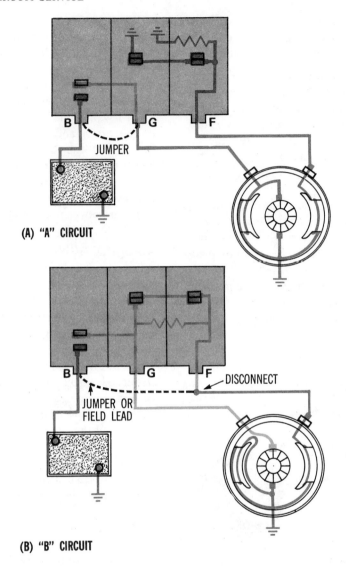

(A) "A" CIRCUIT

(B) "B" CIRCUIT

Fig. 46-6   Polarizing a Generator

46-5 REGULATOR QUICK CHECKS

When abnormal conditions are indicated, the following procedures may be used to determine the cause of the malfunction.

A Fully Charged Battery and a High Charging Rate. Such a condition, if allowed to continue, will damage the battery. If the high charging rate is accompanied by a high voltage, other electrical units in the system will also be damaged.

While the improper operation may be caused by the regulator, the battery should be considered as a possible cause. If the battery becomes very hot, as a result of either internal or external conditions,

its cemf decreases greatly. In this condition the battery will accept a high charging rate, even at a so-called normal voltage-control unit setting and with the other equipment operating properly. To check this possibility, determine the temperature of the battery electrolyte with a suitable thermometer.

If the battery electrolyte temperature is within the normal range, then a test ammeter should be connected into the circuit at the battery terminal of the regulator and the field lead disconnected from the field terminal of the regulator. This check will indicate whether the regulator or some other unit of the electrical system is at fault. The disconnecting of the field lead removes the regulator completely from the generator field circuit and the generator output should drop to zero. If the output does drop to zero when the lead is disconnected from the field terminal, the regulator should be checked for a high voltage setting or for grounds or shorts within the regulator.

If the output does not drop to zero when the field lead is disconnected, then the generator field circuit is grounded. The ground can be either in the wiring or in the generator itself. To determine the location of the ground, disconnect the field lead from the generator field terminal. If the output remains high, the generator is at fault and must be removed for additional checking. If the output drops to zero, the fault is in the wiring between the generator and the regulator, and the wiring should be tested.

A Low Battery with a Low Charging Rate. This condition may be caused by loose connections, frayed or damaged leads, a defective battery, high resistance in the charging circuit, a low regulator setting, oxidized regulator contact points, or defects within the generator.

To check for a low voltage-control unit setting or for dirty or oxidized regulator contact points, connect a test ammeter into the circuit at the battery terminal of the regulator. Operate the generator at medium speed and momentarily ground the field terminal of the regulator. If the output rises, then the voltage setting is too low or the points are dirty or oxidized. To clean the contact points, use a spoon or *riffler file*. Never use emery cloth or sandpaper to clean contact points.

If the output remains low, momentarily ground the generator field terminal. An increase in output indicates defective wiring between the generator and the regulator. If the output remains low, the generator is at fault and it should be removed for careful checking.

Excessive resistance in the charging system between the regulator and the battery causes the voltage-control unit of the regulator to operate and reduce the generator output, even though the battery is in a discharged condition. Since the voltage-control unit setting is measured at the battery terminal of the regulator, any resistance between the regulator and the battery will decrease the effective charging voltage at the battery. If the loss is exces-

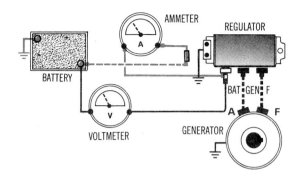

Fig. 46-7   Checking Charging Circuit for Resistance

sive, the charging rate to the battery will be reduced greatly, and undercharging will occur.

Every connection and junction point in an electric circuit is a potential source of resistance and should be inspected carefully when trouble occurs. Connections not only must be tight, but clean. A rusty lockwasher, or a corroded terminal clip, nut, or terminal post can be the cause of difficulty, since rust and corrosion act as insulators.

The condition of the wiring is also very important. Wires with damaged insulation or broken and frayed strands should be replaced. Broken strands in the wire reduce the current-carrying capacity of the wire, thus introducing resistance. Wiring near, or directly connected to, the battery should be inspected frequently because of the tendency for damaging corrosion to develop at this location.

Keep battery cables in good condition, with terminal connections clean and tight. If corrosion develops at the battery terminals, remove the clamps and the battery terminal posts and clean the cable clamps thoroughly with a wire brush. After replacing the clamp terminal on the battery posts, it is good practice to grease them with a heavy-bodied mineral grease to retard corrosion.

No Charging Rate. When no charging rate is obtained, the cut-out relay should be checked since it may not be closing, because of a high voltage setting or an open shunt winding. Dirty or oxidized points on the cut-out relay might also cause an open circuit.

If the cut-out relay is functioning properly, the generator output should be checked. If the generator shows no output whatsoever, then it must be removed for careful checking.

46-6 REGULATOR ELECTRICAL CHECKS AND ADJUSTMENTS

After completing the regulator quick checks, it may be necessary to accurately check the regulator for proper setting. To check the settings the following procedures may be used.

Cut-Out Relay Closing Voltage. Make the necessary meter connections as shown in Fig. 46-8.

To check the closing voltage of the cut-out relay, slowly increase the generator speed and note the relay closing voltage. If an adjustment is required, there are three checks to be made on the cut-out relay; the air-gap check, the point-opening check, and the closing-voltage check.

Before making any adjustments on the cut-out relay, disconnect the battery lead from the regulator battery terminal. Do not allow the battery lead to short against any of the metal parts.

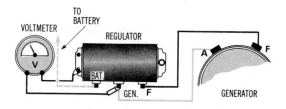

Fig. 46-8   Checking Cut-Out Relay Closing Voltage

To check the air gap—place a finger on the armature directly above the winding core and move the armature down until the cut-out contact points just close. Measure the air gap between the armature and the centre of the core. Do not press down on the armature any harder than is necessary to just close the contact points. If both sets of contact points do not close at the same instant, bend the spring fingers on the armature slightly until both sets do meet simultaneously. To adjust the air gap, loosen the two adjusting screws and raise or lower the armature as required. Securely tighten the adjusting screws after adjustment, making sure that the contact points are still properly aligned.

To check the cut-out relay contact-point opening—the armature must be at rest against the upper armature stop. Measure the contact-point opening between the fixed and movable points. To adjust the contact-point opening, bend the upper armature stop up to increase the opening, or down to decrease it.

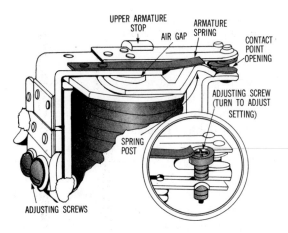

Fig. 46-9   Cut-Out Relay Adjustments

To set the closing voltage—reconnect the regulator in the normal manner to the generator and battery. Momentarily connect a jumper lead between the regulator battery and generator terminals to correctly polarize the generator before operating it.

The closing voltage is then checked as outlined previously. To adjust the closing voltage, increase the armature spring tension to increase the closing voltage, and decrease the armature spring tension to decrease the closing voltage. The spring tension may be varied by bending the spring post on some types of cut-out relays, or by adjusting the adjusting screw provided on other types.

Voltage-Control Unit Checking. Make the necessary meter connections as shown in Fig. 46-10.

To check the voltage-control unit setting, operate the generator at medium speed and note the voltage setting. The regulator must be at operating temperature and the cover must be in place when readings are taken. If adjustment is required, see the section headed regulator adjustments.

Current-Control Unit Checking. Make the necessary meter connections as shown in Fig. 46-10.

To check the current-control setting, the voltage-control unit must be prevented from operating. Operation of the voltage-control unit will reduce the generator output to a value below that required to make the current-control unit operate. There are several ways to prevent the voltage-control unit from operating. One is the *jumper-lead method.*

To use the jumper-lead method, connect a jumper lead across the voltage-control unit contact points to prevent its operation. The output will then increase with generator speed to the value for which the current-control unit is set. The test ammeter

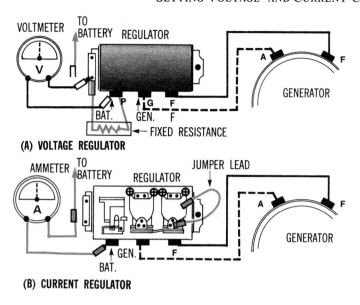

Fig. 46-10   Checking Voltage and Current Regulator Units

that has been connected into the circuit will measure the current setting. The lights, radio, heater, and other accessories should be turned on during this test to avoid high voltage in the system.

Another method of checking the current-control unit setting does not require the removal of the regulator cover and the installation of the jumper lead across the voltage-control unit points. In this method, the battery is first partially discharged by operating the cranking motor for a period not longer than 30 seconds. During cranking, the high-tension lead must be removed from the ignition coil to prevent the engine from starting. After using the cranking motor for the brief period of time, the voltage-control unit will not operate since the voltage in the system will not increase sufficiently to cause it to operate. In fact, the voltage-control unit will not operate until such time as the generator has recharged the battery to compensate for the electrical energy used in operating the cranking motor. During this interval the current output will increase sufficiently to cause the current-control unit to operate. Note the current setting on the test ammeter. As in previous tests, the regulator must be at operating temperature when being checked.

46-7 SETTING VOLTAGE- AND CURRENT-CONTROL UNITS

Before attempting to set either the voltage- or current-control units, the air gap must be checked and set to proper specifications.

Checking Air Gap. To check the air gap, push down the armature until the contact points just

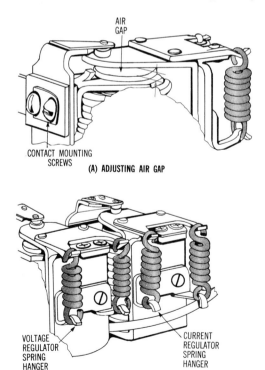

Fig. 46-11   Adjusting DC Generator Regulator Units

open, then slowly release until the contact points barely touch. With the contact points just touching, measure the air gap between the centre of the winding core and the armature. If adjustment is required, then disconnect the regulator from the battery and, preferably, remove from the vehicle. To adjust, loosen the contact mounting screws slightly to allow movement of the contact support. Insert a feeler gauge between the armature and the winding core and press the armature down against the gauge. Adjust the contact support up or down until the contact points just barely touch. Secure the adjustment by tightening the contact mounting screws.

After the air gap has been set, the regulator may be reconnected to the generator and battery, so that the electrical settings can be checked.

Setting the current- and voltage-control units. The electrical setting of the current- and voltage-control units may be adjusted by increasing or decreasing the armature spring tension. This is accomplished by bending the spring hangers on some models or by adjusting screws on others.

To adjust the current-control unit—operate the generator, under proper conditions, at a speed sufficient to produce current in excess of the specified setting. By turning the adjusting screw or by bending the spring hanger, adjust the current output to the specified setting. After each adjustment and before taking the current reading, replace the regulator cover, reduce the generator speed until the relay points open, and then bring the generator back to speed again.

To adjust the voltage-control unit—operate the generator under proper conditions, at a speed sufficient to produce voltage in excess of the specified setting. By turning the adjusting screw or bending the spring hanger, adjust the voltage to the desired setting. The generator must be cycled after each

adjustment in the same manner as was done after the current-control unit adjustments.

The final voltage- or current-control unit setting should always be approached by increasing the spring tension, never by reducing it. If the setting is too high, adjust the unit below the required value, and then raise it to the exact setting by increasing spring tension.

REVIEW QUESTIONS

1. State the necessary field connections for testing (a) "A"-type (b) "B"-type generators for maximum output.
2. Name and describe briefly the three tests performed on a generator armature in order to determine if it is serviceable.
3. What is the purpose of undercutting a generator commutator?
4. When testing generator field-current draw, if the ammeter readings are below that specified, what effect will this have on generator maximum output? Why?
5. What effect will too much generator brush-spring tension have on generator service life? Why?
6. How is an "A"-type generator polarized?
7. Why is it important to check battery state of charge and mechanical condition before proceeding with regulator service work?
8. State four causes of a low state of charge of the battery and a low charging rate.
9. What effect does high resistance between the battery and the voltage-regulator battery terminal have on voltage-regulator operation? Why?
10. Why must the air gap be checked and adjusted as required before attempting to adjust any of the regulator units?
11. State two methods of adjusting voltage- and current-unit settings.
12. Why must the voltage-control unit be shunted out of the circuit while testing or adjusting the current-control unit.

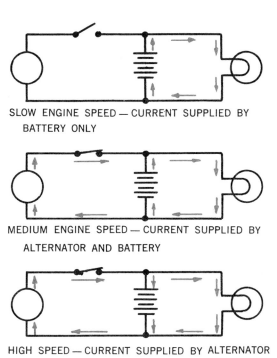

SLOW ENGINE SPEED — CURRENT SUPPLIED BY
BATTERY ONLY

MEDIUM ENGINE SPEED — CURRENT SUPPLIED BY
ALTERNATOR AND BATTERY

HIGH SPEED — CURRENT SUPPLIED BY ALTERNATOR
— RECHARGING BATTERY

Fig. 47-2   Current Flow During Engine Operation

Chapter 47
THE AC CHARGING CIRCUIT

The ac charging circuit consists of: a mechanical device, an *alternator*, which converts mechanical energy to electric energy; a *control* or *regulator* to regulate the amount of electric energy being produced in accordance with the amount being used and the state of charge of the battery; the *battery*; an *ammeter* or *indicating device* to indicate whether the charging circuit is operating properly; and the *wiring* to connect these various units.

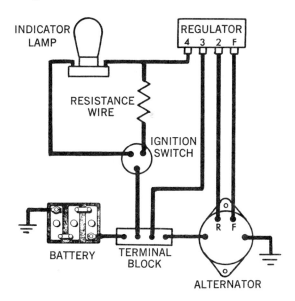

Fig. 47-1   AC Charging Circuit

The purpose of the alternator is to convert mechanical energy to electric energy that is required to operate the electrical devices in the automobile and to recharge the battery.

When the engine is cranked by the cranking

motor, or operated at very low speeds, the battery is the source of electric energy for all of the electrical units. When the engine is operating at off-idle or faster speeds, the alternator supplies part or all of the required electric energy. Any electric energy produced in excess of that required by the electrical units is used to recharge the battery. This recharging compensates the battery for the electric energy used during the cranking or idling periods. The alternator is usually located near the front of the engine, either to one side of or above the engine block. It is driven by a V-belt. In some automobiles, this belt also drives the water pump and fan.

47-1 ALTERNATOR OPERATING PRINCIPLES

Magnetic Induction. The alternator operates on the basic electromagnetic principle that when a magnetic field is moved past a conductor, the movement of the field will cause a current to be induced to flow in the conductor. This is because, as the field moves, it is distorted and tends to wrap around the conductor. Whenever a magnetic field surrounds a conductor, the field will induce a current to flow in the conductor.

When the field moves in one direction, it will induce the current to flow in one direction. This

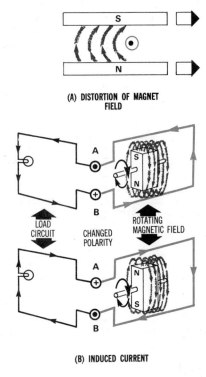

(A) DISTORTION OF MAGNET FIELD

LOAD CIRCUIT   CHANGED POLARITY   ROTATING MAGNETIC FIELD

(B) INDUCED CURRENT

Fig. 47-3   Magnetic Induction

direction of current flow can be determined by the left-hand generator rule. This rule states: that by placing the index finger of the left hand in the direction of the magnetic field, and the second finger in the direction of the field movement, then the thumb will indicate the direction of the induced current flow.

Alternators produce voltage in stationary conductors by rotating a magnetic field across them. Movement of a magnetic field, with the conductor held stationary, causes lines of force to be built up in such a direction that the induced voltage will cause a current to flow in one direction. Changing the field polarity or changing the direction of field motion will change the direction of current flow.

The strength of the induced current depends upon: the strength of the magnetic field; the number of turns of wire in the coil or conductor; and the speed with which the magnetic field passes by the conductor. The higher the speed of the field, the greater the distortion of the magnetic field; the more it surrounds the conductor, the greater will be the induced current.

Since the alternator utilizes rotating components, the induced current flows first in one direction and then the other. In the alternator the magnetic field rotates, resulting in a reversal of polarity since first

the north pole then the south pole passes by the conductor.

Since the induced current is alternating (ac) in nature it must be rectified (changed) to direct (dc) current before entering the automotive electric circuit. This is accomplished by the *diodes* of the alternator.

47-2 AC GENERATORS OR ALTERNATORS

The ac generator or alternator has replaced the dc generator on most modern motor vehicles. The alternator provides for increased output at lower engine speeds, and at the same time maintains high output at cruising speeds. The increase in output at lower speeds is advantageous in today's stop-and-start type of city driving.

The alternator works on the principle that voltage is induced in a coil or coils of wire (stator) when a rotating magnetic field passes by. Diodes are used to convert the ac current produced to dc current required by the automotive electric system.

47-3 ALTERNATOR CONSTRUCTION

An alternator consists of a *stator winding*, a *rotor assembly*, two *end-frame assemblies*, a set of *brushes*, and the necessary *diodes*.

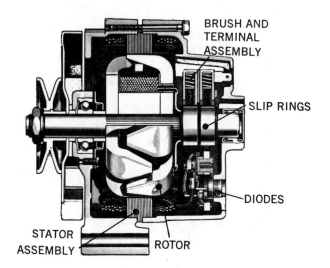

BRUSH AND TERMINAL ASSEMBLY

SLIP RINGS

DIODES

STATOR ASSEMBLY   ROTOR

Fig. 47-4   The Alternator

The Stator Assembly. The stator assembly is made up of a laminated iron frame and a series of stator or output windings assembled into a stator frame. The windings are assembled into slots cut into the laminated iron frame.

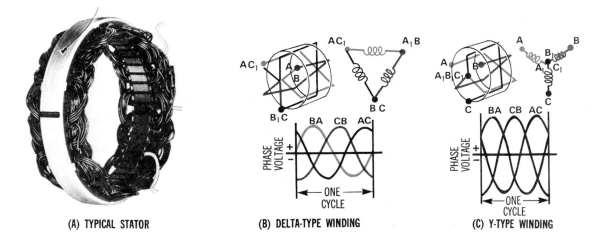

(A) TYPICAL STATOR   (B) DELTA-TYPE WINDING   (C) Y-TYPE WINDING

Fig. 47-5   Typical Stator Construction

Each stator winding consists of seven coils and each coil consists of many loops of wire. The individual loops are in series, and the voltage developed in each loop is added to the voltage developed in all the other loops to produce a total coil voltage. The seven coils are also in series; therefore, the voltage induced in each coil is added to obtain the total winding voltage.

There are three separate windings in a stator assembly. Each winding is known as a *phase*, hence a three-winding stator is known as a three-phase unit. The three-phase windings may be connected to form a "Y," or Delta-type (a triangle) of connected formation, the "Y"-type formation being the most popular.

There are two basic reasons for using three stator windings rather than just one winding. First, more voltage can be developed. The total voltage between any two terminal ends, or phase voltage, is always made up of the voltage of at least two individual windings instead of one. Secondly, the use of three separate windings produces a more constant voltage between phases. The arrangement of the windings is such that each phase reaches its maximum developed voltage at a different time. Therefore, a more constant voltage is available at the diodes.

The stator windings carry the output current and perform the same function as the rotating armature windings of a dc armature.

The Rotor Assembly. The rotor assembly is made up of a doughnut-shaped field coil that is fitted over the rotor shaft and mounted between two iron seg-

ments. Each iron segment has several fingers. The fingers are interlaced and form north and south pole pieces. The coil and iron segments are held together by a press fit on the shaft.

When current is passed through the coil, it creates an electromagnet with a north and south pole. This magnetism is transferred to the iron segments, causing the fingers or poles of one segment to assume a north polarity and the other segment to assume a south polarity. The interlacing of the fingers or poles produces a north pole, south pole, north pole sequence around the circumference of the rotor.

The rotor shaft is supported by bearings in each end frame—a ball bearing in the drive end frame and a roller bearing in the opposite end frame. The ends of the rotor winding are attached to two slip

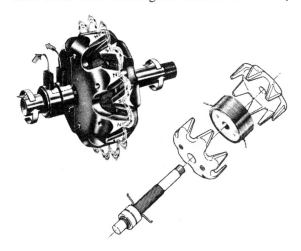

Fig. 47-6   Typical Rotor Construction

rings which in turn are mounted on yet insulated from the rotor shaft. A brush rides against each slip ring to conduct current to and from the rotor winding. The rotor rotates inside the stator and performs the same function as the field windings of a dc generator, that is, to produce a magnetic field.

Diodes. A diode is an electronic device made of materials that will conduct current in one direction only. Diode principles are discussed in Chapter 39.

There must be a positive and a negative diode for each phase of the alternator. Therefore, most automotive alternators require three positive and three negative diodes. The diodes are mounted in the slip-ring end frame of the alternator. The three negative diodes are mounted directly into the end frame. The three positive diodes are mounted in a heat sink that is attached to but insulated from

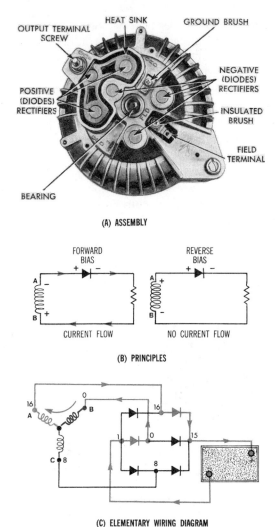

(A) ASSEMBLY

(B) PRINCIPLES

(C) ELEMENTARY WIRING DIAGRAM

Fig. 47-7   Diodes

the slip-ring end frame. These diodes when connected serve as a rectifier assembly that changes the alternating voltage developed in the stator windings to a single unidirectional or dc voltage as required for the automotive electrical system.

The diodes also prevent the battery from discharging back through the alternator, thus eliminating the need for a cut-out relay. A capacitor is usually connected between the battery terminal of the alternator and ground, to protect the diodes from voltage surges that could develop because of the action of the diode.

47-4 OPERATING PRINCIPLES

To illustrate the operating principles of an ac generator or alternator, a permanent magnet and a single conductor will be used. The permanent magnet is used in place of the rotor and the conductor forms a single-phase type of stator winding. The basic principle involved is the principle that if a magnetic field is moved across a conductor, a voltage will be induced in the conductor.

With the magnet at one of the neutral points (the point midway between the conductors), no voltage will be induced in the conductors. As the magnet rotates in a clockwise direction, the south pole of the magnet approaches the top conductor; the rather weak field at the tip of the rotor magnet starts to cut across the conductor, and a voltage is developed. As the magnet continues to turn, the voltage increases and reaches its maximum value when the rotor magnet has turned 90° and the south pole is directly below the top conductor. In this position the loop of wire is being cut by the heaviest concentration of magnetic lines of force. As the rotor continues to turn, the induced voltage in the conductor reduces as the stronger magnetic field moves away from the conductor. The induced voltage in the conductor reaches zero again after 90° of magnet rotation. The direction of current flow in the conductor may be determined by the left-hand generator rule, which states that if the index finger indicates the direction of the magnetic field, the second finger the direction of motion, then the thumb indicates the direction of induced current flow.

While the south pole was passing the top conductor, the north pole was passing the lower conductor and inducing a similar voltage in that portion of the conductor.

As the south pole of the magnet rotates through

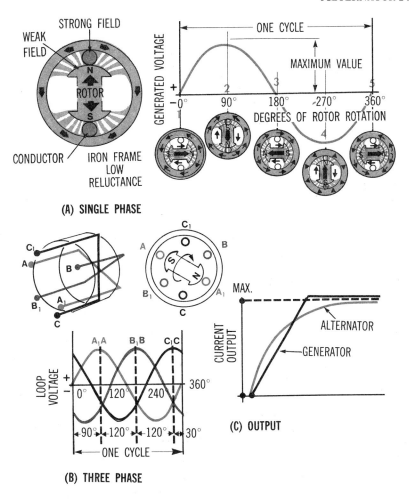

(A) SINGLE PHASE

(B) THREE PHASE

(C) OUTPUT

Fig. 47-8   Alternator Principles

the next 90°, it induces a voltage in the lower conductor. This induced voltage is in the opposite direction to the one produced by the south pole in the top conductor. Again the maximum voltage is reached when the highest concentration of the magnetic field is in line with the conductor. As the permanent magnet rotates through the next 90°, the induced voltage again drops to zero.

Since the top and bottom conductors are influenced alternately by the south and north poles of the rotating magnet, the current will flow through the conductor first in one direction and then in the other. Hence an alternating voltage such as shown in Fig. 47-8 is induced in the conductor.

The rectifying diodes are placed in the stator circuit (the conductor) in such a manner that each end of the stator winding is connected to a diode.

The positive diode permits the induced current to flow toward the battery only while the negative diode allows current to flow through the ground return from the battery to the winding only. In this manner the diodes rectify or change the current from ac to dc.

Since in the automotive alternator, the alternator rotor has many north and south pole fingers, and since the stator has three phases, therefore, in one rotation of the rotor, three separate pulses or phases of current are produced. The peak voltage of each phase occurs at equal intervals as the rotor turns. Figure 47-8 shows graphically how the maximum voltage of each phase is related to the other phases. The method by which the diodes are connected to the stator provides a smooth flow of direct current to the electrical system of the vehicle.

47-5 RECTIFYING ACTION OF THE DIODE

The action of the diodes in rectifying the ac current to dc current during one revolution of the rotor is as follows: in Fig. 47-9 the path of current flow is shown from the A terminal of the stator winding to the diode rectifier, when a voltage is induced in the stator windings A and C. The current then flows through the positive diode which is connected in the proper manner to permit current flow through the diode to the battery terminal of the alternator. From the battery terminal of the alternator the current flows to the battery, then through the

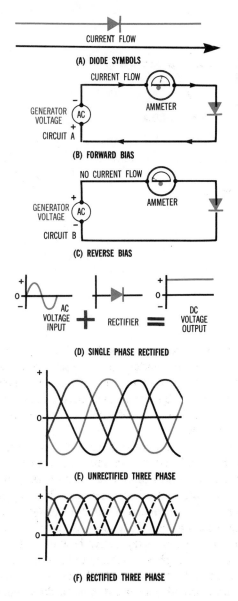

(A) DIODE SYMBOLS

(B) FORWARD BIAS

(C) REVERSE BIAS

(D) SINGLE PHASE RECTIFIED

(E) UNRECTIFIED THREE PHASE

(F) RECTIFIED THREE PHASE

Fig. 47-9   Rectifying Action

ground return circuit to the negative diode of the rectifier. It flows through this diode and then to the C winding of the stator.

When the rotor has rotated 180° the opposite pole is now affecting windings A and C resulting in a current flow in the opposite direction. The current now flows from terminal C of the stator winding to a different positive diode in the rectifier. Since this rectifier is connected in the proper manner to permit current flow, the current flows to the battery terminal of the alternator, to the battery, and returns through the ground return circuit to a negative diode, and through this diode to the A stator winding.

Similar actions take place when the current flows in either direction through the stator windings A and B or B and C. There are, however, other instances during the rotor rotation where a current flow is prevalent in all three windings at the same time. Since this occurs only for very brief periods of time it is not considered to be of a major importance. The diode function during these periods remains the same and results in a dc voltage and current always being prevalent at the battery terminal of the alternator.

As a result of the diode action regardless of the direction of current flow in the stator windings, the direction of current flow through the battery is always the same.

The output of an alternator, like the generator, depends upon the magnetic field strength and the speed of the rotor. The stronger the magnetic field and/or the higher the speed of rotation of the rotor, the higher the alternator output.

47-6 FIELD EXCITATION

The electric current required for the electromagnetic field of the rotor comes from the battery or the direct current side of the rectifier. The connection is made through the brushes and the slip rings of the rotor. The output of the alternator is controlled by varying the amount of current which excites the rotor windings.

47-7 TYPES OF RECTIFIERS

There are several different types of rectifiers that can be used to change the ac current to dc current. These include the *magnesium-copper sulphide, selenium* and *silicone-* diode types, the silicone-diode type being the most popular today.

Both the magnesium-copper sulphate and the

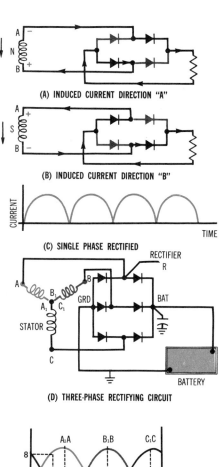

(A) INDUCED CURRENT DIRECTION "A"

(B) INDUCED CURRENT DIRECTION "B"

(C) SINGLE PHASE RECTIFIED

(D) THREE-PHASE RECTIFYING CIRCUIT

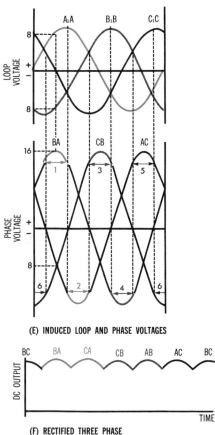

(E) INDUCED LOOP AND PHASE VOLTAGES

(F) RECTIFIED THREE PHASE

Fig. 47-10   Rectifying AC Current

selenium rectifiers use rather large plates made of their respective materials and connected in what is known as a three-phase bridge connection. These large units when used are attached to the rear of the ac generator or in a location where the radiator cooling fan could help dissipate the heat that the rectifiers produce.

The magnesium-copper sulphate type has a comparatively high carrying capacity per unit of area, but 3 volts is the maximum voltage that each plate can withstand. For this reason this type of rectifier is only used on 6-volt type alternators.

Fig. 47-11   External-Type Rectifier

The selenium rectifier has a comparatively low current-carrying capacity per unit of area, but it operates satisfactorily at higher voltages and can be used on 12-volt alternators.

The silicone or silicone-diode type rectifier, because of its small size, high voltage, and current-carrying ability, is therefore the most commonly used type today. See other sections of this text for the construction and operation of this type of rectifier.

47-8 AC GENERATOR OR ALTERNATOR REGULATORS

The ac generator or alternator control is an electromagnetic device used to control the output of the alternator. Unlike the dc generator regulator which requires three units, a cut-out relay, a current-control unit and a voltage-control unit, the alternator only requires a *voltage-control unit*.

The cut-out relay is replaced by the diode. The diode action prevents current from flowing in the reverse direction from the battery to the stator

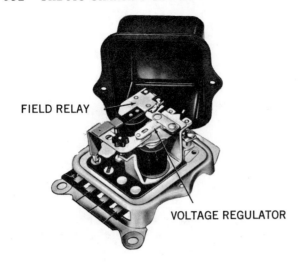

FIELD RELAY

VOLTAGE REGULATOR

Fig. 47-12   Typical Two-Stage AC Regulator

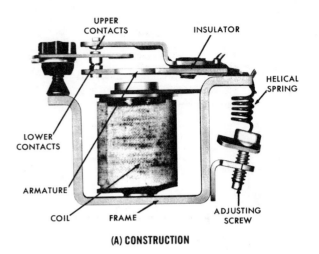

UPPER CONTACTS

INSULATOR

HELICAL SPRING

LOWER CONTACTS

ARMATURE

COIL   FRAME

ADJUSTING SCREW

(A) CONSTRUCTION

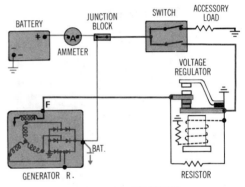

BATTERY

JUNCTION BLOCK

SWITCH

ACCESSORY LOAD

AMMETER

VOLTAGE REGULATOR

F

BAT.

GENERATOR R.

RESISTOR

(B) ELEMENTARY WIRING DIAGRAM

Fig. 47-13   Voltage-Control Unit

windings. The reverse flow of current through the rotor windings is prevented by the opening of the ignition switch which is interconnected with the rotor circuit.

The current-control unit is not required because the alternator rotor fields are not self-excited. That is, the alternator does not produce the electric energy used by the rotor fields, within the unit itself. The rotor field current is supplied by the battery. Since the voltage of the battery and the electrical system is controlled by the voltage-control unit, it therefore remains more or less constant. Using Ohm's Law, which states that it takes 1 volt of pressure to push 1 ampere of current through 1 ohm of resistance, then the maximum amount of current flow through the rotor field winding is determined by the voltage in the system, and the resistance of the rotor field windings. The designing engineer selects a total resistance for the field circuit which is sufficient to limit the maximum output of the alternator to within safe limits.

The amount of current that the unit actually produces is therefore controlled by the voltage applied to the rotor field windings.

Although the voltage-control unit is the only unit required to control the alternator output, the alternator control frequently contains other magnetic relays. These are a field relay used to reduce the current flow through the ignition switch, and an indicator-lamp relay to control the charging-circuit indicator lamp which is mounted on the instrument panel. These additional relays may be mounted on the same base as the voltage-control unit or on separate bases.

47-9 VOLTAGE-CONTROL UNIT

The alternator regulator uses a double-contact vibrating type of voltage-control unit.

Construction. The unit consists of a *shunt coil* wound around an iron core, an *armature* which is "U" shaped with each leg insulated from the other, and a *contact point* mounted at the end of each leg. A double-fixed contact is mounted in line with and between the movable contacts. Spring tension on the end of the armature keeps the armature away from the core and keeps the lower set of contacts closed. A resistor, mounted in a circuit through which the current must flow when the lower points are open, is used to reduce the current flow to the rotor fields. A capacitor or condenser is included in most units to supress radio interference.

Operation. When the ignition switch is closed, and before the engine is started, current flows from the battery through the ignition switch to the regulator, and on through the lower contacts of the voltage

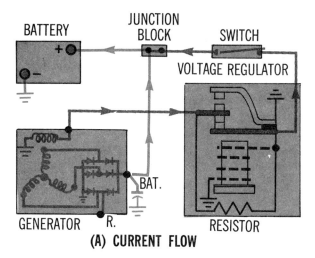

(A) CURRENT FLOW

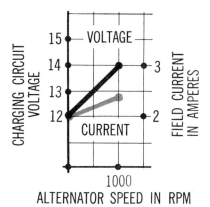

(B) VOLTAGE AND CURRENT REQUIREMENTS

Fig. 47-14 Voltage-Control Operation (Low Speed)

control unit to the rotor field coil, through the coil to ground. The current flow is then completed through ground back to the battery.

When the engine starts and the alternator rotor begins to rotate, the magnetism created in the field coil by the field current induces an alternating voltage in the stator windings. The diodes change the alternating voltage to dc voltage. This voltage and resulting current flow is available to charge the battery and operate the electrical system.

As the speed of the alternator rotor increases, the voltage available from the alternator also increases. This higher voltage increases the current flow through the voltage-control unit's shunt winding, thus increasing the winding's magnetic strength. When the magnetic field strength is sufficient to overcome the armature spring tension, the armature is pulled toward the winding core, opening the lower

set of contact points. With the lower set of contact points open, the rotor field current must now pass through the resistor, thus reducing the rotor field-coil current. This reduced field-coil current reduces the strength of the rotor field which results in reduced voltage in the stator winding, and therefore alternator output. The reduced circuit voltage

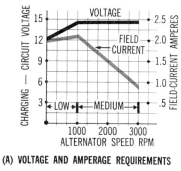

(A) VOLTAGE AND AMPERAGE REQUIREMENTS

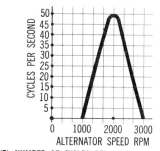

(B) NUMBER OF CYCLES PER SECOND

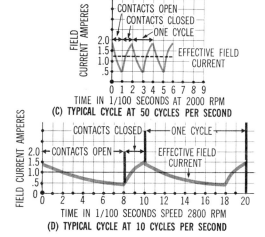

(C) TYPICAL CYCLE AT 50 CYCLES PER SECOND

(D) TYPICAL CYCLE AT 10 CYCLES PER SECOND

Fig. 47-15 Voltage-Control Unit Operating Principles (Lower Contacts Vibrating Medium-Speed Range)

reduces the current flow through the shunt windings of the voltage-control unit weakening its magnetic pull. The spring tension then overcomes the magnetic attraction of the armature and the lower contact points close. The rotor field-coil circuit is again re-established without the resistance in series with the field windings, thereby increasing the output of the alternator. This cycle is repeated many

times per second to limit the alternator voltage to a preset value.

As the speed of the alternator increases further, its output voltage also increases. The higher voltage causes additional current flow through the shunt windings of the voltage-control unit. The increased magnetic strength of the coil attracts the armature down closer to the winding core, which results in the closing of the upper set of contacts. When this happens both ends of the rotor field-coil circuit are placed at ground potential, and no current passes through the coil.

With no current flow through the rotor field coil, the output voltage of the alternator drops. The reduced voltage decreases the magnetism of the voltage-control unit shunt coil and the upper contact points open. With these points open, the rotor field current again flows through the resistance circuit to the field windings. As the voltage output of the alternator again increases, the upper contacts again reclose. This cycle is repeated many times a second to limit the output voltage of the alternator to a preset value at higher engine operating speeds.

The output of an alternator is also determined by the state of charge of the battery and the number of accessories in operation. As the state of charge of the battery decreases and/or as more accessories are turned on, the voltage in the electrical system decreases. As the circuit voltage decreases, the voltage-control unit does not put the resistance in the circuit as frequently. Rotor field-current flow therefore will increase, resulting in increased alternator output to maintain an output sufficiently high to compensate for the electrical requirements. The maximum output of the alternator is controlled by the maximum allowable voltage in the circuit. The maximum amount of current flow in the field wind-

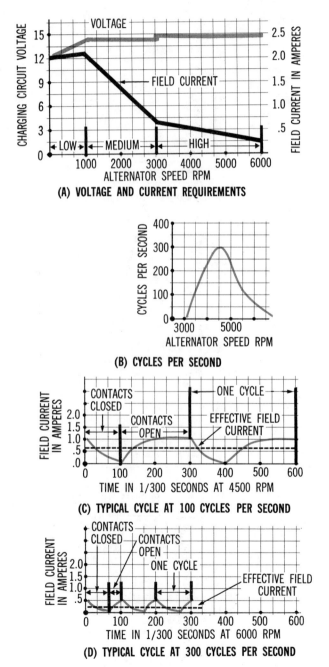

(A) VOLTAGE AND CURRENT REQUIREMENTS

(B) CYCLES PER SECOND

(C) TYPICAL CYCLE AT 100 CYCLES PER SECOND

(D) TYPICAL CYCLE AT 300 CYCLES PER SECOND

*Fig. 47-16   Voltage-Control Operating Principles
(Upper Contacts Vibrating High-Speed Range)*

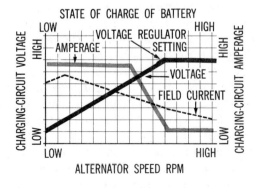

Fig. 47-17   Relationship of Charging Circuit Factors

ing is in relationship to the resistance of the field windings and the circuit voltage.

Regardless of the number of additional relays included in the alternator regulator, the operation of the voltage-control unit remains the same.

47-10 FIELD-RELAY UNIT

The field-relay unit is an electromagnetic relay switch inserted in the rotor field circuit in such a manner so as to bypass the ignition switch. Its purpose is to reduce the amount of current flow across the contacts of the ignition switch. It accomplishes its purpose, since only the small amount of current required to energize the relay windings flows through the ignition-switch contacts.

Construction. The field-relay unit consists of a *coil* of many turns of fine wire wound on an iron core, an *armature* with a contact point on one end, a *fixed contact point* mounted below the movable contact, and an *armature spring*.

This unit is usually mounted on the same base as the voltage-control unit.

Operation. When the field relay is used in charging circuits which include an ammeter, its operation is as follows: when the ignition switch is closed, current from the battery flows through the ignition switch to the field-relay shunt-winding coil. The current flow produces a magnetic field of sufficient strength to overcome the armature spring tension and close the relay contact points. When the relay contact points close, current flows from the battery, through the contact points to the rotor field coil windings, through the windings, and returns to the battery through ground. As long as the ignition switch is closed the rotor field windings are energized.

Opening the ignition switch breaks the current flow to the field-relay winding, cancelling the magnetic field; the armature spring then opens the contact points thereby breaking the rotor field circuit and preventing current flow through the field windings.

When the field relay is used in a charging circuit that includes an indicator lamp, the relay points are not placed directly in the rotor field circuit but in a type of bypass circuit connected to the rotor field circuit. The current required to engage the relay shunt-winding coil is obtained from a special relay terminal located on the alternator unit.

When the ignition switch is closed and before the engine is started, the rotor field current flows from the battery, through the ignition switch, through the indicator lamp which is in parallel with a resistor, to the voltage control unit, through the voltage-control contact points to the rotor field winding, through the winding and returns to the battery through ground. This causes the indicator lamp to light and the rotor field winding to be energized to form a weak magnetic field. The weak rotor field results because of the small amount of current that can pass through the indicator lamp and the resistor. This small current flow protects the ignition-switch contacts.

When the engine starts and the alternator rotor rotates and the alternator produces voltage, this voltage is applied to the relay and battery terminals of the alternator. The relay terminal of the alternator is connected to the shunt winding of the field-relay unit. When the current flow in the field-relay shunt-winding is sufficient to create a magnetic field strong enough to overcome the armature spring tension, the armature is pulled down and closes the relay contact points. The rotor field current now flows from the battery through the relay contact points, bypassing the ignition switch and indicator lamp. Since the indicator lamp now has system voltage in both sides of the bulb, no current will flow through the bulb and the lamp will go out.

If trouble should develop in the system to cause the voltage at the alternator relay terminal to decrease to a low value, the field-relay contact points will open, causing the indicator lamp to come on which indicates trouble in the system.

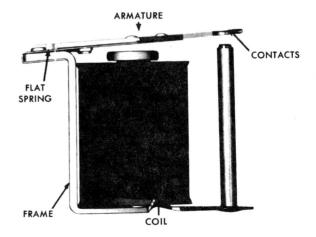

Fig. 47-18A   Field-Relay Unit Construction

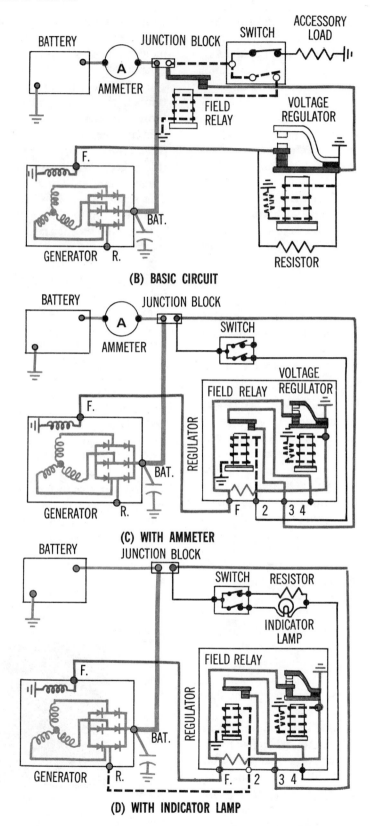

(B) BASIC CIRCUIT

(C) WITH AMMETER

(D) WITH INDICATOR LAMP

Fig. 47-18B   Field Relay Unit

47-11 INDICATOR-LAMP RELAY

The indicator-lamp relay is an electromagnetic relay used to control the indicator lamp mounted on the instrument panel. The unit may be mounted on the same base as the voltage-control unit and field-relay unit or on a separate base.

Construction. The unit consists of a *shunt winding* of many turns of fine wire wound on an iron core, an *armature* with a contact point on one end, a *fixed contact point* mounted above the armature contact, and an *armature spring*. The control contact points are connected into the indicator-lamp circuit between the lamp, which is connected to the ignition switch, and ground. The shunt winding is connected between the relay terminal of the alternator and ground.

Operation. When the ignition switch is closed, and before the engine is started, current flows from the battery through the ignition switch, through the indicator lamp, the indicator-lamp relay contact points to ground, and returns to the battery through ground. The lighted indicator lamp indicates that the alternator is not operating.

When the engine starts and the alternator begins to operate, the voltage which is developed at the relay terminal of the alternator is impressed across the winding of the indicator-lamp relay shunt windings. The magnetism created in the winding causes the armature to be pulled down separating the con-

tact points and breaking the indicator-lamp circuit. The indicator lamp goes out to indicate that the alternator is operating.

If trouble develops in the system to cause the voltage at the alternator relay terminal to drop to a low value, the indicator-lamp relay armature spring recloses the contacts, and causes the lamp to come on, indicating trouble in the system.

The voltage-control unit, the field-relay unit, and the indicator-lamp relay unit are used in varying combinations and interconnected by various wiring schemes by different manufacturers. The operating principles in each case are the same.

47-12 TRANSISTOR-TYPE VOLTAGE REGULATOR (TVR)

The transistor-type voltage regulator contains two PNP *transistors*, a series of *diodes*, a *zener diode*, a number of *resistors*, a *capacitor*, and a *thermistor*.

Principle Of Operation. The basic theory of operation is dependent upon the operating characteristics of the transistors and the zener diode. When the emitter-base circuit of a transistor is forward biased by the battery current, the entire transistor has very low resistance and the current will flow through both the emitter-base and emitter-collector circuits, the major portion of the current flowing through the emitter-collector circuit to the rotor field windings.

If the battery is connected to the emitter-base circuit in reversed bias, the transistor has a very high resistance and no current will flow through the emitter-collector circuit to the rotor field windings. Therefore, by reversing the bias of the base current, a transistor can be made to operate like a relay to control the flow of current through the emitter-collector circuit.

A zener diode is nonconductive until a specified voltage is reached. When this voltage is reached the device breaks down or becomes conductive, and current can flow through it. The zener diode is located in the emitter-base circuit of the first transistor. When the specific voltage is reached and the zener diode breaks down, current flows through both emitter-base and the emitter-collector circuits of this first transistor. The manner in which this transistor is wired into the circuit is such that when current flows through its emitter-collector circuit this current reverses the bias of the base current of the second transistor. As previously pointed out,

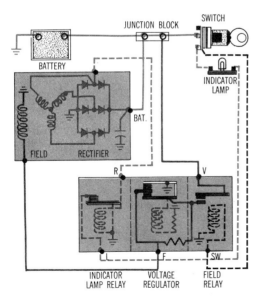

Fig. 47-19   Elementary Wiring Diagram of AC Charging Circuit with Indicator-Lamp Relay

reversing the bias of the base current stops current flow through the transistor emitter-collector circuit. Since the emitter-collector circuit of the second transistor controls the flow of current to the rotor field winding, breaking this circuit collapses the rotor magnetic field and stops alternator output.

Reduced alternator-output voltage reduces the voltage on the zener diode below the break-down point, at which time the diode becomes nonconductive again. This in turn stops the current flow in the base circuit of the first transistor, which in turn permits the base current of the second transistor to return to forward bias and current again flows through the emitter-collector circuit of the second transistor to the rotor field coils. This cycle is repeated over and over again as fast as 2,000 times per second to maintain the proper regulated voltage.

A variable resistor or *potentiometer* in the zener diode circuit permits adjusting of the regulator to limit the alternator output voltage to different values.

A thermistor, a special resistor that decreases its resistance with increases in temperature, is also included in the zener diode circuit. The thermistor will permit the regulator to operate at a lower setting during hot weather and a higher setting during cold weather, automatically.

A capacitor is incorporated into the circuit to smooth out the system voltage variation resulting in more stable voltage control.

There are many variations of transistor-type voltage regulators. For complete details see the manufacturers' manuals.

47-13 TRANSISTORIZED VOLTAGE REGULATORS

The transistorized- (not transistor) type voltage regulator uses a single transistor working in conjunction with a vibrating set of contact points, which are in the emitter-base circuit of the transistor. The field-winding circuit of the alternator is connected to the emitter-collector circuit of the transistor. When the emitter-base circuit is broken, so is the emitter-collector circuit. Because of the small amount of current in the emitter-base circuit, the use of a transistor makes possible reduced current flow across the contacts of the vibrating control, thereby prolonging contact point life.

Fig. 47-20   Transistor-Type Voltage Regulators

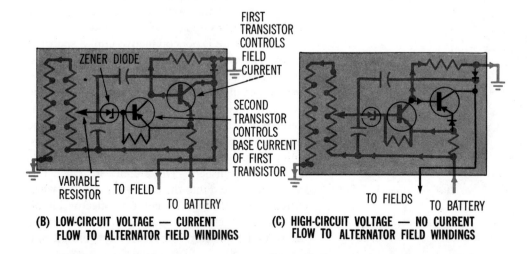

(A) TRANSISTOR-TYPE ALTERNATOR REGULATOR

(B) LOW-CIRCUIT VOLTAGE — CURRENT FLOW TO ALTERNATOR FIELD WINDINGS

(C) HIGH-CIRCUIT VOLTAGE — NO CURRENT FLOW TO ALTERNATOR FIELD WINDINGS

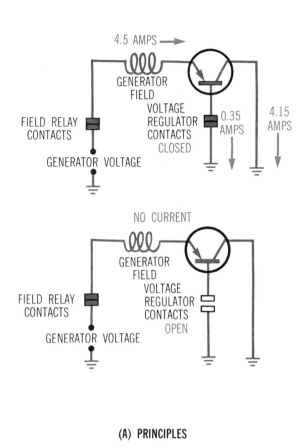

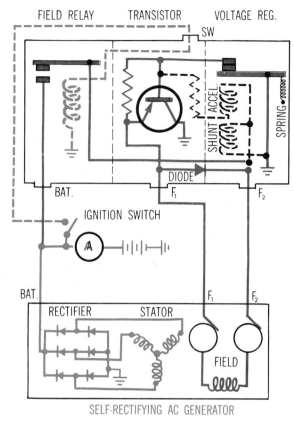

(A) PRINCIPLES

(B) ELEMENTARY WIRING DIAGRAM

Fig. 47-21 Transistorized Voltage Regulators

47-14 INTEGRAL-TYPE REGULATORS

The integral-type regulator is a hybrid unit consisting of solid state devices which are technically referred to as *integrated circuits* and *discrete components*. An integrated voltage-regulator circuit is composed of *transistors*, *diodes*, and *resistors* all fabricated within a single piece of silicon crystal measuring about ⅛ inch square. All these components are interconnected by means of very small aluminum conductors. This circuitry is not repairable or adjustable. If the voltage regulator unit is not operating properly, it must be replaced.

The size of the voltage-regulator housing is determined by the need for connections to the alternator. Terminals built into the regulator housing furnish the circuit connecting points. The ignition-switch connection provides the current for energizing the integrated circuit, which in turn controls the alternator field circuit and regulates the alternator voltage.

REVIEW QUESTIONS

1. List the units of an ac charging circuit.
2. What is the purpose of an alternator?
3. State the basic operating principle of an alternator.
4. Why is the current produced in the stator winding of an alternator always ac in nature?
5. State the rule used to determine the direction of flow of the induced current of the stator windings.
6. State three factors which determine the strength of the induced current in an alternator.
7. Explain how the diodes convert the ac current of the stator winding to the dc current required by the electrical system.
8. State two reasons why three-phase stator windings are used.
9. By means of sketches, illustrate (a) delta (b) Y-type three-phase stator windings.
10. Describe the construction of the rotor.
11. Describe the magnetic actions and reactions that take place in one stator coil as a two-pole rotor unit is rotated 360°.

12. Describe the action of the diodes of one stator winding while the rotor north pole, then the south pole passes by the stator winding.

13. How is the rotor excited?

14. What effect does the amount of current flowing through the rotor have on alternator output? Why?

15. Name three types of rectifiers.

16. Explain why a cut-out relay is not required when an alternator is used.

17. Explain why a current-control unit is not required when an alternator is used.

18. Describe the operation of a double-contact type voltage-control unit as used with an alternator when (a) the ignition switch is turned on and the engine is not running (b) the engine is running at moderate speed and the battery is fully charged (c) the engine is running at high speed and the current usage is high.

19. What is the purpose of the field-relay unit?

20. Describe briefly the operation of the field-relay unit.

21. State the path followed by the current through the indicator-lamp circuit when (a) the ignition switch is turned on and the engine is not running (b) the ignition switch is turned on and the alternator is operating satisfactorily.

22. Describe the basic operating principles of a transistor-type voltage control.

23. Explain how a transistor-type regulator functions as a cut-out relay.

24. Explain the function of a zener diode of a transistor-type regulator.

25. How may the proper voltage setting be obtained in a transistor-type regulator?

26. What is the purpose of the thermistor in a transistor-type regulator?

27. How does a transistorized regulator differ from a transistor-type regulator?

28. Describe briefly the construction of a solid-state type regulator.

Chapter 48
AC CHARGING-CIRCUIT SERVICE

The problem indications for both dc and ac generator systems are quite similar, and result from many common malfunctions. Check the ac charging system for conductor condition, terminal tightness, loose drive belt, etc. Check the battery condition and state of charge. Replace a faulty battery or recharge a discharged, but sound, battery. The battery cable terminals should be clean and tight. It is important to have a fully charged battery and good connections in order to have accurate testing of the ac charging system.

Always disconnect the battery ground cable before making or breaking any test lead connection or before removing any of the system units or wire connections. The ignition switch must be in the "off" position until ready to start the engine to perform any test. Failure to follow these procedures can result in serious damage to the system.

After a visual inspection of the wiring for breaks, and for loose, dirty or corroded connections, check the alternator for maximum output.

48-1 CHECKING ALTERNATOR OUTPUT

This test is performed to measure the alternator's ability to produce its rated output at a specified speed and voltage at operating temperature.

To perform the test, follow manufacturers' instructions regarding the use of equipment and connections. With the engine running at its specified rpm and the voltage limited to the specified amount, observe the ammeter reading. If no output is indicated, stop the test. If the reading is within 5 amps of the rated output, the unit is satisfactory. The re-

duction of 5 amps is utilized by the ignition system and the instruments and is not recorded on the ammeter. The test should be completed as quickly as possible to avoid damage to the automatic transmission.

Circuit Resistance Test. If the current output test indicates a malfunction in the alternator system, the circuit resistance tests should be performed. These tests will indicate whether the trouble is in the circuits or in the alternator. To perform the tests follow the manufacturers' procedures.

If the alternator output is below specifications and the circuit resistance is within specifications, then the alternator must be removed, disassembled, and bench tested to locate the trouble.

48-2 ALTERNATOR OVERHAUL

Before disassembling the unit, it is advisable to place scribe marks on the front and rear housings to aid in reassembly. Follow the manufacturers' instructions for disassembly.

Cleaning. Clean all parts except the rotor and the stator windings in a suitable solvent. Wipe the rotor and stator windings with a damp solvent-dipped wiper.

Testing the Rotor
The rotor must be tested for an open circuit, a grounded circuit, or a short circuit.

Open circuit test—is performed by using a 110-volt test lamp or an ohmmeter.

To perform the test using a test lamp, one lamp lead is placed on each slip ring. If the lamp lights, the circuit is complete or closed. If the lamp fails to light, then the circuit is open.

To perform the test using an ohmmeter, place one lead on each slip ring. If the reading is high (infinite) then the circuit is open. No reading indicates the circuit is complete.

Ground test—is performed by using the 110-volt test lamp or an ohmmeter.

To perform the test using a test lamp, one lead is placed on a slip ring, the other on the rotor shaft. If the lamp lights, then the windings are grounded. When using a test lamp, the leads should never be placed on that portion of the slip ring which is in contact with the brush, or on the bearing portion of the rotor shaft. To do so may result in pitting the surfaces because of arcing.

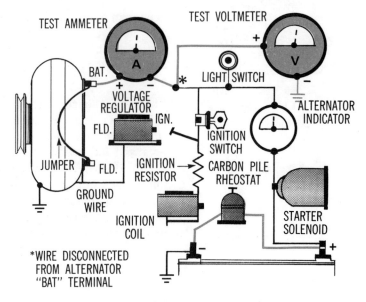

(A) ALTERNATOR-OUTPUT TEST

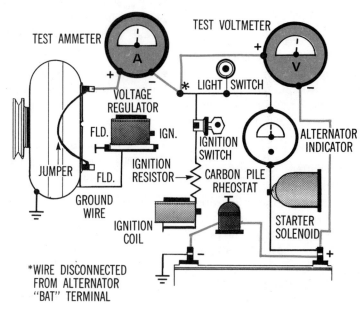

(B) CHARGING-CIRCUIT RESISTANCE TEST

Fig. 48-1   Typical Alternator on Vehicle Tests

To perform the test using an ohmmeter, place one lead on one of the slip rings and the other on the rotor shaft. If the meter reading is high, then the windings are not grounded. Low readings indicate grounded windings.

Short test—is performed by using an ohmmeter. One ohmmeter lead is placed on each slip ring and the meter reading is observed. If the reading is below specifications then the windings are shorted. Readings slightly higher then specifications indicates resistance in the windings.

If the rotor fails any test, then it should be replaced.

Slip ring and rotor shaft tests. Slip rings and rotor

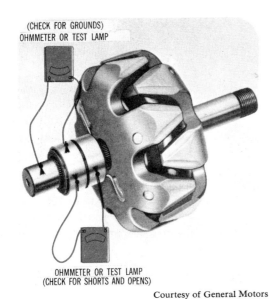

(CHECK FOR GROUNDS)
OHMMETER OR TEST LAMP

OHMMETER OR TEST LAMP
(CHECK FOR SHORTS AND OPENS)

Courtesy of General Motors

Fig. 48-2 Checking Rotor for Grounds on Shorts

shaft must be smooth and round. If the slip rings are dirty, clean by holding 400 grit polishing cloth (do not use emery cloth because its material is an electrical conductor) against the slip ring and rotate the rotor.

If the slip rings are scored or out-of-round they should be turned down until true, then polished with 400 grit polishing cloth.

Check the rotor shaft bearing areas for signs of wear, scoring, etc. If the shaft is in poor shape, the rotor assembly must be replaced.

Testing the Stator

The stator windings must be checked for grounds, shorts, and continuity (opens).

Continuity test—is performed with a 110-volt test lamp or an ohmmeter.

To perform the test using a test lamp, connect the test-lamp leads to each of the three stator leads in turn, two at a time. If the lamp lights when each connection is made, then the circuit is complete or has continuity.

To perform the test using an ohmmeter, connect the ohmmeter leads to each of the three stator leads in turn, two at a time. The meter readings should show the specified resistance when each connection is made. Infinite resistance readings indicate an open circuit.

Ground test—to perform this test a 110-volt test lamp or an ohmmeter may be used.

To perform the test using the test lamp, place one lead on the stator core, the other lead on each of the stator windings in turn. The lamp should not light; if it does, then the windings are grounded.

To perform the test using an ohmmeter, place one lead on the stator core, the other lead on each of the stator windings in turn. A low meter reading indicates the circuit is grounded.

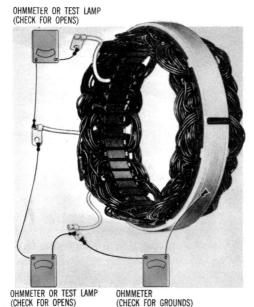

OHMMETER OR TEST LAMP
(CHECK FOR OPENS)

OHMMETER OR TEST LAMP
(CHECK FOR OPENS)

OHMMETER
(CHECK FOR GROUNDS)

(A) TESTING STATOR

TEST LAMP   TEST LAMP

(B) TESTING DIODES

Fig. 48-3 Testing Stator and Diodes   Courtesy of General Motors

Short tests—to check the stator windings for shorts requires special test equipment. Follow the manufacturers' instructions to perform the tests. However, if the windings show no signs of overheating or physical damage, the possibility of shorted stator windings is small. If after reassembly, the unit output is below specifications, then the stator windings could be suspected of being shorted.

Capacitor test—The capacitor (condenser) should be disconnected and then tested by placing an ohmmeter across the leads. An infinite reading indicates a good condenser, while a low reading indicates a defective condenser. Test the condenser's capacity by using a condenser tester.

NOTE: DO NOT POLARIZE AN ALTERNATOR. An alternator polarizes itself automatically each time the ignition switch is turned on. Do not attempt to polarize—serious damage can be done!

48-3 AC GENERATOR- OR ALTERNATOR- REGULATOR SERVICE

Troubles in the ac charging circuit are usually indicated by either an undercharged or an overcharged battery. On applications where an indicator lamp is used, indicator lamp operation will usually indicate a fault in the system. On other applications that have an ammeter or voltmeter instead of an indicator lamp, consistently high readings or consistently low meter readings may also indicate a fault in the system.

Since there can be many causes of charging system troubles, it is wise to consider them all before condemning any one unit in the system—perhaps erroneously.

48-4 SERVICE PRECAUTIONS

Before attempting any service work on an ac charging system, it is important to keep in mind that the alternator and regulator are designed for use on a specific polarity system. The following precautions must, therefore, be observed. Failure to observe these precautions will result in serious damage to the electrical equipment:

1. When installing a battery, make sure the ground polarity of the battery and the ground polarity of the alternator are the same. If a battery of the wrong polarity is connected into the charging system or if the battery is reversed when installing it, the battery is directly shortened

through the diodes. Consequently, the diodes and the vehicle wiring are endangered by high current flow. Burned wiring harness and burned "open" diodes, or both, will result.

2. When using a booster or "slave" battery, make certain to connect the negative battery terminals together and the positive battery terminals together. Failure to observe this precaution will result in the same damage as described in precaution No. 1.

3. When connecting a charger to the battery, connect the charger positive lead to the battery positive lead and the charger negative lead to the battery negative terminal. Failure to follow this procedure will result in the same damage as described in precaution No. 1.

4. Never operate an alternator on open circuit. With no battery or electrical load in the circuit (open circuit), the alternator can build up very high voltages which could damage the diodes. Before making tests or "on-the-vehicle" checks, it is important to make sure that all connections in the circuit, and including the test equipment leads, are tight and secure.

5. Do not short across or ground any of the terminals on the alternator or regulator. Any artificial circuit set up by grounding or shorting any of the alternator or regulator terminals can cause serious damage to one or more of the electrical units in the charging system. When analyzing and troubleshooting the charging circuit, it is important to follow established procedures as described in the manufacturers' service manuals or the manuals pertaining to the electrical test equipment being used.

6. Do not attempt to polarize an alternator. Polarizing the dc type of generator is necessary to ensure that the generator and the battery parity are the same. Alternator polarizing is not necessary, since the voltage developed within the alternator is of both polarities, and the diode rectifier automatically controls the direction of current flow. It is important, however, that the battery ground and the alternator ground be of the same polarity for the protection of the diodes and the charging circuit wiring.

48-5 OVERCHARGING

An overcharged battery can be caused by:

1. A shorted battery cell or an overheated battery. Batteries located in extremely hot areas or

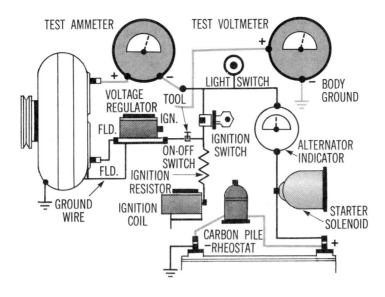

Fig. 48-4   Typical Voltage-Regulator Test

batteries with internal short circuits will accept a high charging rate. Therefore, a battery that has been overcharged should be examined and tested to make sure it is in satisfactory operating condition.

2. Excessive resistance within the charging circuit can be the cause of an overcharged battery. This resistance in the operating circuit of the voltage regulator can increase the charging current and be the cause of an overcharged battery. The procedure to be followed when checking this possibility is outlined in the applicable manufacturers' service manual for the circuit to be tested.

3. A high-voltage control-unit setting can be the cause of an overcharged battery. If no circuit defects are found during the checking procedure and the battery remains in an overcharged condition, then the voltage-control unit setting will have to be lowered. This should be done in accordance with the instructions given in the manufacturers' service manual.

48-6 UNDERCHARGING

An undercharged battery can be caused by:

1. A loose or slipping drive belt can be the cause of an undercharged battery. If the rotor of the alternator is not driven at sufficient speed, the voltage developed within the alternator will not

be sufficient to provide the necessary charging current for the battery. The drive belt should be tightened in accordance with the engine or vehicle manufacturers' recommendations.

2. A battery which is sulphated, or one with an intermittent open circuit at a terminal post or in one of the cell connectors, will remain in an undercharged condition under normal operating conditions. Therefore, when a chronic

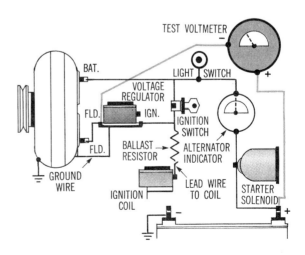

Fig. 48-5   Checking Field-Circuit Resistance

undercharged battery problem presents itself, a thorough check of the battery should be made.

3. A malfunction of the field-relay unit within the regulator can be the cause of an undercharged battery. This possibility can be quickly checked by using the procedures outlined in the manufacturers' service manual.

4. Excessive resistance within the charging circuit can be the cause of an undercharged battery. This resistance in either the battery circuit or the field circuit can decrease the charging current and be the cause of a discharged battery. For the proper procedure to be followed in checking for this condition refer to the manufacturers' service manual.

5. If no circuit defects are found and an undercharged battery persists, the cause most likely will be a low voltage-control unit setting. Refer to the proper manufacturers' instructions for the setting and adjusting procedures.

6. A malfunctioning alternator can be the cause of an uncharged battery. The checking procedures of the alternator are outlined in the beginning of this chapter.

REVIEW QUESTIONS

1. List the items that should be checked and/or repaired in order to have accurate testing of an ac charging circuit.

2. Why is it important to determine the battery's state of charge and mechanical condition before proceeding with regulator service work?

3. Why must the ground battery cable be disconnected and the ignition switch in the off position before making or breaking any test lead connections?

4. Name and describe briefly the test used to determine the serviceability of the alternator.

5. Name and describe briefly the tests performed on an alternator (a) rotor (b) stator, in order to determine their serviceability.

6. Why is it not necessary to polarize an alternator?

7. List four precautions which must be observed when servicing ac charging circuits.

8. What defects in the charging circuit can result in (a) overcharging (b) undercharging of the battery?

Chapter 49
WIRING, LIGHTS, INSTRUMENTS, AND ACCESSORY CIRCUITS

49-1 AUTOMOTIVE WIRING

The increased number of electrically operated components of the modern automobile has made the wiring circuits very complex. The wires between these components are usually bound together to form a wiring *harness*. Each wire is identified by colour, either a plain, solid colour, or a solid colour and a second colour line or tracer. The circuits between the engine-compartment components and the instrument panel are completed by connector plugs at the fire wall.

The wire used in different circuits varies in size and current-carrying capacity; the current requirements of the circuit and the length of the conductor will determine the correct size of wire to be used. The smaller the diameter of the wire or cable, the greater its resistance; also, the longer the wire or cable, the greater its resistance. Wire and cable sizes are expressed by a gauge number, which indicates the cross-sectional area, not the diameter of the conductor. This area is given in *circular mils*. A circular mil is a unit of area equal to the area of a circle that is one mil in diameter. A mil is a unit of length equal to .001″. Therefore, a No. 10 gauge wire will have a circular mil area of 10380 circular mils. In the case of stranded-type wire, the cross-sectional area of the wire is equal to the circular mil area of a single strand, times the number of strands.

When comparing the size of wire, it is important that only the size of the metal conductors be compared. The thickness of the insulation has nothing to do with the current-carrying capacity of the

wire. A battery cable, because of the large amount of current required for cranking motor operation, is usually an American Wire Gauge No. 1 or 2 cable; while the dash or courtesy lights which require very little current use No. 16 or 18 gauge wire. The most common type of wire used in automotive wiring is the stranded or flexible type. It is covered with a suitable type and amount of insulation to prevent the possibility of a short circuit.

In order to attach the wires to the different units of the electrical system, a wide variety of clips and connectors are used.

WIRE SIZE FOR LIGHTING CIRCUITS

TOTAL LOAD	LENGTH IN FEET FROM BATTERY TO FARTHEST LAMP			
	5 ft.	15 ft.	25 ft.	35 ft.
3 cp	16	16	16	16
5 cp	16	16	16	16
10 cp	16	16	16	15
15 cp	16	16	15	14
20 cp	16	16	14	13
25 cp	16	15	14	12
50 cp	16	12	10	9
75 cp	14	10	8	7
100 cp	13	9	7	6

WIRE GAUGE TABLE
Common Automotive Sizes

AMERICAN WIRE GAUGE	WIRE DIAMETER	CIRCULAR MIL AREA
00	.3648	133100
0	.3249	105500
1	.2893	83690
2	.2576	66370
3	.2294	52640
4	.2043	41740
6	.1620	26250
8	.1285	16510
10	.1019	10380
12	.0808	6530
14	.0640	4107
16	.0508	2583
18	.0403	1624
20	.0319	1022
22	.0253	642

Fig. 49-1   Wire Sizes and Gauges

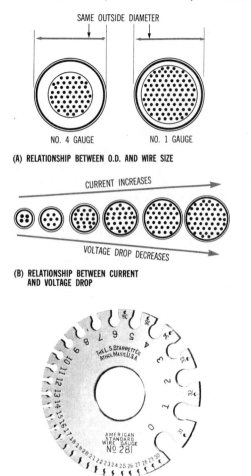

Fig. 49-2   *Wire Gauges*

49-2 FUSES OR CIRCUIT BREAKERS

To protect the circuit from an overload, either a fuse or a circuit breaker is used; these devices are capable of carrying only a certain amount of current. The heat developed by additional current causes either the small strip of metal inside the fuse to melt and break the circuit, or the bimetal strip in the circuit breaker to move and separate the contact points, thus breaking the circuit. Both units prevent damage to the wiring or to the units in the circuit.

Fusible Links. A fusible link is a special type of wire placed in the wiring harness. It has a special type of nonflammable insulation which will bubble or blister if excessive current should flow through the wire and cause it to overheat. The fusible link is used in place of a fuse or circuit breaker and serves the same purpose, that is, to prevent major damage to the wiring should a short circuit, grounded, or overloaded condition develop.

49-3 LIGHTING AND SIGNAL SYSTEMS

Various lighting and signal devices are used in the automobile; parking lights, headlights, brakelights, dashlights, courtesy lights, directional signals, and backup lights are common to most vehicles. All of these lights and signalling devices operate on a ground-return circuit. When more than one bulb is used in a circuit, the bulbs are connected in parallel, but usually they are in series with the switch or control.

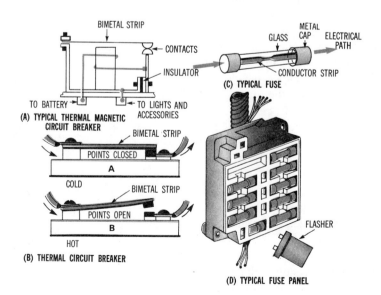

Fig. 49-3   *Circuit Protectors*

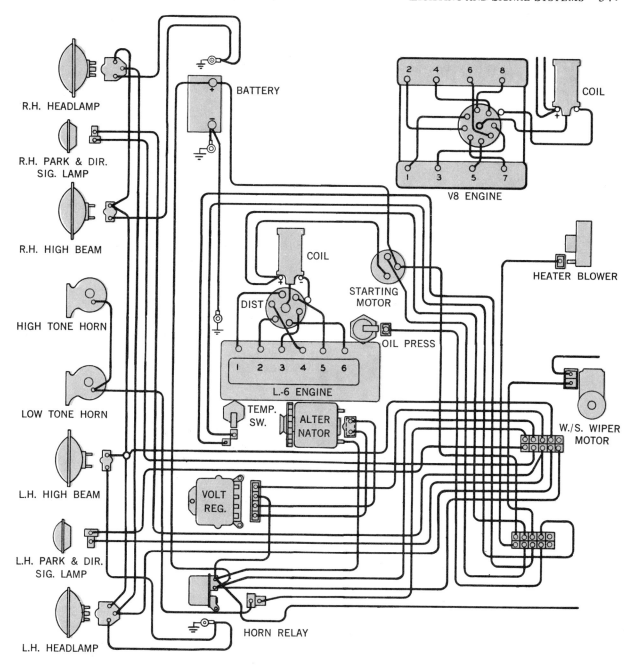

Fig. 49-4 Electrical Diagram of Front Lighting and Engine Compartment

49-4 PARKING, TAIL, AND STOPLIGHTS

The parking, tail, and dashlights are controlled by pulling the light switch out to the first stop.

The parking lights—consist of two front lights mounted in either the front fenders, grill or bumper. Each front parking light uses a two-filament bulb, with the brighter filament being used as the directional signal light.

The tail lights—may consist of two lamps mounted in the rear of each rear fender, or a series of lamps arranged across the rear of the vehicle in the fenders and trunk lid. Each tail lamp contains a two-filament bulb, the brighter filament serving as a combination stop and directional signal light.

The licence plate lamp or lamps—are usually

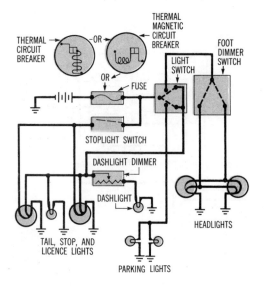

Fig. 49-5   Simplified Lighting Circuits

attached to the centre area of the rear bumper or licence plate holder.

The dashlights—consist of one or more lights attached to the instrument panel in such a manner as to provide diffused light to illuminate the instrument, controls, and dash accessories.

The brightness of the dashlights can be controlled by turning either the knob of the headlight switch or a separate dashlight dimmer switch. Either method operates a variable resistance that is in series with the dashlights. This control, when turned to one end, also frequently controls the passenger compartment courtesy lights.

The courtesy lights—are also controlled by switches mounted in the door posts so that the lamp comes on each time the door is opened.

Stoplights. The stoplights use the bright filament of the tail lamp bulbs and are controlled either by a mechanical switch operated by the brake-pedal

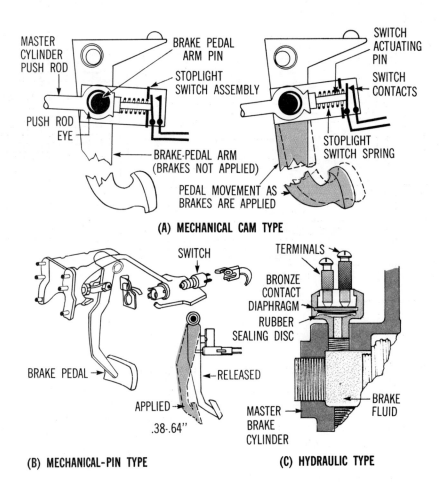

Fig. 49-6   Stoplight Switches

linkage or by a hydraulic switch mounted at the master cylinder. The mechanical switch closes the stoplight circuit the instant the brake pedal is depressed. The hydraulic switch closes the circuit as soon as hydraulic pressure is built up in the brake system when the brakes are applied.

49-5 HEADLIGHTS

When the light switch is pulled out to the second stop, the electric circuit between the battery and the headlights, tail lights, and dashlights is completed. The headlight circuit passes through a foot switch which, when operated, selects either high or low driving beam.

Each headlight consists of electrical *filaments* placed between a highly polished *reflector* and a glass *lens*. The shape of the lens concentrates the light rays to give the best illumination of the road ahead. The sealed-beam headlight unit consists of a hermetically sealed, highly polished reflector and lens assembly, inside of which is placed one or two filaments. A one-filament lamp is identified by the number 1 moulded into the glass near the top of the lens. Two-filament lamps are identified by the number 2 moulded into the lens.

The two filaments in the lamp are used to provide a high and low beam. The high beam is used on the open highway; the low beam is used in the city, and also on the highway when following another vehicle at a distance of less than 500 feet, or when within 1,000 feet of a vehicle approaching from the opposite direction.

When four sealed-beam units are used, the outer units contain two filaments, one each for high and low beam, while the inner ones contain only one filament which is used for high beam only. When only two headlights are used, they contain both high and low beams.

Headlights must be focused or aligned to give

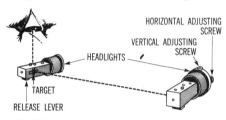

(A) TYPICAL HEADLIGHT ALIGNMENT EQUIPMENT

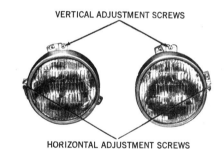

(B) HEADLIGHT ADJUSTING POINTS

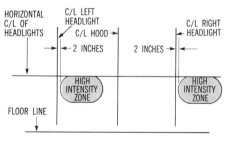

(C) LOW BEAM ADJUSTMENT PATTERN

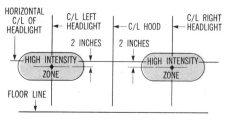

(D) HIGH BEAM ADJUSTMENT PATTERN

Chrysler of Canada

Fig. 49-8   Headlight Alignment

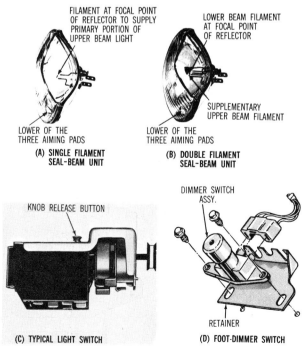

(A) SINGLE FILAMENT SEAL-BEAM UNIT

(B) DOUBLE FILAMENT SEAL-BEAM UNIT

(C) TYPICAL LIGHT SWITCH

(D) FOOT-DIMMER SWITCH

(C) Ford of Canada

Fig. 49-7   Headlight Circuit Components

the best lighting efficiency and the least glare to oncoming drivers. Special headlight alignment patterns are supplied by the automotive manufacturers, and the headlights must be adjusted to conform to the patterns.

Headlight Covers. Some vehicles are equipped with vacuum-operated headlight covers that are raised to expose the headlights when the lights are turned on and are lowered when the headlights are turned off. The raising and lowering of the covers is accomplished by linking the covers to either one or two vacuum motors. The vacuum motors are controlled by a distribution valve attached to the back of the light switch. When the light switch is pulled full out, the distribution valve directs engine vacuum to the vacuum motors. The vacuum is applied to one side of the diaphragm of the vacuum motor to raise the covers. The distribution valve also provides a vacuum relief or exhaust port which permits atmospheric pressure to enter the side of the vacuum-motor diaphragm to which vacuum is not applied.

When the headlight switch is pushed in to turn off the headlights, the vacuum supply and exhaust port positions of the distribution valve are reversed. This subjects the opposite side of the vacuum-motor diaphragm to engine vacuum, and at the same time vents the vacuum at the other side of the diaphragm to atmospheric pressure. This reverses the action of the vacuum motor to close the cover. In another method of closing the covers, when the headlights are turned off, the distribution valve is moved to a position where the exhaust port permits atmospheric pressure to enter the vacuum side of the vacuum motor. Then springs are used to close the covers.

The system includes a vacuum reservoir which provides vacuum storage to permit limited cycling of the headlight covers when the vehicle's engine is stopped. A check valve mounted between the engine manifold and the reservoir prevents the vacuum leaking from the reservoir back through the engine. Sometimes an over-centre type cover spring is used to help hold the covers in either the open or closed position.

If the headlight covers do not open automatically, a bypass valve vents the system and permits the covers to be opened by hand.

49-6 BACKUP LIGHTS

Backup lights are located at the rear of the car and come on when the driver places the shift lever in the reverse-gear position. This closes a switch which is operated by the shifter lever and connects the battery to the backup lights.

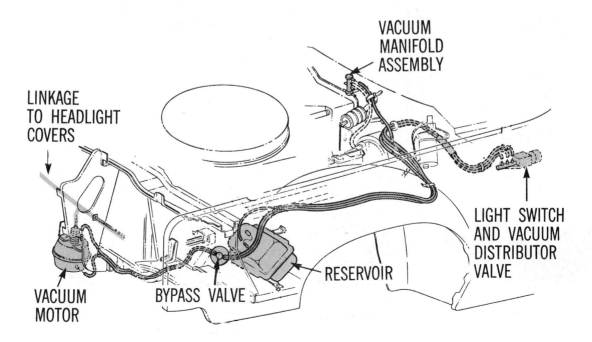

Fig. 49-9 Typical Headlight Cover System

Ford of Canada

49-7 DIRECTIONAL SIGNALS, EMERGENCY WARNING, AND CORNERING LIGHTS

Directional Signals. The directional signals use the bright filament of both the parking and tail lamp bulbs. When the signal switch, mounted on the steering column, is moved to the right or left turning position, the corresponding lamps are connected into the circuit which is controlled by the flasher. This causes the lamps on the side of the vehicle nearest to the direction of turn to flash on and off at a rate of about 60 to 120 times per minute. An indicator lamp or lamps mounted on the dash also flash to indicate to the driver the direction for which the signal has been set. After the turn has been completed, and as the steering wheels nears the straight-ahead position, a cam and striker self-cancelling device built into the steering column moves the switch lever back to the off position.

The flasher unit contains two sets of points that are actuated by the flow of current. Both contacts are open when the control switch is in the off position. When the control lever is moved to the right or left, it completes the circuit between the flasher

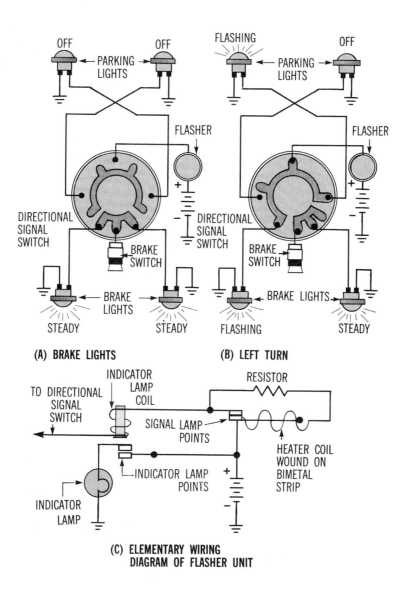

(A) BRAKE LIGHTS

(B) LEFT TURN

(C) ELEMENTARY WIRING DIAGRAM OF FLASHER UNIT

Fig. 49-10   Directional-Signal Circuits

and the proper directional signal bulbs. The current now flows from the battery through the flasher resistor wire coil mounted on a bimetal spring, a resistor, an electromagnetic coil, the signal lights, and then through ground back to the battery. The resistor impedes the flow of current to the extent that there is insufficient current to light the lamps or energize the electromagnetic coil, but is sufficient to heat up the resistance-wire coil to the extent that the bimetal spring moves and closes the signal-lamp contacts. The resistance coil and resistor are then shunted out of the circuit, and sufficient current flows through the electromagnetic coil to light the signal lights. Since this current must pass through the electromagnetic coil, it energizes it and closes the indicator-light contacts, thereby lighting the indicator lamp. Should either the front or rear directional-signal bulb be burnt out, then insufficient current would flow through the electromagnetic coil, and its magnetizing force would be insufficient to overcome the indicator-lamp point spring tension and the lamp would not light. This then would indicate a malfunction in the system.

As soon as current stops flowing through the resistance coil and the resistor, the coil cools down and the bimetal spring moves in the opposite direction to open the indicator-lamp contact points. This opens the indicator-lamp circuit until the resistance coil heats up again and the cycle is repeated.

Emergency Warning Lights. An emergency warning-light system operated by a separate hazard-warning switch mounted either on the dash or the steering column is used to connect all four directional signal lamps to a separate flasher. A separate flasher is required because of the difference in circuit resistance when all four lamps are used rather than just two.

Cornering Lights. Some vehicles include cornering lights. These are lights that are mounted in the side of each front fender and are used to illuminate the side of the road into which the vehicle is turning. These lights are also controlled by the directional-signal lever. When the directional-signal lever is moved, it directs current to a relay switch at each light. This relay keeps the circuit in the on position as long as a turn is being made. Returning of the steering wheel to the straight-ahead position causes the self-cancelling device to return the control lever to the off position.

49-8 HORNS

The automotive horn consists of a vibrating magnetic switch which sets a diaphragm into rapid vibration when connected to a battery. The horn uses a winding that is connected in series with a set of contact points. When the circuit to the battery is completed by actuating the horn button or ring, current flows through the points and winding creating a magnetic field around the winding. The magnetic field attracts a heavy iron armature. This armature is attached to the horn diaphragm so that movement of the armature causes distortion of the diaphragm and also opens the contact points, thus breaking the electric circuit to the winding. The magnetic field then collapses and the armature and diaphragm return to their original position. The electric circuit to the winding is completed again, and the cycle is repeated many times per second. The repeated distortion of the horn diaphragm produces the warning signal. The faster the diaphragm vibrates, the higher the pitch of the warning signal.

Since automotive horns have a high current draw, the horn circuit includes a horn relay. The relay is constructed and operates in a normal manner and is used to reduce the amount of current required at the horn button in the steering wheel.

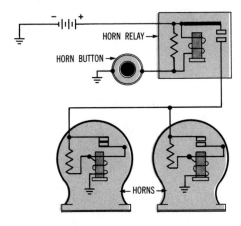

Fig. 49-11   Typical Horn Circuit

Horn-Relay Buzzer System. A warning buzzer which operates when the key is left in the ignition switch when the driver's door is opened is used to remind the driver to remove the keys before leaving the vehicle.

When the key is fully inserted in the ignition switch, it closes contacts at the base of the key hole to complete a circuit between the courtesy-light

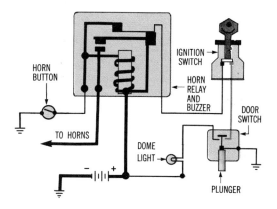

Fig. 49-12 Typical Elementary Drawing of Horn Relay-Buzzer Circuit

door switch of the driver's door and a special terminal on the horn relay. When the driver's door is opened, sufficient current flows through the horn-relay coil winding producing sufficient magnetism to open the buzzer contacts. This breaks the coil

winding circuit and the contacts close. This cycle is repeated many times per second, thus producing the buzzing sound. Removing the key or closing the door will open the circuit and shut off the buzzer.

49-9 WINDSHIELD WIPERS

Most windshield-wiper motors today are electrically operated, although some vehicles may use vacuum-type motors. The electric-motor type may be of the one- or two-speed type, or may be equipped with a variable-resistance type switch and have variable speed.

The wiper motor operates a gear train and crank arm that drives the wiper linkage, which in turn drives the wiper-arm pivot. The rotation of the motor crank arm imparts a reciprocating movement to the linkage, then to the wiper-arm pivots. As the pivots turn, they move the wiper blades back and forth across the windshield.

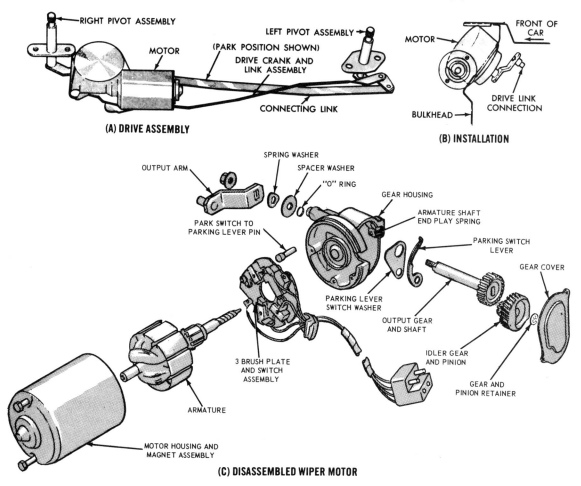

Fig. 49-13 Windshield Wipers

(A) and (B) Chrysler Canada Ltd.
(C) Ford of Canada

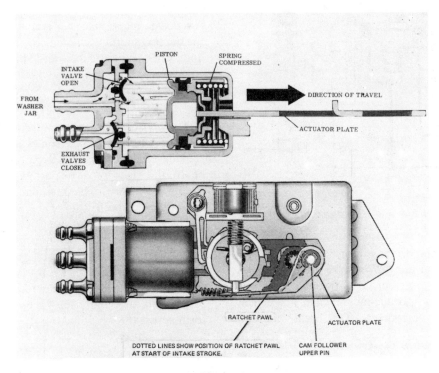

(A) INTAKE STROKE

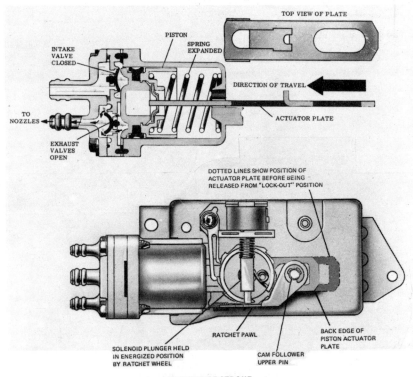

(B) EXHAUST STROKE

Fig. 49-14A   Wiper Motor-Type Pump   Courtesy of General Motors

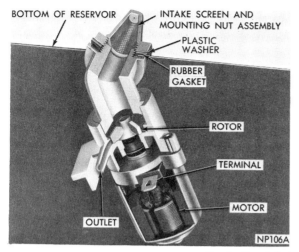

Fig. 49-14B   Reservoir-Type Pump

Chrysler Canada Ltd.

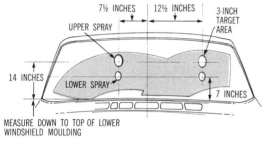

Chrysler Canada Ltd.

Fig. 49-14C   Typical Washer-Aiming Diagram

Windshield wipers are classified as either *depressed* or *nondepressed* types. The depressed type has the wiper blades located below the windshield trim moulding when not in use. The nondepressed type has the wiper blades 1½ to 2″ above the windshield trim moulding when not in use.

Some depressed-type blades are concealed by cover panels when not in use. These panels are operated by a vacuum motor, actuated by a vacuum valve which is operated by a solenoid controlled by the windshield-wiper dash switch. The operation of the covers is similar to that of headlight covers.

49-10 WINDSHIELD WASHERS

The windshield-washer system includes the following components: a *reservoir*, a *pump*, two *nozzles*, a *control*, and the necessary *connecting hoses*. The reservoir is usually mounted under the hood on one of the front fender wheel wells. The nozzles usually extend through the air grille just ahead of the wind-

shield and direct the stream of cleaning liquid onto the windshield.

Two different pumping systems are used. In one type a diaphragm or piston-type pump is mounted adjacent to and operated by a cam device driven by the windshield-wiper motor. The other type is mounted in the base of the reservoir and uses a small electric motor to drive a rotor-type pump. The control switch may be integral with the wiper motor control or mounted separately on the dash.

49-11 INSTRUMENTS

Instrument Voltage Regulator. Some manufacturers use a simple voltage-regulating device consisting of a *bimetal spring*, a *heating coil*, and a pair of *contact points* to maintain a constant voltage to the indicating instruments.

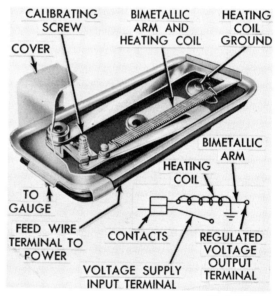

Ford of Canada

Fig. 49-15   Instrument Constant Voltage Regulator

When the ignition switch is turned on, the current for the fuel, oil, and temperature gauges flows through the regulator. This current flows through the heating coil and heats up the bimetal spring, causing it to bend and open the contacts. With the contacts open, no current flows through the coil and the bimetal spring coils, thus permitting the contacts to close and start the cycle over again. The rapid opening and closing of the contacts results in a pulsating voltage with an effective average value regardless of the input voltage created by the battery or the charging circuit.

The regulator, therefore, ensures accurate reading gauges regardless of the electrical conditions within the other electric circuits.

49-12 DASH INSTRUMENTS

When a vehicle is equipped with dash gauges for temperature, oil pressure, and fuel, they may be of either the *thermostatic* type or the *electromagnetic* type.

The thermostatic type of dash gauge—consists of a heating coil wound around a bimetal hair pin which is attached to the instrument needle. The current flowing to the sending unit passes through the heating coil causing it to heat up. The amount of heat produced by the coil is controlled by the amount of current flowing in the circuit, which in turn is controlled by the amount of resistance offered by the variable resistor in the sending unit. The greater the amount of current flowing, the greater the heat —thus causing expansion of the dissimilar metals in the hair pin causing it to bend. This bending of the hair pin actuates the needle of the gauge, causing it to move across the face of the instrument. Therefore, any changes in the resistance of the sending unit will cause changes in the current flow, the heat of the coil, the expansion of the hair pin, and the location of the needle on the face of the gauge.

The electromagnetic or balancing-coil type of dash gauge—consists of two electromagnets with a needle pivoted between them. One electromagnet is internally grounded and maintains constant magnetic strength. The other electromagnet is grounded through the variable resistor of the sending unit, and its magnetic strength is varied depending upon the resistance in the circuit. The needle is moved across the face of the gauge by being attracted to the strongest of the two magnetic fields. Therefore, any changes in the resistance in the one electromagnet circuit will change the position of the needle on the face of the gauge.

Temperature Gauges. The temperature gauge is used to indicate the temperature of the coolant in the water jackets. The gauge type is comprised of a *sending unit* and a *dash unit*.

The sending unit consists of a flat disc that changes its electrical resistance as the temperature

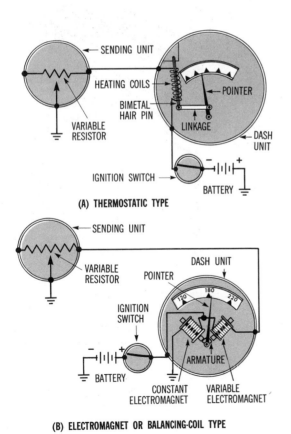

(A) THERMOSTATIC TYPE

(B) ELECTROMAGNET OR BALANCING-COIL TYPE

Fig. 49-16   Typical Dash-Gauge Units

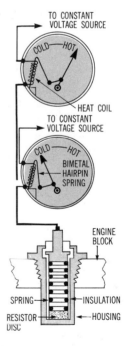

Fig. 49-17   Typical Thermostatic-Type Temperature Gauge Circuit

changes. As the coolant temperature increases, the resistance of the sending unit decreases; thus more current will flow through the circuit. When the coolant in the cooling system cools, the electrical resistance of the disc will increase; thus reducing the current flow through the circuit.

When the electromagnetic or balancing-coil type of dash unit is used, the resistance changes in the sending unit alter the magnetic strength of one of the two coils in the dash unit. The needle is then attracted to the stronger field, thus indicating an increase in engine operating temperature.

When the thermostatic bimetal hair pin-spring type of dash unit is used, the resistance changes in the sending unit change the amount of current flowing through the heat coil, thereby changing the amount of heat it produces. The changes in heat affect the bimetal spring, which in turn causes the needle to move across the face of the gauge to indicate engine operating temperature.

Oil-Pressure Gauges. Some vehicles are equipped with an oil-pressure gauge that indicates in pounds per square inch.

The sending unit of the pressure-type gauge contains a pressure diaphragm which is attached to the sliding contact of a variable resistor. As the oil pressure increases, the diaphragm moves inward, causing the contact to move along the resistor winding, thus increasing the resistance in the circuit.

When the electromagnetic or balancing-coil type of dash unit is used, the resistance changes in the sending unit alter the magnetic strength of one of the two coils in the dash unit. The needle is then attracted to the stronger field, thus indicating the oil pressure.

When the thermostatic bimetal hair pin-spring type of dash gauge unit is used, the resistance changes in the sending unit change the amount of current flowing through the heat coil, thus changing the amount of heat it produces. The changes in heat affect the bimetal spring which in turn causes the needle to move across the face of the gauge to indicate engine oil pressure.

Fuel Gauges. The fuel-gauge system consists of a *float-type sending unit* which is actuated by the level of the fuel in the tank and a *dash unit*.

The sending unit consists of a float-operated variable resistor. It is mounted in either the top or side of the fuel tank with the float and float arm extending into the tank. The unit may also include the fuel pick-up tube for the fuel line to the fuel pump. Since the float always follows the level of fuel in the tank, the position of the float will determine the electrical resistance offered by the variable resistor. When the fuel tank is empty, the variable resistor in the tank offers maximum resistance; therefore the amount of current flowing in the circuit is at its minimum. When the fuel tank is full, the variable resistor is in the position which

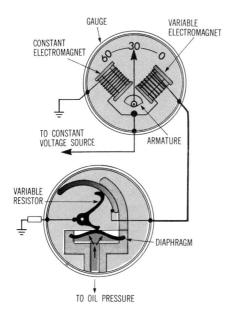

Fig. 49-18   Typical Electromagnetic-Type Oil Pressure Gauge Circuit

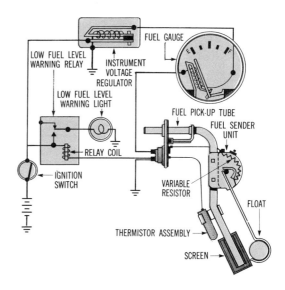

Fig. 49-19   Typical Thermostatic Fuel Gauge with Low-Fuel Indicator-Light Circuit

offers the minimum resistance and the current flow through the circuit is high. Since the float follows the level of fuel in the tank, the amount of resistance in the circuit will vary. By sensing the amount of current in the circuit, the dash unit will register the level of fuel in the tank.

When the electromagnetic or balancing-coil type of dash unit is used, the resistance changes in the sending unit alter the magnetic strength of one of the two coils in the dash unit. The needle is then attracted to the stronger field, thus indicating the amount of fuel in the tank.

When the thermostatic bimetal hair pin-spring type of dash unit is used, the resistance changes in the sending unit change the amount of current flowing through the heat coil, thereby changing the amount of heat it produces. The changes in heat affect the bimetal spring, which in turn causes the needle to move across the face of the gauge to indicate the amount of fuel in the tank.

49-13 INDICATOR LAMPS

Some vehicles are equipped with temperature and/or oil-pressure indicator lights instead of gauges.

Temperature Indicator Light. When cold and hot indicator lights are used, the sending unit contains a bimetal spring which, when cold, closes a set of contacts to complete the circuit to the cold indicator light. As the engine warms up to the normal operating temperature, the circuit to the cold indicator light is broken by the change in position of the bimetal spring, and the light is turned off. Should the engine overheat, the bimetal spring moves farther and closes a second set of contacts, which completes the circuit to the hot indicator light.

Oil-Pressure Indicating Lights. When an oil-pressure indicating light is used, the light is connected to a pressure-operated switch. When the oil pressure in the engine is above the setting of the switch, the electrical contact through the switch is broken and the light remains off. When engine oil pressure falls below the setting of the switch, the electric circuit is completed and the light goes on. This indicates that there is not sufficient oil pressure for safe operation of the engine.

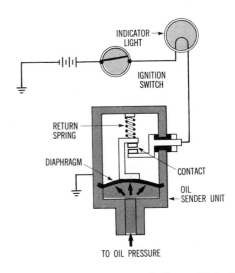

Fig. 49-21   Typical Oil Pressure Indicator Light Circuit

Low-Fuel Level Indicator Light. The low-fuel indicator light will glow just before the fuel gauge pointer indicates empty.

The low-fuel level indicating system consists of the *thermistor assembly* attached to the fuel pick-up tube located in the fuel tank, a *low-fuel relay*, a *ballast resistor* in parallel with the relay coil, and the *low-fuel light* located on the dash.

The thermistor assembly is attached to the fuel pick-up tube and is kept cool when covered by gasoline. When the fuel level drops low enough to expose the thermistor to air, the thermistor heats up. The thermistor resistance then decreases and allows current to flow through the low-fuel signal

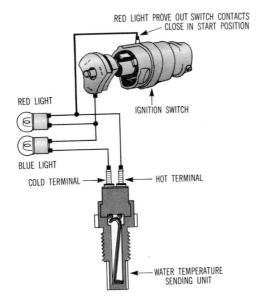

Ford of Canada

Fig. 49-20   Typical Cold and Hot Temperature Indicator Light Circuit

relay. The relay contacts then close, to light the low-fuel indicator light.

Ammeters. The ammeter or charge indicator used on motor vehicles is of much simpler design than the meters used in automotive service work. Two common types are used, the *moving-vane type* and the *loop type*.

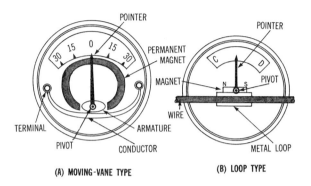

Fig. 49-22   Ammeters

The moving-vane type ammeter contains a steel armature mounted on the same shaft as the pointer and pivoted between the poles of a permanent horseshoe magnet. The magnet holds the armature in such a position that the pointer indicates zero when no current is flowing through the meter. When a current is flowing, it passes through a plate or conductor connected between the ammeter terminals. This current produces a secondary magnetic field which bucks the magnetic field of the permanent magnet. The secondary magnetic field acts upon the armature on the pointer shaft, causing it to swing, moving the pointer away from zero. The amount of swing is determined by the strength of the second magnetic field, which in turn depends upon the amount of current flowing. The direction of pointer movement depends upon the direction of current flow.

The loop-type ammeter consists of a magnetic and pointer assembly and a loop formed by the conductor as it passes across the back of the instrument. When current flows through the conductor, the reaction between the magnetic fields of the magnet and those around the conductor cause the pointer to move. The direction and amount of movement depends upon the amount and direction of the current flowing in the conductor.

Ammeters are connected into the wiring circuit so that if the charging circuit is producing more current than is being used, the pointer will move to indicate a charge. If more current is being used than is being produced by the charging circuit, then the pointer will indicate discharge.

Charge Indicator Lamps. Some manufacturers connect a charge indicator lamp into the field circuit of ac charging circuits. When the ignition key is turned to the on position and the engine started, current flows through the indicator lamp bulb and its parallel resistor to the alternator field winding. This current lights the lamp and also energizes the winding to establish the alternator field which allows the alternator to start producing current.

When the alternator builds up sufficient voltage to close the field-relay contact points, current will then flow through the relay to the alternator fields, bypassing the resistor and indicator lamp bulb. The lamp will then go out.

When a dc charging circuit includes an indicator lamp, the lamp is connected in parallel with the cut-out relay contact points. When the ignition switch is turned on and the cut-out points are open, the lamp lights. When the engine is started and the generator builds up sufficient voltage to close the cut-out contacts, the bulb circuit is bypassed and the lamp goes out.

Speedometer. The speedometer is driven by a flexible cable enclosed in a casing or housing. One end of the cable is connected to a shaft and gear assembly that is driven by another gear assembled on the transmission rear main shaft. The other end of the cable is connected to the speedometer head. The speedometer head includes the *mechanism* required to move the pointer across the speedometer face to indicate vehicle speed and the *odometer*, a unit which records the distance the vehicle travels.

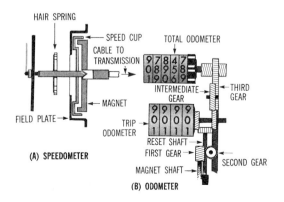

Fig. 49-23   Speed and Mileage Indicators

To record vehicle speed, the drive cable rotates a permanent magnet which is inside a bearing-supported nonmetallic speed cup to which the pointer shaft and pointer is attached. A field plate or cover which surrounds the cup and rotating magnet completes the field to produce eddy currents from the rotating magnet. These eddy currents exert a definite pull on the speed cup, causing it to move in a direct ratio to the speed of the revolving magnet. A 1,000 rpm of the magnet is equal to an approximate reading on the speedometer face of 60 mph. As the speed of the rotating magnet increases, the magnetic drag produced by the eddy currents pulls the speed cup and pointer farther around, indicating a faster speed. A finely adjusted hair spring is used to maintain the proper relationship between the magnetic pull and the true vehicle speed. This spring also returns the pointer to zero when the vehicle is stopped.

The odometer face consists of five wheels each numbered with digits from 1 to 10. The right-hand wheel is connected through gears and a worm drive to the same shaft that drives the speedometer rotating magnet. A complete revolution of any one wheel turns the next wheel to the left one-tenth of a revolution.

Some speedometer assemblies also include a trip odometer. This unit operates in the same manner as the odometer, except that it has a reset device which will return the wheels to zero whenever it is desired.

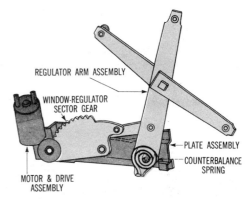

Fig. 49-24   Typical Power Window Unit

Power Windows. Each power-operated window has an internal-circuit breaker protected reversible electric motor, which operates the window-regulator mechanism through a self-locking, rubber-coupled gear drive. Each power window can be controlled by either the master switch located on the left front door or by an individual switch mounted on the respective door of the vehicle.

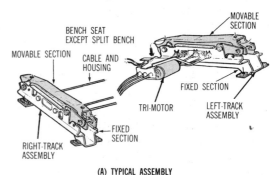

(A) TYPICAL ASSEMBLY

(B) TYPICAL SEAT RAIL ASSEMBLY

Fig. 49-25   Typical Power Seat Unit

Ford of Canada

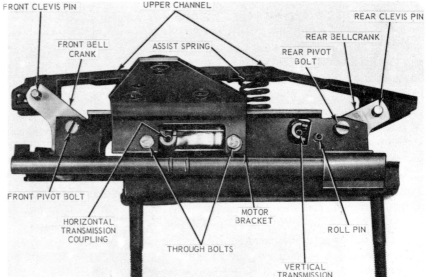

Most manufacturers include a main-circuit relay which prevents the operation of the windows until the ignition switch is turned on.

Power Seats. Power seats are operated by an electric motor which operates a gear train to supply power through flexible cables to the individual slave units. The seat may be raised or lowered by turning a gear nut in the proper direction; it may be moved forward or backward by turning a pinion, which is engaged with the rack strip mounted in the seat tracks, in the proper direction. The desired movement is selected by operating the multitype master control switch. This switch energizes the proper solenoid which in turn engages the solenoid plunger dog with the proper drive mechanism. After engaging the proper dog, the solenoid completes the electric circuit to the motor-control relay, energizing its coil and closing the relay contacts. This completes the circuit to the motor, causing it to operate. The circuit is protected by a circuit breaker and may also include a relay to prevent seat operation unless the ignition switch is turned on.

Heater and Defroster Units. The heating and defrosting system consists of one or two electric motors, a heater radiator core supplied with heated coolant from the vehicle's cooling system; damper-type control valves to regulate the amount of heat desired, the amount of fresh air desired, and to direct this heated air either to the passenger compartment or to the windshield defroster outlets; and the necessary duct work and connections.

The forced air effect is produced by axial flow fans connected to the fan motor shafts. A two- or three-speed motor control switch provides air control by regulating the fan's speed. Flexible core and conduit type cables connect the driver-operated controls mounted on the dash to the proper damper control valve to produce the desired heating or defrosting.

49-14 AIR CONDITIONING

Air conditioning can be defined as a method whereby the air entering the passenger compartment of a vehicle is cleaned, dehumidified, and maintained at a selected temperature. During the four seasons of the year the air may be both heated or cooled as required. The system uses hot liquid from the engine cooling system to heat the air, and a refrigeration system to cool the air. The two systems are interconnected to provide heating or cooling as required.

The cooling section of an automobile air conditioner is a heat transfer unit. Its operation is based on the thermal law that fluids absorb heat while changing from a liquid to a gas and give up heat when changing from a gas to a liquid. The liquid used in automotive refrigeration systems is Refrigerant-12 (R-12) which is actually Dichlorodifluoromethane or CCl_2F_2. R-12 is nontoxic, noncorrosive, noninflammable, nonexplosive, and odourless under normal usage. It will boil or vaporize at $-21.7°F$ at atmospheric pressure. If the pressure of the liquid is raised high enough, the

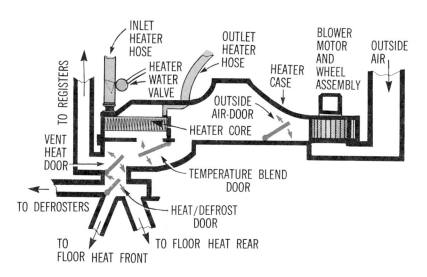

Fig. 49-26   Typical Schematic of Air Passages in Heater Unit

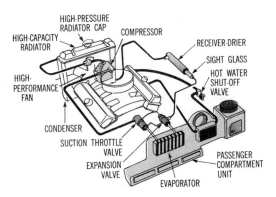

Fig. 49-27   Typical Air-Conditioning Installation

boiling point can be raised well beyond the temperature encountered on the hottest day. It can be circulated endlessly through the system, without any loss of efficiency.

The refrigeration system consists of a *compressor*, *condenser*, *receiver*, *expansion valve*, *evaporator*, and a *suction throttling valve*, which are interconnected by high-pressure lines.

The Compressor. The compressor is mounted on the engine and belt-driven from the crankshaft. It is used to compress and concentrate the heat molecules in the refrigerant vapour and to circulate the refrigerant through the sealed system. The action of the compressor places hot refrigerant gas under high pressure and circulates the gas to the condenser.

Condenser. The condenser consists of a long tube passed back and forth through numerous cooling fins. It is mounted in front of the radiator so that sufficient air can be forced through the fins for cooling. As the hot refrigerant, under pressure, passes through the condenser it gives up its heat to the cooling air stream, cools and condenses back into a high pressure liquid. It then flows into the receiver-dehydrator.

Receiver-Dehydrator. The receiver-dehydrator is a metal tank that collects the liquified refrigerant from the condenser. The unit strains the refrigerant and removes any moisture by means of a special drying agent. The receiver may include a sight glass. This glass provides a means of inspecting the refrigerant for bubbles or foam which indicates the system might be low on refrigerant and require recharging. Also the glass provides a means of examining the refrigerant for moisture content. Excessive moisture causes a moisture-sensitive ingredient in the refrigerant to turn pink. If the moisture level is within limits, the moisture-sensitive ingredient remains blue.

From the receiver the refrigerant passes to the expansion valve.

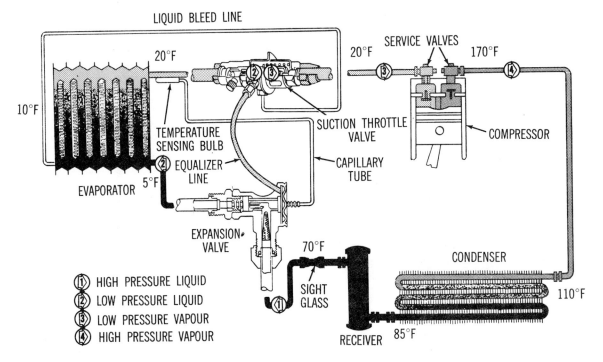

Fig. 49-28   Air-Conditioning Refrigeration Circuit

Ford of Canada

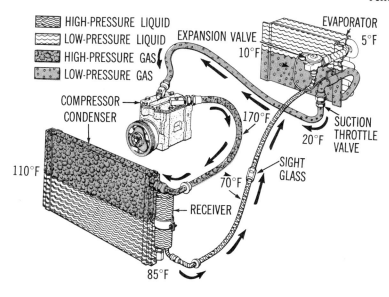

Fig. 49-29   Typical Air-Conditioning System

Expansion Valve. The expansion valve serves two purposes. It reduces the pressure of the refrigerant, and meters the refrigerant into the evaporation coils. It must admit the correct amount of refrigerant into the evaporator coils so that a careful balance is maintained between the evaporator cooling efficiency and the heat load.

Evaporator. The evaporator consists of a long tube passing back and forth through a series of cooling fins. A blower fan forces air from the passenger compartment through the fins and around the coil. In the evaporator the refrigerant has been subjected to decreased pressure and exposed to an increased area. Under these conditions the refriger-

(A) Courtesy of General Motors
(B) Ford of Canada

Fig. 49-30   Air-Conditioning Control Valves

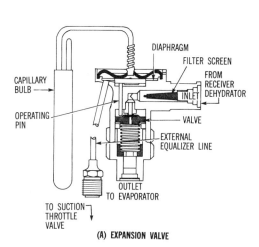

(A) EXPANSION VALVE

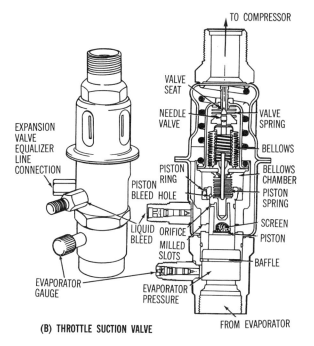

(B) THROTTLE SUCTION VALVE

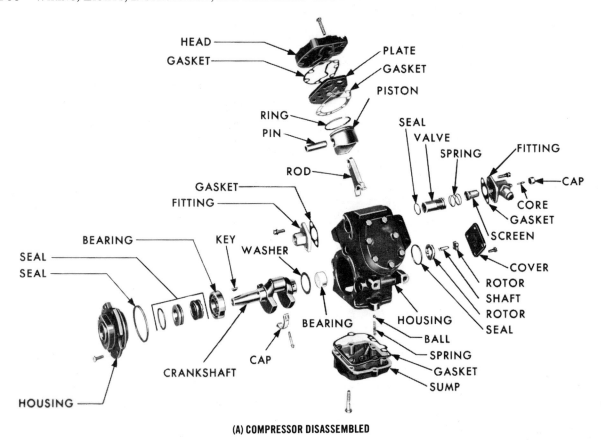

(A) COMPRESSOR DISASSEMBLED

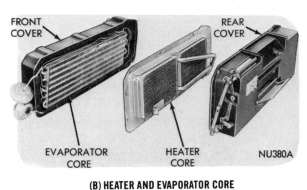

(B) HEATER AND EVAPORATOR CORE

Chrysler Canada Ltd.

Fig. 49-31 Air-Conditioning Components

(C) RECEIVER DRIER

ant will boil and turn into a vapour. In doing so, it absorbs heat from the coil and fins, which in turn absorb heat from the air stream, resulting in the cooling of the air stream.

The heat-laden refrigerant then flows through the suction throttling valve and is drawn into the compressor to complete the cycle.

Suction Thottling Valve. The suction throttling valve is installed in the evaporator outlet and is used as a means of controlling the evaporator temperature. It does this by regulating the pressure of the refrigerant in the evaporator.

Discharge and Suction Service Valves. All systems include discharge and suction service valves so that the refrigerant may be emptied or charged (filled) and checked with pressure gauges.

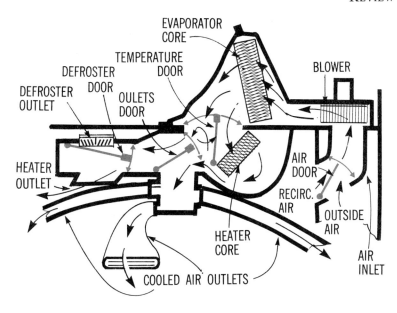

Courtesy of General Motors

Fig. 49-32   Typical Air-Conditioning Air Flow Schematic

Air Circulation. Air, either outside air or recirculated air, enters the system and is forced through the system by the blower fan. As the air passes through the evaporator, it receives the maximum cooling if the manual controls are set for cooling. From the evaporator, the air enters a selector duct where, by means of manually operated diverter doors, it may flow through or bypass the heater core in proportions necessary to provide the desired outlet temperature.

When warm air only is required, the evaporator will not be in operation and the air flow will be heated to the desired level in the same manner as used in a standard automotive heater.

For service procedure and precautions follow carefully the manufacturers' service manual.

REVIEW QUESTIONS

1. What factors determine the size of wire required for a specific electric circuit? Why?
2. How are wire-gauge sizes calculated?
3. Is the outside diameter of a conductor a good indicator of the wire size? Why?
4. State how the three types of circuit breakers protect the circuit.
5. Why are the lamps which are connected together in parallel usually connected in series with the switch?
6. State two methods of controlling stoplights.
7. What is the purpose of the headlight lens?
8. Why must headlights be properly aligned?
9. Describe briefly the operation of headlight covers.
10. Describe the operation of a directional-system flasher.
11. Why does the directional-signal indicator lamp not flash if one signal lamp bulb is burned out?
12. Why is a separate flasher required for the emergency warning light system?
13. Why would high resistance in the horn circuit lower the pitch of the horn?
14. Trace the path followed by the current through the horn-relay buzzer circuits.
15. How are windshield wipers classified?
16. Describe briefly each type of windshield-washer system.
17. Why are instrument voltage regulators used?
18. What is the operating principle of an instrument voltage regulator?
19. Explain the operation of a balancing-coil type of instrument.
20. Explain the operation of a bimetal-hair pin type instrument.
21. How is the current in the temperature-gauge circuit varied by the sending unit in accordance with engine temperature?
22. Describe the operation of the sender unit of a hot- and cold-lamp type of temperature indicator as the engine temperature rises from cold to hot.
23. How is the current flow related to engine oil pressure in a pressure-gauge type oil gauge?

24. Explain the operation of a fuel-gauge tank unit.
25. What is the operating principle of an ammeter?
26. Name and describe briefly the construction of two types of vehicle ammeters.
27. Describe the operation of the charge indicator lamp in an ac type charging circuit.
28. How are magnetic fields used by the speedometer to indicate vehicle speed?
29. What type of electric circuit would be used to control power windows, a series circuit, or a parallel circuit? Why?
30. How are solenoids used to control power seat movement?
31. How is the (a) temperature (b) amount (c) distribution of heated air from the heater controlled?
32. State the thermal law as used in air-conditioning units.
33. Why is the refrigerant R-12 considered to be a good refrigerant?
34. State the path of the refrigerant through the cooling section of an automobile air conditioning unit.
35. What is the purpose of the sight glass?
36. What is the purpose of the expansion valve?
37. Describe the air-circulation system of an automobile air-conditioning system.

Chapter 50
TEST EQUIPMENT AND ENGINE TUNE UP

Snap-On Tools of Canada, Ltd., Toronto, Ont.

Fig. 50-1   Typical Automotive Test Equipment Panel

The trend in automotive service work today is toward preventive service rather than the repair of breakdowns. This is particularly evident in regard to the electrical and fuel systems. Various electrical and mechanical adjustments must be maintained within close accuracy in order to get the maximum performance and economy from an engine. This work, known as engine tune-up work, is performed at regular intervals of mileage and in a systematic manner. Essentially, the aim is to restore the original standards of adjustment in the electrical and fuel systems, for a gradual change in these systems results in a corresponding decrease in engine performance and efficiency. A regular tune up also minimizes the possibility of breakdown on the road by detecting faults in the mechanisms at early stages of development. Neglect results in abnormal wear and deterioration.

What constitutes an engine tune up is somewhat indefinite. Various authorities have different ideas as to exactly what service operations should be included. The items may vary from merely cleaning and adjusting the spark plugs and ignition breaker points, the ignition timing, and minor carburetor adjustments, to a complete reconditioning of all the electrical and fuel system units. Therefore, there are both minor and major tune ups.

The minor engine tune up consists mainly of battery inspection and adjustments to the ignition and fuel systems. The major tune up includes all the items of the minor tune up and additional inspection and adjustments, with some reconditioning of individual units.

The performing of an engine tune up requires the knowledge and use of a variety of pieces of test equipment. There is a great variety of this equipment on the market for testing cylinder compression, batteries, ignition system, fuel system, charging system, and the starter system. The equipment includes compression testers, vacuum gauges, voltmeters, ammeters, ohmmeters, distributor testers, coil testers, condenser testers, battery testers, exhaust gas analyzers, and oscilloscopes. Any of these instruments may be obtained individually or combined in groups to form test panels. Before using any of this equipment, carefully study the manufacturers' operating instructions.

50-1 ENGINE-TESTING EQUIPMENT

Compression Tester. A compression tester is designed to measure the pressure in the cylinder at the end of the compression stroke. It indicates the pressure in pounds per square inch (psi). The correct pressure for any engine may be found in the manufacturers' manual. While it is important that the cylinder pressure should be nearly that specified for the engine concerned, it is even more important that the pressure be nearly the same for all cylinders.

To perform a compression test:
1. Check the battery to ensure it will maintain an even cranking speed throughout the test.

2. Remove all the spark plugs. Loosen the spark plugs half a turn and then start the engine to remove any loose particles of carbon which may have fallen off the combustion chamber when the spark plugs were loosened. These particles could cause false readings if they became lodged between the valve face and seat.

3. Block the choke and throttle valves in a wide open position to ensure that a full charge of air enters the cylinder.

4. Remove the high-tension wire from the centre of the distributor cap and ground it, to prevent high-tension sparks.

5. Insert the gauge in a spark-plug hole and crank the engine until the gauge pointer no longer rises. This usually requires six or seven compression strokes. Record the compression readings. Repeat for all cylinders.

50-2 ANALYSIS OF COMPRESSION READINGS

Normal—if the readings are the same within 10 psi and close to manufacturers' specifications, the difference in compression usually will not be noticeable in engine performance.

Above normal—if the compression of any or all cylinders is 10 or more psi above normal, this indicates the presence of layers of carbon in the combustion chamber. Remove the cylinder heads; scrape off the carbon. Too high compression results in detonation.

Below normal—if below normal readings are obtained on one, several, or all cylinders, inject a small amount of engine lubricating oil into each cylinder through the spark-plug hole and repeat the compression test. If the compression test readings rise considerably, then compression loss past the piston rings is indicated. If the compression readings remain approximately the same, then leakage past the valves is indicated. In either case additional mechanical repair work is required. Two adjacent cylinders with low compression may indicate a blown head gasket.

Remember, in order for an engine to perform properly, the first requirement is even and good compression.

50-3 VACUUM GAUGE

The vacuum gauge is an instrument used to measure pressure lower than atmospheric pressure (14.7 psi) in the intake manifold between the throttle valve of the carburetor and the intake valves, when the engine is running.

The intake-manifold vacuum varies with different engine operating conditions, and also varies with different engine defects.

50-4 ANALYSIS OF ENGINE VACUUM GAUGE READINGS

1. A steady and fairly high vacuum reading (17 to 22" depending on the engine; late model engines with high-lift cams and more valve

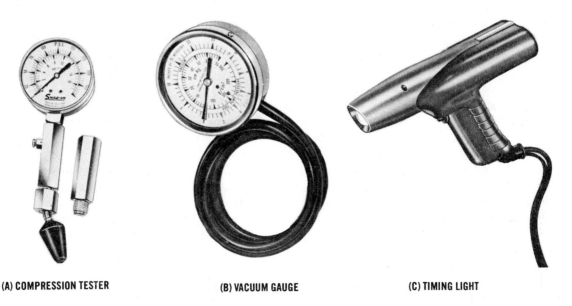

(A) COMPRESSION TESTER   (B) VACUUM GAUGE   (C) TIMING LIGHT

Fig. 50-2   Basic Tune-Up Equipment

Snap-On Tools of Canada, Ltd., Toronto, Ont.

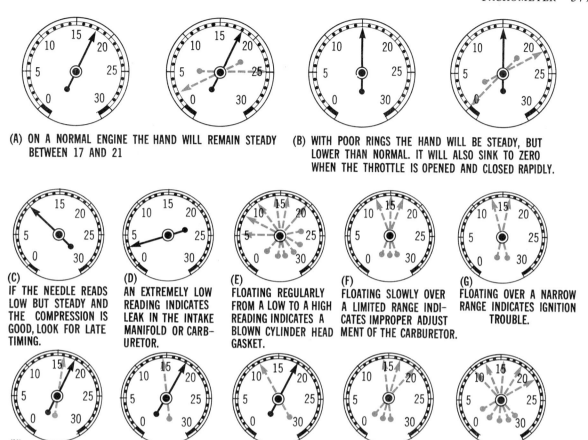

(A) ON A NORMAL ENGINE THE HAND WILL REMAIN STEADY BETWEEN 17 AND 21

(B) WITH POOR RINGS THE HAND WILL BE STEADY, BUT LOWER THAN NORMAL. IT WILL ALSO SINK TO ZERO WHEN THE THROTTLE IS OPENED AND CLOSED RAPIDLY.

(C) IF THE NEEDLE READS LOW BUT STEADY AND THE COMPRESSION IS GOOD, LOOK FOR LATE TIMING.

(D) AN EXTREMELY LOW READING INDICATES LEAK IN THE INTAKE MANIFOLD OR CARB-URETOR.

(E) FLOATING REGULARLY FROM A LOW TO A HIGH READING INDICATES A BLOWN CYLINDER HEAD GASKET.

(F) FLOATING SLOWLY OVER A LIMITED RANGE INDI-CATES IMPROPER ADJUST MENT OF THE CARBURETOR.

(G) FLOATING OVER A NARROW RANGE INDICATES IGNITION TROUBLE.

(H)
A-LEAKY VALVE.-STEADY DROP.

B-STICKING VALVE. -OCCASIONAL DROP.

C-BURNED VALVE. -REGULAR DROP.

D-LOOSE VALVE GUIDES. -FAST VIBRATION.

E-WEAK VALVE SPRINGS. -WIDE VARIATION AS ENGINE IS ACCELERATED.

Fig. 50-3   Interpreting Vacuum-Gauge Readings

overlap are apt to have lower and more erratic intake-manifold vacuum readings) indicates normal engine operation.

2. A low, steady vacuum reading indicates late ignition timing or leakage around the piston rings and/or valves.

3. A very low reading indicates air leaks usually around the manifold or carburetor gaskets or around the throttle-valve shaft.

4. Oscillations of the pointer, increasing with engine speed, indicate weak valve springs.

5. A gradual dropping back of the pointer indicates a clogged muffler.

6. A regular dropping back of the pointer indicates a missing condition in one cylinder.

7. A floating motion or slow oscillations of the pointer indicates improper setting of the carburetor fuel mixture.

50-5 TACHOMETER

A tachometer is an instrument used to measure engine speed in revolutions per minute (rpm). The instrument is connected to the ignition primary circuit and measures the number of times per minute the primary circuit is interrupted. The unit then translates this information into engine rpm.

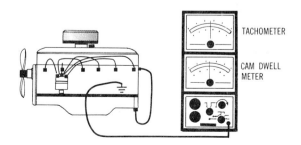

Fig. 50-4   Cam Dwell, Tachometer and Connections

50-6 COMBUSTION OR EXHAUST GAS ANALYZERS

The combustion or exhaust gas analyzer tests the exhaust gas to determine what percentage of gasoline has not been burnt. The analyzer draws a small part of the exhaust gas from the exhaust tail pipe into the tester probe and through the analyzer. Particulate matter and water are first removed from the sample by a trap and filter. The sample then flows through a three-way valve and a gas flow indicator before reaching the detector units. Several types of detectors are used; the *Wheatstone Bridge* type, the *Infrared* type and the *Ultraviolet* type.

The Wheatstone Bridge Type. A Wheatstone Bridge is an electrical device which operates on the principle of the thermal conductivity of gases.

The gasoline air mixture burned in the engine is made up of hydrogen, carbon, and oxygen. During perfect combustion, each atom of carbon unites with two atoms of oxygen to form carbon dioxide. Each two atoms of hydrogen combine with one atom of oxygen to form water. When the mixture is rich, the combustion is imperfect and some of the hydrogen does not combine with oxygen. The pure hydrogen is a good coolant. The cooling effect of the hydrogen gas affects the Wheatstone Bridge in such a manner as to change the resistance value of some of the bridge components. The lack of the cooling effect of the hydrogen in a lean mixture changes the resistance value of other bridge components. The change in resistance values of the components of the bridge are recorded on the meter to indicate a rich or lean fuel-air ratio.

The Wheatstone Bridge type of analyzer is not considered suitable for the modern emission-controlled engine since it uses the carbon dioxide content of the exhaust gases to determine the percentage of complete combustion.

The modern combustion analyzer uses the carbon monoxide and hydrocarbon content of the exhaust gases to determine the state of combustion. The carbon monoxide content gives a more accurate indication of the fuel-air ratio. The new analyzers indicate two conditions, the carbon monoxide content and the quantity, in parts per million, of the unburned hydrocarbons.

Infrared-Radiation Type. The operation of this type of analyzer is based on the infrared absorption characteristics of hydrocarbons. Different types of hydrocarbons absorb infrared radiation at different

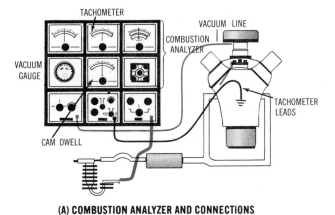

(A) COMBUSTION ANALYZER AND CONNECTIONS

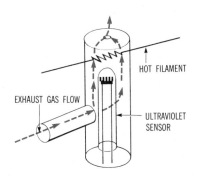

(B) DETECTOR CELL ULTRAVIOLET-TYPE ANALYZER

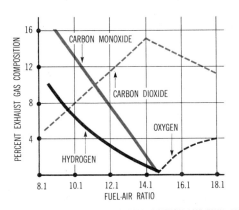

(C) COMPARISON OF EXHAUST GAS COMPOSITION AND FUEL-AIR RATIO

Fig. 50-5   Combustion Analyzer and Connections

wave lengths. When a gas absorbs infrared radiation, its temperature and pressure is increased. In the analyzer, a detector is used to pick up this information and relay it to an indicator device.

The analyzer unit contains two detector cells. The detector cells consist of two chambers which are separated by a pressure-sensitive diaphragm. The two chambers are filled to identical pressures with a "sensitizer" gas, usually n-hexane. N-hexane is one of the approximately 150 chemicals found in internal combustion engine exhaust gases. It has infrared absorption characteristics similar to those of the troublesome hydrocarbons. One of the two cells in the analyzer is an air cell, while the other is an exhaust gas cell.

During operation equal amounts of infrared radiation are directed through each cell to the sensitizer gas. The radiation passing through the air cell is not diminished by the air, and full radiation reaches each chamber of the cell resulting in no change of pressure in either cell. The exhaust gas passing through the other cell absorbs radiation at the same wave length as that of the sensitizer gas, reducing the amount of radiation reaching the gas in one chamber of the cell. The sensitizer gas in this chamber cools, and its pressure drops in accordance with the amount of radiation absorption that has taken place in the exhaust gases. The diaphragm between the two chambers of the exhaust cell moves in accordance with the difference in pressures, and the movement operates a variable resistor in the meter circuit causing a deflection of the needle proportionate to the change in current flow.

Ultraviolet-Radiation Type. This type of analyzer uses ultraviolet radiation to determine the carbon monoxide and hydrocarbon content of the exhaust gas.

The analyzer consists of one detector cell which includes a heater filament and an ultraviolet radiation sensor. As the exhaust gases flow through the detector cell they are oxidized or burned by the heat filament. Both carbon monoxide and hydrocarbons are combustible gases which, when burned, emit ultraviolet radiation. The amount of ultraviolet radiation emitted is proportional to the concentration of carbon monoxide and hydrocarbon in the exhaust gases. The ultraviolet sensor picks up this radiation and relays the signal by electronic devices to the two meters.

Most new type combustion analyzers are equipped with a test probe which can be used to detect gasoline odours and exhaust leaks.

In order to operate the analyzer, follow the manufacturers' instructions carefully as this test requires a great deal of care in order to produce usable results.

50-7 ELECTRICAL TEST EQUIPMENT

Electrical test equipment such as the high-rate discharge tester, voltmeter, ammeter, ohmmeter, distributor stroboscope machine, timing light, and oscilloscope units are used extensively in testing engine performance and servicability. The construction, operation, and use of each of these units has been covered in the appropriate chapter of this text.

50-8 CHASSIS DYNAMOMETER

The chassis dynamometer is used to test the engine in the car under a variety of simulated operating conditions. With the engine running and the transmission in gear, the rear wheels spin the dynamometer rollers. By placing a load on the rollers, the engine is forced to operate as though the vehicle were actually on the road.

Various instruments can be connected to the engine being tested so that engine horsepower, speed, intake-manifold vacuum, fuel-air ratios, etc., can be tested under normal driving conditions.

50-9 MAJOR ENGINE TUNE UP

Listed below, in brief form, are the items that should be included in a major tune up. Additional information regarding the service work involved will be found in the various service chapters included in this text.

Procedure:

1. Clean, inspect, and tighten battery cables.
2. Test battery. Both state of charge and battery mechanical condition tests should be performed to determine the condition of the battery. Batteries below specifications should be recharged or replaced as required. A starting motor draw test can also be conveniently performed at this time.
3. Compression Test. Since repairs of engine proper, such as valves and piston rings, are not included in an engine tune up, the compression test should be performed early in the tune-up procedure. If the compression is not within the specified range, it will be impossible to have satisfactory results from the tune up.
4. Tighten all cylinder-head and manifold bolts or nuts to specified torque.
5. Clean, adjust, test, and replace as required all spark plugs.
6. Inspect and check spark-plug wires; replace those showing signs of deterioration. Resistance-type wiring should be checked for proper resistance value.

7. Inspect distributor rotor and cap for signs of damage because of burning, cracking, or resistance. Clean or replace as required.

8. Check the distributor shaft and housing for wear, and the advance mechanisms for proper operating range. If the shaft and housing are worn or the advance mechanisms are not within the proper operating range, the distributor should be removed and overhauled.

9. Check the ignition breaker points for pitting, burning, cleanliness, and worn rubbing block. Clean or replace as required and set the breaker points to the proper point-gap or cam dwell angle.

10. Inspect the ignition primary circuit wiring for resistance and the available voltage at the coil. Repair as required.

11. Test the ignition coil on an ignition-coil tester or with an oscilloscope.

12. Set the ignition timing according to the manufacturers' specification.

13. Test the fuel pump pressure and vacuum. Replace the pump if it is below specifications.

14. Clean the fuel pump sediment bowl and screens or the fuel filter, if applicable.

15. Remove, clean, repair, and adjust carburetor. The carburetor should be disassembled and cleaned to remove gum and sediments, the needle and seat valve should be checked and replaced if necessary, and the float level set to specifications.

16. The air cleaner should be cleaned and serviced as required.

17. Adjust the carburetor mixture and idle adjustments to specifications.

18. Analyze the engine combustion.

19. Road or dynamometer test.

INDEX